THE CAMBRIDGE HISTORY OF EARLY INNER ASIA

The Cambridge History of Early Inner Asia introduces the geographical setting of the region and follows its history from the paleolithic era to the rise of the Mongol empire in the thirteenth century.

From earliest times Inner Asia has linked and separated the great sedentary civilisations of Europe and Asia. In the pre-modern period it was definable more as a cultural than a geographical entity, its frontiers shifting according to the changing balances of power. Before the advent of efficient firearms, it was their almost irresistible light cavalry which enabled the nomadic people of the steppes to take by force what they could neither produce themselves nor procure through trade. Their sedentary neighbours retaliated with constant attempts to dehumanise this nomad enemy, and created the concept of the 'barbarian' bent on destroying the civilised world. The early history of Inner Asia is, therefore, the history of the barbarian.

Written by distinguished international scholars who have pioneered the exploration of Inner Asia's poorly documented past, this book chronologically traces the varying historical achievements of the disparate population-groups in the region. These include the Scythians and Sarmatians, the Hsiung-nu, the Huns and Avars, the people of the Russian steppes, the Türk empire, the Uighurs and the Tibetan empire. It is the editor's hope that this book will bring Inner Asia more closely into the fabric of world history.

The Cambridge History of Early Inner Asia

Edited by
DENIS SINOR
Distinguished Professor Emeritus of Uralic and Altaic Studies
Indiana University

CAMBRIDGE
UNIVERSITY PRESS

Published by the Press Syndicate of the University of Cambridge
The Pitt Building, Trumpington Street, Cambridge CB2 1RP
40 West 20th Street, New York, NY 10011-4211, USA
10 Stamford Road, Oakleigh, Melbourne 3166, Australia

First published 1990
Reprinted 1994

British Library cataloguing in publication data

The Cambridge history of early Inner Asia.
From earliest times to the rise of
the Mongols
1. Asia. Inner Asia, to 1987
I. Sinor, Denis
951

Library of Congress cataloguing in publication data

The Cambridge history of early Inner Asia.
Bibliography.
Includes index.
Contents: v. 1. From earliest times to the rise
of the Mongols.
1. Asia, Central – History. I. Sinor, Denis.
DS329.4.C35 1988 958 88-18887

ISBN 0 521 24304 1

Transferred to digital printing 2004

SE

Contents

Preface

Inner Asia as presented in this volume is a cultural rather than a geographical concept: to some extent it is coterminous with the area called "the geographical pivot of history" by the late Sir George Mackinder. Therefore it should come as no surprise to the reader that the histories of some, strictly speaking "European" nations (such as the Huns, the Avars, or the Khazars) have found their proper place in this work. The first chapter of this book should give more ample detail on the definition of the area.

Contributors to this volume are distinguished scholars from many parts of the world who often pioneered in exploring early Inner Asia's poorly documented past. While presenting the specialist not only with new insights but, in many instances, also with hitherto unknown facts, they have attempted to open up for the benefit of the interested general reader a little-known chapter of human history. Because of the scarcity and variety of written sources, and with archeological explorations only recently begun, Inner Asian historiography is in its infancy. We could do no better than attempting to provide a relatively secure framework of political history which, I hope, will mark an important step in the incorporation of Inner Asia into the fabric of world history. No attempt has been made to whip the contributors into line; I do believe that there is value in allowing differences in approach to be noticeable, but great efforts were made to bring uniformity to the spelling of proper names. To justify each and every one of the forms adopted would need a special, lengthy article.

This is not a definitive history of pre-Mongol Inner Asia. It is an honest presentation of what we know at this stage of scholarship. We have tried to eliminate details which throw no light on the main events and to concentrate on the more important facts: those which bore consequences for the future course of history. Anyhow, such was the intention; it is up to the reader to judge to what extent it has been achieved by the individual authors.

I am deeply grateful to the John Simon Guggenheim Foundation for a

second fellowship which allowed me to concentrate my efforts on this work, and also to the Rockefeller Foundation for one month spent in the haven of its study center in Bellagio for the same purpose.

The competent translation from Russian of chapters of chapters 3 and 4 was the work of Julia Crookenden.

My thanks are due to the staff of Cambridge University Press for their smooth co-operation.

Denis Sinor

I

Introduction: the concept of Inner Asia

Unless they coincide with clearly defined physical boundaries – as is the case, for instance, with Australia – the borders of a cultural area can rarely be established with ease and accuracy. To some extent the problem lies with the highly subjective and often purely emotional criteria by which a civilization is defined. Thus, for example, as these lines are written, many nations would place themselves within a larger community which they call the "free world," while no attempt is made to define what freedom may mean to human beings with a cultural background different from their own. If there is a "free world" then, presumably, there must exist, in the minds of those who use the term, another world, "not free," and the differentiation is contingent on an emotionally charged interpretation of the ill-defined term of "freedom." It is a well-known rule of logic that classifications made on the basis of a single attribute are artificial and of limited use. So there must be a cluster of attributes by which a human group is defined, and these must be specific and essential, if they are to serve a useful purpose. Yet what is essential to one observer is not to another. Some would opt for language, others for race, religion, or shared destiny in the past or the present. It is also quite common to find that individuals tend to identify their own community by criteria which may be different from those used for the same purpose by outsiders. Particularly artificial are distinctions made on the basis of, often ephemeral, political arrangements which are given priority in defining an area over more lasting, deeply rooted national or cultural traits. The virtual disappearance from public consciousness of the valid cultural concept of Central Europe is a good modern case in point. Prompted by short-term political motives, and on the basis of one single attribute, Europe has been divided into an eastern and western part, and in the process the cultural entity of Central Europe has all but disappeared. This has led to the ludicrous situation in which the two Germanies are now considered by the public at large to be on the opposite sides of a divide whereas, of course, they share the same culture.

The problem of establishing the limits of cultural areas is not one that has

only recently emerged. Europe and Asia are also correlative terms neither of which can be understood without reference to the other. The division of the Old World into Asia, Europe, and Africa predates Herodotus, who was puzzled by the seeming illogicality of such division and could not conceive "why three names... should ever have been given to a tract of land which is in reality one."[1] The impossibility of drawing any clear, logical dividing line between Europe and Asia rests to some extent on the fact that the latter term is not autochthonous in origin, and until recently was not used by the Asians themselves. Quite understandably, no group solidarity existed among peoples living in a territory whose unity was not perceived. The slow emergence of a concept called Europe – for a long time closely associated with Christendom – brought about the gradual crystallization in European minds of the concept of Asia. The geographical delimitation of that continent is purely conventional and, even today, is subject to fluctuations. Very few Americans would think of Israel as an Asian state.

If the continents of Europe and Asia are conceptual entities, Eurasia – the combined land mass of the two – is a physiogeographical one. A cursory glance at any map of Eurasia will show that the major, sedentary civilizations developed on the periphery of the huge continent, while the cultural evolution of its heartland remained slow. Each of the sedentary civilizations – in loose terminology Europe, the Middle East, India, Southeast Asia and East Asia – is a unique combination of cultural features. Some of these may appear in more than one area; yet an association of various components, moulded by a unique historical process and greatly influenced by national environment, made each of these regions different from the others. The definition in geographical terms of some of the cultural spheres is not always easy. Such is the case, for example, of the Muslim and Hindu civilizations, flourishing simultaneously in the Indian Subcontinent. In the course of time the sphere of any civilization is subject to change; it may expand or shrink for reasons sometimes known and sometimes unknown; new civilizations arise while others disappear or undergo changes so substantial that their very core is affected. Yet there is one, constant, special mark, characteristic of all the cultural areas located on what we may call the external boundaries of Eurasia, namely their agricultural economic basis. Between them, in the central part of the Eurasian continent, and distinct from them in this respect, lies the cultural area with which we are here concerned: Central Eurasia or, to use a less cumbersome though less accurate term, Inner Asia.

[1] *The Histories*, Book IV, 45.

The frontier of Inner Asia is unstable; it has varied from age to age, shifting according to the balance of power between its own population and that of the surrounding, sedentary civilizations. The Roman province of Pannonia and the Greek territories in Asia Minor became "Inner Asia" when occupied respectively by the Huns (5th century A.D.) and the Saljuk Turks (11th century A.D.). Northern China became, for a while, "Inner Asia" under occupation by the Kitan, the Jurchen, the Mongols, and the Manchus.

The manner and the length of the process by which each Inner Asian attack was neutralized varied from case to case, but the sedentary people's victory was seldom achieved by brute force. Rarely was the successful invader and occupier overcome decisively by arms and expelled: in most instances he was assimilated, absorbed by the local population. One might say that, almost invariably a superior fertility rate was the crucial factor in the outcome of the confrontation.

In the endemic conflict between peoples of Inner Asia and the sedentary populations, the former have usually, though not always, taken the role of the aggressor. Military conquest played a relatively modest part in the gradual expansion of the sedentary world, a notable exception being, in modern times, the Russian advance into and permanent occupation of the lands which still remain within the cultural boundaries of Inner Asia. Though pre-emptive strikes or retaliatory campaigns against Inner Asian peoples were – mainly on the Chinese border – a constant feature of interaction, the gradual expansion from the periphery towards the heartland was, first and foremost, the result of the increase – either from natural causes or by immigration – of the sedentary populations. Thus, although the area of Inner Asia is subject to fluctuations, the general trend has been towards contraction, although the sedentary civilizations have suffered setbacks. Some of these remain largely unexplained as, for instance, the disappearance in the 2nd millenium B.C. of the flourishing urban life of southern Central Asia, as exemplified by the ruins of Altyn Tepe and other sites. Some encroachments by Inner Asia happened in historical times and are better documented, as for example the turcization of Anatolia, a region once imbued with Hellenistic culture.

In the preceding pages the fairly obvious point has been stressed that in the course of history the shifting nature of the borders of Inner Asia was due to interactions with the regions around it. The question now arises what caused Inner Asia to exist as a separate cultural entity and what made the conflict between it and the surrounding civilizations inevitable. As stated earlier, the most important common factor of the civilizations surrounding Inner Asia is their agricultural economy, whereas with regard to Inner Asia Robert Taaffe

has listed (see p. 26) "inadequate supplies of water, the brevity of growing seasons, edaphic problems, and difficult terrain" as being "the most important physical-geographic impediments to the development of sedentary agriculture" there. To be sure, in suitable and relatively small areas farming has been and is being practised, but it has played only a marginal role in the economy of the whole region. The vast stretches of the steppe – the only natural region in Central Eurasia capable of supporting a polity of some sophistication and power – are favorable only to extensive animal husbandry, which has remained the most characteristic occupation of the Inner Asian peoples down to modern times. But, in the words of Rhoads Murphey, "Rivalry between the steppe and the sown, between nomads and sedentary farmers, may well be one of the oldest conflicts of modern civilization."[2] The natural conditions prevailing in the three other Inner Asian zones – the arctic tundra, the forest region (*taiga*), and the desert – do not allow the formation of powerful states, as none of them can provide food for a population large enough to muster the political power necessary to initiate conquest.

In political conflicts humans oppose humans and the motives for action are multiple and difficult to define. Yet the complexity characteristic of such actions should not be allowed to obscure the basic nature of the opposition between Inner Asia on the one hand and any of the sedentary civilizations on the other. In its essence, it was one between haves and have-nots, the latter trying to reach the proverbial flesh-pots defended by those who had been lucky enough to place themselves close to the hearth. First and foremost, the conflict was thus economically motivated, one group trying to improve its living conditions at the expense of the other, the outsiders' attacks being contained or repulsed by those inside: the natural course of action of the two opposing segments of human society, if – indeed – those who are "outside" may really be considered "human." The *fundamentum divisionis* is the relative economic standard of the two areas, one being Inner Asia, any of the sedentary civilizations the other. The fear that the Barbarian may come and take away the fruits of sedentary toil permeates these civilizations, well aware of the lure of their own riches, which had to be protected from Barbarian greed, a favorite *topos* of statesmen and historians, whether Chinese or Roman.[3] The great Chinese historian Ssu-ma Ch'ien called the Hsiung-nu greedy and avaricious (*t'an lan*), thus echoing an opinion recorded in the *Tso-chuan* as early as the third century B.C.: "The Barbarians of the west (Jung) and of the north (Ti) are ravenous wolves who cannot be satiated." According

[2] Murphey, Rhoads, 1961, p. 505.
[3] See Sinor, 1978, pp. 171–82, with exact references to the texts cited.

to the *Hsin T'ang-shu* "The Northern Barbarians are greedy and grasping; they care only about profit." The Huns, in the words of Ammianus Marcellinus (XXXI,2,11), "burn with an infinite thirst for gold," and in his *Strategikon* Maurice describes the Avars as "dominated by an insatiable desire for money." The adjective ἄπληστος ("insatiable") is often used to qualify the Barbarians' character. It is favored by the emperor Constantine II Porphyrogenitus in his manual of statecraft normally cited by the Latin title *De administrando imperio*. On the Pechenegs he has this to say: "Now these Pechenegs, who are ravenous and keenly covetous of articles rare among them, are shameless in their demands for generous gifts."[4] He gives some vigorous advice to his son: "Know therefore that all the tribes of the north have, as it were implanted in them by nature, a ravening greed for money, never satiated, and so they demand everything and hanker after everything and have desires that know no limit or circumscription."[5]

Here, as in many other testimonies, what appear to be standard comments were rooted in personal experience. When, in the 13th century, John of Plano Carpini described the Mongols as "most grasping and avaricious, exacting in their demands, most tenacious in holding on to what they have and most niggardly in giving"[6] he was not following literary conventions but writing from bitter, first-hand knowledge. This was true also of his contemporary, the Dominican Simon of Saint-Quentin who stated: "Such greed burns in them [the Mongols] that when they see something that pleases, they will immediately either obtain it through forceful insistence or they will take it away from the owner with violence, whether he likes it or not."[7] Greedy they certainly were, those Mongols who created an empire greater than any which had existed before them, yet even at the height of their power, they were poor, often lacking in basic commodities. The Franciscan Rubruck, himself no stranger to poverty, could truthfully report to Louis IX of France: "I say to you with confidence, if your peasants, I will not say kings and knights, were willing to go as do the kings of the Tartars and to be content with the same kind of food, they could take possession of the whole world."[8]

What, it may be asked, were the reasons for such poverty, why could Inner Asia not give its population a living standard similar to those enjoyed in the surrounding civilizations? The key to the problem is the absence of substantial farming caused, as already mentioned, by a combination of physical–geographic factors, perhaps first of all the climate, which, in simple terms, is too cold and too dry to allow a thriving agriculture. To characterize Inner

[4] Moravcsik, 1967, p. 54. [5] *Ibid*, pp. 66–7. [6] Dawson, 1966, p. 16.
[7] Richard, 1965, p. 35. [8] Dawson, 1965, p. 220.

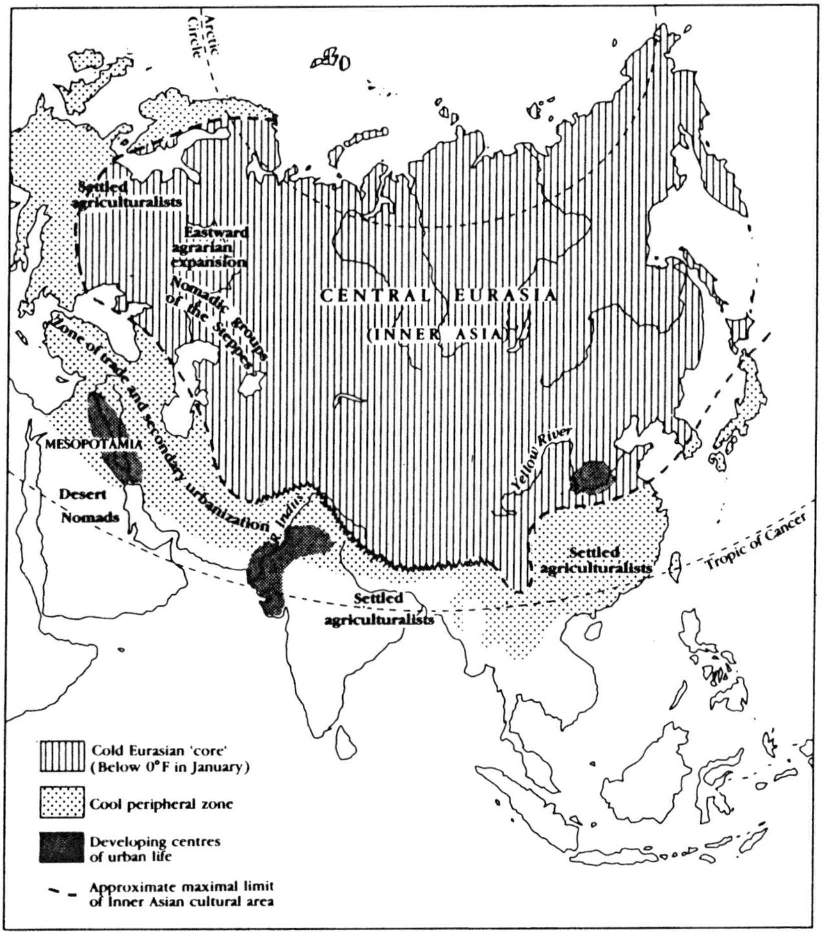

Asia, Chinese sources often use the phrase "where the killing frosts come early."[9]

The economy of the tundra, the northernmost natural zone of Inner Asia, could never provide its inhabitants with more than a subsistence-level existence, and this only on condition that they lived dispersed over vast territories. The political power of the population (usually only a dozen or so families operating within each circumscribed area), which was all the limited

[9] On *topoi* relative to the Barbarians' land see Meserve, 1982.

hunting and reindeer-breeding economy of the tundra could support, was negligible. The gap between the minimal population figure (below which a group cannot go without danger to its survival in a hostile environment) and the maximal one (above which it cannot go because the environment cannot then provide for even its basic needs in food) was very narrow.

The situation prevailing in the forest belt (*taiga*) was, in some ways, analogous but here the natural resources could support a hunting-fishing-gathering population with relative ease. When practiced on a large enough scale to provide for the basic needs of a community, hunting and fishing both require tools of considerable sophistication, technologically more advanced than those used in primitive agriculture. Also, collective fishing and hunting, especially the latter, demand a social organization capable of carrying out joint actions of some complexity. However, because a hunting economy is essentially predatory, it cannot serve as a basis for high-density populations, and so by definition it cannot muster the collective power required for conquest. In 17th-century Siberia, Tunguz hunting clans numbered between 15 and 25 men, though there are records of clans 300–700 head strong – still a minuscule force.[10]

So it is the steppe which is the key to the understanding of the role of Inner Asia in world history. On this vast pasture-land, cattle-breeding, whether of horned cattle, camels, sheep, goats or horses (the five categories of domestic animals, *tabun qosiyun mal* of the Mongols), was always extensive. To ensure economic self-sufficiency, and to avoid overgrazing, the herds had to be continually on the move, normally within a given perimeter but, on occasion wherever grass could be found. "They follow the grass and water" is the Chinese stereotype used to characterize the nomad. But, unlike the inhabitants of the tundra or the taiga, the nomads could congregate with great speed and important masses of men and beasts could stay together for relatively long periods of time. In other words, the population-carrying capacity of the steppe, within a fixed area, is superior to that of either the tundra or the forest. The environment could and did allow the creation of strongly centralized states and was able to maintain such a political superstructure for as long as the community could complement its basic production with commodities obtained from other, mostly agricultural regions. In Owen Lattimore's words, steppe life

> is based on an economy which is capable of being entirely self-sufficient. Its own resources provide the essentials of food, housing, clothing and transport, even fuel

[10] Dolgikh, 1960, p. 619. See also Sinor, 1965.

(from cattle dung). Nor does it prevent the mining and working of metals on a small scale, as is known from archaeological evidence. The steppe-nomad can withdraw into the steppe if he needs to, and remain completely out of contact with other societies. He can; but so rarely does he so that this pure condition of nomadic life can fairly be called hypothetical. For every historical level of which we have any knowledge there is evidence that exchange of some kind, through trade or tribute, has been important in steppe-nomad life.[11]

If the steppe-based state no longer enjoyed the quasi-autarchy of a small-scale pastoralist tribe, it had the capability of compensating for any deficiency either by trade or by military means. Horse breeding on a large scale provided the basis for both activities.

The exceptional qualities of the Inner Asian horse have been praised by all, beginning with Herodotus, who never had the opportunity to become acquainted, directly or indirectly, with its powers of endurance, its resistance to cold, its frugality. These animals are rather ugly to western eyes but they are capable of digging their food out from under the snow and, in case of need, can survive by eating twigs, tree bark, or any other vegetal matter. At the height of their power the great nomadic states disposed of huge horse herds; in fact it may be said that their might depended on the number of mounts they could command. Foreign travelers were amazed by their multitude. The Mongols had – as John of Plano Carpini put it – "such a number of horses and mares that I do not believe there are so many in all the rest of the world." There is a fairly rich documentation on the number of horses sold at various times to the Chinese, and the figures are impressive. The sale of 10,000 head on any one occasion was a routine transaction, but much more substantial deals were also common. Thus for example in A.D. 222 the Hsien-pi sold 70,000 head to the kingdom of Wei.[12]

The horse was the mainstay of steppe economy, the principal commodity produced, and in it lay the wealth of the nation. Unless some natural disaster struck – such as the dreaded *jud*, the freezing of the pastures – the steppe could and did produce horses far in excess of domestic needs, which were rather modest; the level of effective internal demand has always fallen short of productive capacity. In the non-monetary society of the steppe, within one social group the determinants of domestic consumption were quasi constant, producers and consumers were the same, and in the absence of technical progress, the law of diminishing returns was fully operative. The continuous

[11] Lattimore, 1938, reprinted in Lattimore, 1962, p. 253.

[12] See Sinor, p. 175. On the trade in horses, spontaneous or imposed, see e.g. S. Jagchid–C.R. Bawden, 1965; Rossabi, 1970; Serruys, 1975.

growth of herds could not directly improve the (individual or collective) owner's living standards, though it most probably added to his prestige, and in the case of collective ownership may have led to economic or political control of other groups. But whatever the size and potential power of the social unit, the non-diversified economy could not by itself bring about a substantial improvement in its members' living standard. The traditional Inner Asian economy was not gain-oriented; the aim was not the accumulation of wealth but the acquisition of goods which, for one reason or another, it was unable to produce. To obtain them, recourse had to be had to external trade, mainly with the sedentary civilizations.

In principle, commercial prospects between the steppe and sedentary civilizations seemed ideal. The former could provide the latter with a commodity of prime importance, the horse, and could receive in exchange much appreciated goods such as textiles (silk and linen), tea and, quite often, grain, desperately needed when the herds had fallen victim to some natural catastrophe. Of course it was possible to raise horses outside Inner Asia, but these, compared with the pony of the steppe, were of inferior quality and insufficient in number. In his description of Darius' campaign against the Scythians Herodotus stated that, "In these combats the Scythian horse always put to flight the horse of the enemy,"[13] and the truth of this opinion was confirmed in countless other encounters. Over many centuries lack of horses plagued successive Chinese administrations. The problem was insoluble not only because the Chinese lacked the expertise in horse-breeding but also, more importantly, because the pastures of their land could not provide for all the horses needed for civilian as well as military purposes. Thus, apparently, there was a constant equilibrium between supply and demand with a commodity needed by the buyer and available to a willing seller. It might seem that circumstances favored the latter who had a virtual monopoly on high quality horses, deemed essential by the Chinese military. Yet in fact the Barbarian's bargaining power was severely limited by the absence of any competition in the bidding for what he had to offer. The steppe was the sole supplier of a distinctive product and thus, in theory, he could have set whatever price he chose had he not been dependent on a monopolist market with economic reserves vastly superior to his own. His case can be compared to that of a hungry man trying to sell a diamond to the only jeweler of a small town. Yet I have referred to the horse-breeding pastoralist's ability to obtain by force what he could not procure through trade. In this aforementioned, imaginary

[13] Herodotus, *The Histories*, IV. 127.

jeweler's shop a gun in the hand of the hungry man would completely alter the picture.

With the horse, the steppe-nomad possessed not only a commodity which was not only of steady use-value and high, though fluctuating, exchange-value, but which was also indispensable in war. Horses were used generally in all wars fought on Eurasian soil, and they were still in service until at least the earlier stages of World War II. Until firearms became generally available, an important mass of nomad light cavalry, if properly led, was virtually irresistible, provided that it was backed by relay horses, essential for the fast troop movements characteristic of its distinctive mode of operation. For each warrior the number of mounts needed varied, according to our sources, between 3 and 18.

The unavoidable reliance of the Chinese military on the horse produced a curious situation in which, to resist the attacks of the steppe-nomads, China needed the horses which only they could provide. At the same time, by purchasing these horses and thereby offering the potential enemy the means to buy the goods they hankered for, the attacks became, as it were, superfluous, and could altogether be avoided. Conversely, to obtain goods needed or coveted, two courses of action were opened to the nomad. In both the horse was the key factor; he could barter it for other commodities or use it to obtain them by force of arms.

The military efficiency of a nomad cavalry force was a function of its size, but the relationship between the number of horses and their military value was not a mathematical constant but a geometric progression. The maintenance of such an army was dependent on the availability of adequate pasture, and so military victory could not resolve the conflict between the pastoral and the sedentary civilizations. The nomads were able to invade but were unable to maintain their hold permanently over the conquered territories without relinquishing their trump card, their strong cavalry. Usually this meant the erosion of their power base with, ultimately, absorption and assimilation into, or ejection by the people they conquered. For their part, the sedentary peoples could not support on a permanent basis a significant force of cavalry and so, for the supply of horses, remained dependent on the pastoral nomads.

It is of some interest to note that in the provision of arms a similar situation obtained, favoring this time the sedentary manufacturers. Although the pastoral nomads were capable of producing the bulk of their armament, there are many instances in which their desire to obtain Chinese or Roman weapons is clearly documented. As a countermeasure, the export of war material was frequently prohibited, as for instance in Han times when strict regulations

forbade the export of strategic goods to the Hsiung-nu, or in the 6th century, when a Byzantine embargo was put on the sale of swords to the Avars. Between Barbarian and Civilized, even more than among modern nations, trade and war were but two aspects of the same policy, and governments were frequently faced with the choice of one or the other.

If was far from easy to take the right decision and quite often emotion rather than reason determined the course adopted. Depending on the temperament of the decision makers, the Barbarians' request for goods was sometimes rejected on the grounds that "if they do not get what they need their power will crumble, they may perish, victims of a famine";[14] an argument prompted by wishful thinking which led to innumerable armed conflicts. Proponents of another policy, that of appeasement, argued that by satisfying the Barbarians' "reasonable" demands peace could be obtained. The success of such a course of action depended very much on whether the demands were genuinely prompted by necessity, and proportionate both to the needs of the applicant and to the resources of the prospective donor, or whether they were dictated by the greed which we have recognized as an essential trait in the Barbarian's portrait. The history of Inner Asia is full of examples of both success and failure resulting from each of these contradictory policies. Sechin Jagchid, who studied with great insight and in detail the consequences of the two types of policy as practised in China towards requests for aid, expressed the view that in many instances the Chinese "failed to discover that poverty and famine caused the nomads to invade China to supply their needs by force."[15] He also showed, by specific examples, that the provision of food could, and on many occasions did, avert invasions. Yet, giving in to the demands of the Barbarian often amounted to nothing else but paying him tribute. The humiliating aspect of such a policy were clearly perceived and resented by many, and perhaps no one was more vocal in his indignation than Salvianus of Marseille:[16]

> The Romans were of old the mightiest of men, now they are without strength; of old they were feared, but now they live in fear, barbarous nations paid tribute to them, but to these same nations they are now tributary. The enemy sells us the very daylight, almost our whole safety is purchased for a price. Alas for our misfortunes! to what a pass we have come! For this we give thanks to the barbarians, that we are allowed to

[14] See for instance the remark quoted by Serruys, 1975, p. 222, from the *Wan-li wu-kung lu*: "The fact that among the Barbarians, clothing, food, and habitations are all the same as in China is like a Heaven-sent support for China: it gives control over life and death."

[15] Jagchid, 1970, p. 40.

[16] *De Gubernatione Dei*, VI, 98–99. Translation by Eva M. Sanford, *On the Government of God*, (New York 1930), p. 188.

ransom ourselves from them at a price. What could be more abjectly wretched than to live on such terms? Yet after all this we think that we are living, we whose lives depend on tribute! We even make ourselves additionally ridiculous by pretending that the gold we pay is merely a gift. We call it a gift, yet it is really a ransom – but a ransom paid on unusually hard and wretched terms . . . we are never free of the payments due: we pay ransom constantly in order to have the privilege of continuing endlessly to pay.

The merits and demerits of providing "foreign aid" to impoverished nations is, in our time more than ever, a subject of constant controversy, a circumstance which ought to induce us to view with some indulgence efforts made by previous generations to solve an insoluble problem.

In the preceding pages, I have tried, however imperfectly, to sketch some basic characteristics of Inner Asian economy in so far as these affected the region's relationship with the sedentary civilizations. It would be a mistake to imagine that at a remote period of prehistory the forest or steppe zones were somehow "backward" in comparison with the sedentary, peripheral areas. One can almost say that the opposite would be true, since sophisticated hunting or stock-breeding demand at least as much ingenuity as primitive farming. The main difference between the three modes of production lies in agriculture's capability to almost unrestricted development, whereas – at least until modern times – neither hunting nor stock-breeding could boast of essential improvements in their methods of production. Also, while hunting is a predatory occupation and stock-breeding relies mainly on the natural instincts of the animals, agriculture adds to the natural resources available to man and in the process often alters the physical environment or harnesses the forces of nature. Through the clearing of land for cultivation, the building of irrigation channels, the use of windmills, or similar activities, the Civilized invests labor in the improvement of a definite piece of land to which he is attached and which he cannot leave if he wishes to see, quite literally, the fruits of his labor. More often than not the Barbarian exploits the natural world which the Civilized tries to improve; there is between the two a basic difference in outlook, rooted in distinct evolutions extending over millennia. There was a time, probably in the late Paleolithic, when differences between the technological levels of various civilizations did not ensure a definite advantage to the one over the other though, as time has shown, they carried in them differing potentials for further development. After the domestication of the horse – wherever this may first have happened – those peoples whose habitats were on the steppe (or who moved there to take advantage of the newly acquired skill) were able to profit from the rich pastures first to increase

their herds, then to adopt them for military use. It is to the credit of the earliest nomad warriors (in recorded history first represented by the Scythians) that they brought virtually to perfection a method of warfare which, for almost two thousand years, held its own against other military systems, without undergoing significant improvements. Yet excellent though it was, it did not contain within itself the possibility of further development: very early in time technological evolution on the steppe reached a dead end.

In periods of success the mounted warrior was happy with his lot; there is plenty of evidence to show that he thought disparagingly of farmers and, in general, of urban populations whom he viewed as prisoners within their own cities. But even at such times of prosperity, the lure of consumer goods, making life a little better, was too strong to resist. Some puritan men, such as the wise Türk minister Tonyuquq (see p. 312) warned in vain against the danger of adopting Chinese ways; his words in the long run went unheeded. It could not be otherwise, since the very *raison d'être* of the campaign was the desire to acquire goods not produced by and on the steppe. So the choice was really between living in "honorable" poverty – at the mercy of nature and in fairly constant conflict with other nomad groups vying for the better pastures – or asking for "admittance" into the civilized world, at the risk of losing one's national identity. Over the centuries, fairly constantly, the majority of those who had an option chose the second alternative. As mentioned earlier, the growth of the sedentary civilizations has been due less to conquest than to voluntary settlement within their borders.

Admittance, however, did not depend on the will of the Barbarian alone, it also needed the consent of the future host which – if it was to be given without constraint – was contingent upon a number of factors. These, besides the whim of the decision-maker, included the availability of free space on which to settle the newcomers, and the ratio of their number to that of the population of the host country. Most often there was no time to consider calmly the pros and cons of such an action, and negotiations had to be conducted in a hurry, frequently under duress. The ultimate outcome of such operations depended almost entirely on demographic factors: would the local, agriculturalist population absorb the newcomers – as it happened in China – or would the latter impose their own, often inferior, civilization on the host land, as happened in Anatolia, or on the Iranian frontier, where turcization resulted in a definite cultural regression.

In the foregoing strong emphasis has been put on economic factors which, so it would appear, are the basis of any definition that can and should be given of

Inner Asia. In them are rooted also the differences which set this region apart from the sedentary civilizations and, in course of time, caused a confrontational relationship to develop between the major division of Eurasia: the agricultural periphery and the central part supported – depending on the natural zones – by hunting/fishing or by pastoral economy.

The question should now be asked whether the region can be defined also in positive terms, i.e. not only by contrast with other cultural areas. Were there any objective criteria specific to Inner Asia taken as a whole? If they once existed, today they are no longer discernible, the links which usually hold together or create a cultural entity – such as script, race, religion, language – played only a very moderate role as factors of cohesion.

The important, often decisive, role of writing in the creation of cultural zones is often overlooked though no one would deny the solidarity created by the use of a common script. The spread of the Latin alphabet in modern times, and that of the Cyrillic script in the last century or so, show vividly the cohesive force which a common alphabet represents, and the official adoption of a new system by a government (as happened for instance in Turkey in 1926) can move a people from one cultural community to another. In some instances the use of a common script can even obviate the obstacle created by different languages, as is the case between China or Japan, or – to some extent – even within China. The peoples of Inner Asia have never shared a common system of writing and none of the various ones used at different times was widely adopted. Moreover, since illiteracy was general, the use of one way of writing or another affected only a minuscule number of people.

As regards physical anthropology, though Mongoloid and Tungusid types may now be considered typically Inner Asian, the presence of Europoid populations in the very heartland of Inner Asia is well attested in the Neolithic period. A case in point is the Afanasievo culture which appeared around 2000 B.C. in the steppe island around Minusinsk. The people of the Andronovo culture which spread from the Altai to the Caspian Sea were also of Europoid race. The first appearance of Mongoloids is possibly around 1200 B.C., when the so-called Karasuk people became dominant over the Europoid population of the Minusinsk region. During the latter part of the 2nd millenium B.C. first the Indo-Aryans and then most of the Iranian peoples moved south off the steppe to conquer and settle in the Indian subcontinent and Iran; but the presence of Iranians (notably the Scythians) is well attested on the steppe in the first millennium B.C., and it is not until the early centuries of the Christian era that the last Iranian elements there disappear, submerged by Turkic peoples. The task of outlining the racial history of Inner Asia cannot be

undertaken here, but it is clear that criteria established by physical anthropology do not figure among the possible distinguishing features of the region.

Inner Asia has not given birth to any great conquering religion, but the Iranian prophet Zarathustra (Zoroaster) is held by some to have lived and taught on the steppe sometime between 1450–1200 B.C., his religion being subsequently carried south by migrating tribes to become "the" Iranian religion.[17] In Inner Asia itself no one faith has ever commanded the allegiance of more than a fraction of its population. In the absence of adequate written sources information on any indigenous religious belief is scanty and difficult to interpret; the worship of Tengri (heaven or sky – the word has both meanings) was obviously widespread at least in the steppe zone in medieval times, but there is no trace of doctrinal development taking place. In the 13th century belief in one supreme God was vigorously asserted by the Mongol rulers who, at the same time, displayed a remarkable tolerance towards all religious beliefs. Possibly herein lay their greatest intellectual and moral achievement. Traces of mythological themes which may have been generally known before the beginning of the process of differentiation survived in Greece and China though – because of lack of written tradition – they may not always have been preserved in Inner Asia itself. There are a few, well documented, cases which convincingly show that identical mythical conceptions found in Greek, Chinese, and Near Eastern writing are not, as it is often thought, borrowings, but all derive independently from a common Inner Asian substratum.[18] It is most likely that the peculiar early art form which for many centuries flourished all across the continent – the so-called "animal art" – is also based on such common, though long-forgotten conceptions. Just as the bodies of mammoths have been preserved in the subsoil of the Siberian permafrost, so remnants of ideologies, or of mythical concepts may yet be unearthed from unfathomed depths of Inner Asia's cultural heritage.

In the absence of written documents – the earliest of these, in a Turkic language, date from the middle of the 8th century A.D. – it is impossible to reconstruct the linguistic history of Inner Asia. It is, however, beyond doubt that there has never been a linguistic unity within its confines and that the diversity of languages within the area was much greater in the past than it is now. In fact since the times when their study caught the interest of European scholars – i.e. since the 18th century – a great number of Inner Asian languages have become extinct. The nature of the relationship between the Uralic

[17] See Chapter I in Boyce 1975, pp. 3–21.

[18] Disregarding many uncritical attempts, one may here cite the works of Meuli, 1935, 1960; Kothe, 1970, pp. 37–53 of Sinor, 1946–7.

(Finno-Ugric and Samoyed) and Altaic (Turkic, Mongol, and Tunguz) languages which, for as far back as the available data allow us to go, have constituted the dominant linguistic group in the forest and tundra zones of Inner Asia, cannot be established with any degree of certainty.[19] While there are those scholars who aver that some or even all of them are genetically related – that is, that they descend from a common, ancestral *Ursprache* – others, including myself, believe that the elements which they unquestionably have in common are due to constant interaction over the centuries if not millennia, and that they result from convergent rather than divergent development. Beyond purely linguistic arguments which cannot be entered upon here, the historically documented absorption by either Uralic or Altaic languages of many of the so-called Paleoasiatic tongues would support such a theory. Be this as it may, many of these languages are not mutually intelligible and, to the best of our knowledge, there never was a time when a Turkic and a Mongol speaker could understand each other. Uralic and Altaic languages may be typical of Inner Asia, but they have certainly never constituted a bond of unity between the mosaic of peoples living there. In so far as historical data are available, it would appear that all the steppe empires had a multilingual population.

If then none of the above-mentioned factors is an essential constituent in the civilization of Inner Asia, it would seem that the most workable definition, the *fundamentum divisionis*, must remain the *relative* economic and cultural standard of the area, not its *absolute* content: it is that part of Eurasia which, at any given time, lay beyond the borders of the sedentary world. To be a part of it involved the practice of specific modes of production and permanent opposition to a more prosperous outer world.

There is no way of knowing how long the almost continuous adding of new layers to the outer fringe of the civilized enclaves has been in progress. Opposition between the two groups may sometimes have arisen from family feuds, setting against each other the successful and unsuccessful branches of the same clan. There were those who "made it" and became settled, perhaps because they were more ruthless or cunning, or less adventurous, than their close kin. History must have produced more sibling pairs like Cain and Abel or Esau and Jacob than we know of, and Isaac's words have a ring of truth for many who feel dispossessed:

[19] See Sinor, 1988.

Your dwelling shall be far from the richness of the
earth far from the dew of heaven above,
By your sword shall you live,
and you shall serve your brother;
but the time will come when you grow restive
and break his yoke from your neck.
(Gen. 27, 39–40)

The Book of Genesis tells us that Jacob thought it wise to listen to his mother's advice and seek refuge out of the reach of his brother, Success does not breed peace of mind. Need may then be felt for a barrier to be erected between winner and loser. They may be built of stone, as the Great Wall of China or Hadrian's Wall, but such constructions may crumble or may be taken by assault. It is better to build a dam in the hearts of men, which can resist the ravages of time and neutralize the assaults even of common sense. Prejudice is virtually impregnable. A permanent hostility towards the "outsider," implanted and carefully tended in the heart of every member of the more successful community, presents the added advantage of strengthening the bonds of solidarity, holding the polity together and making it more amenable to a government which – the individuals are led to believe – is alone capable of protecting them against the dangers lurking in the Outer Darkness and threatening to despoil them of the fruits of their labor. The fear is permanent and pervasive; the division must be maintained at all costs. In a well-ordered universe, to quote Ssu-ma Ch'ien "inside are those who don the cap and the girdle [i.e. the Chinese], outside are the Barbarians." While for "Chinese" one may substitute other civilizations such as "Greek" or "Roman," no such substitution is possible in the case of the Barbarian, he is *sui generis*, the enemy of all the others. To combat him is the foremost duty of the ruler, in fact it may be the justification of his power over his own people. It is in combating the outsider, the real challenger of the established order, that the ruler is able to show his mettle, that he is able to convince his subjects of his own fitness to rule and, hence, of the legality of his power. Faced with him, the Barbarian ought to be awe-stricken, overcome by fear and reluctant to act. If, as Eustathios of Thessalonica put it, wars are like the illnesses of nations, a war waged by a Barbarian against Byzantium is as if a disease were to defy the omnipotence of God.[20]

We have seen that the Barbarian is driven by insatiable greed. This is so, we

[20] As cited by Lechner, 1954, p. 81. On the Barbarian viewed from the Inner Asian point of view, see Sinor, 1957.

are told, because he does not know his proper place in the universe, he acts *κατα κόςμου* in disorder, without propriety, he is "irresolute as a rat" and ignores the rules of etiquette. "The rules of conduct" – states the Book of Rites (*Li chi*) – "allows the Civilized to keep his feelings under control . . . to follow one's inclinations is the way of the Barbarian." For Salvianus of Marseille, the Barbarians are "void not only of Roman but of human wisdom" and in the words of Albertus Magnus "They are called Barbarians who are not ordered for virtue by law or government or the discipline of any other system." For Roger Bacon the world is divided into two parts: the region of the Barbarian and that of "reasonable men".[21]

On rare occasions, and temporarily, a compromise is conceivable, but it rarely lasts and is, in some ways, unnatural. The aim of the Civilized cannot but be the banishment of the Barbarian beyond the borders of the *oikoumene*, the prevention of further intrusions. This was the spirit which prompted, for instance, Alexander the Great of legend to shut out, beyond iron gates, set into impenetrable mountains, the "impure" people of Gog and Magog, mythical embodiment of the quintessential Barbarian. Yet there can never be certainty that he will not emerge from his northern lairs, if not earlier then at doomsday, when the hosts of Gog and Magog will bring universal devastation to a world from which they have been excluded.

The history of Inner Asia (and it may be necessary to recall once more that the correct term would be Central Eurasia) began at some unspecified time when the differentiation between various occupational groups and their respective levels of prosperity became sufficiently marked to call for the erection of physical and moral barriers for the defence of the more prosperous. With sudden outbursts of activity and with lulls, mostly due to exhaustion, these conflicts have continued until modern times, perhaps, in some aspects, even to our own day. It could hardly be otherwise, since the Barbarian and the Civilized are opposed and complementary, neither can be defined without an understanding of the other and the gap between the two has proved unbridgeable: "What peace can there be between hyena and dog? And what peace between rich man and poor?"[22] Inner Asia is the antithesis to "our" civilized world. Its history is that of the Barbarian.

[21] *Opus majus*, ed. J.H. Bridges, I, 301. [22] *Ecclesiasticus*, 13, 18.

2

The geographic setting

The areal extent and diversity of the natural landscapes of Inner Asia impel a survey of the geographic background of this region to concentrate on the environmental characteristics which seem to contribute most to an understanding of the even greater complexities of the human use of these lands. To this end, attention will be focused initially on five general geographic features of Inner Asia: its size; the effects of distance from maritime influences on movement and climate; the problems of its rivers; geographic diversity and uniformity; and, the limited capabilities for areally extensive crop agriculture. This will be followed by a discussion of the major environmental components of the natural zones of Inner Asia.

General geographic characteristics

The Inner Asian region occupies an immense area in the interior and northerly reaches of the Eurasian land mass and encompasses a territory of more than eight million square miles or about one-seventh of the land area of the world. The east–west dimensions of this region extend some 6,000 miles, which is slightly more than twice as long as the maximum north–south axis. These distances are comparable to those traversed by only a few of the most adventurous maritime vessels in the European "Age of Discovery." Within Inner Asia, however, the pre-eminent means of long-distance communication has been overland movement inasmuch as no region on earth is as landlocked by the absence of feasible maritime alternatives. The major movements of peoples, cultural innovations, and goods has been on Inner Asian land routes far removed from the Pacific, the ice-covered Arctic and the Indian Ocean.[1] In the European portions of this region, substantial use has been made of Black

[1] It might be noted, however, that parts of the early Silk Road traffic was channeled through Indian Ocean ports. See Boulnois, 1966, pp. 40–60.

Sea and Caspian Sea routes, but this has been confined essentially to the margins of Inner Asia.

In addition to the limited role of maritime routes, the use of rivers as an alternative to land movement has been constrained by a number of serious problems. The most obvious of these is the absence of navigable waterways over a large part of the arid and semi-arid zones. Moreover, the extensive areas of interior drainage in Inner Asia extending from the Caspian Basin in the west to the Khingan ranges in the east do not provide a river approach to the world ocean. Unfortunately, some of the rivers which reach oceans flow in directions which scarcely are conducive to a major transport role. The most important examples are the massive rivers of Siberia, including the Ob-Irtysh, Yenisey, and Lena systems, which empty into the Arctic Ocean, which is ice-bound most of the year. Even the eastward flowing Amur bends to the north rather than the south at Khabarovsk and flows into the Taiga rather than southwards through the fertile Ussuri–Khanka lowlands which terminate at the excellent natural harbors of Vladivostok and Nakhodka. Fortunately, the northward flowing Ussuri River tributary of the Amur passes through these lowlands. To a considerable extent, movement in the Siberian and European portions of Inner Asia has been able to compensate for these directional debilities by use of land routes between river systems. Relatively short portages connected the long, latitudinally oriented tributaries of the major north-flowing Siberian rivers to form east-west avenues of movement. Although the limited navigational season on these rivers, ranging from six months in southern Siberia to only three months in the northern parts, also was a serious handicap to transportation, pathways formed by the frozen surfaces of rivers frequently were used for overland type movement. West of the Urals, the rivers of the Volga Basin draining into the enclosed Caspian Sea are linked to the other river systems flowing through the Russian Plains by easily traversed land routes. The Volga, however, is blocked by ice from three to five months a year.

By contrast, passage through most of the extensive interior zone of arid and semi-arid lands could not employ river and portage routeways and overland transportation had virtually unchallenged pre-eminence. Fortunately, the grasslands of Inner Asia have few natural obstacles to movement. In many ways, the elongated steppe zones, the isolated oases, and the major mountain passes and corridors of Inner Asia have been the overland equivalents of ocean routes, ports-of-call, and canals.

From a different point of view, the modest importance of maritime influences and the northerly latitudes of Inner Asia have a far-reaching effect on its

climate. This region is characterized by the highest degree of continentality on the surface of the earth, which means that the greatest differences in average temperatures between cold and warm seasons are encountered here. The winters in most of Inner Asia are cold or extremely cold and the summers are either warm or hot. The distance from oceans in conjunction with mountain barriers has impeded the flow of maritime air masses and has led to a pervasive deficit of moisture in the parts of Inner Asia south of the forest zone. To make the aridity and temperature problems worse, the interior portion of the Eurasian land mass is the site of the annual winter appearance of a massive and stable zone of high pressure centered on Mongolia which brings clear skies, sub-zero temperatures, and precipitation-free weather. Dry and cold winds emanate from this high pressure ridge and influence the winter weather of a large part of Inner Asia.

As could be anticipated from an awareness of the imposing physical dimensions of this region, Inner Asia embraces a wide variety of physical-geographic landscapes between the barren deserts and snow-covered peaks on its southern margins to the desolate, tundra-fringed shores of the Arctic Ocean in the north. The forests, steppes and deserts, which are separated by transitional areas, are aligned in broad, latitudinally oriented natural zones. It is difficult to imagine two areas which differ more in appearance than the waterlogged forests of the West Siberian Taiga and the bare sand dunes of the Taklamakan desert.

In addition to locational factors, the geographic diversity of Inner Asia is intensified by the effects of mountainous terrain. The broad ecological zonation of the natural features distributed over geographic space is encountered on a condensed vertical scale in the mountains of this region where altitudinal differences in vegetation, soils, and moisture combinations replace the latitudinal variations in natural zones. The northern ranges of the eastern T'ien Shan exemplify the vertical zonation of landscapes.[2] On the windward, or northern slopes of these mountains, the steppe grasses on the lower slopes are found up to elevations of 1,600 meters where they mix with scattered stands of trees. This pattern is replaced farther up the slopes by a solid band of coniferous trees which continues up to the tree line of 2,600 meters. Above that elevation, the vegetation cover begins to diminish and changes from alpine meadows to a zone of barren rock and primitive mountain soils above 3,600 meters which is covered by a permanent cap of snow on the highest peaks and ridges. On the dry leeward, or southern side of these same ridges,

[2] Institute of Geography, 1969, vol. 1, pp. 236–7.

deserts rise up the slopes to elevations comparable to the start of forests on the opposite, windward side. These high-altitude deserts yield to subalpine steppes and eventually slopes devoid of vegetation.

In addition to the formation of vertically layered natural zones and, of course, the striking differences in relief caused by mountains rising far above adjacent basins, the mountains of Inner Asia have added to the geographic variety of this region by contributing to the formation of the commonly encountered landscapes in the dry zones in which verdant oases on rivers flowing down from adjacent mountain ranges stand in sharp contrast to surrounding deserts or steppes. This type of landscape is most evident on the margins of the Tarim Basin, the plains of Zungaria next to the northern slopes of the T'ien Shan, and on the loessial piedmont plains which fringe the southern mountain borders of Central Asia.

The oases of Inner Asia depend primarily on the mountains for their water lifelines. When air masses which yield little or no precipitation over the plains rise over the windward slopes of mountains, they cool and acquire a lower saturation point which often leads to heavy precipitation on these slopes and in the core of the mountains with relatively little precipitation on the leeward side. As a result of this process, the high mountain ranges serve as reservoirs in which water is collected and stored in the form of seasonal snows or more persistent mountain glaciers until it thaws in the warm season and descends by mountain streams through gravel piedmonts to the oases. Even the oases farther downstream or in deltas, such as that of the Amu Darya, are dependent upon mountain-originated water. In addition to the orographic moisture effects, the fertile soils of the oases are usually those of alluvial plains created by mountain rivers as they reduce their gradient and deposit their sediments. In a sense, the mountain-dependent oases represent a type of localized compensation for the aridity of much of Chinese Turkestan and Mongolia induced in part by the enclosure of this area on virtually all sides by mountains.

A distinction should be drawn between the oases of deserts, including those within the Tarim Basin, and the oases located in the steppe. Adjacent to mountain ranges, such as along the northern margins of the T'ien Shan or Zungaria. The desert oases are isolated and self-contained in a geographic sense whereas the steppe oases are interconnected by easily traversed grasslands. Complementary trade developed between the sedentary and intensive agriculture found in both types of oases and the pastoral nomadism of the steppe. However, the steppe oases have had even more difficulty than their

desert counterparts in resisting the periodic conquests of nomadic steppe invaders.[3]

At the other extreme of elevation and relief, some of the geographic diversity of Inner Asia can be attributed either to landscapes below sea level or the existence of land areas which are close to possessing the attribute of perfect flatness. The best example of the former is the Turfan Depression at the northeastern edge of the Tarim Basin where the floor level is 505 feet below sea level.[4] The combination of topographic protection against extreme cold, the long and hot growing season and the existence of oases have made this depression a particularly fertile area of ancient settlement, renowned for its fruit, melons, and cotton.

On a different scale, the flat West Siberian Lowlands have the dubious distinction of possessing the most extensive swamps on the surface of the earth. They occupy most of the immense territory from the Vasyuganye Swamp, located between the Ob and Irtysh rivers, to the Arctic shores. One of the evident geographic anomalies is the existence of this massive, water-surplus area to the immediate north of the deserts of the Turanian Lowlands. Although the desirability of transferring West Siberian water to these deserts, which would partially recreate their geological past, has been apparent for centuries, the resolution of this problem, thus far, has even defied the technology of the twentieth century.

Paradoxically, the region of Inner Asia is sufficiently large to encompass both geographic diversity and uniformity on an impressive scale. The clearest manifestation of spatial homogeneity is the relative uniformity of the natural zonation of the environment along similar latitudinal bands. For example, journeys of six thousand miles could be made in a westerly direction from the Pacific coast without leaving the taiga. South of the forests, the steppe areas extend from Manchuria to the Hungarian Basin. Although regional variations are found in the nature of the grass cover of the sprawling steppe lands, the physical-geographic similarities of the areal subdivisions of the steppe are far more evident than their disparities.

With respect to terrain, the two most important examples of geographic uniformity in Inner Asia are the dominance of land with relatively gentle relief and the striking areal continuity of the mountain zone. The Russian Plain coalesces with the West Siberian and Turanian lowlands to form an immense

[3] Lattimore, 1940, p. 155–8. Often accompanying the conquests of steppe oases was the intrusion of pastoral nomadism to replace crop farming.

[4] Institute of Geography, 1969, vol. II, p. 4.

plain embracing most of the territory between the Carpathians in the west and the deeply dissected uplands bordering the Yenisey system in the east. By convention, the Ural Mountains are regarded as the boundary between European and Asiatic portions of this plain. However, the low elevations and ease of crossing the Urals make them only a modest physiographic interruption of the plains. To the east of Central Asia, an elongated zone of dry, elevated plains and plateaus stretches from the mountains bordering Chinese Turkestan on the west to the center of Manchuria and the Amur Basin on the Pacific coast and, also, passes through the tablelands in the southern and eastern parts of Mongolia. This belt of relatively low relief is broken by the ranges of the T'ien Shan and Altai Mountains, ribbons of mountainous terrain on the desert edges of the Mongolian Plateau and by the Greater Khingan Mountains which separate this plateau from the Manchurian lowlands.

The mountain zone of Inner Asia consists of a large number of mountain chains of diverse geological structure and age. Nonetheless, these mountains have a substantial degree of homogeneity with respect to geographic location. With some exceptions, the mountain ranges of this region are aligned in a sinuous and occasionally discontinuous band trending thousands of miles from the southwest to the northwest and reaching from the Caucasus and southern margins of Central Asia to the northeastern tip of Siberia with major mountain chains branching off this axis and penetrating deeply into Sinkiang, Mongolia, and Manchuria. The major exceptions to this striking geographic continuity are the Carpathians, which border the Hungarian Plains and the low-lying Urals, which resemble true mountains only in their northern extremities.

The highest elevations in the zone of mountains are found in the Pamir, "the roof of the world," where peaks of almost 25,000 feet are encountered. In a sense, many of the mountain ranges of Inner Asia are linked geographically, although not necessarily structurally, in the form of arcs spiralling outward from the Pamir core. Toward the west, an arc of mountain ranges includes the Caucasus Mountains, the Elburz south of the Caspian Sea, and the Central Asian borders of the Nebit-Dag and Hindukush. Maximum elevations in these mountains are between 10,000 and 18,900 feet. Although outside the study area, it might be noted that the Karakorum and Himalaya ranges also emanate from the Pamir core. Toward the east, a major band of mountains radiating from this core encompasses the towering Kunlun and Astyn-Tagh margins of the Tarim Basin, the Nan Shan edge of the Kansu Corridor, and the mountain borders of the Mongolian Plateau. The Pamir Mountains and their

Trans-Altai extension also are adjacent to the origin of the lofty and snow-capped ranges of the T'ien Shan which extend 1,100 miles into Sinkiang and attain maximum elevations in excess of 24,000 feet. The continuous zone of mountains extends from the Pamir–T'ien Shan interface toward the northeast in the form of smaller ranges separated by important corridors until the Altai Mountains are reached. The Altai ranges penetrate into western Mongolia and have maximum elevations of approximately 14,600 feet. Between the Altai and the Sayan Mountains, which form an arc between the western origins of the Altai and Lake Baikal, are the extensive Hangai ranges of Mongolia, with maximum elevations somewhat less than 13,000 feet, and the Tannu–Ola ranges directly south of the Sayans. The mountain zone is continued to the east through the ranges of the Trans-Baikal, Yablonovy, and Stanovoi Mountains until it veers toward the northeast and passes through the taiga and tundra until the shores of the Bering Straits are reached. Many mountain ranges branch off this Siberian axis and extend deeply into Mongolia, Manchuria and the southern part of the Russian Far East. Included in this category are the Kentei ranges of northern Mongolia, which is a southerly geographic extension of the Yablonovy Mountains and the mountainous borders of Manchuria. This region is separated from Mongolia by the relatively low Greater Khingan Mountains, which do not rise over 6,500 feet, and the even lower Jehol ranges impede access to the North Chinese Plain. The Lesser Khingan ranges enclose Manchuria from the north and the Sikhote–Alin and East Manchurian mountains block the Manchurian and Ussuri lowlands from the shores of the Pacific to the east. If it were not for the outlets provided by the Sungari River flowing to the Amur through the Lesser Khingan, the Liao Valley passage through the Greater Khingan ranges, and the narrow coastal lowland leading into northern China, the Manchurian steppe would have been far more isolated from neighboring lands than has been the case.

One of the most important manifestations of climatic uniformity in Inner Asia is the existence of an extensive zone of aridity occupied by deserts from the eastern shores of the Caspian Sea to the western edge of the Gobi desert. In many respects, this is a middle-latitude continuation of the massive area of Saharan and Middle Eastern deserts in which interior location and orographic barriers replace the dry trade winds of lower-latitude deserts as primary sources of aridity. Another type of geographic uniformity with respect to climate is the predominance of long winters which are either cold or bitterly cold throughout Inner Asia. Apart from Antarctica, the coldest average temperatures on earth have been recorded in northeastern Siberia. For

example, the mean January temperature at Verkhoyansk in this region is −59° F. and on some days the temperature dips to less than −100° F. Even in the Mongolian city of Ulan-Bator (Urga) far to the south, the mean January temperature is a frigid −17° F.[5] On similar latitudes, the average winter temperatures tend to increase toward the west and less severe winters are encountered in Central Asia and the European areas. For example, Alma-Ata and Odessa have mean January temperatures of 20° F. and 28° F. respectively.[6] Nonetheless, only the southern margins of Central Asia and the lowlands and littorals of the Caucasus have average January temperatures above freezing. As noted above, the combination of these cold winters and the warm or hot summers are described as the continentality effect, which is the most pervasive thermal characteristic of Inner Asia.

One of the lessons which can be drawn from the diminution of the territorial extent of the culture region of Inner Asia through the encroachment of sedentary civilizations and the ploughing of grasslands for crops is that the physical-geographic constraints on sedentary agriculture are neither precise nor immutable. Rather, the pattern of land use reflects the complex interaction of historical precedents, societal features, and the prevailing state of technology as well as the physical characteristics. With these admonitions in mind, some generalizations still might be made about the agricultural limitations of Inner Asia which might be ascribed to the dominant features of the natural environment. The most important physical-geographic impediments to the development of sedentary agriculture in this region are the inadequate supplies of water, the brevity of growing seasons, edaphic problems, and difficult terrain.

In the extensive deserts and most of the steppes of this region, the growing of crops has been confined to scattered oases because of the impossibility or impracticality of either rain-farming or an extensive expansion of irrigation networks. Historically, the frequently cited periodic incursions of crop agriculture into the steppe occurred primarily in the moister grasslands next to the Great Wall of China whereas most of the steppe lands were untouched by these changes until recent times. Another physical problem hindering agricultural development in the arid and semi-arid zones is wind erosion stemming from the frequent windstorms in the deserts and desert-steppes or from the strong, hot winds, known as Sukhovei, which emanate in the vicinity of the Caspian Sea and dessicate the steppe lands in their path. The widespread salinization of soils in the arid zone is an additional difficulty which has

[5] Murzaev, 1954, p. 237. [6] Wernstedt, 1972, vol. IV, pp. 283 and 288.

prevented the expansion of farming and also has been a persistent problem for oases agriculture.

The tundra and the taiga zones are even more inhospitable to sedentary agriculture than the dry areas to the south. Among the obstacles to farming in these bitterly cold regions are the short growing seasons, permanently frozen soils, and extensive swamps and marshes. These impediments to crop cultivation in these sparsely inhabited northerly areas have not been surmounted even in the present day.

By contrast to the interrelated problems of inadequate water supplies, soils which are salty, waterlogged, or frozen, and dry and cold climates, the agricultural problems posed by difficult terrain are relatively modest. As discussed above the positive role of mountains as elevated grazing lands and sources of water in the arid regions outweighs the negative aspects of mountainous terrain in restricting the areal extent of agricultural land and impeding trade. In many areas of Inner Asia with pronounced differences in relief, including the frozen northlands and the deserts, the terrain factor is the least of the problems confronting potential sedentary agriculture.

Conversely, the lands of Inner Asia have been far more suited for areally extensive forms of agriculture activity than for the intensive types of the adjacent sedentary civilizations. The dominance of pastoral nomadism in the rich grasslands and the forest zone equivalent of reindeer-herding and hunting reflect quite well the land-use constraints and opportunities derived from physical geography as well as from the technology, organization and values of Inner Asian societies.

The natural zones of Inner Asia

The most important type of physical-geographic regionalization in Inner Asia is the subdivision of this area into natural zones which can be regarded as large-scale ecological complexes embracing interrelated components of the physical environment. Although these zones are designated by their dominant form of natural vegetation, they represent integrated physical systems encompassing climatic factors, soils, and vegetation as well as certain aspects of water resources and terrain.[7] The controlling physical component of these zones is climate, which exercises a decisive effect on most of the other natural features. The central role of climate also is reflected in the virtually coterminuous boundaries of broad natural zones and those of the major

[7] The classic study of natural zones is Berg 1950.

climatic types distinguished by Koeppen and others in the most widely used system of climatic classification.[8] In many ways, the single most important climatic indicator of variations in natural zonation is the ratio of precipitation to evaporation or what might be termed effective moisture. A consideration of one of these elements without the other could be quite misleading. For example, four inches of precipitation in the tundra could lead to excessive moisture because of low evaporation whereas the same amount of precipitation can be encountered in the Gobi Desert where the intensity of solar radiation and evaporation is much higher. In general, the degree of effective moisture diminishes from north to south in broad bands corresponding, to a considerable degree, to the natural zones of Inner Asia.[9] In the northern, tundra margins of this region, actual precipitation is more than 50 percent greater than evaporation. At the other extreme, the precipitation in the desert zone is less than one-eighth of the potential rate of evaporation and even in the steppe, the precipitation–evaporation ratios are quite low. The boundary between the tall-grass steppe and the wooded steppe corresponds to an effective-moisture line indicating that precipitation is only 60 percent as great as the thermally induced rate of evaporation. This particular effective-moisture line stretches from the northern edges of the Ukrainian steppe to Lake Baikal and the northern fringe of the Manchurian Plain. Between this line and the southern boundaries of Inner Asia moisture problems are pervasive, although of varying types and intensity. North of this 60 percent effective-moisture line, thermal impediments to human activity are more restrictive than moisture constraints.[10]

Before discussing individual natural zones, mention should be made of four aspects of this physical-geographic regionalization of Inner Asia which make these zones less sharply defined than might be presumed from a cursory examination of their clearly distinguished cartographic delimitation. One of these features, the vertical zonation of landscapes in mountainous terrain, already has been treated. The others are: human modification of natural zones; natural boundary changes; and, the existence of distinctive natural regions and transitional types.

Because human activities in general have had a profound effect on natural landscapes, reflected in such changes as the clearing of forest, the ploughing of grasslands and wooded steppes, and the geographic redistribution of water resources, the determination of natural zones in many of the more populous

[8] Koeppen–Geiger 1930.
[9] The precipitation–evaporation ratios in this section are derived from Grigoriev–Rudyko, 1960. [10] Hooson, 1966, p. 38.

regions of the world can be derived more easily from historical evidence than from the present appearance of the landscapes. For example, the grasslands of the Hungarian Basin apparently represent an old man-made steppe which replaced an original cover of forests.[11] Despite certain exceptions, Inner Asia has been one of the most extensive areas of the world in which the human alteration of the natural environment has been only of modest importance. For the most part, the encroachment of large-scale and permanent dry

[11] Pounds, 1961.

farming on the moister steppe and wooded steppe margins of this region did not take place until the Nineteenth and Twentieth Centuries. To a remarkable extent, a large part of the tundra, forests, grasslands, and deserts of Inner Asia have retained their original character.

Another type of change in these zonal ecological complexes can be attributed to relatively short-term climatic fluctuations. The boundaries of climatic regions often migrate according to temporal variations in moisture and, to a lesser extent, thermal conditions. Corresponding alterations occur in the natural zones. Although by no means restricted to drier regions, these boundary changes are particularly evident in the semi-arid and arid zones of Inner Asia and reflect a climatological law which states that the annual variability of precipitation is inversely related to its magnitude. Thus, the low average amount of precipitation in the steppe and deserts is associated with sharp variations in effective moisture from year to year and with frequent shifts in the zonal boundaries but not in their core. In some cases, it is difficult to distinguish between naturally induced boundary shifts and those brought about by such activities as the removal of the natural vegetation cover by farming or the overgrazing of grasslands. It might also be noted that these climatic variations are short-term and often compensatory in nature. By no means do they lend credence to some of the earlier, imaginative theories which sought facile explanations for historical change in Inner Asia by reference to unsubstantiated, long-term climatic changes.[12]

A useful approach to the system of natural zonation in Inner Asia is to distinguish between distinctive zones and those which are transitional types separating the more clearly defined ecological complexes of the tundra, forest zone, steppe and desert. From north to south, the stunted vegetation cover of the tundra gives way gradually to the extensive coniferous forests of the taiga, which, in turn, is bordered on the south by belts of mixed and deciduous forests. The transitional area between the forests and the grasslands of the steppe is occupied by a band of wooded steppe. The intermittent tree cover of this zone diminishes toward the south and is replaced by the tall grasses of the steppe. In the drier borderlands of the steppe, the luxuriant grasslands are supplanted by the short and relatively sparse grasses of the transitional zone of desert steppe or, as it is sometimes termed, the semi-desert. Because of the bordering of the steppe on all sides by closely related transitional zones and the lack of precise or stable demarcations between zones, the term steppe is often applied, with considerable justification, to the area embracing all three

[12] An example of this approach is Huntington, 1917.

zonal types of steppe. The desert steppe gradually merges into a massive belt of Inner Asian deserts. Even within the desert zone a distinction can be made between the extremely arid or extra-arid deserts, such as the Takla-Makan, which often has no annual precipitation, and the somewhat moister deserts of Central Asia.[13] To be sure, internal variations occur within all the natural zones but rarely are they of a sufficient magnitude to disrupt the essential territorial uniformity of these zones.

Tundra[14]

The tundra is the northernmost natural region of Inner Asia and occupies the coastal plains and mountains bordering the Arctic Ocean from Lapland to the Bering Straits as well as the northeastern corner of Siberia down to the start of the Kamchatka Peninsula. For the most part, the tundra is an Arctic wasteland characterized by sparse and essentially treeless vegetation consisting primarily of perennial plants, such as moss, lichens, dwarf shrubs, and berry-carrying bushes. In some areas, midget birch trees are encountered. The tundra has a bitterly cold climate in which temperatures during the long winter may drop below − 100° F. The summers are short and cool with average July temperatures less than 60° F. Strong arctic winds often sweep across the unprotected tundra landscapes. Proximity to the cold currents of the Arctic also contributes to a high frequency of cloudiness and fogs over the adjacent land areas. Although the tundra receives relatively little precipitation, the minimal degree of evaporation has contributed to the waterlogging of their thin and permanently frozen soils, and, also, to the formation of an extremely deep and persistent snow cover in certain sections of this zone, particularly in the West Siberian tundra. The reindeer, which thrives on the sparse tundra vegetation, is the dominant animal of this zone and supplies an extraordinary variety of needs for the hardy peoples of this lightly settled region. Reindeer herding is supplemented by the hunting of such animals as fur-bearing foxes and lemmings.

The tundra zone exhibits the type of transitional changes characteristic of the system of natural regions. The barren Arctic tundra in the north gradually is replaced by a shrub tundra, dominated by thickets of shrubs, which in turn gives way to wooded tundra landscapes in which scattered taiga-type forests are found.

[13] Meigs, 1953, pp. 203–10.

[14] Much of the discussion of this region is based on: Berg 1950; Suslov 1961; Murzaev 1954 and 1958; Anuchin 1948; Wang 1961. In addition, two atlases were particularly useful: Hsieh 1973, and Academy of Sciences, 1974.

Forest zone

The coniferous forests of the taiga not only constitute the dominant natural feature of this zone but also form the most extensive tree cover in the world. The arboreal landscapes of the taiga extend in a continuous and gradually widening zone from Scandinavia to the Sea of Okhotsk, a distance of approximately 6,000 miles. In a north–south direction they stretch some 1,700 miles in their maximum width between the Arctic Circle and the Upper Amur Basin and Lake Baikal in the south. In addition, the mountainous taiga penetrates into the northern margins of Mongolia and Manchuria. In the enormous forest zone substantial regional variations occur in the dominant species of trees. Norway spruce, pine and fir trees predominate in the European parts whereas east of the Urals, the hardy Siberian and Dahurian larches, which are well-adapted to permanently frozen soil, are pre-eminent. To the immediate south of the taiga in the forest zone are found either mixed forest, as in European Russia and northeastern Manchuria, or relatively narrow bands of broadleaf deciduous trees characteristic of the Asiatic margins. One of the most striking biotic features of Siberia is the elongated belt of birch trees which separate the taiga from the wooded steppe over a distance in excess of 1,500 miles. Farther east, the prairies of the Manchurian Plain and the Ussuri Basin are insulated from the mountainous taiga by extensive borderlands of oak and birch forests as well as mixed coniferous–deciduous forest areas. Major differences on a regional and smaller scales also occur in the density of tree cover in the taiga and other parts of the forest zone. Large areas have only scattered forests or thin stands of trees which do not inhibit communication in contrast to some of the northern sections where a thick forest cover, rugged terrain, or waterlogged soils act as deterrents to local movement.

The taiga has a subarctic climate marked by long frigid winters with average January temperatures ranging from −40° F. at Yakutsk in the north to −14° F. at Chita in the south and brief, cool summers with a fairly uniform July average temperature of approximately 65° F. In general, this is a relatively moist area because low evaporation compensates for modest amounts of precipitation. The severity of the climate of the forest regions and tundra also has given rise to the development of the permafrost zone, which is an immense area of permanently frozen soils occupying a large part of the taiga. These soils consist of a thaw zone at the surface layers and an underlying rock-hard band of frozen soils which never thaw. Because of the drainage problems created by this frozen soil-horizon, the thaw zone becomes a veritable sea of mud during the summer which impedes overland transportation. In the

central and northern parts of the East Siberian taiga, major land routes are designated for primary use during the cold season. Conversely, the thawing of the extensive network of rivers during the warm period has led to their transport pre-eminence during this season. Fortunately, Western Siberia has only its northern margins in this frozen-soil zone and even in the lands east of the Yenisei where permafrost is predominant, substantial variations occur in its intensity. A continuous band of perpetually frozen land in the north gradually breaks up toward the south until the permafrost is found only in scattered islands surrounded by the thawed ground of the southern taiga. Even in areas devoid of constantly frozen land, however, the heavily leached podzolic soils, which pervade the entire taiga, are quite infertile.[15]

The forest zone can be divided into four major physiographic regions east of the Urals: the massive West Siberian Lowlands drained by the Ob–Irtysh system; the deeply dissected Central Siberian Uplands from the Yenisei River to the extensive basin of the Lena River as well as the mountainous southern borderlands of this region; the chains of snow-covered mountains dominating the landscapes east and southeast of the Lena; and the lowlands bordering the Pacific and Sea of Okhotsk which extend into the basins of the Amur–Ussuri River systems. As discussed above, these geographic sub-regions have been linked with one another by use of the east–west branches of north flowing Siberian rivers and the relatively short land divides which have been spanned for centuries by portage routes. However, the Siberian rivers are frozen at least one-half the year in their upper courses and nine months near their Arctic mouths. The blocking of their lower courses by ice for longer periods than the upper courses leads to extensive annual floodings.

Traditionally, the forest zone has been a region of reindeer herding and hunting. It is inhabited by many species of large animals, including elk, deer, bear and lynx as well as the renowned tigers in the southern margins of Siberia and Manchuria. However, the small, fur-bearing animals, such as sable, fox, ermine, marten and the ubiquitous squirrels were much more important in providing incentives for early Russian movement into this area.

Steppe zones

The steppe zones center on the grasslands or prairies of the typical steppe. To the north, the moister transitional zone of wooded steppe separates these

[15] The areas of deciduous trees and a large part of the mixed-forest zone have more fertile grey-brown podzolic soils which are less leached (i.e. their upper layers are less deprived of mineral nutrients) than the podzolic soils of the taiga.

grasslands from the continuous belts of deciduous trees or mixed forests and combines vegetative features of both zones. On the drier southern margins of the steppe, the short grasses of the desert steppe act as a biotic divide between the prairies and deserts of Inner Asia. Generally, the richness of the grass cover of the steppes increases directly with their distance from the deserts of Inner Asia. This generalization also extends to the altitudinal zonation of landscapes up to the start of mountain forests.

The wooded or forest steppe forms a contorted and narrow band extending from the northern Ukraine through northern Kazakhstan, to the southern margins of the West Siberian plains and Mongolia, where the intermingling of grass and deciduous trees occurs on the moderately elevated slopes of the Hangai and Kentei mountains and, to a lesser extent, the Altai Mountains. The Hungarian Basin also could be classified as a wooded steppe.

Virtually every characteristic of this zone indicates its intermediate position between forest and steppe zones. The typical landscape consists of meadow steppes, or mixed herbaceous steppes, and, originally, feather grasses interrupted by scattered stands of deciduous trees. The oak trees in the west are supplanted by birch and aspen groves in the east. Most of the wooded steppe landscapes have fertile degraded chernozem soils. The climate also has features of both the forest and steppe regions. The winters are cold and dry and the summers are moderately warm. The wooded steppe has higher evaporation rates than the adjacent forest areas and more precipitation than the steppe, which has led to a relatively low degree of effective moisture with average precipitation equal to 60 percent to 99 percent of evaporation rates.

The steppe region, as opposed to its transitional borderlands, is a distinctive ecological system which encompasses a broad belt of grasslands from the lands north of the Black Sea to the plains of Manchuria. In the western parts of Inner Asia, the major sub-regions of the steppe include the Ukraine, the northern Caucasus and southern Urals, and the immense Kazakh, or Kirgiz, steppe. The eastern steppes encompass the extensive grasslands in the eastern and central areas of Mongolia and the Manchurian prairies. In addition, the elevated steppes in the T'ien Shan and Altai borders of Zungaria also should be cited as should the lush valley of the Ili River.

The virtually continuous cover of grasses is the most distinguishing characteristic of the steppe. Although these grasslands vary in type and quality, a common feature is that they have provided an abundant and easily utilized fodder base for pastoral nomadism. The black-earth soil regions in the steppe typically are covered by tall pinnate feather grasses, fescue, and mixed grasses. In the drier southern portions of the steppe, different varieties of feather

grasses and other cereal grasses dominate the biotic structure. Very often, an area in the steppe will have a succession of different varieties of grasses from May to autumn providing a wide range of fodder opportunities.

In addition to its luxuriant grasses, the steppe is characterized by the fertility of its soils. Extremely rich chernozem or black-earth soils are found in a band from the Ukraine to the start of the Altai Mountains in Western Siberia. A substantial black-earth belt reappears in the heart of the Manchurian Lowlands in the east. The southern parts of the Ukrainian and Kazakh steppes have relatively fertile dark chestnut soils as do virtually all the grasslands of Mongolia. In the dry, southern margins of the steppe, light chestnut soils prevail.

The steppe climate is continental and semi-arid. Arctic air masses intrude into the steppe lands during the prolonged winter and bring average January temperatures down to a level ranging between − 10° F. and 10° F. over most of this zone. The European grasslands with average January temperatures of 20° F. are the warmest part of this region. The most severe steppe winters are in Mongolia because of its interior location, mountain borders, and the clear skies and freezing weather induced by the Mongolian high pressure belt. As mentioned above, Ulan Bator has a mean January temperature of − 17° F. and average monthly temperatures below freezing for six months (October–March). At Urumchi in the Zungarian steppe, January temperatures average 5° F. and at the Manchurian city of Harbin, this figure drops to − 4° F. At both sites, the average number of sub-freezing months is five. By contrast, summers in the steppe are universally warm with virtually the entire zone having an average July temperature in the range of 65°F. to 75°F., although the summers are longer in the European steppe than elsewhere in this zone. Special note should be made of the anomalous temperatures of Manchuria. In winter, taiga-type weather prevails as the cold winds from the seasonal Mongolian anticyclone blow over land to the Pacific. Conversely, warm and moist summers occur as the Pacific air masses move toward the adjacent lands. These summer monsoonal effects quickly dissipate toward the interior and most of the Mongolian and Sinkiang steppe lands have only moderate summer rainfall and most of this is of Atlantic origin.

The steppe is a moisture-deficient region with annual average precipitation between 10 inches and 20 inches. The European and Manchurian grasslands are at the upper level whereas most of the Mongolian and Sinkiang steppes are closer to the lower figure. In the steppe as a whole, precipitation is only 30 percent to 59 percent as great as the rate of evaporation. Fortunately, the moisture problem is not as serious as might be surmised from these data. The

western steppes are traversed by many major river systems with a dense network of tributaries. These include the Danube, Dnieper, Don, and Volga systems, among others, in the European parts. To the east, the Ob–Irtysh system drains the Kazakh steppe. Most of the eastern steppes are in the zone of interior drainage and only the Black Irtysh, the rivers of the northern edge of Mongolia, particularly the Orkhon and Selenga, and the Liao and Sungari tributaries of the Amur are linked to oceans. However, other hydrological compensations exist. The Zungarian steppe, which benefits somewhat from moist European air masses, has frequent, elongated steppe oases receiving their water from rivers flowing down from the adjacent northern slopes of the T'ien Shan. In the Mongolian grasslands, the water table is quite close to the surface and has been tapped for centuries. Finally, the moisture problems of the steppe pertain primarily to crop agriculture and not to the type of pastoral nomadism which has thrived in this zone.

In addition to its vegetative cover, the relatively gentle relief of most of the steppe lands also has contributed to the general ease of movement in the grasslands. Even the low-altitude steppe bands of mountains have been easily accessible. A major terrain distinction is the high elevation of the eastern section of the steppe, Although these elevated lands are virtually enclosed by mountain borders, local relief is relatively flat or gently rolling. For example, the Mongolian Plateau ascends steeply from the floor of adjacent plains and has an average elevation of 5,000 feet. However, most of its grasslands, excluding the mountainous steppe, extend over areas with only modest variations in relief.

On their dry borders toward the south, the prairies of the steppe merge into the intermittent short-grass meadows of the desert steppe, or semi-desert, which is the natural transition from steppe to desert. The desert steppe zone starts north of the Caspian Sea and occupies a broad band through the plains of Sinkiang, Kansu, and the southern and northwestern regions of Mongolia. In Central Asia, this zone separates the steppe from the Turanian deserts whereas in the east it divides the underlying Gobi desert and its extensions from the Mongolian grasslands. Feathergrass meadows and sagebrush (wormwood) predominate in the desert steppes on a soil cover of the light chestnut type. The climate is continental but the summers are a little warmer than the steppe, as can be seen in July temperature averages of 75° F. to 80° F., and the winters are somewhat less severe or prolonged. Yearly precipitation is between six to ten inches, which amounts to only 13 percent to 29 percent of the evaporation rate. This places the desert steppe region into the arid category. Although the famed Kansu Corridor, a structural depression less

than 50 miles wide and over 600 miles long, is located between parallel mountain ranges in this dry zone, it is occupied by a series of productive oases deriving their water primarily from the neighboring Nan Shan Mountains. This enchanced the role of this corridor as a major routeway through arid lands. At its drier margins, the desert steppe is difficult to distinguish from the true desert which is comparable to the problem of separating the moister desert steppe from the adjacent grasslands of the steppe. The three regions of the steppe support a variety of fauna. By far the most important, however, are the domesticated animals of the pastoral nomads. The horses of the steppe, of course, are world renowned and in the deserts and such desert-steppe areas as the Kansu Corridor, the breeding of Bactrian camels has been important. The grazing of cattle, sheep and goats has been particularly well suited to the natural conditions of the steppe zone.

Desert zone

A massive zone of deserts occupies most of the southern portions of Inner Asia from the Caspian Sea to the eastern edges of the Gobi and Ordos deserts in Mongolia. The Central Asian portion of this desert zone is dominated by the Turanian lowland which encompasses the extensive sand dunes of the Karakum and the stabilized sands and stoney floors of the Kyzylkum. The densely vegetated alluvial plain of the Amu Darya separates these two major deserts and the band of deciduous forests along the Syr Darya performs a similar role between the Kyzylkum and the sandy Muyunkum to the north-west. This belt of aridity extends to the desolate Betpak-Dala upland west of Lake Balkhash and to the sandy expanses of the Sary-Ishikotrau Desert south of the lake. At the western end of Central Asia, the Ustyurt Plateau rises steeply from the western shores of the Aral Sea and eastern margins of the Kara-Bogaz-Gol inlet of the Caspian Sea and is even more barren than the adjacent Karakum Desert.

Less than four inches of precipitation annually are received in the core of the Karakum and Kyzylkum deserts, east and south of the Aral Sea. However, some of the outer margins of the Central Asia desert zone receive as much as 8 inches of precipitation annually, with a spring maximum. But even this is only about 15 percent of evaporation rates. The general aridity of Central Asia has led to the appearance of saline and highly alkaline soils. However, grey desert soils, which can be made fertile with irrigation are much more common. Fortunately, the best soils in Central Asia are found in the oases at the foot of the mountains in the south and in the alluvial plains of major rivers. The fertile

oases have developed primarily on the loessial piedmont plains drained by the Syr Darya, including the Fergana Basin and Tashkent oases, the Amu Darya, and the Zerafshan, which flows through the Samarkand and Bukhara oases. In addition, the alluvial soils of the delta of the Amu Darya have supported human occupance at the delta of the Khorezm oasis since antiquity. The Central Asian rivers have a double flow maxima with the first occurring in spring, based on rainfall peaks and lower-slope snows melting, and the second occurring in mid-summer when mountain glaciers thaw. The oases are surrounded by sparsely vegetated deserts in which shrubs and semi-shrubs predominate.

Pronounced seasonal and diurnal variations in temperature characterize these middle-latitude Central Asian deserts. However, the winters generally are short and, in the southern margins, have only one or two months in which the average temperatures are below freezing. Summers are hot with mean July temperatures over 85° F. in the south. On individual days, temperatures rise as high as 120° F.

After a mountainous interruption, the desert zone continues toward the east in two bands, separated by the T'ien Shan and its adjacent desert steppe. These bands converge at the eastern outlet of the Tarim Basin and extend eastwards in a continuous series of deserts, of which the Gobi in the southern part of the Mongolian Plateau is the most prominent. These high-altitude, middle-latitude deserts are characterized by their pervasive aridity, cold winters, and hot summers as well as by striking differences in temperatures between daylight hours and the desert nights in all seasons. Although a complex mixture of desert types is common, generally, the surface of these deserts is covered by sand in the west, stone and gravel in the central Gobi regions, and by sands and gravels in the eastern deserts of the Ala Shan and Ordos.

The Taklamakan Desert occupies the center of the enclosed Tarim Basin and contains migrating sand dunes (barkhans) with heights occasionally reaching 300 feet to 400 feet. This enormous zone of sands is virtually devoid of vegetation except for the dense "tugay" vegetation along the Tarim River and its tributaries which empty into the Lobnor lake. Because of its remoteness from oceans and the surrounding orographic barriers to the movement of maritime air masses, the Taklamakan Desert is one of the driest regions on earth. It receives less than two inches of precipitation a year and in many years, no precipitation at all. By contrast, the southern and northern edges of this desert contain a stepping-stone series of fertile oases bordering the Kunlun and Astyn Tag, the Pamir, and T'ien Shan inner mountainous edges of

the Tarim Basin. In the south and west, these include the oases of Kashgar, Yarkand, Khotan, Keriya and others located on intermittent tributaries of the Tarim River. Smaller oases, such as Kucha and Aksu, border the southern slopes of the T'ien Shan at the northern boundary of the basin. A less extensive sand and gravel desert is found between the T'ien Shan and Altai Mountains in the heart of the Zungarian Basin and is separated from both mountain ranges by grasslands.

The transition between the sandy deserts and the stone-gravel types is in the desolate Pei Shan desert, just outside the Tarim Basin. This waterless desert as well as adjacent desert areas, including the western margins of the Kansu Corridor, have a shiny black pebble surface which has given rise to the name of Black Gobi for these barren desert lands. Among other problems, this area also has frequent and strong windstorms, particularly in intermediate seasons.

Despite sandy dunes which cover a small part of its surface, the seemingly boundless desert plains of the Mongolian Gobi, which receives less than four inches of precipitation a year, essentially have stone and gravel surfaces resulting in a desert pavement. To a considerable extent, the underlying sands and silt have been removed by wind erosion and, apparently, deposited as loessial foothills to the south of the Great Wall of China. The surface of the Gobi exhibits substantial variations in terrain patterns. Typically, these lands are divided into broad basins separated by relatively low mountains and hills. These basins, in turn, have many relatively shallow, undrained hollows in which intermittent lakes, or playas, are formed. Certain parts of the Gobi have neither vegetation nor soil whereas other sections have saksaul shrubs and grass patches.

Toward the south, the Gobi merges into the Ala Shan Desert, north of the Kansu Corridor, and the Ordos Desert, located in the bend of the Yellow River north of the Great Wall. The western part of the Ala Shan is referred to as the Little Gobi and consists of extensive sand and gravel surfaces with scanty vegetation. In its eastern margins, sand dunes with shrub vegetation predominate. The Ordos Desert is a vast, virtually unbroken, expanse of stabilized sands and dunes largely bare of vegetation. Some dried-up lake beds in this desert form depressions (*tsaidam*) with a sparse grass cover.

In discussing the physical-geographic differences and similarities of the arid and semi-arid natural zones located on opposite sides of the mountainous divide from the Pamir to the Altai, the feasibility of movement and interaction across these mountains also should be emphasized. Despite their imposing elevations and relief patterns, major corridors of movement through them

exist and have been used intensively. The desert and oasis routes through the Tarim Basin are continued from Kashgar through the mighty Pamir by way of the high Terek Pass and the broad and winding valleys of the Pamir until the productive Fergana Basin is reached. A more northerly route through Kulja traverses the rich grasslands of the Ili River, flowing through parallel ranges of the T'ien Shan, and connects Lake Balkhash with the long and important route through the Kansu Corridor, the Turfan Depression, and Urumchi. An even more important variant of this route uses Urumchi as a way-station for movement passing through the famed valley of the Zungarian Gates, which lies between the Zungarian Ala-Tau extension of the T'ien Shan and the Barlyk Maili ranges. The Zungarian Gates open into the Semirechye region and the massive grasslands of Kazakhstan. This historic pass has strong local winds emanating in the vicinity of the eastern approaches around Lake Ebi-Nor which are sufficiently warm in winter to melt the ground snows.

Between the Barlyk Maili and the Altai Mountains are located two additional intermontane corridors. One of these is the Chuguchak (Tacheng) route bordered on the north by the Tarbagatay ranges. A more heavily used route to the northeast traverses the grasslands along the southern slopes of the Altai and the valley of the Black Irtysh in a wide avenue to Lake Zaisan and ultimately to the steppes of Kazakhstan and Western Siberia. Generally, north–south movement among different natural zones in Inner Asia either encounters few natural obstacles or when such problems as difficult terrain intervene, solutions comparable to those discussed above for east–west communication have been obtained without great difficulty.

3

Inner Asia at the dawn of history

The end of the 19th and the beginning of the 20th centuries brought to light exceedingly important discoveries by archeologists on the continent of Asia. For the first time Asia appeared to the students of the distant past as a land where complex events had occurred which were related to the beginnings of the human race and where cultures, frequently high cultures, had come into being, displaced each other, and left profound imprints on world history.

The countries in which these discoveries were made are lands related to the general concept of the Far and Near East: India, Mesopotamia, Palestine, in the west; and China, Japan, parts of Korea, Indochina, and the Malayan Archipelago in the east.

All that lay deeper within Asia, to the north and east of China and India, however, in one way or another remained outside the image of world history during its earliest stages as viewed by the majority of scholars and people in general.

History, it would seem, had actually halted before the high barriers of the mountain ranges, these grandiose mountainous structures and the lands which partitioned off the world of the high agricultural cultures of the Near and Far East as known to European scholarship. Actually, however, beyond these frontiers there existed a world of history which, although unknown, was just as great.

Even a desultory glance at a physical map of the continent of Asia allows a graphic view of this frontier, allows us to sense and realize its grandiose dimensions, hence to conceive its very real effect on the course of the historical development of those who during antiquity lived here behind these natural and historical barriers in the very depths of the continent. These barriers were, most important and to the south, the Himalayan ranges with the highest peak in the world, Gaurishankar or Everest, which separate Inner Asia from India and the Indian Ocean with its monsoons, warmth, and abundant summer precipitations.

But there are other barriers beside those in the south. These extend along the frontiers of Inner Asia to the west. No less impressive, no less majestic, are the mountain massifs of the Pamirs and the T'ien Shan ranges which separate Inner Asia from the vast steppes of Turan: Soviet Central Asia, from the steppes of Kazakhstan, the deserts of Turkmenia, and the steppes of the Volga.

To the north this natural barrier is formed, in the western part of the continent, by the mountain peaks of the Sayan–Altai system; in the east by the Vitim–Patomsk uplands.

Within the boundaries of this orographic system Inner Asia appears against a background of the rest of the planet as an enclosed unit with its own characteristic terrains and peculiar flora and fauna. This is no lowland, however, but a land raised high above sea level, a terrain characterized by a dry, and in winter rather severe continental climate. This is the land of forestless steppes and countless mountain ranges and hills which alternate with deep depressions within which are found lakes, large and often saline.

Further to the north, beyond the Sayans, extends the taiga, a boundless sea of forests; further on – the forest tundra, and beyond this, finally, on the very shores of the Arctic Seas, the tundra which extends from the Bering Straits to the Kola Peninsula.

To the extreme east, beginning in the upper reaches of the Amur, the Ussurian taiga extends in the direction of the Great Wall of China. It is here that we find broad-leaved forests with their flora and fauna which combine elements from both north and south, and here that the tiger hunts the reindeer and the wild grape and the lianas of the magnolia vine twine about the trunks and branches of the blue Jeddo spruce. This, altogether, is Inner Asia.

It would seem to go without saying, one might almost say it would be a priori, that these lands on the Asian continent would be of special interest to the historian from the standpoint of the interaction between man and nature. The peculiarities of natural conditions there would of necessity have left their mark on the course of historical development, on the nature of cultural creativity, and on man's struggle for existence.

Nor would the manner in which the interaction of local peoples and the environment took place be of less importance. This interaction would certainly be far from uninteresting to anyone interested in the course of the world historical process during antiquity. Suffice it to recall the upheaval that brought about the eruption of the Huns into Europe, or the dramatic events connected with the eruption of Chinggis Khan's forces into that selfsame Europe seven centuries later.

Nor should it be without interest to world history that the fates of such enormous and widespread linguistic families and ethnic groups as the Tunguz, Mongols, Turks, or the Finno–Ugrians, and Paleoasiatics are connected with Inner Asia. And, again from the standpoint of world history, it is not unnatural that one of the most important problems related to Inner Asia's past has been that of its place in the origin of man and man's first conquest of the planet.

As we know, proceeding on the assumption that the evolution of the ape-ancestors of man who first led a forest life must have taken place in terrain where there occurred a gradual change from forest conditions: tropical or subtropical forest to open terrain, during the 19th and the beginning of the 20th century many outstanding scholars believed that the most favorable conditions for this existed at the end of the Tertiary and the beginning of the Quaternary in Inner Asia. Theories, grandiose as regards space and time, were subsequently developed concerning the rise of the human race in Inner Asia and its later emigration thence to the rest of the world: the contemporary ecumenes.[1]

Even at the beginning of the 20th century, however, expectations of sensational discoveries concerning the ancestors of man in Inner Asia had given way to equally great disappointments and pessimism caused by the failures in the search for paleolithic man and his culture by an expedition as great as the Central Asiatic Expedition led by Roy Chapman Andrews which, like the Sino–Swedish Expedition led by Sven Hedin, failed to find such remains in Mongolia.[2] Unusually interesting finds in the neighboring regions of China beginning with the Sinanthropus, the Lantian man, and ending with the discovery of a Lower Pleistocene or Middle Pleistocene culture at Kekhe, only increased pessimism as to prospects of finding aboriginal man and his culture in Inner Asia. The same was true of Japan where during the two previous decades not only had an ancient pre-ceramic culture been unexpectedly discovered, but monuments such as the Hosino, Nyui, and the cave of Fukui, which were forty or perhaps even sixty-thousand years old and far exceeded anything yet found in Siberia or Mongolia.

The factor which decisively altered these concepts was the exploration of the Soviet–Mongol Paleolithic Expedition which was carried on over a period of several years (1949, 1960–70) by the Academy of Sciences of the U.S.S.R. and the Academy of Sciences of the Mongolian People's Republic. During this period new, important data were obtained by Soviet archeologists in the north

[1] V.E. Larichev, 1969. [2] J. Marunger, 1950, A.P. Okladnikov, 1951.

of Asia, in Siberia, and in the Far East.[3] At the present time Soviet science is in possession of two data which are of fundamental importance concerning the ancient history of this part of the continent of Asia, data which permit a deeper penetration into the past of Inner Asia, back to a period which may be called the epoch of the Lower and Middle Paleolithic.

The first such datum is the existence in Mongolia of exceedingly ancient sites, archaic in appearance and containing typical flint artifacts. One such site is located twenty kilometers to the west of the city of Sain-Shand on the road to Mandakh Somon.

A second site containing similar flint workings was found on the road from Mandakh Somon to Saikhan Dulan and Undurshil. Both sites, as well as several others between Sain-Shand and Burun-Urt and Dalan-Dzadagada in Southern Mongolia (southern Gobi) are connected with a specific geological situation which proves their great antiquity. The flints which have been worked by man are scattered over the surfaces of terrace-like spurs of hills which consist of flint rock which shows great abrasion and their composition shows that they are not local but were transported from a great distance by powerful fluvial currents the existence of which in these arid regions is out of the question. It is to be presumed that the formation of these strata of flints goes back to periods during which there occurred energetic thawing of massifs of ice and snow which had formed during a maximum glaciation in the mountainous regions of Asia, i.e. during some interglacial period.

In these flint deposits there are found many quartzitic flints of a yellow or whitish hue which are exceedingly hard and durable. When chipped, even with a minimum expenditure of labor, they would produce a sharp cutting edge with which man might do his work: chopping, cleaving, cutting, and chipping.

The flint was used here in its original, natural state and without special chipping. Frequently it was simply split along the smooth surface by a powerful blow and left in that condition. A single, massive, sharp working edge, without further processing, satisfied the toolmaker. Occasionally the edge would be re-worked on one side by several blows thus producing a chopper or axe-like tool the handle of which would be the opposite unworked smooth surface of the flint. Thus primitive flint tools were produced. Also worthy of note is a group of instruments of the chopping-tool type, made of the same flint but struck from both sides, the remainder of the surface remaining untouched.

[3] A.P. Okladnikov, 1949, 1964a, 1964b, 1970. *Istorija Sibiri* I, 1968.

Special variants of these flint tools are chopping tools or choppers of flint with a cutting point in place of a transverse cutting edge. These are no longer merely choppers; they are "proto-adzes".

One characteristic feature of these flint workings in Mongolia is a total absence of flaking and the almost complete absence of chippings, a factor which sharply distinguishes them from the Paleolithic of Europe and Africa where flakings and flaked tools are as a rule found alongside the large flint objects or pieces of rock where the flakings, not the flint itself from which they were struck, were the tools and the object of the toolmaker's work. We find a similar situation in Western Mongolia where, at several locations, especially in the vicinity of Kobdo and Mankhan-Somon, on terraces along the courses of mountain streams and brooks, there are found extensive fields of worked flints among which there are scattered comparatively recent, lightly-flaked flint artifacts as well as tools which are clearly of an earlier origin. Characteristic of the latter is a peculiar, thick, yellowish or brownish patina with the distinct, often oily, luster of struck flint. Outstanding here are typical chopping tools with transverse cutting edges produced by broad, heavy cleavages.

The Paleolithic flint tools of Mongolia are not an isolated phenomenon nor are they in any way unique. Paleolithic tools, choppers and chopping tools are well known in neighboring Siberia, in Central Asia, and in the Soviet Far East, as well as in China, Burma, the Near East, Europe, and Africa. It was H.L. Movius who first posed the problem of flint workings being characteristic of the Lower and Middle Paleolithic over a certain broad area of Eastern Asia.[4] In the west and south–west of Asia, beginning with India (the Madras workings and adze culture), and also in Java, according to Movius, the bifacial hand adze culture was predominant in Lower Paleolithic techniques. Movius also assumed that the area of flint tools, choppers, and chopping instruments existed in the Punjab, in Burma, and extended further to the east in Asia.

However at the time that Movius was propounding his theory vast regions of Asia were still little studied or not studied at all archeologically and this included the Paleolithic. With the accumulation of new data, new facts and problems appeared which substantially altered the nature of things. A new, more complex, and richer picture came into view of the ancient cultures of Central and Northern Asia and of their mutual relations with the ancient cultures of other countries, including the Near East, Europe, and Africa.

The first such fact is the existence, among the most ancient monuments of

[4] H.L. Movius, 1944.

human culture on the continent of Africa, of an ancient flint industry as well as an industry in which materials other than flint were used, various kinds of rock, in the famous Oldoway pit in Tanganyika. Here were found choppers and chopping tools. Actually, this type of proto-adze was discovered in the lower stratum of the Oldoway. Crude flint tools discovered in the high terraces of the river Vaal, which are the same type of South African proto-adzes, are similar to these. Similar artifacts were discovered under faultless geomorphological and stratigraphical conditions by László Vértes at Vértesszöllő near Budapest along with fauna of the Upper Bikharien (Mindel) and the skeletal remains of Archanthropus-Hungaricus Pithecanthropus. Chronologically approximating these are the stone tools and the Heidelberg jawbones of Germany from the strata of the Mauern period. It is quite possible that the flint tools from Romania, collected by Nicolaescu-Plopşor, also belong to this same chronological group. In Asia, flint tools from both Cambodia and Vietnam are of ancient origin.

Proceeding to Siberia, we must first of all make mention of two sites: Ulalinka and Kyzyl-Ozek, which are located in the immediate vicinity of each other on the river Mayme, a tributary of the Katun', near Gorno-Altaisk. Both sites have interesting and indicative (in the sense of determination of geological age) homogeneous stratigraphy. The stratum with which they are connected is divided into two individual strata, the upper consisting of loess-like loam. Throughout the entire territory of Southern Siberia Upper Paleolithic settlements which are geologically dated as belonging to the Sartan glacial period and have been dated by radio carbon tests as being 21–10 thousand years old, are connected with these loams. These are underlayed by a thick stratum of glacial loam which geologists have determined as Lower Pleistocene (O.M. Adamenko), or early Middle Pleistocene (perhaps Riss Würm, or early Würm according to Western terminology), i.e. not younger than 100–150 thousand years. In this stratum there occur innumerable chipped flints of yellow quartzite which were used to make stone tools. The latter are represented by peculiar "tablets" or "lobes" which were formed by chipping the flints into two halves along their length, typical choppers and chopping tools, "proto-adzes," massive scrapers made of these lobes, and curious instruments with projections or "bills" and indentations on the cutting edges. There are also cores of an unusual type which are flat and have a bevelled surface with a flint incrustation at the end opposite the striking edge.[5]

The next group of ancient flint-culture sites in Siberia is in the Far East and

[5] A.P. Okladnikov, 1969b. O.M. Adamenko 1970, pp. 57–62.

is represented by the well-known site at Ust'-Tu and another on the river Zeya. Both sites underlie heavy strata of porous deposits and are the outcroppings of ancient flint deposits, buried sandbars or alluvia from the tributaries of the Zeya. A similar series of ancient sites is to be found on the Amur near the village of Kumara and at the tributary of the Lower Amur, the Amgun', where the geological situation is identical with that at Filimoshki and at Ust'-Tu on the Zeya.[6]

The Ulalin settlement-workshop which has been studied most thoroughly by geologists in cooperation with archeologists places this series of ancient flint artifacts chronologically. They go back, or at least the oldest monuments do, to the end of the Lower Pleistocene or the Middle Pleistocene.

Evidence of this early date is the fact that at Ulalinka the stratum which contains flint tools corresponds in age with strata in China which contain the earliest man-made stone objects. Both are earlier than the loess formations; both are pre-loess. The same is true of the sites on the Amur where later deposits of sandy loam and argillaceous soil (which corresponds to the loess of other parts of Asia) overlay the strata containing the flint workings. It would be quite safe to similarly date the earliest flint instruments of Mongolia, i.e. sites in the east of the MPR, in the areas of Sain-Shand and Mandakh-Somon.

The second data of prime importance to an understanding of the historical processes which took place during the Lower Paleolithic in Inner Asia are the finds at Yarkh Mountain on the road from Mandakh-Somon to Undurshil. Yarkh Mountain, the mention of which is tabu, is, with its cupola-like peak of limestone, visible from afar. On the anticline of this mountain, near the rocky cupola, there was discovered an occurrence of stone artifacts which included tools of white quartzite and flint. These were found lying on the surface of the ground and are of the Paleolithic or Neolithic type. At approximately four kilometers from Yarkh Mountain innumerable chips and pieces of yellow jasper which had been worked by men of the Stone Age were found. Here there had once been an enormous workshop where pieces of yellow flint rock, taken from the surface or quarried from the vein outcroppings, had been used.

Essentially, the remnants of the stone tool workings consist of the first semi-finished materials which as a rule retain a porous, generally irregular lumpy crust which was removed by a series of blows from one or both sides. There are many chippings which retain this nodular crust on their surface. Some do not have it. Flakings are comparatively rare. The best of these are of a triangular form, have a more or less convex striking platform, and two, less

[6] A.P. Okladnikov, 1959c, 1964a,b, 1969d.

frequently three, planes along the reverse side. Found among these semi-finished tools are cores, occasionally large ones, with characteristic beveled edges along their axes. These are all single-edged, the flakes and chippings being removed from one side only. Such cores might be classified as proto-Levalloisian as they do not yet exhibit the regular methods for forming cores which are characteristic of the Levallois.

Of greatest importance are the many semi-finished, bifaced tools which have been struck from both sides. In form these are typically Acheulean, Abbevillian hand cutters. They are usually oval, less commonly cordiform or triangular. As a rule these bifaces were formed by broad cleavages from the ends. The cutting edges are undulating or of zig-zag form. The majority of them are large, massive; some, however, are small and delicate. These objects might be called hand tools. The discovery of this workshop in which Acheulean bifaces were produced was the greatest surprise in all my years of fieldwork in Mongolia.

As mentioned, it has generally been supposed that flint tools and the corresponding techniques of stone working were predominant in Eastern Asia. Here, however, in the very heart of the continent, was an obvious site of Acheulean bifacial tools and, judging from the form of these tools, probably belonged to the Middle Acheulean period. Nor do the proto-Levalloisian forms of the cores, characteristic of a still immature Levalloisian technique, contradict this dating.

Here mention should be made of the fact that this site, with its clearly expressed features of Acheulean workings which are also found in Europe, the Caucasus, India, and Africa, is the first and only one of its kind to have been found in Eastern Asia. Certainly, however, the finds at Yarkh Mountain cannot, because of the express Acheulean techniques and forms of the cutters, be compared in any way with the unique tools which are bifacial quite by chance, from Northern China and Korea (Dintsun, Kekhe, Kulpho).

Thus a new problem arises concerning the development of the ancient techniques of stoneworking and the ancient technological and cultural traditions in the east and north of the continent of Asia. At the present time this problem may be formulated in the following way. It is highly probable that during the Lower Paleolithic two different cultural-technical traditions existed here at the level of development of Archanthropus-pre-Neanderthal man. The first of these, which is most clearly expressed by finds at the settlements of the Ulalinka and Kyzil-Ozek type in the High Altai, was a flint tradition, indigenous to these regions. As we shall later see, it also existed here much later, during the Upper Paleolithic.

The second tradition, which may be called Acheulean, is evidently genetically related to those regions of the Ancient World where there occurred a development in ancient times of this type of bifacial toolmaking (Abbevillian-Acheulean). Most probably this culture was brought into the heart of Asia, by a group of Archanthropes who moved from west to east during an interglacial period (a period most favorable for this sort of movement), probably during pre-Riss times, the Mindel-Riss.

Quite naturally, another problem arises in connection with the new finds: the problem relating to the Lower Paleolithic past of Inner Asia. This has to do with possible routes over which the Acheuleans of Yarkh Mountain penetrated into the east from the west. The first thing that strikes our attention when looking at a geomorphological map of Asia is, of course, the high mountain barrier of the Himalayas which separates the spaces of Inner Asia from the nearest regions where are found, in the Lower Paleolithic, cutters of the Abbevillian (Chellean) and Acheulean type.

These regions are, first, India and the Punjab, then the Indonesian Archipelago with its Javanese tools of the Patjitan type. The rare finds of primitive tools in Japan (Gongeniyama, Ivaidzuku) may be an offshoot of this western type of cutter culture or, in the given instance Patjitan; but these unique objects are not typical as to form and contrast greatly with the monuments of classical flint tools such as Niyu in Japan. Nor are there to be found genuine bifacial tools in the other ancient monuments such as Hosino and the Fukui caves, as is well known from the publications of Seridzawa. As we know, in the lowest strata of these monuments the basic material used in toolmaking was not fluvial or marine pebbles, but flaked pieces of flint rock. No bifaced cutters are to be found there. Nor could the Caucasus with its frequent tools of this type (Ossetia, Armenia, Georgia) have been the place from which Eastern Mongolia obtained the cutters found at Yarkh Mountain. The absence of genuine Acheulean cutters in Central Asia, where artifacts of the Acheulean type, or approximating this type, are found only in the area around Mangishlak or, rarely, in the vicinity of Krasnovodsk, (i.e. in the immediate vicinity of the Caucasus and Trans-Caucasia), speaks against such an hypothesis.[7] The bearers of the Acheulean culture did not, evidently, penetrate further north or east where the flint techniques of the Ulalinka type, indigenous to Northern Asia and its inner regions, must have predominated.

Concerning the regions immediately joining the Himalayas and taking into consideration the distance, as the crow flies, from there to Mongolia, which is

[7] I.N. Klapchuk, 1970, pp. 217–26. A.G. Medoedov, 1970, pp. 200–16. N.K. Anisjutkin–S.N. Astakhov, 1970, pp. 27–33. A.P. Okladnikov 1966; V.A. Ranov, 1970, pp. 17–26.

not great, we must consider two factors. First, that at that time the mountains may have been lower, and second, that the people of the cutter culture might have overcome the obstacles through the mountain passes and valleys during interglacial periods when the climate in the mountains was less severe than now and passages leading to the north were not blocked by ice massifs.

This group of western emigrants, one is led to believe, wandered, if not through totally uninhabited regions, at least through sparsely-settled territories which were abundant in game. The natives of these enormous spaces would certainly have been groups of peoples who employed the indigenous Asiatic flint techniques, the same peoples who left traces of their activities in the High Altai at Ulalinka and still further to the east in the Amur Basin, at Filimoshki, Kumary, and at Ust'-Tu.

Consequently, what occurred was not an emigration of large and compact masses of ancient peoples, but a sort of disorderly and elemental displacement of the "atoms" of aboriginal communities, of human hordes, which followed the hunt. Each had its own peculiar technical traditions inherited from the ancestors; some, as already mentioned, with the traditions of the East Asian flint techniques, others, and this was rare and exceptional, the Abbevillian or Acheulean traditions. The correlations between these two traditions which so greatly differed determines a basic outline of the entire historical picture which we are now able to restore from the very real data at our disposal which, although disparate, is indicative.

The next great stage in the history of Inner Asia was the Middle Paleolithic, that period during which in the Occident: Europe and the Near East, the cultures of the Mousterian type were passing through their cycle of development.

That the territory of Mongolia was inhabited by men who employed a purely Mousterian method of working stone, using the same principles as in Europe, is born out by the widely distributed, although few, objects of the Mousterian type: disk-like cores and typical flakes of elongated, triangular form, and occasionally scrapers of the Mousterian type with their characteristic sharp, tapering, fractured working edges. Such objects have been found on the high terraces of a now dry river bed in the southern Gobi at the foot of one of the highest mountains of the Gobi Altai, Ikh Bogdo, at Bogd-Somon. They have also been found in the far east of Mongolia, in the area between Sain-Shand and Barun-Urt, near Delgerekh Somon. Everywhere here, under milder climatic conditions than now obtain, there must have wandered sparse, mobile groups of Mousterians, the hunters of steppe game. The conditions under which their remains have been found near Delgerekh Somon show that

their favorite camping grounds were the southern slopes of rocky protuberances from which they could observe the surrounding country, broad valleys between mountains, and the great craters of now-extinct volcanoes. It was not only the herds of game which attracted to these parts the Mousterians, who in physical appearance were probably similar to the Neanderthal man of Central Asia and Palestine, but the deposits of workable stone. This stone which they highly valued was, in addition to various types of siliceous igneous rock, an excellent white flint which is now covered with a lovely bluish patina.

The Middle Paleolithic peoples of Inner Asia achieved their highest culture probably somewhat later, as is evidenced by a series of rich finds in the south of the Mongolian Peoples' Republic, in the southern Gobi, and in the west at the foot of the Mongol Altai. These finds are of an unusual nature and are connected with the geological structure of the Gobi Altai mountains where, in several locations, there are outcroppings of thick strata of silicified rock which includes high quality jasper-type rock suitable for stone toolmaking. It was from this yellow and waxy-red jasper-type rock that the people of the Middle Paleolithic in the south of Mongolia made their tools. At several locations at the eastern extremity of the Artsa-Bogdo mountains, where they turn abruptly to the south, workshops have been found where stone raw material was worked by men of the Middle Paleolithic. Occasionally the Stone Age toolmakers settled directly over the veins which cut through the rocky massif. This was the case, for instance, at Suji, where at the outcroppings of excellent yellow jasper there have been found many chippings and semi-worked tools of this stone which remained from the preliminary "rough" working of flints. The worked stone "blocks", the cores, were taken away to be used as required, although a few still remain at the site. These are cores of a very definite Middle Paleolithic form. Outstanding among these is one which had been left behind, probably because its size made it difficult to transport (it is approximately thirty centimeters in diameter). In form it is a marvelous bifaced core-disk, typically Mousterian, which has been flaked from the edges to the center on both sides.

Frequently the ancient toolmakers of the southern Gobi who worked at the foot of the Artsa-Bogdo did not find their materials at the foot of the mountains or in the deep and narrow ravines, but much further below, on the gently sloping surfaces of the piedmont deposits which descend to the lowlands, and on the terraces along the dry riverbeds, the *sairs*. Evidently this is to be explained by the fact that the people of the Paleolithic collected their material for making tools (red jasper) in the alluvial fans of the beds of mountain streams but did not break them off directly from the outcroppings

as did the workers in the valley of the Suji. This is probably because when red jasper is transported and washed it becomes more durable and is free of the clefts which marred the rock which was found in the outcroppings. Actually, the people of the Paleolithic did exactly the same as their contemporaries, the toolworkers of the Stone Age, who gathered their flints in the valleys of the Orkhon and Tola. This material, washed by the river, was handy and of better quality and its durability had been tested by nature herself. These worked cores of red, less frequently yellow, jasper-like rock are found scattered over an enormous area of approximately a hundred square kilometers in the Artsa-Bogdo mountains. They cover an area of approximately ten kilometers in the mountains themselves and some ten or fifteen kilometers to the side. Individual "clusters" of these are found in the lowlands in the vicinity of what are now the high lakes and nearby wells, e.g. at Tugrik-shiret and other localities from the Artsa-Bogdo mountains to Bulgan Somon. Thus there was located here in the mountains of Artsa-Bogdo a large production center in which ancient man processed stone raw materials and to which, over the millenia, Paleolithic man came to obtain the stone which he prized.

Another locality which contains workshops of this type is to be found on the boundaries of Mongolia and China, eastward from the Gobi Altai, at the border-outpost of Ottson-Mant. The outpost sites are situated in a wide valley near springs of pure, fresh water, surrounded by picturesque buttes of granite which bring to mind the ruins of an ancient city with its towers and walls. Paleolithic man came here, as to the mountains of Artsa-Bogdo, not so much in search of the wild game which pastured and drank in this vicinity, as to obtain the stone raw materials which he so highly valued. The source of these materials was a thick vein of black volcanic rock which had at one time interrupted a stratum of granite, then been released by arid weathering. At present this vein emerges on the level floor of the valley in the shape of a sharp ridge, five or six meters high, which is visible from afar. Beside it in the sand are hundreds of bits of rock which have been worked by man. Such accumulations of stone workings are to be found in at least six other localities where ancient artisans maintained their camps. At all these sites the material is the same. All artifacts were prepared from the same black silica shale which crops out in veins from a granite stratum on the floor of a hollow. Typologically they are also alike.

The stone tools at all six sites near Ottson-Mant consist of cores, chippings, and flakings. The cores are typically Levalloisian, and are usually triangular with single or double surfaces and one or, more rarely, two, cleaved surfaces. The working side of the cores, the cleaved surface, is usually convex and has

facets, "negatives", of chippings used for flakings or chippings. The striking surfaces of the cores are beveled and rectified by retouching. Some of the cores are practically rectangular. The flakings and chippings correspond in form to the cores and are elongated-triangular with three facets on the back and a comparatively large striking platform. Occasionally scrapers are found with a sharp Mousterian retouch and points of the Mousterian type, retouched on one side.

To evaluate in the fullest degree the importance of these finds in relation to the history of Inner Asia, we must take into consideration the fact that the appearance of this technique, which was more perfect than the previous flint techniques or even that of the Mousterian culture, indicates enormous progress, and progress not only in the strictly technical sense.

The Levalloisian core, before it was actually used, not only underwent elaborate processing, but had an overall different form. It was designated to have long, narrow chippings and flakings removed from it, not broad, triangular ones as formerly. So accurate were the profiles of these flakes that each might be used as a knife or arrowhead without further rectification. The possibility of producing these accurate flakings depended upon several factors connected with the progressive physical development of man himself and the workings of his mind. The strokes on the cores had now become bolder and more accurate and better-aimed. This shows evolution of man's wrist in the direction of flexibility and maneuverability. An evolution of labor and of the hand developed simultaneously with the evolution of man's mental powers. Both the cores and the flakings are indicators of a far-reaching development of the powers of understanding of the human mind, of a clearer recognition of the task which the worker set himself. In short, this is evidence of a far reaching, progressive, process of sapientization in man, the surmounting of the original animal elements in him, and the attainment of new, purely human traits and qualities as well as new laws, not only biological, but social.

Here mention should be made of an attitude which has become commonplace: that a certain fatal backwardness and stagnation are peculiar to the history of the culture of innermost Asia. Such a concept, at the sight of the crude and primitive tools of Sinanthropus, arose in the mind of so bold and clear a thinker as André Breil. But millenia separate Sinanthropus from the people of the Middle Paleolithic. The existence of the progressive Levalloisian as the basis for the techniques of the peoples of Inner Asia during the Middle Paleolithic is an express proof of the fact that there was no absolute standstill or stagnation in the evolution of techniques of toolmaking nor, consequently, of man.

Nor, during the Paleolithic, were the inhabitants of this part of Asia totally isolated from other parts of Asia. We may judge this from the broadly-dispersed Levalloisian techniques as well as from the existence of hand choppers of the Acheulean type. Purely Levalloisian stone tools which might be called classic models have been found in the Altai at the Ust'-Kansk caves on the Charysh and Strashnaya rivers (in the Tigerek mountains).[8]

The common source of the Levalloisian techniques in Mongolia and Siberia must have been the Levallois-Mousterian culture of Central Asia (upper strata of the Teshik-Tash and the Khojikent caves in Tashkent),[9] which, in turn, were probably genetically connected with the Levallois-Mousterian of Iran (the Bisitun cave), and the Mediterranean (the Levallois-Mousterian cave on Mt. Carmel).[10] Everywhere here there are found the same methods of stone chipping and the same Levalloisian cores and narrow, well-proportioned flakings of elongated, triangular form. Thus at the end of the Riss-Würm and the beginning of the Würm of European classification, i.e. 100–40 thousand years ago, Inner Asia saw the rise and flourish of the Middle Paleolithic culture.

The history of this culture during the subsequent Paleolithic period within the territory of Central Asia and in Mongolia is most clearly revealed by the materials from the famous multistratified settlement of Moltyn-Am (Birdcherry Hollow) in the valley of the river Orkhon opposite the ruins of the capital of the Mongol khans, Karakorum, and the ancient monastery of Erdeni Juu.[11] Here the Upper Paleolithic begins with conditions of predominantly Levalloisian techniques. Nor are these techniques less clearly expressed in the abundant materials from the Upper Paleolithic settlements in the valley of the Tola, for example in the lower strata of the bistratified settlement of Zaisan-Tologoi on the northern slope of Mt. Bogdo-uul, or at Sangino on the opposite, right bank of the Tola sixty kilometers below Ulan Bator. The lower stratum at Sangino produced a good collection of Levalloisian cores with both single and double surfaces. Judging from finds in the valley of the Katun', at Biysk, the Upper Paleolithic tribes of the Altai also chipped their flints by purely Levalloisian methods. They also possessed the same types of cores and flakes as the toolmakers of Bird Cherry Hollow on the Orkhon.

The Levalloisian tradition is also distinctly expressed in Siberia and to the east of Baikal in the Trans-Baikal region. No less indicative than the Altai

[8] S.I. Rudenko, 1960.

[9] A.P. Okladnikov, 1949, 1961, pp. 68–76, A.P. Okladnikov–A.P. Derevjanko, 1968, 1969, p. 114. [10] C.S. Coon, 1951. D.A. Garrod–D.M. Bate, 1937.

[11] A.P. Okladnikov–S.L. Troickij, 1967, pp. 4–23.

finds are the Upper Paleolithic settlements beyond Baikal in the valley of the river Uda: the multistratified settlements of Sanny Mys and Khotogoi-Khabsagai, where there have been discovered (at Sanny Mys) typical Levalloisian cores and the flakings that correspond with them along with the bones of a rhinoceros and a curved-horned antelope. The Trans-Baikal, Levalloisian-type finds from the valley of the Uda river and the Selenga (e.g. at Nyangi and Fofanovo) are geographically and culturally a direct continuation of the Upper Paleolithic of the Tola and the Orkhon valley. Traveling down these rivers which later form the Selenga, the bearers of the Levalloisian culture of the Upper Paleolithic of Inner Asia were very early able to reach the shores of Lake Baikal and even penetrated further westward, to Pre-Baikal. Proof of this are the typical Levalloisian cores from Mal'ta (basic lower horizon of this settlement) and from settlements of the Verkholenskaya Gora type on the Angara. Levalloisian techniques are also clearly represented at one location on the river Ingoda: at the Titovskaya mound near Chita.[12]

One outstanding phenomenon having to do with the history of Inner Asia is the fact that during the Upper Paleolithic, against the background of the general predominance of the Levalloisian tradition, there appears yet another technological trend, that of an ancient flint technique indigenous to Asia, found now in more perfect, one might say refined, forms. In the Upper Paleolithic settlements of Mongolia (Moltyn-am on the Orkhon, at the estuary of the Tuin-Gol river near lake Orok-Nor, settlements along the Tola river near Ulan Bator and Nalaikha) flint weapons are being increasingly found: choppers and flint scrapers.[13] Monuments also exist, possible specialized workshops, for example the site on the left bank of the Tola which is forty kilometers below Ulan Bator at the Altan-Bulak Somon, or on the cliff at the airport of that city, or at the promontory two kilometers above the village of Kharakhorin on the Orkhon river where there are found "pure" flint tools (semi-finished tools of various sorts as well as flint cores and choppers).

Thus we may conclude that the flint techniques of toolmaking did not irrevocably disappear, but continued to exist in retreats or refuges of sorts, and not for dozens of millenia, but for many hundreds. It is most probable that these refuges were located somewhere in the north where the bearers of the southern Levalloisian traditions did not, for long, penetrate.

Quite exceptional because of their singularity against the background of Levalloisian and flint traditions in Inner Asia are the two Angara Paleolithic settlements of Mal'ta and Buret' which contain stone implements of an

[12] A.P. Okladnikov–I.I. Kirillov, 1968, pp. 111–114.

[13] M.M. Gerasimov, 1958. A.P. Okladnikov, 1962, pp. 169–75. A.P. Okladnikov, 1965b.

expressly occidental type. These are neither chipped flints nor large Levalloisian flakings, but tiny flaked instruments which consist of flakes struck from actual cores which were prismatic. They include small end scrapers and curved cutting blades and drills which are characteristic of those found at Mezina in the Ukraine and in the Hamburg and Arensburg cultures of North Germany. There also exist here indicative examples of flakings with lateral depressions which are exact replicas of Aurignacian prototypes in the west. One tends to believe that the culture of Mal'ta and Buret' developed from an original Aurignacian starting point in the far west, then, after several millenia, continued to steadily maintain the traditions inherited from the Upper Paleolithic of the west in a new location and during later times (the absolute age of Mal'ta is fourteen thousand years, i.e. the Magdalenian period.)

On the banks of the Angara these immigrants from the west continued to live the life of their ancestors. They constructed durable winter dwellings from the bones of the mammoth and rhinoceros, ethnographically similar to those of the Eskimos; they hunted these animals and also the reindeer with spears having large points made of mammoth tusk or deer horn. In the dwellings of Mal'ta and Buret' there have been preserved rich collections of artistic bone carvings which include a large group of sculpted female figures which are basically the same as the Aurignacian statuettes of Eastern and Western Europe; like them, they are magnificent nude mother-figures. Local variations exist, however, which are peculiar to a local school and distinguish them from the European figures, e.g. they are not faceless, but have elaborately carved physiognomies. Beside the nude figures there are those with clothing. The clothing is sewn and consists of a sort of double skin coverall which tightly envelopes the body and a hood which covers the head. The most perfect figure of this type and the one with the most detailed dress comes from excavations made at Buret' in 1936. An unusual feature of the Angara Paleolithic bone carvings are peculiar statuettes which portray flying birds with short wings which are probably loons or geese.[14]

During the Upper Paleolithic of Siberia there existed not only small, portable, art forms, but monumental cliff drawings. These have been preserved on the high cliffs in the valley of the Upper Lena between Kachug and Verkholensk where realistic figures of wild horses of almost natural size have been traced in broad stripes with red paint. There are also two smaller

[14] A.P. Okladnikov, 1959c.

drawings (each about a meter in length) which represent a wild horses and a bull or bison.

Mention should also be made of the amazing cave frescoes in the Mankhan-Somon region of Western Mongolia which are found in the Khoit-Tsenker cave on the bank of the river of the same name. In the depths of this cave, in the eternal semidarkness, are found innumerable drawings in color which portray antelopes, mountain goats and sheep, a horse, a camel, a pelican, strange birds which resemble ostriches, and massive animals with trunks and tusks, obviously elephants or perhaps mammoths or *namadici*.

In the Khoit-Tsenker cave the same dark red, brownish, or pale red, almost rose-colored paint also portrays the partial representations of animal heads, the antlers of a deer, most probably a *maral* [a Siberian stag], and symbols in the form of trees, arrowshafts or darts, and a snake. These drawings often overlay and intersect each other and appear almost like a palimpsest. Both because of its explicit animalism (there is not a single human figure nor anything even remotely resembling a man) and because of its obvious character of magic of the hunt, this art of the ancient peoples of Western Mongolia points toward an intimate link with the art of the painted Paleolithic caves of Western Europe. The symbols themselves are also reminiscent of the Paleolithic cave paintings of the West. The same symbols are found in the famous caves of France and Spain: Liasco, Altamira, and Castillo. No less characteristic of Western Paleolithic art is the "transparence" or "palimpsest-like" overlay of certain figures upon each other, the purpose of which was magic, and the repetition of the same rites of the hunt on the same sacred spot. The stylization of the murals at Khoit-Tsenker, the line drawings, the restrained, dry treatment of the animal figures, the lack of movement and frozen poses – all correspond to the Paleolithic of the West, more specifically to the Aurignacian.

The cave paintings at Khoit-Tsenker, the cliff drawings at Shishkino (the oldest in Northern Asia), and the drawings in the Shakhty grotto in the Pamirs, prove that the art of cave painting was not an inheritance from the West alone, but that, beside the Mal'ta–Buret' nidus of small or portable art, Innermost Asia had, during the Upper Paleolithic, its own home of monumental art which included cave art. In accordance with the finds in the Khoit-Tsenker cave, this nidus may be called Central Asiatic; nor is it inferior, from the standpoint of artistic value, aesthetics, and perhaps even antiquity, to the early Aurignacian art of Western Europe.[15]

[15] A.P. Okladnikov, 1966d, pp. 96–104.

In many ways the culture of the Upper Paleolithic in the Far East, on the Amur, and along the littoral, developed independently. One of the most ancient Stone Age monuments in the littoral is a settlement-workshop in the Suifun basin at the village of Osinovka near Ussuriysk. In an overlayed crust of erosion, in a stratum of brown-red clay formed during an interglacial period, possibly before the maximal glacial period in the Sikhote-Alin' mountains, i.e. approximately forty thousand years ago, there have been preserved types of work platforms where Stone Age toolmakers worked. From nodules of whitish-grey volcanic tuff they made strange and unusual instruments which combine the characteristics of cores similar to the Levalloisian cores with the characteristics of chopping instruments. It would seem that flint and Levalloisian techniques were combined when working on the same tool. Similar finds have been made in other localities of the littoral: on the river Mo near lake Khanko, and at the Ilyushknia mound in the city of Ussuriysk. And, most interesting of all, on the Middle Amur, near the village of Bibikov above Blagoveshchensk, something quite similar has been found.[16]

The same process of development of the Stone Age culture, based on the flint technique, is to be seen in new finds from the littoral, cave finds, from a cave called the Cave of the Geographic Society near the city of Nakhodka at the estuary of the Suchan river. Together with the bones of a cave hyena and a wild horse, there were found large chippings formed by the characteristic method of cleaving the flints by transverse blows directly along the flint surface, the surface itself remaining unworked. Also found were the cores, flints, from which these were chipped. The finds in the Cave of the Geographic Society, the ages of which are probably of the glacial period, i.e. somewhat younger than the interglacial Osinovka (35–25 thousand years), are worthy of note as they indicate the routes along which the mammoth and, following him, primeval man, penetrated to Sakhalin and Hokkaido over the land bridge which during the glacial age connected the littoral with the islands of Japan and the continent of America.

The end of the Paleolithic in Northern Asia is indicated by two very widely disseminated elements of Paleolithic or Mesolithic tools.

The first of these is foliated blades worked on both sides by surface retouching of the "Solutrean figure." These blades were first found on the Angara at the village of Verkholenskaya Gora and in the Ushkanka Depression. They have also been found in Mongolia, in the latest Paleolithic settlements on the Orkhon in the locality of Birdcherry Hollow. The same

[16] A.P. Okladnikov, 1959.

type of blade has also been found in the Dyuktai Cave in the valley of the river Aldan. They show an element characteristic of the Late Paleolithic settlements of Japan which were contemporary with the Magdalenian of the West, their age being 17–12 thousand years. It would follow that similar blades found in the littoral in the upper stratum of the settlement-workshop on the river Tadush near the village of Ustinovka would be of the same age.[17] At Ustinovka, as well as in the Dyuktai Cave and at Verkholenskaya Gora, these foliated bifacial retouched blades are accompanied by cores which are called "Gobi cores" although they were probably not cores at all, but scrapers or cutters. In the strata of Birdcherry Hollow these tools are characteristic of the final stages of this unique coremaking in the Paleolithic deposits in the valley of the Orkhon. A settlement is also known on Mt. Khere-uul in the valley of the Khalkhin Gol in Mongolia where these Gobi cores comprise the greater part of the stone tools.

Consequently, there occurred a peculiar integration of cultures during the final stage of the Paleolithic or Mesolithic from Yakutia to Eastern Mongolia. The phenomenon was more widespread, as pointed out by Nelson according to whom the Gobi cores comprise the connecting link between the pre-ceramic cultures of Alaska and of Central Asia. It is perhaps not by chance that during this same period, i.e. approximately ten or eleven thousand years ago, the Folsom culture of wandering hunters was spreading, the most characteristic features of which were these points worked by retouch on both sides.

It is highly probable that at the end of the Paleolithic not only Inner Asia, but also America, participated in these movements to which these characteristic items, so unusual for Europe, testify.

The recent period in the history of the culture of Inner Asia begins with an enormous crisis in nature. Between 10 and 13 millenia ago the final stage of the glacial period came to an end. In Northern Asia (where this period has been studied more completely than in Central Asia) the taiga emerges on a massive scale over the former steppes and tundra which extended from the British Isles to the Bering Straits. The last of the mammoths still lived in the Taimyr Peninsula (the age of the Taimyr mammoths is eleven thousand years), but their days were numbered as were those of other representatives of the mammoth fauna with whom the first inhabitants of Siberia, the people of the Upper Paleolithic, were connected. The people of Mal'ta, Buret', and Afontova Gora belonged to the glacial period.

[17] A.P. Okladnikov, 1966, pp. 352–72.

The Holocene begins, and with it the emergence of new fauna: the roe, elk, and red deer. The slowly-oncoming changes in conditions of life and the change from an arctic climate to the contemporary one created a crisis in the ancient way of life of the hunters of mammoth and reindeer which is effectively portrayed at Mal'ta and Buret'. The culture created by the Mal'ta people disappeared, including their marvelous realistic art. Their first architecture perished, and light, temporary structures, tents or wigwams, covered with skins or bark now take the place of the durable semi-subterranean Paleolithic houses of the people of Mal'ta and Buret'. But we see not only decline in the life of the aboriginal Siberians during this truly great crisis. Actually, the life of the Siberian tribes moved forward steadily in the direction of new forms which found their expression in the way of life of the mature Neolithic, in a new culture created by the descendants of the Paleolithic peoples.

The great crisis of the Holocene provided a powerful impetus toward the search for new forms of life and toward the energetic creation of a new culture, especially as regards the material culture, economy, and techniques. The changes in the techniques of toolmaking reflect, of course, only partially and indirectly, the overall shifts in the life of the ancient tribes during the transition from the Paleolithic to the more advanced stages of their history. Nevertheless, they are very real indicators which show the scope of these changes. Such, for instance, is the general changeover from the techniques of the Upper Paleolithic to those of the new Mesolithic in Europe and the Near East which are expressed in the widely disseminated and specific techniques of making microlithic tools of geometrical form: segments, trapezia, and triangles. This change took place against a background of still deeper and more far-reaching changes in the economy. A primitive agriculture was born and the entire economic and existential structure of life was reorganized.

Things were quite different in Northern and Central Asia where there were no microlithic tools of geometric form. The wave of geometrization halted at the Urals in the north and at the Syr Darya in the south.

In the Altai and in Siberia archaic flint, and obsolete Levalloisian techniques continued side by side.

The basic material for toolmaking continued to be river flint which was struck lengthwise or transversely, then chipped at one end, to produce a series of sharp, cutting tools which could successfully chop a tree, dismember the carcass of a slaughtered animal, cut hides, and sew them into garments. Such tools have been found at the station of Ust'-Seminsk in the valley of the river Katun' in the Altai together with bifacial, retouched miniature arrowheads!

In Mongolia and on the Yenisei flint tools, choppers and chopping tools, as well as flint cores, continued in their stable, unchangeable form in many localities until the very end of the Neolithic. Such a locality is one of the settlements at the "Truba" on the Yenisei. The finds at the famous Biryusinskaya camp are also related and the excavations by G.P. Sosnovsky, N.K. Auerbach, and V.I. Gromov at the latter location established something quite unexpected: the flint choppers and characteristic crescent-shaped scrapers were used by the peoples of this multi-stratified settlement from beginning to end. The strata which contained these crude, massive tools were directly overlaid by a stratum which contained the remnants of a mature Neolithic culture. These observations have been corroborated by the recent work of N.N. Gurina, who found on the Biryus the identical picture of stability of the Paleolithic culture in all its stages until the rise of the Neolithic. The flint tools, especially the scrapers, are of a definitely archaic coloration at multi-stratified settlements of the early Holocene in the Baikal region as well as at the settlement at the estuary of the Belaya river near Irkutsk, and the large stone tools found here are not basically different from the Late Pleistocene scrapers or choppers from the Yenisei which are dated as early Pleistocene and are approximately 20–12 thousand years old.

The ancient Levalloisian chipping techniques, the classic forms of which are found in neighboring Central Asia, continued as persistently in the Altai and are well represented in the pre-ceramic settlements of the Selenga and the Altai, and, finally, at the multi-stratified settlement at the estuary of the Belaya, the latter being representative of the Baikal region. This is understandable, as the Levalloisian core, which was basically the same flint, produced, even during the Paleolithic, large, broad flakes: knives and points, which could be used without preliminary processing or retouching. Nevertheless, the extent of change was considerable and included many vitally important aspects of the activities of the peoples of Northern and Central Asia. In order to conquer the taiga, the forest steppes, and the new, no longer Arctic, steppes, innumerable innovations were essential.

The first of these was the bow and arrow and also pottery. These are the basic elements of the overall Neolithic culture as we know them throughout the entire region inhabited by man on our planet during the Neolithic stage of cultural development.

Of no less importance, as an overall characteristic of the course of historical development, is the fact that now, under different conditions of terrain and geography, there came into being different economic and living conditions which were compounded by purely ethnographic peculiarities, not directly

dependent upon natural circumstances, which definitely determined the features of the great cultural-ethnographical fields or provinces which arose during the Neolithic. Even at the Mesolithic level, during the Early Holocene, we find the beginnings of future local variations in the cultures of individual groups among the peoples of Inner Asia which are the forerunners of future peculiarities in the realm of ethnoculture. In the Altai, for instance, at the excavations near the Kugom landmark, there has been detected a special kind of technique of stoneworking. Whereas at the Paleolithic settlements such as the famous camp at the village of Srostka the basic technique was a flint technique in which large scrapers and blades predominate, here, with the passing of time, chipping and flaking techniques assumed increasing importance. Large flint tools became the exception and the general trend of development is expressed by the fact that flakings and small tools made from these flakings dominate absolutely. Even the small flint tools become increasingly smaller, more and more miniature. The same would seem to be true of neighboring Kazakhstan as shown by the excavations of S.S. Chernikov in one of the caves at Semipalatinsk on the Irtysh (the "Peshchery" campground). It is by no means impossible that in these two variations of the development of stoneworking techniques there is to be seen a single continuity with two cultures of the Upper Paleolithic which had different origins. One of these may be termed the Mal'ta–Buret' culture, the other the Afontov culture.

The progressive microlithization of the stone tools, the appearance of the first miniature arrowheads, and the unexpected emergence of actual bows and arrows (no longer simply javelins), show the transition from the old, Paleolithic, to the new, Neolithic culture. Development was quite similar in Kazakhstan and in Western Mongolia.

In Western Mongolia there has been discovered still another pre-ceramic culture characterized not only by light stone tools of the round scraper type, but also by tools formed by the characteristic serrate technique. These have sharp teeth or projections and the corresponding depressions on the blades. This same technique was later to be developed in the South-Gobi during the early Neolithic.

Finally, two other characteristic variations of the maturation of the new culture, two genetically different traditions, are to be found in the Far East. The first of these is represented by the extremely rich complex of artifacts from the famous bistratified settlement-workshop on the Tadush river near the (littoral) village of Ustinovka. Here we find two types of cores and core-like tools. The first type is Levalloisian and certainly goes back to the Levalloisian Paleolithic of Inner Asia. The second type are the original Gobi-

(or as they are otherwise called in the terminology of B.E. Petri, "wedge-shaped cores" and core-scrapers). The culture of the peoples of the pre-ceramic settlement at Ustinovka is intimately connected with the late pre-ceramic cultures of the islands of Japan where radio-carbon tests have determined an exceedingly ancient age (17–14 thousand years). No less important is its connection with the pre-ceramic culture in the valley of Khalkhin Gol (the settlement on the Khere uul mountain). The Gobi cores connect this with the Trans-Baikal region as well as with Alaska. The third characteristic of the Ustinovka tools and culture are the flaked cutters with long edges which are worked with light retouch, although the cleavage is made diagonally along the long axis of the flaking, obliquely. These cutters have been named after Araya in Japan where they were first found and described.

The second variant of the Mesolithic of the Far East is represented by a group of settlements on the Amur at Khabarovsk (at the settlement above the railway line at Sakachi-Alyan), and on the Ussuri (Venykovo). Here the most common forms of stone tools are the bifacial, retouched objects of flint which are in the form of cutting tools with serrated blades worked not by polishing, but by retouch only. Also characteristic of these tools are bifacial, retouched wedges which are mostly foliate and amygdaloid in form and are in many ways reminiscent of the wedges from the upper horizon at Ustinovka. Occasionally hefts are found, among them tools of flat flint one end of which has been transformed by retouch, on one or both sides, into sharp blades. Also found here are flaked knives retouched at one end and Gobi cores.

The ancient culture of Kamchatka also developed in its own peculiar way. Remains have been discovered at the multi-stratified settlement on the Ushakov Lake where the strata of the various cultures are separated by inter-stratifications of volcanic ash. The lowest stratum (the sixth) of this settlement was deposited at a time when the forestless, bush-moss tundra predominated, i.e. earlier than ten thousand years ago. (The radio carbon date of the fifth stratum is B.P. 10360 ± 345.) At that time the inhabitants of Kamchatka used Gobi cores extensively and also made bifacial retouched wedges of darts which had hefts, similar to those used by the Paleo-Indian tribes of North America. As far back as the Mesolithic there were contacts between the peoples of the Old and the New Worlds, most probably by way of the Aleutian Islands.

The diversity in the development of cultures of the ancient peoples of Inner Asia is expressed even more fully during the Neolithic. It was, in all certainty, during this period that the great local cultures of Inner Asia developed. These

may be subdivided, with more or less certainty, into lesser local variants.

During the Neolithic the forest belt of European Russia which extends from the Urals to the Baltic Sea was inhabited by tribes of hunters and fishermen. The most characteristic features of their material culture were sharp-bottomed clay vessels entirely, or almost entirely, covered with horizontal rows of depressions frequently inlaid with fossil belemnites. These "comblike" impressions, so characteristic of these vessels, were made with a multi-serrated stamp or comb.

In sharp contrast to the culture of the Comb-Marked Pottery was another culture of Central Eurasia which has been called the Kelteminar culture, prevalent in the Aral region from the lower reaches of the Amu Darya, where it was discovered by S.P. Tolstov, to regions as distant as the lower reaches of the Zerafshan and beyond in northern Kazakhstan.[18] Its earliest monuments date from the fourth millenium; its later monuments from the beginning of the second millenium B.C. The people of this culture, the Kelteminars, hunted the giraffe, wild horse, and wild boar which inhabited the taiga thickets along the rivers and lakeshores. They fished for pike, carp, and sheatfish, not only with harpoons, but with nets. Fishing provided a comparatively stable and sedentary way of life. At Janbas-kal there was discovered a house, ovaloid in form and of an area of 270 square meters, which contained a large hearth in the center, possibly a sacred hearth where burned the sacred flame. Ordinary hearths, those used by families, were constructed in several rows on the periphery. The dwelling had a framework of wooden posts and beams, covered by a light reed roof. At the settlement of Darbazykyr in the lower reaches of the Zerafshan remnants have been found of a four-cornered dwelling of 81 square meters. Here the hearths for cooking were constructed on the outside of the dwelling. The Kelteminar people, like the Neolithic tribes of Eastern Europe, used vessels with round bottoms although the latter were more varied as concerns composition and were somewhat different in form. They include elongated, semi-ovoid and semi-spheroid vessels, low, wide cups, and dishes in the form of a boat. The most characteristic feature of the Kelteminar pottery is its ornamentation, which consists of wavy-striated parallel lines which were applied with a moving stick. Such ornamentation indicates connections with the neighbors of the Kelteminars, agricultural tribes who used clay vessels painted with identical undulating lines (the settlements of Jeitun, Namazga-depe, and Kara-depe in Turkmenistan). Some

[18] S.P. Tolstov, 1948, pp. 59–66. Ja.G. Guljamov, C. Islamov, A. Askarov, 1966.

vessels of the Kelteminars show traces of having been covered with paint or yellow ochre on their surfaces.

Contacts with the agricultural south are also evident from the stone tools of this people. Large polished tools, axes or adzes, are rare. Most of the stone tools consist of flakings struck from superbly cut prismatic cores. Arrowheads with serrated edges were made from the flakings. The scrapers, drills, and chip axes with alternate indentations are identical to those from the early Neolithic strata of the Jebel cave on the shores of the Caspian in Turkmenistan and the purely agricultural settlements of the Jeitun culture. Here, however, not a single segment has been discovered and only several trapezia, the latter from excavated materials.

The Kelteminar culture was, as it were, a transmitter of cultural elements to the further north, in the direction of the Urals. There, along the shores of the many lakes and rivers lived the people of the Shigir culture who, like the Kelteminars, were hunters and fishermen but were forest dwellers. Indicative of the material culture of the Shigir tribes is an archeological stratum which links it with the Neolithic of the Comb-Marked Pottery and contains sheathed bone daggers with flint blades, needles and awl-like points of bone, some with curious biconical or spindle-like heads. Ceramic vessels are identical in form to those of the Comb-Marked Pottery although their ornamentation is, both from the standpoint of ornamental structure and the presence of undulating lines, pure Kelteminar.

To the east of the Urals there begins a series of other, purely Siberian, Neolithic forest cultures. Beginning with the Ural range in the west, the first of these extended as far as the Yenisei. Here the people were semi-sedentary or sedentary tribes of fishermen and hunters of the western Siberian taiga.[19] In winter they constructed durable semi-underground dugouts which were joined together and fortified into settlements where entire tribes lived. Inside these dwellings are found round-bottomed vessels similar in form and design to the Comb-Marked Pottery of the forest belt of European Russia and decorated with the stylized figures of flying ducks. Undulating lines drawn with a stick were the most popular design and, like the ducks, indicated water. Similar designs have been preserved on the inscribed cliffs of the Urals and in Western Siberia. Worthy of note is the fact that these ornamental motifs and the mythological concepts expressed in them coincide with the art and mythology of the Finno-Ugrian tribes of Eastern Europe and Western Siberia.

[19] V.N. Chernecov, 1953.

Here also, among the primordial elements of Finno-Ugrian culture are found signs of the highly-developed cult of the bear which is represented in the Neolithic of Western Siberia by sculptures unusual in their realism. From ancient times the bear occupied an outstanding position in the art and mythology and religious practices of the Finno-Ugrians. It was connected with the supreme deity, hence enjoyed highest honors in the cult. It would follow that the Neolithic region of Western Siberia was that region where the eastern branch of the Finno-Ugrians originated, more concretely the ancestors of the Ob-Ugrians (Ostiaks and Voguls) and the Hungarians, their western relatives, who later branched off from them.

Still another great cultural-ethnic region which we may call the Pre-Baikalic or Baikalic[20] extended eastward from the right bank of the Yenisei. From materials found in burial grounds along the Angara and the Upper Lena there has been traced the uninterrupted development of a Neolithic and early Bronze Age culture of the Baikal region which passed through several stages: the Khin, Isakov, Serev, and the Kitoi (the early Bronze period).

During the initial stage, the early Mesolithic, there were no ceramics. Judging, however, from finds at the estuary of the Belaya river, there were the rudiments of stone polishing for the production of stone chopping tools including tools of nephrite. There also appear the first arrowheads made by the ancient techniques of sharp flaking and improved only slightly by retouching at the ends. Arrowheads of the same type, typical of the Mesolithic, have also been found in the low-lands of the Chastaya and Khinskaya rivers.

It was during the following period, the Isakov, that the mature cultural complex of the Baikal Neolithic was formed. Here we find specifically local forms of polished adzes which are triangular and trapezoidal. The vessels are paraboloid in a vertical profile and are covered with netlike impressions. Arrowheads are asymmetrical with cores and bases in the form of a swallow-tail.

Certain elements in this complex, e.g. crescent-shaped scrapers, large arrowheads and knives, as well as an obvious preference for mammoth bone for the making of hunting weapons, indicate a strong Paleolithic tradition. The next stage in the development of this culture was the Serov. Here the forms of the vessels become more differentiated (mitre-like vessels with necks), and the ornamentation becomes more profuse. Instead of a simple horizontal band of indentations below the rim, the vessels have bands of parallel lines made with a comb-like stippled stamp or a zig-zag band. There is

[20] A.P. Okladnikov, 1950, 1957.

[20a] [No doubt the author had in mind works such as Debec, 1948 and 1956. D.S.]

also a design in the form of rythmically placed indentations which are round or crescent shaped. There is also another ornamental composition consisting of horizontal bands and short vertical lines descending from them. The surfaces of the vessels are smoothed and covered with reticular impressions. Of the latter there remain only indentations which are remnants of the depressions made in the clay. The old form of triangular adzes and axes now gives way to a new type which is rectangular. In addition to grey, flinty slate, green Sayan nephrite was used increasingly as the material for making tools. Figures of fish carved from stone and bone (and intended as lures) are common in the finds of the burial grounds. Also found are fortified bows with bone facings.

The Kitoi stage is indicated by the occurrence of burial sites which contain no stone tools. The skeletons are thickly coated with ochre which was symbolic of the source of life, the "blood of the dead." Indicative of implements of the Kitoi burials are unusual stems for fishhooks which have crescent shaped projections at both ends. Nephrite adzes are found in profusion among the tools, as are triangular knife blades which are of nephrite and lenticular in profile, flat knives of argillite, the surfaces of which are depressed by broad diagonal facets of pressed retouching, sandstone "rectifiers" for arrows, polishers, round stone slabs, and other typical items. Unusual here as concerns ornamentation are stone rings of white marble, the sides of which are decorated with ornamental incisions. These were the predecessors of the later Glazkov rings of white nephrite. The common characteristic of the Kitoi artifacts is the masterly perfection of the press technique of working flints. The Kitoi people also achieved great perfection in the working of such unusual material as nephrite. From that period there have come down to us artistically cut fragments and indeed blocks of this stone from which were made adzes, knives, and even ornaments. M.P. Ovchinnikov found at Glazkov a workshop in which white nephrite was processed and in which, in addition to blocks in various stages of processing, he found the sandstone slabs which were used as saws.

Realistic art also developed and was basically animistic. In the Kitoi burials there have been found representations of fish, including flat images of bone, which were probably shamanistic amulets. There are also representations of elk heads which were, in all probability, the heads of shamans' staffs and are similar to the Buriat horsehead staffs. But there is also anthropomorphic sculpture, the forerunner of sculpture of the human form which is characteristic of the Glazkov period. One of the outstanding works of the Kitoi sculptures is the head of a bearded man with an elaborately and skillfully

modeled face, cut from white marble. It has a small, low forehead, long, straight nose, well-expressed nasal bridge, deeply sunken eye sockets, and a short, triangular beard. The overall appearance of the face is Europoid rather than Mongoloid and recalls the Europoid factor in the skulls of the Neolithic peoples of the Baikal region which were noted by G.F. Debets.[21]

The above-described features, which connect the artifacts of the Kitoi period with those of the Glazkov period, and the many burial sites found at the estuary of the Belaya River whose artifacts are definitely transitional and have to do with ritual, verify the fact that the Kitoi culture gave birth to a new one: the Glazkov culture. It was during the Glazkov period that metals, copper and bronze, were first extensively used in the Baikal region. Connected therewith there came into being many new elements of material and spiritual culture. During the time of its existence the Glazkov culture displayed a definite continuity and common characteristics.

The many hearths in the Neolithic camps of the Baikal region belonged to comparatively small groups of hunters and fishermen who migrated from place to place, from river to river, in dependence upon the seasons and the presence of fish or game; they did not belong to the large communal collectives which have left their traces at the settlements of the Neolithic Ob region. This inference is affirmed by the character of the Neolithic graves of the Baikal region which are frequently found on the grounds of the settlements themselves. These graves belong to different periods. Sometimes not centuries, but millenia, separate them. The ceramics are a singular indicator of a mobile way of life: the vessels of the Neolithic Baikal region never attained the large size or thickness that they did on the Ob. Occasionally the fragility of the vessels' sides is astonishing and is connected with a peculiar technique of making clay vessels not on a form, as did the Ob people, but by forcing out the sides by means of a special rammer which was mounted on a massive stand and placed inside the vessel. Still more characteristic are the small pots with handles for suspension. These are smokers which protected the hunters in the taiga from the terrible scourge of those parts: gnats and mosquitoes.

It is still too early to assess the culture of these wandering, or perhaps more correctly semi-sedentary, hunters of the taiga as more primitive than the culture of their Western Siberian neighbors who were firmly attached to their camps and to their dugout dwellings. This culture was not one of a lower level, but qualitatively and specifically different, and, in certain respects, even more refined, more complex. A case in point is the Neolithic bow of the Baikal

[21] A.P. Okladnikov, 1965.

region, the evolution of which at the Serov stage of development was at least a thousand years in advance of the development of the bow in other countries, e.g. Egypt. Even more indicative is the level of artistic development. In power of expression and aesthetics the Neolithic sculpture of Eastern Siberia, the realistic images of elk and fish of the Kamenny Islands, and the "writings" of the Lena may be favorably compared with the works of the Paleolithic artists of Eastern and Western Europe.[22]

The final, most conclusive, and most unusual feature by which we may characterize the peculiarities of the life of the Baikal tribes who were a part of the taiga scene of Eastern Siberia, and their economy, are the remnants of their dress. Judging from the spacing of ornaments of shell, beads, and nephrite discs or rings among the skeletons of the Neolithic and earliest Bronze stage of the Glazov, the dress of these people consisted of a short caftan which came down to the knees and was similar to a frock or camisole. The flap of the caftan, which was open in the front, was drawn to or gathered together with laces on a frontpiece which hung downward from the neck. This frontpiece was elegantly decorated with the greatest care and probably not only with shell beads and nephrite discs, but also with embroidery done with the magic subcervical hair of the reindeer which was the most important ornament of the "hyperborean" tribes of Asia and America.

This dress is an integral component of a specific ethnographical complex and is an indicator of its way of life, that of hunters wandering on foot through the taiga and the forest tundra, an existence basically different from the life of the arctic hunters of sea animals. Suitable of this life was the light frock-type dress with a slit in front, moccasins, skis, which were the basic means of transport in the snowy forests, birchbark boats, the pirogue, dwellings of skin or bark, or wigwam or teepee type dwellings.

The dress is a characteristic feature of ethnic appurtenances. It belongs to the Tunguz tribes and their near neighbors, the Yukagirs. Identical connections between the ancient Neolithic and Eneolithic and later ethnographical cultures are to be detected in other areas: in the economy, way of life, and, finally, in art and mythology. Such, for example, are skin tent dwellings, birchbark canoes, rectilinear-geometrical ornaments which among the Tunguz tribes and the Yukagirs are practically identical with Neolithic ornamentation, the cult of the elk, the legends of the River of the Dead which explain the fluvial orientation of the Glazkov burials. The entire Neolithic ethnographical complex of the Baikal presents a concept which has the basic

[22] A.P. Okladnikov, 1946, 1950, 1955. S.A. Fedoseeva, 1968.

characteristics of that culture which in the 17th–20th centuries was typical of the Tunguz tribes of Siberia and comprised their traditional inheritance.

Eastward from Baikal, along the middle and lower reaches of the Lena, but also to the east and west of the lower reaches of the same river, there lived, during the Neolithic, other tribes whose culture and way of life, although in many ways different,[23] were similar to that of their Baikal neighbors.

Excavations of multistratified settlements in the valley of the Aldan in Yakutia and work in the valley of the Lena have shown Neolithic shift processes in the making and finishing of the surfaces of clay vessels. Characteristic of the first stage (the Sylakh) are reticular designs; of the second (the Belkachansk), are hatches made with a buffer and covered with filaments; of the third (the Ymyjakhtakh), are artificial textile traces made with a trowel and incised as grooves. Here there has also been found an admixture of wool in the clay of the vessels, multifaceted core-like incisions, and artifacts of stone.

As in the Baikal region, here the overall historical development took place autochthonously and without any great changes in the ethnic make-up of the basic population which might have influenced the form of its culture. These people were evidently wandering reindeer hunters, the ancestors of the Yukagirs and the Nganasans. These Neolithic tribes followed their own mode of life in the steppes and forest-steppes of Trans-Baikal and Eastern Mongolia.[24] Their history is clearly divided into two successive stages. During the first stage, in the Trans-Baikal region and the eastern part of the Mongolian People's Republic, there existed a culture of tribes which still did not possess bifacial retouched Neolithic arrowheads, but employed awl-like points, less frequently flaked stone ones. Seemingly, they had no ceramics or, at any rate, rarely used them, employing instead cores of a peculiar type with a struck beveled surface. Their specific tools were adze- and scraper-like instruments of a trapezoidal form and vessels made from flat rock or stone slabs retouched on one side only and only along the edge. It is of great interest to note that rectangular semi-underground dwellings, similar to those of the Amur, were characteristic of this period in Mongolia.

Of great importance is the presence of agricultural implements, massive slabs of grain-hullers and grinders, the latter having an unusually peculiar form which recalls the metatarsal or metacarpal bones of bulls or horses. This indicates a fact of enormous significance, namely, that the early Neolithic inhabitants of Mongolia practised agriculture; that here, today a land of

[23] A.P. Derevjanko, A.P. Okladnikov 1969, pp. 141–56. Ju.A. Mochanov, 1969.
[24] A.P. Okladnikov, 1969.

nomadic cattle breeding, there once was an ancient and unquestionably independent seat of agriculture which determined the sedentary way of life of these tribes.

Nor can we exclude the possibility of the beginnings of domestic cattle breeding: horses, and cows. Indirect indications of this are the many bones of animals and the special place which they occupied in the religion of the Neolithic tribes of Mongolia as shown by the ritual burials of the skulls or bones of bulls which have been found on the banks of the Kerulen and at Tamtsak-bulak.

Also unusual are the human burials from the Neolithic period found along the Kerulen and at Tamtsak-bulak. The dead were placed, in a seated position, in narrow burial pits which, as observed at Tamtsak-bulak, were dug into the floor of the dwelling. Here they sit in pit-tombs, like weary travelers, exhausted to death, their heads folded on their arms.

Gradually, during the second stage, there appear indications of connections with Eastern Siberia. The tendency to wander becomes stronger, and two-edged, retouched arrowheads become prominent as during the Neolithic of the Baikal region. The influence of the Baikal tribes, judging from the spread of stone tools and ceramics with reticular impressions, reached as far as the southern regions of the Gobi and even further south, to the Great Wall of China.

The Neolithic of the Amur also developed in its own peculiar way. To the east of the Yablonovy Range, along the central Amur, and further to the south along the same river, a new country begins. Beginning with the area around present-day Blagoveshchensk, the white birch gives way to the black birch of Erman. Throughout the vast prairies of the Amur oak thickets replace the pine and larch. Here grow groves of wild apple, pear, and grape, and on the distant, remote lakes grow the lotus, the most northerly and westerly ones in the world. In short, it is here that the world of the Ussuri taiga and Manchurian flora, amazing in its diversity, begins. It is the world which, because of its wealth of curious forms peculiar to both north and south, astonished the first Russian traveler-naturalists: Maksimovich, Moak, Przhevalsky, and Komarov.

But there is another aspect of nature which was of even greater importance in the development of the Neolithic culture of the Russian Far East, one which set its specific and characteristic mark on the economy and the entire way of life of the local inhabitants of the Stone Age. At a certain season of the year, following the instinct of propagation of the species, countless schools of ocean fish: the chum salmon, humpbacked salmon, and chinook salmon, rise from

the ocean depths and come up the rivers in search of spawning grounds. From ancient times the fat, tender flesh of these fish has been the staple diet of the local inhabitants, their "bread," and the primary source of existence of the peoples along the coast. The peoples of the Far East: Nanays, Ulchas, and Nivkhi-Gilyaks, even within the memory of the living, not only fed upon chum salmon and were primarily ichthyophagists, but even dressed in fishskins. Fishing placed its stamp upon the domestic lives of these peoples, on their dwellings and settlements, and even on the beliefs and mythology of these "fish-skinned" inhabitants of the Amur. It was not due to chance that among the Gilyaks the beginning of the universe, the origin of the race, and the fate of its first ancestor were linked with the ancient myth of the marriage of an unknown youth, the first man on earth, with a fish-woman who came forth from the waves to give birth to mankind.

From time beyond recall the characteristic feature of the Neolithic settlements on the Amur was a sedentary way of life which was perhaps more thoroughly grounded and more stable than that on the Ob. The country of the Neolithic dugouts and large settlements in which dwelt dozens or hundreds of persons begins near Blagoveshchensk at the mouth of the river Amazar. Such, for instance, is the Novopetrovsk settlement which consisted of at least a dozen or so dwellings, each of which had its foundation trench dug into the ground, solid, durable walls of upright beams, and roof covered with sand or earth to retain the heat. The further one goes down the Amur in the direction of the ocean, the thicker these settlements become (especially below Khabarovsk), and in places, e.g. on the Island of Suchu at Marinsk, or at Kondon near Lake Evoron, they become Stone Age towns like the "ostrozhki" (islets) of the Kamchadals about which Stepan Krasheninnikov wrote, having seen them, during the flourishing of the Stone Age, with his own eyes.

In connection with the sedentary life of the fishermen mention must be made of the most important factor of the Neolithic cultures: ceramics. None of the ancient ceramics of the Amur, with the exception of vessels of the Late Neolithic at Sargol, obviously brought to the Amur from the north, are conical-bottomed as in the taiga zone of Eastern and Western Siberia. They are all flat-bottomed. The hunters who lived in tents had neither shelves nor benches, sat directly on the earthen floor, and inserted the bottoms of these vessels into the ground. Here on the Amur, however, household furnishings were more complex and included wooden shelves on which the clay vessels were placed.

Certain other elements among the stone artifacts from the Neolithic settlements on the Amur may be explained by the requirements of a fishing

economy, e.g. the knuckle-clubs which are identical to those of the Ob Neolithic peoples, and the knives with a worked handle or "knob," suitable for splitting and cleaning fish. In many instances there have been found not only the simplest type of net plumbs which are simply stones with indentations, but heavy weights. Such examples suffice to indicate the extent to which the specifically Amur type of fishing influenced the overall cultural form of the local tribes during the Neolithic.

As we go on to the littoral and, to a lesser extent, to the territory of the central Amur the overall picture of the life of the tribes of the Far East becomes more complex. From ancient times there existed on this fertile soil, especially on the prairies of the Amur, a rather highly-developed form of agriculture. Domestic cattle were also bred. This is well known from the ancient chronicles and from the archeological materials from the metal age. This is the more interesting in view of the fact that the beginnings of a productive agricultural economy are found here incomparably earlier than might have been expected, i.e. during the Neolithic, and not only in the southern littoral, but in the north as well. For example, a large slab belonging to a grain huller, carefully "forged" and ornamented, was found in one of the Neolithic dwellings in the vicinity of the Tetyukhe Cove on the banks of the Tetyukhe River. Also found there, along with flaked axes, flint wedges, and scrapers, were typical grinders in the form of segments. An entire series of similar grinders has been discovered at the excavations of Neolithic dwellings at the Maikhe settlement No. 1 near Vladivostok. Alongside the first indications of the use of metal in the Kharinskaya Depression near Lake Khanka and at the Korovsk settlement near the city of Artem, there appear for the first time different types of grinders which are scaphoid. Also characteristic of the Late Neolithic settlements along the littoral are other objects used in agriculture, such as shoulder-strap mattocks for the tilling of the soil, crescent-shaped sickles made of schist which contain apertures for attachment to a handle. Further, indirect, but very convincing evidence of the existence of agriculture are fragments of the bottoms of clay vessels which contain many apertures, such vessels being used to steam grain foods. At the settlements of the Early Metal period (village of Kirovsky) there have also been found the charred remnants of millet.

Thus the emergence of agriculture forms a definite link in the Far East between the Neolithic agriculturists of the littoral and those of the Central Amur region (settlement on Osinoveo Ozero near Novopetrovka) on one hand, and their contemporaries and neighbors who remained at the level of a gathering economy of primitive hunters, on the other. Moreover, the Neo-

lithic art of the Lower Amur, which is similar to no other in Northern Asia,[25] is an exceedingly peculiar feature in the life of the Neolithic tribes of the Far East. Ornamentation, above all, differs from that of other Siberian art and is based on curved, not straight, lines: tight spirals, the complex ligatures of the Amur reticular designs. The Amur meanders are, it is true, rectilinear, but there is nothing like them to be found in the simple ornamentation of Siberia. Even more outstanding is the contrast between the simple animal style art of the Siberian forest hunters and the art of the sedentary fishermen of the Amur with its enigmatic anthropomorphic masks such as found on a vessel from Voznesenovka and on the cliffs of Sakachi-Alyan. The preponderance of anthropomorphic forms in the art of the Amur and its characteristic static nature point to a totally different world of aesthetics and a qualitatively different world outlook. Thus two antithetic styles face each other on the Amur and in the Baikal region, styles which, following G. Kjun, we call the sensory and imaginative, in other words, abstract and concrete-realistic.

It is quite possible that the soil upon which this peculiar art of the Amur Neolithic flourished was the sedentary way of life of the inhabitants. The overall picture of the Far Eastern Neolithic, rich as it is in bright details, becomes even more complex and fecund when we approach its localized and chronological variants.[26] The first of these is the Gromatukhinsk, which appeared against the background of the Mesolithic of the Lower Amur and is represented by bifacial wedges and chopping tools which were worked from whole rocks, the latter bearing features similar to the Hoa-binh stone tools of Indo-China, so similar, in fact, that it might seem that they had been brought north from the south. The Gromatukhin people were hunters and fishermen who lived in tents of hide or bark containing the same type of stone hearth that we find in the Baikal region. They had ceramics which oddly combined the aboriginal features of the Amur with those of the Arctic, Yakutia, and the Baikal region. The contribution of the Yakut Neolithic to the emergence of this culture is especially evident from the admixture of wool with the clay used in making vessels. The Baikal contribution was the stamped decoration.

Another culture which may have existed simultaneously with the Gromatukhinsk culture, if not earlier, is represented by the settlements at Novopetrovka. Along with flint tools, Mesolithic in design, which have been found in the dwellings here there have been found a few polished adzes. However, there are no bifacial arrowheads, typical of the developed Neolithic. In their place we find only archaic flaked points. The Novopetrovka

[25] A.P. Derevjanko, 1971a, 1970b. A.P. Okladnikov, 1966, pp. 32–41.
[26] A.P. Derevjanko, 1969.

pottery is surprising in its simplicity and crude forms and is represented by flat-bottomed, bucket-like vessels, innocent of all ornamentation or decorative bands at the upper rim.[27]

This pottery definitely connects the Novopetrovka culture with the following Osinovozersk culture, so-called from Osinovo Lake near Novopetrovka. In the remains of semi-underground dwellings with shallow trenches discovered here there have been found, alongside vessels decorated with attached cylinders, large half-finished cores of chalcedony and jasper and typically Neolithic arrowheads of chalcedony which are not found at Novopetrovka. There have also been found blades for bone or wooden spears and daggers expertly worked by the finest retouching. The stone raw materials used in the production of weapons and tools also differ from those at Novopetrovka. The rich spectrum of stone used here contrasts strikingly with the monotonous hue of the stone tools from the Novopetrovka dwellings. In place of the Novopetrovka cores used for flakings, we have here only amorphous block-nodules which were struck at random from different sides.

There existed another Neolithic world below Khabarovsk where, on the Lower Amur, near the village of Voznesenovka, excavations have produced a multistratified settlement which exhibits several stages of a local Neolithic.[28] The earliest stage is represented by the lowest stratum of the multistratified settlement at the village of Voznesenovka near the mouth of the Khungara River, and by finds at the village of Kazakevichevo on the Ussuri, at the Amursk sanatorium in Khabarovsk, and at the village of Malyshevskoe below Khabarovsk. As usual, the most indicative material is pottery. The vessels are flat-bottomed, frequently covered on the exterior with a thin coating of purple-reddish paint which is rather like engobe, and polished to a lustre. Characteristic of this stage are stamped and perforated designs, some of them applied with a comb-stamp with large teeth. The motifs consist of broad horizontal bands and scallops as well as triangular elements the interior of which are filled with oblique stripes. Indicative of the way of life of these people is the fact that no traces of semi-underground dwellings have been found. Evidently their shelters consisted of hide tents or huts.

Above this, at Voznesenovka, is found a stratum with still more richly decorated pottery. Here the vessels are also flat-bottomed and have clearly outlined meanders and, as a variation, a meander-like pattern with roundish

[27] A.P. Okladnikov, 1966c, pp. 175–8.

[28] N.N. Dikov, 1977, 1979, 1964, S.I. Rudenko, 1947 = (English version) 1961. L. Krader, 1952. A.P. Okladnikov, 1956, 1969c. O.S. Chard, 1958a, 1958b. S.A. Arutjunov–D.A. Sergeev, 1969. R.S. Vasil'evskij, 1961. J.B. Griffin, 0000.

projections, the forerunner of the spiral. This latter is of enormous importance: before our eyes the spiral comes into being out of the ordinary meander and is actually the meander itself, but circular. In addition to pottery decorated with meanders, there are also vessels ornamented with relief, the typical Amur reticular design, on a background of deeply impressed rhombi. Along with these vessels there have been found large square or rectangular adzes and arrowheads, worked on both sides by pressed retouching and with assymetrical veins; also amulets of white nephrite.

Above this have been found traces of semi-underground dwellings and trenches of dugouts of the typical Amur type. Connected with these are those ceramics which were most prevalent and characteristic of the Lower Amur: large, flat-bottomed vessels the surfaces of which are covered with punctuate comblike patterns in the form of vertical parallel zig-zags. Over this stamped background broad, unfolding concentric spirals have been incised. Fragments of still more elegantly decorated vessels exhibit strange masks which have been sculpted on a lustrous red glazed background. Many large and small stone tools have been found with these pots. These include single-faced convex adzes and axes, flint arrowheads with the usual notched base and haft. At Kondon hafted points of an unusual type have been discovered, archaic in technique and form, not bifacial or retouched, but flaked, and worked on one side only and only along the edge.

The series of Neolithic deposits at Voznesenovka terminates in a stratum containing rectangular stone axes and convex, semi-finished adzes which have been struck from one side only. There are also narrow-mouthed vase-like vessels with tall necks, which are completely devoid of any ornamentation. Along with these ceramics at the Nizhnaya Tambovka station have been found a shale knife, in form similar to the Karasuk knives, a "paste" bead, (made of pyrophyllite?), and a small disc of white nephrite. These are obviously relics of the Metal Age.

At Kondon (Sargol' settlement) it was observed that the people of the spiral-ornamented ceramics dug semi-underground dwellings in which there have been discovered not flat, but round-bottomed vessels similar to those of the Baikal region. Both the ornamentation and the composition of these vessels are surprisingly similar to those of the Baikal region. It would consequently follow that during the Neolithic or by the beginning of the Bronze Age there was an incursion into the lower reaches of the Amur, around Lake Evoron, of new cultural elements, obviously due to the penetration into this region of a group of people from the north who brought with them ceramics of the Baikal type.

One of the most ancient Neolithic settlements in the littoral, and one which contains large pit-dugouts, is to be found on the northern side of a hill at the village of Tetyukha. Here have been found flat-bottomed vessels with decorative borders around the rims similar to the Amur reticular designs as well as various types of stone artifacts such as double-edged convex flaked axes, retouched scrapers and knives of volcanic tuff, and triangular arrowheads of flint.

In the south of the littoral there were settlements of the Gladkaya I or Zaysanovka type where ovaloid flaked axes, small retouched tools of pitch-black obsidian, and arrowheads of the same material were used. Ceramics are represented by wide cups, tall, truncated, conical vessels, and vessels with convex sides. Unusual are the decorative vessels whose thin sides and black lustre are similar to the Lushchansk ceramics. Such vessels are commonly ornamented with horizontal bands incised in parallel lines or vertical zig-zags, occasionally interrupted by a "spruce tree" (herringbone design). These decorative vessels are decorated with a fine meander.

The next, third, group of Neolithic settlements has been most thoroughly investigated around and to the north of the city of Nakhodka. Characteristic of these are flat-bottomed vessels with incised vertical zig-zags and, less frequently, meanders. These settlements belonged to agriculturists as is shown by a series of shoulder-mattocks and grain grinders found in the semi-underground dwellings. Broad, triangular obsidian knives, in form and retouching similar to the Mustersk points, have also been found.

The Neolithic tribes of the Far East had connections with Korea and the Islands of Japan: with the Jomon Ainu culture. Such connections were, seemingly, of long duration and many-sided. Thus, for example, in the lower reaches of the Amur there have been found richly ornamented ceramics which in many ways are identical to the late Jomon ceramics and, contrariwise, at the settlement of Niseko on Hokkaido there are Neolithic vessels with spiral bands which have obviously been copied from late Amur ceramics.

Analyzing all known materials from the Neolithic of the Amur, we may state with certainty that this ancient culture shows unexpectedly strong ties with the contemporary local inhabitants, the Nanays, Ulchas, and other aboriginal tribes of the Far East. Indicative of this are the curved-line decorations: spirals, and the "Amur reticular design" as well as many subjects in the cliff carvings characteristic of the modern ethnographic art of these peoples of the Amur. Thus, some of the ancestors of these tribes of the Lower Amur lived here as far back as the Neolithic.

Any overall picture of the economic and cultural-ethnic life of Northern

Asia would be incomplete without mention of the littoral regions and the Pacific islands to the north of the Amur.[29] As the archeological monuments show, the ancestors of the Koryaks, littoral hunters and fishermen, lived here and have left the remains of enormous semi-underground dwellings. Kamchatka was settled by the ancestors of the Itel'men–Kamchadal who for centuries lived in practically the same manner as observed by Stepan Krashennikov and G. Shteller in the eighteenth century. The materials from the multistratified settlement at Lake Ushkovskoe show gradual stages in the history of the cultures of the Kamchatka tribes following the Mesolithic. These strata, as we know, are separated by layers of volcanic ash. Related to the Neolithic at Lake Ushkovskoe are cultural remains dating from the time of the post-glacial inundation, a climatic optimum, which are found at a depth of 1.15 meters from the surface. These consist of knife-like flakings, prismatic cores of rectilinear form, cutting tools of the same flakings, and several retouched arrowheads. The material from which these were made is black obsidian and flint. Evidently there was no pottery. Later, toward the end of the inundation period, approximately in the second century B.C., the first clay vessels appeared along with polished axes and a various assortment of stone knives, scrapers, arrowheads and spears, all finely worked with retouching. Widely prevalent during this period were different types of stone figured knives, scrapers, and even figures of little men and animals which had been worked by retouching. The curious figured scrapers and knives, and also the elongated sharp-edged polished adzes, were widely used on Kamchatka and, in all probability, found their way from there to the Aleutian Islands.

The second stratum of the Ushkov settlement, the dugout dwellings on the shore of Tarya Bay at Petropavlovsk, and the dugout dwellings at Kultuk on Lake Ushkovskoe belong to the Middle Neolithic. At Kultuk there has been found a trench approximately 10 meters in diameter, which was the foundation for a semi-underground dwelling. Among the dwellings there is a hearth which is surrounded by a supplementary circle of smaller hearths. This, according to N.N. Dikov, was a dwelling of the Itel'men type. The trusses of the roof rested on the edges of the pit, the upper ends on a square which rested on the central posts. The roof was evidently of birchbark and was then covered with turf and earth. The entrance, in the form of a short corridor, was from the direction of the river. Above the fire was a smokehole in the roof (which among the Itel'mens served as a second entrance). The hearth occupied

[29] S.A. Teploukhov, 1927. S.V. Kiselev, 1950.

a third of the living space of the dugout and proved to be a mass of ashes and burnt bones of fish, fowl, and animals, a meter in depth.

The thick layers of burnt fish-bones in the hearth of the dugout indicate the length of residence of the people at this rich source of fish. Here supplies of chum and other large salmon were prepared for future use. Here also were brought offerings to the deity, the protector of fishermen, who was evidently half man, half fish. The remnants of a wooden image of such a deity which consisted of pieces of wood and birchbark in the form of a fish were found in the pit beneath the ruins of a tent which had been erected above it. Beneath and above this fish-like image were found the remains of sacrificial fires and near its head the bones of fishheads which had been offered. These monuments on Kamchatka were followed by the late Neolithic which, in the same form, continued until the eighteenth century when it was described by G. Shteller and S.P. Krashennikov.

Further to the north, along the shores of the Bering Straits, and also toward the estuary of the Kolyma and on the nearby islands, there existed for a period of two thousand years a highly specialized and wealthy culture of hunters of sea animals: the ancestors of the present-day Eskimos. Outstanding features of this culture are the rotary harpoon, a lamp which burned fat, and the skin boat. These inventions not only allowed the people to create a culture on a rim of ice in the Arctic seas along the coast of Asia, but to become masters of the spaces of Arctic America and distant Greenland. The early Eskimos not only performed this outstanding historical feat, but also accomplished a true Arctic miracle by their astounding, fantastically inventive art of carving walrus tusks. These carvings are of two distinctive trends: abstract ornamentalism, and realistically-sculptured forms.

The next great step forward in the history of Inner Asia came about as the result of the introduction of a new material for the fashioning of implements and weapons: metal, (more concretely, copper and bronze). This transition and the earliest monuments of copper and bronze have been studied most thoroughly in the Minusinsk Basin.[30]

Here the earliest culture, which was copper-stone or eneolithic, has been called the Afanasevo culture. Its monuments are well known in the Altai. The Afanasevo peoples still employed stone axes, beaters, spear- and arrowheads for their daily needs. They did not know how to melt or cast metal, and what

[30] G.A. Maksikenkov, 1963.

metal they did use was probably from native ore. Copper instruments are represented only by needles, awls, small knives, and fittings for wooden vessels. Silver, gold, and meteorite iron were also used for ornaments. Thus we find a leather bracelet on the arm of a woman in a grave near Afanas'eva gora framed with iron rings. Ceramics still resemble those of the Neolithic, the vessels, often bulky and with a large holding capacity, have conical bottoms and their surfaces are completely covered with band-like designs which are primarily horizontal bands of the "herringbone" type, undulating lines, and zig-zags. Culturally, the most important achievement of the Afanasevo tribes was the beginning of cattle breeding (sheep, horses, and cows), and, probably of agriculture. Their social structure remained as before, similar to that of the Neolithic tribes. Equality of Kinsmen is shown by absence of any indication of the primary position of any one individual. Important in their religion was the cult of the sun with which were connected strange censer-vessels which contained compartments and were in the form of cups resting on trays. Ochre also played a role and may have represented the "blood of the dead."

Physically, the Afanasevo peoples belonged to the Europoid race and resembled the Cro-Magnon peoples of Eastern Europe to whom are attributed the monuments of the Pit-grave culture. In their material culture we can detect contacts with the neighboring regions of the Urals, Central Asia, and the Black Sea steppes, to wit the Pit-grave culture, the Kelteminar, the Zamanbabin culture on the Zerafshan, and the Shigir culture of the Urals.

Of all these cultures, the Zamanbabin, which is dated the first half of the second millennium B.C., is of special interest because of its connections with the agricultural tribes of Central Asia. The Zamanbabin people who during this period replaced the Kelteminars in the lower reaches of the Zerafshan at Makhan-Karye, in addition to flint arrowheads, used copper extensively, to fashion various utensils such as simple knives, mirrors, fishhooks, unless they obtained these things from other tribes. This copper is arsenide with no admixture of tin. The Zamanbabin people not only bred large and small cattle, but successfully practiced agriculture. Remnants of wheat and barley have been found. An intimate relation with the agriculturalists of the south is to be seen in a small image, a statuette of the Mother Goddess. The square clay vessels containing partitions must also be attributed to the south. These are "bird feeders" and are related to the concept of the soul being in the form of a bird. One half of the feeder contained grain, the other water, for the bird-souls of the departed.

Evidently the Zamanbabin culture originated with a colony of southern people who appeared in the midst of the hunter-fishermen and early cattle-

breeding tribes. It is not impossible that from here radiated the influences which affected such complex cultural-historical entities as the Afanasevo culture on the Yenisei and in the Altai where besides distinct Kelteminar features also more southern elements such as paintings on various vessels, "censers," bird feeders, and the first metal tools and ornaments may be found.

The Afanasevo culture which flourished toward the end of the third millenium gave way, during the beginning of the second millenium B.C., to the Okunev culture.[31] This is shown by Okunev graves found in the Afanasevo burial grounds. It is assumed that the appearance of the Okunev culture at Minus is related to a new people, not Europoid, but Mongoloid. With the advent of this new people, the burial rites were altered, in place of the round burial enclosures characteristic of the Afanasevo culture, there now appeared rectangular ones. The dead were buried within the enclosures in caskets made of stone slabs. Like their predecessors, the Afanasevo people, the Okunev people were cattle-breeders. Technically, the Okunev culture had a great deal in common with the Afanasevo. Stone was still used to make tools and weapons such as axes, arrowheads, marble discs, but forged items were also used (fishhooks, knives, temporal rings) and so were objects made by casting. In one of the Okunev graves the first cast copper hatchet to be found in Southern Siberia was discovered. Pottery showed great differentiation: the vessels are flat-bottomed and are either of a "jar" type or have the form of a pot with convex sides. The amazing art of the Okunev people contrasts vividly with their comparatively primitive level of material culture.[32] It is represented especially by monumental sculpture: stelae which were formerly believed to be of the age of the Karasuk. On these stelae are figures in relief masks which are half anthropomorphic, half zoomorphic, in many instances reminiscent of the muzzles of bulls to which have been added the horns of bulls or deer, and snakes. Radiating head ornaments are also to be seen. This complex symbolism of the Okunev stelae is increased by solar or cosmic symbols which are in the form of circles with branches: rays or crosses, inside them. Similar representations are also to be found on the slabs which were frequently used to construct the Okunev graves. On one such slab there was carved the figure of a being with a magnificent "corona," holding a spear in each hand. The faces vary from realistically executed sculpture to abstract representations with three symmetrically placed eyes and a mysterious stripe which divides the face. Frequently the mouth is either lacking or is astonishingly large. In two instances at the top of the stelae there is the sculptured head of a ram. Several

[31] E.B. Badeckaja, 1967. M.P. Grjaznov–E.P. Shnejder, 1929.
[32] V.I. Matjushenko, G.B. Lozhnikova 1969, plates 6–16.

of the figures have enormous bellies like those of a pregnant woman. On the belly of one figure there has been drawn the realistic snout of a predatory animal. Also carved on the Okunev grave slabs are the figures of predatory animals, panthers or tigers, to judge by their coiled tails. Sun symbols, circles, which contain cross marks, indicate the solar, cosmic nature of these figures of predatory animals. There are also realistic images of bulls with huge, curved horns. One tends to believe that the semantics of the Okunev stelae express a complex cycle of cosmic concepts which are related to the worship of the forces of nature common to cattle-breeding tribes and include the sun and fertility cult. Also connected with the fertility cult are miniature figurines of steatite and bone with human faces, including those of women with long, loosely-flowing hair. These are similar to the ethnographic dolls of the Ugric tribes of Siberia, the fertility fetishes. During this same period as well as later, there existed on the Upper Ob the Samus' culture which was related to the Okunev. Characteristic of the former are vessels with the same fantastic beings with coronas and a highly-developed production of bronze items, the latter certainly representing a later stage of development which was simultaneous with the development of the Andronovo culture to the west of them in the steppes of Southern Siberia.

These bronze items, including worked axe-celts, and superb spearheads, also worked, are practically exact replicas of the well-known Seymin-Turbin type, although there are a few differences, e.g. spearheads with hooks at the base. The knives and daggers are also similar to the Seymin-Turbin metals. One of these has an unusual handle in the form of a sculpted figure of a man on skis(?) who is holding a rope attached to the figure of a horse. It would seem that this amazing scene represents the taming of a horse and symbolizes the transition from hunting to cattle breeding.[33] Also worthy of note is the fact that similar scenes of skiers following elk or deer are to be found carved on several petroglyphs in Karelia, on the Kammeny Islands, and in the valley of the Angara.

Also interesting is the fact that individual items of the Seymin-Turbin type, celts and spearheads, and a leaf-shaped axe, are found far to the east as well as in the west of Western Siberia: in Yakutia, at Vilyu, on the shores of Baikal, and even in Manchuria. On the shores of Baikal, on the Bay of Sagan-Zaba, there are cliff drawings in blindingly-white marble in which anthropomorphic figures are visible which recall the figures on the vessels from the valley of the Ob, one of which holds a hammer(?) in its hands. These monuments of the

[33] A.I. Martinov, 1964, pp. 249–61.

Bronze Age point to extensive contacts with the south of Russia (the Borodin treasure), the valley of the Volga (the Seymen finds), and the Vilyu region of Yakutia, as well as the Urals and the region around Baikal.

It is quite possible that the emergence of the Bronze culture of the Yin period in Northern China is somehow connected with these extensive contacts of the bearers of early metallurgy of the Bronze Age which moved from west to east through the forest belt of Eastern Europe and Siberia.

In the history of Southern Siberia the Andronovo culture was of special importance. Its most southerly monuments are to be found in the foothills of the Altai; the most northerly ones are in the Ob region in the zones between the forest and the steppe. The Andronovo people avoided the taiga.[34]

One of the most important centers of the Andronovo culture was the Minusinsk Basin, although it extended from west of the Altai to the Yenisei and even included Kazakhstan and the steppes of the southern Urals. A more advanced development of the cattle-breeding economy and primitive agriculture were characteristic of this culture in which horned cattle played the most important role although small cattle, sheep, were also important and produced meat and wool for clothing and also, probably, felt. The wool was processed, "pounded" with special "beaters" made from the jawbone of a cow. Wool was used for knitted caps, the remains of which have been found in graves. Horses were also bred and probably used for riding, although there is no direct proof of this. The earth was worked by hand with mattocks. Grain was ground with grinders made of stone slabs.

The most important material progress was realized in metallurgy. Metal was obtained in the Altai and the Kalbin ranges in Northern Kazakhstan from shallow open shafts. The basic source of raw metal was oxidized ore from surface deposits. The ore was beaten with stone hammers, then smelted in primitive furnaces. The metalworkers used pouring-moulds of clay, also composite stone moulds, and often a combination of the two in which celts, spearheads, and other objects were simultaneously moulded.[35]

The Andronovo agriculturalists and cattle breeders lived a more or less sedentary life in permanent settlements near their plowlands or cattle corrals. The dwellings, whose foundations were sunk into the earth, contained plank beds, hearths, and special pits for the storage of provisions. The regular, sedentary life necessitated many clay vessels, flat-bottomed jar-like pots with straight sides, and vessels with convex sides. As a rule such vessels were ornamented by a comb-like stamp with zig-zags, triangles, and rhombs. Meanders were especially popular.

[34] S.S. Chernikov, 1949. [35] O.A. Kricova-Grakova, 1952.

The development of cattle breeding as a primary occupation and the accumulation of surplus products introduced serious changes into the social structure. This is shown by the double burials which now become common. The wife accompanied her husband to the grave as did, and this even more frequently, the second wife. Authority in the family now belonged to the husband, the patriarch.

In religion, as formerly, the cult of nature (the elements) and the ancestors remained of prime importance. But the agrarian religion of the Bronze Age agriculturalists now appears in different forms than formerly. Indicative of this is the place of offerings in the Alekseev burials on the river Tobol where fifty-nine vessels with milk and vegetable foods were placed in the ground and five other special pits were filled with earth and charcoal, straw and wheat grains as offerings.[36]

The burial rites of the Andronovo people included both burial (on the left side with the feet and hands drawn up, more rarely on the right side), and cremation.[37]

Judging from their skulls, the Andronovo people belonged to a peculiar type of Europoids called the Andronovs. They came to Southern Siberia, as shown by the decorations on their vessels, sometime during the so-called Alakul period, i.e. during the 16th–14th centuries B.C.

In spite of the comparatively dense population and wide dissemination of the Andronovo culture, it was short-lived on the steppes of Western Siberia, on the Yenisei, and in the Ob region where a new culture, the Karasuk, soon appeared (13th–10th centuries B.C.). The latter brought new, substantial changes which affected all aspects of life of Southern Siberia and Kazakhstan where their monuments are now to be found.[38]

The latter are represented by many burial structures of a new type. The graves are in the form of a chest of unworked stone slabs, covered by another slab. Around the burial chest there was constructed a circular enclosure. The traditional ritual included sending food to the other world with the deceased. At his head was placed a pot of liquid food; at his feet four pieces of meat which included the shoulder, breast, and two hind legs. Often the graves were placed side by side and formed rather large tribal or family cemeteries. The mortuary pottery of the Karasuks is basically different from the Andronovo pottery in form, and quite different in ornamentation. Beside the flat-bot-

[36] V.S. Sorokin, 1962.

[37] M.P. Grjaznov, 1929, 1952, 1956, 1961. S.S. Chernikov, 1960. N.L. Chlenova, 1964, pp. 263–78. E.A. Novgorodova, 1969.

[38] G.P. Sosnovckij, 1941, pp. 273–309. N.N. Dikov, 1958, 1964.

tomed vessels, round-bottomed ones are very prevalent and are decorated with designs in the form of zig-zags, rhombs, isosceles triangles, less frequently with meanders and herringbone designs. Outstanding are the vessels with a surface of shining black lustre upon which designs have been drawn with a contrasting white paste.

The products of the Karasuk metal workers show a high degree of technical perfection and the wide use of metals testifies to an unusually broad scale of metallurgical production. The same is true of the mine workings in Kazakhistan, most of which, evidently, is related to the Karasuk period. At Jezkazgan, for example, approximately a million tons of ore had been mined by the miners of the Bronze Age before Scythian times. The Karasuk foundrymen also mastered the techniques of afterchanging copper, adding arsenic and tin, which improved substantially the properties of the alloy and the technical qualities of the metal-work. These foundry-masters reached a high level of perfection in their work. This may be seen especially in the knife and dagger hilts. The most simple of these have figured tops in the form of a button or mushroom. Knives and daggers are also found with tiny bells and with the sculpted heads of mountain goats, rams, horses, and deer on the handles. The daggers do not have guards and the hilt is separated from the blade only by a projection in the form of a dowel. Also common were bronze axe-celts, hexagonal at the insert, with convex band shafts on the upper edge. The jewelers of the Karasuk culture fashioned many ornaments, including copper and bronze clips for leather breastplates, bracelets, finger rings, palmate hair pendants, and temporal rings.

Researchers believe that the economy of the Karasuk tribes of Southern Siberia was based upon cattle breeding. Archeologists have discovered indications of horse riding: a psalion for a bridle carved from bone or horn. Hard bits, however, have not yet been discovered.

This, however, was a far cry from true nomadic cattle breeding. Proof of a permanent sedentary way of life are the rectangular dugout dwellings with an area of 150–160 square meters and with plank beds along the walls and hearths which were used to heat the dwelling and for cooking. Occasionally these dwellings were constructed in pairs and connected by a passageway. The smaller of these may have been used as a storehouse for supplies and household utensils.

The Karasuk culture, however, was far from being a uniform whole. Recent researches on the Yenisei have shown that it consisted of two stages, the Karasuk proper, and the Kammenolozh. Concerning the latter scholars are still divided in opinion.

The Kammenolozh stage which, according to M.P. Griaznov, was the later of the two, contains angular knives and daggers, massive bracelet-cuffs richly ornamented with geometric designs, spearheads with notches in place of sockets, and bone psalia. The form of the burial structures also changes. The burial enclosures which were placed beside each other now disappear as do the trapezoidal burial chests made of slabs.

Local variants are very diversified, no less than ten of them having been observed. These include the Karasuk settlements on the Ob, which are unusual by reason of their specific peculiarities. Judging from the large grain grinders, agriculture was more important here than in the steppes of the Upper Yenisei.

Also of interest are the monuments which are closely related to the Karasuk monuments and are found far to the south and west of the Yenisei and Ob, in Central Kazakhistan (the Dyndybayev burial ground), and in the Urals (Tagisken). Characteristic of these burial mounds, which have produced valuable ceramics, including vessels with cracks joined by gold clips, are such purely Karasuk decorations on clay vessels as traced designs, the grooves of which are filled with white paste and vessels with attached knobs.

Even more interesting is the wide occurrence of metal objects with specifically Karasuk form and ornamentation. Such items have been found in the west of Southern Siberia in localities where the Seymin-Turbin metal occurs, specifically in Kazakhistan and along the Volga as well as in the Urals in curious proximity to the Seymin-Turbin metal. These are the characteristic curved daggers and knives with handles sculptured in the form of a ram's head or pairs of horses' heads. The connection with Karasuk metallurgy is even more obvious in the east, beginning with the Trans-Baikal region and terminating with Yin China where at Anyang the daggers and knives are identical with those of Siberia and are found in the earliest burial sites together with archaic Chinese bronzes. Seemingly the Karasuk type of metal was disseminated as the result of some sort of contact which occurred from west to east and extended as far as Northern China.

Of great importance also are the monuments of the Bronze Age from the second and first millenia B.C. which are found beyond Lake Baikal in the territory of the Buriat Autonomous Socialist Republic and in Mongolia.[39]

On both shores of Lake Baikal, there was disseminated the same early Bronze culture of the Glazkov people as on the Upper Lena and the Angara between Irkutsk and Bratsk. One of the most interesting monuments belonging to this culture is a large burial ground on the high Fofanov mountain in the

[39] A.P. Okladnikov, 1959, pp. 114–36.

valley of the Selenga at the beginning of the delta of the Selenga. Of special interest among the other, typically Glazkov burials here, is the grave of a child in which, along with Glazkov type axes of nephrite, there has been preserved a bronze or copper dagger of the archaic Karasuk type which has the characteristic cusps at the base of the handle. From this find we may infer that in the Trans-Baikal region there took place a local process of independent maturation of the Karasuk metallurgy.

Throughout the entire territory of the Trans-Baikal region and from Baikal to the Mongolian border, and in Mongolia from Ulan Bator and on to Tibet and Inner Mongolia, there occurred a singular culture characterized by graves built of stone slabs. These constitute the most characteristic features of the cultural-historical landscape of these regions. They are constructed of huge, undressed, native stone slabs, erected vertically; they are usually rectangular and are oriented from east to west, i.e. with the sun. Usually these slab graves are grouped together in a line which is oriented from south to north. The corner-stones rise higher than the other slabs and occasionally have deeply carved representations of deer and other figures. To the east, at a short distance from the graves, are found deeply-buried "guard stones" or "hitching posts" which in many instances are also ornamented with the same designs in which may be discerned what are evidently details of ornament or dress, e.g. necklaces and the forms of stylized battle-axes. The upper portions of these figures recall the heads of anthropomorphic statues. Perhaps we may see in these figures the early predecessors of the later "stone *babas*" which may have represented the people buried in the slab graves or their servants, the "grooms."

Wherever the slab graves have been discovered it is evident that they were frequently and totally pilfered, even in ancient times. The little that the grave robbers have left us, however, gives us valuable information concerning the culture of the builders of these monuments, first of all on their economy. The builders of the slab graves, judging from the remnants of the bones of domestic animals which are found in the graves, appear to have been true cattle breeders who raised horses and sheep. The bones of large cattle are also found in the slab graves, but much less frequently. This is probably due to the nature of the terrain occupied by the people of the slab graves. It was devoid of the lush pastures favored by horned cattle. Also, all year round, they relied entirely on range grazing, with no provisions made for putting aside fodder for the winter. The animals had to dig up grass from under the snow. Then as now, horses and sheep were more tolerant of such methods of feeding than cattle.

We may assume that in locations suitable for agriculture there were plowlands. The vessels in the graves suggest the possibility of a comparatively sedentary way of life and the existence of agriculture. These vessels are of two types: flat-bottomed ones of the "jar" form, and tripod vessels similar to three cow or mare udders sewn together. Such leather vessels made of udders and with teats exist among the Altaic peoples even today. Also indicative of the indigenous steppe origin of the Trans-Baikal tripods and the tripods of the Bronze Age of Mongolia is their specific ornamentation which imitates hair plaits and is similar to that which decorates the ritual kumiss vessels of the Yakuts, the *chorons*, which were used at the spring horse-fertility festival, the *ysyakha*.[40]

The mineral wealth of the Mongolo-Okhotsk region, which included tin and gold, was the basis for a highly developed metallurgy. Even in the plundered graves, e.g. on the Tapkhor mountain near Ulan-Ude, marvelous examples of casting which belong to that period have been preserved: a celt with a square socket, a dagger, and ornaments of bronze and gold. Many objects of the Karasuk type belong to the slab grave culture, e.g. such outstanding examples of this style as the dagger with a sculptured hilt in the form of a ram's head which was found on Lake Kotokel', and the unique bronze sword from the river Shilka at Sretsnsk (village of Boty).

The monumental slab graves, majestic, elevated sarcophagi, also throw light on the social relations and the social structure of that period. The precious ornaments of gold and gems, the valuable weapons, and the dimensions of the graves themselves are direct indicators of the outstanding positions of the people buried inside them. By this time there must have existed social inequality and an aristocracy of patriarchal tribal clans. The placing of the graves in rows would seem to indicate individual aristocratic families who influenced the life of their tribes. There is still no indication of the existence of a still higher stratum of society: princes or khans.

The spiritual life of the people of the slab grave culture can be seen from their art-monuments such as the cliff drawings which were made with red paint and the stag stones.[41]

In the petroglyphs the same traditional subjects appear with astonishing regularity: enclosures, "courts," with spots in and around them, soaring birds which are like eagles, vultures, or falcons, schematically-drawn little men and, less frequently, horses. Such figures are obviously connected with the fertility cult, above all with milch mares and an abundance of milk products. They are

[40] A.P. Okladnikov–V.D. Zaporozhskaja, 1970.
[41] A.P. Okladnikov, 1954. N.L. Chlenova, 1962, V.V. Volkov, 1967.

also related to concern for the welfare of the tribal community which is symbolized by the "enclosures." The soaring predatory birds recall the important function of the eagle in the shamanistic mythology of the ancient Mongols, both as totem and culture hero.

In the petroglyphs the eagle, ancestor and culture hero, must also have been the protector and defender of his tribe. The decorated cliffs themselves, which occur frequently in the Trans-Baikal region, were evidently sanctuaries of the individual tribes, their local religious centers, where the spring, and perhaps also the autumn fertility rites were performed and which are similar to the Yakut *ysyakha*, the function of which is to assure the victory of the universal forces of light over darkness, the conquest of winter by summer, the victory of life over death.

The Bronze Age peoples of Trans-Baikal and Mongolia also had their common tribal religious centers. Occasionally these are indicated by entire groups of stag stones around which the collective solemn religious rites were performed. These were based on the same cult of the beneficient elements, the sky and sun, the fertility cult.

The stag stones are so-called because of the curious stylized figures of stags which appear on them in high relief. There also appear circles which are obviously sun symbols and mirrors, bows, quivers, daggers, and battle-axes.[42]

Judging from the dress and armaments, the stag stones were originally an expression of the cult of the heroized ancestor-warriors, the tribal leaders, and, possibly, were originally placed over their graves. But the cult of the sun was also expressed on them and is indicated by the disk-mirrors and the figures of the sun deer which were, as V.I. Abaev has pointed out, some of the most popular "totems" among the Scythians of Central Asia and the Black Sea region.

The stag stones are also interesting in view of the fact that the daggers represented on them have sculptured Karasuk hilts. This indicates that the culture of the slab graves had deep roots and came into being not later than the first half of the second millenium B.C. Judging from the sepulchral finds, which include some iron objects, the slab grave culture continued to exist even during the first half of the first millenium B.C.

Thus it is obvious that the histories of the tribes of the Bronze Age in Western Siberia, on one hand, and of Eastern Siberia and Mongolia, on the other, developed along different lines. As the monuments of the Minusinsk region and the Altai show, beginning with the Afanasevo period, complex

[42] A.P. Okladnikov, 1963.

ethnic movements took place in Western Siberia, and several times the different tribes and their cultures gave way to others. In the east, however, during an entire millenium the overall cultural-ethnic picture remained stable and without any great changes in the composition of the local population.

While the tribes of the greater part of Siberia were passing through the Bronze Age and metal in the form of copper and bronze became their basic material for producing tools in the Far East, a curious situation arose among the peoples of the Amur and the littoral. Here there were no rich and easily-available copper deposits such as existed in the Trans-Baikal region, at Minuse, or in the Altai. For this reason stone tools continued to be used over a longer period of time. The first indication of an acquaintance with metal here is the appearance of stone (most frequently polished slate) tools which imitated bronze knife blades, daggers, spearheads, and arrowheads.

One of the most ancient and interesting monuments of this type is a settlement on the Bay of Pkhusun. It consists of two strata, the lower of which contains the "Amur reticular design," the upper containing square, polished axes and fragments of dagger-like blades of slate and even real daggers with handles, which are copies of metal ones. Unexpected here are flaked arrow-heads with hafts like those found at Kondon. The pottery in the upper stratum is totally different from that in the lower where the vessels are flat-bottomed, miniature, thin-walled, and practically free of ornamentation, show the characteristic bulging rims which are edged with a curious cornice. Most curious in this stratum are small discs cut from soft stone, one side of which is convex, the other flat. What these stone "checkers" were used for remains a mystery. The settlement is especially interesting because it has been dated by the radio-carbon method and proves to be 4170 ± 60 years old.

Another ancient settlement on the Kharinskaya Mound near Lake Khanka goes back to the second and first millenia B.C. At some distance from the lake, in wild, picturesque terrain among mountains covered with heavy virgin forest, the remains of a large settlement have been preserved. This consists of several dozen dwellings of the dugout type, all of which were constructed according to a single plan. On the level top of the mound, in porous deposits of sandy loam, there was excavated a depression in the form of a circle or oval with steep, almost perpendicular, walls. In places the depression was fortified with slabs of unworked rock which had been removed from the craggy slopes of the mound. In the center were small hearths and in one of the dwellings which was made of stone slabs there was found a real stove. Along the edges of the pits, as was common in the Far East, columns were placed at short intervals which supported the walls of the dwelling. In these dwellings, along

with stone axes and polished arrowheads, were found a stone imitation of a bronze wedge, and an imitation in stone of a small, half-spherical metal plate: a "button." The tribes of the littoral were consequently well-acquainted with metal and had contacts with peoples whose way of life included the use of metal. This was now the culture of the Bronze Age, although here, in the littoral, metal was still a rarity, otherwise there would have been no need to imitate it in stone.

Evidently it was not due to mere chance that the settlement on the Kharinskaya Mound was established in so wild a location and one so difficult of access – the top of an isolated mound naturally protected by steep slopes. This was a mountain fortress. The inhabitants, however, were not satisfied with the natural defenses. With enormous effort they had excavated a deep trench on the top of the mound which ran across it transversely. But neither the trench nor the steep, cliff-like walls were able to save this ancient settlement from a cruel fate. When the earth which covered the foundations of the ancient dwellings had been removed and the floors came into view, the excavators were faced with a rare and touching picture: before them lay the remnants of a settlement which had suddenly been deserted by its people while in the midst of activity – a Pompeii of the Stone Age. On the floors and around the walls lay piles of cup-phials from which these people ate and drank. Beside these were found perfectly-preserved large, narrow-mouthed vessels which were deeply sunken into the ground and which contained supplies. In practically every house, at the end of the "shelves" were still to be seen boat-shaped millstones and the flat slabs of grain grinders. Also found there were flat, square, stone axes, polished arrowheads, and crescent-shaped sickle-like knives. In short, everything that this community of ancient Stone-Age agriculturists, which has disappeared without a trace, possessed. In a corner of one of the dwellings, hidden away, there was an unusual treasure: a pile of round pebbles of various colored chalcedony, snow-white, amber, yellow, brown, waxy-red, and olive-green. Most astonishing was a typical Neolithic flint point of chalcedony, the only one of its kind to be found in the entire excavation of the dwellings on the Kharinskaya Mound. It was obtained, evidently, from some far-distant place, then buried in a secret place along with the other playthings and treasures of a child of long ago. This settlement on the Kharinskaya Mound was evidently the victim of a catastrophe, probably an unexpected attack by enemies who mercilessly destroyed the entire population, including the children.

Echoes of a similar violent and tragic event are to be found in another region of the littoral not far distant from Vladivostok, near the village of Kirovsk in

the Artemgres district where there was once a similar settlement of agriculturists who lived at approximately the same time as the people of the Kharinskaya Mound. As was the case at the Kharinskaya Mound, the settlement near Kirovsk was suddenly abandoned by its masters. All their property, their supplies and wealth, grain grinders, pots and vessels were left. Even the millet gruel, recently boiled on the fire, was left uneaten. Charred nuts and the burnt remnants of ancient wooden constructions – all this casts an ill-omened light on the fate of the masters of this ancient settlement.

Evidently the disappearance of this culture occurred not only quickly, but suddenly and violently. This is indicated by the conflagration in which the settlement perished, its inhabitants along with it. What took place after this is told us by the monuments of a new type: settlements which contain piles of shells and which are the monuments of the new, Sidemin culture which used, alongside stone axes, cast iron celts.[44]

The Sidemin culture, as well as the Uril Early Iron culture which existed simultaneously and had much in common with it, belonged to a people whose economic life was centered around agriculture. This is shown by many grain grinders of a new type which were now not segmented, but scaphoid. There was a difference, however. The Sidemin people who lived along the coast from Korea in the south (Island of Chkhodo) to the Suchan River in the north, in addition to agriculture, worked the sea. They fished, harvested sea kale, and caught edible mollusks. Their settlements are accompanied by thick layers of shells which in places cover the floors of their dwellings.

The next period along the littoral and the Amur is characterized by the supremacy of iron, a further development of the economy and social relations along the lines of a civilized class-society, and a government which came into being about the third century B.C., first in Korea, then, several centuries later, in the littoral (the Pohai Kingdom).

Let us now analyze the results of our journey into the depths of ancient Inner Asia. As far as the facts at our disposal at the present time allow us to judge, man, at the level of development of Archanthropus–Sinanthropus, penetrated to the north and east beyond the great barrier of the Asian continent far earlier than might have been supposed. In all probability this occurred during one of the interglacial periods of the Middle Pleistocene, perhaps even earlier, between the Middle and Lower Pleistocene. He came here, to the Altai and the Gobi, even to the Amur, equipped with the knowledge of cleaving stone and making tools: choppers, chopping tools, and tools with "bills," primitive, but sufficient to his needs.

During the next stage and also, probably, under the more favorable conditions of an interglacial climate, another group of primitive people, Paleoanthropus, most probably early Neanderthals who were at the level of development of the Acheulean culture, left to posterity the unique workshop of Acheulean cutters at Yarkh Mountain in Eastern Mongolia. This entire period was one of small and uncoordinated communities, atoms of a sort, which moved freely over the immense uninhabited areas which abounded in the game which was their food. It is for this reason that the remnants of their culture are so rare.

It was during the Middle Paleolithic that the greatest progressive breakthrough took place when, in North and Central Asia, but also in southern Siberia from the Altai to the Amur, the new, Levalloisian technique of working stone was disseminated. It was during this period that man's labor underwent fundamental changes. Man himself consequently changed. Under the new conditions the population of Inner Asia rapidly increased and it was during this period that the basis was laid for all future development of Paleolithic man: his society and his culture.

The next stage was the Upper Paleolithic during which man became master of the spaces of Inner Asia on an even larger scale. It was during this stage that he reached as far as Yakutsk, Aldan, and the Bering Straits. It was also during this period, if not earlier, that man crossed the land-bridge to the islands of Japan which during the glacial period, i.e. approximately 40–30 thousand years ago, were part of the continent, and continued on to the adjacent continent, which then comprised a part of the single Asian–American continent. While becoming master of the spaces of Inner Asia during the glacial period, man of the Upper Paleolithic made many necessary inventions, created his own art media, and his own world.

His constructions were of two kinds. The first variant we find at Mal'ta and Buret'. The people of these settlements built solid, semi-subterranean dwellings which allowed them to pass the long, cold winter in comfort. They sewed bag-like, double clothing which could not be penetrated by the Arctic winds. They acquired valuable working experience in the working of bone and stone which allowed them to make the necessary weapons for the hunt as well as everything essential to a comfortable life.

The other variant of adaptation to the conditions of the hunter's life during the glacial period is seen in the materials from such dwellings as the one at Afontova Mountain and from other monuments of this type. This was not a sedentary world, rather one of more or less mobile Paleolithic hunters. Here we also see the creativity of these people and their inventive capacities, above

all in their dwellings, which were in the form of light, portable tents, probably conical, which could be easily struck, moved to a new location, and as easily set up again. All that remained from the old encampment was a hearth of slabs or stones in the form of a ring or tub. Here the wandering mode of life and the constant pursuit of game probably created a different type of dress: a light caftan with a frontpiece, long fur boots with knee pieces, and short pants. Both of these ethnographic variants of the material culture of the Upper Paleolithic in Inner Asia proved to be so practical that they have continued to exist, practically unchanged, down to the present time. They have thus stood the test of time for 15–20 millenia. One variant may still be seen in the coastal regions of the Arctic, among the Eskimos and the sedentary Chukchis; another among the Tunguz and Yukagirs as well as among the Nganasan tribes of Siberia and the Indians of North America.

The next change in the history of the Neolithic peoples of Inner Asia begins against the background of further great natural changes in this land, when the glacial period came to an end and the contemporary terrains were formed. It was during this period that the great economic-cultural and ethnic domains came into being which correspond to the original homelands of the later Uralic and Altaic linguistic and ethnographic families.

Simultaneously there occurred important changes in the economies of various peoples of Inner Asia. These were not only specializations which had to do with the terrain, (fishing on the Ob and Amur, deer hunting in the tundra), but a phenomenon which was basically new: agriculture and the beginning of a productive economy among several of the Neolithic tribes of the Far East and Mongolia. As documented by the cliff drawings, religion and art continued to develop.

It was during the Bronze Age that metallurgy came into being bringing about a breakthrough in the techniques of toolmaking as well as actual progress in the economy. In southern Siberia there appeared a complex way of life based on agriculture and cattle breeding, one example of which was the Tagar culture on the Yenisei. But even before this, in the steppes of Mongolia and the Trans-Baikal region among the tribes of the slab grave culture, there had developed a basically different economy and way of life which was to become that of the nomad steppe tribes of Central Eurasia, during the following four milennia. Of outstanding importance was the invention of the bronze bit which made possible the use of horses for riding. The nomads developed a completely new material culture, one which was adapted to a mobile life with cattle in the steppes. This included the felt tent, the hooded

cart, a complex and highly productive milk economy with dairy foods, kumiss and lactic alcohol, cheese, and much else concerning which the hunters and their fishermen neighbors had no concept. The people of this culture had guaranteed supplies of food not only in the form of meat, but also of milk products. They produced wool for felt and cloth which replaced the former animal pelts as the material for clothing.

The steppe nomads of Inner Asia also created their own spiritual world. In religion this was a rich dualistic mythology based on the heavenly gods of light and the evil gods of the underworld. Heaven was honored as the highest divinity. In art they created the dynamic animal style and monumental epic poems, astonishing in their scope of fantasy. Echoes of this wealth of folklore are still to be heard in the Yakut heroic poems, the *olonkho*, and in the Buriat and Mongol *üliger*.

In the social structure of the nomads there was also unquestionable progress, tribal alliances, predecessors of governments, came into being. The first such alliance was evidently among the tribes of the slab-grave culture, as evidenced by the astonishing uniformity of their monuments from the Baikal to Tibet.

Contrary to popular opinion, the nomads were not simply the enemies of progress; they were an influential force in universal history and the catalysts of many events. They not only took, but also gave a great deal to their neighbors. We see an example of this in the history of the aesthetics of China where, under the influence of the nomadic tribes, a new style of art, dynamic and penetrated by the spirit of live realism, the Huai style, displaced the stiff, priestly style of the Yin(or Shang)–Chou era.

Because of their mobility, the nomadic tribes of Inner Asia played an important role as intermediaries between various countries and nations. The rise of metallurgy gave a powerful stimulus to broad contacts, because metals, especially rare metals such as tin, may be found in only a few localities. Not only the exchange of raw materials, but technical experience was necessary for the development of metallurgy, as we can see from the extensive occurrence of Karasuk, Seimensk–Turbin, and the later Scythian bronzes.

The nomads of Inner Asia also created and took to different countries the elements of a spiritual culture, including the peripatetic subjects of folklore and myths. On the cliffs of the Altai and the Gobi–Altai in Mongolia the figures of sun chariots have been preserved. The same sun chariots are to be found in Kirghizia, in Scandinavia (Skiberg, Bohuslän, Vestergotland, and Skone), and in Italy (Val Camonica). One such chariot at D'yalangash in the

Altai is drawn not by horses or oxen, but by goats, a picture reminiscent of the chariot of Donar-Thor and his goats.

It was during the following stage, that of the Scytho-Sarmatians and the Hsiung-nu, with its rich and complex cultural inheritance, that history met the nomadic tribes of Inner Asia at the beginning of the first millenium B.C.

4

The Scythians and Sarmatians

From the end of the 7th century B.C. to the 4th century B.C. the Central-Eurasian steppes were inhabited by two large groups of kin Iranian-speaking tribes – the Scythians and Sarmatians. While these two groups were ethnically close and their ways of life were very similar, each of them had their own historical destinies and characteristics, in economic and social development, as well as in culture. The periods of their greatest development and greatest significance in world history do not coincide.

The basic sources for the study of both these tribes are the testimonies of the Greek and Roman authors who were interested in different aspects of the life of barbarians, archeological and ancient epigraphical data. Written sources describing the Scythians are more numerous, but they contain only fragmentary and often contradictory evidence.[1] The archeological materials dating back to the Scythians and Sarmatians are now enormous; thousands of burial sites have been examined, helping us to formulate and to resolve a number of questions about the Scythian and Sarmatian tribes, their material and spiritual culture. Along with this it must be said that the available written and archeological sources still do not enable us to give any definitive answer to certain important questions about both Scythian and Sarmatian history and archeology. These questions are still being discussed and are explained in different ways by different scholars.

However, the study of the Scythians and Sarmatians in the Soviet era has made very considerable advances, particularly through the accumulation of new archeological sources in the post-war period.

The Scythians

Our most important information about the Scythians is contained in the work of Herodotus, who around the middle of the 5th century B.C. visited the Greek

[1] See Latyshev, 1893–1947. [The texts used for this venerable and still useful compilation are not always the best available. D.S.]

town of Olbia on the Bug–Dnieper estuary. Almost all of the fourth book of Herodotus' *History* is devoted to the Scythians. And a number of important facts about the life of the Scythians can be found in the works of Greek writers, poets and historians who lived both before and after Herodotus, as well as in the works of Roman authors who used the accounts of their predecessors.

Following the written tradition of antiquity it may be confidently stated that from the end of the 7th century to the 3rd century B.C. the Scythians occupied the steppe expanses of the north Black Sea area, from the Don in the east to the Danube in the west. Herodotus stresses the unity of the whole Scythian world in this territory and distinguishes the Scythians from their neighboring tribes. But in the literature of antiquity, particularly that dating to the Hellenistic period, there existed another conception of Scythia. Not only the tribes of the north Black Sea area, but others living far beyond – in the forest-steppe and even the forest zone of Eastern Europe, and also in Asia – were often thought to be Scythians. For example, Hecataeus was already referring to the European Melanchlaeni and Asian Issedones as Scythians.

At the end of the 8th century B.C. the Scythians began to drive the Cimmerians out of the area. But it is very possible that already in the 9th–8th centuries B.C. some Scythian tribes, together with Cimmerians, were roaming the steppes of the north Black Sea area. This assumption is based on the fact that in his *Iliad* Homer writes of "milkers of mares – milk consumers." Hesiod, who is thought to have lived in the 8th or 7th century B.C., refers to the Scythians by name and gives a graphic description, similar to Homer's, of their life. However, the presently available archeological materials dating from the 9th to the first half of the 7th centuries B.C. from the steppes of the north Black Sea are similar enough; they cannot be divided into Cimmerian and Scythian. The most probable explanation for this is that the Cimmerians and Scythians were kindred peoples, indistinguishable in origins and culture. Many archeologists, also leading authorities on the Iranian languages, nowadays adhere to this point of view. The definitive establishment of the Scythians took place in the second half of the 7th century B.C.

There does exist another opinion about the appearance of the Scythians in the north Black Sea area which, in my view, has less foundation. A.I. Terenozhkin considers that Hesiod's reference to the Scythians is merely an anachronism, resulting from a confusion of ethnic names, which is common in the authors of antiquity. He believes that the Greeks of the Mycenaean and early post-Mycenaean periods knew only the Cimmerians, not the Scythians, of whom they heard no earlier than the 7th century B.C. He correspondingly associates all archeological sites from the 9th to the first half of the 7th

centuries B.C. in the steppes of the north Black Sea area exclusively with the Cimmerians. Adherents of this view place the appearance of the Scythians in the 7th century B.C. Furthermore, they regard the Scythians as an alien people who supplanted the Cimmerians, bringing with them a new, fully developed culture which in its complex manifested no local traditions.[2]

It is true that Scythian archeological culture was established in the north Black Sea area only in the second half and up to the end of the 7th century B.C. However, a change of culture does not necessarily indicate an entire change of population. Moreover, a number of elements in Scythian culture – the distinct characteristics of the funeral rite, ceramics, horse equipment and some types of weapons – go back to those which had existed in the north Black Sea area in the Persian epoch and originated in the Srubnaya culture of the Bronze Age.

The written sources do not allow us to draw any single conclusion about where the Scythians of the north Black Sea area came from. The three legends – versions of the origins of the Scythians related by Herodotus – are contradictory and can be interpreted in different ways. Archeological sources are still insufficient and, moreover, not as illuminating as the written ones. M.I. Rostovtsev has advanced the hypothesis that the Scythians–Iranians came from Asia. This hypothesis has been particularly staunchly defended and developed over the last ten years by Terenozhkin, who believes that the Scythians originally came from the steppe expanses of Inner Asia.[3] At present his point of view has many adherents. However, in my view, there is another more convincing hypothesis according to which the Scythians were descendants of tribes of the Srubnaya culture who, between the middle of the 2nd millenium B.C. and the end of the 7th century B.C., moved in several waves from the Volga–Ural steppes into the north Black Sea area and assimilated the remaining Cimmerians.[4]

The early history of the Scythians is bound up with military expeditions into the countries of Western Asia. Testimony of this fact is to be found both in writers of antiquity and in Assyro-Babylonian cuneiform documents. The first reference to the Scythians (*Ishkuzai* or *Ashguzai* of cuneiform documents) in the ancient East dates to the seventies of the 7th century B.C. Here also Scythians are mentioned alongside Cimmerians but, more often, individually, until the beginning of the 6th century B.C. when they were partially exterminated by the Medes. Those who were left returned to the Black Sea steppes. Scythian detachments, first under Partatua (Protothyes to the writers of antiquity), then under Madyes, carried out devastating raids; they aroused

[2] See Terenozhkin, 1971, p. 8. [3] Cf. Rostovcev, 1918; Terenozhkin, 1971, pp. 183, 208.
[4] Artamonov, 1950; Grakov, 1971, pp. 23–5.

terror amongst the local population and exacted tribute from the people they conquered. In Mesopotamia, Syria and Egypt, in the sites of the 7th to the beginning of the 6th centuries B.C., particularly in the defensive walls of towns, bronze arrowheads of the Scythian type have been found – the direct result of invasions and sieges. And it was the Scythians who took, destroyed and burned one of the northern Urartean fortresses, Karmir-Blur near Yerevan. Scythian arrowheads have been found here, stuck into the clay walls; and there are other traces of the Scythian invasion of this fortress.

The Scythians conducted their advances into Western Asia by way of the Caucasus. At that time the plains to the north of the Caucasus served as a base, as it were, from which detachments of nomads set out further south. It is in this area that archeologists have discovered kurgans dating to the middle of the 7th century B.C. with burials of Scythian chiefs and their mounted bodyguard (at Krasnoe Znamya Khutor in Stavropol, some kurgans at Kelermes Stanitsa on the Kuban). The Scythian advances through the Caucasus are reflected in archeological materials relating to the indigenous Caucasian tribes. In the burial grounds of the peoples of 7th–6th century B.C. Koban-Colchidic culture who lived in the foothills and mountain regions of the Caucasus, weapons and horse equipment of the Scythian type are frequently found.

The relatively long period spent by the Scythians in the countries of Western Asia exerted a strong influence on Scythian society and culture. The Scythian chiefs learned to appreciate luxury and strove to imitate oriental sovereigns. Scythian material culture was enriched by Western Asian elements, while Scythian art absorbed many Western Asian subjects and devices for communicating them.

Returning to the Black Sea from their expeditions in Western Asia, the Scythians, according to Herodotus, had to fight a war, "no smaller than the Median one," against descendants of slaves, with whom Scythian women had intermarried, wearied by the protracted absence of their husbands. It would appear from the legend told by Herodotus that the Scythians once again had to subjugate some of the tribes which had fallen away from them. According to Herodotus this happened in the Crimea.

Archeological materials testify to the fact that some of the returning Scythians were delayed in the steppes bordering the Caucasus, in what today is Stravropol, and along the Kuban. The famous Kelermes kurgans and the kurgans at Ulskij Aul and Kostromskaya Stanitsa, dating to the 6th and beginning of the 5th centuries B.C., are remarkable for the richness of the objects they contain, quite a number of which are of Western Asian origin.

Although these kurgans are situated in areas which, Herodotus claims, were inhabited by the Maeots, they most probably belong to Scythian chiefs who had returned from distant military expeditions. In the north Black Sea area itself only about twenty kurgans from the 7th–6th centuries B.C. are known, while we know of hundreds from the 4th century B.C. Furthermore, none of them, the Melgunov kurgans excepted, can compare with the richness of the Kuban kurgans. This fact is hard to explain.

Towards the end of the 6th century B.C. (about 514 or 512 B.C.) the most heroic events in the history of the Scythians took place. The king of Persia, Darius, with an enormous army (consisting of 700,000 soldiers, according to Herodotus, 800,000, according to Ctesias) invaded Scythia. The Scythians were determined not to fight an open battle with the well organized army of Darius. They adopted the tactics of partisan warfare, avoided decisive confrontation and enticed Darius into the depths of their country. The Persian army, in pursuit of the Scythians, appears to have crossed the Tanais (Don) and entered the territory of the Sauromatae; here Darius proceeded to build huge wall-like constructions against the Scythians. But the Scythians soon returned to their own territory and once again Darius moved after them. It was only with the greatest difficulty that the king of Persia managed to get out of Scythia, but he had to leave his base and weakened soldiers there. After this the fame of the Scythians as the unconquerable was firmly established in the ancient world. Modern historians do not accept all of Herodotus' account as fact. But from his information we can establish real events, distinguish the basic stages of the war, mark out the route taken by the Persian army and evaluate the results of the war between the Scythians and the Persians.

In 496 B.C., in order to secure themselves against fresh Persian encroachments, the Scythians invaded Thrace and reached Thracian Chersonese.

The war with the Persians furthered the unification of the Scythian tribes and the growth of a national self-consciousness and, perhaps, gave a more clear-cut definition to the territory of the Scythian kingdom. In all likelihood, it was after the war with Darius that the picture of the distribution of the Scythian tribes which Herodotus learned when he was in Olbia receiving information from Scythian spokesmen finally took shape.

The dominant position in Scythia belonged to the Royal Scythians. King Idanthyrsus thus proclaimed his Scythian army at the time of the war with Darius. Nomad Scythians, the Callipidae, the Alizones, agricultural Scythians (the Georgi) and ploughing Scythians occupied a submissive position. Evidently only Royal Scythians and Nomad Scythians were pure nomads, while the Callipidae and Alizones seem to have led a semi-nomadic way of life, and

ploughing Scythians definitely were sedentary agriculturalists. Until recently agricultural Scythians were thought to have been similar to ploughing Scythians in way of life and occupation. Then an original theory about the description of this tribe was put forward by V.I. Abaev. He believes that the name of the tribe, the "Georgi," is not a descriptive name, but that the Greeks adopted the barbarian designation of the tribe, which should be translated as "esteeming livestock."[5] If Abaev is right, then it would seem that this Scythian tribe was nomadic or semi-nomadic.

Unfortunately, we cannot uncritically transfer all Herodotus' geographical data onto the contemporary map of the north Black Sea area, nor does the latter permit us to establish the exact location of all the tribes which made up the Scythian kingdom. The written accounts and archeological data are hard to reconcile. For this reason there is still no one accepted view amongst scholars about the ethnography of Scythia. The most controversial question is the location of the ploughing Scythians and agricultural Scythians (the Georgi).

Herodotus begins his enumeration of the tribes at Olbia. Not far from Olbia, at the mouth of the Bug, live the Callipidae or Graeco-Scythians; to the north the Alizones; and further north the ploughing Scythians. According to Herodotus, the northern border of Scythia is unclear. However, no archeological sites of sedentary agricultural tribes, which might be associated with Herodotus' ploughing Scythians, have been discovered in the steppe zone of the Bug. Therefore, many contemporary archeologists are inclined to place the ploughing Scythians in the forest-steppe between the Dnieper and Bug. This theory is contradicted by the fact that the tribes of the forest-steppe zone, which includes the area between the Bug and the Dnieper, in the view of most scholars were not Scythians, that is of the Iranian linguistic group, and most probably had to do with the ancestors of the ancient Slavs. Herodotus himself emphasizes the unity of the Scythian tribes. However, the contradiction disappears when we look at Scythia not purely as an ethnic unit, but primarily as a political one, which could have included some non-Scythian tribes.

The steppes of the Azov Sea area and the left and right banks of the Dnieper were the lands inhabited by the nomadic tribes of Scythia. It is extremely difficult to distinguish a boundary between the Royal Scythians and Nomad Scythians. Most scholars believe that both banks of the lower Bug as far as the River Konka were the lands of the Nomad Scythians. The Royal Scythians roamed lands further east and south as far as the Don. Some scholars assign

[5] In *Diskussionye problemi*, 1980, pp. 23–5.

the Crimean steppes to the Nomad Scythians, others to the Royal Scythians.

Strictly according to Herodotus, the tribe of agricultural Scythians (the Georgi) should be located in the lower Dnieper area, up to the River Ingulets. The absence of 6th–5th century B.C. sites in the steppes of the lower Dnieper which might be associated with sedentary agriculturalists has prompted archeologists to look for the agricultural Scythians on the left bank of the Dnieper in the forest-steppe. However, as long ago as the 1950s B.N. Grakov suggested that the agricultural Scythians might well have been semi-nomadic, rather than purely sedentary, which would explain the absence of traces of their settled life on the banks of the lower Dnieper.[6] Abaev's hypothesis, which is discussed above, substantiates Grakov's suggestion.

Scythia was surrounded on all sides by non-Scythian tribes: to the west, beyond the Danube, by the Getae; to the east, beyond the Tanais, by the Sauromatae; and north of the Sauromatae lived the Budini and Geloni. The area of the Dnieper rapids was apparently inhabited by the Androphagi (Maneaters), who had their own language, different from that of the Scythians, but who were nomadic and wore Scythians dress. North of the Royal Scythians, on the left bank of the Dnieper, lived the Melanchlaeni, a non-Scythian tribe, although their way of life was Scythian. North of the ploughing Scythians lived the Neuri, and west of the Neuri lived the Agathyrsi. All the non-Scythian tribes, apart from the Getae and the Sauromatae, lived in the forest-steppe zone of Eastern Europe where archeologists have uncovered several local groups of sites from the 6th–4th centuries B.C. These sites can be linked with Herodotus' list of non-Scythian tribes, the nearest neighbors of the Scythians. However, once again scholars are still not agreed on this question.

Archeologists have been unable to find the land of Gerrhi which, according to Herodotus, was the burial-place of the Scythian kings. Some scholars link it to the River Gerrhus, which they equate sometimes with the River Molochna of today, and sometimes with the Konka. Others are inclined to look for it in the forest-steppe on the left bank of the middle Dnieper. But no indicative group of royal Scythian kurgans from the 6th–5th centuries B.C., which could be equated with the royal burial-place described by Herodotus, have been discovered in either of these two areas. Such a burial-ground, dating only from the 4th century B.C., clearly stands out in the Nikopol and Zaporozhe region on the lower Dnieper where the most famous "royal" Scythian kurgans – Solokha, Chertomlyk, Krasnokutsk, Aleksandropol, etc. – are situated. The

[6] Grakov, 1954, p. 169.

few kurgans in this region dating from the 5th century B.C. are those of members of the Scythian aristocracy (Baby, Raskopana Mogila, Zavadovskaya Mogila 1).

At the end of the 5th and, particularly, in the 4th century B.C. the picture of life in the north Black Sea area alters radically. Many nomads became sedentary. This process was most intense in the east Crimea near the towns of the Bosporan Kingdom. But numerous village sites are emerging on the left bank of the Dniester estuary, not far from the Greek town of Niconium (at Roksolany in the Odessa region). In the lower Dnieper area of central Scythia there grew up at the end of the 5th century B.C. a huge, well fortified town (at the villages of Kamenka and Znamenka in the Zaporozhe region). The metalsmiths who supplied the people of the surrounding steppes with iron and bronze artifacts lived there. And, apparently, the royal headquarters were situated in an additionally fortified part of the town. Kamenskoe Gorodishche was, in the 4th and first half of the 3rd centuries B.C., the economic, political and trading capital of Scythia. At the same time, along the banks of the lower Dnieper and of the small steppe rivers, in places suitable for agriculture, there were small settlements of nomadic Scythians who had become sedentary.

On the eastern edge of Scythian territory, on the main island of the Don delta at Elizavetinskaya Stanitsa another well fortified site has appeared. In the 4th and the beginning of the 3rd centuries B.C. this was the large administrative, trading and handicraft center of the lower Don and the north Azov Sea area; it was also the home of the local clan-tribal leaders.

Along with all this it must be said that in the 4th–3rd centuries B.C. the nomads of the north Black Sea area between the Don and the Danube made up the majority of the population of Scythia. Furthermore, kurgans clearly left by nomadic Scythians of the 4th–3rd centuries B.C. have been excavated at Borispol, near Kiev, indicating that Scythian nomads had taken lands from the forest-steppe tribes.

There was considerable property and social differentiation in Scythian society. But in the 7th–5th centuries B.C. the Scythians continued to live in tribes, headed by chiefs. The main chief, the king, was descended from the dominant tribe of Royal Scythians. The king's power was hereditary, although limited by an assembly of warriors. Subject Scythians paid tribute to the royal tribe and provided servants for the king and tribal aristocracy. Herodotus also talks of slave labor amongst the Scythians, but says that slaves were used only domestically. Evidently there was no developed form of

slavery. Some scholars regard Scythian society of the 7th–5th centuries B.C. as an early class society,[7] while others maintain that it was only on the threshold of class relations to the state.[8]

In the history of the Scythian kingdom the 4th century B.C. was the period of greatest economic, political, social and cultural development. This may be surmised from written and, most importantly, archeological sources – materials from the numerous Scythian burials which date to this period. From Strabo we know that in the 4th century B.C. King Atheas united all the tribes of Scythia under his personal power. During the long reign of Atheas a series of new phenomena can be observed in Scythia, both in the internal life of the kingdom and in its external policy, which show quite clearly that a state, although insufficiently developed, did exist amongst the Scythians.

The economy of this primitive state polity was based on the exploitation of free members of the community. An important source of revenue for the king and Scythian aristocracy was the corn trade supplying the Greek colonies of the north Black Sea area. In the 4th century B.C., partly because of the Peloponnesian War, the Bosporus became Greece's main supplier of corn and the corn trade between the Scythians and the Bosporus grew considerably. The Scythian nomadic aristocracy adopted the role of mediator in the supplying of corn to the towns of the Bosporan Kingdom and was interested in increasing the amount of grain produced in Scythia. This, evidently, was largely responsible for nomads becoming partially sedentary. But, as in the past, most of the grain procured by the Scythian aristocracy for selling to the Greeks probably came from fertile, traditionally agricultural areas, that is from the forest-steppe of Eastern Europe. Enormous benefits were reaped from this trade by the Scythian aristocracy while ordinary members of the community stood aside. Kurgans of the Scythian aristocracy dating to the 4th and beginning of the 3rd centuries B.C. are full of gold and silver artifacts, including many excellent works by Greek tauretic artists and jewelers specially made to Scythian orders. In kurgans of ordinary members of the community there are no signs of luxury. Furthermore, judging from both categories of burials, there was considerable property and social gradation amongst both the aristocracy and ordinary nomads, which reflects the fairly complex structure of Scythian society in the 4th and beginning of the 3rd centuries B.C. Scythian art, which reflects the interests of the higher stratum of society, demonstrates a large gulf between the aristocracy and the rest of the

[7] Terenozhkin, 1966, pp. 33–49; Khazanov, 1975.
[8] Grakov, 1971, pp. 33–6; Artamonov, 1972, p. 62.

population of Scythia in the social as well as in the cultural sphere. In the art prestigious elements, the deification of royal power, and the cults of hero-worshipped ancestors and of military valor clearly emerge.

In the last decade a considerable quantity of female burials with weapons dating from the 4th century B.C. have been uncovered. For the most part they are amongst the burials of ordinary nomads, more rarely amongst those of more well-to-do nomads. In a number of burial grounds the graves of armed women make up as much as 37 percent of the overall number of female graves. Most often, as is also the case with the male burials of ordinary Scythians, only arrows are found in these burials; but there are female burials which contain a more or less full range of weapons including, along with arrows, one or two spears and, rarely, a sword. Until recently this phenomenon was discussed only in the context of Sarmatian sites and was regarded as one of the indications that survivals of a matriarchy existed amongst the Sauromatae. However, this conclusion is hardly acceptable in the context of Scythian society which was more developed than that of the Sauromatae. The presence of armed women in the ranks of nomadic societies of the Middle Ages allows us to suppose that the presence of armed women in Scythian society is to be explained by a specific historical situation, associated first and foremost with the particularities of the life of nomads. When the free male population was engaged in fighting wars, the organization of the herds and nomadic home rested with the women. So it was necessary for women to have weapons and to know how to use them.

The most important external political event in King Atheas' reign in the 4th century B.C. was the Scythian harassment of the Thracian border. Around the middle of the century Atheas firmly established himself on the right bank of the Danube, having seized some lands from the Getae. An expression of this king's might in these western borderlands is the fact he had his own coins struck in one of the west Pontic towns, most probably in Byzantium. But in 339 B.C., at the age of ninety, Atheas was killed in battle with Philip of Macedon. Philip captured 20,000 women and children and more than 2,000 pedigree stallions. This event is described, albeit briefly, by Strabo, Trogus Pompeius (extracts of his account appear in Justin's work), Frontinus and some other writers of antiquity.

After the defeat of Atheas the Getae crossed over to the left bank of the Danube and moved into a number of places in the area between the Prut and the Dniester. However, the Scythians continued as in the past to roam these lands, as is testified by burials in kurgans in the northwest Black Sea area dating to the end of the 4th century B.C. No real weakening, still less any

disintegration of the kingdom created by Atheas ensued. Kamenskoe Gorodishche was preserved on its former scale and the wealth contained in kurgans of the Scythian aristocracy of the last third of the 4th century and the beginning of the 3rd century B.C. is little different from that in kurgans dating from the time of Atheas. Chertomlyk, Tolstaya Mogila near Ordzhonikidze in the Ukraine, Aleksandropolsk kurgan and a few others indicate this clearly. Only in the second half of the 3rd century B.C., when the Celts and the Thracians swept in from the west and the Sarmatians from the east, did the Scythian kingdom in the lands between the Danube and the Don cease to exist.

Instead, in the last two centuries B.C. and in the 1st century A.D., as described by Strabo, two Little Scythias arose. One of them was situated in what today is Dobruja and was founded, apparently, by those Scythians who remained on the right bank of the Danube after the death of Atheas. The Scythians were always in the minority amongst the Geto-Thracian tribes of this area; but Scythian kings ruled over some of the Getae, creating an independent state which existed from the end of the 3rd to the beginning of the 1st century B.C.

The second Little Scythia comprised the foothills and steppes of the Crimea as far as Taurida, the lower Dnieper and the lower Bug. The capital of the Scythian kingdom was transferred to the Salgir valley, not far from what is today Simferopol, and called Neapolis. It was here that the Scythian royal headquarters, the focus of the Scythian aristocracy, were situated. The stone relief depicting two 2nd-century-B.C. Scythian kings, Scilurus and his son Palacus, comes from this site. From written sources we know of two other Scythian towns in the Crimea – Chabum and Palacum. Archeologists have located three, apart from Neapolis. Ten earthworks and at least fifty small sites are also known. The lower Dnieper was another area in which a large number of nomads became sedentary. In the 2nd century B.C. a whole network of small well fortified towns and settlements appeared; and from the 2nd century B.C. Scythia became a primarily agricultural country, although the kings and aristocracy continued as before to lead a nomadic life.

The 2nd century B.C. was the time of the greatest flourishing of the late Scythian kingdom centered in the Crimea. The Scythian kings wanted to dispense with mediators in their trade with the Mediterranean and thereby gain greater revenue from this trade, so they conducted a series of successful offensives against Greek towns. Thus, thanks to the war with Scilurus, the Chersonese lost some of its lands and towards approximately the middle of the 2nd century B.C. all the northwest Crimea was in Scythian hands. Chersonese settlements were destroyed, Scythian fortresses built on the sites

of some of them, and Kerkinitida and Calos Limen were crushed and destroyed. Olbia became subject to the Scythian king. And Scilurus struck his own coins in this Greek city. At the same time close ties were established between Scythian Neapolis and Olbia. There are reasons for us to believe that from the time of Scilurus the Scythians had their own fleet, which enabled Scythian merchants to transport their agricultural produce independently to Mediterranean markets.

At the end of the 2nd century B.C. the Chersonese turned to the king of Pontus, Mithridates VI Eupator, for assistance. Under the successor of Scilurus, Palacus, the Scythians were defeated by the Pontic king's army, led by Diophantes, but only after three expeditions had been led against them. Thus the Chersonese was spared overwhelming defeat. However, it was never able to recover all its lands.

In the 1st century A.D. the Scythians once again became restless, increased their harassment of the Chersonese and frequently waged war on the Bosporan Kingdom. The expedition of the Roman general Platinus Silvanus against the Scythians in 63 liberated the Chersonese from Scythian siege. Scholars attribute the burning and destruction of a number of fortified Scythian settlements in the northwest Crimea in the 1st and beginning of the 2nd centuries A.D. to the Roman army.

However, in the 2nd and the first half of the 3rd centuries A.D. once again some development is discernible in the life of the late Scythian kingdom. Only around the middle of the 3rd century did the Scythian settlements in the Crimea and lower Dnieper cease to exist, as a result of the invasion of the Goths. During the period of the great migration of different peoples the Scythians finally dissolved into the multitude of tribes and lost their ethnic distinction.

In both the history and culture of the Scythians two basic periods can be singled out: the Scythian of the end of the 7th–3rd centuries B.C.; and the Sarmatian of the 2nd century B.C. to the 3rd century A.D., which dates to the period when the Sarmatians dominated the steppes of the north Black Sea area.

The culture of the Scythian period was created and existed in an era when the leading role in the Scythian kingdom belonged to nomads and it conformed to nomadic life.

A vivid description of the burial of the Scythian kings and of ordinary members of the Scythian community is contained in Herodotus' *History*. Archeological data concretize and supplement his description. The basic characteristics of the Scythian funeral ritual (burials beneath kurgans accord-

ing to a rite for laying the body in its grave) remained unchanged throughout the entire Scythian period. In the construction of burial buildings and in the burial environment there were developments and new elements gradually appeared.

The striking and characteristic tokens of Scythian material culture of the end of the 7th–3rd centuries B.C. – weapons, horse equipment, the so-called animal style of art – represent the particular Scythian variant of the material culture of nomads in the huge area of the Central-Eurasian steppes. As time passed forms of things changed, the result both of internal development and of influence from the outside. In the early period of Scythian history the most noticeable influence is that of Western Asia. But already in the 6th–5th centuries B.C. and, particularly, in the 4th century B.C. Greek influence was very strong, enriching Scythian culture as a whole, although primarily the culture of the Scythian aristocracy. A number of items made of precious metals found in the kurgans of the Scythian aristocracy dating to the 4th century B.C. also show signs of Thracian influence. In turn Scythian elements passed on and gained currency amongst peoples living far beyond the borders of strictly Scythian lands. They became most firmly established amongst the Scythians' sedentary agricultural neighbors in the forest-steppes, the Maeots of the Kuban. Weapons and articles of horse equipment were in great demand amongst the Geto-Thracian tribes of the Carpatho-Balkan area, while Scythian arrowheads have been found in a number of places, both in Central and Western Europe. Scythian influence is very marked in the ancient towns of the north Black Sea area. The arms of the soldiers from these towns included Scythian bows and arrows and *akinakes* swords. All of these cross-influences are easily explained by the course of the historical process which has been discussed above.

The changes in material life which took place in the Sarmatian period also changed the face of Scythian culture, although old traditions were preserved in some individual forms. The role of Greek civilization further increased owing to the proximity of Scythian settlements to the Greek towns of the north Black Sea and there were close contacts, at times peaceful, and at times of war, between the inhabitants of these towns and the Scythians. At settlements in the lower Dnieper, the lower Bug and the Crimea, traces of an urban environment are now clearly visible. These appear in the lay-out of the settlements, the way in which defensive walls were constructed, the prevalence of stone dwellings and the development of urban trades. In the funeral ritual we can observe a transition from burials beneath kurgans to urban and village earth cemeteries and there are changes in the contents of the burials,

although the character of the burial according to a rite for laying the body in its grave is preserved. Signs of traditional customs of Scythian burials can be observed more clearly than anywhere in the mausoleum at Neapolis, where the king and members of his family were interred in a stone tomb. The central burial of the king, like the royal burials in the 4th century B.C., was accompanied by the interment of horses and grooms.

Greek influence also touched on the military affairs of the late Scythians. This is reflected in the Scythians' use of battering rams. In the Sarmatian period the animal style disappears from the art of the Scythians, although anthropomorphic images, particularly the horseman, wall-paintings and grave reliefs are very widespread.

Apart from the influence of Greek culture, that of Sarmatian culture is noticeable, and in the lower Dnieper area the influence also of Thracian and Celtic cultures may be discerned. But along with the disappearance of the late Scythian kingdom, late Scythian culture also disappeared.

The Sarmatians

The first period of the historical development of the Sarmatians, which embraces the 6th–4th centuries B.C., is associated with the Sauromatae – the eastern neighbors of the Scythians, occupying lands beyond the Tanais which are "fifteen days journey northward from the northern tip of Lake Maeotis."[9] Herodotus supplies no other details about the location of the Sauromatian tribes. Nor are any supplied by other writers of antiquity. Contemporary scholars, allowing for the fact that the Father of History got his geography wrong when he believed the Tanais flows directly north, locate the Sauromatae to the northeast of the mouth of the Don, in a territory 550–600 kilometers long. On the basis of archeological materials two local groups or areas of a single culture of the 6th–4th centuries B.C., conditionally called Sauromatian, can be singled out: the lower Volga (between the Volga and the Don, and the Trans-Volga); and the Samara-Ural. The territory of Herodotus' Sauromatae fully corresponds only with the first. As yet we are unable to identify the Samara-Ural group with the specific tribes known to ancient writers that inhabited the east of what is today the Soviet Union. But the fact that the sites of both local groups are so close means that we can talk about close kin ties between the members of both.[10]

From the legend about the origins of the Sauromatae told by Herodotus we

[9] Herodotus, IV. 21. [10] Cf. Smirnov, 1975, p. 153; Machinskij, 1972, pp. 30–7.

can conclude that the Sauromatae and the Scythians were kindred tribes. The pseudo-Hippocrates calls the Sauromatae a Scythian tribe. On the basis of written sources and analysis of archeological materials scholars today believe that the ancestors of the Sauromatae, as well as the Scythians, were the people of the Srubnaya culture of the Bronze Age. But these were the "Srubnites" who until the end of the Bronze Age remained on the Volga and who early on began to co-operate actively with their eastern neighbors of the Andronovo culture. The participation of the latter in the development of the Sauromatae probably explains why "the Sauromatae spoke the Scythian language, but from the earliest times a corrupt form."[11]

In the 6th–5th centuries B.C. the Sauromatae comprised, both ethnically and politically, a single group of tribes whose territory was bordered on the west by the Don. But already at the end of the 5th century B.C. some of the Sauromatae had crossed to the right bank of the Don and settled around Lake Maeotis (the Azov Sea), apparently alongside the Royal Scythians and Maeots.

Relations between the Sauromatae and the Scythians were peaceful in the 6th–4th centuries B.C. This is clearly indicated by the existence of a long overland route from Scythia to the East through the land of the Sauromatae and the fact that the Sauromatae fought with the Scythians against Darius, which we read about in Herodotus.

In level of social and economic development as well as in culture the Sauromatian tribes were somewhat more primitive than the Scythian, although a number of common characteristics can be found. The Sauromatian kurgans which have been excavated are as a whole poorer than those of the Scythians; they also show that there was less social and property differentiation between the Sauromatian aristocracy and the ordinary members of the community. More developed, evidently, were the tribes from the southern foothills of the Urals, where the large and rich kurgans of a military aristocracy dating to the 5th century B.C. – such as the Pyatimary group on the River Ilek – are known. No such burial grounds have to date been discovered in the Volga area. This has led scholars to suppose that the clan structure disintegrated more slowly amongst the Sauromatae in the area between the Volga and the Don and that the clan-tribal aristocracy here was economically and militarily weaker than the aristocracy near the Urals.

From written sources we learn that in Sauromatian society a special role belonged to women. They actively participated in military operations and in

[11] Herodotus, IV. 177.

social life. Archeological materials seem to confirm this phenomenon. Burials of armed Sauromatian women comprise no less than 20 percent of the military graves with arms known to date. In a number of places kurgans with a female burial in the group occupy the central position and appear to be the richest. It is in female Sauromatian graves that stone sacrificial altars, thought by some archeologists to be associated with the following of some kinds of cults, have been found. Mention has already been made of the fact that scholars have explained this phenomenon as the survivals of a matriarchy in Sauromatian society. Also concurrent is the view that possibly a matriarchal clan at a late stage of development existed amongst the Sauromatae. And some scholars incline to the opinion discussed earlier in relation to the burials of Scythian armed women.[12] At present it is hard to say which of these views most corresponds to the truth. It must be pointed out, however, that the position of Sauromatian women nevertheless does seem to have been higher, for it attracted the attention of ancient writers. Indeed, there is no mention in ancient literature of any special position for Scythian women. Such a position is attributed to women in the tribes of the Massagetae and Issedones as well as to Sauromatian women.

In the 3rd century B.C. the ethnic term "Sarmat" first appears in ancient written sources. However, by force of literary tradition many Greek and Roman writers frequently substitute for this term and use the customary name "Sauromat." Comparison of data provided by the writers of antiquity shows that the basis for this substitution was not so much the proximity of the names of the tribes as the existence of genetic links between them. Archeological sources enable us to clarify certain points about the origins of the Sarmatians. Archeologists have established that no direct line of development can be drawn from Herodotus' Sauromatae, that is the 6th–4th centuries B.C. population of the area between the Volga and the Don, to the Sarmatians of the 3rd century B.C. It appears that the nucleus of the Sarmatian people formed in the foothills of the south Urals, with the participation of migrants from the forest-steppes beyond the Urals. In the 4th–3rd centuries B.C. part of the population of the south Urals moved into the lower Volga and the trans-Urals steppes and conquered the Sauromatae living here. As a result new Sarmatian polities – known to the ancient world as the Aorsi, the Roxolani, the Alans and the Iazyges – were formed. These were the threatening and militarily powerful unions of tribes which from the 3rd century B.C. began their great advance westwards, across the Don and into the steppes of the north Black Sea area,

[12] *Problemy skifskoj arkheologii*, 1971, pp. 188–90.

where they "devastated a considerable part of Scythia and, exterminating the conquered to the last man, they turned the greater part of the country into a desert."[13] They also moved southwards, into the north Caucasus. From Strabo's *Geography* we know that in the 2nd century B.C. the Iazyges settled between the Don and the Dnieper, while Ovid at the beginning of the 1st century A.D. encountered them on the right bank of the Ister (the Danube) where they had laid waste lands adjacent to the town of Tomi and terrorized local inhabitants. Pliny talks of Iazyges living in the Tisza valley in the middle of the 1st century A.D.

In the 2nd century B.C. the Roxolani who, in all probability, followed the Iazyges, occupied the Black Sea steppes as far as the Dnieper and conducted raids on Taurida (the Crimea). In the middle of the 1st century A.D. the Roxolani had already reached the area between the Dnieper and the Danube. In the same period they moved on further to the west and attacked Moesia, thereby threatening the eastern provinces of Rome.

The active advance of the Sarmatian tribes into the foothills of the north Caucasus dates to the 3rd–1st centuries B.C. Judging from what Strabo says, the Siraces and Aorsi, two Sarmatian tribes who were independent of one another and frequently at odds, were operating here. In A.D. 49 the Romans went into battle alongside the Aorsi against the Siraces, who had formed an alliance with Mithridates. The Siraces were routed and lost control of the greater part of their lands. Soon after this event, in the 50–60s A.D., the Alans appeared in the foothills of the Caucasus. Prior to this, in the beginning of the 1st century A.D., the Alans had occupied lands in the northeast Azov Sea area, along the Don. In the 2nd century A.D. they were already supreme in the steppes of the north Caucasus as well as in the north Black Sea area, having created a powerful confederation of tribes in the territory they had conquered. A graphic description of this confederation can be found in Ammianus Marcellinus.

In the 3rd century A.D. the Goths, surging down from the Baltic, seriously weakened Sarmatian supremacy in the north Black Sea area. But the shattering blow to the Sarmatians was dealt by the Huns in 375. A considerable percentage of the Sarmatian population was slaughtered and some Sarmatians were absorbed by the Hunnic tribal polity, but some of the Alans from the north Caucasian steppes moved up into mountainous regions of the Caucasus and remained there, playing an important role in the ethnic origin of certain contemporary Caucasian tribes, such as the Ossets, Kabardians and others.

[13] Diodorus Siculus, *Bibliotheca*, II, 43.3.

Archeological materials directly correspond to data supplied by the written tradition, although it is hard to single out a picture of the material culture of one or other Sarmatian tribe. Sarmatian kurgan burials dating from the end of the 3rd century B.C. onwards are to be found all over the steppes of the north Black Sea area and in the north Caucasus. But the majority of Sarmatian graves date from the 1st century B.C. to the 3rd century A.D. Furthermore, Sarmatian burials of the 2nd–4th centuries A.D. are not only known in the steppes of the north Black Sea area, but also in the forest-steppe, the Poltava area, the Orel and Vorskla basins, and in the north Donets. These testify to the fact that a group of Sarmatian tribes from the steppe settled fairly far north. Sarmatian sites of the 1st century A.D. unearthed along the Tisza in Hungary, also in Romania, confirm the reports of ancient writers that the Iazyges and Roxolani penetrated areas far beyond the north Black Sea.

Sarmatian burials in the north Black Sea area and along the Volga show that the Sarmatians living here led a nomadic life. Another picture emerges of the north Caucasus where, according to Strabo, some of the Sarmatians were nomadic, while others were sedentary and occupied with agriculture. Sites of the 1st century B.C. and the 1st century A.D. excavated by archeologists in the Terek basin and in the area between the Terek and Sunzha rivers, which most probably belong to the Siraces, confirm Strabo's report. Sites of the Sarmatian period known on the Kuban and in the lower reaches of the Don contain Sarmatian archeological materials together with the local ones. These sites were evidently inhabited, alongside Maeots and other local people, by Sarmatians who had become sedentary. Some scholars believe that these sites also are Sarmatian.[14]

The burial buildings, burial rite and basic range of objects in the Sarmatian burials in the lands they conquered are similar to those in the Volga area. Archeologists single out three consecutive stages in the history of Sarmatian culture, which were anticipated by the Sauromatian stage or culture of the 6th–4th centuries B.C. The three stages are: the early stage, which has been called Prokhorovka culture, dating from the end of the 4th–2nd century B.C.; the middle stage, or Susly culture, dating to the 1st century B.C. and the 1st century A.D.; and the late stage, embracing the 2nd–4th centuries A.D. Each of these stages demonstrates its own particularities in the building of graves, burial customs and contents of burials. Weapons, horse equipment, ornaments and pottery were most susceptible to change as time passed. Apart from the chronological, local differences emerge owing to the influence of local,

[14] Vinogradov, 1963.

ancient cultures and also the influence of the peoples with whom different groups of Sarmatian tribes had most to be in contact. Thus, in Sarmatian sites of the north Black Sea area the influence of late Scythian and of ancient cultures is discernible. It must be pointed out, however, that the Sarmatians did not experience the multi-faceted influence of antiquity on their culture, art and ideology which the late Scythians did. Such an influence is indicated only by the appearance in Sarmatian circles of pottery and individual imported items. These came to the Sarmatians through their trade links with Greek and Roman merchants. A considerable proportion of these imports – wine, pottery, ornaments, including gold and silver ware – came from the ancient towns of the north Black Sea area. But some artifacts, such as Italian bronze vessels or some brooches, apparently reached the Sarmatians, bypassing Greek towns, along the Danube–Pannonian trade-route. It is not impossible that some of the valuable items found in Sarmatian kurgans came to Sarmatian chiefs as tribute or payment for their participation in wars, or that they had been plundered from ancient centers.

Sarmatian culture appears to have been most homogeneous over its entire territory during the late Sarmatian period, which was one consequence of the closer economic and political unification of the Sarmatian tribes with the Alans at the head.

In their turn the Sarmatians, like the Scythians in an earlier period, played a very important role in the life both of neighboring and more distant tribes and of those ancient states with which they had contacts, sometimes friendly, sometimes antagonistic. Archeological materials indicate that the Sarmatians began to infiltrate the capital of the late Scythian kingdom, Neapolis, and the northwest Crimea in the 1st–3rd centuries A.D.; they also show the profound influence of Sarmatian culture on late Scythian culture. Also very strongly influenced by Sarmatian culture were the Maeotian tribes of the Kuban who played a considerable role in the history of the northeast Black Sea area in the Scythian period and who, owing to Sarmatian influence in the earliest centuries A.D., ceased to be an independent and ethno-cultural force.

Sarmatian influence can be observed in the tribes of Chernyakhiv culture, amongst which many scholars discern the ancestors of the ancient Slavs. It is even thought that the late Scythians and Sarmatians played a considerable role in the forming of Chernyakhiv culture.

In the last centuries B.C. and the first centuries A.D. there was an influx of Sarmatians into the ancient towns of the north and northeast Black Sea. Archeological and epigraphical materials show that many went to Olbia, Panticapaeum, Tanais and even to Tyras. Furthermore, ethnic Sarmatians

were to be found in all sections of the population of these towns, right up to the ruling elite. The newcomers brought with them their traditions of daily life, culture, art and religion which could not but influence the general aspect of these ancient towns. Sarmatian influence can be traced in literally all spheres of their political and cultural life.

As yet we are unable to draw any precise and well-founded conclusions about the social system of the Sarmatian tribes from archeological and written sources. Nevertheless, very rich burials dating to the first centuries A.D. have been discovered in the north Black Sea area and in the north Caucasus, some of which are catalogued in scholarship and treasuries (Zolotoe Kladbishche [Golden Cemetery] on the Kuban, Khokhlach kurgan near Rostov-on-Don, the Voronezh, Starobelsk and Yanchokrakshkij Treasuries, etc.). The amount of gold and other valuable items in these burials considerably exceeds that in earlier Sarmatian burials. This testifies to the fact that property and social differentiation increased in Sarmatian society as time passed and that wealth accumulated in the hands of the chiefs and their military bodyguards who broke with the traditions of a primitive-communal system. The mass burial-places of ordinary Sarmatians, which date to the same time as the rich kurgans and contain modest collections of items, emphasize the differences in material situation between the Sarmatian aristocracy and ordinary members of the community.

The Sarmatians knew about slavery, but, like the Scythians, they only used slaves as domestic servants and also as articles to trade. Polybius writes that many slaves were exported from the lands around Pontus and that one of the markets where they were sold was the town of Tanais.

It seems that Sarmatian society as a whole, even in the period of its greatest development, did not transgress the boundaries of a clan-tribal system and was not in the process of class organization and transition to a state.

A number of rich burials without kurgans, dating to the end of the 4th century A.D., have been discovered in the lower reaches of the Dnieper, along the Volga, in the north Azov Sea area, the Prut basin and in some other places. The burial rite of these sites is somewhat reminiscent of the Sarmatian rite and a number of items found in them have a Sarmatian look. At the same time in these burials there are things which are uncharacteristic of Sarmatian culture; ornaments and other objects of Hunnic character have been found in them. Not so long ago some scholars thought that these burials were late Sarmatian.[15] However, there is more foundation to the view that they are Hunnic.[16] Sarmatian, Alan burials of the Hunnic epoch have been discovered

[15] Rutkivska, 1969. [16] Zaseckaja, 1971.

which show that the Sarmatians in the south Russian steppes were not completely destroyed by the Huns.

All contemporary historians, archeologists and linguists are agreed that since the Scythian and Sarmatian tribes were of the Iranian linguistic group neither could have played a direct role in the ethnogenesis of the Slavic tribes that, in the second half of the first millenium A.D., settled in the lands of Eastern Europe, which include the north Black Sea area. At the same time, in the culture and especially in the art of the Slavic peoples, right up to the Middle Ages, the preservation of some traditions of Scythian and Sarmatian culture can be observed. Reminders of the art of the Scythian animal style and of Sarmatian zoomorphic art survive, especially in the art of ancient Rus.

5

The Hsiung-nu

The Chinese written tradition traces the beginnings of the Hsiung-nu back to times immemorial. It is reported that the Hsiung-nu had been known in remote antiquity under a number of different names such as Hun-chu, Hsien-yün, Jung, Ti, etc. In modern times even the name Kuei-fang of the Shang period is added to the list. From a strictly historical point of view, however, all these identifications must remain conjectural in status. The present state of our historical knowledge does not permit us to give any reliable account of the Hsiung-nu much beyond the 3rd century B.C.; and the only other name with which the Hsiung-nu can be safely identified in early Chinese sources is Hu. In other words, the Hsiung-nu made their earliest formal appearance on the stage of Inner Asian history when Chinese history was just about to turn a new page – at the end of the Warring States period.

Interestingly enough, from early Chinese sources we know how China defended herself against the Hsiung-nu before we actually encounter the Hsiung-nu's armed incursions into China. In the late Warring States period three major states, Ch'in, Chao, and Yen, were all southern neighbors of the Hsiung-nu, and each as a defense against the nomads built a wall along its northern border. Of the three, Ch'in was the first to do so, probably no later than in 324 B.C.; but its entire walled defense system – in Lung-hsi (Kansu), Pei-ti (parts of Kansu and Ninghsia), and the Shang Commandery (parts of Shensi and Suiyuan) – was not completed until around 270 B.C. Next came the northern border wall of Chao, stretching from Yün-chung (in Suiyuan) through Yen-men to Tai (both in Shansi), which was built around 300. Lastly, about a decade later than Chao, King Chao of Yen also constructed a long wall from Tsao-yang (in Chahar) to Hsiang-p'ing (in Liao-ning) to guard against the attacks, not only of the Hsiung-nu, but of the Tung-hu (Eastern Barbarians) as well.

During this period the state of Chao in particular had close contacts with the Hsiung-nu. In order to meet the Hsiung-nu's military challenge on their

own ground, King Wu-ling issued, in 307 B.C., a decree formally adopting the barbarian form of dress and instructing his people to learn the arts of horseback riding and archery. This policy of "barbarization" bore immediate fruit, for the Chao forces were able to penetrate into the lands of the Hsiung-nu as far as Yü-chung (in Kansu) within only about a year's time. Chao had still another brilliant victory over the Hsiung-nu to its credit later in the mid-3rd century. The famous general Li Mu, who was responsible for garrisoning the northern frontier of Chao at Yen-men (near modern Ta-t'ung, Shansi), routed the Hsiung-nu in a large-scale battle. After he had lured the nomads deep into Chao territory, Li made a surprise attack with a combined army of chariots, cavalry, and archers over 160,000 strong, and defeated a Hsiung-nu army of more than 100,000 horsemen. The *shan-yü* (leader of the Hsiung-nu) fled with his forces and for about ten years thereafter did not, as the Chinese report goes, even dare get near the Chao frontier cities. This defeat was apparently a serious setback to the early expansion of the Hsiung-nu.

The state of Yen also had contacts with the Hsiung-nu as is illustrated by the following story. In 227 B.C. the Ch'in general Fan Yü-ch'i defected to Yen and the Yen heir-apparent named Tan granted him asylum. A senior advisor at the court of Yen, however, urged that General Fan be sent to the Hsiung-nu. According to his calculation, this would serve two purposes. First, it would prevent Ch'in from knowing that Fan had fled to Yen. Second, Yen could take this opportunity to seek an alliance with the *shan-yü* of the Hsiung-nu in order to unite against their common enemy, the state of Ch'in, which was becoming increasingly aggressive. That the counsel was not heeded is not that important to our discussion. What is significant is the fact that the counsel itself clearly reveals that by this time the Hsiung-nu were already a great political power in the north.

However, of the three Chinese states, it was Ch'in that really held the southward expansion of the Hsiung-nu in check. The unification of China by the First Emperor of Ch'in in 221 B.C. pushed the sphere of influence of the Hsiung-nu back farther north. In 214 B.C. the Ch'in general Meng T'ien succeeded in taking the Ordos from the Hsiung-nu. Immediately following that Ch'in connected, repaired, and extended the three separate walls of Ch'in, Chao, and Yen which had been built in the Warring States period, so that one long Great Wall was finally formed, stretching from Lin T'ao in Kansu all the way to Chieh-shih, north of present day P'yŏngyang. The Hsiung-nu were therefore forced to retreat into the Yin Mountains north of the Ordos. In the next few years the Hsiung-nu were not only prevented by the Ch'in from southward expansion, they also faced the powerful Tung-hu on

their eastern flank, the Yüeh-chih in western Kansu and eastern Sinkiang, and the Ting-ling and other tribes in the north. The Ting-ling, it may be noted, inhabited the area from around Lake Baikal in southern Siberia to slightly beyond the Yenisei River. Thus, before the breakup of the Ch'in empire at the end of the 3rd century B.C. the Hsiung-nu were surrounded by powerful neighbors on virtually all sides.

On the other hand, however, the unification of China and the completion of the Great Wall also produced positive results for the Hsiung-nu. These two events acted as stimuli to their nomadic society, wakening within it a sense of solidarity. This newly-aroused feeling must have aided the *shan-yü* Tumen in asserting his leadership and weaving the various Hsiung-nu tribes into a unified political network after the model, more or less, of the Ch'in empire.

The rise of Motun

It was right at this time of initial expansion, in 209 B.C., that Motun took the throne and became *shan-yü*. The story of his succession is indicative of the kind of unswerving loyalty which he commanded, and the method of rule he used. Although Motun was the eldest son of Tumen, his father favored another son, and sought to dispose of Motun by sending him as a hostage to the Yüeh-chih in the west, then attacking them. Before the Yüeh-chih could kill Motun, however, he stole one of their best horses and escaped. Tumen was impressed with his son's courage and rewarded him by giving him command of 10,000 mounted bowmen. Motun disciplined these archers to shoot without question at whatever he himself hit with a special whistling arrow. Those who did not do so immediately were killed on the spot. Motun began by eliminating those men who hesitated when he fired a whistling arrow, first at his favorite horse, and then at his favorite wife. When not one of the men balked when he shot his father's finest horse, he knew they were trained to perfection. Assured of unbroken discipline, he then shot at his father, and his men obediently followed. Next Motun did away with the rest of the family who had plotted against him, and any uncooperative officials. His leadership thus firmly established within the Hsiung-nu empire, Motun was free to turn his attention outward.

The eastern neighbors of the Hsiung-nu, the Tung-hu, hearing of Motun's succession, evidently tried to test the new ruler. They asked Motun to give them, first a prized horse, then one of his beautiful concubines. Both of these he gave without much hesitation, for the Tung-hu were quite powerful at this time and equal to, if not stronger than, the Hsiung-nu. But when the Tung-hu,

thinking that Motun was afraid of them, became bolder and demanded some territory lying between their two countries, Motun was enraged and suddenly attacked the Tung-hu, catching them off guard and totally defeating them. He killed their leader and took a great number of prisoners and livestock. Following this victory he turned west and defeated the Yüeh-chih, then south to finish recovering the Hsiung-nu lands taken from them by China under the Ch'in.

There are two obvious reasons which help explain how the Hsiung-nu were able to reoccupy the Ordos region. The first was the death of the Chinese general Meng T'ien. During the First Emperor's time Meng T'ien had commanded an army numbering slightly over 300,000 in guarding the Great Wall. His headquarters were established in the Shang Commandery, in present day Inner Mongolia. This location reflects the fact that the principal area of defense was the Ordos. After Meng T'ien was forced to commit suicide in 210 B.C., however, the defense system in the Ordos region fell completely apart. Secondly, in the First Emperor's time a great number of Chinese had been forced to migrate to the Ordos region to fill the land and guard the frontier. After civil war broke out all of these people fled inland and returned home, leaving the land empty and giving the Hsiung-nu an opportunity to gradually move in.

Motun's power was rapidly expanding during the early years of the Han dynasty. To try to ward off the Hsiung-nu invasions, Emperor Kao-tsu sent King Hsin of Han[1] in the spring of 201 B.C. to guard the border, with his headquarters established in the city of Ma-i. King Hsin was besieged for a long time by Motun's forces in the autumn of that same year, and therefore sent envoys several times to the Hsiung-nu to seek peace. These frequent contacts with the Hsiung-nu caused the Han court to suspect that Hsin was disloyal. Fearing that the court might take action against him, Hsin surrendered the city of Ma-i to the Hsiung-nu and also helped them to attack T'ai-yuan (in modern Shansi). In the winter of 200 B.C. Han Kao-tsu personally led an army to defeat Hsin. The emperor then advanced farther to attack the Hsiung-nu, going as far as P'ing-ch'eng (near modern Ta-t'ung in Shansi). The Han forces numbered over 300,000 altogether, but before all of the Han soldiers could reach the city, Motun surrounded P'ing-ch'eng with an equal number of his best cavalry. Emperor Kao-tsu was trapped in the besieged city for seven days, and then only narrowly escaped. After this test of strength Han Kao-tsu no longer thought the war was working to his advantage, and gave up the idea of

[1] Hang Wang Hsin, not to be confused with Han Hsin, Marquis of Huai-yin.

overcoming the Hsiung-nu with force. We can see from this incident that in terms of military power the Hsiung-nu were superior to the Han at this time. Their superiority lay primarily in their fast-moving cavalry and their lightning attacks, which were the principal Hsiung-nu tactics. In contrast, the Han relied mainly on slower-moving infantry.

The case of King Hsin of Han's defection is indicative of an important fact, namely that the Hsiung-nu threat to China in the early years of the Han dynasty was not only military but also political. During this period, several other powerful men on the northern border equal in standing to King Hsin joined the ranks of defectors, notably Lu Wan, King of Yen, and Ch'en Hsi, prime minister and general of Tai. Moreover, many of the Han frontier generals, like Wang Huang, had previously been merchants, and as merchants they had long established good relations with the Hsiung-nu. It is only natural that these men were all political amphibians, and whether they looked to the Han or to the Hsiung-nu for leadership depended very much on the situation in the border areas. At any rate, the Han court could by no means count on their faithfulness.[2] Even the Chinese common people had yet to develop their sense of loyalty toward Han China. There was a saying among fugitives in China: "Northward we can flee to the Hsiung-nu, southward we can run to the Yüeh." Thus the danger of defections at all levels was always present, and such defections constantly affected the balance of power between the Han and the Hsiung-nu. Before the establishment of its supreme authority at home, the Han court's continued hostilities with the Hsiung-nu could only work toward weakening the foundation of Han imperial order.

The Hsiung-nu and the Han under the *Ho-ch'in* treaties

Under these circumstances Han Kao-tsu had no choice but to take the advice of Liu Ching and seek the well-known *ho-ch'in* peace alliance with the Hsiung-nu in 198 B.C. The original form of the *ho-ch'in* alliance was rather simple. The two parties agreed that: a Han princess would be married to the *shan-yü*; several times a year the Han would send gifts of various kinds, including fixed amounts of silk, wine, and food, to the Hsiung-nu; the Hsiung-nu was a brother state equal in status to the Han. For their part the Hsiung-nu promised not to invade Han lands. In the winter of 198 B.C. Liu Ching escorted a daughter from the royal clan under the name of an imperial princess to the Hsiung-nu and signed the first *ho-ch'in* treaty.[3]

[2] On the problem of defection, see Owen Lattimore, *Inner Asian Frontiers of China*, pp. 477–80.

[3] On the *ho-ch'in* alliance between the Han and the Hsiung-nu from Han Kao-tsu down to Emperor Wu, see the article by Tezuka Tayayoshi in *Shien*, vol. XII, no. 2 (Dec., 1948).

With the expansion of the Hsiung-nu empire, however, Motun became more and more dissatisfied with the conditions of the original *ho-ch'in* treaty, and he also became increasingly arrogant. In 192 B.C., when Emperor Hui came to the throne, another so-called princess was sent to marry Motun. During Emperor Hui's reign, the actual government was in the hands of his mother, Empress Lü. Motun wrote her a letter around this time saying,

> I am a lonely widowed ruler, born amidst the marshes and brought up on the wild steppes in the land of cattle and horses. I have often come to the border wishing to travel in China. Your majesty is also a widowed ruler living a life of solitude. The both of us are without pleasures and lack any way to amuse ourselves. It is my hope that we can exchange that which we have for that which we are lacking.

In Empress Lü's reply to this insulting letter she says,

> My age is advanced and my vitality weakening. Both my hair and teeth are falling out, and I cannot even walk steadily. The *shan-yü* must have heard exaggerated reports. I am not worthy of his lowering himself. But my country has done nothing wrong, and I hope that he will spare it.[4]

Motun then sent an envoy to thank the Empress, together with his apology. The *ho-ch'in* treaty was once again resumed.

Some fifteen years later, in 176 B.C., Motun sent a letter to Emperor Wen which shows his boldness even more vividly. Motun begins by calling himself the "Great *shan-yü* of the Hsiung-nu Established by Heaven." The letter continues:

> Through the aid of Heaven, the excellence of our fighting men, and the strength of our horses, we have succeeded in wiping out the Yüeh-chih, slaughtering or forcing to submission every member of the tribe. In addition we have conquered the Lou-lan, Wu-sun, and Hu-chieh tribes as well as the twenty-six states nearby, so that all of them have become a part of the Hsiung-nu nation. All the people who live by drawing the bow are now united into one family, and the entire region of the north is at peace. Thus I wish now to lay down my weapons, rest my soldiers, and turn my horses to pasture, to forget the recent affair and to restore our old pact.[5]

We can detect a threatening tone in this letter. Obviously, after the Hsiung-nu's conquest of the Yüeh-chih and other groups, Motun's position was very much strengthened and the Hsiung-nu control over the north consolidated. When Emperor Wen received this letter he discussed it with his ministers in a court conference. It was the consensus of opinion that the Han must comply with Motun's wishes to renew the *ho-ch'in* treaty.

[4] For Motun's letter to Empress Lü see the *Han Shu*, 94A: 4b; for the reply, *Han Shu*, 94A:5a.

[5] Watson, II, p. 168, slightly modified. The twenty-six states should be thirty-six, according to Matsuda Hisao. See his *Kodai Tenzan no rekishi chirigaku teki Kenkyū*, Tokyo, 1956, pp. 36–8.

Motun died in 174 B.C. His son Lao-shang (also called Chi-chu) succeeded him as *shan-yü*. Lao-shang appeared to be even more aggressive than his father. In 166 B.C. he personally led 140,000 cavalry in an invasion of An-ting (in modern Kansu). When Lao-shang was succeeded by his son Chün-ch'en in 160 B.C., the latter also showed no respect for the peace treaty. In 158 B.C. Chün-ch'en *shan-yü* sent 30,000 cavalry to invade the Shang Commandery, and another 30,000 to attack Yün-chung. The mountain-top warning beacons were burning as far back as Ch'ang-an, the Han capital. We can more or less discern a pattern in these attacks. Each time a new *shan-yü* ascended the throne he managed to establish his own authority among the Hsiung-nu through military achievements.

These continuing invasions eventually forced Emperor Wen to revise the conditions of the *ho-ch'in* treaty. According to historian Pan Ku, "Emperor Wen opened border trade with the Hsiung-nu, sent a Han daughter to marry the *shan-yü*, and increased the gifts to the Hsiung-nu to 1,000 pieces of gold a year."[6] Among these revisions the opening of border trade, which took the form of the establishment of border markets, is particularly noteworthy. Previously historians all have believed that the formal opening of border markets in the north began in the time of Emperor Ching (156–140 B.C.). Actually, the establishment of border markets was imposed on the Chinese by the Hsiung-nu in Emperor Wen's time. The statesman and scholar Chia I, who died in 169 B.C., has left us with a brief account concerning the border markets:

> It is the border markets [*kuan-shih*] which the Hsiung-nu need most badly, and they have sought desperately to obtain them from us, even resorting to force. I urge your majesty to send envoys with lavish gifts to make peace with [the Hsiung-nu], using this opportunity to inform them of our decision, made not without reluctance, to grant their request of establishing large-sized border markets. Upon the return of our envoys, we should immediately open up many [markets] in locations of strategic importance. In each of these market places sufficient military forces must be stationed for [our] self-protection. Every large border market should include shops which specialize in selling raw meat, wine, cooked rice, and delicious barbecues. All the shops must be of a size capable of serving one or two hundred people. In this way our markets beneath the Great Wall will surely swarm with the Hsiung-nu. Moreover, if their kings and generals [try to] force the Hsiung-nu to return to the north, it is inevitable that they would turn to attack their kings. When the Hsiung-nu have developed a craving for our rice, stew, barbecues, and wine, this will have become their fatal weakness.[7]

During the reign of Emperor Ching and in the early years of Emperor Wu (from roughly 156 to 135 B.C.) the Hsiung-nu stopped their large-scale inroads

[6] See Pan Ku's "Remarks" in *Han Shu*, 94B:12b.

[7] Chia I, *Hsin Shu*, (Ts'ung-shu chi-ch'eng edition) *chüan* 4, p. 41.

into China. But this temporary and relative peace was not without its price. Under the *ho-ch'in* system the Han court never ceased to increase the gifts which formed part of the peace treaty, in order to keep the Hsiung-nu interested in observing the agreement. When Emperor Wu came to the throne the price paid by the Han court for the *ho-ch'in* treaty reached its highest point. According to Chinese accounts, among the first things that Emperor Wu did was to "reaffirm the *ho-ch'in* peace alliance. He treated the Hsiung-nu with great generosity, allowing them to trade in border markets, and sending them lavish gifts. From the *shan-yü* on down, all the Hsiung-nu grew friendly with the Han, coming and going along the Great Wall".[8] From this statement we can see that in the early days of Emperor Wu not only did the Han give the Hsiung-nu more gifts, but the official border trade was also widened in scale. Imperial gifts were to satisfy the Hsiung-nu nobility, while official border trade met the needs of the Hsiung-nu people.

Altogether from 198 to 135 B.C. the Han and the Hsiung-nu signed no fewer than ten *ho-ch'in* treaties.[9] Almost each time a new pact was signed something was lost by the Han, and gained by the Hsiung-nu. To Han China, the *ho-ch'in* treaties had become a constant and increasing financial drain. All these gifts, however, did not completely prevent the Hsiung-nu from raiding the border. For instance, in 144 B.C. the Hsiung-nu penetrated well into the Shang Commandery, and took horses from the imperial stables there. Again, the Hsiung-nu invaded Yen-men in 142 B.C. and fought with the commandant Feng Ching, who died in battle. With the increasing cost, and decreasing effectiveness of the *ho-ch'in* treaty, it was almost inevitable that the Han court would decide to change its policy from the defensive to the offensive, and do away with the Hsiung-nu threat once and for all.

The Hsiung-nu and their non-Chinese neighbors

At this point we must retrace our steps to review the relations between the Hsiung-nu and other neighboring peoples. We first come to the Tung-hu, or Eastern Barbarians, comprised mainly of the Wu-huan and Hsien-pi[10] peoples. Towards the end of the 3rd century B.C. the territories under Tung-hu control extended from the southern part of Inner Mongolia to southern Manchuria. The Tung-hu were very powerful at this time, and constantly

[8] Watson, II, p. 176.

[9] The recorded *ho-ch'in* treaties are as follows (all B.C.): 198, 192, 179, 174 (twice), 162, 161, 156, 155, 135.

[10] [Professor Yü uses this spelling of the name transcribed Hsien-pei elsewhere in this volume. D.S.]

raided the Hsiung-nu lands to their west. We have seen that around the beginning of the Han Empire in 206 B.C., after Motun had murdered his father and made himself *shan-yü*, he was able to defeat the Tung-hu in a decisive battle, and captured numerous Tung-hu people, cattle, and much property. After this defeat, both the Wu-huan and the Hsien-pi migrated from Inner Mongolia to Manchuria, and settled in what we now call the Shira Muren River valley and the Lao-ha River valley (two upper branches of the Liao River) respectively. From that time on the Wu-huan became subject to the control of the Hsiung-nu, and every year sent them oxen, horses, sheep, and sable skins as tribute. If they failed to send tribute to the Hsiung-nu in time, the Hsiung-nu would enslave their wives and children. We do not have enough information about the Hsien-pi during this period, but in all likelihood they were treated in a similar way by the Hsiung-nu.

The fact that the Wu-huan had to send annual tribute to the Hsiung-nu, even as late as toward the end of the Former Han, can be seen in the following incident. In A.D. 2 the Han court, under Wang Mang's influence, promulgated new regulations concerning the Hsiung-nu's relations with the Chinese and other peoples. One of the regulations forbade the Hsiung-nu to take captive any Wu-huan people who surrendered to them. In enforcing this new regulation the Chinese office in charge of Wu-huan affairs therefore told the Wu-huan to stop paying skin and cloth taxes to the Hsiung-nu. Nevertheless, the Hsiung-nu as usual sent envoys to collect the taxes from the Wu-huan, and this year the envoys were followed by a large number of ordinary Hsiung-nu men and women who wanted to trade with the Wu-huan. When the Wu-huan refused to yield to the Hsiung-nu demands the envoy arrested the Wu-huan chieftain and hung him upside down. The chieftain's brothers were infuriated and killed the Hsiung-nu envoy and his followers, keeping the Hsiung-nu women and the cattle which they had brought along. When the *shan-yü* heard of this he sent the Wise King of the Left to attack the Wu-huan offenders. At this the Wu-huan people scattered. Some of them went up into the hills, and others hid themselves in fortified areas. The Hsiung-nu killed many of the Wu-huan who did not go into hiding, and took prisoner 1,000 women and children, placing them in the area ruled by the Wise King of the Left. The Hsiung-nu told the Wu-huan to bring horses, cattle, skins, and cloth to ransom back their people. The relatives of these Wu-huan captives, over 2,000 in number, brought money and cattle to the Hsiung-nu, but the Hsiung-nu kept not only the money and the cattle but the people as well. This story is a clear example of the long-standing obligation which the Tung-hu people had

to pay regular taxes to the Hsiung-nu after their defeat in Motun's time. These taxes probably became an important part of the Hsiung-nu's revenue.

With the conquest of the Tung-hu completed, Motun turned westward toward the Yüeh-chih, a nomadic empire like the Hsiung-nu. They originally lived in the Kansu area and at the height of their power are reported to have possessed military forces of over 100,000 bowmen. Since Motun in his early days had been a hostage among the Yüeh-chih it seems that he had developed a kind of hatred against them. In his first war with the Yüeh-chi shortly after his succession, Motun took much of the Kansu corridor from the Yüeh-chih. Some twenty years later, in 175 B.C., Motun ordered the Wise King of the Right to attack the Yüeh-chih again on an even greater scale. This time the Yüeh-chih were utterly routed.

After this defeat the Yüeh-chih could no longer hold their position in the Kansu corridor, and split into two groups known as the Great and Small Yüeh-chih. The Small Yüeh-chih retreated into the southern part of the Ch'i-lien Mountains (bordering the Kansu corridor), and mixed with the Ch'iang people. The Great Yüeh-chih went westward and settled in the Ili River valley. But later, in 162 B.C., Lao-shang *shan-yü*, jointly with the Wu-sun (a state on the northeast side of the T'ien Shan which had just been conquered by the Hsiung-nu), attacked them again and killed the king of the Great Yüeh-chih and made his skull into a drinking vessel. The Wu-sun then moved into the Ili Valley themselves while the Great Yüeh-chih went farther west to the south of Sogdiana (K'ang-chü). After the Hsiung-nu had occupied the Kansu corridor, two Hsiung-nu kings named Hun-yeh and Hsiu-t'u were stationed there.

The Hsiung-nu then went on to conquer the Western Regions, an area centering around the Tarim basin. The first states of the Western Regions conquered by the Hsiung-nu were Lou-lan (south of Lobnor), Wu-sun, and Hu-chieh, whose people may be identified with the Uighurs of later days. The Hsiung-nu control would soon be extended over the entire Western Regions, strengthening further the political and economic foundations of their empire.

In general the peoples in the Western Regions led sedentary lives. They built cities, farmed the land, and domesticated animals. Economically they were in a more advanced state than the nomadic Tung-hu. To govern these states in the Western Regions, the Hsiung-nu established an office known as the *T'ung-p'u tu-wei* (Commandant in charge of slaves) under the jurisdiction of the *Jih-chu* King. The *T'ung-p'u tu-wei* headquarters were situated between the three states known as Yen-ch'i (Karashahr), Wei-hsü (northwest of Yen-ch'i), and Yü-li (Kalmagan). This office had the power to tax the various

states, and it also had the authority to conscript corvée labor. We thus know from the establishment of this office that the Western Regions provided the Hsiung-nu with both material and human resources.

The office of the *T'ung-p'u tu-wei* lasted until 60 B.C., when the *Jih-chu* King surrendered to the Han and the office was abolished. Evidence shows, however, that after this year, whenever possible, the Hsiung-nu still continued to collect taxes and labor services from the various states of the Western Regions. For example, the state Sha-ch'a (Yarkand) presented annual tribute to the Hsiung-nu. To give another illustration, between A.D. 107 and 123 the Northern Hsiung-nu demanded that all the states of the Western Regions pay tax arrears before a specified date. Thus we can see that whenever the Han control over that region weakened, the Hsiung-nu hastened back to claim their lost rights.

Presumably for historical reasons, even after the Han influence had penetrated into the area, there were still states which showed a clear inclination towards the Hsiung-nu, notably Wu-sun and Lou-lan. As a matter of fact, from Motun's day up to the submission of Hu-han-yeh to the Han court in 53 B.C., the states in the Western Regions west of Wu-sun as far as Parthia (An-hsi) as a rule treated the Hsiung-nu better than they did the Han. For instance, Hsiung-nu envoys needed only to carry with them their credentials from the *shan-yü* to obtain complete supplies everywhere. In contrast, the Han envoys could get neither food nor horses without paying handsomely. It did not take long for the Han court to realize that the Hsiung-nu could not be defeated without their major sources of strength – the Western Regions – first being taken away. It was precisely this realization which prompted Emperor Wu's decision to establish relations with states in the Western Regions, in order "to cut off the right arm of the Hsiung-nu."

The Han offensive

The year 134 B.C. was a decisive turning point in the history of Hsiung-nu–Han relations. In this year, a frontier merchant by the name of Nieh Weng-i of Ma-i city proposed to the Han court a plot to lure the Hsiung-nu forces into a Chinese ambush in Ma-i, which, after heated debate in a court conference, was finally adopted by the young Emperor Wu. The next year Nieh slipped out to the Hsiung-nu and said to the *shan-yü*, "I can kill the magistrate and military officer of Ma-i and surrender the city to you, so that you can obtain all the wealth and goods there." The *shan-yü* liked him and believed him, so he promised to follow Nieh's advice. Then Nieh killed a prisoner awaiting the

death sentence, and hung his head outside of the city as a signal to the *shan-yü*'s envoy, and said to him, "the magistrate of Ma-i is now dead, please move quickly." Thereupon the *shan-yü* came through the pass into China with 100,000 cavalrymen. Meanwhile, the Han mixed forces of chariots, cavalry, and infantry, altogether numbering more than 300,000, were waiting in the valleys around Ma-i. But before the Hsiung-nu had come within 100 *li* (a *li* is about one third of a mile) of Ma-i the *shan-yü* discovered that he was about to fall into a trap, and immediately turned back. This single event decisively ended the *ho-ch'in* relations between the Han and the Hsiung-nu which had lasted for over 70 years.

Nevertheless, full-scale war did not break out until 129 B.C., five years later. In the autumn of that year the Han court dispatched four generals – Wei Ch'ing, Kung-sun Ho, Kung-sun Ao, and Li Kuang – each with 10,000 cavalrymen, to attack the Hsiung-nu by surprise at the border markets. Nothing was gained by these attacks; it is interesting to note, however, that the Han forces chose the border markets to attack the Hsiung-nu because, as we have seen, the Hsiung-nu often came in large numbers to these markets to buy things and obtain food and drink. The first severe blow which the Han dealt the Hsiung-nu came in 127 B.C. General Wei Ch'ing led an army across the border from Yün-chung towards Lung-hsi and took the lands in the Ordos, where the Han then established the two commandaries of Shuo-fang and Wu-yüan, sending in 100,000 Chinese to populate the area. From this time on the Ordos returned permanently to China. The Hsiung-nu received their second major defeat at the hands of General Ho Ch'ü-ping in 121 B.C. General Ho led his light cavalry westward out of Lung-hsi and penetrated deeply into the Hsiung-nu lands of the Right. Ho fought his way through five Hsiung-nu kingdoms and killed the Hsiung-nu kings Che-lan and Lu-hou, and captured the son of King Hun-yeh (who was guarding the Kansu corridor as mentioned above). He took both the Yen-chih and Ch'i-lien Mountains from the Hsiung-nu. He even forced King Hun-yeh to surrender to China with 40,000 men. In 119 B.C. both generals Ho Ch'ü-ping and Wei Ch'ing, each with 50,000 cavalrymen followed by thirty to fifty thousand footsoldiers, pursued the *shan-yü* north of the Gobi, each following a different route. Wei Ch'ing chased the *shan-yü* northward as far as the Chao Hsin fort in the Tien-yen Mountains before turning back. Ho Ch'ü-ping reached the vicinity of Han Hai (Lake Baikal) where he performed the *feng* and *shan* sacrifices at Lang-chü-hsü Mountain (between Ho-lan Mountain and the Yin Mountains) and at Ku-yen, respectively.

As a result of these campaigns the Hsiung-nu moved their court from south

of the Gobi, near Han lands, to north of the desert. The two generals had killed or captured altogether about eighty to ninety thousand Hsiung-nu, but this number was matched by the loss of Han soldiers. Much more significant to the Chinese, however, was the loss of horses. When both generals left the border they had with them altogether 140,000 government and privately owned horses, but by the time they returned to China the horses numbered fewer than 30,000. Henceforth, due to a shortage of horses, the Han made no further attempt to attack the Hsiung-nu in the desert.

According to an official of Wang Mang's time (A.D. 9–23) there were several difficulties which the Han forces faced in going out of the border to attack the Hsiung-nu. Among these difficulties was the problem of food supplies. One soldier alone would need eighteen bushels of dried rice for a 300 days' march. This rice had to be carried by ox. But the food for the ox meant adding another twenty bushels of wheat to the beast. It was known from experience that the ox would die within 100 days in the desert. The rice which remained would still be too heavy for the soldier to carry. Another difficulty was the weather in the Hsiung-nu lands. In autumn and winter it was extremely cold, and in the spring and summer very windy. The soldiers could never carry enough fuel for these northerly expeditions. Therefore in the past, as the official went on to explain, no single Han campaign against the Hsiung-nu had ever exceeded 100 days.[11]

The two great battles of 121 and 119 B.C. produced at least two far-reaching consequences as far as the lives of the Hsiung-nu were concerned. One was the loss of the Ch'i-lien and Yen-chih Mountains, which for many years had been the cherished homelands and favorite pastures of the Hsiung-nu. A Hsiung-nu song mourns their loss:

> Since we have lost our Ch'i-lien Mountains, our animals
> have ceased to proliferate.
> Since we have lost our Yen-chih Mountains, our women
> have no rouge to brighten their cheeks.[12]

Another change was the loss of the lands stretching west from the Kansu corridor to Lobnor. The Han established the Chiu-ch'üan Commandery in this region, thus separating the Hsiung-nu from the Ch'iang peoples to the south, who had been their allies since Motun's time. With the establishment of

[11] *Han Shu* 94B:10b.

[12] The Chinese word *yen-chih*, which means rouge, was linguistically of a possible Tokharian origin. It is believed that *yen-chih* was made from safflower, which was said to grow in abundance on the Yen-chih Mountains. See E.G. Pulleyblank, "Chinese and Indo-Europeans," *Journal of the Royal Asiatic Society*, April, 1966, p. 20.

this commandery Han gained access to the Western Regions for the first time. The age of the Hsiung-nu's sole domination of the Western Regions was over.

The struggle for the Western Regions

The half-century that stretched from 115 to 60 B.C. was a period in which the Hsiung-nu and the Han struggled for mastery over the Western Regions. The Han court was keenly aware of the fact that the Western Regions provided an important military, political, and economic base for the Hsiung-nu; they therefore used all possible means to wrest the Western Regions from Hsiung-nu hands.

In the early years of his reign, Emperor Wu (140–87 B.C.) sent Chang Ch'ien to the Western Regions in search of the Great Yüeh-chih, in hopes that a Han–Yüeh-chih military alliance could be made to attack the Hsiung-nu from two flanks. Chang Ch'ien failed in this mission. Nevertheless, his imprisonment among the Hsiung-nu for about a decade, and the year or so he spent traveling in the Western Regions, including the state of the Great Yüeh-chih and Bactria (Ta Hsia), were not completely wasted. He brought back to China first-hand information of the Western Regions and he also had familiarized himself with the geography of the Hsiung-nu territory. Chang's knowledge of Hsiung-nu terrain later proved to be of great military value. In 123 B.C. he served as the guide to General Wei Ch'ing's army and helped the general win a brilliant battle over the Hsiung-nu's Wise King of the Right.

Han Wu-ti did not give up the search for allies against the Hsiung-nu. In 115 B.C. Chang Ch'ien was sent to the Western Regions for the second time in the capacity of a Han envoy. He succeeded in establishing initial contacts with such states as Ferghana (Ta Yüan), Sogdiana (K'ang-chü), and Wu-sun. In their dealings with states of the Western Regions the Han made use of gifts of gold and silk, but sometimes marriage was also an important bargaining point. For example, in 105 B.C. the Han sent a Han "princess" to marry K'un-mo, the aged king of Wu-sun, another state which had been the Hsiung-nu's ally since Motun's days. The Hsiung-nu quickly saw the significance of this marriage, so the *shan-yü* also sent one of his daughters to marry the king. K'un-mo made the Han princess the Bride of the Right, and the Hsiung-nu princess the Bride of the Left. If the Wu-sun people, like the Hsiung-nu, considered the seat on the left side to be the place of honor, however, then we must say that the Han did not exactly win the first battle on the marital ground.

The struggle between the Hsiung-nu and the Han for supremacy in the

Western Regions also took political forms, such as the hostage system. In 108 B.C. General Chao P'o-nu defeated Lou-lan, which surrendered to the Han. When the Hsiung-nu heard of this they attacked Lou-lan, so that the king of Lou-lan finally was forced to send one son as hostage to the Han, and another son as hostage to the Hsiung-nu. That these hostage sons played important political roles can be seen in the following situation. Several decades after 108 B.C., the king of Lou-lan died. As soon as they learned of his death the Hsiung-nu rushed their hostage prince back to Lou-lan and put him on the throne, thus seating someone favorable to them in power. This instance clearly demonstrates the Hsiung-nu's skill in playing the game of politics.

But the decisive victories in the struggle were to be determined on the battlefield. We will take Chü-shih (actually two states, one in the Turfan depression, the other over the mountains bordering the depression on the north) as an illustration. Chü-shih was the key area for both the Hsiung-nu and the Han in exercising control over the Western Regions, since the Hsiung-nu could control the Western Region peoples only through their military base in Chü-shih, and the Han had to go through there in order to reach such western states as Ferghana and Wu-sun. Chü-shih had been a faithful ally of the Hsiung-nu for a long time. In 108 B.C., therefore, immediately after General Chao P'o-nu occupied Lou-lan, he advanced north to defeat Chü-shih. With this state under Han's control, states as far away as Wu-sun and Ferghana could feel China's military influence. The fact that the Han was able to establish its first marital ties with Wu-sun in 105 B.C. was directly related to the Han victory over Chü-shih.

Nevertheless, the Hsiung-nu also realized the vital military and economic importance of this area to them, so in the first quarter of the 1st century B.C. they made repeated attacks to win Chü-shih back. After 60 B.C., when the Hsiung-nu finally lost their absolute control of Chü-shih, their uncontested domination of the Western Regions also came to an end. Throughout the period of the two Han dynasties, however, the ties between the Hsiung-nu and Chü-shih were never completely broken. In centuries after 60 B.C., if the Han influence in the Western Regions ever weakened, the Hsiung-nu immediately came back to seize Chü-shih. As late as A.D. 123 evidence shows that Chü-shih was still the Hsiung-nu's military and economic base. As a matter of fact, the Northern Hsiung-nu under the Later Han dynasty were always trying to develop their control over the Western Regions from their base at Chü-shih.

Another important battle which helped the Han to wrest control of the Western Regions from the Hsiung-nu was the conquest of Ferghana (Ta Yüan) in 101 B.C. by the Han Erh-shih General, Li Kuang-li. The Hsiung-nu,

when they learned about the Han military movement westward, tried to intercept the army, only to be outnumbered by the Han forces. Emperor Wu's determination to conquer Ferghana was motivated by two important considerations. First, Han wanted to obtain more of Ferghana's "blood-sweating" horses to use in fighting the Hsiung-nu. Second, the Han wanted to demonstrate its military strength to the peoples in the west. Ferghana was very far from Han China (12,550 *li* from Ch'ang-an), and situated to the west of Wu-sun. If Han could subdue Ferghana, then all the states in the Western Regions would be at the mercy of China. As the History of the Han Dynasty says, "After the Erh-shih General /Li Kuang-li/ conquered Ta Yüan, all of the states of the Western Regions were shocked and frightened. Most states sent envoys to present tribute to the Han."[13]

The Hsiung-nu lose control of the Western Regions

The Hsiung-nu's repeated defeats on the battlefields of the Western Regions eventually led to Han dominance in the area. The Han hegemony is marked by the establishment of the office of the Protector General of the Western Regions (*Hsi-yü Tu-hu*) in 60 B.C. Previously we have seen that the *Jih-chu* King, named Hsien-hsien-t'ien, surrendered to the Han in 60 B.C. With his surrender the Hsiung-nu office of *T'ung-p'u tu-wei* was abolished. We have every reason to believe that the function of the Hsiung-nu's office of *T'ung-p'u tu-wei* was taken over by the Han office of Protector General (*Tu-hu*). The Han general Cheng Chi, after receiving the *Jih-chu* King's surrender, was immediately appointed the first Chinese Protector General. In addition, the office of *Tu-hu* was not only the Han military headquarters in the Western Regions, it also possessed a general political authority to keep the whole area under Han control on the one hand, and regulate relations among most of the states there on the other. The office of the *T'ung-p'u tu-wei* is reported to have been located somewhere between Yen-ch'i, Wei-hsü, and Yü-li. The Han office of the *Tu-hu* was set up in the city of Wu-lei (Chadir), which was only 300 to 500 *li* away from each of these three states. It is quite reasonable to assume that Chadir had been the site of the Hsiung-nu's *T'ung-p'u tu-wei*. In other words, the Han simply took over the Hsiung-nu's office and transformed it into that of the Protector General.

After the Han gained access to the Western Regions the Hsiung-nu suffered an economic loss as well as a political defeat. As early as after the conquest of

[13] *Han Shu* 96A:1b.

Ferghana, the Han began to establish military agricultural colonies (*t'un-t'ien*) in various parts of the Western Regions, forcing out the Hsiung-nu. Each of these *t'un-t'ien* establishments normally included about 500 soldier-farmers. The purpose of the settlements was the production of sufficient food supplies for both Han soldiers and envoys in the Western Regions. Again Chü-shih played a key role in the struggle, since in addition to its strategic value, Chü-shih was also known for the fertility of its agricultural land, and had been the Hsiung-nu's ricebowl. This explains why Chü-shih particularly became the focal point of armed struggle between the Hsiung-nu and the Han for over two decades in the early part of the 1st century B.C.

In Emperor Chao's time (86–74 B.C.) the Hsiung-nu had been in full control of the cultivated lands in Chü-shih. After Chü-shih surrendered to the Han in 67 B.C., however, the Han began to set up *t'un-t'ien* settlements there. The Hsiung-nu leaders quickly realized the gravity of this development, and they made repeated attacks on the Han *t'un-t'ien* settlements in Chü-shih after 67 B.C. As a result of these raids, the Han were compelled to evacuate Chü-shih in 64 B.C. and let the Hsiung-nu take the lands back. But as the Han withdrew from the area they forced most if not all of the people of Chü-shih to migrate to Ch'ü-li (Kurla), thus leaving the Hsiung-nu practically without land cultivators. But in 48 B.C., five years after *shan-yü* Hu-han-yeh had submitted to the Han, however, the Han re-established the *t'un-t'ien* system in Chü-shih. This time an office known as the *Wu-chi* Colonel was created to take formal charge of all the *t'un-t'ien* settlements in the whole of the Western Regions. The Hsiung-nu domination of the Western Regions had at long last come to an end.

The century and a half between 209 and 60 B.C. witnessed the rapid rise and expansion of the Hsiung-nu empire, as well as the waning of its influence in the Western Regions. Expansion strengthened the regionalistic tendencies within the empire, which in turn sowed the seeds of internal strife, while severance from the Western Regions stripped the Hsiung-nu of much of their military and economic resources. We shall come to the problem of regionalism later. For the moment, let us define more clearly what the loss of the Western Regions meant to the Hsiung-nu. First, many of the states in the Western Regions, especially Chü-shih, had developed agrarian economies. Before the Han gained control over the area, the Hsiung-nu had relied heavily on grain produced in these states for food supplies. Second, the Western Regions had also provided the Hsiung-nu with various kinds of war materials, including iron weapons. Third, the Western Regions had contributed greatly to the manpower of the Hsiung-nu, as indicated by the existence of the office

of the *T'ung-p'u tu-wei*. Finally, the Hsiung-nu had collected taxes from the Western Regions. The total tax revenue must have been considerable when we take into account the large amount of transit trade that had been passing through the Western Regions between China and the far west. The beginning of Han domination in the Western Regions meant the end of all these benefits for the Hsiung-nu.

The Hsiung-nu's military defeats at the hands of the Han also encouraged rebellions among peoples who had previously been enslaved by the Hsiung-nu. These rebellions further shook the Hsiung-nu's economic foundations. For instance, in 72 B.C. Wu-sun mounted soldiers, with the help of a Han army, were able to sack the headquarters of the Hsiung-nu's Lu-li King of the Right, and captured not only 40,000 Hsiung-nu people, including nobles, but also horses, oxen, sheep, donkeys, and camels totalling 750,000 head. In 71 B.C., taking advantage of the Hsiung-nu's already weakened position, the Ting-ling from the north, the Wu-sun from the west, and the Wu-huan from the east made a concerted attack on the Hsiung-nu and caused them even heavier losses, which reportedly amounted to thirty percent of their population, and half of their livestock. From this time on the Hsiung-nu's control over their subject states totally collapsed.

Regionalism and leadership crisis

As the Hsiung-nu empire initially expanded to encompass the Tung-hu lands in the east and the Western Regions in the west, it was impossible for the *shan-yü* alone to govern the vast territories of his empire. As early as Motun's time therefore, the Hsiung-nu had already developed a dualistic political system. Under the *shan-yü*, the most powerful leaders were the Wise Kings of the Left and Right and the Left and Right Lu-li Kings. In addition to the central territory under the direct control of the *shan-yü*, the eastern part of the empire was controlled by the Left group and the western part by the Right group. Within each kingdom, the king possessed a very high degree of autonomy, having the power to appoint his subordinate officers and officials. It is this kind of decentralization that has led some historians to believe that the Hsiung-nu empire always preserved a certain element of "feudalism."[14]

As expansion continued, moreover, more kingdoms had to be created to

[14] W.M. McGovern, *The Early Empires of Central Asia*, University of North Carolina Press, 1939, p. 118. See also a recent study by Hsieh Jiann, "A Study of the Political Organization of the Hsiung-nu," (in Chinese) in *Bulletin of the Institute of History and Philology, Academia Sinica*, vol. 41, part 2 (1969).

incorporate the newly annexed territories. It is important to note that such newly created kingdoms were not necessarily assigned a place within the original dualistic system. For instance, around 120 B.C. there appeared in the western part of the Hsiung-nu territory (in the Kansu corridor) two powerful Hsiung-nu kings known as Hun-yeh and Hsiu-t'u, each of whom had his own people and lands. Obviously neither was assigned by the *shan-yü* to the Left or Right group. Later under *shan-yü* Hu-tu-erh-shih (A.D. 18–46), the *Jih-chu* King of the Right was given the power to control not the western part, interestingly enough, but the southern part of the Hsiung-nu empire. This case further shows that regionalism among the Hsiung-nu caused them eventually to outgrow the dualistic structure. There is also evidence that the Hsiung-nu dualistic organization had been expanding over the centuries. *The History of the Later Han Dynasty*, for example, lists six additional Left and Right Kings who are not found in the preceeding historical sources.

From the middle of the 1st century B.C. on, two other developments also seem to have testified to the growth of regionalism. First, there were cases in which local kings refused to attend the annual meetings held at the *shan-yü*'s court. Second, several of the *shan-yü* developed their power bases first in regions which had been originally under their jurisdictions. Almost all the five *shan-yü* contending for power in 57 B.C., for instance, had their own regional followings. In A.D. 48 the first *shan-yü* of the Southern Hsiung-nu, Pi, was set up jointly by chieftains of the eight tribes in the southern part of the empire, which had been the territory directly under Pi's control.

The growth of regionalism was greatly facilitated by what may be called a leadership crisis among the Hsiung-nu, which lasted from 114 to 60 B.C. During this half-century, the Hsiung-nu throne was occupied by seven *shan-yü* in succession, namely: Wu-wei (114–105), Chan-shih-lu (105–103), Kou-li-hu (102–101), Ts'ü-ti-hou (101–97), Hu-lu-ku (96–85), Hu-yen-t'i (85–69), and Hsü-lü-ch'üan-ch'ü (68–60). On the average the reigns were short-lived. With the exceptions of Hu-lu-ku and Hu-yen-t'i, each *shan-yü* did not last longer than ten years, the shortest reign being one year. This contrasted sharply with the long rules of the earlier *shan-yü*, especially Motun (209–174) and Chün-ch'en (160–126). In addition, none of these seven *shan-yü* provided his people with strong leadership. Two of them, Chan-shih-lu and Hu-yen-t'i, came to the throne perhaps even before coming of age. The former was nicknamed the boy *shan-yü*, and the latter was very much under the influence of his mother. In fact, during the last two reigns, from 85 to 60 B.C., internal factional strife had already begun and regionalism visibly asserted itself.

At this juncture, a word about the institutional background of the Hsiung-

nu's leadership crisis is in order. The leadership crisis was closely related to the problem of the succession to *shan-yü*. Admittedly, it is very difficult to generalize about the principles that underlaid the transfer of the throne of the Hsiung-nu. Historically speaking, however, between the time Motun became *shan-yü* in 209 B.C., and the first split of the Hsiung-nu in the middle of the 2nd century B.C., two basic conditions seem to have been established practice. First, the title of *shan-yü* normally passed from father to son. Out of ten cases of succession from Lao-shang (174–160) to Hsü-lü-ch'üan-ch'ü (68–60), for instance, only four deviated from the father-to-son pattern. Of these four cases, I-ch'ih-hsia (126–114) who followed his brother Chün-ch'en (160–126) took over the *shan-yü* throne from his nephew, the heir-apparent named Yü-tan, through rebellion; Kou-li-hu succeeded his nephew Chan-shih-lu (105–102) because the latter's son was still a minor and could not function as *shan-yü*; and since Kou-li-hu died in the next year (101) his brother named Ts'ü-t'i-hou stepped in, presumably for the same reason Kou-li-hu had. Only in the case of Hsü-lü-ch'üan-ch'ü do we find the circumstances under which he took over from his brother Hu-yen-t'i to be rather ordinary. But by this time (68 B.C.) the Hsiung-nu were already seriously plagued with the problem of a crisis in leadership and this change in the succession pattern could have been made as a rational response to the crisis.

Second, in the appointment of an heir-apparent, the reigning *shan-yü* usually had the final say. For instance, in spite of the cruelty and unpopularity of the boy *shan-yü*, the Hsiung-nu nobility nevertheless accepted his rule without questioning the legitimacy of his authority, which apparently derived from his father's will. The case of *shan-yü* Hu-lu-ku may serve as another example. Hu-lu-ku was the elder son of Ts'ü-t'i-hou and had been appointed the rightful heir by his dying father. But Hu-lu-ku failed to come to the *shan-yü*'s court in time and the Hsiung-nu nobility therefore made his younger brother the *shan-yü*, thinking that Hu-lu-ku might be seriously ill. Upon learning that Hu-lu-ku was in good health, the younger brother insisted on giving the throne back to Hu-lu-ku, suggesting, however, that Hu-lu-ku return the favor by appointing him the next legitimate heir. This case particularly shows the extent to which the reigning *shan-yü*'s will was respected as far as the succession was concerned. Clearly it outweighed the collective decision of the Hsiung-nu nobility.

It seems that this kind of succession system tended to create, or at least aggravate, the leadership crisis among the Hsiung-nu. More often than not, the man on the throne was unworthy of the position of *shan-yü*. In cases when the successor was an immature youngster, such as the boy *shan-yü* (Chan-

shih-lu) and Hu-yen-t'i, the result could be disastrous. The boy *shan-yü* created general tension and unrest among the Hsiung-nu ruling class because of his fondness for killing. His tyrannical rule even led to the rebellion of a powerful group under the leadership of the Commandant of the Left. Hu-yen-t'i, being a weakling and under the domination of his mother, also alienated a large part of the Hsiung-nu nobility and caused a general fear among the Hsiung-nu people of attacks by the Han. At any rate, this old pattern of the father-to-son succession not only proved to be increasingly ineffective in coping with wartime situations, but also became a major source of power struggles among members of the Hsiung-nu royal house. The split of the Hsiung-nu into five rival groups in 57 B.C., for instance, resulted directly from the struggle over the right to succession. It was obviously because of this painful experience that *shan-yü* Hu-han-yeh (58–31 B.C.) laid down a new rule that in the future his eldest son who would take over his throne must pass it on to a younger brother. On the whole, brother-to-brother succession appeared to be the dominant pattern from Hu-han-yeh's time to about the middle of the 2nd century A.D.

From split to submission

The internal struggles of the Hsiung-nu came completely into the open after 60 B.C. With the assistance of the deposed queen of the late *shan-yü* Hsü-lü-ch'üan-ch'ü, the Wise King of the Right, T'u-ch'i-tang, became *shan-yü* (taking the name Wu-yen-chü-t'i) in 60 B.C. The queen had been in love with T'u-ch'i-tang before Hsü-lü-ch'üan-ch'ü died. She made her lover *shan-yü* because, according to Hsiung-nu custom, a new *shan-yü* had the right to take over the queen of the deceased *shan-yü* as his own legitimate wife. The first thing Wu-yen-chü-t'i did was to eliminate all those who had been powerful under *shan-yü* Hsü-lü-ch'üan-ch'ü, whose power base had been in the Left group. It seems certain that the purge had a regional background. By this action, however, *shan-yü* Wu-yen-chü-t'i antagonized all the nobility of the Left, who therefore made Ch'i-hou-shan their own *shan-yü* (known as Hu-han-yeh) in 58 B.C. In the same year, Hu-han-yeh defeated Wu-yen-chü-t'i in battle and forced him to commit suicide. Hu-han-yeh's initial victory turned out to be only the beginning of a great schism in the Hsiung-nu ranks. In the following year (57 B.C.) the Hsiung-nu split into five regional power groups, each having its own *shan-yü*. Finally, in 54 B.C., the breakup was reduced to two major contending factions headed by *shan-yü* Hu-han-yeh and *shan-yü* Chih-chih.

In 54 B.C. Hu-han-yeh suffered a military defeat at the hands of his rival

brother Chih-chih. He therefore was forced to give up the Hsiung-nu capital in the north, and moved southward toward China. In the next two decades the two brothers divided Mongolia into two separate Hsiung-nu kingdoms, with Hu-han-yeh in Inner Mongolia, and Chih-chih in Outer Mongolia.

Hard pressed by Chih-chih from the north, the idea of submission to China for military and economic aid began to look increasingly attractive to Hu-han-yeh. As early as toward the end of *shan-yü* I-ch'ih-hsia's reign (126–114 B.C.) the Hsiung-nu had already begun to explore the possibility of renewing the *ho-ch'in* peace alliance with the Han. But the Han court's decision to impose the Chinese tributary system on the Hsiung-nu nipped the negotiations in the bud. When *shan-yü* Wu-wei (114–105 B.C.) came to the throne, he restrained the Hsiung-nu raids along the border in the hope that a *ho-ch'in* peace might be secured from the Han. Again the Han tributary terms stood in the way of any fruitful exchange. As the Hsiung-nu's military and financial situation further deteriorated, both *shan-yü* Hu-yen-t'i (85–69 B.C.) and Hsü-lü-ch'üan-ch'ü (68–60 B.C.) also expressed genuine interest in renewing a peace agreement with China. In the light of this background, it is not in the least surprising to see Hu-han-yeh's inclination to participate in the Han tributary system.

But the Hsiung-nu were a proud and defiant people. Acceptance of the status of a vassal of the Han was a bitter pill for them to swallow. At a court meeting in 53 B.C. at which Hu-han-yeh presided, there was a heated debate between King I-ch'ih-tzu of the Left, who advocated submission to the Han, and a group of opposing Hsiung-nu nobility. The nobility considered submission very humiliating to the Hsiung-nu and maintained that it would cost the Hsiung-nu their heretofore unquestioned leadership of all non-Chinese peoples. Responding to this argument, King I-ch'ih-tzu pointed out:

> The Han's power is now at its peak. Wu-sun and other states have all become China's vassals. In contrast, we Hsiung-nu have been declining in power since the days of *shan-yü* Ts'ü-t'i-hou [101–97 B.C.] and there is no way for us to restore our fallen fortune. In spite of all our exertions, we have experienced scarcely a single day of tranquility. At present our very security depends upon whether we submit to the Han or not. What better course is there for us to follow?[15]

This realistic account totally won over Hu-han-yeh, and the decision to accept the Han tributary peace was finally reached.

The Han tributary terms imposed on the Hsiung-nu may be briefly described as follows: first, the *shan-yü* would pay homage to the Han emperor at the Chinese court; second, the *shan-yü* would send a son to the Han court as

[15] *Han Shu* 94B:2a.

hostage; third, the Hsiung-nu should send tribute to China to return the favor of imperial gifts. In return the Han had the obligation to offer the Hsiung-nu military protection whenever necessary. Moreover, the Han also had to supply the Hsiung-nu with Chinese goods, especially silk and food.

Hu-han-yeh fulfilled all of his part of the tributary requirements in the next few years. In 53 B.C. he sent a son to the capital of China as hostage, and then in 51 B.C. he attended the Han court at Ch'ang-an in person, with tribute, to pay his first homage to the Chinese emperor. Hu-han-yeh's submission to the Han was an event of the first magnitude in the history of Han–Hsiung-nu relations. According to the *Han Shu*, it was only after Hu-han-yeh had paid homage at the Han court that the peoples in the Western Regions switched their loyalties from the Hsiung-nu to the Han.[16]

Hu-han-yeh was amply rewarded for his participation in the Han tributary system, however. While at Ch'ang-an the Han emperor gave him 20 catties of gold, 200,000 copper cash, 77 suits of clothes, 8,000 pieces of various kinds of silken fabrics, and 6,000 catties of silk floss. Most important of all, China also supplied the Hsiung-nu with much-needed food provisions. Thus, later in the year 51 B.C. some 34,000 bushels of dried rice were forwarded to the Hsiung-nu after Hu-han-yeh's return to Inner Mongolia, and in 48 B.C., at the request of the *shan-yü*, the Han court again sent 20,000 bushels of grain to the Hsiung-nu from two frontier provinces. During the half century between 51 and 1 B.C., the Hsiung-nu received financial aid from the Han on a steadily increasing scale.

In addition to financial assistance, the Han also gave Hu-han-yeh military support. In 51 B.C. two Han generals with 16,000 Chinese mounted soldiers escorted Hu-han-yeh back to the *shan-yü*'s court. The Han army was then ordered to stay with Hu-han-yeh and help him to quell the rebellious Hsiung-nu, obviously a reference to the defiant Chih-chih group in the north. Admittedly, the Han forces must also have been given secret instructions by the Han emperor to keep an eye on the newly submitted Hu-han-yeh. Nevertheless, the Han forces did greatly strengthen Hu-han-yeh's military position in his bid for leadership against Chih-chih. It is reported that when he learned that the Han had assisted Hu-han-yeh with both armed forces and food provisions, Chih-chih knew that he had no chance of unifying the Hsiung-nu under his rule, and therefore moved westward to the vicinity of Wu-sun, who inhabited the Ili River valley.

In 44 or 43 B.C., the Hsiung-nu, under Hu-han-yeh, and the Han signed a military alliance, which reads as follows:

[16] *Han Shu* 96A:8b.

From the day this treaty is signed, the Han and the Hsiung-nu will be united into one family. The two parties shall not, from now to all future generations, deceive or attack one another. In case of robberies [i.e. the Han robbing the Hsiung-nu or *vice versa*], governments on both sides must notify each other, and take up the responsibilities of punishment and compensation. When one side is invaded by an enemy [third party], the other side must send rescue troops to help. If the Han or the Hsiung-nu should dare to violate this treaty, Heaven will bring misfortune to them. Descendants of the Han and the Hsiung-nu should honor this agreement throughout all future generations.[17]

Needless to say this treaty, like all other treaties in human history, did not last forever. Nevertheless, it proved to be more effective than the previous *ho-ch'in* treaties, and on the whole regulated the Hsiung-nu and Han relations until the beginning of the Hsin dynasty of Wang Mang (A.D. 9–23).

It was probably under this treaty commitment that the Han general Ch'en T'ang defeated and killed Chih-chih in Sogdiana (K'ang-chü) in 36 B.C. with a combined army of Han and Hsiung-nu soldiers. In gratitude, Hu-han-yeh then expressed his willingness to pay homage to the Han emperor at the court. The homage trip, Hu-han-yeh's last, took place in 33 B.C. This time Hu-han-yeh also requested to become the son-in-law of the Han. Instead of honoring the *shan-yü* with a "princess" the Han emperor gave him the imperial court lady-in-waiting named Wang Ch'iang (Chao-chün), one of the most famous beauties in Chinese history. This is a sure indication of the fact that the *shan-yü* now was assigned a lower status under the tributary system than he had had under the previous *ho-ch'in* system.

Hu-han-yeh's marriage to Wang Ch'iang proved to be politically fruitful, however, for after Hu-han-yeh's death (around 33 B.C.), not only did one of his sons by Wang Ch'iang become Lu-li King of the Right, but Wang's son-in-law named Hsü-pu-tang was also in power in the *shan-yü*'s court and pursued a firm pro-Han foreign policy. According to Chinese records, relations between the Hsiung-nu and the Han had never been more cordial than in the years between 33 B.C. and A.D. 11. These friendly contacts are also borne out by recent archeological excavations. From Han tombs of this period unearthed along the old sites of the Great Wall in Inner Mongolia, numerous Han tiles have been found. A great many of these tiles bear inscriptions such as "Peace with the *shan-yü*" or "Heaven brings about the *shan-yü*'s submission."

The final split: the Southern and Northern Hsiung-nu

The political schism in the middle of the 1st century B.C. left a permanent scar on the Hsiung-nu people. From that time on, the cohesive solidarity which

[17] *Han Shu* 94B:3a.

had characterized the Hsiung-nu empire under Motun, Lao-shang and Chün-ch'en was lost forever. During the rule of *shan-yü* Hu-tu-erh-shih (A.D. 18–46), however, when China was busy, first with civil wars and then with the restoration of political order, the Hsiung-nu were still strong enough to seize the opportunity to reclaim much of their authority among not only peoples of the Western Regions, but also the Eastern Barbarians (Tung-hu), especially the Wu-huan.

The Hsiung-nu also tried to revive their previous standing in relation to the Han. In A.D. 24 when, during his brief rule (A.D. 23–5), Emperor Keng-shih sent an envoy to the Hsiung-nu asking them to return to the Han tributary system, Hu-tu-erh-shih insisted that it was time to reverse the tributary system, and that the Chinese emperor must pay homage to the *shan-yü*. Hu-tu-erh-shih claimed that he had helped the Han overthrow the Hsin dynasty of Wang Mang, just as the Han court had supported Hu-han-yeh's struggle against Chih-chih. In the early years of Emperor Kuang-wu's reign (A.D. 25–57), the *shan-yü* persistently held to his earlier position. Moreover, Hu-tu-erh-shih even compared himself to his illustrious ancestor Motun, and wanted to impose the *ho-ch'in* terms of two centuries before on the Later Han.

In many ways, the relations between the Hsiung-nu and the Later Han in the first two decades of Emperor Kuang-wu's reign did bear resemblance to those between Motun and Emperor Kao-tsu of the Former Han. First, Emperor Kuang-wu made repeated attempts to appease the Hsiung-nu with humble language and large amounts of money. Second, the Hsiung-nu found many allies in several powerful Chinese generals from the northern border who defected to their side, notably P'eng Ch'ung and Lu Fang. Third, during these two decades the Hsiung-nu raided and plundered the Han provinces from time to time, in spite of the lavish imperial gifts which the Han showered on them.

But by this time, regionalism among the Hsiung-nu had grown to such an extent that Hu-tu-erh-shih's control over the local magnates was far from complete. Earlier, under the short-lived Hsin dynasty, Wang Mang had made a serious attempt to divide the Hsiung-nu empire into fifteen parts to be headed, respectively, by the fifteen sons of Hu-han-yeh. An envoy had been sent to the Hsiung-nu with large quantities of valuables, to bestow on each of the sons the title of *shan-yü*. The move achieved a rather limited success: only three out of the fifteen accepted Wang Mang's offer. Nevertheless, this scheme attests fully to the divisibility of the Hsiung-nu, otherwise the very idea of simultaneously creating fifteen *shan-yü* among the Hsiung-nu would not have occurred even to a politically imaginative person like Wang Mang. *Shan-yü*

Hu-tu-erh-shih's self-image as a reincarnated Motun thus was unrealistic and self-deceptive. Toward the end of Hu-tu-erh-shih's reign, his appointment of his own son as the heir-apparent, a violation of the late Hu-han-yeh's principle of brother-to-brother succession, aroused the resentment of his nephew named Pi, the *Jih-chu* King of the Right, who was the elder son of the preceding *shan-yü*. Pi's own power base was then in the southern part of the Hsiung-nu empire, and he even refused to attend the annual meeting at his uncle's court, demonstrating once more the divisibility of the Hsiung-nu.

In A.D. 46 Hu-tu-erh-shih died and his son P'u-nu took the *shan-yü* throne. Pi then decided to follow the example of his grandfather Hu-han-yeh and submitted himself to the Later Han the following year. He had the full support of the eight Hsiung-nu tribes in the south, whose military forces totalled 40,000 to 50,000 men. In A.D. 48 the nobility of the eight tribes made Pi their own *shan-yü* and from this date they collectively came to be known in Chinese history under the official name of the Southern Hsiung-nu, as distinguished from the Northern Hsiung-nu under *shan-yü* P'u-nu.

The Southern Hsiung-nu under the Han tributary system

The Southern Hsiung-nu formally returned to the Chinese tributary system in A.D. 50. In that year *shan-yü* Pi sent a hostage son, as well as envoys representing himself and carrying tribute, to the Later Han court to pay homage. In return, Emperor Kuang-wu gave the Hsiung-nu, among other gifts, 10,000 pieces of silken fabric, 10,000 catties of silk, 25,000 bushels of dried rice, and 36,000 head of cattle and sheep. These tributary relations between the Southern Hsiung-nu and the Later Han became more rigidly regularized than before. On the one hand, the Hsiung-nu were required to send annual tribute and a new hostage son at the end of the year. On the other hand, the Han was responsible for escorting the *shan-yü*'s hostage son of the previous year back to the Hsiung-nu's court. Moreover, annual Han gifts to the Hsiung-nu were also more or less set at a fixed amount. For instance, a Chinese memorialist reported in A.D. 91 that according to the established practice of the Later Han, the annual provisions for the Southern Hsiung-nu amounted to 100,900,000 cash in value.

Hard pressed by P'u-nu's northern group, the Southern Hsiung-nu moved farther south to seek protection from the Later Han. In A.D. 50 many of the Hsiung-nu tribes were taken into the Han empire and scattered within the frontier provinces (in today's Inner Mongolia, Kansu, and Shansi). Toward the end of the 1st century A.D. the Hsiung-nu population inside China already

exceeded 200,000. The Later Han government also forced large numbers of Chinese to migrate to these frontier provinces and mixed settlements of Hsiung-nu and Chinese began to grow up. After the 1st century A.D., the developments of the Southern Hsiung-nu became part of Chinese history rather than the history of Inner Asia. It must be further noted, however, that it was the descendants of the Southern Hsiung-nu under the leadership of *shan-yü* Liu Yüan that overthrew the Chinese dynasty of Western Chin in A.D. 317 and established the first alien dynasty in Chinese history.

The Northern Hsiung-nu

The submission of the Southern Hsiung-nu to the Later Han put their northern brothers in a very difficult position. With China's military and economic backing, the Southern Hsiung-nu gradually consolidated their power in Inner Mongolia and the Northern *shan-yü* P'u-nu no longer found it possible to realize his dream of re-establishing a unified Hsiung-nu empire. From the very beginning the Later Han court adopted a policy of isolating and containing the Northern Hsiung-nu. The court's long-range goal was to cut off all of the Northern Hsiung-nu's political and economic ties with not only the Southern Hsiung-nu but also the entire Western Regions.

Fully aware of the gravity of their situation, the Northern Hsiung-nu made repeated attempts to seek a reconciliation with the Later Han. In A.D. 51 they sent envoys with tribute to the Chinese frontier province of Wu-wei (in Kansu) to seek to negotiate a peace. After discussion in a court conference, Emperor Kuang-wu finally turned down their proposal for fear of alienating the Southern Hsiung-nu. In the judgment of the Han Emperor, China's resumption of peace with the Northern Hsiung-nu might eventually lead to a Hsiung-nu re-unification.

The next year, A.D. 52, *shan-yü* P'u-nu made another important move towards peace. This time the Northern Hsiung-nu envoys brought to the Later Han court not only tribute of great value, including horses and furs, but also many representatives from states in the Western Regions. It is also interesting to note that they asked the Han court to give them new Chinese musical instruments (such as *yü*, *se*, *k'ung*, and *hou*), on the grounds that the old ones given to Hu-han-yeh a century ago had all worn out.

It is not difficult to understand why the Hsiung-nu envoys had in their company representatives from states of the Western Regions. The Northern Hsiung-nu obviously thought that these representatives would strengthen their own bargaining position *vis-à-vis* the Later Han court. Their request for

musical instruments, however, contained at least two messages which require a word of explanation. First the Hsiung-nu wanted to show through their conspicuous interest in Chinese music their sincerity to establish peaceful relations with the Later Han; for by now the Hsiung-nu had already become thoroughly familiar with the Chinese conception that rites (*li*) and music (*yüeh*) were the two major symbols of peace. In addition, the "worn out" Han musical instruments had originally been given to Hu-han-yeh in recognition of the legitimacy of his position as *shan-yü*. Had the Later Han complied with the Northern Hsiung-nu's request to replace the old musical instruments with new ones, it would have meant Chinese recognition of *shan-yü* P'u-nu's claim to be the legitimate successor of Hu-han-yeh. This incident fully reveals the degree of sophistication which the Hsiung-nu had reached in playing the subtle game of politics.

In his official reply to *shan-yü* P'u-nu, Emperor Kuang-wu specifically commented on two points: representatives from Western Region states, and the request for musical instruments. The emperor was not happy that the Northern Hsiung-nu had involved the Western Regions in their "tribute mission." From his point of view, the states in the Western Regions were all under the suzerainty of the Han. It was not proper for the Northern Hsiung-nu to present these states to the Han court, as if they only followed the Northern Hsiung-nu's lead. The Emperor also turned down the request for new musical instruments saying that what the Northern Hsiung-nu needed right then was not musical instruments but weapons. It is obvious from this reply that the Han court was determined not to yield to the Northern Hsiung-nu's display of strength.

In fact, throughout the Later Han period, the Chinese government only took the Northern Hsiung-nu as a *de facto* economic and military force, but persistently refused to recognize them as a *de jure* political entity. This attitude is clearly shown in the fact that although the Later Han government often dispatched officials to negotiate frontier trade with the Northern Hsiung-nu, they were nevertheless very reluctant to reciprocate the Northern Hsiung-nu's "tributary missions" by sending imperial envoys to the *shan-yü*'s court.

Having failed to obtain a satisfactory peace settlement with the Later Han, the Northern Hsiung-nu therefore turned their attention fully to the Western Regions. Throughout Emperor Kuang-wu's reign (25–57), China was busy with her internal affairs and found neither time nor sufficient strength to take care of the Western Regions. In the early years of the Later Han, Emperor Kuang-wu even rejected requests from many states in the Western Regions to

participate actively in the Han tributary system. He refused not only to accept hostages from these states, but also to re-establish the office of Protector-General in the area. This policy of non-involvement in the first decades of the Later Han therefore gave the Northern Hsiung-nu plenty of room for political and military maneuvers in the Western Regions.

From toward the end of Emperor Kuang-wu's reign to about A.D. 73, several states rose to power in the Western Regions. The first state which became a dominant force in the Western Regions was Sha-ch'a (Yarkand). The King of Sha-ch'a, named Hsien (reigned A.D. 33–61), was very ambitious and attempted to conquer the entire Western Region while the Later Han was still occupied with setting its own house in order and the Hsiung-nu's power was much weakened as a result of natural calamities such as droughts and plagues. In A.D. 45 eighteen Western Region states – including Chü-shih, Shan-shan (around Lobnor), and Yen-ch'i (Karashahr) – sent hostages and valuables to the Later Han court asking for military protection from Sha-ch'a's oppression. They even bluntly told Emperor Kuang-wu that if China could not protect them from annexation by Sha-ch'a their only alternative was to turn to the Hsiung-nu. Being powerless to deal with the situation, Emperor Kuang-wu had to let these states go to the Hsiung-nu's side. This development initially helped the Northern Hsiung-nu re-establish their power base in the Western Regions.

Later, in the sixth decade of the 1st century A.D., the power of Sha-ch'a declined rapidly. Other states, like Yü-t'ien (Khotan), Shan-shan, and Chü-shih rose to contend for supremacy in the Western Regions. But when the Northern Hsiung-nu eventually intervened, they forced all these major powers in the Western Regions to be their subject states. For example, immediately after Yü-t'ien had subdued Sha-ch'a, five Northern Hsiung-nu generals led an army of over 30,000, composed of soldiers from fifteen western states, to attack Yü-t'ien. As a result the king of Yü-t'ien capitulated to the Northern Hsiung-nu. He not only sent a son as hostage to the Northern Hsiung-nu, he also promised to pay them annual taxes. With the support of the human and material resources of the Western Regions, the Northern Hsiung-nu from time to time made incursions beyond the northwestern frontiers of Han China. The four frontier provinces in the Ho-hsi region (in Kansu) – Tun-huang, Chiu-ch'üan, Chang-yeh, and Wu-wei – became so unsafe that the gates of all major cities had to be closed even during the day. This situation left the Later Han court no other choice but to decide, in A.D. 73, to take the Western Regions away from the Northern Hsiung-nu by force.

In the spring of 73, the Later Han court sent four separate armies of mounted soldiers to attack the Northern Hsiung-nu. Of the four armies, the one led by General Tou Ku accomplished the most. Tou Ku's army went north out of the border from Chiu-ch'üan and heavily defeated the Hsiung-nu army under the command of the Hu-yen King in Barkol dawan (an eastern portion of the T'ien shan). Tou Ku chased the Hu-yen King as far as Lake P'u-lei (Barkol nor) and as he returned to the Han, he left some officers and soldiers to establish *t'un-t'ien* settlements in the vicinity of I-wu-lu (Hami). The next year, 74, Tou Ku again defeated the Northern Hsiung-nu in the area around Barkol nor and advanced to the state of Chü-shih. Following the conquest of Chü-shih Tou Ku obtained the approval of the Han court to re-establish, after an interval of some 60 years, the offices of the Protector-General and *Wu-chi* Colonels there. Thus for the first time under the Later Han dynasty, China effectively cut off the Northern Hsiung-nu's ties with the Western Regions. It may be pointed out that I-wu-lu as well as Chü-shih were known for the fertility of its land; both states were therefore of great economic value to the Hsiung-nu. It was precisely for this reason that the Later Han's re-conquest of the Western Regions began with these two key areas.

The Northern Hsiung-nu suffered their greatest military defeat at the hands of the Chinese General Tou Hsien. In a battle fought at Ch'i-lo Mountain (in Outer Mongolia), over 13,000 Hsiung-nu, including high-ranking nobles, were killed. The *shan-yü* himself took refuge in Chin-wei Mountain (southern range of the Altai Mountains) and eighty-one Hsiung-nu tribes consisting of more than 200,000 people surrendered to the Han. In 91 the Northern *shan-yü* was again defeated at Chin-wei Mountain and fled westward to the Ili valley. As a result of these defeats the Northern Hsiung-nu empire in Outer Mongolia and the Western Regions collapsed.

The Northern Hsiung-nu's collapse was caused, however, not as much by military defeats as by several other forces which were also at work. The ingenious diplomacy of Pan Ch'ao was one of those forces. General Tou Ku sent Pan Ch'ao to the Western Regions as a Han envoy in 73, with the mission of winning over the Northern Hsiung-nu's allies in the Western Regions. By using highly unconventional strategems, Pan Ch'ao succeeded in separating the Northern Hsiung-nu from several of the leading states there, including Shan-shan, Yü-tien, and Su-le (Kashgar). As a result, many states formally returned to the Han tributary system. Pan Ch'ao's efforts thus were mainly responsible for undermining the Northern Hsiung-nu's power base in the Western Regions. Later, between 91 and 102, when Pan Ch'ao was appointed

Protector-General of the Western Regions, headquartered at Ch'iu-tz'u (Kucha), the Later Han's control over the whole Tarim basin became firmly established.

A second contribution to the Northern Hsiung-nu's collapse in the eighth decade of the 1st century A.D. was heavy losses of manpower resulting from large-scale desertions. Probably owing to material hardships, large groups of people began to run away from the Northern Hsiung-nu in Outer Mongolia. Many of them surrendered to the Later Han, while others joined the Southern Hsiung-nu, Wu-huan, Hsien-pi, or Ting-ling. The largest single surrender took place in 87, in which it is reported that some 58 tribes, consisting altogether of 200,000 civilians and 8,000 soldiers, sought Chinese protection in four Han frontier provinces: Yün-chung, Wu-yüan, and Shuo-fang in modern Suiyuan, and Pei-ti in modern Ninghsia. We do not know whether these deserters were themselves Hsiung-nu or peoples conquered by the Northern Hsiung-nu. According to a later source, however, runaways from the Northern Hsiung-nu did include large numbers of people of the Western Regions, the Ch'iang, and the Ting-ling, who had been enslaved by the Hsiung-nu since the Former Han. Needless to say, these continuing losses of manpower must have greatly weakened the Northern Hsiung-nu.[18]

Third, during this same troubled time, other non-Chinese peoples on the northern border of Han China began to play a much more active role than before. They included the Southern Hsiung-nu, the Hsien-pi, the Wu-huan, the Ting-ling, as well as peoples in the Western Regions. For instance, according to the *Hou Han-Shu*, in 85:

> When it became known that the Northern Barbarians had declined in power as a result of large-scale desertions, the Southern Hsiung-nu attacked them in the front, the Ting-ling in the rear, the Hsien-pi on their left side, and [the states of] the Western Regions on their right side. The *shan-yü* [of the Northern Hsiung-nu] was not able to hold his position any longer and therefore fled to far-away places.[19]

In fact, the two Han expeditions against the Northern Hsiung-nu in 73 and 89, mentioned above, were not battles fought between the Northern Hsiung-nu and Chinese exclusively. The Han forces had been assisted not only by cavalrymen of the Southern Hsiung-nu but also by those of the Ch'iang, the Wu-huan, and the Hsien-pi.

The Hsien-pi, it must be noted, was an important rising power in Inner Asia. In 87 they alone inflicted a heavy defeat on the Northern Hsiung-nu. They killed the Northern *shan-yü* (Yu-liu) in battle and then flayed his body.

[18] Ma Chiang-Shou, *Pei-Ti yü Hsiung-nu*, pp. 39–40. [19] *Hou Han Shu* 119:5a.

This Hsien-pi attack wreaked havoc among the Northern Hsiung-nu, the above-mentioned surrender of 58 Hsiung-nu tribes to the Han being one direct major consequence. In 91, when the Northern *shan-yü* moved his court to the Ili Valley, it was the Hsien-pi who migrated into the territories in Outer Mongolia vacated by the Northern Hsiung-nu. In the latter half of the 2nd century, under the able leadership of T'an-shih-huai, the Hsien-pi expanded rapidly. Around this time, it is reported that the Hsien-pi "plundered the border of the Han in the south, blocked the Ting-ling in the north, pushed back barbarians in Fu-yü [in Manchuria] in the east, and attacked the Wu-sun in the west. They occupied all the former lands of the Hsiung-nu." The role of the Northern Hsiung-nu in Inner Asia was thus entirely taken over by the Hsien-pi.[20]

The Northern Hsiung-nu made a brief comeback in the Western Regions between 107 and 123, as the Later Han forces withdrew almost completely from the area due to financial difficulties. But by this time the base of operations for the Northern Hsiung-nu was no longer in the Tarim Basin or in Outer Mongolia.

[20] Wang Shen, *Wei Shu* quoted in *San-kuo chih*, po-na edition (ed. Ch'en Shou), *wei* 30:6a. For the Hsien-pi, see Ishiguro Tomio, "The Territory of the Nomad Tribe Hsien-pei," *Hokudai Shigaku*. October, 1957, pp. 80–91. The author wishes to thank the Institute of Chinese Studies, the Chinese University of Hong Kong for providing him with research assistance, 1974–5, which facilitated the preparation of this chapter. He is also indebted to Miss Susan Converse for her excellent editorial help.

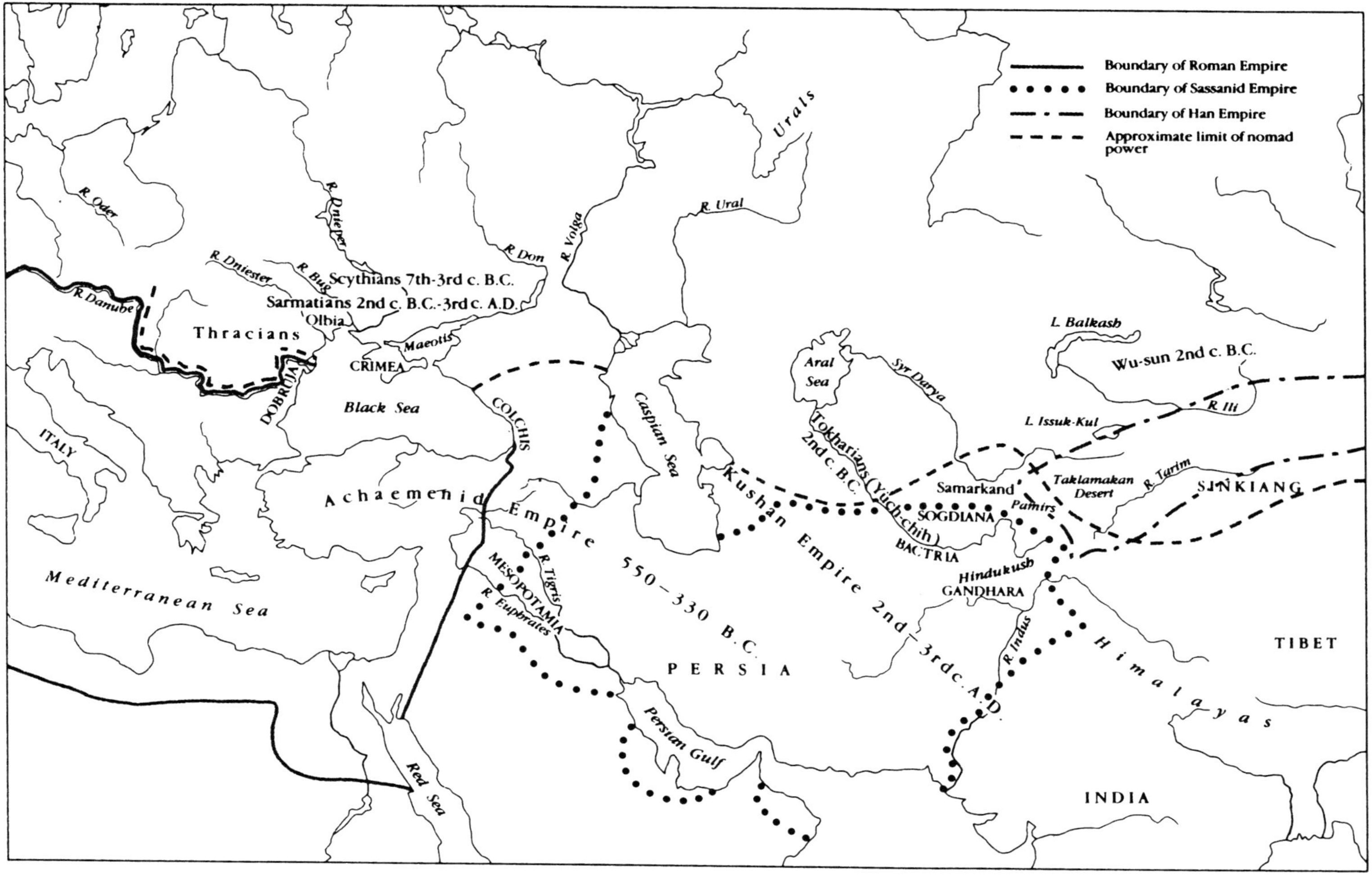
Boundary of Roman Empire
Boundary of Sassanid Empire
Boundary of Han Empire
Approximate limit of nomad power
Urals
R. Ural
R. Volga
R. Don
R. Dnieper
R. Oder
R. Dniester
R. Bug
R. Danube
Scythians 7th-3rd c. B.C.
Sarmatians 2nd c. B.C.-3rd c. A.D.
Olbia
Thracians
Maeotis
CRIMEA
DOBRUJA
Black Sea
ITALY
COLCHIS
Caspian Sea
Achaemenid Empire 550–330 B.C.
Mediterranean Sea
MESOPOTAMIA
R. Tigris
R. Euphrates
PERSIA
Persian Gulf
Red Sea
Aral Sea
Syr Darya
L. Balkash
Wu-sun 2nd c. B.C.
R. Ili
L. Issuk-Kul
Tokharians (Yuch-chih) 2nd c. B.C.
Kushan Empire 2nd–3rd c. A.D.
Samarkand
SOGDIANA
BACTRIA
Pamirs
Taklamakan Desert
R. Tarim
SINKIANG
Hindukush
GANDHARA
R. Indus
Himalayas
TIBET
INDIA

6

Indo-Europeans in Inner Asia

No barbarians survived so long and became so famous as those who are conventionally known as the Indo-Europeans. No discovery has created such a mirage as the possibility that so many languages of Europe and Asia are derived from a common origin and that we must look for the original people and their home in antiquity. For more than a century, this pursuit has withstood the challenges of science and prejudice alike. The truth may defy us, but the lure of it is still there. This gift of the comparative philologist is yet to be accepted by the archeologist, and the task of the historian is unenviable. While the original home of the Indo-Europeans remains to be finally settled, the charm of Chinese links with them has not ceased to attract. Perhaps Inner Asia holds the key.

The earliest linguistic remains of the Indo-Europeans in this area date from about the third quarter of the first millenium A.D. This consists of a literature, largely of Indic origin, Buddhistic in content, mostly translations or adaptations of religio-philosophical works, and a few commercial documents. They are written in a variety of the Indian syllabic script known as Brāhmī, remains of which have been recovered in various states of preservation from the ruins in the region of the modern cities of Kucha, Karashahr and Turfan. This linguistic relic, which is demonstrably Indo-European, strangely enough bears close affinity with the Western languages of the so-called "centum" group, rather than with the Indic and Iranian, the so-called "satem," languages of the geographically contiguous areas. However, a remarkable influx of loan words from various languages and influence of non-IE languages, confirm a gap of centuries – maybe, of even two millenia – between the time when it was first spoken and when it was first committed to writing. It also emphasizes the notorious mobility of the speakers and their interaction with others in Inner Asia, a "corridor" area in the huge Eurasian mass of land.

This Indo-European language has been known as Tokharian,[1] on the basis

[1] See Bailey, 1937 and 1947; Burrow, 1935; Henning, 1938; Krause, 1955; Lane, 1958, 1964, 1970. [Also Pelliot, 1934].

of the word *twyry* found in a Turkic Uighur colophon of a Buddhist work, *Maitrisimit*. The discovery of a Sanskrit word *Tokhārikā*, for "a woman of Kucha," in a bilingual text fragment of this language, now preserved in Leningrad, also confirms this designation of the people.[2] Two dialects of the language have been distinguished, "A" and "B". The first is known from texts found in Turfan and Karashahr (Agni) in the east, and was probably a dead liturgical language preserved in monasteries. The second, known from Kucha in the west, was perhaps a vernacular language used for commercial as well as religious purposes. Besides these two dialects of Tokharian, it needs to be noted that the Kharosthī documents from Chinese Turkestan, dating from the 3rd century A.D. also contain Tokharian linguistic elements. Undoubtedly Tokharian elements, linguistic as well as ethnic, were present in Inner Asia all through the first millenium A.D.

In the classical literature of India, the word Tuṣāra or Tukhāra has been used for a barbarian people before the 4th century A.D. In the Purāṇas their kings are listed after the Yavanas. Similarly, Tou-ch'u-lo is familiar in Chinese Buddhist literature and in the dynastic annals as the name of a country, and a people with their own language, from the 4th century A.D. Hsüan-tsang, the famous Chinese Buddhist pilgrim in the 7th century A.D., described the country of Tu-huo-lo as limited by the Pamirs on the east, Persia on the west, the Hindukush on the south and the Iron Gate on the north, with the river Oxus flowing through the middle of it. He added that the people had a peculiar spoken language and an alphabet of 25 letters and their writing was horizontal from left to right. This is no doubt a reference to the old Bactrian kingdom of the Yavanas north of the Hindukush, which became well known to al-Bīrunī much later, as Tokharistan.

But Ptolemy, in the 2nd century A.D., already refers to Thagouroi in Kansu Takoraioi north of Imaus, Taguouraioi near Issyk-kul, Tachoroi in Sogdiana and Tocharoi in Bactria. This is indeed the odyssey of one and the same people. If Pliny's Focari is a mistake for Thocari, we have a reference there too. Strabo, who used Apollodorus, included the *Taxapoi*, among the best known nomads, who along with the Asii, Pasiani, and Sakarauli, were responsible for taking away Bactriana from the Greeks. The *Prologues* of Trogus also refers to the Asiani as the kings of Thocara. The presence of the Tokharians in the Oxus valley is thus vouchsafed in the 2nd century B.C. But their history acquires real meaning only when their existence is noted in the Tarim Basin and farther east even earlier. For this we must identify them with the Yüeh-chih of the Chinese sources.

[2] Vorob'ev-Desjatovskij 1958; Bailey 1970b.

The ancient historical literature of China[3] informs that the Yüeh-chih people, who lived between Ch'i-lien mountain and Tun-huang, were forced to move out of their homeland on account of the pressure from the Hsiung-nu, and that they finally reached the Oxus valley in the 2nd century B.C. They also add that while the "Great" Yüeh-chih moved west, the "Small" Yüeh-chih remained behind. In fact, a trickle of the Yüeh-chih people dropping out here and there on their long and arduous march can very well be imagined.

While consensus of scholarly opinion identifies the Yüeh-chih with the Tokharians, the attempt to include some other peoples of Inner Asia, like the Wu-sun, the Kang-chu and the Ta-yüan, in the Tokharian ambit must await further research and more discoveries.[4]

The possibility that the Tokharian language could be adopted by speakers of a non-Indo-European language and adapted to the structure of their former speech cannot be excluded. But the Indo-European ethnic origin of the Yüeh-chih = Tokharians is generally accepted. It has been suggested that originally they had lived in the West and had migrated to the borderlands of China in a much earlier period so that their movement in the 2nd century B.C. was, in fact, a rebound journey to the West.[5] Archeology, however, has not yet substantiated any such theory. The trend of new discoveries seems to weaken the theories which seek a European home of the Indo-Europeans. Recent studies of Kurgan cultures indicate in the direction of the southern steppes of Russia. A careful re-examination of the Andronovo culture and its relationship with other cultures as well as meticulous paleo-anthropological analysis of the burial finds may not exclude the possibility of a more easterly homeland for the Indo-Europeans in Inner Asia. Suggestions have already been made to identify as Tokharian the Ch'i-ch'ia culture in Kansu which was "corresponding in time to the Lungshanoid horizon to the east but possibly of a different ethnic strain and definitely of a distinctive cultural tradition."[6] An Indo-European impact as a reason for the so-called "sudden" growth of civilization in China has been denied, and it is considered as settled that "the Chinese civilization, on the whole, was built upon Chinese neolithic foundation."[7] Once the *raison d'être* for the western influence is removed, it is not difficult to appreciate the recent argument that "there probably was no Indo-European

[3] For most of the relevant passages from Chinese historical, geographical and Buddhist sources bearing on the Yüeh-chih = Kuṣāṇa problem see the translations in Zürcher, 1968. Unless stated otherwise, I have used Zürcher's translations and the editions used by him. See also Watson, 1961, Hulsevé, 1979, and Chavannes, 1907.

[4] Pulleyblank, 1966. I find it difficult to include the Wu-sun, who were the deadly enemies of the Yüeh-chih and the K'ang-chü who were perhaps the Sogdians of Iranian stock, in the Tokharian category of Indo-European.

[5] Pulleyblank, 1966, pp. 14ff.

[6] Chang, 1963, p. 235.

[7] Chang, 1963, p. 138; Cheng, 1973.

invasion on the western frontiers of China in the early years of the first millenium B.C. causing the barbarians to migrate either to the west or to the northwest, for the single reason that the Indo-Europeans had been there since time immemorial."[8] In fact "there was a remarkable continuity in the development of the ceramic art of Kansu during two thousand years from 2500–500 B.C."[9] A possibility need not be ruled out that the Yüeh-chih = Tokharian people, speaking the archaic Indo-European language, lived in the Inner Asian region, as a powerful local tribe, and possessed superior knowledge and better techniques then their neighbors, from unknown times until they were noted by the earliest historical records of China. One need not be surprised if, one day, the spade of an archeologist digs out the necessary evidence of these first Indo-Europeans of Inner Asia.

Even in purely linguistic terms, the greater antiquity of Tokharian in relation to other Indo-European dialects has been suggested by quite a few philologists, and agreements between Tokharian and Hittite have been pointed out. This is interesting in view of the general acceptance of Hittite as antedating all other Indo-European dialects. The relationship between Tokharian and Hittite has been considered so close that they could have separated from the parent speech earlier than, and independent of, the rest of the Indo-European family. In view of this linguistic antiquity of Tokharian, its being the starting stage of the Indo-European language family and migration cannot be dismissed out of hand. Certainly, the linguistic evidence does not stand in the way of taking the Inner Asian "Tokharian-land" as the original home of the Indo-Europeans, and their moving westward seems more reasonable than the other way round. In fact, this provides a better solution to the vexing problem of the lack of geographical correlation of the "satem" and "centum" dichotomy. Starting from the Tokharian homeland with an original *K*, it is easier to explain its retention in its essentially westward movement. The other outlying areas closer home show a different development (namely, *S*), which can simply be treated as a reflex of original dialectal non-significant phonetic variation. It is a commonly noticeable phenomenon of dialect geography that a language tends to show greater variety closer home in its essential linguistic features than in its country of migration.

It is significant therefore that the linguistic remains of Tokharian are found in Inner Asia and not in Bactria. For it was preserved orally there by those among the Yüeh-chih who were left behind in the east. They were not obliged to adopt an Indo-Iranian language and use a modified Greek script, like the

[8] Prušek, 1971, p. 72. [9] Anderson, 1943.

leaders of the ethnicon, the Great Yüeh-chih, on account of their interaction with the Graeco-Irano-Indian civilization in Bactria. It is only later in the first millenium A.D., with the spread of Buddhism in Inner Asia, in which the Great Yüeh-chih played a significant role, that the original Tokharian language received its scriptual clothing; and this must be distinguished from the later "Tokharian" language of the Indo-Iranian category known from the inscriptions and coins of the Kuṣāṇas.

If the earlier forms of Yüeh-chih, e.g. Yü-chih, Nu-shih (or chih) and Yü-shih, are taken into consideration, we find these Yüeh-chih = Tokharians mentioned in the *I Chou Shu* in a list of tribute-bearers said to have arrived at the Chou court around 1000 B.C.;[10] this may be fiction but it does show that the name was known in the Pre-Han period. Undoubtedly, the Tokharians were already settled in the area between the Ch'i-lien mountains and Tun-huang, before the beginning of the 3rd century B.C., and were the neighbors of Ch'in on the one hand and the Hsiung-nu on the other.

The *Shih-chi* reports that the Yüeh-chih were strong and flourishing, while the Hsiung-nu power, which was treated with contempt by the Yüeh-chih, was just being founded by Tumen, who could not withstand the Ch'in and had migrated to the north. Tumen sent his son Motun as a hostage to the Yüeh-chih. Because Tumen wanted to get rid of his father, he attacked the Yüeh-chih, whereupon the latter wanted to kill the hostage prince. But Motun escaped and in 209 B.C. he killed his father and became the *shan-yü*. Shortly afterwards he routed the Eastern Hu. He then rode westward and smote and chased the Yüeh-chih. In 162 B.C. the *shan-yü* Lao-shang attacked and killed the king of the Yüeh-chih and made his skull into a drinking cup. By this time, the Hsiung-nu had succeeded in pacifying Lou-lan, Wu-sun, Hu-ch'ien and "twenty-six adjoining countries" and all these had become part of the Hsiung-nu so that they could claim "all the peoples who draw bows have been united into one family."

After their ignominious defeat, the Yüeh-chih, or at least their ruling faction, the "Great" Yüeh-chih, were obliged to leave their homeland and move westward. They "bore a constant grudge against the Hsiung-nu, though, as yet, they had been unable to find anyone to join them in an attack on their enemy." The Han, who were at this time, engaged in a concerted effort to destroy the Hsiung-nu, naturally wanted to establish relations with the Yüeh-chih. Ch'ang Ch'ien, who was a palace-attendant during the Chien-yüan era (140–135 B.C.), was made an envoy entrusted with this mission. He

[10] Cf. *I Chou Shu* vol. 130, 7: 11–13; Haloun, 1937; Pulleyblank, 1966, p. 19.

set out from Lung-hsi in c. 139/138 B.C., but traveling west he had to pass through the territory of the Hsiung-nu. The *shan-yü* refused to let him proceed. "The Yüeh-chih people live north of me," he said, "what does the Han mean by trying to send an envoy to them?" Do you suppose that if I tried to send an embassy to the Kingdom of Yüeh in the southeast, the Han would let my men pass through China?"[11] Ch'ang Ch'ien was accordingly detained by the Hsiung-nu for "over ten years," before he could escape to proceed toward the Yüeh-chih.

Since the king of the Great Yüeh-chih had been killed by the Hsiung-nu, his son had succeeded him as ruler. Under his leadership the Yüeh-chih people had, in the meanwhile, moved "far away to the west, beyond Ta Yüan where they attacked and conquered the people of Ta Hsia and set up the court of their king on the northern bank of the Kuei river." So, Ch'ang Ch'ien after "hastening west for twenty or thirty days" reached the kingdom of Ta Yüan in c. 129/128 B.C. The king of Ta Yüan gave him guides to take him to the state of K'ang-chü, and from there he was able to make his way to the land of the Ta Yüeh-chih in c. 128 B.C. Their state was then bordered on the east by Ta Yüan, on the west by An-hsi, on the north by K'ang-chü and on the south by Ta Hsia.

On the basis of the evidence of the *Han-shu* it is possible to divide the long journey of the Yüeh-chih into two stages, the first, which took them from their homeland in the Tun-huang area to the Upper Ili, and the second, which took them from the Upper Ili to Ta Hsia. While the first movement was due to the Hsiung-nu, the second was due to the Wu-sun, probably encouraged and supported by the Hsiung-nu. It is difficult, however, to determine when exactly the first stage of the movement ended and how long the occupation of the Upper Ili, which resulted in the dispersal of the Sai people southward, lasted. It is likely that the Yüeh-chih had already reached the Upper Ili before Ch'ang Ch'ien started his journey in c. 139/138 B.C., and that they had already passed through Ta Yüan, on their way to Ta Hsia, before Ch'ang Ch'ien reached Ta Yüan in c. 129/128 B.C. The *Shih-chi* does not refer to the defeat of the Yüeh-chih by the Wu-sun; nor does it refer to the southward movement of the Sai Wang. What both the *Shih-chi* and the *Han-shu* agree is that the Yüeh-chih did pass through Ta Yüan before they subjugated Ta Hsia. But about Ta Yüan borders, there are two statements in the *Shih-chi*; one, that "Ta Yüan lies southwest of the territory of the Hsiung-nu," and two, that "Ta Yüan is bordered on the northeast by the land of the Wu-sun." Since the Wu-sun acknowledged themselves "as part of the Hsiung-nu," the two statements can

[11] Cf. Watson, 1961, II, pp. 264–5.

be reconciled. Ch'ang Ch'ien states that K'ang-chü "acknowledges nominal sovereignty to the Yüeh-chih people in the south and the Hsiung-nu in the east." So, if there has to be a demarcation between the two stages of the Yüeh-chih movement, it should be located in what must have been the K'ang-chü state, perhaps inclusive of Upper Ili, of which the eastern part changed hands between the Yüeh-chih and the Wu-sun, as dependents of the Hsiung-nu. The K'ang-chü, however, continued to acknowledge the nominal sovereignty of the Yüeh-chih, who had moved their government to Ta Hsia in the south. The Wu-sun were for some time under the hegemony of the Hsiung-nu and were "ordered to guard the western forts;" they became independent only before they received the mission of Ch'ang Ch'ien in c. 115 B.C. If the Wu-sun inflicted a defeat on the Yüeh-chih before or after they passed through Ta Yüan, in the K'ang-chü state, they must have done so as agents, and at the behest, of the Hsiung-nu. The K'ang-chü acted as a buffer state between the Yüeh-chih on the one hand, and the Hsiung-nu and later the Wu-sun, on the other.

Be that as it may, when Ch'ang Ch'ien reached the Ta Yüeh-chih in c. 128 B.C., he found them "still a nation of nomads, moving from place to place with their herds." They had "some one or two hundred thousand archer warriors." The Yüeh-chih king had forced the kingdom of Ta Hsia to recognize his sovereignty. The region he ruled was rich and fertile and seldom troubled by invaders, and the king thought only of his own enjoyment. He considered the Han too far away to bother with and had no particular intention of avenging his father's death by attacking the Hsiung-nu. Having failed "to interest the Yüeh-chih in his proposals," Ch'ang Ch'ien spent "a year or so in the area," and returned to China in c. 125 B.C. following a route "along the Nan Shan" and "through the territory of the Chiang barbarians." On his way he was once more captured by the Hsiung-nu and detained for over a year.

We need not blame the Yüeh-chih king for his lack of response to the Han king. In fact it was wise of him to do so. This unnamed Yüeh-chih king, who led his people through the arduous march, spread over thirty years, from Tun-huang to Ta Hsia, through the domains of nomadic tribes, each zealously guarding its own "territorial imperative," was certainly endowed with qualities of unfailing courage and great endurance. Having succeeded ultimately in carving out his own principality in the fertile Oxus valley, he was, naturally, content with the nominal sovereignty over the K'ang-chü in the north and Ta Hsia in the south. He deserved the security and peace, to which was added the prosperity arising out of the commercial genius of the people of Ta Hsia. His policy certainly paid dividends. The strength and prestige of the

Great Yüeh-chih were recognized by the neighboring states. The Chinese also continued to keep in touch with them by sending emissaries. This had its desired effect on the Hsiung-nu, their common enemy.

We do not know how long this wise and brave king ruled. The *Shih-chi* does not refer to a succeeding son. He may indeed have had a long reign of about sixty years, lasting probably until the end of the 2nd century B.C. For, when the curtain rises in the 1st century B.C., we learn from the *Han-shu* not only that the Ta Yüeh-chih had "completely subdued and tamed" the Ta Hsia and they supported the envoys of the Han together, but that there were five *hsi-hou* (*yabghu*) in their kingdom, namely, the Hsiu-mi, the Shuang-mi, the Kuei-shuang, the Hsi-tun and the Kao-fu, which "all belong to the Great Yüeh-chih."[12] Doubts have been expressed whether or not all of these *yabghus* were ethnically Yüeh-chih, but they do not seem to be well founded. This administrative organization was designed to ensure internal unity by satisfying the growing ambitions of the younger leadership and it helped consolidate their territorial power. We do not know whether this was the last achievement of the same Yüeh-chih king or this happened soon after his death. In any case, with the beginning of the 1st century B.C., the second phase in the growth of the Yüeh-chih power had begun.

The Yüeh-chih movement from the Upper Ili to the Oxus had forced some of the tribes, for whom the generic word "Scythian" had been used by Strabo, to move into the areas held by the Parthians. The nomadic pressure in a desperate situation was indeed difficult to handle. Two Parthian kings, Phraates II and Artabanus II, lost their lives in their encounter with the Scythians. Finally Mithridates II, who came to the throne in c. 124 B.C., succeeded in providing them a habitat, by containing them, in Seistan. Before the 2nd century B.C. was out, Mithridates II was indubitably a power of world standing, having sent embassies to Sulla of Rome and Wu-ti of China. The Yüeh-chih were their immediate neighbors in the east and it was in their mutual interest to remain peaceful and friendly, if for no other reason than to make the best use of the newly opened silk trade route between China and the western world. The last years of Mithridates II, however, were disturbed by rebellions. His death in c. 88 B.C. was the signal for further troubles. What was happening in Parthia, an older and much more stabilized state as compared to the new one of the Yüeh-chih, must have been a lesson to the latter, and so wisely they took steps to contain the restive ambitions of tribal leadership by dividing their kingdom into five *hsi-hou*.

[12] *Han shu* 96A: 14b; Zürcher 1968, p. 367.

Apollodorus, who in c. 100 B.C. knew that the Tokhari were among those who destroyed the Graeco-Bactrian power, does not provide us with the name of their king and his achievements. Also he is not aware of the five *yabghus* into which the erstwhile kingdom of Bactria, north of the Hindukush was divided, unless a veiled or confused reference to all or some of them are implied in the names of the other tribes who are listed with the Tokhari. Trogus, in c. 85 B.C. surely has reasons to report that the Tokhari were ruled by the Asiani, which, if emended into Cuseni, may refer to the Kuṣāṇa, the Kuei-shuang, who no doubt prove to be the most pre-eminent among the Yüeh-chih so that they did succeed in unifying the Yüeh-chih power later.

The success of the Kuei-shuang, or the Kuṣāṇa, is known from the *Hou Han-shu*, compiled by Fan Yeh. For the description of the Western Regions, Fan Yeh relied on what Pan Yung recorded at the end of the reign of Han emperor An (A.D. 107–25). But Pan Yung's record, certainly about the Yüeh-chih, was based on the information he had obtained from his father's campaigns before 100 A.D. when the latter sent his last "memorial" to the Han court. Pan Yung was able to return to the Western Regions only in 123 A.D. but he could not stay for more than four years in the area, and never came in contact with the Yüeh-chih.

Now, according to the *Hou Han-shu*, more than a hundred years after the formation of the five *yabghus*, "the *yabghu* of Kuei-shuang [named] Ch'iu-chiu-ch'üeh attacked and destroyed the [other] four *yabghu* and established himself as [their] king; the kingdom was named Kuei-shuang. [This] king invaded An-hsi, took the country of Kao-fu, and, moreover, destroyed P'u-ta and Chi-pin and completely possessed their territory. Ch'iu-chiu-ch'üeh died at the age of more than eighty years, and his son Yen-kao-chen succeeded him as king. He in his turn destroyed T'ien-chu [Northern India] and placed there a general to control it. Since then the Yüeh-chih have been extremely rich and strong. In the various [Western] countries [their ruler] is always referred to as 'the king of Kuei-shuang,' but the Han, basing themselves upon the old appellation, speak about 'the Great Yüeh-chih.'"[13]

Thus three phases of the Yüeh-chih history after their dispersal from their homeland are reported in the Chinese historical annals. The *terminus post quem* for these are c. 90 B.C., c. A.D. 25 and c. A.D. 100 respectively. The first phase, therefore lasted from c. 160 B.C. to c. 90 B.C., the second from c. 90 B.C. to c. A.D. 25, and the third from c. A.D. 25 to c. A.D. 100.

We have already noted the failure of Ch'ang Ch'ien's mission to win over

[13] *Hou Han shu* 118: 9a; Hulsewé 1979, p. 122.

the Yüeh-chih. He also failed in his second mission of 115 B.C. to woo the Wu-sun against the Hsiung-nu. But he set the basic policy of having a "tributary system" in the Western Region, which was originally meant to contain the influence and power of the Hsiung-nu, on account of Ch'ang Ch'ien's discovery of the West, became imperative in order to keep the trade routes safe and open. However, it was not until the success of the Er-shih general Li-kuang-li against Ta Yüan in 101 B.C. that the states of the Western Regions were frightened and started sending "envoys to present tributes" to China. But it took another fifty years for the Han, after the surrender of the southern group of the Hsiung-nu under Hu Han-yeh in 53 B.C., to establish real influence in Inner Asia. The office of *tu-hu*, Protector General of the Western Regions, was first created in 59 or 60 B.C. under the reign of Hsüan. Now, instead of dealing with a strong and unified nomadic power of the Hsiung-nu, the Chinese found themselves involved in handling a multitude of smaller states. It was not easy to keep all of them in good humor, even when the fear of the Hsiung-nu was reduced. By the time Wang Meng died in A.D. 23, all the states of the Western Regions had revolted and had eventually severed their relations with China. And in the meanwhile, the Yüeh-chih, at the other end of the Western Regions, were not only enjoying peace and prosperity but, after c. 90 B.C., had expanded their political power and consolidated their economic position. According to the *Han-shu* in the fifty kingdoms "under subjection to China" in the Western Regions there were "in all 376 persons holding the seal and ribbon of investiture from China"; but "K'ang-chü, Ta Yüeh-chih, An-hsi, Chi-pin and Wu-li, being all at an extreme distance," were not included in the number. "When envoys came from there bearing tributes, they were cordially recompensed; but no oversight was exercised, nor were they under control." The Yüeh-chih had so much gained in strength and prestige that when, under emperor Ming (A.D. 58–75), the Later Han once again wanted to implement their policy of "tributary system" in the Western Regions, they had to seek help of the Yüeh-chih, the "great" as well as the "small." In A.D. 78 in his memorial to the throne the general Pan Ch'ao expressed his desire to defeat and destroy Ch'iu-tz'u (Kucha) with the help of the Yüeh-chih and others. In A.D. 84 Pan Ch'ao sent an "envoy with a lot of colorful silk" to the king of the Yüeh-chih so that the K'ang-chü king, with whom the Yüeh-chih were on good terms on account of matrimonial relations, could be persuaded to withdraw his troops, which were supporting Chung, a rebel king of Su-lê (Kashgar). The Yüeh-chih helped the Han also to attack Chü-shih (in the Turfan area), and in A.D. 86, in return for their services, they "offered as tribute precious stones, *fu-pa* [antelopes] and lions," and they also "used the

occasion to ask for a Han princess." But Pan Ch'ao "stopped their envoy and sent him back, and from that moment they bore a grudge [against the Han]." In A.D. 87 when Pan Ch'ao defeated So-chü (Yarkand) they became more cautious. In A.D. 88 when the Yüeh-chih in Ch'iang-yeh (Kansu) were under attack of the Ch'iang and when they asked for protection of the Han they did not get it. In A.D. 89, it is true that a group of Yüeh-chih was made into the I-ts'ung Hu or "voluntary barbarian followers" by Teng Hsün, the Protector-Colonel of the Ch'iang, but the fact remains that after the Chinese obtained success in their designs under Pan Ch'ao, the relationship between them and the Yüeh-chih deteriorated fast. In fact they were now the two great powers at the two ends of the Western Regions and their temporary friendship turned into rivalry. And so, in A.D. 90, the Yüeh-chih sent their *fu-wang* Hsieh to attack Pan Ch'ao. But because his "provisions were almost exhausted" and he could not get timely help from Ch'iu-tz'u (Kucha), Hsieh could not defeat Pan Ch'ao. According to *Hou Han-chi*, however, Hsieh was not a *fu-wang* (sub-king) but a *wang* (king) and that the event took place in the second year of Yung-ho and not in the second year of Yung-yüan.[14] Be that as it may, the success of Pan Ch'ao tilted the balance of power in favor of China at least for a decade. But Pan Ch'ao had become old and died within a month of his return in c. A.D. 102. Soon the states of the Western Regions became truant again. Some of them even transferred their allegiance to the Great Yüeh-chih.

The evidence of coinage generally confirms and supplements our knowledge about the Yüeh-chih = Kuṣāṇa history from the Chinese sources. Before the Great Yüeh-chih settled themselves north of the Oxus, the Yavanas had already ruled there for about one hundred and twenty-five years, and had minted one of the most beautiful series of coinage for circulation in the area. When the Yüeh-chih replaced them politically they naturally felt the need to mint their own money, but they had no tradition of their own in this regard. They therefore issued rude imitations of the most popular coins which were then current. It is significant that the latest among the monolingual Graeco-Bactrian coin-types imitated by them is that of Heliokles I, whose rule probably ended by c. 140 B.C.[15] No name, in fact nothing whatsoever, indicative of a Yüeh-chih king is found in all these "imitation" coins. A few of these, which bear fragments of illegible non-Greek inscriptions, might have been issued by the Scythians for a brief period before they moved to Seistan. But the bulk of these barbaric imitations certainly belong to the Great Yüeh-chih.

[14] Enoki, 1968. [15] Narain, 1962 pp. 105–6, 181.

These barbaric imitations were followed by coins which bear the names of Heraus, Hyrcodes, Sapadbizes, Phseigacharis as well as one or two other kings whose names are not legible. This coin-series seems to belong to the Five-*Yabghu* period, when individual identity became imperative. At least Heraus made it clear by announcing it on his money; the corrupt Greek letters which read *KOPCANOY* certainly stand for his *yabghu* Kuei-shuang = Kuṣāṇa. His impressive portrait on the obverse and a mounted and armed king being crowned by Nike on the reverse are remarkable.[16] None of the others, however, mention their *yabghu* names on their issues. But the individuality of their types is evident, and so also their personalities. The provenance of these coins suggest that the territories of the Kuṣāṇa Heraus lay in the eastern part of the Yüeh-chih kingdom on both sides of the Oxus; those of Hyrcodes adjoined Parthia and Sogdia; and Sapadbizes and Phseigacharis ruled the Termez and Bamiyan regions respectively.

Heraus, the Kuṣāṇa, the most pre-eminent among the Great Yüeh-chih, was probably succeeded by Kujula Kadphises, the Ch'iu-chiu-chü'eh (Ancient Chinese: **Kilu dzilu Kiak*) of the *Hou Han-shu*. He vanquished the other four *yabghus* and, having unified the Yüeh-chih power, conquered Kao-fu (Kabul), Pu-ta (Peshawar) and Chi-pin (Swat valley). His coins indicate a judicious selection of types from among those which circulated in the newly acquired kingdom. Thus, we have the "Hermaeus and Herakles," "Bust of Augustus (or Tiberius) and the seated figure on curule chair," "Helmeted head and the Macedonian soldier," and "Bull and Bactrian camel" types. A coin-type showing "a figure seated cross-legged with his right hand uplifted" is probably the first attempt to introduce the Buddha in human form. His Buddhist leanings are manifest from his epithet "*Sacadhramathidasa*" (lit. "Steadfast in the true Faith") on coins. All these coin-types were probably meant for circulation in territories south of the Oxus as well as south of the Hindukush; they have not been found in Soviet Central Asia. But, if the coins of the so-called "nameless king" were issued by Kujula Kadphises, we have in them the popular coinage for the whole of his empire including the territories north of the Oxus, where they alone among his coins have been reported.

Epithets used by Kujula on his money, e.g. XOPANCY ZAOOY, BACIΛEWC BACIΛEWN CWTHP MEΓAC in Greek and *Yauga*, *Maharajasa rajadirajasa* in Kharoṣthi, are indicative of the phases of growth

[16] Cunningham, 1888.

[17] Basham, 1968, p. 434; note my remark "the evidence justified any date between A.D. 100 and 120." I have found no new evidence to modify my opinion, except that the later limit may be extended to A.D. 130. I cannot accept any date before A.D. 100 or after A.D. 130. My preference is for an earlier date in the first quarter of the 2nd century A.D., and I strongly believe that it was Kaniṣka who received the Kashgarian prince Ch'en-p'an in the years 114–19.

of his political career. So also are the titles, *erjhuna* (prince), *maharaya Guṣaṇa*, *maharaya rajatiraja Khuṣaṇa*, used with reference to him in the three epigraphs of Takht-i-Bahi, Panjtar and Taxila, datable in the first half of the 1st century A.D. The Roman coin-type of Kujula not only confirms the continuation of his rule in the third quarter of the 1st century A.D. but also friendly relations with Rome. Perhaps with the independence of Hyrcania, the road sought for by the Romans and the Kuṣāṇas alike was opened for mutual prosperity; and there are reports about "Indian" embassies in Rome. Kujula Kadphises died when he was over eighty. He probably ruled at least for about fifty years, from c. A.D. 25 to 75.

Kujula was succeeded by his son Yen-kao-chen, who is identified with Vima Kadphises of coins and inscriptions. He continued the aggressive policy of his father and conquered T'ien-chu, i.e. the Upper Indus valley; and he appointed a *ch'iang* (lit. "general") to supervise the administration. Encouraged by success in the south and southeast, the Yüeh-chih were naturally interested in extending their power and influence more effectively in Eastern Turkestan where the influence of the Han had ceased to exist after the death of Wang Mang. But the Chinese revived their *locus standi* in the region about the same time Vima came to the throne. So Hsieh, probably the Yüeh-chih *fu-wang* (lit. "sub-king") of Vima had his confrontation in A.D. 90 with Pan Ch'ao, the Han Protector-General for the Western Regions. As we have stated earlier, Hsieh's attempt was foiled by Pan Ch'ao's strategy. The Yüeh-chih did not succeed in their political designs until a generation later. But economically they had acquired prosperity not only by their annexation of Kabul and the Upper Indus valley, but also by controlling the entrance to trade-routes at the western end of the Taklamakan. Political and economic stability are reflected in the coinage of Vima Kadphises. He issued a large number of gold and copper coins, of fixed metrology and firm types. With troubles in Parthia, the Kuṣāṇa exploited their role of middlemen between the Chinese and the Romans to the maximum, and a brisk trade in silk, spices, gems and other articles was carried on by traders of Indian, Iranian and other nationalities. Pliny refers to the flourishing commerce between the Indian and the Roman empires in the 1st century A.D., and deplores the heavy drain of gold from Rome to India to pay for luxuries imported for the use of Roman nobles and ladies. The Roman gold coins, which poured into India, appear to have been melted down and recoined by Vima and his successors, for their own use and for the use of the trading magnates in their empire. This also resulted in the fixation of the metrology of the Kuṣāṇa coins on the Roman standard. Vima continued using the titles adopted by his father on coins and in inscriptions. But instead of the Buddhist leanings of his father, he showed his favor to the

Pāśupata or Māheśvara creed of Śaivism by depicting Śiva standing by the side of a bull and using the coin legend *maharajasa rajadirajasa sarvaloga iśvarasa mahiśvarasa Vima Kathphisasa tradara* (lit. "A great king, king of kings, Lord of all the worlds, a Māheśvara, Vima Kadphises, the protector"). He also used the title *Devaputra* (lit. "the son of Divine being") which is known from his coins as well as from the Brāhmī inscription on his statue found at Mathurā. If a fragmentary inscription of Khalatse, a village in Ladakh, 52 miles below Leh on the trade route, bearing the name of Vima is dated A.D. 96 or 99, he may well have ruled, having succeeded an octogenerian, for about twenty-five years, up to the closing years of the 1st century A.D.

It is generally agreed that Vima was succeeded by Kaniṣka. In spite of several international symposia held this century, there is no conclusive decision on his date. But, on circumstantial evidence, he seems to have certainly ruled for most of the first half of the 2nd century A.D. While it is not possible to give an absolute date for the beginning of his reign, it would be quite reasonable to look for it during the first thirty years of the 2nd century, but the earlier the better, preferably in the first decade.[17] With Kaniṣka, the Yüeh-chih = Kuṣāṇa history enters the fourth phase, which must be counted as one of the great periods of world history.

In the beginning of the 2nd century A.D., the four great powers of the contemporary world were Rome, Parthia, India, and China. Rome was strong under Trajan (89–117) and Hadrian (117–138). Parthia was weak and torn after the death of Vologases I (A.D. 80) on account of internal dissensions and Roman invasions. China, after the death of Pan Ch'ao (102 A.D.), had lost influence in Eastern Turkestan and was busy settling her own problems. All this augured well for Kaniṣka, the Tuṣāra King of India and Inner Asia.

From the Annals of the Later Han we learn that a prince of Kashgar went to the Yüeh-chih king during A.D. 114–19 and the latter helped him, with his army, to get the throne of Kashgar in A.D. 119. If the testimony of the Chinese pilgrim Hsüan-tsang is correct this king could be no other than Kaniṣka. The pilgrim also informs that "from the earlier memoirs I have learned that anciently king Chia-ni-se-chia [Kaniṣka] of the country of Ch'ien-t'o-lo [Gandhāra], whose majesty spread over the neighbouring kingdoms and whose transforming [influence] penetrated the far away regions, led his troops to enlarge his territory [even] to the east of the Ts'ung-ling [Pamirs]. [The rulers of] the frontier tribes in the region west of the [Yellow] River [Ho-hsi] stood in awe of him and sent 'their sons as hostages to him.'"[18]

[18] Hsüan-tsang. I have used the translation of the relevant passages made by Zürcher, 1968, p. 377. See also Watters, pp. 122–30, 294, and Beal, pp. 54–68, 173–5.

In the Chinese and Tibetan Buddhist tradition there are stories about Kaniṣka's conquest of Sāketa and Magadha (Eastern India): the latter surrendered the sacred alms bowl of the Buddha, the famous scholar Aśvaghoṣa and a miraculous cock to him. We are also told how a "cruel and obstinate" Parthian king attacked Kaniṣka, but the latter gained victory after killing "altogether 900,000" people and felt remorse over the sin he committed thereby. Finally, there is a tradition about his projected campaign in the north and how the ministers and the people, tired of his waging wars, "smothered him when he was lying ill." These stories, shorn of all embellishments, at least point to an active career of aggrandisement in all directions as well as his failure towards the end of his reign in expanding further in the north beyond the Pamirs; which may be true because Pan Yung, the son of Pan Ch'ao, had succeeded in reviving the Chinese influence in the Western Regions about the same time as Kaniṣka was in the last years of his reign. But there is no record of Kaniṣka losing any part of his empire during his lifetime. Kaniṣka was probably at the height of his power, when, in A.D. 117, Trajan, having reached the Persian Gulf, did not venture, ostensibly on account of his age, to repeat Alexander's march further east, and instead received an Indian embassy; the policy started by Kujula was continued and the two powerful emperors of the East and the West were pleased to extend their hands in friendship over a much weakened and shattered Parthia. The geographical distribution of the coins and inscriptions of Kaniṣka, as well as the archeological evidence, affirm his vast empire, which included the whole of Tajikistan, a large part of Uzbekistan, possibly a portion of Kirgizia and southern Turkmenistan, almost the whole of Afghanistan and Pakistan, a part of Eastern Turkestan north of the Pamirs, and the whole of Northern India as well as parts of Eastern and Central India.[19] He proudly took the title of *Devaputra* (lit. "son of Divine Being") and established the cult of ruler-worship; and thus, statues of the Kuṣāṇa emperors were installed, in what was known then as *Devakula*, at Mathurā, and in the "sanctuary" at Surkh-Kotal.[20] No better expression of royal majesty and divine strength can be found than in the Mathurā statue of Kaniṣka – even though it is headless. On his coins, the *Shaonano Shao Kaneshko Koshano* (lit. "the King of Kings, King Kaniṣka, the Kuṣāṇa"), is represented by a robust bearded figure with Central Asian peaked headdress and long boots and heavy coat, making offering at an altar. Sometimes his

[19] There is some controversy about the eastern limits in South Asia and the northern limits in Central Asia of the Kuṣāṇa empire. See Puri, 1965, pp. 50ff.; M.E. Masson, 1968, pp. 14–25; Staviskij, 1968, pp. 202–5.

[20] For the Mathurā statues cf. Agrawala, 1950, pp. 72–9. For Surkh Kotal see the articles of Schlumberger. Also, Rosenfield, 1967, chapters 6–8.

bust is shown as if emerging from clouds, as are those of his predecessor Vima Kadphises, on his coinage, a visual indication of the divinity of the king.

But Kaniṣka's greatness rests not so much on his military exploits as on his peaceful pursuits, his achievements in the field of religion, art and culture. Buddhist tradition eulogizes his role in the history of Buddhism, which is next only to Aśoka. The momentous Fourth Buddhist Council was held under his patronage and a great reorientation of Buddhism took place; the sacred literature was reorganized, explanatory treatises were composed, and recognition was extended to as many as eighteen sects. Hsüan-tsang informs us that Kaniṣka had the new extensive literature engraved on copper plates, enclosed in stone coffers and deposited in a stupa specially built for the purpose. While these copper plates have yet to be exhumed, the pilgrims' testimony in respect of the building of a relic tower and a monastery by Kaniṣka is confirmed by the unearthing of a gilt relic casket with a Kharoṣṭhī inscription referring to the "Kaniṣka vihāra." Literary sources, too, associate such Buddhist celebrities with him as Aśvaghosa, his *Kalyāṇa-mitra* (i.e. "the friend, philosopher and guide"), Pārśva, Vasumitra and Sangharakṣa. His personal predilection for Buddhism, especially the Sarvāstivāda School, need not be doubted. But, like Aśoka, he pursued a policy of religious toleration, which took into account the multi-cultural elements of his empire. This fact is characteristically proved by the large number of deities, appertaining mainly to the Zoroastrian but partly to the Hindu, Greek and Roman pantheon, in addition to the Buddha, which figure as the reverse devices on his gold and copper coins. The list includes Mithro, Mao, Nana, Athsho, Oado, Arooaspo, Farro, Orlagno, Ardoksho, and Oesho (=Śiva), and Helios, Selene and Hephaestus.[21]

The Kuṣāṇa inscriptions following a system of reckoning from the first year of Kaniṣka's reign, give dates up to year 23 for Kaniṣka, from 22 to 28 for Vaśiṣka, from 28 to 60 for Huviṣka, from 30 (?) to 41 for another Kaniṣka, and from 60 to 98 for a Vāsudeva. Thus, from Kaniṣka I to Vāsudeva I, the Kuṣāṇa kings ruled for about one hundred years, that is from the first decade of the 2nd century to the first decade of the 3rd century A.D. Definite relationships between them are not mentioned. The dates which are the first and last known of the kings are inclusive of their reigns; and they overlap. A collateral succession and some form of joint rulership or association of a sub-king in the imperial administration cannot be ruled out. No coins of Vaśiṣka and Kaniṣka II are known, nor do inscriptions provide information about their achievements. Probably Kaniṣka I ruled until year 28 when he was succeeded by

[21] For the coins of the Kuṣāṇas see Cunningham, 1892; Gardner, 1886, pp. xlvii–liii, plates 24–9; Whitehead 1914, pp. 171–214, plates xvii–xx.

Huviṣka; and Vaśiṣka and Kaniṣka II were associated with them respectively as joint rulers. It is interesting to note, however, that both Vaśiṣka and Kaniṣka II use the same imperial titles as Kaniṣka I and Huviṣka. Kaniṣka II goes a step further and adds one more, that of Kaisara, emulating the Roman Caesar.

Huviṣka, whose Brāhmī and Kharoṣṭhī inscriptions have been found in the Uttar Pradesh in India, in northwest Pakistan, and in Afghanistan was thus the king from the 28th year of the Kaniṣka's reckoning. Kalhaṇa's *Rājataranginī* which confirms the rule of Kaniṣka and Huviṣka over Kashmir, reports the foundation of a town Huṣkapura by Huviṣka[22] (modern village of Ushkur, the Ūshkārā of al-Biruni). The important "Bactrian" inscription found at Surkh-Kotal, dated in the 31st year of the Kuṣāṇa reckoning, which records the repair and adornment of a sanctuary, built by Kaniṣka I, by one Nokonzoko, a high official, indicates the firm hold and vigilant administration of Huviṣka in northern Afghanistan.[23] A Mathurā inscription refers to endowments made by a "lord" of Kharāsalera and Vakana, probably of the Wakhan region. The provenance of Huviṣka's coins is the same as that of Kaniṣka and they have been found in large numbers. The obverse of the gold coins usually bears the imperial bust dressed in garments decked with jewels, and an ornamental headdress, with the sceptre in his hand. The obverses of his copper coins show him in various attitudes, such as riding on an elephant, reclining on a couch etc. The reverse contains, like the coins of Kaniṣka, figures of deities belonging to various pantheons, but many new deities are now added to the list, e.g. the Indian divinities like Skanda-Kumāra, Viśākha, Mahāsena and Umā, the Alexandrian Serapis, Riom (Roma), the Greek Herakles and Zoroastrian Shahrevar, Luhrasp, Oanindo and others. Huviṣka seems to have ruled over the entire Kuṣāṇa empire of Kaniṣka effectively and the economic prosperity of his times is more than reflected in his money.

The liberal policy of Kaniṣka, which was continued by Huviṣka, set the pace for the syncretic culture of the Kuṣāṇa realm, which, more variegated than anything before or after, yet blended in harmony, was hardly matched in history. This may be seen clearly in the art objects. The widespread contacts may be deduced from the discovery of plaster plaques with Greek profiles, Chinese lacquer, Indian carved ivories and Egyptian glassware in the Kuṣāṇa territories. While Rome was being ravished by the material luxuries of the east and had begun draining itself economically, the best of the west and of the east performed a wholesome exercise in coexistence under the leadership of the

[22] Sir M.A. Stein, 1, p. 30. [23] Maricq, 1958; Henning, 1960.

Kuṣāṇas. The credit goes to the unnoticed hands of the local genius and to a cultural soil which had an unfathomable capacity to absorb extraneous elements. The impact of the Kuṣāṇa syncretism was indeed great throughout the empire, including the Indo-Gangetic valley. But, it was greater in Inner Asia where mobility and nomadic adventurism discovered in and through it a new cultural identity which transcended self-contained ethnocentrism without making compromises, because it was more inclusive than exclusive in content.

By the 2nd century A.D. the Arsacid Parthians had lost their vitality and the Later Han China had withdrawn into its own shell. Thus, the Kuṣāṇas had a free hand in Inner Asia not only for regulating trade but also for shaping its cultural contour. Whereas in the Indo-Gangetic plains they had accepted both the language and the script prevailing there, and in Afghanistan they modified the Greek script to suit the local Iranian language they had chosen for their coin legends and official documents in that region along with the use of Aramaic and Kharoṣṭhī; for the inscriptions in Inner Asia, which had no literate tradition of its own, they introduced first Kharoṣṭhī, and later Brāhmī also, probably for administrative work to start with, but soon they were used for religious texts and commercial documents. Monks as well as traders helped the state in this process of providing Inner Asia with its earliest script and the spoken Tokharian language its written garb. It is interesting to note that in the list of translators of Buddhist literature into Chinese, up to the end of the Western Chin dynasty (A.D. 316), there are only six or seven each from India and China, while some sixteen others are traditionally linked with Central Asia (6 Yüeh-chih, 4 Parthians, 3 Sogdians, 2 Kucheans and 1 Khotanese). The "barbarian" had already learned the role of the civilizer.

About A.D. 160 or a little later, Huviṣka was succeeded by Vāsudeva, the only purely Indian name among the Kuṣāṇa kings. The dates in the epigraphs show that he ruled for about forty years. If the 105 year duration of the rule of the Tuṣāra kings as given in the Purāṇas[24] is true, his reign must have ended about or a little later than A.D. 205. No remarkable events of his reign are known and his coins no longer depict the multitude of divinities represented on those of his predecessors. The reverse device *par excellence* is now Śiva, though Nana and Ardoksho also appear rarely. With a Vaiṣṇava name but with Śiva leanings he no doubt continued the spirit of religious toleration so characteristic of the Kuṣāṇa kings, though in a limited sense. The absence of Kharoṣṭhī inscriptions indicates either a weakening of Kuṣāṇa economy in the

[24] Pargiter, 1962, p. 72.

northwest or an inertia in religious acts and building activities. The Brāhmī inscriptions of Mathurā, on the other hand indicate the area of activity and prove that the empire did not suffer diminution in the east. Vāsudeva probably succeeded in maintaining the *status quo* and managed to rule over the entire empire he inherited by virtue of the sheer tempo which was generated earlier, and which was sufficient to take even an unambitious king such as himself in its stride. But the signs were obviously not bright, and with him ends the fourth phase of the Yüeh-chih–Kuṣāṇa history, the period of the Great Kuṣāṇas.

The fifth phase, after Vāsudeva, is a story of definite decline of the Kuṣāṇa glory. Barely one or two inscriptions belonging to this period can be dated and the coinage shows unmistakable signs of deterioration. They lack the minimum quality of artistic engraving and even the obverse legend is rudely executed. But, at least two kings, if not more, can be identified on these coins; a Kaniṣka III and a Vāsudeva II. It has been suggested that the Kuṣāṇa empire was divided after the death of Vāsudeva I, but we have no means to substantiate the hypothesis or work out the details. However, it is clear from the archeological, numismatic and epigraphical evidence that the Kuṣāṇas lost all their territories in northern India to the Nāghas, Maghas, Yaudheyas and other monarchical and republican states by the end of the first quarter of the 3rd century A.D. An inscription dated in the year 114 of the Kuṣāṇa reckoning refers to a Kaniṣka. Probably Vāsudeva I was followed by this Kaniṣka III, who probably ruled from sometime after c. A.D. 205 to about A.D. 225. After Kaniṣka III, we have no evidence of a Kuṣāṇa king ruling from Mathurā. Vāsudeva II, who seems to have followed Kaniṣka III, was probably ruling over the western and northern parts of the erstwhile Kuṣāṇa empire, while Ardashir-i-Babegan (A.D. 226–40) was busy carving out a Sassanian empire at the cost of his neighbors. According to Ṭabāri, the king of the Kuṣāṇas offered his submission to Ardashir. It is possible that Vāsudeva II stood in a vassal relationship to Ardashir. But no doubt the core of the Kuṣāṇa empire in the west was included in the Sassanian empire of Shāpūr I (A.D. 240–70). It is difficult to fix the exact date of the Kuṣāṇa defeat and the actual annexation of parts of their kingdom in the northwest by the Sassanians. Begram was destroyed during the reign of Vāsudeva II, whose dates overlap with Ardashir as well as with Shāpūr I. All evidence can be satisfactorily reconciled by putting the first defeat and submission of the Kuṣāṇas under Ardashir while the incorporation of the *Kushansahr* in the Sassanian empire would date from Shāpūr I's reign.[25]

[25] Henning, 1962, Maricq, 1968; Bivar, 1963, p. 499; Frye, 1966, pp. 235–65.

It is significant that Chinese historians also begin to mention the Yüeh-chih about this time. We are told that on January 6, A.D. 230, the king of the great Yüeh-chih, Po T'iao, sent an envoy with tribute to the court of the Wei emperor. "[Po] T'iao was made [given the honorary title of] king of the Great Yüeh-chih [who shows] affection towards the Wei."[26] Po T'iao's identification with a Vāsudeva has not been doubted. If it is Vāsudeva II, the Chinese information is quite probable in view of the Sassanian aggression. Probably to justify his "affection" for the Chinese, Vāsudeva II struck some copper coins with his name in Brāhmī written vertically in the Chinese style;[27] this practice which was first introduced by him on the Kuṣāṇa coinage was followed by later Kuṣāṇas, and even by the Guptas. But, anyway, this friendship was not sufficient to contain the Sassanian growth of power.

It seems that after Vāsudeva II, whatever was left of the Kuṣāṇa empire in the northern and northeastern peripheries, some splinter Kuṣāṇa families continued to rule for some time in the hill enclaves and other isolated pockets with real or nominal independence. And the Yüeh-chih prestige was not totally lost in Inner Asia. When the political power of the *Great* Yüeh-chih declined, the *other* Yüeh-chih, who certainly were proud of their links with the Kuṣāṇas and who had in the meanwhile acquired confidence and prosperity, thought that it was their turn now to revitalize the Yüeh-chih power. Already, in A.D. 184 there was a serious revolt, of the Little Yüeh-chih in Kansu and Ch'ing Hai, who had previously been loyal to the Chinese; and this revolt had still not been suppressed in A.D. 221. The Chinese sources do not give clear reasons for the uprising. But this event brings us close to the beginning of the period of Kharoṣṭhī documents in Inner Asia. It has been suggested that Po T'iao, who sent an embassy to the Wei court in A.D. 230, could have belonged to "one of the splinter kingdoms, one of the fragments in which the Kuṣāṇa empire fell apart. At the beginning of the Three Kingdoms, it might well have seemed that a small local ruler would look to the Wei as a better prospect of protection than was offered by the old Bactrian kingdom."[28] But we do not know of any king of the name of Po T'iao from this region, and there is no compelling reason to reject the general agreement of his identity with a Vāsudeva of the great Kuṣāṇa dynasty. But the idea that the Kuṣāṇas probably ruled the Shan-shan, at least for a short period, and introduced the northwest Indian Prākrit and the Kharoṣṭhī script for governmental purposes may be accepted.[29] From this region and period no forms of writing other than Chinese and Kharoṣṭhī are known to have been in common

[26] *San-kuo chih* 3: 6a; Zürcher, 1968, p. 371.
[27] Cunningham, 1892, p. 123, plate XXIV.1. [28] Brough, 1965. [29] Brough, 1965, p. 598.

use. There are five kings of the Shan-shan mentioned in the Kharoṣṭhī documents, namely Pepiya, Tajaka, Amgoka, Mahiri, and Vasmana. The earliest and the latest dates available for these kings are A.D. 235–6 and A.D. 321. We have no evidence to connect these kings with the Kuṣāṇa family of Kaniṣka. No indication has yet been found in the Kharoṣṭhī documents themselves of a name used for the inhabitants of the country. The possibility of an Indian colony in the Shan-shan has also been discounted in spite of the evidence of the Sogdian "Ancient Letters."[30] But, for the Chinese, these people were Yüeh-chih and we see no reason to doubt that these kings belonged to one of the Yüeh-chih branches. We do not have much material about the political careers and achievements of these Yüeh-chih kings, who ruled in Shan-shan until the middle of the 4th century A.D. But certainly their active roles in the field of religion and commerce, as well as their relationship of coexistence with their Chinese neighbors, are very well attested to by their epigraphs.

In the west, after the death of Shāpūr I in A.D. 272, during the succeeding generations, the Kuṣāṇas, who were living a life of precarious freedom in the peripheries, became restive again. Claudius Mamertinus records the help given by the Kuṣāṇas, among others, to Hormizd against Bahram II (276–93).[31] The Paikuli inscription counts the Kingdom of the Kuṣāṇas at the top of independent states and is called "*Kusānsahr*";[32] this independence was probably obtained after A.D. 290. But the exact location of the Kuṣāṇas at that time cannot be fixed. However, in the time of Shāpūr II (309–79), reports of invasions by the "Cuseni," probably another branch of the Kuṣāṇas, between A.D. 356 and 358, are noted. In 367–8, Shāpūr II again fought a battle with the Kuṣāṇas of Pahl (Balkh) and, according to Faustus, severe damage was done to the Sassanian troops.[33]

These instances do indicate that the Kuṣāṇas had not given up, and that more than one branch of them were struggling to maintain their independence and enhance their political power during the century-long period of decline. But they were, on the whole, contained by the Sassanians, until the death of Shāpūr II in A.D. 379. The strength of the Kuṣāṇa power was, however, soon to be felt under the new leadership of the Kidarites, known after Kidāra, the founder of a new Kuṣāṇa royalty.

That the Kidarites were connected with the Great Yüeh-chih in the west is clear from the account in the *Wei-shu* (= *Pei-shih*).[34] We are informed that the country of the Great Yüeh-chih lay to the west of Fu-ti-sha (Badakhshan); that

[30] Henning, 1948, p. 603. [31] Enoki, 1970, p. 30. [32] Herzfeld, 1924, pp. 119, 204–5.
[33] Enoki, 1970, p. 31. [34] *Wei shu* 102: 1321–3; *Pei shih* 97: 1295–6.

because of repeated invasions of the Juan-juan they moved westward away from Fu-ti-sha; that their king, Chi-to-lo (Kidāra), a brave warrior, marched to the south and invaded northern India; and that he crossed the Hindukush and completely subjugated five countries to the north of Chien-to-lo (Gandhāra). In its report on the Little Yüeh-chih, the *Wei-shu* informs us that their capital was at Fu-lou-sha (Puruṣapura, which is the modern Peshawar); that the king was originally the son of Chi-to-lo, king of the Great Yüeh-chih; that Chi-to-lo had been forced to move westwards by the attack of the Hsiung-nu, and that he made his son guard this city; and that "for this reason the kingdom was named the Little Yüeh-chih." This son was probably Kouncha mentioned by Priscus.[35]

It has been shown that the commonly accepted view which places the Kidarites in the second half of the 4th century A.D., and dates their expulsion by the Hephthalites in c. A.D. 400, must be revised because it is based on a misunderstanding of the *Records* left by Fa-hsien.[36] The *Wei-shu* account is based on the report of Tung Wan, who was sent to the western kingdoms in A.D. 437, and this may be accepted as the *terminus post quem* for the rise of the family of Kidāra. The *terminus ante quem* may be fixed at A.D. 412 on the basis of the evidence of Fa-hsien, Kumārajīva and Dharmavikrama. Thus, the unification of the north and the south of the Hindukush under the Kidarites must have taken place between 412 and 437. This was the period when the Northern Wei had revived its contacts with the western kingdoms, and not only were two ambassadors, Tung Wan and Kao Ming, sent to them, but merchants from the Great Yüeh-chih also came to Tai, during the reign of T'ai Wu (432–52), and taught the Chinese how to make glass.

The Kidarite branch of the Great Yüeh-chih became independent during the reign of Bahram V (420–38). But, in less than fifty years, the Sassanid king, Peroz, defeated Kouncha, probably a son of Kidāra, in A.D. 468. It is interesting to note that three embassies from the Yüeh-chih kingdoms visited China between A.D. 459 and 477. It is likely that the Kidarites lost their territories north of the Hindukush to the Sassanians after Kouncha's defeat, but they continued to be in the possession of the territories south of the Hindukush at least until A.D. 477 and possibly afterwards. But by the end of the 5th century or in the beginning of the 6th, the Kidarite dominance in the south of the Hindukush was removed by the inroads of the Hephthalites.

Some Chinese sources treat the Hephthalites too as Yüeh-chih.[37] A striking resemblance may also be noted in the deformed heads of the early Yüeh-chih

[35] Enoki, 1969, p. 20. [36] Enoki, 1970, pp. 13–38.
[37] For a discussion of the Chinese sources see especially Enoki, 1959.

and Hephthalite kings on their coinage.[38] But while scholarly consensus is still needed to include them in the Tokharian Yüeh-chih fold, their Iranian links have been considered seriously even when the Altaic or Hun elements in them cannot be denied.[39] Be that as it may, the Hephthalites were a potent factor in Transoxiana during the last quarter of the 5th and the first half of the 6th centuries A.D.

But, Tokharians were not the only Indo-Europeans of Inner Asia. There were the Sakas and the Sogdians among others of the Iranian stock. On the northern route from Tun-huang westward, skirting the Tarim basin and the Taklamakan, the Tokharian element seems to have predominated, and the Sakas occupied the Upper Ili and the western part of the southern route. The Chinese accounts and the archeological and linguistic remains confirm this. *The History of the Former Han* informs that when the Yüeh-chih went to the West and became rulers of Bactria the Saka king of the Upper Ili went southwards and became king of Chi-pin. It also reports that the Sakas, having dispersed southwards after their encounter with the Yüeh-chih, founded several kingdoms and that "the kingdoms to the northwest of Su-le (Kashgar) such as Hsiu-hsün and Yüan-tu, all belong to the original Sai race."[40] Probably the city states of Kashgar, Yarkand, Khotan and some of the others on the southern route were of Saka origin, although the Chinese sources do not specify their ethnic composition. But in Central Asia a Saka-rāja is known, being possibly the ruler of Saka, the older name of Yarkand.[41] And the founders of the Kingdom of Khotan, whose language, as the Chinese records state, was similar to that of Yarkand, were almost certainly also Saka. So also the languages of Kashgar and Tumshuk were similar to those of Yarkand and Khotan and thus belonged to the Iranian family of the Indo-Europeans.

To narrate the history of these Saka city states of Inner Asia before the Turks occupied them is a difficult task indeed. Naturally the Chinese dynastic annals report on them only when these states are relevant to the vicissitudes of Chinese political power and military strength. There are no means of verifying their account, and thus it is also impossible to identify the kings whose names are known only in Chinese form. No doubt these states came into existence before the end of the 2nd century B.C. But already, by the middle of the 1st century A.D., they are found not only fighting among themselves but also in their roles as pawns in the game of balance of power in Inner Asia between the Chinese on the one hand and the Yüeh-chih and the Hsiung-nu on

[38] Compare for example the figures of Vima Kadphises (Cunningham, 1892, plate XV) and those of the "White Hun" kings (Cunningham, 1894, plates VII–IX).

[39] Enoki, 1959, p. 56; also Enoki, 1955. [40] Zürcher, 1968, p. 363. [41] Bailey, 1971.

the other. The successful campaigns of the Chinese general Pan Ch'ao brought them under the Chinese hegemony by the end of the 1st century A.D., but soon after his return and death these states looked up to the Yüeh-chih–Kuṣāṇas and the latter exercised their supremacy in Inner Asia during the first half of the 2nd century A.D. The Sino-Kharoṣṭhī coins found in this area probably belong to this period.[42]

For one of these Saka states, that of Khotan, other sources than Chinese have become available; these are the literary documents in the Saka language and the Tibetan tradition.[43] From these indigenous documents the names of eight kings of Khotan have been recovered, some only as names in the dating of documents, others, as in the case of Viśa Saṃgrāma, in long compositions, others again in colophons to manuscripts. One name, that of Vijita Saṃbhava, is written within a Buddhist Sanskrit manuscript of a religious text, the *Sitātapatrá-dhārani* (= the Spell of the Lady with the White Umbrella), with a prayer for the king's protection, the *rakṣā*, which is often stressed. All the royal names in these documents are of Indian origin: Kīrti, Dharma, Vaham, Vikrram, Sura, Saṃgrāma, Saṃbhava, and Siṃhg. The *Annals of Li Yul*, i.e. Khotan, record other similar Indian names in Tibetan. Some of these names appear in Chinese translations in the Chinese dynastic histories as ruling in the 10th century A.D. The variety of linguistic remains in the Saka language provides what amounts to a veritable index to the high civilization of the Sakas in Inner Asia.

In the Iranian complex the closest settled neighbors of the nomadic Sakas were the Sogdians, who inhabited the oases of Bukhara, Samarkand and probably part of Ferghana valley and other adjoining areas. They had put up some of the toughest resistance to Alexander, who married one of their girls, Roxane, his only wife, who bore him his only son. They remained untamed until, along with the Bactrians, they became an independent state by the middle of the 3rd century B.C. But in less than a hundred years, we notice them breaking away from the Bactrians while the latter get more involved south of the Oxus in the valleys of Kabul and Indus. This is clear from the coins bearing Sogdian letters but imitating the types of Seleucid and early Bactrian Greek coinage. By 128 B.C., when Ch'ang Ch'ien visited the West, the Sogdians, known as K'ang-chü to the Chinese, were again reduced to an only quasi-independent status acknowledging nominal sovereignty to the Yüeh-chih in

[42] Thomas, 1944; Enoki, 1965; Zejmal, 1971. For the view adopted here cf. A.K. Narain and J.C. Cribb, "The Sino-Kharoṣṭhī Coins of Central Asia", read at the 29th International Congress of Orientalists, Paris, 1973.

[43] Bailey, 1970, 1971. See the bibliography at the end of these two papers.

the south and to the Hsiung-nu in the east. But when at the close of the 2nd century B.C. the Yüeh-chih moved to the south of the Oxus and divided their kingdom into five *yabghu* perhaps the southern part of the Sogdian territory was integrated into it, while the northern part remained independent but friendly to them. At times while the Sogdians paid only a forced servitude to the Hsiung-nu in the east and took care to live in peace with other neighbors, they refused to look up to China like the other nations, and their hostage prince in the time of Emperor Ch'eng is known to have been haughty and insolent. When Pan Ch'ao attacked Chung, a rebel king of Kashgar but could not defeat him, it was because the latter was strengthened by auxiliary troops from K'ang-chü; and the Sogdian king withdrew his support only after the Yüeh-chih, who had established bonds of marriage with the K'ang-chü, persuaded him to do so. By the end of the 1st century A.D. the Sogdians seem to have come under the hegemony of the Kuṣāṇas, and probably continued to be so under their successors. With the rise of the Hephthalites a progressive erosion of the Sogdian frontiers took place and, by the end of the 5th century A.D., Sogdiana had probably ceased to exist as a single political state. But the Sogdians survived in a series of small city-states, Samarkand being one of them, until they were finally conquered by the Arabs.

For the Sogdians, however, economic matters were more important than political ones and commerce more rewarding than war. The men of Sogdiana, says the New T'ang History, "have gone wherever profit is to be found."[44] Indeed, they had extensive trade relations with China for over half a millenium before the Arab conquest. Sogdian merchants and colonists were found as far apart as Mongolia and Merv. It was in their hands that the silk trade effectively rested under the Hephthalites, and they did not cease to influence their Türk Kaghan in matters of commercial policy in relation to Persia and Byzantium. If they were good entrepreneurs of trade they were also alert observers of political happenings; the "ancient letter" of Nanaivandak to Nanai-dvar of Samarkand bears witness to Chinese catastrophe in A.D. 311 when the Hsiung-nu captured the capital city of Lo-yang, took the emperor prisoner, and burned the city to the ground.[45] Culture goes with commerce, and the Sogdians are known for their transmission of religious ideas and items of culture. If their role in disseminating Buddhism into Inner Asia is evident from their participation in the translation of the doctrinal texts, that in spreading Iranian culture to the Turks is amply attested by Sogdian words in Old Turkic. It was in Sogdiana that Manichaeism found its refuge when it was

[44] *Hsin T'ang shu* 221 B: 1a. [45] Henning, 1948, pp. 603–7.

persecuted on all sides; its syncretism found a good vehicle in the Sogdian merchant who traveled far and wide amidst people belonging to various religions and faiths.

The political history of the Indo-Europeans of Inner Asia from the 2nd century B.C. to the 5th century A.D. is indeed a glorious period. It is their movement which brought China into contact with the Western world as well as with India. These Indo-Europeans held the key to world trade for a long period and introduced a new gold in the form of silk. They acted as carriers of religious doctrines and artistic traditions from the east to the west and vice versa. They were instrumental in creating a syncretic culture in which the styles of Inner Asia found an expression and received not only a recognition but a sophistication which at once broadened the outlook of the Iranian, the Greek, the Indian and the Chinese. The new eclecticism generated new trends of thought and they were reflected in religion, art and literature. In the process of their own transformation, these Indo-Europeans influenced the world around them more than any other people before the rise of Islam.

7

The Hun period

No people of Inner Asia, not even the Mongols, have acquired in European historiography a notoriety similar to that of the Huns, whose name has become synonymous with that of cruel, destructive invaders. Just as the name of the Germanic Vandals has given us the term "vandalism," the name Hun has been used pejoratively to stigmatize any ferocious, savage enemy. Their greatest ruler, Attila, "the scourge of God," has become the legendary embodiment of a cruel, merciless leader of barbarians.

There are several reasons why the Huns caught the Western imagination. Firstly, not since Scythian times had any Inner Asian people seriously challenged the equilibrium of the Western World. The Germanic menace to Rome, serious though it was, presented nothing unusual or unexpected – it was part and parcel of Roman political life; the limits of conflict and the patterns of resolution were clearly established. The Huns presented a challenge of a different type: they did not fit into any conventional political category; their very looks, their mode of waging war set them apart from humanity as known to Europe. Secondly, they appeared on the European scene at a time when both the eastern and the western parts of the Roman Empire had to contend with serious internal disorders which weakened their military preparedness. Thirdly, the status quo of the period was disturbed not only by their direct action but even more by their being instrumental in setting into motion the great upheaval of peoples commonly known as the *Völkerwanderung*. Finally, the enduring reputation of the Huns is due in no small measure to some excellent descriptions given by contemporary writers, even poets whose imagination was caught by this, quite literally, extraordinary people.

According to a widely accepted but unproven theory, the Huns are the descendants of the Hsiung-nu, an identification first suggested in the 18th century by the eminent French orientalist Deguignes, which has little else in its favor than the fortuitous consonance of the two names, one known only in

Chinese transcription. The political power of the Northern Hsiung-nu was completely broken by the middle of the 2nd century A.D., and – although the history of some Southern Hsiung-nu can be followed well into the 4th century – there is no evidence of any westward migration of these tribes. On the contrary, its course leads to complete absorption by the Chinese. If we admit the Hsiung-nu–Hun identity, there is no accounting for the two centuries that elapsed between the eclipse of the Northern Hsiung-nu in Mongolia and the appearance of the Huns on the European horizon. The disintegration of the Hsiung-nu empire was not tantamount to the disappearance of its population. It can be taken for granted that descendants of former Hsiung-nu subjects were incorporated into other bodies politic just as the Romans' progenies may be found today in a number of countries. In the constantly shifting composition of Inner Asian ethnic units Hsiung-nu elements could be, and perhaps were, present in the ranks of the Huns. Whether they were aware of their Hsiung-nu origin must remain an unanswered question. In the words of Rafe de Crespigny[1] "... it seems sensible to recognize that the expression *Xiongnu* [Hsiung-nu] in the texts of the Han period possesses a double meaning. On the one hand, *Xiongnu* referred to a specific group, of specific ethnic origin, language and culture. At the same time, in extended meaning, *Xiongnu* refers to the political entity which was established under the dominance of that tribe." What is here said about the Hsiung-nu applies to most, if not all, Inner Asian nomad-type states, including that of the Huns. The important point is to remember that there is no evidence to show that the dominant element in the Hun state was historically connected with that of the Hsiung-nu.

The question of the origin of the Huns greatly intrigued contemporary writers. Ammianus Marcellinus, one of our most reliable and richest sources, admits that the people of the Huns is "but little known from ancient records." The only *extant* record prior to Ammianus' time is Ptolemy (2nd century A.D.) who lists the Khounoi (*χοῦνοι*) among the peoples of European Sarmatia. The indication is vague not only in absolute terms but even within the framework of Ptolemy's own view of the world. It is probably safe to postulate that the name Khounoi is the equivalent of the Latin name of the Huns; it is less certain that it was applied to *the* Huns, that is, to the people appearing on Europe's eastern border two centuries later.

Chronologically, the next, second mention of the name Hun appears in a letter written in Sogdian shortly after 311. In it a Sogdian merchant living at the eastern end of the great trade route, probably in Su-chou, informs another

[1] De Crespigny, 1984, p. 174.

merchant living in Samarkand of the destruction of the Chinese capital Lo-yang by the Huns (the name is spelt: *xwn*)[2]. The letter obviously refers to the occupation of Lo-yang by the Southern Hsiung-nu, and some consider its contents proof of the Hsiung-nu–Hun identity. The flaw in this argument is its disregard of the fact that the name Hun has been used consistently as a generic for many barbarian or barbarous peoples – for example in Byzantine sources in which Hungarians or Ottomans are often called Huns. The Germans are neither Huns nor Hsiung-nu, though in his correspondence with Franklin D. Roosevelt, Winston Churchill calls them Huns. The people who sacked Lo-yang in 311 could not be the same as that which fought the Goths some sixty years later. One cannot but admire J.B. Bury who – although unable to check the accuracy or the weaknesses of theories propounded by Orientalist scholars – relying only on his own, exceptionally sound judgment declared that "... the immediate events which precipitated the Huns into Europe had nothing to do with the collapse of the Hiung-nu [sic!] power which had occurred in the distant past."[3]

The name Hyaona, which appears in Avestan and Pahlavi texts, has often been linked with that of the Huns. A barbarian people, enemy of the sedentary Iranians, the Hyons cannot be dissociated from the Chionitae mentioned in Latin texts, a people of similar customs who in the middle of the 4th century was alternately enemy or ally of the Persians. The Chionitae were certainly not Huns; Ammianus Marcellinus, our main source on both peoples, does not link them. In the Pahlavi heroic poem *Āyadgār i Zarērān* – a later compilation which contains elements harking back to Parthian time and even earlier, and which has moreover many anachronisms – the Hyons are considered Turks.

In Greek sources the standard spelling of the name of the Huns is Ounnoi (*Οὖννοι*); Latin texts would usually indicate an initial *h*-, thus Huni, Hunni, Chuni, though on occasion readings such as Unni or even Ugni occur.

When it comes to the origin of the Huns, modern scholarship cannot really go beyond the statement of Ammianus, according to which before their appearance the nation of the Huns "dwelt beyond the Maeotic marshes [i.e. the Sea of Azov], beside the frozen Ocean." Reference to the "frozen ocean" should not be taken literally, this being the term for the body of water encircling the flat surface of the earth and constituting the outer limits of the world, a truly proper place for a people "surpassing every extreme in ferocity" to come from. There can be no quarrel with the statement that, before their coming into contact with the Roman world, the Huns lived east of the Azov

[2] Henning, 1948. [3] J.B. Bury 1958, I, p. 101.

Sea, on the south Russian steppe, or perhaps even further east in the not clearly circumscribed, measureless lands of "Scythia," whence all bad things come. The first to bear the brunt of a Hun attack were the Alans nomadizing along the Don (Tanais), a people whose way of life was in many ways similar to that of the Huns, but who were not filled with the fury of aggression. The paucity of available information does not allow the compilation of a precise account of the clashes between Huns and Alans but it is clear that the former were victorious and that the surviving Alans joined the victors in their further warlike undertakings. These events took place in the early 370s.

The joint forces of Huns and Alans now turned against the Eastern Goths (Ostrogoths) whose powerful Germanic state occupied the south Russian steppe from the Don to the Dniester, and from the shores of the Black Sea far north to the Pripet Marshes. Their king Ermanaric, unable to withstand the repeated attacks by the joint forces of Huns and Alans, killed himself in despair and Vithimeris, his successor, fell in battle soon afterwards. The Ostrogoths now came under Hun domination though they were still ruled by a king of their own, Hunimund "protégé of the Huns." Not all Ostrogoths acquiesced in this arrangement, Alatheus and Saphrax "experienced generals known for their courage," with such fighting forces as were willing to follow them retreated to the river Dniester where they established contacts with the troops of Athanaric, chief of the Western Goths (Visigoths). Most probably they meant to join forces with those of their Visigothic brethren for a joint action against the oncoming Huns. Athanaric was certainly not ready to surrender and prepared for battle. But the Huns, unexpectedly crossing the river by night, outflanked the Goths, who hastily retreated and attempted to build a second, fortified line of resistance between the Prút and the Danube. This makeshift barrier was strong enough to withstand an attack by the Huns who were so laden with booty that they made no new attempt to break through it.

It is not for us to relate in any detail the further destinies of the Visigoths, some seeking refuge in the Carpathian basin, some in Thrace where, in the fall of 376, they were permitted to settle. Their growing discontent with Roman administration was but one of the many causes which ultimately (on 9 August 378), led them to engage at Adrianople the hastily assembled forces of the Emperor Valens and to inflict upon them a crushing defeat. We must limit our investigation to the Huns' share in the tumultuous events of the early phase of the *Völkerwanderung*. If abstraction is made of the fact that they provided the initial impetus to the events just outlined, the role of the Huns in them seems almost insignificant. Their victory over the Alans would not normally qualify

as an important event, it was just one episode in the endless succession of clashes between peoples of the steppe. There is no indication of a strong, conquering personality leading the moves. Beyond his name, nothing is known of Balamber, the Hun ruler who may have initiated the conflict. To the eminent historian E.A. Thompson[4] "It seems reasonably certain that Balamber never existed: the Goths invented him in order to explain who it was that conquered them." This is perhaps an extreme view but it is safe to assume that, at the most, Balamber was merely the leader either of a tribe or of an *ad hoc* group of warriors. Ammianus' statement (XXXI,2,7) that the Huns "are subject to no royal restraint, but they are content with the disorderly government of their important men [*tumultuario primatum ductu contenti*], and led by them they force their way through every obstacle"[5] is no more *topos*. Our authorities reveal no evidence of marked national consciousness among the Huns, not even a strong feeling of solidarity. Against his Hun aggressors Vithimeris can set Hun mercenaries; in the course of the campaigns against the Goths, Huns and Alans are indistinguishable, and modern historians cannot ascertain with certainty whether or not Hun contingents took part in the pillage of the Balkans preceding and following the battle of Adrianople. If present, the Huns were certainly auxiliaries rather than actuators.

The autonomy of various Hun groups is exemplified by the readiness of some to accept the status of federates and – together with Goths and Alans serving under Alatheius and Saphrax – to settle in Pannonia. This happened in 380 and the decision to do so must have been taken on the local level; consultation with any higher, geographically distant authority can safely be ruled out. From their new base these Huns could help or harass provinces, and were able to interfere in the persistent internal conflicts of the Roman Empire. Thus, for example, in 384 in the service of Bauto, Master of the Soldiers under Valentinian II, the Huns fought the Juthungi in Raetia and, having beaten them, were said to be approaching Gaul when, against payment, they returned to their base, presumably in Pannonia. In 388 Huns helped Theodosius I to defeat the usurper Maximus, while in 394, as John of Antioch reports, Hun warriors from Thrace were again to lend him support, this time against Eugenius, another usurper. Actions such as these presuppose prompt decisions taken by local leaders and one may wonder whether there was any central authority directing Hun policies and if so, who was in charge of it and where it had its seat.

The first of these questions is easy to answer. While our sources do name

[4] E.A. Thompson, 1948, p. 57. [5] ed. Rolfe, III, pp. 384–5.

Goth and Alan leaders, those of the Huns remain anonymous, a clear indication of their relative insignificance. For the period extending from the Huns' victory over the Alans to 395 – with the exception of the disembodied Balamber – no Hun is mentioned by name, a clear indication that none of them was a leader of influence. It is probably correct to surmise that Hun detachments, though certainly led by men of their own stock, operated under either Gothic or Alan commanders. The first Hun leaders known by name are Basikh and Koursikh who in 395 led an important military campaign into Asia, one we shall examine in the sequel. For the moment it suffices to say that neither of these two men was, or claimed to be, ruler of the Huns, the sources refer to them as *arkhontes*, high ranking military commanders. At the turn of the 5th century no one man could claim authority over all the Hun factions.

The Hun campaign into Asia provides an answer to the second of the questions raised above, that which concerns the location of the center of gravity of Hun power. The size of the forces mobilized, the purposefulness of its execution, indicate that the raid was conceived and executed on a scale much larger than the military actions undertaken by Huns further west. There are good reasons to believe that, though they set in motion the *Völkerwanderung*, the Huns were not really participating in it, and that the bulk of the Huns continued to occupy the Pontic steppe where they had first appeared a quarter of a century earlier and whence they now swarmed into Asia Minor.

The great Hun raid of 395–6 across the Caucasus into Armenia, Syria, Palestine, and Northern Mesopotamia was a traumatic event for the inhabitants of these thoroughly civilized regions. No wonder that the shock caused many to write about it, though the concrete data they provide are but small islands in a torrent of apocalyptic prose bemoaning the devastations, dreading their recurrence. Perhaps the most telling piece is by St. Jerome:

> Lo, suddenly messengers ran to and fro and the whole East trembled, for swarms of Huns had broken forth from the far distant Maeotis between the icy Tanais and the monstrous peoples of the Massagetae, where the Gates of Alexander pen in the wild nations behind the rocks of the Caucasus. They filled the whole earth with slaughter and panic alike as they flitted hither and thither on their swift horses . . . May Jesus avert such beasts from the Roman world in the future! They were at hand everywhere before they were expected: by their speed they outstripped rumour, and they took pity neither upon religion nor rank nor age nor wailing childhood. Those who had just begun to live were compelled to die and, in ignorance of their plight, would smile amid the drawn sword of the enemy.[6]

[6] Quoted after Thompson, 1948, p. 27.

One can but speculate on the causes which prompted the invasion, though that much is clear that conquest of territory was not its aim – the Huns showed no intention of settling down at any of the places to which they paid an unwelcome visit. In an account based on earlier sources, the Syriac chronicle of Joshua the Stylite attributes the invasion to the tyranny of the praetorian prefect Rufinus – favorite whipping boy of bad poets and others of those days – without, however, specifying the link between presumed cause and effect.[7] Some contemporaries accused the Georgian pretender Pharasmanios of having enlisted Hun help to foster his personal projects.[8] Such charges, though common, are difficult to substantiate and, at all events, do not explain the reason why the Huns should have accepted such an offer. Be that as it may, it is obvious that it was the lure of booty that prompted this and many other Hun campaigns.

That the Anatolian campaign was no mean affair may be deduced from a conversation in 449, in Attila's camp, between Priscus – who recorded it – and his West Roman counterpart Romulus. More than half a century after the event the raid was said to have been caused by a famine among the Huns: a very credible explanation offered by a well-informed person who also knew that Basikh and Koursikh, at some later date, visited Rome to conclude an alliance. The Huns retraced their steps heavily laden with booty, carrying away into slavery a multitude of captives. If one can believe Claudian – an approach not devoid of risks – herds constituted an important part of the booty:

> ... stolen from the stalls of their homesteads, the captive herds drink the snowy streams of the Caucasus, and the flocks exchange the pastures of Mount Argaeus for the woods of Scythia. Beyond the Cimmerian marshes, defence of the Tauric tribes, the youth of Syria are slaves.[9]

If such really was the case, one may view it as additional evidence pointing to a famine among the Huns. In normal circumstances driving cattle onto the steppe may be likened to carrying coals to Newcastle but if, as it sometimes happens, the pastures were ruined by the frost *jud*, cattle might indeed have been the most valuable commodity for the Huns to appropriate.

The duration of the Hun raid cannot be established with any certainty, it may even be that the Huns' operations were not continuous and that at least some contingents left earlier than others. This much is certain: that the total evacuation occurred probably late in 396 and certainly sometime before the

[7] Markwart, 1930, p. 99. [8] Marquart, 1901, p. 96.
[9] *In Eutropium*, I, 247–250; ed. Platnauer I, p. 157.

end of 398. The withdrawal, I presume, had nothing to do with the troops painfully assembled by the eunuch Eutropius and, for once, one can sympathize with Claudian's scoffing at his claim to have put the invaders to flight. One can take it for granted that our sources would have made much ado about any victory on the battlefield, and their silence about any such occurrence indicates that the Huns – as was their wont – withdrew of their own volition, having won their objective: a good time spent in a land of plenty, a rich loot to take back home. As a matter of fact, on their return the Huns were to be deprived of most of the accumulated booty. According to a Syriac chronicle normally referred to by the most inappropriate title of *Liber Calipharum*, on their return from Anatolia the Huns went on an ill-advised foray into Persia where they reached the approaches of the capital Ctesiphon. Attacked by the Persians, they suffered heavy losses and had to abandon most of their plunder, including 18,000 [!] prisoners.[10] The episode is recalled by Priscus (fragm.8) who, quoting Romulus, describes these Huns as returning to their home by the Derbend Pass.

Hun activity was not limited to Anatolia. Simultaneously with the southern campaign hostilities flared up also on the Danube border. Claudian refers to both events: "Some [Huns] pour across the frozen surface of swift-flowing Danube and break with the chariot wheel that which erstwhile knew but the oar; others invade the wealthy East, led through the Caspian Gates and over the Armenian snows by a newly-discovered path."[11] The question may be asked whether the two military actions – one through the Caucasus, the other across the Danube into Thrace – were in any way coordinated, whether it would be justified to speak of an attempt to mount a concerted attack against Byzantium. The sources do not support such a supposition. At this stage of Hun history there is no trace of a strong, unified Hun leadership capable of strategic planning on a large scale. The Huns operating in Asia Minor or in the Danubian provinces aimed at no more than pillage, and if there was a common motive force behind the predatory expeditions it was of an economic nature, possibly the famine to which allusion has already been made.

It is generally, and probably correctly, assumed that at the turn of the 4th century Huns continued to occupy the Pontic steppe. Regrettably none of the available sources say so, and what meagre evidence there is on their habitats points only to two regions with more or less permanent Hun settlements. One of these is Pannonia, the other the land north of the lower reaches of the Danube, in what is today eastern Romania. This region was the base of

[10] On this episode see Maenchen-Helfen, 1973, p. 58, and the important remarks made by Czeglédy, 1957, p. 238. [11] *In Rufinum* II. 26–30; ed. Platnauer, I, p. 61.

operation of Uldin (Uldis), only the second Hun chief (*regulus*) following Balamber to be known by name. When the Goth chief Gainas in the wake of his unsuccessful rebellion fled across the Danube with what remained of his army, "intending to return to his original home and there live out the rest of his life"[12] he was engaged by the forces of Uldin, and defeated (December 400). Gainas' severed head was sent to the Emperor Arcadius, Uldin was rewarded, and a treaty was concluded between Huns and Romans. The terms of this agreement are unknown but in 404–5 Huns led by Uldin again invaded Thrace, as usual, with no intention of permanent conquest. A year later, in April 406, this time in the service of Stilicho, Huns were instrumental in the defeat near Fiesole of the Goth king Radagaisus, in fact they formed the bodyguard of the mighty Master of the Soldiers. Following Stilicho's fall and execution (27 August 408) an elite corps of three hundred Huns – possibly the same unit which had served Stilicho – was stationed in Ravenna under the orders of Olympius, minister of Honorius, who in the spring of 409 dispatched them to intercept the mixed Gothic and Hun army of Athaulf coming to the rescue of Alaric. If we are to believe Zosimus (V,45), in an engagement, possibly near Pisa, these three hundred defeated 1100 Goths with a loss of only 17 men. There is no way of knowing whether such mercenary troops hailed from Pannonia or the Dobrudja, and whether – in either case – they were Uldin's men. The "three hundred" of Ravenna operated probably independently because in the summer of 408 Uldin personally led another attack on Thrace, took possession of Castra Martis (present-day Kula) in Moesia and, according to Sozomen (IX,5), boasted that "it would be easy for him, if he desired to do so, to subjugate every region of the earth." A short while after, many of his troops were induced by the "philanthropy of the emperor" to desert him, others were slain, and Uldin himself escaped only with difficulty to the northern bank of the river, not to be heard of again. With his disappearance the curtain falls on the further history of the Huns in Dobrudja.

Huns constituted a military reserve to be counted upon by anyone willing and able to pay the price (in cash and devastation). Following the disgrace of Olympius in the Spring of 409, his successor Jovius is said to have hired ten thousand Huns on behalf of Honorius (Zosimus V,50). It would appear, however, that this important army never reached Italy.

In 412–13 Olympiodorus of Thebes was head of a mission sent to the Huns, and wrote a description of his experiences. Unfortunately only fragments have survived and even these have often been misinterpreted. For a part of his journey Olympiodorus traveled northwards by sea, and on the assumption

[12] Zosimus V, 21; translation p. 215

that he was an envoy of the East Romans it has normally been taken for granted that he sailed across the Black Sea and met the king of the Huns, called Kharaton, somewhere on the Pontic steppe. A more careful sifting of the available evidence suggests that Olympiodorus' mission was undertaken on behalf of Honorius, that he sailed northwards on the Adriatic and that Pannonia was the place of his encounter with Kharaton. While with the Huns, Olympiodorus met a certain Donatus, taken for a Hun king by certain modern historians. Yet the text calls Donatus neither a Hun nor a king and – though repeated efforts have been made to provide it with a contorted Altaic etymology – the name is, of course, Christian, much in use in the 4th and 5th centuries. Among the more illustrious bearers of this name at that time one can mention St. Donatus (d. 361), bishop of Arezzo; Aelius Donatus, grammarian and preceptor of St. Jerome (4th c.); and Donatus, bishop of Casa Nigrae in Numidia (4th c.), founder of what is known as the Donatist heresy. We learn from Olympiodorus that, deceived by an oath, Donatus was killed and that his death angered the Hun king who then had to be appeased by presents from the emperor. It is thus safe to assume that Olympiodorus' party was responsible for the murder. The pattern of the action is very clear and in some respects very "modern"; a government dispatches its agents to dispose of a possibly inconvenient émigré who had taken refuge in a foreign country. The motives which prompted the action, Donatus' guilt in the eyes of his murderers, must remain a secret. The displeasure shown by Kharaton is proof that he held Donatus in esteem; that he did not react with greater violence would suggest that, though deploring the action, he considered it a settlement of accounts between Romans. As a piece of fanciful speculation may we not presume that Donatus was a Donatist of importance, seeking refuge among the Huns from the religious persecution which – condoned even by St. Augustine – caused grave disturbances before and after the council of bishops held in Carthage in 411, and which was at its height at the time of Olympiodorus' visit to the Huns? Donatist or not, the presence of a Roman in Kharaton's entourage should not cause surprise, for there must have been many who sought asylum or, simply, a different, perhaps better, life among the Huns. A noted case is that of Eudoxius, a well-known doctor involved in the revolt of the Bagaudae, who in 448 fled to Attila's court. It was also there that Priscus met a Greek émigré who had chosen to stay with his former captors among whom, so he said, he had a better life than he had had formerly in his country of birth.

For a decade after Olympiodorus' visit to Kharaton nothing is heard of the Huns, until in 422 there was a major incursion into Thrace. The campaign

launched across the Danube and menacing even Constantinople ended with a peace treaty in which the Romans agreed to pay the Huns an annual subsidy of 350 pounds of gold. The Hun ruler responsible for this invasion – and presumably reaping the benefits derived from it – was Ruga (Rua, Rugila) who, according to Theodoret, was struck by lightning in the course of the campaign. If any credence is to be given to this story aimed at showing divine protection accorded to Theodosius II, death must have struck another, unnamed, Hun leader participating in the campaign, for Ruga died in 434.

Imperium over the Huns was divided. Ruga's domain was the eastern part of the empire – if the use of this term is at all justified – comprising the land south of the Carpathians and north of the Danube whence in 422 he launched his attack against Thrace. The territory north and west of the Carpathians, comprising the Great Hungarian Plain, was ruled by Ruga's brother Octar. Since the date of his accession is unknown, it cannot be established whether the reconquest by the Romans of Pannonia Secunda in 427 – hailed by several chroniclers – was accomplished in his time. Octar died in 430 during a campaign against the Burgundians, who were living at that time on the right bank of the Rhine between the Main and the Neckar. There is no indication that his place was taken by anyone, so one must assume that his apanage was taken over by Ruga, to whom in 433 Pannonia Prima was surrendered by Aetius. It was a reasonable enough compensation for the massive help given him the previous year by Ruga which allowed him to reassert his authority in Ravenna.

In his youth – probably between 405 and 408 – Aetius was a hostage among the Huns and learned – besides the art of their superb horsemanship and skill in the use of the bow – one must assume, also their language. Literally as well as figuratively, Aetius knew how to speak with the Huns among whom he sent his son, Carpilio, as a hostage and apprentice. In 425 Aetius used Hun auxiliaries, said to number 60,000, in the service of the usurper John the Tyrant who was fighting against the forces of Theodosius II. Succor came too late, John had been captured and executed a few days before the arrival of Aetius. Adaptable, his bargaining position no doubt strengthened by the presence of his Hun friends, Aetius now accepted a charge from the formidable Galla Placidia and, without delay, could once again demonstrate his skill in handling the Huns. He induced them to return whence they came, if not empty-handed, at least without doing any damage.

In 432 or 433 Ruga – now assured of peace with the West Romans – let it be known that he intended to go to war against some tribes whom he considered to be his own subjects, who had taken refuge on East Roman territory. The

menace was taken seriously and Plinthas, a Goth and Master of the Soldiers, an experienced trouble-shooter, volunteered to travel to Ruga to open negotiations. He did not have to leave; to the jubilation of the people of Constantinople the news of Ruga's death arrived and it seemed that with his mortal remains the whole matter could be put to rest. It was not to be. *Le roi est mort, vive le roi* – the throne of Ruga did not remain vacant. Our sources speak of two successors, two brothers, both nephews of the defunct Ruga, Bleda the elder, Attila the younger. In view of the role Attila was to assume in history, and also because of the early death of his brother, it is not surprising that some sources consider Attila the sole heir of Ruga, and, with a few exceptions, Bleda appears only as a shadowy co-ruler besides his spectacular younger brother. The Gallic Chronicle puts the true situation in the simple statement: Ruga's successor was Bleda. Clearly, he inherited the eastern parts of the empire, while Attila, we do not know when, stepped into the place of Octar. Viewed from an Inner Asian perspective, it makes no sense to imagine that two persons should accede to the throne left vacant by one, whereas it would not be unusual to see two brothers ruling simultaneously over two parts of an extended empire. In the Ruga–Octar double kingship the former was the senior partner probably in age and certainly in importance. On his death his place was taken by Bleda, and one can assume that Attila had been in charge of the Western Regions ever since the death of Octar.

Apparently, Bleda did not deviate from his uncle's political line, and the East Romans found it necessary to send Plintha, accompanied by the *quaestor* Epigenes, to meet their Hun counterparts. The meeting took place near the city of Margus. The Hun envoys – and not Bleda and Attila in person as suggested by some – who negotiated mounted on their horses, a practice the Greek envoys felt obliged to conform to, drove a hard bargain. Their aim was twofold: to exact a higher tribute and to obtain the extradition of Hun deserters. The negotiations ended by the doubling to 700 pounds of gold of the annual payment agreed upon in 422, and wide-ranging measures were also taken to regulate the destinies of Hun fugitives and of Roman prisoners of war escaping without having been ransomed. A trade agreement was negotiated as well. Though the Treaty of Margus favored the Huns, for about five years it did give a respite from the constant Hun inroads into the East Roman border areas, notwithstanding some dilatoriness by Theodosius in the payment of the annual dues. In the meanwhile, the Huns turned their attention to some minor military campaigns against "Scythian" tribes.

At first, the change in Hun leadership did not alter the line of Hun activities in the West. Hun auxiliaries continued to operate as in the past, and it is

unlikely that they were taking any direct orders from either Bleda or Attila. If any centralized planning has to be conjectured, it should be linked with the destructive attack in 436 against the Burgundians which, though instigated by Aetius, may well have been a follow-up on the stand-off of 430, and thus a retaliation for the death of Octar. The destruction of the Burgundian kingdom of Worms caught the imagination of generations to come and constitutes the principal historical core of the Niebelungenlied. Another reasonably well documented case of Hun activity in the West is their participation in the war against the Visigoths. Probably at the end of 436, under the command of Litorius, a general under Aetius, the Huns relieved Narbonne, which was besieged by Theodoric. After this success they continued to operate in the south of France principally against the Bagaudae, an activity which indicates their operational autonomy, for no central authority had anything to gain from such expeditions. In 439, so the story goes, Litorius made an unwise choice. If we are to believe Salvianus "he laid his hopes in the Huns" while Theodoric's Visigoths "laid theirs in God"; the siege of the Visigothic capital Toulouse ended with the annihilation of the Hun troops and the capture and subsequent death of Litorius.

It is not known when, how, and how thoroughly Attila got hold of the reins of power. The oft-voiced opinion that he simply stepped into the place left vacant by Ruga is – as we have seen – untenable. With the murder of his brother Bleda, in 444 or 445, he became the sole ruler of the Huns and at the time of Priscus' visit, in 448 or 449, he was clearly in full command. How far his power extended – did it really reach the "islands in the sea" as suggested by Priscus? – how effective was his control over the populations who recognized his supremacy, cannot be established. Possibly under the influence of Priscus' splendid description, modern historians tend to ascribe to Attila any action undertaken by Huns, even though his name may not appear in the relevant sources. The fact is that, apart from Priscus' report and works derived from it, Attila's name does not seem to occur in Greek sources. A survey of Latin sources yields different results but it is good to remember that not every Hun action they describe was inspired, led, or even willed by Attila.

It is difficult to discover behind Attila's deeds the outlines of a grand political design. If there was one, it certainly did not include the overthrow of the East European empire; his policy towards Byzantium is marked by caution and the wars waged against it have a retaliatory motivation and clearly circumscribed objectives. These did not include permanent annexation of territories and, in the main, were economical.

The initial Hun attack, in 441, was provoked by the objectionable action of

the bishop of Margus, who surreptitiously crossed the Danube in search of treasures buried in Hun princely tombs. Roman refusal to extradite the bishop brought upon the land a Hun invasion resulting in the destruction of the prosperous cities of Viminacium, Margus (treacherously handed over to the Huns by the aforementioned bishop), Singidunum (Belgrade) and Sirmium, a key location in the defense of the frontier. A truce was then negotiated which lasted all through 442, but during the respite nothing was done to remove the causes of friction: the payment of the annual tributes was overdue, the fugitives were neither handed over nor redeemed through ransom. So, once again, the Huns took the offensive. The relation of their victories, devastations and rare reverses presents grave problems of chronology which it should not be our task here to resolve. On several occasions in the course of the war the Huns displayed considerable skill in siegecraft. I would accept the date of 447 suggested by Maenchen-Helfen as that of the end of this great Balkan war and also share his way of thinking that *sub specie aeternitatis* the exact dating of each and every action is of trifling importance. What has to be underscored is the magnitude of the East Roman defeat, best shown by the harsh terms of the peace treaty negotiated once again by Anatolius, a skillful diplomat, to be sure; but he had no cards left to play and had to agree that the annual payment to Attila be set at 2,100 pounds of gold (a sixfold increase of the sum agreed on in 422), that the arrears in tribute amounting to 6,000 pounds of gold be paid forthwith, and that the Romans evacuate a stretch of land south of the Danube, five day's journey wide, thus creating a no man's land over which control of movements of individuals or armies could easily be exercised.

Although, not surprisingly, western (Latin and Greek) sources deal principally with Hun activities in the Balkans or further west, there is no reason to believe that the Huns relinquished their hold over the Pontic regions. It is safe to assume that their activity there was reduced in scope, Hun policy, at least since Ruga, being focused on the two Roman empires, sources of wealth. By chance, a fragment of Priscus' report lifts the curtain on a minor incident involving Theodosius, Attila, and the people of the Akatzir (Akatir), located in "Scythia" bordering on the Black Sea. We are told that the latter were approached by Theodosius in an attempt to establish an alliance with a people situated in the rear of the Huns. But the Roman ambassador, whose name is not revealed, botched the job, antagonized the senior chief, a certain Kouridakhos, who informed Attila, securing thereby for himself the independence of his own dominion while the other Akatzir chiefs had to submit and henceforth be governed by Attila's eldest son Ellac. The campaign against the Akatzirs may tentatively be dated 445, a time when the bulk of the Hun

forces were engaged in the Balkans. Most probably it was conducted by Huns stationed in the steppe region. Priscus tells us that the Akatzirs were of Scythian ethnicity (ἔθνος) but, another time, refers to them as Huns; neither of these terms had, at that time, a clearly defined content. Frantic etymologizing of the Akatzirs' name has not yielded anything more likely than the old, simple explanation, that it renders Turkic *ayač eri* "woodman," a well attested ethnonym. A century after Priscus, Jordanes calls the Akatzirs a mighty people (*gens Acatzirorum fortissima*), with no agriculture but only cattle and hunting to provide their sustenance. In all likelihood the old theory is still the good one, the Akatzirs were a people of the forest belt, indomitable, perhaps, but with imperial ambitions of their own. In the 460s they were to be absorbed by the Saraghurs, a more mobile people pushed, and pushing, towards the Byzantine border.

In 449 yet another Hun embassy journeyed to Constantinople charged with communicating to the Romans Attila's current displeasures caused, as usual, by asylum being offered to deserters but also by the Romans' apparent reluctance to evacuate, as they had agreed, a large tract of land lying south of the Danube. While in the capital, Edeco, the leader of the Hun mission, was approached by the powerful eunuch Chrysaphius with the suggestion that – taking advantage of his free access to the Hun ruler – on his return he murder Attila. The deed accomplished, Edeco would come back to Constantinople to spend there the rest of his life in plenty. The conversations were pursued through an interpreter in Roman service called Bigilas, and Edeco feigned to accept the assignment. He and his Hun companions then joined the Roman counter-embassy which – in accordance with prevailing diplomatic practice – was to convey Theodosius' reply to the points raised by Attila. The mission led by a certain Maximus included the interpreter Bigilas and, to the immense benefit of any later historian of the Huns, the rhetor Priscus whose masterful description remains our principal source on the Huns.

The cloak and dagger tale of this aborted attempt on Attila's life has been described so often that one can dispense here with yet another summary of Priscus' description of it. The salient points are that the plot was unsuccessful, Edeco did not betray his lord but revealed the conspiracy, and – quite surprisingly – Attila showed great moderation, even sparing Bigilas' life. The interpreter was relieved of the fifty pounds of gold he carried to pay the alleged accomplices, and had to be redeemed with an equal sum. Edeco must have made it clear that Bigilas was but a supernumerary in the extravaganza produced by Chrysaphius, whose extradition Attila now demanded.

The ransom for Bigilas was taken to Attila by the veteran East Roman

diplomat Anatolius, now about to negotiate his third treaty with the Huns, accompanied by Nomus, another major figure in Byzantine politics. Attila had repeatedly and vigorously insisted that only high-ranking envoys be sent to him; the inconclusiveness of Maximinus' mission – not limited to the assassination attempt gone awry of which the ambassador himself was unaware – convinced Constantinople of the necessity to honor this wish. The agreement arrived at by Attila and Anatolius, possibly in the spring of 450, represents the last successful Hun attempt of extortion from the Eastern Empire. On 28 July of the same year Theodosius died, Marcian was crowned, and the execution of Chrysaphius heralded the beginning of a new course of responsible fiscal policy involving outright refusal to pay the annual tribute to the Huns. The court's previous, conciliatory policy towards them came to an abrupt end.

It has often been suggested, and it may well be the case, that the last treaty with Anatolius allowed Attila to concentrate his efforts on the forthcoming campaign against the West Romans. While it is impossible to determine the thoughts and plans of Attila at that, or at any other, time, I would suggest that all along his ambition was to set foot within the West Roman empire, physically to be sure, but also and principally in the political sense, by becoming a major if not the principal potentate in the west. If ever Attila had imperial dreams, they were of the throne not of Constantinople but of Ravenna; history was there to show him that the West rather than the East was the ambitious barbarian's Land of Promise, though it seems unlikely that he ever envisaged its conquest. He was ready to accept a charge – that of Master of the Soldiers – from Valentinian III, and though the subsidies he received under the guise of military provisions supplied to generals were no doubt welcome, their acceptance implied the recognition of the emperor's pre-eminence. The relationship was not that which would prevail between two sovereign rulers and Attila was certainly aware of this. He set his aim no higher than to supplant Aetius; it is to be doubted that he wished to dethrone Valentinian.

A bizarre incident nearly opened for Attila a side-door to the imperial quarters. In 450, the Augusta Honoria, sister of Valentinian III, angered by the execution of her lover Eugenius, turned to Attila for help. What the lady really had in mind is not clear; the ring which accompanied her written message may well have had no other function than to authenticate the document; it could also, and perhaps was meant to, imply her readiness to marry Attila. This certainly was the way the Hun ruler interpreted the gesture and, very properly, he asked for the hand of Honoria by writing to her uncle, the senior Emperor Theodosius. He, always ready to appease, urged Valentinian to accept the

offer and dispatch Honoria to Attila, but his suggestion was not followed officially on the grounds that she was already betrothed to someone else. Attila's claim to half of Valentinian's domain as Honoria's inheritance and dowry was probably not overlooked when the decision was made.

We know that at that time Attila prepared for war and – contrary to what happened in the Balkans, where his personal involvement is never mentioned – this time he himself took command of the invading forces. It would have been natural to direct the invasion against Valentinian, if for no other reason than to avenge the rebuff suffered. It would have been sensible to lead his hosts straight to Italy, to secure for himself the hand of the woman whom, at least for diplomatic purposes, he considered his wife. But Attila adopted another course of action, more challenging, dictated by a strategic conception on a par with those motivating the Mongol military campaigns of the 13th century. Instead of choosing the obvious option, from his base in Pannonia Attila moved west, probably up the Danube valley, and reached the Rhine somewhere near Mainz. The Hun invasion struck the Romans in the western provinces and from the north. John of Antioch, in all likelihood on the basis of information culled from Priscus, expressly states that Attila "wanted to capture Aetius first, for he thought he would not otherwise attain his ends unless he put him out of the way."[13] Strategically the plan had several advantages. It aimed at destroying, possibly with the help of Theoderic's Visigoths, the main West Roman combat force commanded by Aetius. Once taken care of, the rest of Valentinian's armies could be neutralized with a lesser effort which would not be beyond the capabilities of the by then war-weary Huns. The plan also allowed the Huns to gather on their way to Gaul Germanic auxiliaries. Sidonius Apollinaris (Carm.VII,321–325) lists eight of these, Jordanes (XXXVIII,198)[14] was to speak of "innumerable peoples of diverse tribes" standing under the command of Attila. Finally, the invaders would pass through a region relatively prosperous, and therefore capable of providing provisions and loot to satisfy the needs and desires of the troops, unlike Italy which was impoverished by constant conflicts. Politically, the course of action adopted had the advantage of not posing a direct threat to the emperor, in fact – if we are to believe Prosper[15] – Attila presented his actions in Gaul as a friendly service to the Romans.

We can dispense here with a detailed description of the Hun campaign in Gaul. The events are as well known as possible on the basis of the available sources, pumped dry by generations of historians. Attila's endeavors to use to

[13] Translation taken from Gordon, 1966, p. 105.
[14] Translation by Mierow, 1915, p. 107.
[15] *Epitoma chronicorum* I, p. 481, 1364 = Aalto-Pekkanen, 1975, I, p. 207.

his own advantage the enmity endemic between Aetius and Theoderic failed, resentments were set aside to face a foe who – as Visigoths and Romans rightly sensed – represented an *outside* attempt to interfere in the West's internal affairs. Their joint effort did, indeed, succeed in halting an enemy who, far from his bases, outnumbered, relying heavily on auxiliaries of doubtful military value, could no longer muster in sufficient number the dreaded light cavalry forces which had assured his earlier victories. On that June day in 451, on the Catalaunian Plains, the Huns constituted a minority in the Hun army, the battle was one in which Goths fought Goths in their own, accustomed way. In the account given by Jordanes no mention is made of Hun cavalry charges which had so impressed those who witnessed them earlier, and the "showers of arrows," again so typical of Hun warfare, are said to have come from the Romans, not from the Huns. Between Romans and Goths armed conflicts had become jousts, well regulated, with limited objectives, a family quarrel one might say, costly and embittered on occasion, perhaps a vendetta, but not a total war. The sack of Rome by Alaric for all its baneful consequences was limited to three days and observed rules in which a St. Augustine could find solace. By choice or by necessity Attila had to play the game according to the rules known to and accepted by both his adversaries and by the majority of the soldiery under his command. Faced with generals as experienced as Aetius and Theoderic, Attila, almost a novice in this type of warfare, acquitted himself well.

Ever since that time historians have argued over the moot question, which party was victorious on the blood-sodden plains near Troyes. Disagreement on the outcome and its consequences arose at once, as shown by the contradictory descriptions given by the chronicles, none of which, of course, was favorable to the Huns. Even so, the picture given by Jordanes does not present a defeated or disheartened Attila, whereas Gregory of Tours represents the opposite view: "Nam nullus ambigat, Chunorum exercitum obtentu memorati antestites fuisse fugatum. Verum Aetius patritius cum Thorismondo victuriam obtinuit hostesque delivit."[16] There is no denying that the campaign in Gaul failed to achieve its aim; it is equally certain that the Hun military potential was not seriously affected by its outcome. The casualty figures given by the chronicles are of no value and there is no basis for calculating the strength of the Hun forces. It would, however, appear from the accounts that the Hun contingent was relatively small; on the battlefield of the locus Mauriacus it constituted the center, the wings being formed by the "innumer-

[16] *Historia Francorum*, 1, 2, 7 = Aalto-Pekkanen, p. 229.

able peoples of diverse tribes." No information is available about the route taken by Attila on his way home, so it can be assumed that – partly perhaps because of the losses sustained – his was a small force, avoiding trouble. Yet, as we shall presently see, the campaign in Gaul neither calmed Attila's martial spirit nor diminished the hitting power of his armies.

That same autumn Attila felt secure enough to refuse to see Appollonius, envoy of Marcian, who dared to come empty-handed, and to launch a small, punitive raid into Illyria. More importantly, at the next campaigning season, in the spring or early summer of 452 – less than a year after the battle of the Catalaunian Plains – he took the field again, this time in the direction of Italy. Much ado has been made by historians about Aetius' alleged failure to fortify the passes of the Ligurian Alps through which Attila was supposed to have passed. There is also a tendency to place imaginary, natural obstacles in the way of the invader. The fact is that the road from the Hungarian or the Danubian Plain to Venezia, between the foothills of the Julian Alps and the head of the Adriatic, leads across comparatively low ground and – if this historian may be allowed to bring a whiff of contemporary air into his story – can be negotiated in an automobile without changing gears. Paulus Diaconus[17] also remarked that Italy, protected from the north and the west by the Alps, "from the eastern side by which it is joined to Pannonia" has "an approach which lies open more broadly and is quite level." In 489 the Ostrogoths were to take this same road to reach the Isonzo river which – as World War I has shown – when flooded constitutes a major natural obstacle in the way of invasions. The Huns laid siege to Aquileia and spent an inordinate amount of time taking this city, which they could easily have bypassed. Once again we see Attila a prisoner of western-type strategy, unduly impressed by walls which, in the concept of Inner Asian warfare, served not so much to keep an enemy out but rather to keep their own defenders in. Aquileia conquered and destroyed, Attila advanced in the Po valley without meeting any serious resistance, the forces of Aetius were nowhere to be seen. In Milan, viewing a picture representing the two Roman *augusti* with slain Barbarians at their feet, Attila had it altered so as to represent himself sitting on the throne with the two emperors pouring the content of sacks of gold at his feet.

The question may be raised why Attila advanced westward instead of moving on to Ravenna whence Valentinian III, expecting such a move, fled to Rome. Could it be that the Hun was still anxious not to attack the emperor

[17] *Historia Langobardorum* II. 9. Translation from Maenchen-Helfen, 1973, p. 135.

openly, or was the loot to be had in the cities of the Po valley too tempting? According to Jordanes, Attila considered the possibility of going to Rome but was dissuaded from doing so partly by the fate of Alaric who, possibly smitten by God's wrath, died soon after the sack of that city, partly also by Pope Leo I who, apparently, was able to muster cogent arguments in favor of a retreat from Roman soil. The view expressed by Bury and espoused by Thompson[18] that the pagan Attila was not likely to be swayed by the "thunders of persuasions" of the head of the Church reflects an unbelieving frame of mind, totally alien to a medieval Inner Asian ruler. Nothing would be more natural for Attila than to listen with respect and interest to the arguments of a high-ranking religious fully clad in his pontificals and predicting the dire consequences of an impious act. The man impressed by Alaric's fate could, with better reasons, be expected to be responsive to the pope's suasion. It is not to deny the merits of the illustrious negotiator to point out that plague and a shortage of food and fodder may have had their part in the final decision: the Hun king returned home having achieved nothing.

Attila's birthdate is unknown but his behavior in Italy is that of a rather burned-out, tired leader groping after aims no longer clearly defined. Jordanes (who does give credit to Attila where credit is due) makes a special point of noting that Attila found it difficult to make up his mind whether or not to move against Rome: "eius animus . . . inter ire et non ire fluctuaret."[19] In connection with the siege of Aquileia we are told about a discontented Hun army, a sure sign of Attila's slipping authority. Perhaps he was plagued by ill-health, hemorrhages, to one of which he was to succumb a few months after his return from Italy. We see an Attila, perhaps more cantankerous than before, feeling the weakening of his grip. While he was in Italy, an East Roman force made a successful foray into Hun territory and the menacing message sent to Marcian did not induce the emperor to resume the payment of tribute. Mention should also be made of the rather obscure attack by Attila against the Visigoths whom he tried to approach by a road different from that used previously.[20] This episode is not mentioned by most recent historians of the Huns, though it should not be disregarded. Jordanes' account is confused but it appears that on his way along the Loire valley Attila had to give battle to the Alans at whose hands he suffered a crushing defeat. Thorismund, king of the Visigoths, was ready to offer help to the Alans but by the time he arrived the outcome was settled and he could return to Toulouse without losing a single

[18] Bury, 1958, I, p. 295; Thompson, 1948, p. 147.
[19] Iordanes, *Getica*, 223, Aalto-Pekkanen, p. 222.
[20] Iordanes, *Getica*, 226, Aalto-Pekkanen, p. 222.

man. A problem exists with the chronology. At the earliest, the Italian campaign ended in the late summer or early autumn of 452. In the first quarter of the following year Attila died, so it is difficult to see how he could have undertaken yet another raid, particularly one leading him to the distant Loire valley. Bernard S. Bachrach,[21] one of the few modern historians to take cognizance of the event, suggests that Attila was not personally involved in the battle which was fought by some Hun bands which remained in Gaul after Attila's withdrawal from the Catalaunian Plains.

One cannot but sympathize with the beautiful girl Ildico who during her bridal night, early in 453, witnessed the fatal hemorrhage which killed her elderly bridegroom. She must have been petrified by fear, the door of the nuptial chamber had to be broken down to discover the body lying unwounded in a pool of blood, with a downcast Ildico sobbing behind her veil.

If in the last years of his life Attila appears not very different from other barbarian kings, his burial – as reported by Jordanes on the basis of Priscus' description – certainly showed the trappings of an Inner Asian funeral. The mourning Huns cut their faces, and raced their horses *in modum circensium* around his body lying in state. He was buried in a triple coffin together with many precious things and to keep secret the location those who buried him were slain. This at least is the explanation given by Priscus. Perhaps one should suspect human sacrifice.

At the time of Attila's death the Huns were facing serious difficulties. If Attila ever had the desire to seek admittance into the Empire or to establish a client state at its borders, he failed to fulfill it. There is no indication of any Hun desire to change a pattern of life in which warfare provided the principal means of income. Priscus' Greek interlocutor could make a good case *for* that type of existence in which "men are accustomed to live at ease after a war, each enjoying what he has, causing very little or no trouble and not being troubled."[22] But Hun leisure was dependent on the methodical pillage of neighboring countries either through direct looting or through taxes imposed on the government. The former method demanded the constant lengthening of the action radius – no place can be plundered indefinitely – the second was often more theoretical than practical. We have seen that even the compliant Theodosius was in arrears with the payment of tribute. Moreover, history does not favor inveterate troublemakers; patience tends to get exhausted. Had Attila lived he might have fallen on evil days; his death may have saved the

[21] Bachrach, 1973, p. 67. [22] Gordon, 1960, p. 86.

Hun state. Neither of the Roman empires intended to pursue an offensive policy towards the Huns. There was neither the intention nor the power to forbid the creation of a permanent Hun state beyond the lines, either in the Carpathian Basin or on the South Russian steppe. Some five hundred years later, once Hungarian incursions into the West had been contained and discouraged, the Hungarian state was allowed to take root and become part of the western community. The Huns could have chosen a similar course but Attila's death left his people leaderless, there was no one to re-orientate their foreign policy. Yet even so, destruction came from within.

The rule of the Huns – the people rather than the territory they occupied – was shared out between the many sons of Attila, a division which must have weakened the genuinely Hun element in each of the successor states. The Huns constituted a minority in an increasingly Germanic population, and there was no cogent reason why the latter should not take over the leading role. Jordanes gives an accurate and telling picture of the gist of events, and displays a curious regret at the passing of a great power: "Kingdoms with their peoples were divided, and out of one body were made many members not responding to a common impulse. Being deprived of their head, they madly strove against each other."[23]

These remarks were made with reference to a battle fought early in 455 in Pannonia near an unidentifiable river called Nedao. Ardaric, king of the Gepids, was the leader of the anti-Hun forces composed of a coalition of peoples which, however, did not include the Goths. Hun losses were very heavy – Jordanes speaks of 30,000 slain – and included Ellac, Attila's first-born. Many of the survivors fled to the shores of the Black Sea where Irnikh (Ernac), Attila's youngest son, assumed command while a brother of his, Dengizikh, seemed to have stepped into the place of Ellac. In 467 the two brothers jointly approached Emperor Leo with the request to conclude a peace treaty and to open a market place where Huns and Romans "according to ancient custom" could exchange their merchandise. Angered by Leo's refusal, Dengizikh suggested that they should go to war, but his brother, engaged in other conflicts, thought otherwise and so the precarious peace was maintained,[24] At that time the curtain falls on the Huns of Irnikh; but Huns survived on the Pontic steppe to form, two centuries later, the core of the Bulghar people who in 680 under the leadership of Asparukh moved to the Balkans, where they founded present-day Bulgaria. There is no way of knowing whether those who followed Irnikh in his withdrawal to the steppe constituted the majority of the Hun people. They must have been numerous

[23] *Getica*, 261, translation by Mierow, p. 125.

[24] Priscus fr. 35 = Gordon, 1960 p. 134.

enough to maintain a historical tradition of their own, since the name of Irnikh – following that of a rather mythical ruler – appears in second place in a list of Bulghar rulers.

Not all the Huns were incorporated into Irnikh's state. Dengizikh must also have had a substantial following which, at least so he thought, allowed him to continue the policies of his father. He made a vain attempt to reconquer Pannonia and sent a peremptory message to Leo asking for land and money. Insolent though the tone may have been, in its essence this was a request for admittance, an attempt to become part of the Roman empire. Dengizikh must have realized that elsewhere there was no future for him or for his followers. The conciliatory tone of Leo's reply reflects the recognition of this changed approach and, had it not been for a seemingly inconsequential act by Dengizikh, a settlement en masse of an important Hun group would have become a reality. Noticing a gathering of Huns on the Danube border, Anagastes, Master of the Soldiers in Thrace, sent an embassy to enquire about the reasons for the move. Dengizikh ignored these envoys and, bypassing Anagastes, sent his own people directly to Constantinople. It is not known what exactly caused the conflict to erupt between the slighted Roman and Dengizikh but in 469 their forces clashed and the Hun fell in the battle. In the words of the *Paschal Chronicle* "His head was brought to Constantinople, carried in procession along the Central Street and fixed on a pole at the gate of the Wooden Circus. The whole city turned out to look at it."[25] The terse description brings to mind parallel passages in Chinese sources registering the demise of a once dreaded barbarian chief. This is the proper way to celebrate the victory of order over disorder; the severed head transported to the capital city to be put on display symbolized, in the East as well as in the West, the triumph of civilization over the forces imprudent enough to challenge it.

There is little benefit to be had from trying to disentangle the fragmentary information given in the sources concerning the remnants of Dengizikh's Huns. For some time, they served in small groups as mercenaries hired by one general or another, or became marauders living off the land. Many must have settled to lead a more peaceful life. In the mid 6th century Jordanes mentions two such groups, the Sacromontisi and the Fossatissii, both said to be descendants of the Huns.

It would appear that the Huns recognizing Irnikh's leadership were but one of the Hun splinter groups which kept their ethnic identity after the disintegration of Attila's empire. Other remnants survived in the Caucasus region or even further east and south, possibly in Iran. The principal cause for confu-

[25] See Maenchen-Helfen, 1973 p. 168; Thompson, 1948, p. 157.

sion is the indiscriminate use of the name Hun by contemporary or later writers. Even if we disregard obviously anachronistic or archaistic cases – such as, for instance, when Hungarians or Ottomans are called Huns – we are still left with a dozen or so peoples who, jointly with their own name, carry also that of the Huns. Some of these had acquired the double appellation through their having been conquered by the Huns, as in the case of the Akatzirs who are also referred to as the Akatzir Huns. In other cases, we may suspect inappropriate transference of the name Hun to peoples so called, as it were, by analogy, because of their general appearance and comportment. For example the Kidarites, a local dynasty which in the 5th century ruled over parts of Tokharistan and Gandhara, are called Huns by Priscus, and Procopius attributes a Hun origin to the Hephthalites, though he notes that they differ in their physical appearance.

More complicated is the case presented by the Sabirs, a probably Turkic speaking people whose earliest traceable abodes extended over some of the western parts of Siberia (to which they gave their name) and parts of the Middle Volga region and who – though quite distinct from the Huns – are very often mentioned under the double name Hun Sabirs or Sabir Huns. Procopius speaks of the "Huns called Sabirs." Their first appearance on the Byzantine horizon is connected with a migration which took place between 461 and 465 and brought them to the region north of the Caucasus where, in the 6th century, they became a major power. They made frequent raids across the mountain range; in 508 they devastated Armenia, and in subsequent years were often found in one or other of the ever-contending Persian and Byzantine camps. In fact, in 555–6 Sabir contingents fought simultaneously on both sides. The question of the true identity of these Sabirs – were they Sabirs, Huns, or a mixture of both – is of particular interest because of evidence of the spread of Christianity among them. Syriac and Armenian sources signal this for the 6th century, but they speak simply of "Huns" and there is no way to know with any degree of certainty whether Huns or Sabirs are meant. The Appendix to the Syriac chronicle of the Pseudo Zacharias Rhetor, written in 555, relates the deeds of a certain Armenian bishop Qardusat who, in company with six other clerics, traveled to the Huns with the primary aim of bringing solace to their Christian slaves. They spent seven years among the Huns, baptized many of them and translated into Hun at least some of the Scriptures.[26]

[26] Cf. Thompson, 1946; Czeglédy, 1971, specially pp. 145–8. Also Pigulevskaya, 1969.

Not quite clear is the ethnic identity of a "Hun" king called Gordas (favored reading), who in 527 visited Constantinople where he was baptized. On his return he set out to destroy the idols worshiped by his people, causing thereby a revolt led by his own brother. Gordas was murdered, and those responsible for this act fearing Roman reprisals – if one is to believe Michael the Syrian who described the events[27] – fled to some unknown destination. As of now, the whereabouts of Gordas' Huns cannot be localized.

More is known about another, more successful attempt to preach the Gospel among the Huns. In 682 the Albanian bishop Israel visited what is known as the Caucasian kingdom of the Huns, a vassal-state of the Khazars, located north of Derbend, near the Caspian Sea. Nothing is known about the beginnings of this epigone state, since our principal source, the Armenian historian Moses Daskhuranci, is mainly concerned with ecclesiastical matters.[28] However, he clearly distinguishes these Huns from the Sabirs, whom he locates further east, and, at this time and place, there is no other likely possibility for another people to have borne the name Hun. On the evidence of some proper names there is good reason to believe that these Huns spoke a Turkic language. How long and to what degree this Hun state was able to maintain a certain autonomy within the Khazar empire, how and when the final absorption of this Hun enclave came about, cannot be established. It is probably safe to say that it is the last identifiable Hun community, unless we count as such the Hun bishopric mentioned in a *Notitia episcopatuum* dated from the mid 8th century.[29]

Our documentation on the Huns is more abundant than that on many other Inner Asian peoples, yet the picture which emerges remains fragmentary and important questions are still unanswered. It could be said that we know more about what the Huns did than about who they were.

To begin with, there is no incontrovertible evidence concerning their language. It is of course certain that many languages were used within the Hun dominion and it can be taken for granted that some of these were Germanic. But only a few words of the Hun language – mostly personal names – were noted down in contemporary sources and their analysis or, should we say, decipherment has not yielded generally accepted or acceptable solutions. We cannot here take up the task of a detailed, linguistic refutation of at least four serious attempts made by outstanding scholars (in chronological order:

[27] See Chabot, II, p. 192. [28] See Dowsett, 1961. [29] Moravcsik, 1946, p. 40.

Németh, Doerfer, Maenchen-Helfen, Pritsak)[30] but I would indicate the main reasons for my own scepticism. It is clear that words beginning with a consonant cluster, such as the proper names Bleda or Scottas, or the word *strava*, a Hun term for a funeral feast, cannot be Altaic. The same verdict would be applicable to proper names with an initial *r-*, such as Ruga. However, some Hun personal names, such as Iliger, Dengizikh, have a decidedly Turkic character and lend support to the a priori assumption that the Huns were Turks or Mongols. The fact that the Bulgars of Asparukh – whom we considered descendants of the Huns led by Irnikh – were Turks is also a strong argument in favor of the hypothesis that at least part of the Hun leadership was Turkic speaking, and so were the Caucasian Huns of the 7th century.

There can be no doubt on one point: the physical appearance of the typical Huns differed markedly from that of the peoples with whom the Romans were familiar. The descriptions are mostly hostile, caricatures rather than portraits, as exemplified by Ammianus' well-known remark: "they are so monstrously ugly and misshapen, that one might take them for two-legged beasts . . ."[31] According to Jordanes "by the terror of their features they [the Huns] inspired great fear in those whom perhaps they did not really surpass in war. They made their foes flee in horror because their swarthy aspect was fearful, and they had, if I may call it so, a sort of shapeless lump, not a head, with pinholes rather than eyes."[32] The eye-witness description of Attila given by Priscus is that of a Mongoloid, the term being here used loosely with no claim to anthropological accuracy. An indirect, comparative reference to the Huns' appearance is given by Procopius (I,3; 2,4) who noted that the Hephthalites were "the only ones among the Huns who have white bodies and countenances which are not ugly."[33]

One would expect physical anthropology to confirm the evidence of written sources. However, the few tombs which, for one reason or another, can be considered Hunnic contain but few Mongoloid skulls, and none of these, nor any other skull, can with certainty be attributed to the Huns. The difficulty is compounded by the fact that many of the skulls presumably Hun had been artificially deformed and do not lend themselves to easy racial diagnosis. The custom of artificial cranial deformation is not necessarily typical of the Huns, it was practiced also, or perhaps predominantly, by the

[30] See Németh, 1940b; Doerfer, 1973; Maenchen-Helfen, 1973; Pritsak, 1982.
[31] XXXI, 2, 2; ed. Rolfe, vol. III, pp. 380–1.
[32] XXIV, 127; Mierow, p. 126.
[33] I, 3; 2, 4;, ed. Dewing, vol. I, pp. 14–15.

Europoid Alans who lived in close symbiosis with the Huns. The large proportion of non-Mongoloid elements found in tombs dating from the Hun period shows the mixed racial character of both the invaders and the conquered local populations. One explanation of the scarcity of Mongoloid remains may be that, perhaps, the Huns cremated their dead, a practice not mentioned in the written sources. Be that as it may, there is no reason to question the basic accuracy of the western descriptions, and the absence of massive supporting evidence by physical anthropology cannot weaken the point they so tellingly make. It is the unusual that most attracts attention, hence it is understandable that western observers were most struck with the Mongoloid appearance of these newcomers to the western world.

Information on the horse, faithful and indispensable companion of the Hun warrior, is also lopsided. Written sources contain many references to the ugly but sturdy Hun horses and the veterinary surgeon Vegatius Renatus described them in some detail. On the basis of contemporary descriptions one may safely conclude that the typical Hun horse was from a breed of the Mongolian pony. There is a strange contrast between the vivid descriptions given by the authors and the absence of any information provided by the burials. To quote S. Bökönyi, a foremost authority on the subject, "We know very little of the Huns' horses. It is interesting that not a single usable horse bone has been found in the territory of the whole empire of the Huns."[34]

There is yet no answer to the question of what happened to the mortal remains of these fearful conquerors and their strange mounts. Hun domination was short-lived and *if* the dead were cremated and the horses' bodies not put into the graves, the likelihood of finding their bones is necessarily limited. Even so, the muteness of archeological evidence is surprising and makes one wonder whether the scarcity of recognizable Hun remains may not be explained by their being looked for at the wrong place. It has been generally assumed that the great Hungarian plain – more specifically the land between the rivers Danube and Tisza – and the immediately surrounding areas constituted the center of Attila's empire. Perhaps this view has to be revised. Hungary has a history of intense archeological investigation and the soil has yielded ample evidence of the presence of pre- and post-Hunnic peoples. It could be that the rarity of Hun remains indicates that the Hun occupation of the region was not only short but also of a low density, and that the bulk of that people remained further east, in territories less thoroughly explored by archeology. While this is a mere hypothesis, the fact remains that there is no textual evidence to contradict it.

[34] Bökönyi, 1974, p. 267.

Even though few, if any, finds of organic origin are clearly attributable to the Huns, a number of artifacts have come to light which are peculiar to this people and which, at the same time, show their Inner Asian provenance. One of these is a reflexed, composite bow, the other a cast bronze cauldron, found mostly in the shape of Chinese bells, resting on a stand and provided with a pair of lugs projecting above the rim of the vessel. The cauldron, of which quite a few were found in Europe, has clear analogies in Central Asia, Siberia, and Northern China. It is depicted on Siberian rock carvings of uncertain dates.

Much of what we know about the daily life of the Huns is not specific to them, or to any other people. It is of course interesting that Priscus speaks of the Huns' dances or songs, but had he not done so we should have guessed their existence anyway. The glimpses we catch of some of their quasi religious practices – reliance on diviners, use of scapulomancy – or of their daily life are more tantalizing than revealing. Perhaps the most valuable information concerns diplomatic practices. Valuable are also the data – already referred to – about Attila's burial. They do not expand our knowledge of Inner Asian funeral rites, but, and herein lies their main value, firmly place the Hun customs within their compass.

The Huns, as known to western observers, were a nation of warriors. Their sole productive activity and, at the same time, their only marketable skill was military action in which they excelled but which – at its highest level of efficiency – depended on the limitless pastures of the steppe. The Huns' military value was in direct proportion to the size of the pastures available to their horses. The Hungarian or Wallachian Plains, even the Bulgarian Plateau could provide pasture for important Hun contingents, but provisionment in Italy caused problems that often proved insoluble, and resulted in the withdrawal of Hun forces. There simply was not enough food in Italy to provide for non-local armies, be they friends or foes. Thus for example, to feed the ten thousand Huns who in 409 were called upon to help Honorius against Alaric (see above), grain, sheep, and oxen had to be brought from Dalmatia. Traditional Hun military technique could not be applied on any terrain, it depended on an ample supply of horses for which Italy or Western Europe could not provide grazing grounds. The Huns on the Catalaunian Plains could be likened to Marines operating deep inland, far from the coast, with their lines of supply broken. Because of its high specialized character the Hun military machine was also highly vulnerable, and Hun might was fatally weakened by the metamorphosis of the Hun centaur into an ordinary combatant.

As a result of either a conscious decision – and if this was the case, it was probably taken by Attila – or, more likely, of a short-sighted policy aimed at short-term advantages, the Hun economy became almost monocultural, with booty and ransoms its main products.

It can be assumed that the lower strata of Hun society (perhaps conquered populations) continued, as they have always done, with the tilling of the soil. One is permitted to doubt that the benefits from booty, tribute, or ransom have ever trickled down to their level. The villagers who offered millet, mead, and a drink made of barley to the traveling Greeks were, apparently, neither better nor worse off than other people of their kind living within the boundaries of the Empire. Priscus calls them Scythians, but there is no way of knowing whether they were really Huns, nor is it possible to locate their whereabouts. They appreciated the exotic and generous gifts offered them by the Greeks, goods which, in Priscus' words "do not often come to them" but such a statement would be applicable to most poor villages at any time, anywhere. Save basic food, for most goods the Huns relied heavily on imports, even some of their arms and the material needed for their manufacture were imported. Their insistence on having open markets on the frontier with Byzantium was constant. No data are available on the merchandise offered for sale by the Huns, it possibly included horses and pelts, but with all the gold and coins reaching them through tribute, ransom, and booty, they could afford to pay cash for whatever they wished to buy. It would be of great interest to find out – if it has not already been done – whether it was not the reflux through trade channels of the money paid to, or taken by, the Huns that made possible the payment of the yearly tribute.

It would appear, then, that in contemporary Europe the Huns were an anachronism. Whether they ever envisaged the possibility of joining the European family, either within the Roman Empire or, beyond the lines, in the Carpathian Basin, must remain an open question. Much is known about the Huns; the essential questions about their history remain unanswered.

8

The Avars

The written sources

Although our sources concerning the Avars are rather poor and their historical interpretation is not beyond dispute, the clearest picture that can be drawn of the European destinies of the Avars must rely, above all, on the testimony of Greek and Latin and – to a smaller extent – on the evidence provided by Oriental (Syriac, Armenian, Coptic, Arabic) and Slavic sources. In spite of the fact that these sources view the Avars from the outside and represent a one-sided, Byzantine, Langobard or Frank point of view, they still constitute the most solid base for an approach to Avar history. There are no Avar records of any importance, and one must make do with such sources that are available. A survey of Avar history best begins with a conspectus of the main data culled from the available written sources.

As early as the 6th century B.C. a shaman-like wonderpriest called Abaris is known in the Hellenic tradition. It is however very questionable whether that name – supposedly a personal name of steppe origin – may be directly connected with the ethnic name of the Avars. The palimpsest of the Vatican, deciphered lately, seems to suggest the ethnonym "Aparnoi" which occurs in some manuscripts of Strabo may be a corrupted reading; and should not be considered a reference to the Avars. It is Priscus, chronicler of the great Eurasian migrations of about A.D. 463, who among the known Greek and Latin authors is the first to mention with certainty the name of the Avar people. According to him the Avars would have caused the Sabirs to leave their abodes, and the fleeing Sabirs, in turn, would have expelled the Ugors (Oghurs), the Onoghurs and the Saraghurs from their former dwelling places causing them to migrate to the Caucasian and Pontic regions. It cannot be decided whether the Avars who appeared in the Caucasus nearly a century later had been called by that name from the outset or else, as Theophylactus Simocatta asserts, they acquired the awe-inspiring Avar name in replacement of their original name Varchunni (or Varchonitae), a compound word which

may have denoted the people resulting from the fusion of two Ogur tribes (Var and Chunni). Likewise it remains an open question whether we ought to consider the Juan-juan of Inner Asia or some nation of the Hephthalite Empire the ancestors of the later, Danubian Avars. Perhaps a combination of both these theories may cover the historical reality.

The only certain fact is, that the Türks, having vanquished the Juan-juan and the Hephthalites, in the middle of the 6th century established a mighty empire, and about twenty thousand Avar warriors with their families and goods fled westwards, away from the supremacy of the Türks. Having reached the vicinity of the Alans during the winter 557–8, they sent ahead envoys headed by Kandikh to Justinian. Their hair, tied in plaits, created a big sensation in Constantinople. With gifts and using the tricks of Byzantine diplomacy, the Emperor incited the newcomers against those nomads who threatened the East Roman Empire and harassed it by invading the frontiers and claiming the payment of annual dues. The Avars, partly by their weapons and partly by the force of their awe-inspiring reputation, made the Onoghurs, the Zali, the Sabirs, the Utighurs, and Kutrighurs submit one by one. Many of the Slavic Antes were sold into slavery by the Avars plundering their land.

The famous Bayan is first referred to as the kaghan of the Avars, by Menander Protector, the main source of the history of that age, in connection with the year 562. Bayan then sent his envoys to the Emperor's capital already from the Lower Danube, to ask permission for his people to settle down inside the boundaries of the East Roman Empire. Justinian's diplomacy seems to have averted the surrender of any significant territories. But his successor Justin II (565–78) acceding to the throne coldly refused the Avar envoys: he stopped paying annual stipends and giving presents. At that time Bayan led two marauding expeditions (c. 562, 566–7) as far as the river Elbe. These led to brushes with Sigebert, King of the Franks. More important than the incursions in Thuringia were, for the future of the Avars, the negotiations with Alboin, king of the Lombards. These resulted in an offensive alliance against the Gepids. Caught between the Avars and the Lombards, Kunimund the king of the Gepids fought a battle against the latter, was beaten and lost his life. His land, according to the terms of the treaty between the Lombards and Avars, was seized by the Avars (567). Next spring the Lombards, with the fragments of some Pannonian peoples and with a number of joining Saxons, migrated to the valley of the Po, and as a consequence, Bayan was able also to occupy the western part of the Carpathian basin. Thus the Avars' conquest of the Middle Danubian regions was in fact completed in 568.

During the following years Bayan by a series of diplomatic negotiations,

but not neglecting military actions – such as in 568, when he made his ten thousand Kutrighur subjects invade Dalmatia across the river Sava – aimed at two targets. Sirmium had been handed to the Byzantine troops by the Gepids in 567, but the kaghan, being now the ruler of Gepidia, demanded the former capital of the conquered country to be transferred to him. Moreover, as master of the subjugated Utighurs and Kutrighurs, set up a claim to the annual payment that they used to get from the Emperor. Justin II, who had concluded an alliance with the Türks, who considered the Avars to be their runaway subjects, turned down both demands of Bayan. The only concession in the peace, supposedly concluded about 570–1, was that the Emperor acknowledged the right of the Avars to settle in Pannonia. Also, by receiving the heir to the crown of the Gepids, who with the king's treasure had fled to Byzantium, the Emperor seemed to acquiesce in the Avar occupation of Gepidia. Unless there is some chronological confusion in the relevant sources, the war between the Avars and Byzantium flared up once more in about 574, and Tiberius the commander of the Guards was defeated. Later this same Tiberius, at the end of the year 574, having taken over the government from the demented Justin II, restored peace with the Avars, accepting the obligation to pay 80,000 gold pieces yearly. As a consequence of this, the Türks broke off all relations with Byzantium ready to compromise with their runaway subjects.

The most spectacular manifestation of the short-lived Avar–Byzantine alliance was in 578 when Bayan's 60,000 mounted Avar warriors, using Imperial ships and military roads, moved against the abodes near the Lower Danube of those Slavic tribes who had been reluctant to pay tribute to the Avars, and had invaded Hellas. Some nebulous sources, such as Iohannes Biclarensis in his chronicle, however make us think that during the general upheaval of the Slavic invasions which struck the Balkans from 576–7 on, the Avars were not always standing so unambiguously on Byzantium's side: they turned the situation of the hard-pressed Empire clandestinely to profit, without openly breaking with the Emperor.

An open breach appeared only in about 579–80. At that time Bayan swore, in his heathen Avar fashion as well as in the Christian way, that the bridge he had ordered to be built across the Sava near Sirmium with the help of engineers originally placed at his disposal by the Emperor with a view to helping him in the building of a palace and a bath, was to serve only in his military operations against the Slavs and not against Byzantium. Yet as soon as the bridge was standing, he called for the surrender of Sirmium which, he felt, threatened his security and facilitated the desertion of his subjects. Tiberius' plans to relieve the besieged town by the sending of his fleet, and by

inciting the Lombards against the Avars did not work. By building a second bridge over the Sava, Bayan made the blockade complete, and reduced the inhabitants to terrible starvation. Finally, in the summer of 582, the imperial government, having secured free withdrawal for the soldiers and the citizens of the city, was forced to surrender Sirmium. The capitulation took place shortly before Tiberius' death and the ensuing peace was concluded by his successor, the Emperor Maurice who agreed to pay, once again, the annual subsidy of 80,000 gold pieces to the Avars. It is in connection with these events that the name of Bayan last appears in our sources.

For the period ending with the surrender of Sirmium, together with the *Ecclesiastical History* of John of Ephesus, the fragments of the work of Menander Protector constitute the principal sources of Avar history. During Maurice's rule (582–602) Theophylact Simocattes is our principal witness. In his historical work we can distinguish two phases of the Avar–Byzantine relations. From 572 the renewal of hostilities with Persia absorbed nearly all of Byzantium's military forces for twenty years; so the Emperor had no adequate military forces available against the marauding Avars and the Slavs invading the Balkans. These circumstances sealed Sirmium's fate and made it possible that the Slavs, supported sometimes openly, sometimes clandestinely by the Avars, could get a lasting foothold even on the southernmost corner of Hellas, on the Peloponnesus. If we are willing to believe some much discussed sources, mainly the report given in the Chronicle of Monemvasia, this happened in about 587–8. Until the victorious ending of the Persian war (591) the information of Theophylact Simocattes, which can be complemented here and there by other sources, shows Byzantium reduced to a defensive position, and being in fact nearly at the mercy of the Avars. Repeatedly the marauding nomads pushed into the heart of the Empire and reached the vicinity of the capital several times; and it happened perhaps in 586 (and not in 597) that they laid siege to Thessalonica, as related in the narrative of St. Demetrius' miracles. Avar aggressions continued in spite of the fact that the hard-pressed Emperor had increased the annual payments to 100,000 gold coins (c. 585). The only factor limiting the Avars' expansion to a certain extent was the Türks' westward push. In 576 Türk troops stood in the town Bosporus in the Crimea, about 579 they were roaming near Cherson and towards the end of 584 (or in the first half of 585) the Avar kaghan, encamped near Anchialus, was compelled to give up his successful campaign and to withdraw hurriedly towards Sirmium, having received a report, that his own country had been threatened by the attack of the Türks. An interesting fact of the history of this period is that the Avars demanded only half the amount of taxes from the

inhabitants of the conquered Balkan territories, than these were obliged to pay according to the assessment of the Imperial government. At the end of this period, the Avar expansion seems to begin moving also towards the southwest. Paulus Diaconus, the main source of the Lombard–Avar connections, tells us about an agreement between the king Agilulf and the kaghan. At the same time the pope's epistles allude to a hostile invasion hitting Illyricum about 591–3.

Theophylact's incoherent chronology makes it disputable whether the Byzantine military forces, having become released on the Persian front, began the war against the Avars in earnest as early as 592, or only later, in about 595–6. The former date seems more probable. Be that as it may, it is certain that until Maurice's fall in 602, notwithstanding some short periods of peace or armistice, the offensive campaigns went on permanently, sometimes directly against the Avars, sometimes against the Slavs near the Lower Danube loosely subjected to the protectorate of the kaghan. These campaigns were, however, at intervals counteracted by the inrushes of the enemy into the Empire, occasionally forcing the Byzantine government to increase the annual payments. While the Emperor's brother Petrus, and one of his favorite generals Comentiolus, gathered but poor glory, Priscus among other Byzantine generals achieved considerable successes; about 599–600 he crossed the Danube and penetrated deeply into the Avar home-country. He is also reported to have crossed the river Tissus. This name probably refers to the river Tisza but, according to some, there is confusion in the source between the Temes and the Tisza, and, accordingly the extreme point of the offensive campaign of the Emperor's troops should be located in the area of the Temes.

Theophylact's books V–VIII relate the story of the Avar–Byzantine wars and negotiations, here and there romantically or anecdotically, but by and large truthfully. Particularly instructive are some casual remarks made on various peoples of the Avar home-country and on the sphere of influence of the kaghan. Occasional Byzantine campaigns against the Slavs north of the Lower Danube are ignored by the Avar ruler, on condition, however, that he obtains his share of the booty. Theophylact mentions also, as a separate ethnic unit subject to the kaghan, the Bulgarians, much more closely attached to the Avars than were the Slavs. An attack against the former by the Emperor's troops, unlike the incursions into the district of the Slavs in the Lower Danube region, was considered a gross violation of the peace with the kaghan and called for retaliatory action. Priscus' army pushed forward to the Tissus, rushed upon villages of Gepidia; one Christian Gepid who joined the Byzantine troops during the military operations in the territories of the Slavs

near the Danube, is reported to have known "Avar songs." Interesting is the mention of Slavic chieftains living near the Baltic Sea, who excused themselves for not sending the kaghan military aid because of the great distance.

If the Byzantine manual of strategy, the *Strategicon*, which in most manuscripts bears the name of Maurice, was really a work written during the reign of Maurice, a most likely hypothesis, then the chapters dealing with the Avars and the Türks, their pastoral life and mainly their nomadic military tactics, mirror the conditions of the period at issue. It is another matter, that the fundamental characteristics of Avar warfare may have been the same, at least partly, also during the earlier and later history of this people, and that the Avars followed military practice on the whole common among the steppe peoples. To get the upper hand by hindering the victualling of the enemy, by surprises, ambushes, encircling, by sudden movements of the troops, by sham flights followed by unexpected turning round, by the ruthless pursuit of the defeated enemy – such was the essence of the military tactics of the nomad horsemen, among them of the Avars. The *Strategicon*, when dealing with the equipment of the Byzantine cavalry, suggests following the Avars' example in several respects, such as in the case of cavalry-pikes fitted with banderoles and of the tunics, the caftans that cover the knees, and that are held down by belts. It is probable that the iron stirrup, which first appears in the *Strategicon* among the equipment of the Byzantine cavalry, also imitates the Avar and Türk examples. Archeological evidence shows that the earliest occurrence of the stirrup in Europe dates from the Avar epoch. Beyond the mention of the strict monarchic order, the maintenance of discipline by cruel punishments, the fear of the desertion, its instance being infectious, let some telling sentences of the *Strategicon*'s portraying the Avar stand here:

> They are equipped with breast-plate, sword, bow and pikes; most of them carry two weapons in the battle, pikes on shoulder, bow in hand, using either of them as necessity requires. Not only they themselves are clad in armor, but also the breasts of the notabilities' horses are covered and protected by iron or felt coating. They are carefully trained in shooting with a bow, while riding a horse. They have a multitude of animals, both male and female with them, partly to secure the food supply, partly because their mass seems more impressive in that way. Unlike the Romans or Persians, they do not use fortified camps, but, dispersed in clans and tribes, they pasture their animals incessantly both summer and winter, until the day of the battle. Then they keep the necessary animals hamshackled near their tents, so they are kept and guarded till the moment of drawing up in battle formation. Assuming battle formation begins in the night.

Concerning the decade 592–602, the sources sporadically mention armed actions of the Avars or raids of the Slavs, acting presumably under the

kaghan's authority, in Dalmatia, Istria, Italy and near Bavaria. The most significant of those events was the invasion by 2,000 Bavarian warriors of the nearby Slavic territory and their subsequent annihilation by the kaghan's army coming to the rescue. Alongside the fighting there are some diplomatic contacts with western peoples. Thus the Franks offered Byzantium assistance against the Avars, while the Lombard king Agilulf joined forces with the kaghan against Maurice by sending Italian shipwrights to the nomad prince preparing the capture of some Thracian islands. When, at the end of 602, the Byzantine army of the Avar–Slavic Danube frontier rose up in revolt and, to overthrow Maurice and to install Phocas on the throne, proceeded to the capital, furthermore when the new Emperor increased the annuity to be paid to the Avars (603–4), the fighting on the eastern Balkans seemed to abate gradually. The poor source-material dealing with Phocas' reign (602–10) and with the first years of Heraclius (610–41) tells us nothing of any concrete military actions – apart from Thessalonica being three times assailed (c. 609?, 612–13?, 614–15?); Thrace's and Hellas' hard-pressed situation is mentioned only in vague, general terms. On the other hand the Avar–Slavic expansion towards the south-west seems to become lively. First (603) the Avars send Slavic auxiliary troops to Agilulf who is gaining ground at the expense of the Exarchate of Ravenna. Later, around 610, the kaghan, said to be in his flourishing youth, is marauding in the land of the Friauli Lombards. He may have been the younger one of Bayan's two sons who ascended the throne, and of his raid there is a romantic narrative by Paulus Diaconus, a late descendant of a Lombard child carried off into Avar captivity at that time. Also the most significant event of the fighting near the Adriatic falls in this period: the seizure and laying waste of Salona by the Avar and Slavic troops (certainly after 612, perhaps in around 614). A Hispanian letter, dated about 610–12, shows that an Avar intervention in the Frankish civil war was imminent in the west.

The Avar influence over the territories lying between the Alps and the river Elbe came to a sudden end. In military operations, the Wendic Slavs were thrown into the first battle-lines by their Avar masters; the Avars themselves were lined up behind, and would fight, if necessary, an enemy already exhausted by the encounter with the first lines. Yet, after victory, the Avars would keep the booty for themselves. There were other grievances against the Avars, who made the Slavs pay taxes, and used their wives and daughters as concubines. The victorious Wendic uprising, which resulted in the shaking off of the yoke of the tyrannical Avar supremacy, was initiated by a youth issuing from Avar–Slavic parents. The leader of the fight for freedom was Samo, said

by the Fredegar chronicle to have been a merchant, coming from the land of the Franks; yet the nationality of the prince, who, like a pagan, had a harem, is a controversial problem of modern historiography. He has been ascribed Slavic, Gallic, Celtic, and Frankish origins. During his reign, which lasted till about 658–9, he continued to fight successfully against the Avar state and barred it from further expeditions to, and conquest in the west.

In the Balkans, the Avar glory waned even more unexpectedly than in the west. About 619, the exact date is uncertain, Heraclius had left for Heraclea to conduct peace negotiations with the kaghan personally, and on this occasion he came very near to being captured by the Avar army laying a cunning trap. The nomads not only got hold of the Emperor's precious belongings and those of his escort, but they swept forward to the walls of Constantinople. According to the sources, they carried off about 270,000 subjects of the Empire to the Avar home-country. Instead of an armed retaliation, the Emperor continued to seek a peaceful settlement during the following years; he practically flattered the kaghan. Thus during the winter 622–3 he sent him 200,000 gold coins, and at the same time he gave him as hostages the most high-born Byzantine children (including his own natural son). At that time the Emperor expended all his strength on preparing and waging the life-and-death war against Sassanid Persia, and wished to protect his rear against the danger of an Avar assault, if necessary at the cost of humiliation. His policy was successful only temporarily. In 626 while Heraclius, far from his capital, was leading his army to victory in the East, the kaghan moved against Byzantium. His advance guard reached the walls at the end of June, the main body of his forces, which unsuccessful Byzantine steps could not divert, on 29 July. The ten days' siege led by the giant army composed of Avar, Slavic, Gepid and Bulgarian units, and the course of the futile negotiations carried on simultaneously, left an indelible impression on the memory of the Byzantine world. It was the superiority of the imperial fleet that decided the outcome of the fight. It thwarted the attempt of Sahrbaraz, the Persian commander encamped in 626–7 on the Asiatic coast of the Bosphorus, to send reinforcements to the Avars located on the European shore; it also annihilated the *monoxyla* of the Slav soldiers, set afloat in the Golden Horn. According to the pious belief of the soldiers and citizens, unflinchingly defending the walls, it was the Blessed Virgin Mary's miraculous intervention that saved the city; and both the Patriarch Sergius and the patrician Bonos(us), in order to enhance the enthusiasm, endeavored to strengthen this belief. Accordingly, a whole series of sermons and of other hagiographically colored writings has preserved every detail of the ten days' siege. The kaghan's Slavic auxiliaries seem to have

begun detaching themselves from the Avars immediately after the defeat sustained in the Golden Horn. If we believe a much disputed record of Constantine Porphyrogenitus to be trustworthy – the ancestors of the Croats and of the Serbs settled in the Balkans as the adherents of the Emperor Heraclius; their establishment there meant the cessation of the Avar supremacy and influence over the southern Slavs. Though about 632 the kaghan once again succeeded in extorting a large sum from the Imperial court as the ransom paid for the high-born children who had remained with him as hostages, of a real Avar success, of a military victory over Byzantium we have no further concrete reports. The kaghan's hand could no longer reach over the Sava.

It was the younger one of Bayan's two sons – who in the meanwhile had acceded to the throne – who was defeated under the walls of Constantinople, and this event seems to have shattered the position of the dynasty. In 631–2 the Bulgars claimed that the kaghan's vacant seat should be filled by one from their ranks. In the civil war ensuing, they were of course defeated by the Avars defending their ruling position; 9,000 Bulgarian families fled to Bavaria where they became the victims of a massacre, carried out on the orders of Dagobert, the Frankish king. Only 700 families escaped and took shelter with a Wendic chieftain. But the victory won in the civil war was insufficient to hold up the further decline of the Avar power. About 632 the Onoghur Kuvrat, the Christian prince of Great Bulgharia situated in the region of the Kuban and of the Sea of Azov, who was allied to Byzantium, drove the Avar kaghan's men out of his country. According to the so-called Nestor Chronicle the Avars, who in Heraclius' time had cruelly oppressed the Dulyebs, disappeared. The Dulyebs may have been the descendants of the Antes, who in Maurice's time had passed over to the Byzantine camp, but who in 602 were brought to heel by an Avar army. The sudden disappearance of the Avars – which became proverbial in Old Russian – may well mean their final evacuation of the land of the Dulyebs. From the region of the Danube delta the Avars were driven out by Asparukh, Kuvrat's third son, who later on founded the Danubian Bulgar state (679–81), and settled part of his Slav subjects in such a way that they should be able to defend the heart of his country against the Avars, forced back perhaps to the line of the rivers Jiu or Timok.

We have no information on whether the Avar state ever succeeded in regaining any of its former sphere of influence in the east and south beyond the limits of the Middle Danubian basin. The Khazars supposedly chased Asparukh's Bulgars, fleeing from under their supremacy, as far as the Danube. And the Avar state wedged between the increasingly powerful Danubian

Bulgar state and the Khazar Empire could no longer expand. The two main sources of Avar history for the period from 602 until 681, the Patriarch Nicephorus and Theophanes Confessor last mention Avar–Byzantine relations with reference to the year 678. Their report plainly shows that no trace remained of the Avar expansion in the Balkans, once so much dreaded. Victory against the Arab fleet and an advantageous peace-treaty concluded with the Muslims had consolidated Byzantine power, and the kaghan's delegation requested the Emperor's gracious benevolence. There are left, of course, some "Avars" in Hellas' southern areas until 805–6, as the Chronicle of Monemvasia has it, but they have surely lost all their connections with the kaghan, residing between the Danube and Tisza. It may be supposed that by that time they were speaking only Slavic: the leading Avar upper class, few in number, had probably become absorbed in the Slavic mass. Unlike in the east and south, in the west Samo's death (658–9) and the disintegration of his Wendic state made a more active foreign policy possible for the kaghanate. In 662–3 the kaghan gave shelter to the prince Perctarit (Bertherus), who had fled to him because of the bloody struggle for the throne. Later – on his becoming the king of the Lombards (672–88) – Perctarit thought again with friendly feelings of his pagan host. Once between 663 and 668 the Lombard king Grimoald called a strong Avar army to Friuli to crush the rebel prince Lupus; but, once the task had been accomplished, only a cunning strategy could induce the nomads, who intended to remain by right of armed conquest, to return home.

Kuvrat's fourth son, presumably identical with the Bulgar general Kuber mentioned in the Miracles of St. Demetrius, drew westwards yielding to Khazar pressure. But unlike his brother Asparukh, he did not fight against the Avars, on the contrary he acknowledged their supremacy. In this way he brought one part of the population of Great Bulgharia into Pannonia. This process can be compared to the migration which, about a century earlier, made some ten thousand warriors and their families of the Tarniakh, Kotzager (Kutrigur?) and perhaps also of the Zabender (Sabir?) tribes fleeing the Türks from the east to settle within the Avar Empire. The kaghan, probably afraid of the repetition of the Bulgar uprising in 631–2, hastened, it would seem, to separate his new vassal, the scion of the renowned Dulo dynasty, from his hereditary subjects. He entrusted Kuber and his suite with the governing of the descendants of the Christian Byzantine prisoners of war, carried off sixty years ago, who were living mixed with Avars and Bulghars north of the Danube, not far from the former province Pannonia Sirmiensis. This regentship however did not hold back Kuber from rebellion; he defeated

the Avar army sent to chastise him, and proceeded to the vicinity of Thessalonica. Thus the Christian descendants of the former prisoners of war could return from the Avars to their fathers' country, the Byzantine Empire.

If Kuber himself moved southward, the greater part of the immigrants from Great Bulgharia apparently settled in the Avar home country. They were probably part of the migration reaching the region around 670–80 and resulted in the change of the ethnic composition of the population of the Carpathian basin. On the basis of the radical transformation of the archeological finds, most Hungarian archeologists assume such a change to have taken place.

There are very few sources dealing with the peoples of the Danubian kaghanate in the period extending from the last decades of the 7th century to the time when Charlemagne established contact with the Avars. Moreover, most records still extant are of rather dubious trustworthiness, their interpretation is much disputed, and they contain but poor information. Thus the period 680–780 is the dim century of Avar history. As a chronicle of the late Carolingian epoch has it, in 692 among other peoples also the Avars sent envoys to the Frankish Mayor of the Palace, Pepin of Heristal. Around the turn of the 7th and 8th centuries some hagiographical narratives deal with the plans and actions of four notable churchmen, Egbert of Ireland, St. Emmeran, Rupert and Corbinian, the founders of respectively the bishoprics of Regensburg, Salzburg and Freising. Parts of these narratives may be interpreted, certainly or hypothetically, as hinting at missionary work undertaken in the Avar country. Historically the most noteworthy is what we read about Emmeran, bishop of Poitiers. He had heard of the pagan Avars, and in 696 set out for the east to convert them. But, the Bavarian prince Theodo held him back in his own country, saying that the Avars were at war with Bavaria, and that the district of the boundary river Enns including the city of Lauriacum located at its mouth had been devastated, and that traveling there was dangerous to life. Hence Emmeran remained in Bavaria and pursued his missionary work among the Bavarians until he died a martyr to the cause. Innocent, he was put to death by torture by Theodo's son Landprecht, who paid with exile for this action. He is said to have fled to the Avars and to have died there perhaps in 706. The narrative raises a question yet unresolved, whether the tradition that the Avars devastated Lauriacum after having seized it from the Bavarians can be trusted. If, as seems likely, the correct answer to this question is affirmative, what date should be assigned to the event which entailed the river Enns becoming the western boundary of the Avar empire. Most experts would date the event between 680 and 700. The notorious faked

documents of Piligrim, bishop of Passau, date the destruction of Lauriacum under the strokes of the Avar arms to a considerably later time (about 735). Paulus Diaconus reports that the Lombard king Liutprand (712–44) took good care to preserve the peace with the Avars and the Franks, and conquered some fortified places only at the expense of the Bavarians. A Salzburg ecclesiastic memorial dealing with the conversion of the Bavarians and Carantans (*Conversio Bagoariorum et Carantanorum*) has trustworthy information according to which in about 741–2 the Avars invaded Carantania, but the Carantan chieftain Boruth asked for the help of a Bavarian army. The Bavarians drove back the Avars, and took the Carantan Slavs under their own protectorate, and later (757?) the missionaries of Virgilius bishop of Salzburg began the evangelizing *en masse*. In the following decades three pagan revolts broke out among the Carantans (763?, 765?, 769–72?) and the question may be asked whether the Avars had anything to do with these movements. In 746 the statute of king Ratchis forbade the Lombard subjects to send envoys without the ruler's permission to the neighboring countries, such as Avaria. In 776 Charlemagne quelled the Friuli Lombards' revolt against the Franks. It happened in all probability that Aio fled to the pagans; after a score of years (796), at the breaking up of the Avar state, he was taken captive by the Frankish army, but he won the pardon and even the benevolence of Charlemagne.

Charlemagne entered into negotiations with the kaghan's and the *yugurus*' envoys first in 782, and from that time on the question of relations with the Avar state holding the Enns line would never be taken off from the agenda of Frankish policy. The tension was increased by the Bavarian prince, Tassilo who, on the prompting of his Lombard wife Liutberga, allied with the heathen Avars in order to shake off Frankish supremacy. And just when Charlemagne deprived his faithless vassal of his country, in the summer of 788, an Avar aggression hit Lombardy at Friuli and two successive Avar attacks were directed against Bavaria near the Danube. These raids were driven back by the *missi* of the Frankish king. The first big Frankish offensive against the Avar state was preceded by large-scale military preparation in the Bavarian border-district, and in 790 by an ineffectual exchange of envoys about disputed boundaries. To begin with, in August 791 Pepin sent his army from Italy against the Avars and in a victorious campaign, his troops forced the entrance into an Avar earthwork. Later (September–October) his father Charlemagne himself proceeded with his main army and with the Bavarians' transport-fleet, along the Danube as far as the mouth of the Raba. The Avars yielded the border land reaching to the Enns and the frontier fortresses at the Vienna

basin almost without striking a blow. While returning home, Charlemagne did not lead the troops under his personal command along the Danube, but through Sabaria, for thus he could conduct a mopping up operation of other Avar territories. In 792 and 793 Charlemagne planned to lead in person further military operations against the Avars; in addition to other measures, he had a movable pontoon-bridge constructed on the Danube. At the same time the Avars found allies in the Saxons revolting against the Frankish rule (792), and the Hispanian Muslims dared to make an assault into the Frankish Empire, believing the bulk of Charlemagne's army to be bogged down in the conflict with the Avars (793). But as things turned out events developed contrary to all expectation, the exacerbation of the Saxon revolt prevented Charlemagne from commanding the Avar campaign in person; at the same time the military force of the Avars became paralyzed by a civil war.

The author of the *Strategicon* going under the name of Maurice recognized that the most important factor in the military successes of the early Avars had been their absolute autocracy, the strict centralization of leadership. Now the Carolingian annals (the *Annales Einhardi* etc.) and the contemporary letters (particularly those of Alcuin) throwing ample light upon the circumstances of Charlemagne's epoch, bear testimony that the strong central rule was replaced by disunity, the frittering away of forces in the structure of the Avar state. The kaghan, the *yugurus*, the *tudun*, and as some researchers have it, the *kapkhan* – not identical with the kaghan – each negotiated with the Frankish court on diverse occasions separately; there could be no consistent Avar foreign policy and no unified conduct of the war.

In 794, if not yet earlier, the disaccord led to an open civil war. The *tudun* endeavored to strengthen his position with the aid of the Franks; together with his escort, he received baptism in Aachen (795), and put his part of the country under Charlemagne's protectorate. The kaghan and the *yugurus* fell victims to the bloody quarrel. Such circumstances made it possible that at the end of 795 the Frankish army, sent by the Margrave Erich of Friuli and accompanied by the Slavic commander Woinimir could break into the heart of Avaria without meeting any serious resistance, and that they could send Charlemagne a great booty out of the treasure accumulated by the Avar leaders during long centuries. Charlemagne bestowed part of the precious spoil on his adherents, both ecclesiastical and secular, as well as on some foreign rulers. Fifteen carts each drawn by four oxen, were filled with gold, silver, and silk during the campaign. In the summer of 796 it was Pepin king of Italy who, on the instructions of his father, took command of the Imperial army drawn from several provinces which was assigned the task of liquidating the remains of the

independent Avar state. On the banks of the Danube an episcopal assembly discussed the problems related to the Avars' conversion, including the question of the validity of occasional, earlier baptisms. The raising of such a problem is in harmony with archeological evidence dating from the epoch of the independent Avar state which shows sporadic traces of Christianity. The successor of the kaghan killed during the civil war, together with his principal wife the *catun*, and with his leading dignitaries holding the title *tarcan*, implored Pepin for their lives. Those Avars, who were unwilling to surrender, were driven by the Frankish army to the left banks of the Tisza, and the Ring, which had been the kaghan's residence, was totally plundered and destroyed. But the plain between the Danube and the Tisza was not taken permanently under the suzerainty of the Frankish Empire; only some of the land lying west of the Danube, approximately as far as the mouth of the Drava, or the environs of Sirmium. After this decisive success, there was nothing left but to quench minor riots. The *tudun*'s desertion may have been the cause of the armed action of Erich, the Friuli prince in 797. In the autumn of 799 he was again preparing to enter the Avar land but lost his life in the siege of Tersatto. At the same time the Bavarian count Gerold, brother in law of Charlemagne, fell in the campaign against the Avars. Notwithstanding all this, the Frankish army ended successfully the Avar war which, according to the tradition, lasted eight years (791–9). In 802 the battle near Kőszeg (Güns) – in which two high-born Frankish nobles lost their lives – represented the last convulsions of the Avar independence in Pannonia.

While fighting the Avars, the Frankish government had called for Slavic support, and after the victory the Slavs began settling down in masses in the dwelling-places of the ethnic groups originated from the steppe. From that time on, on several occasions the sources mentioned together the Slav and Avar chieftains (tudun, Canizauci = ? khan Isaac) and envoys appearing before the Frankish rulers, or in the imperial assemblies (803, 811, 822). Frequently, Avars and Slavs appear together in Carolingian documents. For instance in 805 when Charlemagne forbade merchants to deliver arms to the eastern, Avar–Slav territories. They appear together also in documents dating from 817 and 821 in which Louis I the Pious divides imperial territories among his successors, or in a donation dated 832 in which Louis the German endows the church of Regensburg with an estate located in the land of the Avars, together with Slavic serfs. More than once clashes between Avars and Slavs had to be smoothed over by the Frankish government. In 811, and perhaps also in 803 and 813, such a pacification was the task of an imperial army entering Pannonia. At the beginning of the year 805 the Christian kapkhan

Theodorus, visiting Aachen, obtained permission for his people to migrate from their abodes exposed to the harassing of Slavs to the territory between Savaria and Carnuntum. In the autumn of 805, after Theodorus' death, the kaghan, baptised by the name of Abraham, induced Charlemagne to permit that in accordance with the ancient custom, he – the kaghan – should wield the supreme power over the Avars. Of course, this form of governing – the Avars and Slavs in little national units, under the rule of their own native chieftains – ceased towards the end of the decade 820–30. It was replaced by direct Frankish administration, and the Avars, the remnants of their statehood having vanished, became mere peasants paying taxes to the Carolingians on the fields that were left to them in the country that had been theirs. Many of the lands passed into the hands of German churches and cloisters.

In the eastern part of the kaghanate, around 805 the Bulgar khan Krum destroyed the last remains of the Avar statehood, and annexed most of the territory, including the Transylvanian salt mines. It is imaginable that on the steppes and flood-plains on both sides of the upper Tisza some remnants of the steppe peoples survived, independent of the Frankish and the Bulgar Empires, but without any formal state-organization, and consequently without any notable historic role. As to the conditions of the declining Avar society, interesting information is provided by the narratives of the Avars taken prisoner by the Bulgarians. They told Krum what led to the ruin of their state: false accusations, corruption, the bribery of the judges, dishonest dealings, drunkenness. While the Avars, serving in Krum's pay (811), or incorporated into his army (814), were taking part in the destruction of the Byzantines, in the Peloponnese the two centuries old Avar–Slav rule was liquidated by the Imperial army before February 806.

However, the end of their statehood did not mean the complete disappearance of the Avars. An ecclesiastic memorial, drafted in Salzburg about 871–3, certifies truthfully that the christianized Avars were living in Pannonia "usque in hodiernum diem." Constantine Porphyrogenitus records with equal authority that in his time Avars were still living in Dalmatia, as a discernible element of the population. As the word *solitudines*, in a passage of Regino's chronicle, clearly refers to the steppe, inhabited by nomads, and not to an unpopulated territory, so the "*Avarum solitudines*", where – according to the contemporary chronicler of Prüm – Árpád's Hungarians first (*primo*) got a foothold during the conquest of Hungary, are imaginably nothing else than steppe-like abodes of the Avars in the region of the upper Tisza, who remained independent of the Frankish and Bulgarian supremacy. Later (*deinde*) the Hungarians started from here to conquer the Pannonian provinces of the Carantanian

margrave Luitpold, and the neighboring territories of the Moravian and Bulgarian states. Avar history in the Middle Danubian basin ends with the Hungarian conquest.

The peoples and languages of the Avar state

It is still not known for certain what the language of the Avars was. Connection with the language of the Avars now living in Daghestan in the Caucasus would be tempting if it could be shown that this people is indeed a remnant of the Avars who migrated to the Danube, and if the possibility of a subsequent change of language could be ruled out. However, this is not the case, and on the basis of evidence provided by Avar words embedded in Greek and Latin texts most experts rightly think that the language of the Danubian Avars belonged to the Altaic group. Indecision, however, remains whether it was closer to Mongol or to Turkic.

It is probable, although it cannot be proven, that the principal titles used in the Avar state continued the tradition established in Bayan's time. Ethnic changes notwithstanding, the later Avar state was linked by an unbroken legal continuity with that ruled by Bayan. All of the Avar titles and designations of rank – *kaghan*, *khan*?, *yugurus*, *kapkhan*, *tudun*, *tarkhan*, *katun* – can be shown to have been used by one or several Altaic peoples, such as the Türks, the Uighurs, the Mongols the Proto-Bulghars. Some of these titles have convincing Altaic etymologies.

Generally speaking the heathen personal names appearing in the sources, Kunimon and Unguimeri excepted, are explained on the basis of Altaic data. The proper names Apsich, Bookolabras, Ermitzis, Kandich, Koch, Samur, Solachos, Targites belong to this category. Yet it is disturbing that in some cases different etymologies are offered by the experts. Such is the case with the name Solachos, derived by some from a Turkic Solak "left-handed," while others, less convincingly, see in it the reflection of a hypothetical *suv-lay*, derived from Turkic *suv* "water" and meaning "supplied with water." In the cases of some other names, however, a reassuring agreement prevails among the adherents of the Altaic etymology. Bayan's name is generally traced back to an Altaic word meaning "rich," the Avar envoy's, Koch's name is explained from the Altaic color-name "blue." Concerning a few of the Avar personal names referred to, it has been suspected that they are really designations of rank, only the authors of the Greek and Latin sources mistook them for proper names. The following may serve as an illustration of the point made. At about the time of the capture of Sirmium an Avar "magus" had a love affair with one

of the kaghan's wives, and later, afraid of punishment, he tried to escape into the Türk Empire. His having been captured by the Byzantines, Avar diplomacy several times requested his extradition. According to Theophylact Simocattes the name (or, perhaps, the title) of the fugitive was Bookolabras. Some linguists suppose the word to be a compound, the first part of which may be identical with an Altaic word meaning "sage, prophet, wizard" and, there is an opinion, according to which the compound really denotes the rank of a "chief shaman." Also in connection with the name Targites, there has arisen the idea that it stands for the dignity of a prince or that of a chieftain.

The ethnic composition of the Avar state was not homogeneous. Bayan was followed by 10,000 Kutrighur warrior subjects already at the time of the conquest of Gepidia. In 568 he sent them to invade Dalmatia, arguing that casualties they may suffer while fighting against the Byzantines would not hurt the Avars themselves. A little later, fleeing from the Türk supremacy, 10,000 further warriors of the tribes Tarniakh, Kotzager (= ? Kutrighur) and perhaps Zabender (= ? Sabir) joined the Avars. It is probable, even if the sources do not say so explicitly, that these tribes joined the Avars in the Carpathian basin, and not on the Pontic steppe. Theophylact Simocattes asserts that Bayan's people had only adopted the awe-inspiring name of the Avars proper and that in fact the two tribes of these Pseudo-Avars, the Var and the Chunni, were of the same origin and spoke the same language, as the peoples joining them later; they belonged to the Oghur (Ogor, Ugor) ethnic group which spoke in all probability an Altaic or to be more exact a Bulghar-Turkic dialect. But even if we were to discard Theophylact's statement that Bayan's people was but Pseudo-Avar – an option which should not be abandoned – the fact remains that it would be impossible to separate from one another the proper names used respectively by the Avars and the Ogur peoples who joined them, as both used an Altaic language. Consequently it is not impossible that one or the other of the personal names mentioned above refers not to a genuine Avar but to an individual belonging to one of the steppe peoples who recognized the suzerainty of the Avar kaghan. It is remarkable in this context that one of the Avar kaghan's councilors during the early fights against the Antes around 561 was a Kutrighur. In 568 a part of the Bulgars, who belonged to the ancient population of the Carpathian basin, departed to Lombardy with Alboin. It is certain that the number of the Bulgars remaining was not large enough to imperil the Avar rule in that region. The magnitude of the Bulgar revolt of 631–2 can be explained only by immigrations from the steppe which increased their number within the Avar state. This is one of the reasons why the Oghur tribes are normally reckoned among the components

of the Bulgar people. In the wake of the civil war of 631–2, the departure of 9,000 families decreased the number of the Bulgars in the Avar land.

Written sources are silent about Sarmatians and Sueves remaining under Avar rule in the region of the Danube, and tell only about those who migrated with Alboin to Italy, while there are some allusions to Lombards who stayed in the region. Their number may have been augmented by that of many women and children carried away from Friuli around 610 when the men, taken prisoners at the same time, were slaughtered by the Avars on the road back to Pannonia. The histories of the Gepids and the Avars are closely linked. An early indication of collaboration dates from 562 when an envoy of Bayan is said to have been won over to the Byzantine cause. His name, Kunimon as it appears in Greek sources, is probably an imperfect transcription of the Gepid personal name Kunimund. In 567, as already mentioned, the bulk of the Gepids fell under the government of the Avars, the sources frequently mention them in the district reaching from the eastern side of the Carpathians to as far as Pannonia. In about 593 one of them, as we mentioned above, as a Christian, rendered services to the Byzantine army during a campaign against the Slavs on the Lower Danube. Near the river Tissus, Gepid villages fell victim to the big Byzantine offensive launched around 599–600. There are some who – comparing the name Unguimeri, that of the councillor of the kaghan paying homage to Pepin in 796, with the Germanic proper name Ingui(o)mer – surmise that the bearer of the name was a Gepid. Traces of a Gepid population in Pannonia can be found as late as 871–3.

The existence of a romanized population in Pannonia at the time of the Avar invasion is a much disputed question. It is made more involved by the fact that the Avars, in the course of their southern expeditions carried into captivity hundreds of thousands of imperial subjects; thus it is easily imaginable that the archeological finds dating from Avar times and mirroring Roman provincial traditions originate from these prisoners of war and not as a result of the Pannonians themselves representing an unbroken cultural continuum going back to Roman times. The presence of Christians at the time of the Frankish conquest – as witnessed by sources relating the missionary activities of the dioceses of Salzburg and of Aquileia – may well be due to the descendants of provincial populations fallen into Avar servitude.

Outside the Carpathian basin, which constituted the center of the Avar state and where – with the exception of the higher mountainous districts – most archeological finds of distinctive Avar character are concentrated – the kaghan's suzerainty or influence stretched over a diversity of Slavic peoples until about the middle of the decade 620–30 when the decline of the Avar

power came about. With the Slavic peoples living farther away, as for example towards the Baltic Sea or in Hellas, the Avars could have but a loose and ephemeral connection, while the Slavs living closer to the center of Avar power – such as the Antes, the Dulyebs and the Wends – received a full measure of Avar oppression. During the decades that lapsed between the waning of the Türks' power and the growing independence of Great Bulgharia – that is, between approximately 602 and 636 – in the eastern direction over the Pontic steppes, Avar supremacy reached as far as the Kuban.

In the Great Bulghar empire of Kuvrat, which shook off the Avar yoke in about 636, Onog(und)urs and Kotrags (=? Kutrighurs), located on the western side of the Don are mentioned by Byzantine sources. The eponymous leading tribes of these peoples undoubtedly came from the Oghur family, already mentioned several times. It may be taken as almost certain, however, that groups speaking other languages lived in Great Bulgharia, including Finno-Ugrians, among them most probably the forefathers of the Hungarians, who until this day are given names by the peoples of Europe which are variants of the ethnic name Onoghur (Hungarians, Hongrois, Ungarn, Ungroi (H)ung(a)ri, etc.). The ethnic unit which, under Kuvrat's fourth son, migrated into the Danubian Avar country, may possibly have contained also Finno-Ugric elements in addition to the Altaic speaking Oghurs (Bulghars). Moreover, if the archeological theory, which cannot be called a certainty, but which likewise cannot be rejected out of hand, should turn out to be true, and if, among the belt ornaments of a *tamga* type, used to denote nationality, those adorned with the vine-scroll motif are the relics of the Finno-Ugrians among the later Avar material in finds, then the overwhelming prevalence of such belt-studdings in the unearthed cemeteries would prove that a Finno–Ugric speaking population had got the upper hand in the Avar state.

This theory, which should be proposed with the greatest caution, would answer, at least in part, a thorny question. In some peripheral regions, such as, among others, the Adriatic, Carinthia in Austria, and in the districts of the southern and western Slavs, relatively numerous linguistic data are to be found referring to the one-time presence of the Avars, e.g. the series of the toponyms formed out of the Avars' Slavic name *ob(a)r*: Abriakh, Obre, Obrov, Obrovac, etc. At the same time, in the core of the Avar state, the relevant Hungarian linguistic researches reveal only extremely sparse toponymic traces of the Avars' presence, even though this lasted a quarter of a millenium. (The compound place-names containing the member "Várkony" may perhaps preserve the contracted denomination of the two tribes of

Bayan's people: Varchunni, or the place-names with the component "Tárkány" may be the derivatives of the title "Tarcan.") This discrepancy may possibly be explained by the fact that the linguistic relics of the Avar conquerors are more easily discernible against the Slavic and German linguistic background of the peripheral regions than in the central areas where the language of Árpád's Finno-Ugric people mixed with Turkic elements does not contrast sharply with the linguistic substratum of the late Avar population, which was Altaic mixed with Finno-Ugric – always supposing that this substratum really did include a Finno-Ugric component. After the eclipse of the Avar state, as we have seen, Slavs streamed to some parts of its central areas. The linguistic traces of these Slavs, especially the toponyms, stand out sharply before the eyes of the philologist.

Nothing could better illuminate the obscure points of the linguistic problems of the Avar epoch than if philology had some Avar literary record, some written Avar texts at its disposal. Some objects have come to light – needle-cases, bone-plates, bow-props, etc. – in the Avar cemeteries of Jánoshida, Szarvas, Környe, and elsewhere, which bear some marks in runic script. But their reading is, at best, uncertain and the possibility cannot be dismissed that the signs engraved sometimes represent no text but are mere *tamga*-like property marks. At least two pieces of the famous gold treasure found near Nagyszentmiklós (the rhyton and the oval bowl) date, in all probability from the Avar epoch. The runic inscriptions they carry seem to be of later origin and cannot be read unambiguously. Thus, for the time being, the linguistic interpretation of the Avar words found in Greek and Latin texts remains the only practical way in the study of the language of the Danubian Avars and of their eastern, nomad federates.

The archeological evidence

More than once in the preceding pages reference has been made to archeological data and hypotheses complementing the testimony of written sources. A summary of the main lessons to be drawn from the archeological finds may be of some use. To begin with it should be emphasized that more or less important differences and even sharp contradictions exist in the evaluation of the finds by the most competent authorities. Opinions are divided, among other points, on chronology, on the ethnic attribution of the finds and on the interpretation, in terms of the social structure of the Avars, of the cemeteries excavated. Many of the incertitudes are rooted, at least partially, in the present state of archeological fieldwork. Although thousands of individual

Avar tombs have been examined, scarcely any of the major cemeteries located in Hungary, the center of the quondam Avar state, has been fully unearthed and investigated with modern, professional methods. Even less advanced is the study of the exceedingly rare remnants of settlements, not one of which could be fully investigated. Thus the sunken huts of Dunaujváros, dating from the early and middle Avar epoch, together with their network of trenches similar to those found in some regions of the steppe, could be examined only in the course of hurried, rescue excavations. The uncovering of a similar settlement has just begun in Kölked. The Rings, circular earthworks mentioned in the written sources, the palaces and baths built by craftsmen sent at Bayan's request from Byzantium cannot as yet be identified by archeology. In the short survey that follows the most probable among the several archeological interpretations of a given find will be followed.

The nomad warrior seems to have been buried in crowded cemeteries, girt with a belt adorned in accordance with his rank and ancestry. A widespread way of marking a military rank consisted in laying beside the corpse one or several arrows. In the early and middle Avar period, in princely burials located outside the cemeteries, insignia made of precious metals – a rhyton, cup, sword, or quiver with arrows – were added to the belts. So far no princely grave dating from the late Avar period has been found. The hypothesis that the skeletons of Avar cemeteries which are not accompanied by the remnants of belts are those of former serfs and provide an indication of the social stratification of Avar society is not without foundation. Until about 670–80 – the date can be established with the help of Byzantine coins found in the graves – the majority of the belt ornaments were either plain or decorated with stampings using Byzantine techniques. The belt decorations used after this date are clearly distinguishable from the earlier ones as they use carvings or inlaid glass. Simultaneously, or somewhat later, appear moulded belt ornaments, characteristic of the late Avar era and in use as late as the 9th century. The most frequent decorative designs represent griffins and vines with the latter becoming prevalent in the later period. The three archeological strata of the Avar period are characterized not only by belt ornaments but also by other grave finds such as bows, arrows, swords, sabres, cuirasses, stirrups, plait clamps and, for women, earrings, beads, etc.

It would seem that in the major cemeteries few are the graves that can be dated earlier than about 600. This would suggest that until the age of Maurice the Avars and their nomad federates had no permanent winter quarters. Their way of life was totally nomadic, pastoral, migrant, marauding. Graveyards, dating from a later period and containing many hundreds and sometimes

thousands of graves bear witness to the existence of permanent winter quarters and a relatively sedentary way of life. Gradual transition to a more sedentary way of life seems to be mirrored also in the differences existing between successive habitational strata of the Avar settlement in Dunaujváros. Yet attached to the belts found in graves appear utensils typical of a pastoral way of life, such as thong-skivers, strike-a-light irons, knife-suspenders with knives, leather bottles, all pointing to the importance of cattle breeding among the Avars. Evidence to the same effect is provided by the study of the distribution of Avar settlements. The most densely populated areas of the Avar epoch seem to have been the steppes, the moist meadow-lands of the Carpathian basin, most suitable for pasture. The very scarcity of archeological traces of Avar settlements may well be due to the pastoral nomadism practiced by the Avars. The yurts of the nomads leave no trace discernible after many centuries.

Of course to a purely nomadic horseman the Central Danubian plain could offer no possibilities similar to those of the great steppe belt extending from Central Asia to the Pontic area. The graves contain abundant traces of a partial change-over to agriculture and to sedentary stock-breeding. This is evidenced by the appearance in the graves of sickles which, together with axes, may have been placed beside the dead to protect the living from nefarious influences. Bones showing the existence of poultry farming and the shells of eggs put into the tombs of women as symbols of fertility point to a sedentary way of life.

The more sedentary way of life was not substantially altered by the wave of eastern immigrants which may be assumed for the later Avar era. However, in other respects, the newly arrived eastern tribes, distinguished by their belt ornaments with the griffin and vine motif, seem to have stood on a somewhat lower level of social and economic development than the ruling people of the early Avar epoch. Monetary circulation is a good case in point. While until about 670–80 not only the coins of the East Roman Empire but sometimes also their locally made counterfeits were in use, the almost total absence of coins in the finds of the later Avar era is a fact of significance. To be sure, the general decline of monetary circulation in 8th-century Byzantium and the cessation of Avar incursions into the Balkans may partially account for this state of affairs, yet it can hardly be doubted that it is also a reflection of a shift in the economy of the Avars towards subsistence-level production and trade through barter.

Another example of the change occurring at about that time in the Avar civilization is provided by the alteration in the style of the belt ornaments. In

early Avar times the *tamga* marks on the belt ornaments – indicative of the lineage of its wearer – show a geometric stylization which points to a far-reaching disintegration of the tribal clan system. In the late Avar period these are replaced by more naturalistic *tamgas* representing, for example, griffins, which mirror with great immediacy ancestral, totemic ideas. Together with other archeological observations, the change in the decoration of belt ornaments may be taken as a sign of the relatively unaltered survival of a primitive social structure based entirely on consanguinity.

Written sources contain but few data concerning the Avars' religion, their rites and customs, such as their way of taking an oath or the evocation of spirits in the course of a battle. Such information as they contain may have been distorted by the clichés of the portrayal of pagans in Christian literature, as for example when a hagiography narrates that the Avar idols brought into battle against the Byzantines turned out to be powerless against Christian arms. When interpreted in the light of the ethnography of the peoples of the steppe, some objects of Avar origin provide direct evidence of shamanistic beliefs. One of the most interesting objects of this kind is a bone jar from Mokrin on which is engraved the world-mountain and the world-column and, above them, the tree of life with nine branches. The number nine has special significance in shamanistic thought. The tree of life, reaching to the sky, is surrounded with representations of the sun and the moon and of mythical animals. The motif of the tree of life appears in the ornamentation of the so-called "saltcellars," made out of antlers, in connection with horse figures wearing bulls' masks which may have represented fights between shamans, and on a late Avar belt-end which also bears the representation of a dragon and other figures. Although, as in the case of many other artifacts of the Avar period, the finish of some of the pieces just mentioned shows Hellenistic or Sassanid influence, their subject matter is taken from the body of beliefs proper to the peoples of the steppe.

Religion is not the only sphere of Avar culture in which the rich and ever increasing archeological material supplements the poor testimony of the written sources. Thus, for example, Theophylact Simocattes' reference to Avar songs may be connected with the evidence provided by the discovery of double flutes made out of the shinbones of cranes. As the majority of these have five holes, the hypothesis that Avar music was pentatonic may not be too far fetched. The tombs of the, probably itinerant, artisans of the early Avar era throw an interesting light on contemporary handicrafts influenced by Byzantine techniques. In some instances these have yielded the tools, embossing blocks and raw materials used by their late owner.

9

The peoples of the Russian forest belt

Below a line running approximately from Kiev through Riazan to Kazan, lie the south Russian steppes. The region north of this line gives way to a transitional forest-steppe (*lesostep'*) zone before becoming the densely wooded tracts of the Russian and Siberian forests. The latter, in turn, become the taiga and tundra zones in the far north. The great contrast in physical setting is reflected in the economic activities that evolved in these regions. The steppe, in historical times, was largely populated by pastoral nomads of Iranian and Altaic speech. The early population of the eastern Russian forests, our area of concern, consisted primarily of fishing and hunting peoples who spoke Uralic languages. The forest-steppe region became the contact zone between the southern nomads and the northern hunters and trappers. The former, when they entered the contact zone, made certain adaptations in their life-style, becoming semi-nomadic with ever greater emphasis placed on sedentary pursuits. Those Uralic elements that entered the forest-steppe zone, in turn, were drawn increasingly to the steppe and its mode of existence, becoming in time stereotypical, equestrian nomads.

The medieval history of the Russian forest belt is largely concerned with three important movements of peoples. The first is the steady expansion of the Eastern Slavic population from the western periphery of the Eurasian forests to the East. This movement was particularly successful in the forest zone and brought the Volga–Oka mesopotamia into their possession. It also led to the absorption and or conquest of the Finnic peoples of Northern and Central Russia. The second movement is that of Turkic peoples who went or were driven to the very border of the steppe, the forest-steppe zone. There, they played a far-reaching role in the ethnogenesis and historical development of some of the Finno-Ugrian peoples. This is best seen in the history of the Oghur Turks, in particular that of the Volga Bulghars whose symbiosis with the Finno-Ugrian peoples of the Middle Volga is of paramount importance for the ethnic and cultural history of the region. The third movement is that of the

Ugric Hungarians into the steppe and their transformation into a steppe people. These latter two movements will be the major focal points of this chapter. The first movement, although not dealt with here specifically, must be taken into account as an important background factor.

The early Uralic community

Proto-historical and ethnogenetic studies have long employed special terms to designate communities of ancient peoples united by a common language, territory and material culture (*Urheimat, Urvolk, Ursprache, pra-rodina, pra-narod, pra-jazyk, őshaza, ősnyelv* etc.). These terms and the "family tree' (*Stammbaum*) conceptualization of ethno- and glottogenesis from which they derive, are useful, but should not be viewed as denoting strictly unilinear developments.[1] The formation of and interaction between different elements within one and the same ethno-linguistic unit as well as between different units is an extremely complicated process. As we are dealing with pre-literate societies whose activities either antedate historical writing amongst their more cultured neighbors or took place well beyond the field of vision of our few sources, the movements of these numerically small groups of peoples, their incorporation by or defection to other dimly perceived groups, cannot be traced with great certainty. Material culture is equally mute on these points as vanished, illiterate societies cannot tell us what language they spoke. Hence, archaeologists are frequently at loggerheads over the attribution of this or that culture to a specific ethnic group. Indeed, some cultures in their broad outlines could be shared by several different groups. Bearing these caveats in mind, we will employ these terms, but they are to be understood in a very loose, schematic sense.

The Uralic peoples today are divided into two large groups: Finno-Ugric and Samoyed. The latter is subdivided into Northern Samoyed comprising Nenets, Enets and Nganasan and Southern Samoyed consisting of Selkup and Sayan Samoyed (now extinct). Finno-Ugric is composed of two major branches. Ugric includes the Hungarians and Ob-Ugrian peoples, the Mańśi (Vogul) and Khanty (Ostiak). Finnic presents a more complicated picture as it has four major sub-divisions: the Lapps (an originally non-Finno-Ugric people who adopted a Finnic tongue), the Baltic Finnic peoples (Finns, Karelians, Ingrians or Izhorians, Vepsians, Vods, Estonians and Livonians) the Volga Finnic peoples (the Mordvins who are subdivided into Moksha and

[1] *See* the salutary comments of Denis Sinor, "The Outlines of Hungarian Prehistory," *Cahiers d'histoire mondiale/Journal of World History*, 4.3, esp. 514–17 (1958).

Erzä and the Mari or Cheremis) and the Permians. The latter are subdivided into Komi-Zyryen, Komi-Permiak and Udmurt, also known as Votiak. It is a common feature of many of these peoples that they are often known by the names given to them by their neighbors and not by their own self-designations.

The question of the location of the Uralic primitive or most ancient habitat (*Urheimat, pra-rodina, őshaza*) has engendered a considerable literature. In recent scholarship, three main theories have been advanced. Gy. László has placed it in the forest zone between Central Poland and the Oka river.[2] This view has been criticized on many points. The "classic" view, reflected in the writings of E.N. Setälä, M. Zsirai, and others, places this "ancient homeland" in the Middle Volga–Kama region, including the Oka, Viatka and Belaia river basins. E. Itkonen would extend it to the Baltic. P. Hajdú, who earlier subscribed to the "classic" view, has recently shifted the Uralic homeland to Western, North-western Siberia, between the lower Ob and the Ural mountains.[3] However this question may ultimately be resolved, the Finno-Ugrians with whom we are concerned are attested historically in both the regions posited in the Setälä and Hajdú theses and inhabit them today, although not in the same configurations as in the past. Their presence here finds some confirmation, albeit as always of an ambiguous nature, in archaeological finds. The latter indicate that the Volga–Kama–Ural–Western Siberian region was relatively uniform in culture from the seventh to the fourth millenium B.C. Some, if not all of these cultures, may be identified with the Uralians. Anthropologically, this culture shows Paleo-Siberian and Paleo-European elements. This tallies well with the "Uralic" anthropological type which displays Europoid and Mongoloid characteristics.

Within this rather far-flung "community," dialects were taking shape which would later evolve into separate languages. The process was hardly "neat" and caution should be exercised in drawing sharp dividing lines. Rather, there were cross-overs and mutual interactions between the slowly diverging linguistic sub-units. Similarly, we should not imagine that this community was necessarily static with respect to the incorporation of new

² D', Laslo (László, Gyula), "K voprosu o formirovanii finno-ugrov," *Problemy arkheologii i drevneĭ istorii ugrov* (henceforth abbreviated as *PADIU*), ed. A.P. Smirnov (Moskva, 1972), p. 9. For a review of current theories, see *Osnovy finno-ugorskogo jazykoznanija* (Voprosy proiskhoždenija i razvitija finno-ugorskikh jazykov), ed. V.I. Lytkin *et al.* (Moskva, 1974), pp. 31ff.

³ Peter Hajdu, *The Finno-Ugrian Languages and Peoples*, trans. G.F. Cushing (London, 1975), pp. 34–6; *Osnovy* (Voprosy), pp. 33–4; Hajdú, Péter, *Bevezetés az uráli nyelvtudományba* (Budapest, 1966), p. 9.

elements. Uralic unity was ended with the separation and moving away of the elements that would come to form Samoyedic sometime between the sixth and fourth millenia B.C. This breakup may perhaps be connected with the migration of tribes from the steppe zone, the Aral Sea area, which moved north and then divided the Uralians.

The Finno-Ugrians

The Finno-Ugrians, as we may now call them, had their homeland in the Volga-Kama-Belaia region where they are well attested in historical times. For reasons that are still unknown, there appears to have been a westward tendency amongst the western groups of the Finno-Ugrians. This brought them across the Volga and into the Oka region and finally to the Baltic Sea. Finno-Ugrian unity gave way in the course of the third to second millenia B.C. in connection with this westward movement. The Ugrians remained in the old Kama–Ural sites with perhaps some movement towards the south. This location of the Ugrians was decisive for the subsequent development of those elements amongst them which came to form the Hungarians.

The period of Ugric unity lasted some 1,500 years, ending about 500 B.C. The dissolution of the Ugric community was probably gradual. The southern elements of the community continued to be oriented towards the steppes. Here they came into contact with Iranian and perhaps Turkic nomads. Some of the Iranian loanwords in the Ugric languages undoubtedly date from this period. Loanwords also show that contact with the Permian branch of Finnic continued.

The introduction of an equestrian culture may be dated, on the basis of linguistic evidence, to the Ugric period or at the very latest to a time when there was still considerable contact between the Ugrians. Thus, the words for "horse" (Hung. *ló*, Vog. *lūw*, Ost. *lau*), "saddle" (Hung. *nyereg*, Vog. *Naɣra*, Ost. *nogər*), "stirrup" (Hung. *kengyel*, Vog. *kēńś*, Ost. *kenč*) etc. are held in common by the modern descendants of the Ugrians.

The origins of this horse-culture cannot be determined. Given the relative absence of loanwords, it may well have been a natural evolution encouraged by the example of the steppe nomads in the south. This early Ugrian horse-culture was probably qualitatively different, as Hajdú has suggested, from that of the steppe nomads. The Ugrians, at this stage, were not transformed into cattle-herding, steppe nomads. Rather, they retained their identity as a forest-people and became "equestrian" hunters and trappers.[4] As long as the

[4] Hajdu, *Finno-Ugrian*, pp. 63–5.

southern Ugrians maintained their orientation towards the steppe, further transformations would be forthcoming. A probable factor in their attraction to the steppe was the lucrative fur trade, a pursuit that often brought steppe and forest dweller into symbiosis. The major routes of the fur trade traversed the forest-steppe regions now occupied by the southern Ugrians.[5] Hence, contact with the nomads in this connection may be presumed.

The disturbances and displacements touched off by the Hunnic movements also brought more nomads into the Western Siberian and Uralian steppes in the first centuries A.D. These nomads, largely Oghur Turkic tribes (see chapter 10), were, as we know from Chinese and Western sources, deeply interested in the fur trade. The nature of early Oghur–Ugrian contacts is unrecorded in the sources at our disposal. Whether elements of the Ugrians were indeed conquered and organized by the Oghurs, as is sometimes claimed, must remain a matter of speculation. In any event, we may safely ascribe the change-over of some of these Ugrians from a forest, hunting-fishing people to steppe nomads, to both internal developments and the influence of these Oghur Turks.

While the southern Ugrians were drawn towards the steppe, their northern kinsmen who remained in their original habitat between the Kama and the Ural mountains, were themselves being subjected to new ethnic influences. Sometime after the breakup of Ugrian unity c. 500 B.C., a Paleo-Siberian, anthropologically Mongoloid, hunting people crossed from Siberia to the Kama region and mixed with the Ugrians. The language of the newcomers is lost to us for they were absorbed by the Ugrians and became Ugric in speech. Culturally, the two groups were compatible. Indeed, the Siberian immigrants may have accented and sustained the forest-dwelling character of the northern Ugrians. The descendants of this mixing of peoples, the present-day Mańśi (Vogul) and Khanty (Ostiak) peoples are divided into two phratries, the *moś* and the *por*. It is believed that the former probably represents the original Ugrians and the latter the newcomers from Siberia.

The dissolution of the Finno-Permian ancient linguistic community, as it has been reconstructed, presents an even more complicated picture. It is generally accepted that this community came into existence c. 2,500–2,000 B.C. Its breakup has been dated to c. 1,500 B.C. It was at this juncture that the ancestors of the Permian group formed a separate entity which endured until c. A.D. 800. The Finnic speakers continued as a community, termed Finno-Volgaic, which may be said to have come into existence in 1,500 B.C. There is no generally accepted opinion regarding the terminal date of this community.

[5] Ligeti, Lajos, "Az uráli magyar őshaza," *A magyarság őstörténete*, ed. L. Ligeti, (Budapest, 1943), pp. 51, 54–5, 59.

Estimates range from c. 1,000 B.C. to the first or second century B.C. Thus, at some as yet undetermined time in the first millenium B.C., Finno-Volgaic split into Common Finnic, the ancestor of the Balto-Finnic linguistic community, and Volga Finnic. The Lapps occupy a special place within the Balto-Finnic group. Originally, they were a people of still unknown ethno-linguistic origins who came into very close contact with the Finnic peoples while the latter were still living within the Finno-Volgaic community. This intense symbiosis led to a period of bilingualism amongst the Lapps and ultimately to the loss of their native tongue and their adoption of Finnic.

Of the various Finnic peoples mentioned above, the Permian and Volga Finnic groupings will be of greatest interest to us. These two communities and the peoples that evolved from them had, as we shall see, deep and long-lasting contacts with Turkic steppe society. Unlike their distant Ugrian "kinsmen," however, they remained, as they are today, a forest people.

The Oghur Turks and Volga Bulgharia

The steppe-dwellers were the principal catalysts for change in the medieval history of the forest zone. Steppe influences here may be traced back to the Scytho-Sarmatian period. It was at this time that Iranian tribes established contacts with the Finno-Ugrians of the Middle Volga–Ural area. The movement of Hunnic tribes and other nomads set in motion by them brought Turkic peoples to this region as well. From this standpoint, the Oghur tribes were most important. When they first appear in our sources, the Oghurs occupied the western Siberian and Kazakh steppes. Their language was sufficiently distinct from Common Turkic so that we may trace some of the effects of their influence through loanwords taken from them by the Finno-Ugrian peoples. This procedure, however, is complicated by the relative lack of Oghur materials, especially from the early period. Moreover, its only living survivor, Chuvash, has been heavily influenced by neighboring Finno-Ugric tongues.

The economic structure of Oghur society and hence attendant modes of cultural expression appear to have been somewhat different from those of most of the Turkic nomads. Greater emphasis came to be placed on agriculture, urban development and generally more pacific pursuits.[6] Although it is possible to overstate this, it is precisely these elements that are most strongly reflected in our sources and confirmed by Oghur loanwords in the languages

[6] Németh, Gyula, *A honfoglaló magyarság kialakulása* (Budapest, 1930), pp. 119–20.

of their neighbors. In addition, proximity to the forest-steppe zone and the rich potential of the fur trade which elements of the Oghur tribes exploited, may be viewed as factors which tended to contribute to this line of development in their society.

The Sabir invasion of Oghur lands c. A.D. 463 brought many of these tribes from Western Siberia to the south-Russian steppes (see Chapter 10). Others, however, remained. Their numbers were reinforced with the collapse of the Oghur Bulghar state in the Pontic steppes c. 650–70. Although the withdrawal of Bulghars to the Middle Volga following their defeat by the Khazars in the late 7th century is generally considered the opening pages of the history of Volga Bulgharia, the process was far more complicated. There is some evidence, although not universally accepted, that from the Hunnic period onward there was a steady movement of Turkic elements, Oghur and Common Turkic in speech, to the Middle Volga. Some of these tribes contained Iranian elements as well. This process did not end with the late seventh-century migration, but continued into the 8th and 9th centuries with nomadic elements coming from the Pontic steppes, the Ural region, Siberia, Kazakhstan and the Aral Sea steppes.[7] These newcomers, also considerably intermixed with Iranian-Alanic elements, now began to interact with the southernmost Ugrians. This is confirmed by archeological finds which indicate three anthropological types in this area: Central Asian, Uralic and Europoid Alano-Sarmatian.

The Bulghars from the Pontic steppes, now in possession of the Volga–Kama region, came with the most sophisticated and developed political and military institutions. Consequently, they became the predominant political force, building upon the local and other foreign elements that were in the region. The state that was thus created, like its nomadic counterparts to the south, was not homogeneous. Other ethnic and linguistic groups continued to exist. Muslim sources of the 9th and 10th centuries have preserved for us the names of some of the other tribal groupings, or more probably subordinate tribal unions, that were under their authority. These were the *Esgil-Isgil* or *Asghil* (our readings are not certain), the *Suwār* and the *Barṣūlā*. The Suwār are to be connected with the Sabirs (Savir/Savar) who are also associated with

[7] The chronology of the advent of the Turkic peoples to the Middle Volga region is still the subject of considerable controversy: V.F. Genning, A. Kh. Khalikov, *Rannie bolgary na Volge* (Moskva, 1964), p. 74; R.G. Kuzeev, *Proiskhoždenie baškirskogo naroda* (Moskva, 1974), pp. 390–3; Fodor, István, *Verecke híres útján* [...] (Budapest, 1975), p. 186; A.P. Smirnov, *Železnyi vek čuvašskogo Povolž'ja* (Materialy i Issledovanija po arkheologii SSSR, 95, Moskva, 1961), pp. 135–6. A.P. Smirnov, in a recent article, "Ob etničeskom sostave Volžskoj Bulgarii," *Novoe v Arkheologii*, ed. V.L. Janin (Moskva, 1972), pp. 302–7, while granting the presence of other Turkic groups here, argues that the Bulghars constituted the largest element.

the North Caucasian steppes. Sabir elements, however, were probably in the Middle Volga region before the advent of the Bulghars. The *Barṣūlā* may be identified with the *Barselt* tribe and the land of *Berzilia* and *Barsalīya* mentioned by Byzantine and Arab sources. This people was also connected with the North Caucasian steppelands. In the 10th century, the Suwār still maintained their own leader whom Ibn Faḍlān calls *Wīrgh*,[8] perhaps **Vuyrigh*, a Bulgharic version of the well-known Turkic title *Buyruq*. We have Ibn Faḍlāl's direct testimony for Suwār–Bulghar hostilities. This is also confirmed by the *Ḥudūd al-ʿĀlam* (comp. A.D. 982) whose author states that the Barṣūlā, Isgil and Bulghar: "are all at war with each other but if an enemy appears they become reconciled."[9] The Suwār also had their own urban center, Suwār. The Isgils, however, were, at this time, more closely attached to the Bulghar ruler, whose daughter was married to their chief. Ibn Faḍlān also mentions another grouping, the *Baranjār*, whose position within the Bulghar state is unclear. Our source calls them "people of the house" (*ahl al-bait*), an ambiguous term which might either indicate a servile status or a very high social rank. The Baranjār are to be identified with the Balanjar of the North Caucasian steppes and the town of that name within the Khazar Kaganate. Given the presence of so many elements with ties to what became the territory of the Khazar state, it is not impossible that they, like the Bulghars, were refugees from the Khazars. It must be borne in mind, however, that these nomads could and frequently did occupy sizable territories. Moreover, as tribes advanced, some elements remained behind. Hence, different units of the same tribal confederation may be found on the middle and lower Volga.

We cannot say with certainty whether the Suwārs or Barsils spoke Oghur or Common Turkic. Amongst the Bulghar tribes themselves there appear to have been several dialects. At least two can be discerned with the scanty data at our disposal.[10] These data largely consist of Bulghar loanwords that entered the languages of the neighboring Finno-Ugric peoples such as the Mari (Cheremis), Udmurt (Votiak), Mordvins and Ugrians.

At the top of the Bulgharian political structure when Ibn Faḍlān journeyed to them, stood Almush the son of Shilki. He was styled the "King of the Ṣaqāliba," a term used to designate the northern peoples. He also bore the

[8] *Kniga Akhmeda ibn Fadlana o ego putešestvii na Volgu v 921–922 gg.*, facs. ed., trans. A.P. Kovalevskiĭ (Khar'kov, 1956), Russ. trans. p. 139, Arab facs. p. 321 (f. 208b); Györffy, György *Tanulmányok a magyar állam eredetéről* (Budapest, 1959), p. 162.

[9] *Ḥudūd al-ʿĀlam* ("The Regions of the World"), trans. V. Minorsky (Gibb Memorial Series, New Series, XI, 2nd rev. ed., London, 1970), p. 162.

[10] A. Róna-Tas, "Some Volga Bulgarian Words in the Volga Kipchak Languages," *Hungaro-Turcica. Studies in Honour of Julius Németh*, ed. Gy. Káldy-Nagy (Budapest, 1976), p. 169.

title, *yiltavar*, the Bulgharic equivalent of the Common Turkic *el-teber*. This was a title given to the rulers of subject tribal unions. It was in this capacity that Almush held this title from the Khazar Kaghan, his overlord.

The early history of Volga Bulgharia can only be conjectured. The scarcity of sources does not allow us to follow the means by which the various tribes that had migrated at different times to the Middle Volga–Kama region coalesced into a tribal union and ultimately a state. Our earliest eye-witness account, that of Ibn Faḍlān who travelled to Volga Bulgharia in 921–2 as part of a Caliphal diplomatic mission, indicates that the Bulghar king had not yet fully extended his authority to all the neighboring tribes. As a vassal of the Khazar ruler, he was forced to provide hostages to their court at Atil. The movement towards Islam, which Almush actively sought to promote, was openly directed against the Khazars. He wished Caliphal help, symbolically, for the construction of a fort against them. Islam, however, could also provide him with the social glue he needed to unite the tribes of his realm. Thus, the 5,000 Baranjār were already converts. Ibn Faḍlān's journey clearly coincided with and helped to promote the final stages leading to the formation of the independent Bulghar state on the Volga.[11] In addition, the Islamicization of Volga Bulgharia could only have a beneficial effect on that country's extensive trading contacts with the Muslim world.

Ibn Faḍlān also mentions four sub-kings, apparently the sons or close kinsmen of the Bulghar ruler. It is unclear from his report what their precise function was. The relative lack of detail regarding Bulghar political institutions in our sources stands in sharp contrast to the informative notices of these same authors regarding the Bulghar economy. This was, of course, a subject of keen interest to the Islamic world which carried on a lively trade with the Middle Volga realm through the Volga–Caspian and Central Asian routes. Our sources indicate a mixed forest and steppe economy. The area is described as densely wooded. Agriculture and cattle-breeding were both important. In later times, Volga Bulgharia was noted as a major agricultural center. Thus, in 1024 when internecine strife in the Rus' principality of Suzdal' led to famine in that region, it was to Bulghar that the Rus' turned to buy grain.[12] Ibn Rusta (early 10th century) notes that "they have fields and arable lands. They cultivate all the grains such as wheat, barley, millet and others."[13]

[11] A.P. Smirnov, "Očerki po istorii drevnikh bulgar," *Trudy Gosudarstvennogo Istoričeskogo Muzeja*, 11, 78–80 (1940).

[12] *Lavrent'evskaja letopis': Polnoe sobranie russkikh letopiseĭ*, 1, 2nd ed. (Leningrad, 1926, henceforth abbreviated as *PSRL*, 1), col. 147.

[13] Ibn Rusta, *Kitāb al-Ā'lāq an-Nafīsa* ("The Book of Precious Gems"), ed. M.J. de Goeje (Bibliotheca Geographicorum Arabicorum, VII, Leiden, 1892), p. 141.

Nomadic traditions, however, were retained. This is reflected in the fact that taxes to the king were paid in cattle and cattle products and not in the harvests of the fields. Moreover, the Bulghars wintered in their cities and spent the spring and summer nomadizing in the steppe.

The fur trade was especially well-developed. Thus, in the 10th century, the Khazar Kaghan was able to demand one sable skin per home as tribute. The Bulghars attempted to maintain a monopoly over the trade with the northern Finno-Ugric peoples, the *Wīsū* and *Yūra* of the Arabic sources, from whom many of these furs were obtained. They, undoubtedly, were the source of some of the fantastic accounts we find in the Arab geographical literature regarding the peoples of the North (see below). The extent of this trade can be seen in a notice on this subject in al-Muqaddasī (c. 985): "From Khwārazm there are imported sable-skins, squirrel-skins, hermine-skins, marten, foxes, beavers, rabbits of all colors, goat-hides, wax, arrows, poplar wood, hats, fish-glue, fish-teeth, castoreum, yellow amber, *kimukht* [a type of hide], Ṣaqlab slaves, sheep and cattle. All this comes from Bulghar via Khwārazm."[14]

Sitting astride the major north–south, east–west routes, the Bulghars became the principal middlemen of the transit trade in the Middle Volga region. The Bulghar ruler, like his Khazar overlord in Atil, tithed all the ships and caravans that passed through his realm. His commercial contacts extended throughout the Islamic world, Khazaria, Rus', Transcaucasia, Central Asia, Byzantium and China. Through Volga Bulgharia the manufactures of the Mediterranean and Central Asian worlds were bartered to the Finno-Ugrian forest peoples in exchange for furs. The latter article was clearly the dominant element in the Bulghar commerce. It was exported in finished form as well as a raw material. Furs were often used as money locally, although Islamic coins did circulate. According to Ibn Rusta, marten skins were the most important of the furs. One skin could bring $2\frac{1}{2}$ dirhams.[15]

The wealth accruing from this trade undoubtedly spurred the growth of towns. Our sources, largely Russian, have preserved the names of a number of them: *Bulghar*, *Biliar* or *Büler* on the Malyi Cheremshan, the capital, *Suwār*, *Oshel'*, *Briakhimov* (perhaps Ibrahimov?), *Chalmat* or *Toretskii Chalmat* as it was styled in Russian, *Isbil* or *Isbol*, *Kermenchük*, *Sobekul'*, *Zhukotin* (Jüke-tau), *Basov*, *Ernas*, *Merkha*, *Nokrat*, *Tetüsh* and other sites. In later Rus' sources some of these towns appear to have been ruled by "princes."

[14] Al-Muqaddasī, *Aḥsan at-Taqāsīm fī Maʿrifat al-Āqālīm* ("The Best of Divisions regarding Knowledge of the Climes"), ed. M.J. de Goeje (Bibliotheca Geographicorum Arabicorum, III, Leiden, 1906, p. 324. [15] Ibn Rusta, ed. de Goeje, p. 142.

The two major cities, Bulghar and Suwār, were not simply collections of nomadic tents. Our sources all state that the Bulghar cities contained houses of wood, particularly pine and oak. In summer, as al-Iṣṭakhrī (10th century) notes, the wooden houses were abandoned for tents.[16] Ibn Faḍlān describes the king's tent as capable of holding 1,000 people and bedecked with Armenian carpets.

The borders of this state, particularly in the southeast and west, were subject to change. Volga Bulgharia does not appear to have been an expansionist or especially aggressive state. Its territorial seizures were probably limited to the lands of neighboring Finno-Ugrian forest peoples who became tributaries. Thus, in the 10th–12th centuries, the northern borders may be placed on the Kama or somewhat beyond it to the lower Viatka and Vetluga rivers. In the west, the Sura river formed its border as did the Belaia in the east. In the south, the Bulghar realm sometimes extended to the Ural river.

Our information regarding the political history of the Volga Bulghars comes almost exclusively from the annals of the various Rus' principalities. These are occasionally supplemented by notices in the Islamic geographical literature. Thus, the Rus' chronicles, unusually laconic in their treatment of Sviatoslav's Volga expeditions in the mid 960s, are completely silent about the fate of the Bulghars in the 965 campaign which ended the Khazar Kaghanate. Ibn Ḥawqal, who mistakenly reports this campaign *sub anno* 967, mentions, in a series of confused notices, that the Bulghars were attacked as well.[17] Whatever the impact of this raid, the Bulghars, if they had not already emancipated themselves from Khazar overlordship, were now able to do so.

In 985, the Rus' under Vladimir I, in alliance with the Oghuz, raided Volga Bulgharia. The raid is described as successful, but the Rus' were duly impressed with the prosperity of the land. Dobrynia, Vladimir's uncle, remarked "I have examined the prisoners. They all wear boots. These [people] will not pay us tribute. Rather, let us seek out [opponents] who wear bast shoes."[18]

The following year, the Bulghars are reported to have sent emissaries to Vladimir enjoining him to embrace Islam. The historicity of this notice may be open to question. Nonetheless, it does indicate that to its neighbors Volga Bulgharia had come to symbolize Islam.

In 1006, the Bulghars requested and were given permission by Vladimir to trade in the Rus' Oka and Volga regions. Rus' merchants were granted

[16] Al-Iṣṭakhrī, *Kitāb Masālik al-Mamālik* ("Viae regnorum"), ed. M.J. de Goeje (Bibliotheca Geographorum Arabicorum, I, Leiden, 1870), p. 225.

[17] Ibn Ḥawqal, *Kitāb Ṣūrat al-Arḍ: Opus Geographicum auctore Ibn Ḥauḳal "Liber Imaginis Terrae"*, ed. J.H. Kramers (Bibliotheca Geographorum Arabicorum II², 2 vols., Leiden, 1938–9), I, p. 15, II, pp. 392–3, 397–8.

[18] *PSRL*, I, col. 84.

reciprocal rights. The Bulghars, however, were not permitted to trade with anyone other than a merchant and entry into the villages was denied them.[19] The question of the safety of merchants was an important one which often had foreign policy ramifications. As such it figure prominently in Bulgharo-Rus' relations. Thus, Bulghar merchants were attacked by Rus' bands (it is unclear whether these were brigands or local lords) in the 1080s. The Bulgars asked that the Rus' authorities take action against the culprits and return the stolen goods. The Rus' refused to do either and in 1088 a Bulghar army marched on them. Murom, a Rus' city in the territory of the Finnic *Murom* people, was the target. Murom had fallen under Rus' control by at least the late tenth century. This is our first indication of combat in this area. Murom was taken, sacked and burned, as were surrounding villages as well.[20] Here, we have highlighted the most consistent theme of Bulgharo-Rus' relations: the great competition for control over the Finno-Ugrian forest peoples, a theme which persisted until the destruction of the Bulghar state.

We have somewhat more information for the first and last quarters of the twelfth century. In 1107, the Bulghars launched an unsuccessful attack on Suzdal', whose Rus' princes were Bulgharia's most constant foes. Once again the mistreatment of merchants may have been the pretext, if not the principal issue. In 1117, a new element (at least from the perspective of our sources) appears. The Cuman khan, *Ayepa*, the father-in-law of Iurii Dolgorukii, the leading Rus' prince of the north, attacked the Bulghars, perhaps at the instigation of his son-in-law. The Bulghars responded by poisoning Ayepa "and the other princes; all of them died."[21] This is a rare glimpse into the nature of the relations between the increasingly urbanized traders and artisans of Bulghar and the steppe-nomads to their south. Clearly, the steppe could be as great a menace as the advancing Rus' with one difference. Although all engaged in raids which aimed solely at the acquisition of prisoners and booty, the Rus' attacks were backed by the steady colonization movement of the Eastern Slavs. In the northern lands in particular, this movement was actively encouraged by the princes. Some three years later, in 1120, we hear of a successful Rus' attack on the Bulghars in which many prisoners were taken. In 1155, the Bulghars attacked Murom and Riazan' with similar results.[22]

This pattern of local raiding with limited objectives changed somewhat during the stormy political career of Andrei Bogoliubskii (d. 1174), the son of

[19] This is only preserved in the 18th-century Russian historian V.N. Tatiščev, *Istorija rossijskaja*, ed. M.N. Tikhomirov *et al*, 7 vols. (Moskva–Leningrad, 1962–8), II, p. 69.

[20] *PSRL*, I, col. 207; Tatiščev, *Ist. ross.*, II, pp. 95–6.

[21] *Ipat'evskaja letopis': Polnoe sobranie russkikh letopiseĭ*, II, 2nd ed. (Moskva, 1962, henceforth abbreviated as *PSRL*, II), col. 285.

[22] Tatiščev, *Ist. ross.*, III, p. 55.

Iurii Dolgorukii and a Cuman princess. Bogoliubskii wanted to become the master of the increasingly fragmented Rus' principalities. He was successful in much of the north and part of the south. In 1169 he took Kiev and returned to the north with the grand-princely title. Prior to this, in either 1160 or 1164 he conducted a series of campaigns against Volga Bulgharia, achieving some limited successes and burning the city of Briakhimov. His campaigns as "Grand Prince" in either 1172 or 1173 attracted considerable Bulghar attention. A large army was raised to counter the Rus' and as a consequence Bogoliubskii was less successful. His assassination in 1174 brought a halt to hostilities for nearly a decade.

In 1183–4, Vsevolod of Suzdal', Bogoliubskii's brother, launched a major attack on the Volga Bulghars. The cities of Sobekul' and Chalmat(a) as well as the *Tetüz* Bulghars were mobilized to meet the attack. Elements of the *Yemek* Cumans (*Polovtsy lemiakove*) also entered the fray, brought in, it appears, by some Bulghar princes to fight Bulghars. This is, perhaps, a reference to internal troubles amongst the Bulghars. Unfortunately, our sources do not tell us more, The Bulghars suffered some setbacks in this campaign as they also did from another Rus' raid in 1186.

The first quarter of the thirteenth century is marked by the now open and rapidly increasing competition between the Rus' and the Bulghars for control over the forest peoples and with them control over the fur trade and its routes. In 1205, a Rus' naval force penetrated Bulghar territory as far as Khomol, taking many prisoners and considerable booty and then returned home. In 1219, the Bulghars struck back, seizing the important trading town of Ustiug. Their attempt to advance further to Unzha was, however, unsuccessful. The Rus' countered by capturing the Bulghar city of Oshel on 15 June 1220 and devastating other areas. Bulghar peace overtures were repeatedly spurned by the Rus' prince Iurii Vsevolodovich. He was finally brought to the peace table by many gifts and a treaty was signed at Gorodets. It resulted in the Bulghars' loss of some trans-Kama territories, an important part of their empire.

Nonetheless, the struggle for hegemony over the Finno-Ugric peoples of the Middle Volga continued. It now came to center largely on a contest to dominate the Mordvin tribes. Both the Rus' and the Bulghars had allies in the two Mordvin tribal confederacies (see below). In 1221, the Rus' constructed the strategically important fort of Nizhnii Novgorod at the mouth of the Oka river in response to these developments. The final act of this great drama was never played out. In 1223, the Mongols, after defeating the Rus' and Cuman princes on the Kalka river, made a brief attempt on the Bulghar lands. The latter, warned well in advance by their intelligence posts on the Ural river, set

up ambushes and traps, inflicting considerable casualties on the invaders. In 1229, a Mongol reconnaissance force sent the people of Saqsin (an important lower Volga commercial town with Bulghar ties) and Cumans fleeing to the Middle Volga. The Bulghar guards on the Ural river were also defeated and fled home. Belatedly, domestic unity and alliances with the Rus' were sought. A further reprieve came in 1232 when a Mongol force was unable to advance to the "great city." More Mongol and allied troops were brought in and in 1236–7 Bulghar was taken amidst great loss of life.

The influence of the Volga Bulghars and other Turkic groups associated with them had, as was earlier noted, a profound and in some instances decisive impact on the fate of a number of the peoples of the forest zone. This was particularly true of the Finno-Ugrian peoples of the Middle Volga and adjoining areas. This is little reflected in the sparse source materials for Bulghar history at our disposal. It is, however, mirrored in the languages, folklore and material cultures of these peoples. The most profoundly affected were the ancestors of the Hungarians. As we have seen, the milieu from which they spring, the southern and southeastern Ugric tribes, had advanced to the steppe and forest-steppe zone and there made contact with the Turkic nomads.

The origins and development of the Hungarians

The process by which the ancestors of the Hungarians were transformed into a steppe people and their migrations from the forest-steppe zone to present-day Hungary still remains a hotly debated subject. It is not our intention to enter into the myriad details of the various theories and hypotheses that have been proposed as solutions to this or that stage of the process. Nonetheless, it will be useful to present, albeit in greatly simplified and reduced form, those current views that have found support and some indication of the evidence on which they rest.

The "classic" formulation of the contours of Hungarian "Pre-history" were presented by Gyula Németh in 1930 and further developed in a collective work edited by Lajos Ligeti in 1943.[23] According to the *schema* traced there, with a wealth of detail, the Hungarians, an originally Ugric people, left their ancient Finno-Ugric homeland and migrated to the Western Siberian forest-steppe zone. Settling along the Tobol and Ishim rivers, they came into contact with Turkic, predominantly Oghur peoples, and in the course of a symbiosis with them were transformed into steppe-nomads. These tribes were, then,

[23] *See* Németh, *A honfoglaló* and Ligeti, *A magyar. óst.*

caught up in the Oghur migration of A.D. 463 and moved south to the North Caucasian–Pontic steppes or more specifically the Kuban river steppe region. Here they were again under Oghur Turkic (Onoghur) as well as Sabir, Türk and Khazar influences. All of these ethnonyms were reflected in the names by which the Hungarians became known in the eastern and western sources. Thus, *Hungarian, hongrois, Ungar* etc. derive ultimately, according to this theory, from *Onoghur*. The *Sabir/Savir–Savar* name is reflected in *Szavárd, Zuard*, the *Savartoi Asfaloi* of Konstantinos Porphyrogenetos. The name *Türk* is similarly applied to them in western and eastern sources as a reflection of their association with the Western Türk empire and its successor state, the Khazar Kaghanate. From the Kuban steppes, the Hungarian tribal union, which contained a number of Turkic tribes or at least tribes bearing Turkic names, progressed toward the Pontic steppes, settling first in *Levedia* and then *Etelköz*. They were ejected from both of these regions by Pecheneg attacks, one in 889 and the other in 895. The last attack drove them into present-day Hungary.

Németh modified his views some 36 years later in light of new evidence regarding their northern abode.[24] According to this new *schema*, the Hungarians left their Ugric homeland for an area slightly to the south, the territory of presentday Bashkiria, or more specifically Western Bashkiria. This region, termed *Magna Hungaria*, was close to the Volga Bulghar state. Here the initial interaction between the Bulghars and Hungarians began. It was continued in the south-Russian steppes, whither the Hungarian tribal union migrated. This migration may be placed between 750–800. Here they were called the *Dentümogyer* or "Hungarians of the Don." This revision, which eliminated the Western Siberian and North Caucasian sojourns, was already anticipated in many respects by Denis Sinor's article which appeared in 1958.[25] Some interesting variants of this basic theme have been suggested. Thus, it has been hypothesized, for example, that two separate and distinct tribal unions, one the *Magyar* and the other the *Onoghur* existed which only joined together at the end of the 9th century to form the Hungarians of the Conquest Period.[26] Finally, it has been argued that speakers of Hungarian were already in Pannonia when Árpád and the Hungarians entered the area, having come there in earlier migrations dating to the Avar period.[27]

[24] Julius Németh, "Ungarische Stammesnamen bei den Baschkiren," *Acta Linguistica Academiae Scientiarum Hungaricae*, 16.1–2: 1–21 (1966) and his "A baskir földi magyar őshazáról," *Élet és Tudomány*, 13: 596–9 (1966). [25] Sinor, "The Outlines."

[26] Imre Boba, *Nomads, Northmen and Slavs* (Slavo-Orientalia, II, The Hague–Wiesbaden, 1967).

[27] For a summary see László, Gyula, *A honfoglalókról* (Budapest, 1973), pp. 66ff. and his *A "kettős honfoglalás"* (Budapest, 1978).

These *schemata* rest largely on linguistic data, supplemented by a few brief written sources and some archeological evidence.

Linguistic data have established, beyond doubt, that Hungarian is derived from the same milieu as the Ob-Ugric languages. The Hungarian self-designation, *Magyar*, has its regular, corresponding form in Ob-Ugric. *Magy-* = *Mańś-Mańśi* ~ *Mоś*, the ethnonym of the Vogul people and of an Ostiak phratry (*Mōš*). The second element, *-ar* or *-er*(*i*) may be Turkic or Finno-Ugric.[28] In either case it signifies "man, human being."

An examination of these data also reveals a sizable number of loanwords from Turkic and to a lesser degree from Iranian and Permian as well as other languages. The Turkic, Iranian and Permian borrowings, however, constitute important clues as to points and periods of contact. Nonetheless, there are many problems associated with them. A substantial number of these loanwords are considered to be of Bulghar (Oghur) Turkic origin. They entered Hungarian, according to an analysis by K. Czeglédy, at four different stages: in Bashkiria (Magna Hungaria), in the Pontic steppes (in two stages) and perhaps through the Kavars (in both the Pontic steppes and in Pannonia).[29] One may argue with a number of the details here (for example, we know that the Kavars taught the Hungarians "Khazar" Turkic, but we do not know if the latter was Bulgharic). Even more important however, is the fact that many of these "Bulghar" Turkic loanwords are neutral in terms of those characteristics which would permit us to classify them within Turkic.[30] Indeed, with regard to some of them we may only say that they are Altaic. Nonetheless, we can be certain that Bulghar Turkic was known to the Hungarians. It was spoken in Hungary proper as late as the tenth century.[31] Bulgharic elements, along with others, may have entered Hungarian during any or all of the stages noted above. The Hungarians, once they migrated to the forest-steppe zone, were, in fact, in contact with a variety of Turkic peoples, speakers of both Bulghar and Common Turkic. Both groups were present in Volga Bulgharia and adjacent areas. While it is possible that some stages of this process of Ugro-Turkic interaction took place in Western

[28] Németh, *A honfoglaló*, pp. 247ff; Hajdú, *Finno-Ugrian*, pp. 69, 111. See also Benkő, Loránd et al., *A magyar nyelv történeti-etimológiai szótára* (Budapest, 1967–78), 3 vols., II, p. 817.

[29] Czeglédy, Károly, "Etimológia és filológia (Bolgár-török jövevényszavaink átvételének történeti hátteréről)," *Az etimológia elmélete és módszere*, eds. Benkő, Loránd and Sál, Éva (Nyelvtudományi Értekezések, 89, Budapest, 1976), pp. 82–9.

[30] *See* Ligeti, Lajos, "A török szókészlet története és török jövevényszavaink, Gyöngy," *Magyar Nyelv*, 32 (1946) and his "Quelques problèmes étymologiques des anciens mots d'emprunt turcs de la langue hongroise," *Acta Orientalia Hungarica*, 29 (1975); "A magyar nyelv török kapcsolatai és ami körülöttük van," *Magyar Nyelv*, 72 (1976). See also Tibor Halasi-Kun, "Kipchak Philology and the Turkic Loanwords in Hungarian, I," *Archivum Eurasiae Medii Aevi*, I (1975).

[31] Györffy, *Tanulmányok*, p. 57.

Siberia, the data at our disposal do not oblige us to place it there. Rather, it seems far more likely that the area of interaction was the territory of the Volga Bulgharian state and its environs. This finds some confirmation in a variety of sources, literary, linguistic and archeological.

Ibn Rusta notes that "between the land of the Bajanāk [Pechenegs] and the land of the Askil Bulgār is the beginning of the borders of the Majgharīya [Magyars]."[32] This clearly places the Hungarian tribes in the eastern region of Volga Bulgharia. It was also here that linguistic contacts with the Permian-speakers could have occurred. A more easterly location of the Hungarians would have made this highly unlikely. Archeological finds have demonstrated that there were culturo-ethnic elements common to both Volga Bulgharia and Hungary after its conquest by the Hungarians. In this regard, the discovery of certain local, specific features is of great importance. Thus, finds of funeral masks and other specific elements in the Tankeev site of Volga Bulgharia have been matched by finds in Hungary. The use of funeral masks seems to have been an Ugric rather than Turkic feature. The custom was preserved by the Ob-Ugrians[33] and hence must have been part of the religious heritage of the Ugrian peoples while they were still in their "homeland" or at least in close contact with it.

The Ugro-Turkic symbiosis is also reflected in a number of clan and tribal names shared by the Conquest-period Hungarians and the Bashkirs (and to a certain degree the Chuvash). Most of these names do not have parallels in Central or Inner Asia; i.e. they are the unique products of a local symbiosis. Thus, the *Gyarmat* (*Gyormatu) of the Kürt-Gyarmat tribe correspond to the Bashkir *Yurmatī*, the *Jenő* to the Bashkir *Yeney*, the *Nyék* (unlike the preceding two, of Finno-Ugric etymology) to the Bashkir *Nägmän*, the *Keszi* to the Bashkir clan name *Kese*. The Hungarian title *gyula* is reflected in the Bashkir clan-name *Yulaman*. The Hungarian tribal name *Tarján*, deriving from the title *tarkhan*, is found as *Tarkhan* amongst the Bashkirs. But, this title is so widespread that it does not necessarily stem from the Bashkir-Hungarian tie. The legendary figure of *Emesu* of the *Gesta Hungarorum* corresponds to *Imes*, a Bashkir sub-grouping which local legend connects with a people of foreign origin and language. Chuvash has also preserved this name in the pagan clan names *Ir-emes, Irch-emes, Arz-emas*.[34]

[32] Ibn Rusta, ed. de Goeje, p. 142.

[33] Ishtvan Fodor, "K voprosu o pogrebal'nom obrjade drevnikh vengrov" *PADIU*, pp. 170–5; E.A. Khalikova, "Pogrebal'nyj obrjad Tankeevskogo mogil'nika i ego vengerskie paralleli," *PADIU*, pp. 158–60.

[34] Kuzeev, *Proiskhoždenie*, pp. 415–17, 422; Németh, "Ungarische Stammesnamen," pp. 8, 10, 12–16.

Finally, it may be noted that the ethnonym *magyar* in the russified form *mozhar* is widely attested in the Middle Volga region as a toponym and as a distinct ethnic grouping.[35]

R.G. Kuzeev, after a painstaking analysis of the Hungarian-Bashkir materials concluded that the "ancient Hungarians lived on the left bank of the Volga, in the valleys of the Bol'shoi Cheremshan, Kundurcha, Sok and Kinel' rivers, in the immediate vicinity of the Bulghars. In the east, their territory reached the region of the watershed of the rivers of the Bugul'minsk hills."[36] This was the territory of Magna Hungaria. Those Hungarian tribes that did not migrate southwards were subsequently absorbed by the Turkic Bashkirs, a separate and distinct ethnos, or other peoples. It may also be noted in this connection that Islamic authors, throughout the Middle Ages, regularly call the Hungarians Bashkirs (*Basjirt, Bashghird* etc.). As a result of their successive changes of abode, the Islamic geographers who either spliced together different accounts from different periods or "updated" older accounts, betray much confusion in their reports on the Hungarians. Typical of the lack of clarity in our sources is the statement of al-Iṣṭakhrī who notes:

> The Basjirt are of two kinds. One kind lives at the edge of the Ghuzz [Oghuz] at the rear of the Bulghārs. They say that they number approximately 2,000 men who are inaccessible in forest areas so that no one can overcome them. They are subjects of the Bulghārs. The other Basjirt border with the Bajanāk [Pechenegs]. They and the Bajanāk are Turks.[37]

This may be interpreted to mean that both of these Basjirts are the Hungarians viewed diachronically, that is, at two different stages, or that the forest Basjirt are the actual Hungarians and the others are the Bashkirs of the steppe.

If the ethnonym Hungarian is to be derived from *Onoghur*, this name could also have been adopted in Bashkiria. Only this would account for the Russian usage in which (in medieval sources), the denazalized form *Ugra, Iugra, ugor, iugor* etc. is applied to both the Hungarians and the Ob-Ugrians. Similarly, it is not necessary to seek a Caucasian provenence for the name *Szavárd*. It was borne by one element of the Hungarian tribal union (the *Savartoi Asfaloi*) at a still undetermined time and was known to the Hungarians in Pannonia in the form of a clan name, *Zuard*. The name is a Hungarianized form (cf. the *-d* ending) of the ethnonym *Sabir–Savir–Savar–Suwār* found within the territory of Bulghar Bulgharia. The name *Türk*, however, points rather to the Pontic steppes, *i.e.* the Levedia-Etelköz period when the Hungarians had close ties

[35] István Vásáry, "The Hungarians or Možars and the Meščers/Mišers of the Middle Volga Region," *Archivum Eurasiae Medii Aevi*, I, 237–275 (1975).
[36] Kuzeev, *Proiskhoždenie*, p. 413. [37] Al-Iṣṭakhrī, ed. de Goeje, p. 225.

with the Khazar Khaghanate. The latter was a successor state of the Western Türk Empire and the Hungarians may be viewed, within the Khazar framework, as perpetuators of this tradition. Indeed, Byzantine sources subsequently refer to Hungary as "Western Turkia" while Khazaria was "Eastern Turkia."

The migration of elements of the Hungarians from Bashkiria to the Pontic steppes probably took place in the late 8th to early 9th century, in connection with disturbances set off by the Oghuz–Pecheneg wars. The construction of the Khazar fort, Sarkel, against the Hungarians clearly shows that they were in the Pontic steppe zone, near the Don, by 839. Of the much debated locations of Levedia and Etelköz, we can only say that the former probably lay to the east of the Dnieper and the latter to the west of it.

In their Pontic steppe abode, the Hungarians were semi-nomadic cattle-breeders. Typically as steppe-nomads, they frequently raided their sedentary neighbors, in this case the Eastern Slavs, and sold their prisoners to slave-merchants, most probably in the Crimea. They are described as capable of fielding an army of 20,000 horsemen. Their system of government evolved under Khazar tutelage and followed the Khazar model. At the head stood the *kende-kündü*, a largely ceremonial, sacral figure. The actual affairs of state and command of the army were in the hands of the *gyula*. The latter title, given the form in which we have it, indicates Bulgharic influences, while the *kende* shows Khazar affinities. In the course of their sojourn in the Pontic steppes, dissident Khazar elements, the Kabars/Kavars, joined them. Following the two Pecheneg attacks, the Kabars went with the Hungarians to Pannonia.[38]

The Hungarian tribal names preserved in Konstantinos Porphyrogenetos and numerous toponyms in Hungary, indicate that a number of Turkic peoples or groups were present within the Hungarian tribal union. In addition to the Turkic (at least in etymology) tribal names such as *Kürt-Gyarmat, Tarján, Jenő, Kér, Keszi*, there were the *Bercel* (*cf. Barṣūlā–Barselt–Berzil*), several tribes (traditionally three) associated with the Kabars and some Irano-Alanic elements. Subsequent additions of Turkic and Iranian tribal groupings were made so that Hungary, throughout its medieval history, had strong ties to the steppe world.

In Pannonia, the upper strata of Hungarian society continued to practice a modified form of nomadism that had been typical of the Khazar ruling elite as well. The power of the sacral *kende-kündü* line appears to have been consider-

[38] For Kabar settlements in Hungary, *see* H. Göckenjan, *Hilfsvölker und Grenzwächter im mittelalterlichen Ungarn* (Quellen und Studien zur Geschichte des östlichen Europa, vol. 5, Wiesbaden, 1972), pp. 39–43.

ably effaced. The kings of medieval Hungary came from the *gyula* line of Árpád. The tribal structure, of which, aside from the names, we know very little, also began to dissolve. The only exception to this were the Kabars, also known as the "Black Hungarians" (*fekete magyarság*) who retained some cohesiveness. Relying on them and other elements within Hungarian society, it took the Árpádian dynasty some 100 years to break down local power centers and create the Hungarian state.[39]

Extinct peoples of the Middle Volga region

The Hungarians were unique amongst the forest peoples in terms of the transformation their society underwent in consequence of contact with the steppe. There is evidence, however, that other Finno-Ugrians experienced similar changes, albeit with different results.

Islamic sources, as well as some later Russian chronicles and literary works, mention the enigmatic *Burṭās–Burdās–Furdās* or *Brutas–Pertas* people. Various attempts have been made to connect them with the Mordvins, Hungarians, Mishar Tatars and Meshchera peoples. The recent tendency is to see in them a mixed people containing Finno-Ugrian, Turkic and perhaps Iranian elements.[40] According to our Muslim authors, their land was located on the Volga, between the Bulghars and Khazaria. They were a subject people of the latter, able to field an army of 10,000 horsemen. This point, as well as the fact that they warred, apparently with some success, against the Bulghars to their north and Pechenegs to their east, indicates that they had mastered the military techniques of the steppe. Their political structure was completely decentralized, being limited to one or two "elders" for each district. Ibn Rusta informs us that they:

> have extensive lands. They live in the forests . . . Their religion is like that of the Ghuzz [Oghuz] . . . They have camels, cattle and much honey. Most of their wealth is from marten-skins. There are two kinds of them, [one] which burns the dead and one type which buries them. They live in the plains . . . They have arable lands. Their greatest wealth is honey and marten-skins and [other] furs . . .[41]

Although Ibn Rusta's account is clearly a pastiche of various reports, the existence of two distinct groups, one connected with the steppe and the other with the forest zone, is obvious. The *Muyjmal at-Tavārīkh* notes that their

[39] Györffy, *Tanulmányok*, pp. 8–10, 30–1, 55–7, 63, 76.

[40] B. Vasil'ev, "Problema Burtasov i Mordvy," *Voprosy ėtničeskoĭ istorii mordovskogo naroda* (Trudy Mordovskoĭ Ėtnografičeskoĭ Ėkspedicii, pt. 1, Trudy Instituta Ėtnografii, 63, 1960) and R.G. Mukhammedova, *Tatary-Mishari* (Moskva, 1972), pp. 11–17.

[41] Ibn Rusta, ed. de Goeje, pp. 141–2.

"king" (*pādshāh* – when they acquired one is not clear) was called *Ṭ-rw*.[42] Al Mas'ūdī terms them a "large people of the Turks" and stresses their importance to the fur trade. The "black foxes, which are the most precious" come from their land.[43] Scattered references to them in later Russian sources almost invariably lump them together with other Finno-Ugrian peoples. It is quite likely that we are dealing with an amalgam of peoples brought together to exploit the fur trade and protect its routes. The "ethnonym" *Burtas*, which has yet to be successfully etymologized, may well mask a technical or social term.[44] They effectively disappear from the Islamic sources after the 10th century, although they continue to surface anachronistically in later compilations. A late reference to them in the *Ustiug Chronicle* places them, *sub anno* 1380, in the Tatar army of Mamai, along with Circassians, Yas, Mordvins, Cheremis and others. Their subsequent fate is unknown.

The 6th-century historian of the Goths, Jordanes, relates a listing of peoples and places allegedly conquered by the Gothic king Hermanarich. The listing, uncritically lifted from some other sources, contains the following: "Golthescytha, Thiudos, Inaunxis, Vasinabroncas, Merens, Mordens, Imniscaris, Rogas, Tadzans, Athaul, Navego, Bubegenas, Coldas."[45] Some of these names, or their corruptions, mask Finnic peoples. The *Thiudos* are the *Chud'* of the Rus' sources. The term Chud' was a general designation for the northwestern and northern Finnic peoples. The *Vas* in *Vas-in-abroncas* are the *Ves'* of the Rus' sources, the *Wīsū* of the Arabs, the Veps or Vepse people, a Finnic group that historically was found in the region of Lakes Ladoga, Onega and Beloozero. The name was also applied to Finnic groups further to the east. *In-abroncas* may refer to some geographical site. The *Merens* are the *Meri* people, *Meria* of our Slavic sources and the *Mirri* noted by Adam of Bremen (c. 1075). They were located near Lake Rostov (Lake Nero) in the province of Iaroslavl' and Lake Kleshchino (Pleshcheevo) in Vladimir province. Together with the Murom, another Finnic group, they were early tributaries of the Rus'. The Murom were located on the Oka river, near its confluence with the Volga. The Meri were probably a branch of the Mari-Cheremis. The Murom, however, are believed to have been a western Mordvin grouping. Both cease to appear in the Rus' sources after 907. They must be presumed to have been

[42] *Mujmal al-Tavārīkh* ("Compendium of the Histories"), ed. M. Bahār (Tehran, 1939), p. 422.

[43] Al-Mas'ūdī, *Kitāb al-Tanbīh wa'l-Ishrāf* ("The Book of Admonition and Recension"), ed. M.J. de Goeje (Bibliotheca Geographorum Arabicorum, VIII, Leiden, 1894), pp. 62–3.

[44] P.D. Stepanov, "Burtasy i Mordva," *Ėtnogenez mordovskogo naroda*, ed. B.A. Rybakov (Saransk, 1965), pp. 202–5.

[45] Jordanes, *Getica*, ed., Russ. trans, E. Ch. Skržinskaja (Moskva, 1960), p. 150, commentary, pp. 265–6.

subsumed and later assimilated by the Slavs. By 988, Vladimir of Kiev had already established his son Gleb in Murom, a Rus' city constructed in the region. The *Mordens* of Jordanes are to be identified with the Mordvins and *Athaul* probably designates the *Atal–Atil* river, the Volga.

Closely related to the Murom region and people was the territory of *Meshchera*, also inhabited by Finno-Ugrians who spoke, in all likelihood, a variant of Mordvin. The "Meshchera" lived on the left bank of the Oka, opposite the right-bank Erzä Mordvins. Archeological finds have shown that this population, like some of its neighbors, was either driven out or assimilated by the large-scale movement of Slavs along the Oka trade routes in the 9th and 10th century. The presence of steppe-nomads to the south played a role in this Slavic colonization movement,[46] indicating, once again, how closely tied the steppe and forest zones of western Eurasia were.

Finally, we may add the data from the 13th-century Russian work, the "Tale of the Destruction of the Rus' Land" (*Slovo o pogibeli russkyja zemli*). In it mention is made of the *Toimitsi* or *Toimichi* a Finnic people of the North and the *Veda* or *Viada*, a probable Finno-Ugric people of the Middle Volga region. The latter, together with the Burtas, Cheremis and Mordvins are portrayed as tribute-payers (in the form of honey) of the Kievan realm under Vladimir Monomakh.[47]

The Volga Finnic peoples

The breakup of the Finno-Permian linguistic community (c. 1500 B.C.) and subsequent dissolution of Finno-Volgaic (first millenium B.C.) gave rise to Volga Finnic. In this new linguistic community consisting of the ancestors of the Mordvins and Mari-Cheremis of today, as well as the now extinct Meria, Muroma and "Meshchera," the Mordvin groupings occupied the western part and the Mari-Cheremis the eastern part of their area of habitation. This encompassed the Volga–Oka mesopotamia and adjacent northern and northwestern regions. This Volga Finnic community ended with the arrival of the Bulghars in the region. The ancestors of the Mari-Cheremis were drawn into Volga Bulgharia while the most westerly groups were slavicized. The Mordvins, on the periphery of the Slavic and Bulghar-Turkic worlds, were better able to maintain themselves as a consequence of their favorable geographic setting.

[46] A.L. Mongaït, *Rjazanskaja zemlja* (Moskva, 1961), pp. 117, 138–9.
[47] Iu.K. Begunov, *Pamjatnik russkoj literatury XIII veka "Slovo o pogibeli russkoĭ zemli"* (Moskva–Leningrad, 1965), pp. 100, 154–7.

The Mordvins of today are the southernmost, geographically, of the Finnic peoples in the Soviet Union. They were not, however, attracted to the steppe. Their location on the southwestern periphery of the Volga Bulghar territory was sufficiently removed from the Bulghar center to minimize Oghur Turkic influences. Hence, they are much less affected by the Turkic world than their linguistic kinsmen the Mari-Cheremis. The Mordvins are presently divided into two groups, the Moksha and Erzä who speak mutually unintelligible dialects. Mordvin groups have been absorbed by their larger neighbors. Thus, the *Teriukhan* ethnic group are believed to be russified Erzä Mordvins and the *Karatay*, a now Tatar-speaking group, appear to have been of mixed Erzä and Moksha origin. The names *Mordva, Mordvin* are russified forms of **Mord*, a word of Iranian origin (meaning "man, human being") found in other Finno-Ugric ethnonyms.

The Mordvins are first mentioned by Jordanes (*Mordens*) in the 6th century and by Konstantinos Porphyrogenetos (*Mordia*) in the 10th century. Early notices in the Rus' chronicles portray them as tributaries of Kiev along with other Finno-Ugrian peoples. The chronology, and indeed the historicity, of these notices are open to question. The Mordvins do not appear, at least under their own names, in the Arabic geographical literature, although attempts have been made to link them with *Artha* (= *Erzä*) and the Burtas. When more reliable notices regarding them begin to appear in the Rus' annals, it is largely in connection with the Volga Bulghar–Rus' struggle to gain control, or at least a sphere of influence, over Mordvin lands. Caught between the princes of Suzdal' and the Bulghars, these territories became a battleground for the larger struggle. In 1103, we learn of an unsuccessful Rus' raid into Mordvin lands. In 1184, the Rus' mounted troops, after completing a campaign against Volga Bulgharia, were sent against the Mordvins.[48] It is not stated whether this attack was in retaliation for Mordvin aid to the Bulghars (which may be conjectured) or simply for booty.

The twelfth and thirteenth centuries witnessed a steady advance of the Rus' into the Oka–Volga mesopotamia reflected in the construction of fortified towns in the region: Gorodets-Radilov in 1152, Kadom (by at least 1209) and Nizhnii Novgorod in 1221. The latter was built on the site of an earlier Mordvin town. Mordvin lands were annexed in the process. In 1226, the Grand Prince, Iurii, sent his brothers Sviatoslav and Ivan to campaign against them. This successful Rus' attack was followed by others. The Mordvins display little unity at this time. The Moksha under Puresh became allies of the

[48] *PSRL*, I, col. 279; *Patriaršaja ili Nikonovskaja letopis'* (*PSRL*, vols. IX–XIII) (Sanktpeterburg, 1862–1904, reprint: Moskva, 1965), X, p. 10.

Rus' while the Erzä led by Purgas sided with the Volga Bulghars. In 1228, Purgas attacked Nizhnii Novgorod but was defeated by Puresh's son who was aided by Cuman auxiliaries. These struggles which continued up to the eve of the Mongol invasion were symptomatic of the general fragmentation of power that contributed to the Mongol conquest.

The *Mari-Cheremis* are now divided into two major groupings on both sides of the Volga and in the Viatka, Vetluga and Sura river regions. Other groupings are found in the area of Gor'ki (Nizhnii Novgorod), Kirov and Sverdlovsk and in the Tatar, Votiak and Bashkir ASSRs. They are mentioned as one of the subject peoples of the Khazar Kaghanate in the 10th century, probably in their capacity as a tributary people of the Volga Bulghars. The influence of the latter, lasting from the 7th century until the Mongol invasion, has been a determinative force in their history. It is reflected in nearly 500 loanwords. Indeed, the name *Cheremis*, for which an acceptable etymology does not exist, probably derives from the Bulghar designation for them (cf. Chuvash *śarmys*, Kazan Tatar *chermesh*).

Bulghar Turkic influence was followed by that of the Kipchakicized Tatars of Kazan which proved to be equally profound. As a consequence, the Mari-Cheremis have undergone the longest and perhaps strongest Turkic influence of all the Finno-Ugric peoples. This is amply reflected in their language, culture and physical features. The outcome of this symbiosis has been that their history has been virtually submerged in that of the peoples who ruled them.

The Permians

The *Udmurt-Votiak* people and the two *Komi* groupings, the *Komi-Zyryen* and the *Komi-Permiak* at present constitute the descendants of the north and north-eastern members of the Finno-Permian linguistic community. The ethnonyn *Komi* is Finno-Ugric and means "human being." Their ancestors originally lived in the Viatka-Middle and Lower Kama region. There they were in contact with Iranian tribes and with the Ugrians as is evidenced by a number of loanwords. The advent of the Volga Bulghars, as with the other peoples of the region, signaled a new cultural influence, one that would play an important role in the formation of the Permian peoples. This influence radiated from the south and hence it was the southern Permian-speakers who were most influenced. The latter became the Udmurt-Votiaks. The Permian linguistic community ended, in a gradual process resulting from Bulghar influences, in the course of the 8th–9th centuries.

The northern Permians, as they shifted northward away from the Volga Bulghars, came into contact with the Finnic Veps-Vepse people from whose language the term *Perm'* may have arisen. This name, originally a toponym, was passed to the Rus' and the Scandinavians (in the latter as *Bjarma, Bjarmaland*). It originally denoted the lower Northern Dvina region and was then extended to the Komi people.[49] The Russians, in their advance along the Dvina, ultimately separated the Komi from the Veps and other northern Finnic peoples. Slavic pressure led to some Komi movement southward, towards the Kama.

The Komi came to play an important role in the northern trade and had commercial relations with Suzdal' and Novgorod. The latter, "Lord Great Novgorod" as it styled itself, was particularly aggressive in gaining control over the fur trade. As a consequence, the Komi were increasingly drawn into the Russian sphere. In the 14th century they were converted to Christianity by the Russian missionary St. Stephan of Perm' (d. 1396) who also created an alphabet for their language.

The internal history of the Udmurt-Votiak people is even less known. Their ethnonym is derived from the tribal name *Od–Odo–Ud* (appearing in Russian as *Vot-iak* with a prothetic *v-*) and the Iranian *murt* "man." Neighboring Turkic peoples call them *Ar* (as do also some medieval Russian sources). There is within the Udmurt-Votiak a special ethnic sub-grouping, the *Besermän* (*cf.* the Russian *Beserman, Besermian*, Turkic *Besermen, Büsürmen* from Arabo-Persian *Musulman* "Muslim"). The Udmurt-Votiak live in the Kama-Viatka and Izh river region. As with other smaller peoples of this area, their history is lost in that of the powerful Turkic states that held sway here.

The Ob-Ugrians

The Medieval Islamic geographers make mention of the *Wīsū* and *Yūra* as peoples who lived beyond the Volga Bulghars in the far north and with whom the latter traded for furs. The *Wīsū* are the Veps-Vepse people (*Ves'* of the Slavic sources) whom we have already mentioned. The *Yūra* are the *Yugra* (*Ugra, Iugra* of the Rus' chronicles), the Ob-Ugrians, the earliest stages of whose history we have already reviewed. At present they consist of two peoples, the *Mańśi-Vogul* and the *Khanty-Ostiak*. Both *Vogul* and *Ostiak* are foreign names apparently based on hydronyms. Their self-designations are

[49] Zsirai, Miklós, *A finnugorság ismertetése* (Budapest, 1958), pp. 19–20; *Osnovy finno-ugorskogo jazykoznanija* (Marijskiĭ, permskie i ugorskie jazyki), ed. V.I. Lytkin et al. (Moskva, 1976), p. 100.

Manśi (cognate with the Hungarian *Magy-ar*) and *Khanty* which probably denotes "people" (cf. the cognate Hungarian *had* "army, host" < *hodu*, < Finn-Ugric **konta*). The question of how the name *Ugra* etc., deriving perhaps from *Onoghur*, came to be applied to them by the Rus' and Arab sources, has not been resolved.

These Ugrians remained in the Ugric homeland and its immediate environs while their southern kin were drawn to the steppe. The Arab geographers who stress their vital role in the fur trade portray them as a wild people, living in the thickets, who are fearful of all strangers. They communicate, for trading purposes, only by sign-language. Fantastic elements are common to both our Muslim and Slavic reports on them. Thus, *sub anno* 1096, the Rus' chronicler inserts a story he heard four years earlier from the Novgorodian Giuriata Rogovich. The latter sent a servant to the Yugra land by way of the Pechera. He later reported various "marvels" that he witnessed there, including trade with a people who live within a mountain. "A small window has been cut open in that mountain and they talk into it. Their language cannot be understood but they point to iron [objects] and gesticulate as if asking for iron. And if someone gives them an iron object, or a knife or an axe, they will give furs in return."[50] Other tales include that of animal cubs falling from the heavens.[51] According to the 18th-century Russian historian V.N. Tatishchev, who had access to now lost materials (but who has also been accused of fabrications), Iurii Dolgorukii, in the course of his town-building program in Suzdal' and other northern Rus' lands c. 1152, populated these new cities with "Bulghars, Mordva and Iugors."[52] The Novgorodians were particularly interested in this region. In 1193, they dispatched an expedition against the "towns" of a Iugor prince. The expedition was a disaster for Novgorod, but the account does mention that the Iugry "gathered silver, gold, sables and other adornments."[53]

Steady pressure from the Rus', the Komi-Zyryens and the Cumans brought about a shift of the Ugrians from the Kama-Bashkirian zone to Siberia. From 1265 onward, Iugra appears as one of the "districts" (*volosti*, i.e. "colonies") of Novgorod. This led to still further eastward movements. By the 15th century, the Yugra center had definitely relocated to Western Siberia. Russian rule ultimately reached them here.

As is clear from the foregoing, the early medieval history of the peoples of the Russian forest zone can be properly understood only within the context of

[50] *PSRL*, I, col. 234–6; *PSRL*, II, cols. 229–35; *PSRL*, IX, p. 127. [51] *PSRL*, II, col. 277.
[52] Tatiščev, *Ist. ross.*, IV, p. 242. Another manuscript of Tatiščev's history (III, p. 441), has, however, "Hungarians" instead of "Iugors"! [53] *PSRL*, X, pp. 21–2.

their symbiosis with the Eurasian steppe peoples. To a certain extent, the ethnogenetic processes which have produced the present-day Finno-Ugrian peoples of the Middle Volga region were determined by interaction with the nomads to their south. Although the latter, as a consequence of their more advanced military technology and social systems, tended to be the politically dominant element, the influences of the forest peoples were profoundly felt in the nomadic economy, material culture and ultimately in the genesis of the present-day Turkic peoples of Central Eurasia as well.

10

The peoples of the south Russian steppes

The rich grasslands and abundant rivers of the Ponto-Caspian steppes, a continuation of the great Inner Asian plains, constituted a natural gravitation-point for the nomad migrating or ejected from the Asian hinterland. Given these favorable conditions, the long-distance nomadism common to Inner Asia tended to be muted and not infrequently transformed into a semi-nomadic system with increasing emphasis on permanent winter camps. Urban life and the practice of agriculture and other settled pursuits were more in evidence amongst the nomads here. A nomadic life-style, as we know from the Khazar and Hungarian models, became more and more the perquisite of the aristocracy, a badge of social distinction. Those tribal groupings that adopted the semi-nomadic model tended to be more stable and better able to withstand the vagaries of steppe life.

In times of turbulence the tribal and ethnic composition of these steppes became a richly hued mosaic, the colors and textures of which are only partially reflected in our sources. The latter largely stem from and were written in the languages of the surrounding sedentary societies. They are frequently incomplete, on occasion ill-informed and universally tend to view the nomad through the prisms of their own cultures.

The Ponto-Caspian steppes after Attila

The movement of the Huns toward Europe undoubtedly introduced new ethnic elements into the Ponto-Caspian steppes. These included Turkic speakers who later became the dominant ethno-linguistic grouping in this region. We have, however, scraps of evidence that appear to indicate that Turkic nomads were present here even before the Huns crossed the Volga. Thus, Jordanes notes that the Huns as they entered "Scythia" conquered the "Alpidzuros, Alcidzuros, Itimaros, Tuncarsos and Boiscos."[1] Some of these

[1] Jordanes, *Getica*, ed., Russ. trans. E. Ch. Skržinskaja (Moskva, 1960), p. 151; cf. the comments of Otto Maenchen-Helfen, *The World of the Huns*, ed. Max Knight (Berkeley, 1973), pp. 23, 402–3.

tribes were undoubtedly Turkic. Later, Attila subdued the *Akatiroi* or *Acatziri*, a powerful nomadic grouping of probable Turkic origin, over whom he placed his son Ellac. With Attila's death in 453 and the subsequent dissolution of the Hunnic tribal union after the Battle of Nedao, in 454 or 455 (in which Ellac perished), Hunnic remnants and closely allied tribes about whom we know only their names (Ultinzures, Bitgorres or Bittugures, Angisciri and Bardores) retreated to "Scythia Minor," present-day Dobrudja and adjacent areas. Two Hunnic groupings remained, led by the surviving sons of Attila, Dengizikh or Dintzic and Hernac. The head of the former was brought to the Byzantine capital in 469 and the fate of the latter is unknown. His name, however, does appear in the Bulgarian Prince-List and it may well be presumed that either he or his "charismatic clan," and most certainly elements of his tribal followers, mixed with tribes that were then entering the western steppe zone and would later form the Bulghar tribal union.

The advent of the Oghur tribes

Sometime about A.D. 463 a series of nomadic migrations was set off in Inner Asia. A very brief account of this is preserved in the fragments of Priskos Rhetor, the Byzantine ambassador to Attila. According to him the Saraghurs, Oghurs and Onoghurs were driven to the Pontic steppe, from whence they then sent ambassadors to Constantinople, by the Sabirs. The latter, in turn, had been forced from their homeland by the Avars. The cause of the Avar migration was unknown to Priskos and his source. Hence, he tells us that they fled before "a great number of griffins" who had determined to make food of humankind,[2] an embellishment lifted from Herodotos.

Archeological and literary evidence permits us to place the homeland of these newcomers, the Oghur tribes, in Western Siberia and the Kazakh steppes. The latter territory came into their possession when the Huns departed for Europe. The Oghurs were part of a large Turkic tribal grouping known in Chinese sources as the *T'ieh-lê*, who were to be found in Inner Asia as well. The immediate catalyst for their westward migration, the Sabirs, have been placed, albeit without great certainty, in Western Siberia and in the western T'ien Shan and Ili river regions before their migration.[3] The expan-

[2] Priskos in *Dexippi, Eunapii, Petri Patricii, Prisci, Malchi, Menandri historiarum quae supersunt*, ed. I. Bekker, B.G. Niebuhr (Corpus Scriptorum Historiae Byzantinae, Bonn, 1829), p. 158.

[3] V.F. Gening, A. Kh. Khalikov, *Rannie bolgary na Volge* (Moskva, 1964), p. 147; Czeglédy, Károly, *A Nomád népek vándorlása Napkelettől Napnyugatig* (Kőrösi Csoma Kiskönyvtár, 8 Budapest, 1969), pp. 19, 91–6; Németh, Gyula, *A honfoglaló magyarság kialakulása* (Budapest, 1930), pp. 183–6. For a dissenting view, see Denis Sinor, "Autour d'une migration de peuples au Ve siècle" *Journal Asiatique*, 235: 1–78 (1946–7).

sion of the Avars has been explained as the consequence of a military defeat suffered at the hands of the Chinese in 460.[4]

Although some of the antecedents of this important migration are still unclear, there can be no doubt that the Oghur tribes now became the dominant element in the Ponto-Caspian steppes. The term *Oghur* denoted "grouping of kindred tribes, tribal union"[5] and figures in their ethnonyms: *Onoghur* ("Ten Oghurs"), *Saraghur* (probably *Shara Oghur* "White" or "Yellow Oghurs") etc. The language of these Oghur tribes, which survives today only in Chuvash, was distinct from that of Common Turkic. In 467 the Saraghurs conquered the Acatziri and other unnamed tribes. The Acatziri now disappear from our sources. Byzantine diplomacy, ever vigilant for new allies in the steppe, quickly drew this apparently powerful tribe into its web and, securing an alliance, sent them off to fight the Persians. Thereafter, their name also vanishes from the accounts at our disposal, surfacing only in a mid-6th-century Syriac source[6] which undoubtedly reflected earlier conditions.

The fluidity of the situation in the steppes is mirrored in our sources, a kaleidoscope of dissolving and reforming tribal unions. In 480 we find our earliest firm notice on the Bulghars ("Mixed Ones"), a large conglomeration of Oghur, Hunnic and other elements. In addition, we have reports about the activities of the Kutrighurs and Utrighurs who appear in our sources under their own names, as "Huns" and perhaps even as "Bulghars." Their precise relationship to the latter cannot be determined with any certainty, but all three clearly originated in the same Hunno-Oghur milieu. The Bulghars, whose name was used generically for many of these tribes, appear to have ranged from the North Caucasian steppes to the Balkans. The Kutrighurs lived between the Don and Dnepr rivers. Immediately to their east were their close kinsmen, the Utrighurs, going towards the Sea of Azov.

Kutrighur raids on the Byzantine Empire alternated with periods of alliance and joint action. Thus, in 530, Kutrighurs served with Byzantine forces in Italy. From Constantinople's standpoint, however, these were fickle and

[4] N.V. Pigulevskaja, *Siriĭskie istočniki po istorii narodov SSSR* (Moskva–Leningrad, 1941), p. 51; Czeglédy, Károly, *IV–IX századi népmozgalmak a steppén* (A magyar nyelvtudományi társaság kiadványai, 84, Budapest, 1954), p. 11.

[5] Peter B. Golden, "The Migrations of the Oğuz", *Archivum Ottomanicum*, 4: 45–47 (1972). For an attempt to connect Oghur with Uighur (the latter were also part of the T'ieh-lê confederacy), see J.R. Hamilton, "Toquz Oγuz et On Uyγur," *Journal Asiatique*, 1962 23–63, pp. 33ff.

[6] This is the "geographical supplement" found in the Syriac translation of the *Ecclesiastical History* ascribed to Zacharias Rhetor, see *Die sogenannte Kirchengeschichte des Zacharias Rhetor*, translated by K. Ahrens, G. Krüger (Leipzig, 1889), p. 253; Pigulevskaja, *Sirijskie istočniki*, pp. 9–11, 83–4; Károly Czeglédy, "Pseudo-Zacharias Rhetor on the Nomads," *Studia Turcica*, ed. L. Ligeti (Budapest, 1971), pp. 137, 141, 143–4.

unpredictable "allies." Hence, the Emperor Justinian, hoping to avoid a repetition of the 558 Kutrighur raid on Imperial territory, induced Sandilkhos, the Utrighur leader, to attack the now booty-laden Kutrighurs. The mutual slaughter, thus touched off, decimated the two peoples.[7]

We are less well informed regarding the details of the early history of the Onoghurs. The probable starting point for their migration to the west was the northern Kazakh steppelands. The Sogdian name and connection of their city, Bakath, which was destroyed by an earthquake[8] would indicate Central Asian ties. From the 460s they appear to be concentrated in the North Caucasian steppe zone, near the Kuban river. Although nomads, they were possessed of a relatively well developed agriculture. They also engaged in trade-especially in marten skins. This latter point indicates ties with the peoples of the forest zone.

The Sabirs

To the east of the Onoghurs were the Sabirs, who had arrived here by 515. Sabir groupings appear not only in the Caucasian steppe area but along the Volga as well in what became Khazar and Volga Bulgharian territories. It is unclear when they advanced to these latter regions. Later Muslim sources, mentioning them under the name *Suwār*, note their presence in both the Volga Bulghar territory and in the North Caucasus.[9] Attempts have also been made to link their name with Siberia.[10] Byzantine sources tell us that their military technology was on a high level and that they were capable of fielding an army of 100,000 (undoubtedly an exaggerated figure).[11] Thus, it is not surprising that the Byzantines sought them as allies in their ongoing struggle with

7 *Agathiae Myrinae, Historiarum libri quinque*, ed. R. Keydell (Corpus Fontium Historiae Byzantinae, II, Berlin, 1967), pp. 196–7; Procopius, *De Bello Gothico*, ed. W. Dindorf (Corpus Scriptorum Historiae Byzantinae, Bonn, 1833–8), pp. 553, 555–6.

8 Theophylactus Simocattes, *Historiae*, ed. Carl de Boer, rev. ed. P. Wirth (Stuttgart, 1972), p. 260.

9 *Géographie de Moïse de Corène*, ed., trans. A. Soukry (Venise, 1881), p. 27; Ibn Khurdadhbih, *Kitāb al-Masālik wa'l-Mamālik* ("Liber viarum et regnorum"), ed. M.J. de Goeje (Bibliotheca Geographicorum Arabicorum, VI, Leiden, 1889), p. 124; Ibn al-Faqīh, *Kitāb al-Buldān* ("The Book of the Lands"), ed. M.J. de Goeje (Bibliotheca Geographicorum Arabicorum, V, Leiden, 1885), p. 297; Al-Muqaddasī, *Aḥsan al-Taqāsīm fī Ma'rifat al-Āqālīm* ("The Best of Divisions regarding Knowledge of the Climes"), ed. M.J. de Goeje (Bibliotheca Geographicorum Arabicorum, III, Leiden, 1906), p. 355; Ibn Faḍlān, *Risāla: Kniga Akhmeda ibn Fadlana o ego putešestvii na Volgu v 921–922 gg.*, ed., trans. A.P. Kovalevskii (Khar'kov, 1956), pp. 139, 321 (f. 208b).

10 Németh, *A honfoglaló*, pp. 183–6; S. Patkanoff, "Über das Volk der Sabiren," *Keleti Szemle*, I: 258–77 (1900).

11 Io. Malalas, *Chronographia*, ed. L. Dindorf (Corpus Scriptorum Historiae Byzantinae, Bonn, 1831), pp. 430–1.

Sassanid Iran for dominion in the Caucasus. Although not adverse to switching sides, the Sabirs, on the whole, maintained a pro-Byzantine posture. This tradition of alliance with Constantinople would be continued by their successors in this area, the Khazars.

In the eastern Caucasian steppes we find a remnant of the Huns (perhaps those that did not go to Europe). They appear in the mid 5th century, in an Armenian source, as the *Khailandur* who raided Transcaucasia through the border fort of Chor (Darband) and were occasionally used by the Sassanids to subdue Transcaucasian Albania.[12]

Avars and Türks

What little equilibrium existed in the western steppe zone was soon disrupted by the advent of yet another Inner Asian people, the Avars. Contact with Constantinople was established by 557 or 558. They quickly established their hegemony over the Sabirs, whose state they destroyed, the Alans, Onoghurs, and remnants of the Kutrighurs and Utrighurs. Their dominion here, however, was short-lived for the Türks were moving against them in deadly pursuit. The Avars quickly moved on to Pannonia which they occupied by 567. They brought with them sizable elements of the Kutrighurs who thus represented a "Bulghar" element in the Danubian region.

As the Avars removed themselves to Pannonia, the Türks initiated contacts with the Byzantine government and a series of embassies was exchanged. An alliance was concluded but both parties, while having common enemies, often pursued different objectives. At the same time the Türks set about conquering the nomads on the western periphery of their expanding empire. The Onoghurs (or perhaps the Utrighurs, our readings are suspect) and the Alans put up some resistance. Nevertheless, the Türks were victorious and set about implanting their rule in the region. The Sabirs and various Oghur tribes were incorporated into the Türk empire and organized into a subject tribal union at the head of which stood Western Türks. This tribal confederation evolved into the Khazar kaghanate.

The Türko-Byzantine alliance was to be directed at Persia. When the Byzantines delayed taking the offensive against the latter, the enraged Türks attacked and conquered the Byzantine possession, Bosporus, in the Crimea in 576. This was not only a blow to Constantinople's commerce but also effectively deprived them of an important and vital intelligence-gathering

[12] Egishe (Ełishe), *O Vardane i voĭne armjanskoĭ*, trans. I.A. Orbeli (Erevan, 1971), pp. 31, 71, 127.

center in the steppe. According to al-Ṭabarī, Türk expansion also extended to the North Caucasus where the "Abkhaz, Banjar and Balanjar" were conquered.[13] The latter was a Turkic group later associated with Khazar territory (the Khazar city of Balanjar) and Volga Bulgharia. Türk assaults on Byzantine-held areas or spheres of influence continued until the outbreak of civil war within the kaghanate. The Türk empire was collapsing as a consequence of severe internal disturbances and Chinese pressure. A reflection of this on the western periphery may be seen in the flight of the *Kotzagers*, *Tarniakh* and *Zabender* to the Avars noted by Theophylaktos Simokattes c. 598. Shortly thereafter we learn of a mass revolt of the T'ieh-lê subject tribal confederation, including the Oghur tribes in the West. This revolt continued into the early years of the 7th century.[14]

Magna Bulgaria

The development of an independent Bulghar state, the *Magna Bulgaria* or *Palaia Bulgaria* of our western sources, situated between the Kuban river and the Sea of Azov was undoubtedly connected with the Tieh-lê uprising. Our sources present an incomplete and confusing account of its origins. Nikephoros Patriarkhos, writing in the early 9th century, states that "Kubrat, the nephew of Organas, the lord of the Unogundurs [i.e. the Onoghurs, P.G.] rebelled against the Avar Kaghan."[15] It may well be that as Türk rule collapsed the Avars briefly reasserted their hegemony in this area. It seems highly unlikely that they had maintained some vestige of their authority here during the earlier years of Türk control. Kubrat's origins are equally murky. In the Bulgarian Prince-List his clan is given as that of the Dulo. This was also a prominent grouping in the Western Türk confederacy, one of the ruling clans. Kubrat, then, may have been a Türk, a representative of the Western Türk ruling families sent to govern a subject tribal union (the usual Türk practice), who then took advantage of the unsettled conditions to strike out on his own. Given the present state of our sources all this must remain conjectural.

In any event, a new state, that of the Bulghars, came into existence. It

[13] Al-Ṭabarī, *Ta'rīkh al-Ṭabarī*, ed. Muḥammad Abu'l-Faḍl Ibrāhīm (Dhakhā'ir al-'Arab, 30, Cairo, 1962–7), 10 vols., II, pp. 100–1.

[14] Czeglédy, *Nomád népek*, pp. 22–3 and his "Ogurok és Türkök Kazáriában," *Magyar őstörténeti tanulmányok*, ed. Bartha Antal *et al.* (Budapest, 1977), pp. 59–63.

[15] *Nicephori Archiepiscopi Constantinopolitani opuscula historica*, ed. Carl de Boer (Bibliotheca Scriptorum Graecorum et Romanorum Teubneriana: Scriptores Graeci, Leipzig, 1880, reprint: 1975), p. 24.

remained independent for some sixty years and established close ties with Constantinople; Kubrat himself even accepting baptism. Despite its auspicious beginning, Magna Bulgaria was subject to the well-known centrifugal forces common to nomadic states as well as steady pressure from external foes. The memory of this is accurately preserved in the ninth century accounts of Theophanes and Nikephoros Patriarkhos who relate the story of Kubrat's "five sons" and successors. According to this tale, they disregarded their paternal admonition "never to separate their place of dwelling from one another"[16] and as a consequence the Bulghar union broke up. In reality, they were under tremendous pressure from the Khazars who were now the political successors of the Western Türks.

Some of the Bulghar tribes remained in or near their traditional territories. This was true of the hordes of *Batbaian* (or *Baian*) and *Kotragos*. They appear in our later sources as the "Black" or "Inner" Bulghars, subjects of the Khazars. Considerable numbers of Bulghars, however, were displaced and forced to abandon the south-Russian steppes entirely. Thus, Bulghar groupings migrated northwards, up the Volga, to the Volga–Kama region where they imposed themselves on the local Finno-Ugrian population (see Chapter 9), giving rise to the Volga or "Silver" Bulghar state. This important and subsequently Islamicized state (10th century) endured until the Mongol invasions, playing a significant role in the ethnogenetic history of the peoples of the Middle Volga.

One Bulghar grouping, under Asparukh, crossed over into the north-eastern Balkans, c. 679, conquered the local Slavic population and formed the Danubian Bulgar khanate. It maintained its Inner Asian language and culture for several centuries, although few monuments of this period have come down to us (cf. the remarkable Bulgharo-Slavic Prince-List[17]). By the late 9th century, in particular following the adoption of Eastern Christianity in 864, the Slavic language and culture of the majority of the country's inhabitants had become predominant.

Sizable Bulghar or Oghur elements were also present in the Avar state in Pannonia. As was noted above, some Kutrighur and other Oghur-Bulghar elements fled with the Avars in 567. Yet others came in the course of the 7th century in the wake of Khazar pressure. They played an active if not always successful role in the political life of the Avar kaghanate. Thus. c. 631–2, a Bulghar grouping in Pannonia was forced to flee to the West, ultimately

[16] Theophanes, *Chronographia*, ed. Carl de Boer (Leipzig, 1883, reprint: Hildesheim, 1963), 2 vols., 1, pp. 356–8; Nikephoros, ed. de Boer, pp. 33–4.

[17] Omeljan Pritsak, *Die bulgarische Fürstenliste und die Sprache der Protobulgaren* (Ural-Altaische Bibliothek, 1, Wiesbaden, 1955).

stopping in Bavaria where most were subsequently slaughtered. In 663, Bulghars led by Alzeco settled in Italy, coming, perhaps, from the Avar domain. In 685, Kuber, a high Bulghar official in the Avar kaghanate, entered the Balkans with his tribal followers and settled in Macedonia. Finally, in 803, Pannonian Bulghars in contact with Krum, the Danubian Bulghar khan, revolted against the tattered remnants of Avar power, ensuring thereby the certain demise of their onetime overlords.

The Khazars

The origins of the Khazar kaghanate, one of the most important political formations of medieval Eurasia, the dominant power in the south-Russian steppe zone, cannot be delineated with precise detail. The picture that emerges from the available data indicates an amalgam of tribes, Sabirs, Oghurs, Türks and others, organized and led by a Türk charismatic clan, perhaps the Ashina clan as the tenth century Persian geographical treatise, the *Ḥudūd al- 'Ālam* would appear to suggest.[18] The name *Khazar*, whatever its etymology, was first and foremost a political designation and only secondarily an ethnonym. Indeed, in the early stages of Khazar history, the Türk period (568–650), we are hard pressed to disentangle Khazar from Türk. Many of our sources use these names interchangeably. Indeed, there may have been no distinction. Prior to the advent of the Türks we cannot find an unimpeacheable source indicating the presence of the Khazars in the area. Despite attempts to do so, they are not to be identified with the Acatziri as has been convincingly demonstrated by O. Maenchen-Helfen.[19] If an actual Khazar people existed at this time, it must have been either a group of the Türks or a tribe closely associated with them. It is, of course, possible that in the welter of tribes produced by the Avar and Türk incursions, a new tribal union was formed. If so, its genesis has not been recorded in our sources. A "Khazar people" did, in time, emerge, in the post-Türk period, but it is impossible at this stage to see anything but their barest contours in the multi-ethnic, multi-lingual state that was the Khazar kaghanate.

Our notices on the Khazar language are both sparse and contradictory. Thus, al-Iṣṭakhrī, in one notice says it is like that of the Bulghars and in another remarks that it is distinct from any other human tongue.[20] The long-

[18] *Ḥudūd al-'Ālam*, trans. V. Minorsky (Gibb Memorial Series, new series, 11, London, 1937, rev. ed., 1970), p. 162.

[19] Otto Maenchen-Helfen, "Akatir," *Central Asiatic Journal*, 11 (1966).

[20] Al-Iṣṭakhrī, *Kitāb Masālik al-Mamālik* ("Viae Regnorum"), ed. M.J. de Goeje (Bibliotheca Geographicorum Arabicorum, 1, Leiden, 1870), pp. 222, 225.

standing debate over whether the Khazars spoke a form of Oghur or Common Turkic cannot be resolved on this basis. The remnants of the Khazar language as preserved in isolated names, titles, toponyms etc. found in a wide variety of sources, eastern and western and considerably complicated by poor transcription systems and scribal errors, appear predominantly Turkic and of the Common Turkic, or at least "neutral" type.[21] In short, incontrovertible proof is still lacking.

At the zenith of its power, the Khazar kaghanate ruled over an immense territory. Its political and economic heartland was composed of the Volga delta and North Caucasian steppes. It extended, then, to the lands of the Burtas (see Chapter 9) to their immediate north on the Volga and to the Volga–Kama lands of the Volga Bulghars. Khazar holdings in the east were not clearly defined, extending into the steppelands approaching the Khwārazmshāh realm. It is doubtful, however, that Khazar power was often effective as far as the Ural river. In the west, the Khazars were firmly in control of the Don–Donets region and in the mid 9th century, if not earlier, had extended their control to the Eastern Slavic lands, including Kiev. In the south, the Khazars fronted on two great empires, the Arabian Caliphate in the Caucasus, where Bāb al-Abwāb formed an uneasy demarcation point, and the Byzantine Empire where Khazars and Byzantines vied for control over the Crimea. In addition to the Khazars and related Turkic peoples, the empire included elements of the Oghur tribes of Magna Bulgaria, Iranians from Khorezm and the Aralo-Caspian steppes, various North Caucasian tribes, the "North Caucasian Huns," Finno-Ugrian and Bulghar peoples on the Volga and Slavs.

The presence of the institution of the kaghanate amongst the Khazars bespeaks close, genetic ties with the Türks. Descriptions of the ceremonies associated with the Khazar kaghanal office, such as investiture, found in Muslim authors are virtually identical to Chinese accounts dealing with these same practices amongst the Eastern Türks. The Khazar kaghan, however, in time became an increasingly sacral, holy figure, a talisman for the good fortune of the state. Living isolated with his harem, he rarely and only ceremonially appeared in public. Nevertheless, should Fortune cease to smile on his realm, it was considered fitting and proper to murder and replace him.

The Khazars began to emerge as an increasingly distinct entity by about 630, as the Western Türks faded on the periphery of their empire. Their immediate neighbor and principal competitor, as we have seen, was the newly

[21] *See* Peter B. Golden, *Khazar Studies* (Bibliotheca Orientalis Hungarica, xxv, Budapest, 1980). 2 vols., i, chapter 4.

emergent Onoghur-Bulghar state. Warfare soon broke out, lasting until the dissolution of Magna Bulgaria in the 670s. Khazar–Bulghar hostilities, given the Western Türk connections of the ruling strata of the two protagonists, may have been a reflection of the larger Tu-lu – Nu-shih-pi struggle within the parent confederation.[22]

In the midst of their wars with the Bulghars, a new threat appeared. As early as 642, the Arabs, following their conquests in Transcaucasia, raided the Khazar possession of Balanjar. This marked the beginning of a protracted Arabo-Khazar war, periodically punctuated by truces, which lasted until 737. In that year, the Arab commander (and future Caliph) Marwān b. Muḥammad, penetrated to the Khazar heartland on the lower Volga and pursued the fleeing kaghan to the territory of the subject Burtas. The surprised and defeated Khazar ruler was compelled to become a Muslim and a subject of the Caliph, a status from which he quickly abjured as soon as the Arab threat was sufficiently removed. Warfare resumed in the course of the 8th century, but on a reduced level. It was clear that neither side was capable of truly defeating the other. In effect, the Khazars had halted the Arab attempt to advance beyond the Muslim border fort of Bāb al-Abwāb (Darband) and thus played a role in world history analogous to that of the Franks in France.

The Khazars were heirs to the Sabir and Türk tradition of alliance with the Byzantine Empire and on occasion, figured prominently in imperial politics. Thus, in 732, Chichek, the daughter of the Khazar Kaghan was married to the son of Leo the Isaurian (711–41), the future emperor Constantine V. Their son Leo, who also wore the purple, was known as "the Khazar." Given the well documented reluctance of Byzantine royal families to marry "barbarians" (i.e. non-Byzantines), this is a concrete illustration of the importance of Khazaria in the world affairs of the mid 8th century. Khazaria constituted Constantinople's principal line of defence against incursions from the steppe. With the Khazars able to halt unruly tribes at the Volga, the Balkan and Caucasian approaches to the Empire were secure. This did not, however, preclude conflict in other areas, especially the Crimea which was coveted by both. The Khazar presence was even more strongly felt in Transcaucasia. Thus, in 786 the Khazars aided Leon II of Ap'khazet'i (medieval Abkhazia and Western Georgia), who was a grandson of the Khazar Kaghan, to end Byzantine suzerainty in his land.[23]

[22] M.I. Artamonov, *Istorija Khazar* (Leningrad, 1962), p. 170; Györffy, György, *Tanulmányok a magyar állam eredetéről* (Budapest, 1959), pp. 77–8.

[23] *K'art'lis Ts'khovreba* ("The Life of Georgia"), ed. S. Qaukhch'ishvili, 2 vols. (T'bilisi, 1955–9), 1, p. 251.

Sometime during the last two decades of the 8th century or early years of the 9th century, the Khazar Kaghan, according to the 10th-century Arab historian al-Mas'ūdī, converted to Judaism.[24] The reasons for the conversion have long been and undoubtedly will remain a matter for speculation. Unfortunately, a work by this same author in which he discusses this event in detail has not come down to us. We have no evidence that Judaism became the "state religion" of Khazaria. Indeed, a state religion as such does not appear to have existed there. Nonetheless, Khazaria was identified with Judaism by its contemporaries and by Jews in distant Spain and Egypt. Alongside of Judaism, Christianity and Islam, as well as various pagan cults, were well-represented in Khazaria. Our sources are vague, and probably biased depending on the religious affiliations of our authors, with respect to the number of adherents each of the three monotheistic faiths enjoyed in the general population. Legal matters were handled according to religious law, the Khazar government having established seven judges for this purpose. Again according to al-Mas'ūdī, two of the judges were for the Muslim population, two for the Khazars, "[these two] render judgments according to the Torah," two for the Christians and one for the pagans.[25] There is no evidence, as has been claimed in some quarters, that the tradition of broad tolerance or indifference common to most nomadic states of this period, was in any way affected or modified by the conversion.[26] After the conversion, however, it appears that only members of the royal clan who had adopted Judaism could become kaghans. On the other hand, the Khazar equivalent of the Near Eastern vezirate became the monopoly of the Muslim Arsīya, the Iranian guard of the Kaghans from Khorezm. The spread of the monotheistic religions should be viewed as a further indication of the increasing sedentarization of elements of the Khazar tribal union.

The role of Khazar Judaism and the Khazars in the shaping of Eastern European Jewry, especially Russian Jewry, has also given rise to much speculation. Contemporary sources do indicate that Jews from Byzantium and the Islamic lands did come to Khazaria and there were old, established Jewish colonies in the Crimea antedating the Khazar conversion. We do not, however, know the number of Jewish immigrants nor the extent to which they mixed with Judaized Khazars. It is fairly clear from our sources that Khazar

[24] Al-Mas'ūdī, *Murūj al-Dhahab wa Ma'ādin al-Jawhar* ("Meadows of Gold and Mines of Precious Stones"), ed. Charles Pellat, 5 vols. (thus far) (Beirut, 1966–70), I, p. 212. Al-Mas'ūdī places the conversion in the reign of Hārūn al-Rashīd (786–809). See also the survey by Omeljan Pritsak, "The Khazar Kingdom's Conversion to Judaism," *Harvard Ukrainian Studies*, 2: 261–81 (1978). [25] Al-Mas'ūdī, *Murūj*, ed. Pellat, I, p. 214.

[26] *Cf.* the conjectures of Artamonov, *Ist. Khazar*, pp. 275–87; 324ff., 372, 457–8.

Judaism, whatever its ritual imperfections, was not of the Qaraite variety and hence the oft-made claim that the present-day Eastern European Qaraim whose Turkic language shows obvious affinities with Cuman and Armeno-Cuman, are the descendants of the Khazars cannot be substantiated.[27]

The conversion did not negatively influence Khazar-Byzantine relations. In 838, Petronas Kamateros, a specialist in steppe affairs, was sent by Constantinople to oversee the construction of Sarkel. The latter, located on the left shore of the Don near Tsimliansk, was part of the Khazaro-Byzantine defence system. It was most probably aimed at the Hungarian tribal union which was entering the South-Russian steppes at this time and the Pechenegs, who under pressure from the Oghuz to their east, had begun to disturb the "Pax Chazarica." This is confirmed by Ibn Rusta, an early 10th-century author, who notes that the Khazars "in the past, built moats around themselves in fear of the Majgharīya and other peoples who bordered on their country."[28] Sarkel, like other forts built in the area, had a deep flowing moat. Byzantine sources, in turn, state that Sarkel was "a staunch bulwark against the attacks of the Pechenegs."[29] The Hungarians were soon brought within the Khazar orbit (see Chapter 9); the Pechenegs, however, became bitter foes.

Although sporadic warfare continued with the Arabs in the Caucasus, the principal danger to the Khazar realm came from the eastern steppe frontier and from a new power emerging in the northwest. In the early spring of 861 a Byzantine mission headed by Constantine (St. Cyril), the future apostle to the Slavs, came to the Khazar capital on the lower Volga. Ostensibly, Constantine's purpose was to take part in a religious debate at the court of the Kaghan. Undoubtedly, this was part of his assignment. On the other hand, we may presume that the Rus' who had just attacked Constantinople (beginning in June 860), were an important topic of discussion. They were an amalgam of Scandinavian, Slavic and Finnic elements organized for trade and plunder. In the 830s elements of them appear to have been within the Khazar orbit and may well have had dynastic ties with the Khazar "charismatic clan." The memory of this "Rus' Kaghan" was preserved centuries later amongst the

[27] See Zvi Ankori, *Karaites in Byzantium* (New York–Jerusalem, 1959), pp. 64–79. For a presentation of the Khazar–Qaraim tie, see Ananiasz Zajączkowski, *Ze studiów nad zagadnieniem chazarskim* (Polska Akademia Umiejętności, Prace komisji orientalistycznej, 36, Kraków–Warszawa, 1947), pp. 62ff. and his *Karaims in Poland* (Warszawa–Le Haye–Paris, 1961), pp. 12–23.

[28] Ibn Rusta, *Kitāb al-Aʿlāq al-Nafīsa* ("The Book of Precious Gems"), ed. M.J. de Goeje (Bibliotheca Geographicorum Arabicorum, VII, Leiden, 1892), p. 143.

[29] Theophanus Continuatus, *Historiae*, ed. J. Bekker (Corpus Scriptorum Historiae Byzantinae, Bonn, 1838), pp. 122ff.; Ioannas Skylitges, *Georgius Cedrenus Ioannis Scylitzae ope*, ed. J. Bekker (Corpus Scriptorum Historiae Byzantinae, Bonn, 1839) 2 vols., II, pp. 129–30.

Eastern Slavs and is noted by many of our Muslim sources.[30] By 885, however, the situation had changed. The Rus' had united the Eastern Slavic tribes and the dynamism of their expansion now brought them into conflict with the Khazars. This came at a time when the Khazar tribal union was experiencing internal difficulties. Our only firm evidence of this manifested itself in the revolt and breakaway of the Kabars in the early 9th century. They joined the Hungarian union and went with the latter to Pannonia. The circumstances that produced the Kabar revolt remain a mystery. Attempts by some scholars[31] to ascribe the revolt to an anti-Judaizing sentiment amongst Khazar elements are based on rather imaginative readings of the Khazar-Hebrew Correspondence, a source which itself is not free of tendentiousness.

The Rus' now embarked on a series of daring raids on the Volga route to the Islamic lands in the Caucasus and along the Caspian Sea. These began sometime during the reign of the Ṭabarīstānian amīr Ḥasan b. Zaid (864–84). Raids continued in 910 and succeeding years and took place, apparently, with Khazar connivance, the Kaghan receiving half of the booty. The raids enraged the Muslim populace of Khazaria and the Kaghan was unable to prevent them from slaughtering the Rus' returning from an expedition in 310/922. Why the Kaghan permitted these raids which disrupted the lucrative commerce and hence considerable revenue which accrued to the kaghanal coffers, remains unclear. Perhaps, it was connected with a Khazar war with the Muslim ruler of Bāb al-Abwāb that had been going on since 901. In 943–4, the Rus' attempted a takeover of Bardha'a (Partaw) in Azerbaijan. Large-scale expeditions such as this undoubtedly led to a reversal of Khazar policy. In a letter of the Khazar ruler Joseph to the Jewish courtier in Muslim Spain, Ḥasdai b. Shaprut, the former writes of the Rus': "I war with them. If I left them [in peace] for one hour they would destroy the entire land of the Ishmaelites up to Baghdad."[32] The letter is probably to be dated to the early 960s. It confirms the notices in Rus' and Muslim sources regarding serious hostilities between the Rus' and Khazars which led to the collapse of the kaghanate. The Rus' chronicles only mention one campaign, that of 965. In that year, Sviatoslav, the ruler in Kiev, warred on the Khazars overcame them and "took their city

[30] Peter B. Golden, "The Question of the Rus' Qağanate", *Archivum Eurasiae Medii Aevi*, II (1982).

[31] Artamonov, *Ist. Khazar*, p. 324. There is some circumstantial evidence to indicate that the Kabars were Muslims or at least had a strong Muslim element in their midst, see P. Nemet (Németh, Péter), "Obrazovanie pograničnoj oblasti Borzhavy," *Problemy arkheologii i drevneĭ istorii ugrov*, ed. A.P. Smirnov (Moskva, 1972), pp. 218–19.

[32] P.K. Kokovcov, *Evreĭsko-khazarskaja perepiska v X veke* (Leningrad, 1932), p. 102.

and Biela Vezha [i.e. Sarkel]."[33] The Khazar Cambridge Document indicates that the Khazars had been at war with the Alans, Oghuz and other neighboring peoples for some time. Ibn Miskawayh and Ibn al-Athīr provide testimony that the Oghuz played a role in the 965 Rus' campaign.[34]

The Khazars did not entirely disappear at this time. They continued, in a greatly reduced form, as a client state of Khorezm while other Khazar areas fell to the surrounding Muslim rulers. Hereafter, we find scattered references to Khazar pockets. Thus in 1016 a Khazar "Georgios Tzulê" was attacked by a Rus'-Byzantine force. We are not appraised as to where this attack took place. In 1023, the Rus' prince Mstislav, engaged in a struggle for the Kievan throne, had Khazar and Kasogian (Circassian) allies. In 1064 some 3,000 "households of the Khazars" settled in Qaḥtan in the North Caucasus, probably the lands of the present day Turkic Qumuqs. Khazars are also mentioned in 1079 and 1083 in the principality of Tmutorokan' where they seem to have enjoyed some local political prominence. References may also be found to individuals of Khazar origin in Rus' service. Some documents from the Cairo Genizah mention messianic movements in "Khazaria" in the eleventh and twelfth centuries. These probably refer to Jewish colonies (perhaps of Khazar origin) in the Crimea. The bulk of the Khazar population blended into surrounding, largely Turkic peoples. The nomadic elements were absorbed by other tribes.

The paucity of our sources precludes an attempt to outline the domestic history of the Khazars. Analogous with other nomadic and semi-nomadic states, we may presume that there were inner tensions which were reflected in the centrifugal tendencies of some clans or tribes. This may be seen in what little we know of the Kabars. This factor probably also played a role in the weakening of the kaghanate. Khazar power rested, to a certain extent, on its control of the major trade arteries in this region. Disruptions from within or without could seriously affect the entire organism. Khazaria fell, then, as a result of the Kabar civil war, and perhaps other unrecorded domestic calamities, as well as the steady pressure of steppe peoples whom the kaghans on the lower Volga were less and less able to repulse.

[33] *Lavrent'evskaja letopis': Polnoe sobranie russkikh letopiseĭ*, I, 2nd ed. (Leningrad, 1926, henceforth abbreviated as *PSRL*, I), col. 65; *Ipat'evskaja letopis': Polnoe sobranie russkikh letopiseĭ*, II, 2nd ed. (Moskva, 1962, henceforth abbreviated as *PSRL*, II), col. 53.

[34] Cambridge University Library, T-S Loan 38, pp. 2–4; Ibn Miskawaih, *Tajārub al-Umam* ("Experiences of the Peoples" = "The Eclipse of the 'Abbasid Caliphate"), ed. H.F. Amedroz, trans. D.S. Margoliouth, 5 vols., Arab text, II, p. 209, Eng. trans. V, p. 223; Ibn al-Athir, *Al-Kāmil fī'l-Ta'rīkh* (Chronicon quod perfectissimum inscribitur), ed. C.J. Tornberg (Leiden, 1851–76, reprint: Beirut, 1965–6), 12 vols, VIII, p. 565.

Before turning to their successors, some word should be said about the Khazar state and its institutions. As was noted earlier, the sacral character of the Kaghanal office became paramount at some as yet undetermined time. The actual, day-to-day handling of governmental affairs became the domain of a figure called "the king" in our Muslim sources, who bore the title Ishad, Kaghan Beg or simply Beg. According to Ibn Faḍlān who visited the Volga Bulghars in 921–922, the Khaghan-Beg also had deputies, the *K-nd-r* (for *Kündü*, *cf.* the Hungarian *Kündü/Kende*) and the *Jawsh-gh-r*.

The ruler and his subjects wintered in the cities and with the coming of spring returned to the steppes, following the modified nomadic life-style widespread in Western Eurasia. The Khazar capital, termed alternately Atil (or Itil) in some sources and Sarighshin in others, was a dual city. The ruler, government and army-bodyguard occupied one area and commercial elements the other. The majority of the dwellings were the felt tents of the nomads interspersed with a few clay homes. The only structure made of brick was the king's castle. The entire city was surrounded by a wall in which gates led to the steppe and the river. Revenue derived from a tithe on the huge volume of trade that flowed through the city as well as other taxes. These revenues were sufficient to permit the kaghans to maintain a permanent, paid, standing army (the Arsīya). The existence of Khazar coinage is still being debated. Nonetheless, the Khazars were vitally interested in trade and the "Pax Chazarica" undoubtedly did much to promote it. Agricultural pursuits were followed when the populace left the cities in the spring for their sojourn in the steppes. Fishing was also an important activity (confirmed archeologically for many nomadic peoples) and fish, along with rice, was a staple of the Khazar diet. Not surprisingly, then, isinglass was the only Khazar "export" that was genuinely produced by them. Straddling the great commercial routes leading to the Islamic world, Khazaria was one of the commercial giants of the period. This accounts for the relatively detailed accounts we have of them in the Arabic and Persian geographical and historical literature.

The Pechenegs

Al-Iṣṭakhrī, the 10th-century Muslim geographer whose notices, as we have seen, constitute a vital segment of our knowledge of the steppe peoples, notes that "a tribe of the Türks was cut off from their homeland and crossed [to an area] between the Khazars and Rum. They are called *Bajanāk*. This was not their dwelling place in olden times, but rather they came to it and conquered

it."[35] The people described here are the Pechenegs whose movements were both the result of other migrations in the Central Asian steppes and the cause of still other displacements in the steppes to their west. The task of tracing these movements is, at best, a hazardous procedure as only scattered aspects of this or that migration have been reflected in our sources. Hence, the following is, perforce, an imperfect reconstruction of only the broadest outlines of these momentous events.

The 7th-century dynastic annals of the Sui, the *Sui-shu*, in a notice on the T'ie-lê tribal confederation, mention the *En-k'ü*, *A-lan* and *Pei-ju*, amongst others, living east of *Fu-lin* ["Rome," i.e. the Byzantine Empire]. The reconstructed ancient pronunciation of the Chinese *Pei-ju* approximates the name Pecheneg.[36] The notice does not shed any real light on the geographical location of these peoples. The *En-k'ü* (=Onghur-Onoghur) and *A-lan* (Alans), depending on the period in question, can be placed anywhere from the North Caucasian to the Kazakh steppes and the border of Sogdia. The latter region, in light of other information found in Islamic sources, seems most likely, in particular the region going towards the Aral Sea–Syr Darya steppes.

Our earliest firm notice mentioning the ethnonym Pecheneg stems from an 8th-century Tibetan translation of an Uighur report on the peoples of the North. This report notes the *Be-ča-nag* as warring with the *Hor*. The latter is usually a designation for the Uighurs but in this instance probably refers to the Oghuz.[37] This notice places them in the Syr Darya region. Further support for this may be seen in the connection of the Pechenegs with the area of *Kang*, the middle Syr Darya and adjoining territories. Konstantinos Porphyrogenetos, in chapter 37 of his *De Administrando Imperio*, notes that three groupings of the Pechenegs are called *Kangar*. However this name is to be etymologized, it is associated with the *Kang* territory and probably with the *Kängäräs* people and the city of *Kängü Tarban* of the Kül Tigin inscription of the Orkhon

[35] Al-Iṣṭakhrī, ed. de Goeje, p. 10.

[36] Paul Pelliot, *Notes sur l'histoire de la Horde d'Or suivies de Quelques noms turcs d'hommes et de peuples finissant en "ar"* (Oeuvres Posthumes de Paul Pelliot, II, Paris, 1949), p. 226, n. 1; Liu Mau-tsai, *Die Chinesischen Nachrichten zur Geschichte der Ost-Türken (T'u-küe)* (Göttinger Asiatische Forschungen, vol. 10; Wiesbaden, 1958), 2 vols., I, p. 128, II, p. 569 where it is identified with *Bashkir*.

[37] J. Bacot, "Reconnaisance en Haute Asie Septentrionale par cinq envoyés Ouïgours au VIII siècle," *Journal Asiatique*, 244: 147 (1956); Louis Ligeti, "À propos du 'Rapport sur les rois demeurant dans le Nord'," *Études Tibétaines dédiées à la mémoire de Marcelle Lalou* (Paris, 1971), pp. 170, 172, 175, 176.

Türks. The Kängäräs were allies of the Eastern Türks against the Türgesh of the Western Türk Confederacy in the early 8th century.[38]

The ethnic origin of the Kangar–Kängäräs people cannot be determined at this stage. Similarly, the process by which the Kangar became part of the Pecheneg union is unrecorded in our sources. How far westward this Kangar–Pecheneg union extended is yet another puzzle. It may have reached the Ural river. Colonies of earlier Kangar movements have been connected with the *Kangārāyē* in the Caucasus mentioned by Armenian and Syriac authors of the fifth and sixth centuries.[39] Finally, the relationship, if any, of the Kangar to the Qanglï, an important Kipchak Turkic tribal union prominent in the politics of the Khwārazmshāh state in the centuries prior to the coming of the Mongols, is equally unclear.

With the movement of the Oghuz tribes into the Syr Darya region in the 8th century, the Pechenegs soon found themselves caught up in the larger struggles of the Central and Inner Asian nomads who were moving into this area. Oghuz pressure, the memory of which was preserved in the Oghuz tales of wars with the *It-Pechene*, forced the Pechenegs into the Volga–Ural mesopotamia by the late 8th or early 9th century. Peace was not to be granted to them here either. According to Islamic accounts they were at war, in this area, with all of their neighbors. In particular, the Khazars and the Oghuz were allied against them and maintained a constant pressure. As a consequence of this, the Pechenegs were compelled to migrate again, c. A.D. 889 and in so doing drove the Hungarian tribal union from Levedia to Etelköz, further west in the Pontic steppes. A second Pecheneg attack on the Hungarians (see Chapter 9), carried out as part of an alliance with Tsar Symeon of Bulgaria, sent the Hungarians to Pannonia and made the Pechenegs masters of the steppes from the Don–Donets region, where they were the uneasy western neighbors of the Khazars, to the Danube. They held this area until the middle of the 11th century.

The broad contours of Pecheneg social and political organization are known to us through the writings of Konstantinos Porphyrogenetos. Substantial portions of his foreign policy handbook, the *De Administrando Imperio* are devoted to them. While in the Pontic steppes, the Pecheneg tribal union was composed of eight distinct tribal units, each occupying a "province" (*thema*) and each under the rule of a "great prince." These latter divisions may

[38] S.G. Kljaštornyĭ, *Drevnetjurkskie runičeskie pamjatniki kak istočnik po istorii Sredneĭ Azii* (Moskva, 1964), pp. 156–78.

[39] Czeglédy, *Népmozgalmak*, pp. 38–45 and his "Monographs on Syriac and Muhammadan Sources in the Literary Remains of M. Kmoskó," *Acta Orientalia Hungarica*, 4: 65–6 (1954).

have reflected sub-tribes or clans. Following well-attested Turkic principles of bipartite political organization, the eight tribal units were evenly divided on either side of the Dnieper river. Our source does not indicate which wing, the right or the left, held supreme political power. A later and non-contemporary Arab source, Abu Sa'īd (d. 1286) whose notice is preserved in Abu'l-Fidā (d. 1331), mentions a royal town, Bajanakīya and the institution of a Pecheneg khaghanate which passed from father to son.[40] Our contemporary sources do not confirm this. The 10th-century *Ḥudūd al-'Ālam* describes the Pecheneg ruler as a *mihtar* ("prince, lord"), a rank considerably lower than *khāqān* which was a well-known *terminus politicus* in Islamic literature. Moreover, the system of succession recorded in the *De Administrando Imperio* was that of cousin to cousin, one similar to that of the Eastern Türks. The Kangars, as described by our imperial informant, may have constituted the "royal" or "inner" clans or tribes but the notice is sufficiently vague to permit a variety of interpretations.

It seems clear that we cannot really speak of a Pecheneg "state" on the model of the Khazars. Some old Türk titles are in evidence amongst them (*chur/chor*, *boyla*, *Yula/jula*), thereby indicating some probable central organization. Nonetheless, the overall impression is that of a loose, unstable tribal confederation. Such a confederation was usually subject to great internal tensions and these are much in evidence in Pecheneg history.

The Pechenegs are first recorded in the Rus' chronicles in 915. By 920, Igor' of Kiev had already taken the field against them. Given the somewhat fragmented nature of the Pecheneg polity (as well as the centrifugal tendencies of elements of the Rus' state), the conflict which this first encounter heralded was rarely the "total" war that some patriotic historians would have us believe. These clashes, interspersed with localized raiding, sometimes involved sizable forces on both sides but more often than not involved only segments of both populations. Relations were not uniformly hostile. Pecheneg groups, on occasion, were "hired" by the Rus' princes to provide light cavalry for their campaigns. This, along with trade and raiding, was, apparently one of the mainstays of the Pecheneg economy. Thus, in 944 this same Igor' had Pecheneg "allies" in his campaign on Byzantium.

The Byzantines and Poles also made use of Pecheneg auxiliaries, as did the Hungarians. It was in this capacity that the Pecheneg prince, Küre, acting as an ally of Byzantium, killed Sviatoslav of Kiev in 972. In keeping with an old nomadic tradition, he had a drinking goblet fashioned out of his erstwhile

[40] *Géographie d'Aboulféda*, Texte arabe publié d'après les manuscrits de Paris et de Leyde par M. Reinaud et M. Le Bon Mac Guckin de Slane (Paris, 1840), pp. 205, 293.

opponent's skull. In 980, the Pechenegs made their debut in Rus' interprincely feuding. Thereafter, successive nomadic peoples in the south Russian steppes found this to be a lucrative and relatively constant enterprise.

Under Vladimir I (c. 980–1015), who repeatedly fought the Pechenegs, the Rus' state began to erect a series of fortifications on their southern frontier in an effort to contain the nomads. In 1036, the latter mounted a substantial effort against Kiev. They were decisively routed by Iaroslav (1036–54) at the site on which, in commemoration, he later had St. Sophia built. According to the Rus' chronicles, those Pechenegs that were not slain or drowned attempting flight, "have disappeared up to the present day."[41]

The Pechenegs did not entirely disappear from Rus'. Rather, they began to move towards Byzantium's Danubian frontier which they subsequently crossed. In part, this migration was in response to the continuing pressure of the Oghuz who were, in turn being pushed both westward and south into the lands of Islam by the Cumans. Elements of the Oghuz soon began to enter the Pontic steppes where they appear as the Torki in the Rus' chronicles. The Pechenegs continue to be noted in the southwestern Rus' principalities and adjacent regions. When they now figure in Rus' accounts, both here and further east, it is most often as hired bands brought in together with other Turkic groups in the service of one or another local Rus' prince. Sizable Pecheneg elements, along with Oghuz and other nomads, were present in the Chërnye Klobuki (see below) auxiliary forces of nomadic origin in service to the Kievan principality. Our last reference to them in the Rus' annals, *sub anno* 1169 finds them in a service capacity. Thus, from the Rus' perspective, the Pechenegs had been controlled and to a certain extent even harnessed.

Large numbers of Pechenegs, however, had crossed the Danubian frontier. They already had a history of involvement with the peoples of this area dating back to the late 9th century. A Pecheneg raid across the Danube had been repulsed by the still mighty Byzantine empire in 1026. But, following their defeat in 1036 and probably because they had no other choice, considerable groupings of Pechenegs began to congregate on the imperial frontier and then cross the border. In 1048, they devastated Byzantine Bulgaria and continued to plague the Balkan region thereafter. Byzantine attempts to exploit their internal dissensions proved to be ephemeral solutions. As with Kievan Rus', hostilities alternated with periods of peace and cooperation. Pecheneg contingents entered Byzantine service but showed themselves to be highly unreliable. This was demonstrated, with devastating consequences for Constantinople, when they defected to the Saljuq Turks at Manzikert in 1071.

[41] *PSRL*, I, cols. 150–1; *PSRL*, II, col. 139.

The growing enmity between the Byzantines and the Pechenegs led the former to an alliance with the Cumans who now controlled the Pontic steppes. In April 1091, a joint Byzantine–Cuman force dealt a disastrous defeat to the Pechenegs, the effects of which were greatly exacerbated by the Byzantine order to slaughter most of the prisoners taken. This defeat broke much of the Pecheneg power. A last attempt on the Byzantine Balkans was repulsed, again amidst great slaughter, in 1122. Thereafter, the Pechenegs faded, blending in with other Turkic groups. Some made their way to Hungary whither groups of their kinsmen had been going since the 10th century. The bulk of these immigrants, however, probably date to the 11th century which was, as we have seen, largely calamitous for them. As in Rus' they were incorporated into the border-guard system.

We possess only scanty details regarding Pecheneg culture. There are some indications that they, like the Bulghars and Khazars, used a variant of the Türk runiform script. Artifacts from the Pontic steppe with such inscriptions have been ascribed to them[42] but these identifications have not been universally accepted. The remnants of their language appear to be Turkic of the Kipchak or at least Common Turkic variety, although here again, there are dissenting opinions.[43] According to al-Bakrī (d. 1094), the Pechenegs up to the year 400/1009–10, were followers of "the religion of the Magi." This statement may indicate some Zoroastrian or Manichaean influences. It may also refer to a shamanistic cult. After that period, according to our sources, Islam began to make some headway amongst them.[44] Christian efforts to proselytize amongst them led by Bruno of Querfurt (1007) were not successful.

The Oghuz (Torki) in the south Russian steppes

The Oghuz tribes had been concentrated in the Syr Darya–Aral Sea steppes and adjacent areas. It was here that their tribal union took shape in the 8th century. Under their *yabghu*, the Oghuz had been allies of the Khazars against

[42] *See*: A.M. Ščerbak, "Neskol'ko slov o priëmakh čtenija runičeskikh nadpiseĭ naĭdennykh na Donu," *Sovetskaja Arkheologija*, 19 (1954), *Idem*, "Znaki na keramike i kirpičakh iz Sarkela-Beloj Vezhy," *Materialy i issledovanija po Arkheologii SSSR*, No. 75 (1959) and Julius Németh, "The Runiform Inscription from Nagy-Szent-Miklós and the Runiform Scripts of Eastern Europe," *Acta Linguistica Academiae Scientiarum Hungaricae*, 21 (1971).

[43] Julius Németh, *Die Inschriften des Schatzes von Nagy-Szent-Miklós* (Bibliotheca Orientalis Hungarica, 2, Budapest, 1932); György Györffy, "Monuments du lexique Petchénègue," *Acta Orientalia Hungarica*, 18 (1965). For a dissenting view see Omeljan Pritsak, "The Pechenegs, A Case of Social and Economic Transformation," *Archivum Eurasiae Medii Aevi*, 1: 229–30 (1975).

[44] A. Kunik, V. Rozen, *Izvestija al-Bekri i drugikh avtorov o Rusi i slavjanakh*, pts. 1–2 (pt. 1, Supplement to the *Zapiski Imperatorskoĭ Akademii Nauk*, XXXII, 1878), p. 43.

the Pechenegs whom they drove westward. They joined with the Rus' in 965 to invade Khazaria and again in 985 to attack the Volga Bulghars. By this time, however, the Oghuz confederation was experiencing pressure from neighboring tribes and the Islamic states of Central Asia. Concomitant with this were severe and explosive internal tensions. The latter found expression frequently in the religious conflict of Muslim Oghuz warring on their still pagan kinsmen. This was highlighted by the Saljuq movement. This unstable Oghuz union was then hit by a series of shockwaves set off throughout the steppes by the "Qūn migration," beginning c. 1017–18 and probably taking place in several stages. This resulted in the migration of elements of the Oghuz to the south Russian steppes, while others entered the Islamic world.

The Oghuz, called *Tork*, plural *Torki* (**Törk, Türk*) in Eastern Slavic, reappear in the Rus' chronicles *sub anno* 1054 or 1055 after an absence of seventy years. Under this date it is recorded that Vsevolod, brother of Iziaslav who had just taken the throne of Kiev, "marched on the Torki, in wintertime, near Voin, and defeated them."[45] The casual tone of the annalist, who did not feel the need to enter into details, indicates that this was not the first such encounter. Individual Oghuz were probably already present in Rus'. Thus, we find that a certain "Torchin" (i.e. "the Tork") took part in the assassination of prince Gleb in 1015. It is very likely that with the fall of Khazaria, Oghuz groupings had crossed the Volga and were already beginning to penetrate the eastern portions of the Caspo-Pontic steppes, exerting, as we have seen, pressure on the Pechenegs.

The Cumans, who will be discussed below, appeared in the same year as Vsevolod's campaign. The Oghuz movement deeper into the south-Russian steppes is connected with them. In 1060, Prince Iziaslav of Kiev and his brothers Sviatoslav and Vsevolod, "gathering innumerable warriors" staged a land and sea assault on the "Torki." The latter, who were probably now located between the Don and Dnieper, were forced to take flight. Thousands died of hunger, cold and an epidemic which broke out amongst them. By 1064–5, they had reached the Byzantine Danubian frontier. Repulsed here and in 1068 in eastern Hungary, some of the Oghuz remained in the Byzantine borderlands following the familiar pattern of alternately raiding Byzantine lands and finding employment in imperial service. Oghuz units, as with the Pechenegs, defected to the Saljuqs, their fellow tribesmen, at Manzikert. Others returned to the Pontic steppes where together with other nomadic

[45] *PSRL*, I, col. 162; *PSRL*, II, col. 151; *Patriarshaja ili Nikonovskaja letopis': Polnoe sobranie russkikh letopisei*, vols. IX–XIII (Sanktpeterburg, 1862–1904, reprint: Moskva, 1965), IX, p. 91 (where the date is given as 1055).

bands they were organized into border guard units in service to the Kievan state. These were the Chërnye Klobuki. (lit. "Black hoods").

The Chërnye Klobuki evolved out of groups of Torki, Pechenegs and the lesser known tribes or clans of the Berendei, Kui (or Kovui), Turpei and Buty. In the period 1060–1140, they were not formally organized within the Rus' state but were rather nomadic groups that cooperated with the princes of Kiev. At different times various elements of them sought refuge within the confines of Rus' in return for sevice. They came to be largely located within the Kievan principality, although smaller bands existed in the other principalities. After 1140, relations with Kiev evolved into a more formal system entailing both vassal and mercenary elements. It is at this point that we can properly speak of the Chërnye Klobuki *per se*. The Chërnye Klobuki tended to follow whoever sat on the Kievan throne, their loyalty, sometimes shaky, focusing on the office rather than a given individual. Independent nomadic groupings of Torki, Pechenegs and Berendei apparently continued to exist, often serving as mercenaries with the Rus'. A number of towns are associated with the Chërnye Klobuki: Torchesk ("Tork-town") and two towns named after chieftains, Chiurnai and Küldür (Kul'diur'). Iur'ev, on the Ros' river at its confluence with the Ruta, marked the beginning of their territory. Torchesk was probably located south of it.

The Rus' campaign of 1060 was followed by a Cuman attack on Rus' in 1061. In this, the first recorded Cuman–Rus' hostilities, the Kievan princes were defeated. Here again, we may presume a link between the Oghuz encroachments which produced the Rus' response of 1060 and the events of the following year. To round out our picture, we must now look more closely at the nomads who set these events in motion.

The Cumans

There are few problems in the history of the nomads of Eurasia on which more erudition has been expended than that of the origins of the Cumans. Nonetheless, a definitive answer is still not at hand. The form *Cuman* is used here to lessen confusion. It is the most commonly found term in our Greek and Latin sources. In addition, this large tribal union appears as the *Qipchaq* (with variants) in the Muslim and Transcaucasian sources, the *Polovtsy* (from Slavic *polovyi* "yellow, pale, pale-yellow," and probably a translation of Turkic *Quman*) in Rus' sources and taken from there into Western Slavic (*Plauci, Plawci*) and Hungarian (*Palóc*). German sources record: *Falones, Phalagi, Valvi* etc., again, interpretations of the Turkic ethnonym. The same

is true for the Armenian *Khartesh*. Hungarian, in addition, has the more widely used *Kún*.

The Cumans were the westernmost grouping of a large and loosely organized tribal confederation that in time came to extend from Danubian Europe to an ill-defined area deep in the present day Kazakh steppe and Western Siberia. Maḥmūd al-Kāshgharī, writing c. 1076, notes "Kenchek Sengir, the name of a town near Talas. This is the Kipchak border."[46] The borders of this turbulence-prone confederation were rarely stable.

The precise relationship of the Cumans to the Kipchaks is unclear. We are relatively well-informed about the latter. They appear in the eighth century Moyun Chur inscription as the *Türk-Qïbchaq* who were part of the Türk state for fifty years. It has not been definitely established that they are to be identified with the Chüeh-yüeh-shih of the Chinese sources.[47] In all likelihood, they were in the Altai region during the period of the Türk Kaghanate. Subsequent to the collapse of the Türk state, they became part of the Kimek tribal union and with it advanced, or had already progressed, to the Irtysh, Ishim and Tobol river areas. It is here that they first come into the view of the Islamic geographers. Ibn Khurdādhbih, writing in the ninth century but basing himself on earlier materials, indicates that they already held an autonomous position within the Kimek confederation. The tenth century *Ḥudūd al-ʿĀlam*, although indicating that they have separated from the Kimek, notes that "their king is [appointed] on behalf of the Kīmāk."[48]

The Kipchak–Kimeks began to encroach on Oghuz grazing lands to their south during the ninth and tenth centuries, helping thereby to create the internal turmoil that we associate with the Oghuz during this period. As the Oghuz began to move southwest and westward, the Kimek union, now crumbling and probably spearheaded by the Kipchaks, followed in their wake. The city of Sighnāq became the Kipchak urban center in the Syr Darya steppe. Elements of the Kipchaks remained in Siberia while other groups were pushed still further westward in association with the "Qūn migration." As a consequence, three major "Kipchak" groupings came into being: the Kipchaks who entered the south-Russian steppes and extended to the Volga–Ural river region, the Syr Darya Kipchaks who became associated with the

[46] Maḥmūd al-Kashgharī, *Divanü Lûgat-it-Türk*, facs. ed. Besim Atalay (Türk Dil Kurumu, Ankara, 1941), p. 241.

[47] This identification has been advanced in a number of works, *cf.* B.E. Kumekov, *Gosudarstvo kimakov IX–XI vv. po arabskim istočnikam* (Alma-Ata, 1972), p. 43; K.Sh. Šanijazov, *K ètničeskoĭ istorii uzbekskogo naroda* (Istoriko-ètnografičeskoe issledovanie na materialakh kipčakskogo komponenta) (Tashkent, 1974), p. 42.

[48] *Ḥudūd al-ʿĀlam*, trans. Minorsky, p. 101; Ibn Khurdādhbih, ed. de Goeje, p. 31.

state of the Khorezmshahs and the Siberian Kipchaks who would later help to compose the "Siberian Tatars" and whose name still figures in the clan-names of the Altaian Turkic peoples.

A number of researchers have attempted to demonstrate the presence of Mongolian ethno-linguistic elements in this Kipchak–Kimek mass at various stages of its development. The evidence is sketchy and while noting its strong possibility, we must refrain from stating it as an established fact. The Kipchak-Cumans, when they appear fully in the light of our sources and judging from the language monuments left behind, such as the *Codex Cumanicus*, appear as a Turkic-speaking people.

It was the "Qūn migration" that brough the Kipchak-Cumans to the south-Russian steppes. As the Hungarian term for Cuman is Kún, the "Qūn" mentioned in our Islamic sources are presumed to be the Cumans. The events of this migration have been preserved in al-Marwazī (writing c. 1120). He recounts that the "Qūn" people came from the northern Chinese borderlands, the "land of Qitay." They migrated from this region out of fear of the Kitan ruler and a shortage of grazing land. They were then evicted from their new pasturelands by the "Qāy" people. This caused them to enter the territory of the "Shāri" or "Sāri" people, causing the latter to migrate to the land of the Türkmen. These, in turn, went to the eastern Oghuz lands. The Oghuz then moved into the Pecheneg lands in the Pontic steppes.[49]

The *dramatis personae* can be identified with certainty only when they reach the Turkic nomads and Islamicized Turks on the borders of the Muslim world. As a consequence, the identity and ethnic affiliations of the Qūn, Qāy and Shārī/Sārī, despite numerous efforts at explication, remain unknown. Clearly, the Qūn ultimately reached the south Russian steppes, although this is not stated anywhere in our sources. Similarly, the Qāy, or elements of them arrived in the Pontic steppes where the Rus' chronicles attest their presence as the Kaepichi, i.e. "sons of the Qay," a russified rendering of a tribal or clan name *Qay-oba.

The first waves of this large-scale nomadic movement were registered in the Karakhanid realm in 1017–18. In addition to our Islamic sources, Syriac and Armenian authors have preserved the outlines of what must have been a massive migration, or more probably a series of migrations. Beginning in the early 11th century, the reverberations of this movement could be felt decades later. We cannot ascertain whether the Cumans conquered the Kipchaks or simply represent this mass of largely Kipchak-Turkic speaking tribes in the

[49] *Sharāf al-Zaman Tahir Marvazī on China, the Turks and India*, ed., trans. V.F. Minorsky (London, 1942), Arab text, p. 18.

West. They came into view, suddenly as we have seen, in 1054–5. The only certain "victim" of the migration was the Kimek ascendancy in the steppes. The Kimek tribal union dissolved and re-grouped under Kipchak–Cuman leadership. Kimek tribal elements continued to be represented amongst them. Thus, the Rus' annals mention the "Yemek Cumans" who were active in the region of Volga Bulgharia. Yemek, Imek in Islamic authors, is a variant of Kimek.[50]

The Cuman steppe, the Dasht-i Qipchāq of our Persian sources and the Polovetskoe Pole of the Rus' annalists, was divided into five tribal or supra-tribal zones: (1) the Central Asian-Kazakhistan region, (2) the Volga–Ural river mesopotamia, (3) the Don river region, (4) the Dnieper river region, (5) the Danubian region. Further subdivisions may be seen in the terms "White" and "Black" Cumania used by al-Idrisī and Simon of Kéza. "White Cumania" may have denoted the Dniester–Dnieper region while "Black Cumania" was perhaps located on the Severskij Donets.

The Rus' distinguished between "Wild" and "Non-Wild" Cumans, the latter being those tribes or units with which they had close political ties and some degree of cooperation. The "Non-Wild" Cumans appear[51] to have been composed of the Burchevichi, a Kipchak tribe elements of which were found in the Mamlūk state (*Burch-oghlu*) and in Hungary (the Kun clan of the Borchol), the Ulashevichi (*Ulash-oghlu*), the Olaas of Hungary, the Itliareva chad' or people of Itoglyi (*It-oghli*), the Itoba of the Mamlūk state and the Urusobichi (*Urusoba*). Other Cuman tribal names that figure in our Rus' sources are: Toksobichi (Mamluk *Ṭoqsoba*), (*I*) *Chitieevichi*, *Kolobichi*, *Etebichi*, *Ter'trobichi* (cf. Bulgarian dynasty of Cuman origin: Terter), *Olperliueve* (*Ölperlü*), *Elobichi*, *Emiakovie* (Yemek).

Cuman towns tended to be named after their khans and hence names could and did change. Thus, the city of Sharukan, a famous Cuman khan, appears as Sharukan, Osenev, Sharuk and Cheshuev. Other towns were Sugrov and Balin.

The absence of a strong, centralized authority so evident in Pecheneg history was equally true of the Cumans. The late 12th-century Jewish traveller, Petaḥia of Ratisbon, who journeyed through Cumania, notes that they "have no king, only princes and noble families."[52] This freedom of action for

[50] Tibor Halasi-Kun, "Orta-Kipçakça *q-*, *k-* ~ Ø meselesi" ("The Problem of Middle Kipchak *q-*, *k-* ~ O"), *Türk Dili ve Tarihi Hakkında Araştırmalar*, ed. Hasan Eren, Tibor Halasi-Kun (Ankara, 1950), I, pp. 52–53.

[51] Omeljan Pritsak, "Non-wild Polovtsians," *To Honor Roman Jakobson* (The Hague–Paris, 1967), 2 volumes, II, pp.1615–23. On the "Wild Cumans" see Peter B. Golden "The 'Polovci Dikii'" *Harvard Ukrainian Studies*, 3–4: 296–309 (1979–80).

[52] *The Travels of Rabbi Petachia of Ratisbon*, ed. trans. A. Benisch (London, 1856), Hebrew text p. 4, translation p. 5.

the various Cuman khans led to very varied and complicated relations with neighboring states. Cuman–Rus' relations were particularly involved, alternating periods of local raiding with large-scale offensives. Conflicts could be very limited, pitting one khan against one Rus' prince, or pan-Rus'–pan-Cuman affairs. Further complications were produced by the marriage alliances that frequently took place. Cuman khans became thus deeply embroiled in the inter-princely feuds of the Rus' princes, not a few of whom were their nephews of grandsons.

As devastating as some of the raids were, we see very little in the way of attempts to conquer and possess sedentary lands. The mutual and frequent raiding that sometimes led to full-scale war, was largely attributable to the conflict of two very different economic systems. The Eastern Slavs sought to bring more and more land under cultivation, including steppe areas while the nomads looked upon local raiding as an integral part of their economy. After their takeover of the steppe zone, we cannot point to any major Cuman seizures, particularly in settled regions. The attachment of the Cumans to their steppes is illustrated by the tale preserved in the Rus' chronicles, of Otrok, son of Sharukan, who was forced to retreat to the North Caucasian steppes by the vigorous and aggressive policies of Vladimir Monomakh (d. 1125). Here, Otrok, in 1118, entered the service of the Georgian king, Davit' Aghmashenebeli (1089–1125) who married his daughter. After the death of Vladimir Monomakh, emissaries arrived from Otrok's kinsmen urging him to return. He agreed to do so after smelling *eyevshan*, the grass of his native steppe, giving up the security and fame he had won in Georgia.

With the elimination of the Oghuz–Torki as serious competitors by 1070, the Cumans now became the masters of the entire south Russian steppe zone. This area still contained Pecheneg, Tork and other nomadic elements who were, unwillingly for the most part, incorporated into the Cuman union. In the Danubian Byzantine borderlands, they briefly collaborated with the Pechenegs whom they subsequently helped to destroy. They were also involved in Hungarian and Galician Rus' affairs. Early Cuman settlements in Hungary probably date to this period. Hostilities with the Rus' state began in 1061. In 1068, the combined forces of the Rus' princes were defeated at the river Al'ta. This coincided with the movement of a number of Oghuz–Torki from Cuman to Rus' overlordship, part of the process of the creation of the Chërnye Klobuki.

Cuman raids into Byzantine, Hungarian and Rus' territories are recorded throughout the period 1070–1100. In 1078 the Cumans first actively became involved in Rus' inter-princely feuding, one of the most consistent features of their relationship with the Kievan state. Although this aspect of their relations

with neighboring states can be seen as well in Hungary and Byzantium, it was never as extensive nor as profound as in Rus'. In 1091, as we have seen, they participated in the slaughter of the Pechenegs. This was the heyday of the great khans, Altunopa, Tugorkan, Sharukan the Elder and Boniak. The Rus' principality of Pereiaslav, in particular, suffered considerable damage. In 1101, a Cumano-Rus' peace was established at Sakov. It proved to be short-lived and in 1103 the combined Rus' forces under Sviatopolk II and Vladimir Monomakh undertook a large-scale expedition against the nomads. Some twenty khans were killed in the ensuing battle. Other Pecheneg and Tork groups were "liberated" and incorporated into the Rus' border-guard system. In 1109, Vladimir Monomakh again penetrated deep into Cuman lands, capturing "1,000 tents." Campaigns followed in 1111, 1113, 1116, marking a serious Rus' offensive and resulting in the retreat of Otrok's horde to the Caucasus and the incorporation of still other Pechenegs and Torki into Rus' service.

As Cuman activities in Rus' decreased, until the death of Vladimir Monomakh in 1125, there are reports of Cuman raids on Byzantine Balkan possessions and Volga Bulgharia. At the same time, the 40,000 Cuman troops of Davit' Aghmashenebeli helped to make Georgia the most powerful kingdom of the region. The Rus' interprincely feuds resumed in 1128 and the Cuman khans, many of whom now had blood ties with the contestants, were again actively involved. Thus, Iurii Dolgorukii of Suzdal' made use of Sevinch (d. 1151), son of the famous Boniak, in his struggles in the south. Sevinch, according to our Rus' sources, expressed the desire to plant his sword in the golden gate of Kiev as his illustrious father had done. The Cuman aspects of the internecine warfare in Rus' could often have Caucasian, Balkan and Danubian European implications.

By the late 1160s, Cuman raids, large and small, had become annual affairs in Rus'. This pressure, which affected trade routes to the Black Sea and Constantinople, forced the Rus' princes to again attempt concerted action. The successful offensives of 1166–9, however, were cut short by Andrei Bogoliubskii, the son of Iurii Dolgorukii and a Cuman princess, who seized Kiev in 1169 and installed Gleb Iur'evich as his creature there. The latter brought in "Wild" Cumans as well as Tork and Berendei units. Later, the Chernigov princes, warring with Kiev and Suzdal', attempted to use the horde of Könchek located in the Donets–Don region. The Chernigovian–Cuman army suffered a disasterous defeat in 1180; Eltut, Könchek's brother, dying in battle. These alliances were short-lived for in 1183, Rus' forces defeated a large Cuman army capturing khan Köbek (Kobiak), his sons and other

notables. Könchek's attempted counter-stroke ended in negotiations. It was in this context that the 1185 campaign, quite minor in scale, of prince Igor' Sviatoslavich of Novgorod-Seversk, took place. This campaign has been immortalized in the "Tale of Igor's Host" (*Slovo o polku Igoreve*), which accurately reflects the status of Cuman–Rus; relations, both military and cultural.

The confusing and ever-changing pattern of raids and counter-raids indicates that both the Cumans and the Rus' were rarely if ever able to gain the internal unity needed to deal a fatal blow. Indeed, with the possible exception of Könchek, the very notion of doing so may have been foreign to their thinking. Könchek and his son Iurii (whose Russian name may indicate his conversion to Christianity) endeavored to create a more cohesive force out of the various Cuman groups. Könchek, who, as the son of Otrok, had his grudges, is credited with the introduction of certain technological improvements such as Greek fire and a special bow which required 50 men to operate. Clearly, he was contemplating serious military action aimed at urban centers. He was, perhaps, amongst the Cumans who aided Riurik Rostislavich's seizure and sack of Kiev in 1202. Könchek, however, faced domestic enemies as well, a rival khan Kza and Cuman unity proved to be as elusive as that of the Rus'.

Wherever these developments might have led, they were cut short by the appearance of the Mongols. Iurii Konchakovich whom the Rus' annalists noted as "greater than all the Cumans,"[53] died in a skirmish preceding the battle on the Kalka in 1223. Here, a Mongol raiding column led by Jebe and Sübetei defeated combined Cuman–Rus' forces. Mongol efforts against the Cumans were renewed in 1229–30 and in 1237 Rus' and the south Russian steppes were invaded.

Some Cuman elements under Khan Köten (Kotian), fled to Hungary in 1238–9, where other Cuman groups had earlier settled. In the early thirteenth century, Hungary, with Papal encouragement, had become very interested in Cuman affairs. In 1227, Robert, the Archbishop of Esztergom was named papal legate in "Cumania" to follow up on earlier successes of Dominican monks in converting the Cumans to the east of Hungary. Again some successes were scored and the Cumans were brought into Hungarian service. In 1228 a Cumanian bishopric was established. Undoubtedly in partial response to these developments, Béla IV (1235–70) added "King of the Cumans" to his titles. He was deeply interested in steppe affairs (hence the

[53] *PSRL*, I, col. 504.

mission to "Magna Hungaria") as part of his defence policy against the Mongols. Köten came to Hungary and was converted. He was murdered in Pest in 1241, probably because the Hungarian magnates feared that the Cuman army gave the crown too powerful a weapon. Many Cumans fled but returned after the Mongols had left the region. They were settled in Greater and Lesser Cumania (Nagy Kunság, Kis Kunság) and together with the Iranian Alan–As elements that had migrated with them, were subsequently magyarized.

The mass of Cumano-Kipchaks, however, did not flee. The Mongols, taking advantage of the fragmentation of power that had been the dominant feature of Cuman political life, incorporated the latter into their empire. The large number of Kipchak tribesmen thus brought into the Golden Horde gave it an overwhelmingly Turkic coloration. The land, as Islamic authors noted, had prevailed over the conquerors.

11

The establishment and dissolution of the Türk empire

In the 540s there appeared on the Chinese horizon a people previously barely known which, within a few years, not only changed the balance of power in Mongolia – the traditional basis of great, nomad empires – but also introduced into the scene of Inner Asian and world history an ethnic and linguistic entity which in earlier times could not be identified or isolated from other groups showing the same cultural characteristics. It bore the name Türk, an appellation left in legacy to most later peoples speaking a Turkic language. It stands to reason that the Türks of Mongolia were not the products of spontaneous generation and that one must, by necessity, reckon with other Turks living there or elsewhere in centuries preceding the foundation of the empire bearing their name. Yet, such considerations notwithstanding, it should not be lost from sight that the Türks are the first people to whom we can attribute with certainty a Turkic text written in a Turkic language, and that their name – so widely used ever since their rise to power – cannot be traced with absolute certainty before the sixth century A.D.

Early mentions of Türks

It could be that the first mention of the name Türk was made in the middle of the first century A.D. Pomponius Mela (I,116) refers to the Turcae in the forests north of the Azov Sea, and Pliny the Elder in his *Natural History* (VI, 19) gives a list of peoples living in the same area among whom figure the Tyrcae. Usually this information is discarded with the argument that the forms are corrupt, and reflect the Herodotian *'Ιυρκαι* (IV.22) located in the same region, a possible explanation but not more likely than its converse, to wit, that Herodotus has the wrong form. The argument most often heard against the identification – namely that the Latin forms cannot be correct because Turks appear much later and in a different part of the world – is fallacious, a school-example of *petitio principii*. Another, perhaps far-

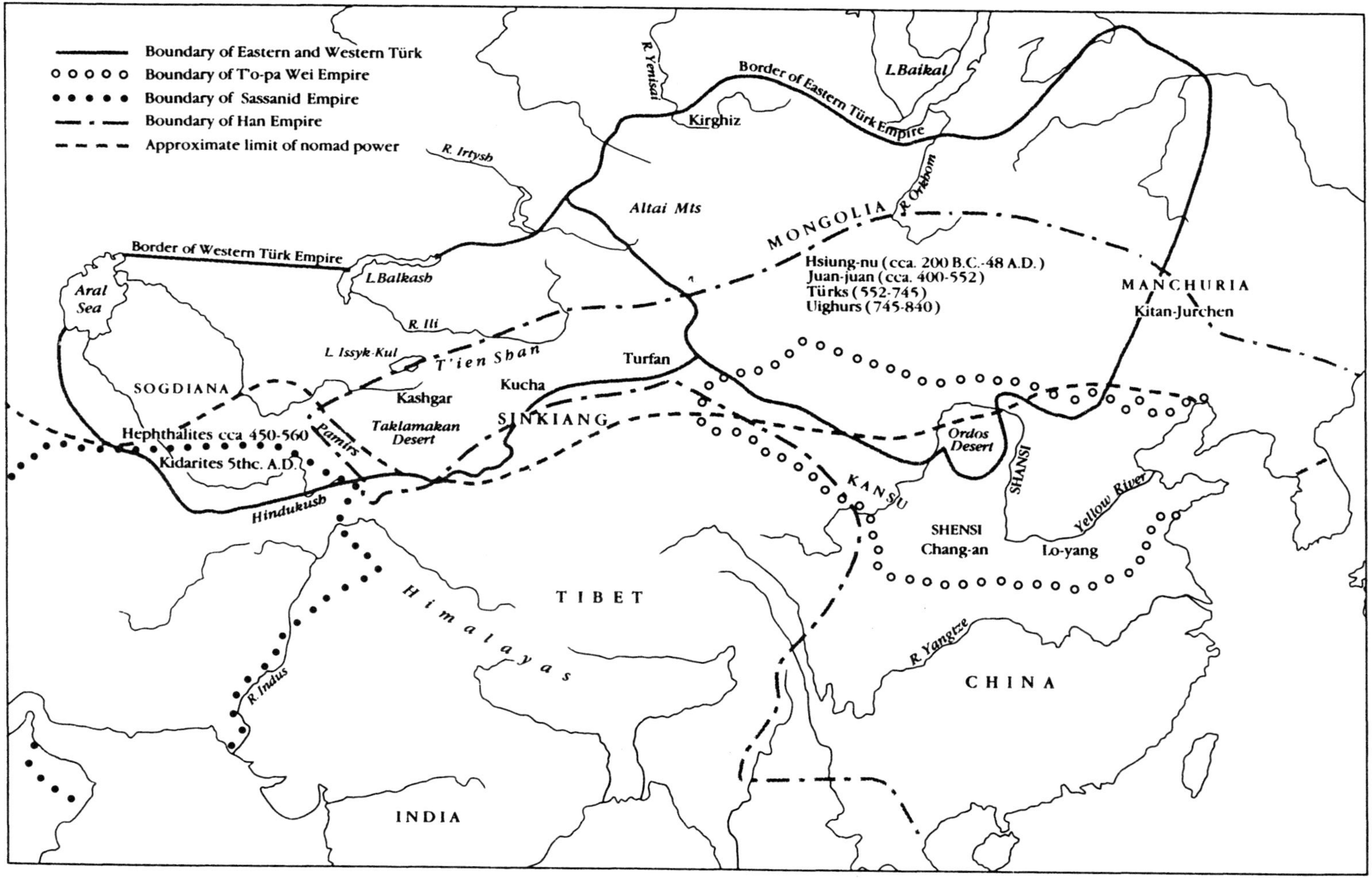
Boundary of Eastern and Western Türk
Boundary of T'o-pa Wei Empire
Boundary of Sassanid Empire
Boundary of Han Empire
Approximate limit of nomad power
R. Yenisai
L.Baikal
Border of Eastern Türk Empire
Kirghiz
R. Irtysh
R. Orkhon
Altai Mts
MONGOLIA
Border of Western Türk Empire
L.Balkash
Hsiung-nu (cca. 200 B.C.-48 A.D.)
Juan-juan (cca. 400-552)
Türks (552-745)
Uighurs (745-840)
MANCHURIA
Kitan-Jurchen
Aral Sea
R. Ili
L. Issyk-Kul
T'ien Shan
Turfan
SOGDIANA
Kucha
Kashgar
Taklamakan Desert
SINKIANG
Pamirs
Hephthalites cca 450-560
Kidarites 5thc. A.D.
Ordos Desert
SHANSI
KANSU
Hindukush
Yellow River
SHENSI
Chang-an
Lo-yang
Himalayas
TIBET
R. Indus
R. Yangtze
CHINA
INDIA

fetched, possibility would be that the Latin authors emended the Greek name to a form familiar to them through other sources. I see no compelling reason to impugn the Latin data. The presence of Turkic-speaking peoples in the Pontic steppe and in the forest belt to the north of it is well established in the fifth century – i.e., well before the Türks' appearance in Mongolia – and Mela's information would simply testify to such presence at an earlier period.

Another pre-Türk reference to Turks may be found in the ninth century *Chronicle* of Ṭabarī. According to him, during the reign of the Sassanid king Bahrām V (420–38), the kaghan of the Turks, at the head of an army of 250,000, invaded Persian territory but his expedition of conquest failed and he himself was killed in battle.[1] Ṭabarī's text – even when complemented by other Arabic sources – does not provide unambiguous information concerning the location of the attack (Khorasan or Sogdiana are the most likely places), nor is there any certainty about the identification of the people called "Turk" by the author. From our present point of view the key question is whether the Turks mentioned in the text were really Turks (perhaps even Türks), or whether we must assume that the historian is guilty of anachronism, projecting into the past an ethnonym he was familiar with. While one cannot completely exclude such a possibility, it is clear that the opposite practice – that of using archaic names for contemporary foreign peoples – is much more common. Be that as it may, the most frequent objection, that "one cannot speak of Turks at such an early date" begs the question and should be rejected.

Origin of Türks; Türk subgroups

Chinese data concerning the origin of the Türks (*T'u-chüeh* in the modern transcription of the Chinese characters used for their names) are contradictory and difficult to interpret. The earliest source, the *Chou shu*, records two traditions.[2] The first of these sees in the Türks the descendants of the Hsiung-nu, a statement that may or may not be accurate. The Chinese were just as prone to link any northern Barbarian with the Hsiung-nu as Byzantine historians were to see Scythians (or later: Huns) in their western counterparts. According to another tradition reported by the same source, the Türks' ancestors originated in the state of So, to the north of the Hsiung-nu. The character *so* designating this people has the meaning of "rope; to bind," and

[1] Th. Nöldeke, 1879, p. 99.

[2] Chapter 50. For a translation of most texts concerning the Eastern Türks see Liu Mau-Tsai, 1958. For the Western Türks the masterpiece of Chavannes, 1903 remains unsurpassed.

the So are called *So-t'ou*, i.e., "So-heads," a term referring to their hair-style. Shiratori[3] refers to them as "Corded Heads" and remarks that they were so called "because of the likeness of their queues to cords." That they wore their hair long (loose or braided) is beyond doubt. The So are linked with the Tabgach (T'o-pa in conventional Chinese transcription) and – through them – with the Hsien-pi whose main group was probably Mongol-speaking. In the *Shi shu* the Türks are said to be mixed Hu from P'ing-liang. Unfortunately the term "Hu" is open to two interpretations: it may be used as a generic for "Barbarians," or, specifically, may designate the Sogdians.

All this is rather nebulous and confusing and allows for only one certain conclusion, namely that the Chinese possessed contradictory evidence concerning the origin of the Türks, and that they were well aware of this fact. Strong corroborative evidence is provided by the Türk ancestral legends noted by the Chinese.[4] There are three versions, showing but a minimal thematic overlap. The differences between them are so essential that these legends cannot possibly be taken to reflect tribal, let along national, tradition. One ethnic entity cannot have several, differing traditions concerning its own origin. Even the *Chou shu* – where two of the three legends are given – remarks on their divergence and comments that they agree only in that in both versions the Türks are said to descend from a she-wolf. The third version gives a story entirely different. Undoubtedly, the Chinese records reflect contemporary information obtained from some Türks and there is no reason to question their authenticity. These legends reflect traditions held by peoples who, from the Chinese point of view, were all Türks (i.e., they lived within the Türk state) but whose own traditions differed from one another.

Historical evidence seems to support the testimony of the legends. Two preliminary questions may be asked. Firstly, was the Türk state ethnically or culturally homogeneous, or, to put it differently, were all those living within its boundaries Türks? Secondly, can we assume that some Türks – and here we mean peoples *called* Türks – lived outside the Türk state, or, if within the empire, did not belong to its ruling stratum? The course of Türk history to be outlined later in this chapter will answer the first of these questions in the negative. The second question – seldom if ever asked in previous research – calls for a nuanced reply.

It is often overlooked that Chinese sources mention more than one Türk (T'u-chüeh) people. Thus they speak of the White Clothed Türks (Pai-fu

[3] Kurakichi Shiratori, "The queue among the peoples of North Asia," *Memoirs of the Research Department of the Toyo Bunko*, 4 (1929), 1–69, p. 1¿2.

[4] A detailed study on the subject: Sinor, 1982.

T'u-chüeh), of the Yellow Head Türks (Huang-t'ou T'u-chüeh), of Skiing Türks (literally Wooden Horse Türks, Mu-ma T'u-chüeh), of Ox-hooved Türks (Niu-t'i T'u-chüeh). The latter were a northern people, living in a very cold country, who were said to have human bodies but the feet of oxen. Somewhat surprisingly, a Tibetan source not only corroborates the Chinese data but also gives the Turkic name of this strange people (*ud qadaqlï* – "ox-footed"). Whatever the origin of their name – which is probably the basis of the legend attached to them – this was a real, as opposed to a mythical, people, probably of the northern (sub-arctic?) regions where the Skiing Türks are also to be located. It would appear that the Chinese knew of what we may call Türk splinter groups, ethnically and linguistically similar to or identical with the Türks proper, but living either on the fringes or beyond the borders of the centrally governed Türk states.[5]

Important differentiations are apparent also among the subjects ruled by the kaghan. First of all there is the clear, but basically administrative and not tribal, dichotomy between Eastern (also called Northern) and Western Türks. Most of the time the latter were divided into two tribal confederations, the Nu-shih-pi and the Tu-lu, each of which consisted of five tribes. We are informed of murderous conflicts opposing "black" and "yellow" tribes, and the Türk inscriptions speak of the Blue Türks, a name not mentioned in Chinese sources. The Toquz Oghuz, the Nine Clans (Chiu hsing) of the Chinese – a confederation of T'ieh-lê tribes – is on occasion called Türk (Chiu hsing T'u-chüeh); there are groups such as the Türks of Mo-cho, or of the *shan-yü* (title of the Hsiung-nu ruler of old, Shan-yü T'u-chüeh), and then, to boot, there are the many peoples such as the Türgesh, the Karluk, and the Uighur, from time to time submissive at other times hostile to the Türks. It stands to reason that groups such as those just listed were constituted on the bases of different criteria. But it is probably safe to assume that they were all Türks (in a sense that Bavarians, Saxons, and Prussians are all Germans), though their civilization was certainly heterogeneous. For at least three of the Türk groups – the Shan-yü, Ox-footed, and Skiing Türks – there is evidence to show that they were forest dwellers, maintaining themselves through fishing and hunting, and living outside the mainstream of the political tussles of the Türk state.

The question may be asked whether all these groups spoke the same language. The Orkhon inscriptions, engraved in the mid eighth century, are certainly Turkic – we refer to their language as Old Turkic, but one may as

[5] Cf. Sinor, 1985.

well call it Türk – and there is no reason to believe that at least the bulk of those who were called Türk used a different language. For example, the *Chiu T'ang shu* clearly states that the languages spoken by respectively the Eastern and Western Türks are only "slightly different." There is, however, some evidence to show that the Türk state incorporated some non-Turkic peoples whose languages left traces in Türk proper names and even in the vocabulary of Türk.

The sources contain a great number of Türk personal names. They appear in a variety of scripts and languages – Chinese, Greek, Sogdian, and, of course, Türk – and sometimes it is possible to recognize the same name in sources written in different languages. The problem caused by the Chinese transcription of foreign names is well known. Yet, difficulties notwithstanding, the reconstruction of the original rendered in Chinese characters is quite often successful, particularly when the native names or other terms are otherwise known, or when the language to which they belong can be identified. On occasion, the reconstruction of the original form of a Türk name given in Chinese transcription causes no major difficulty, as for instance in the case of Ishtemi, the co-founder of the Türk state, whose name is transcribed by the Chinese as Shih-tieh-mi. This name, however, points to a curious problem. In the Türk inscriptions of the Orkhon the name is spelt either with or without the initial *i*-, thus *ištmi* or *štmi*, and Byzantine sources give it in the form Stembis (Στεμβισχάγαν). There is no reason for the Romans to drop an initial *i*-, while there are good reasons why the Türks should put a prosthetic vowel before a consonant cluster such as *st*-, with which no Turkic or Altaic word can begin. We thus are bound to conclude that one of the founding fathers of the Türk empire had a non-Turkic name. The name of Bumin – Ishtemi's co-ruler – is not Turkic either, and it remains unexplained why the Chinese transcribe his name with an initial *t*-: T'u-men. Of the fifty odd names given to Türk rulers in Chinese sources, only a handful have Turkic equivalents and even fewer are genuinely Turkic. The same can be said of the Türk personal names appearing in Byzantine sources. Few of them are identifiably Turkic and in two cases (one of them being that of Stembis) a Turkic origin cannot even be envisaged. Yet it is certain that at least the Türk ruling class in the mid-eighth century (to which the Orkhon inscriptions belong) was Turkic-speaking.

Since, as we shall see, the Türk state replaced that of the Juan-juan, it would be tempting – and probably correct – to assume that the Juan-juan language continued in use among the subjects of the newly formed Türk empire. Unfortunately we do not know what Juan-juan was like. In spite of repeated

attempts to reconstruct them on the basis of Chinese transcriptions, Juan-juan proper names show no trace of being Turkic, nor can they consistently be explained from Mongol. It is probably safe to say that within the perimeter of the Juan-juan state a number of partly unrelated languages were in use, and that the Türks, together with the political power, inherited the linguistic status quo. Scattered but convincing data support such a hypothesis.

The inscriptions of the Orkhon, written in Türk in rune-type characters, contain a number of words not common to Turkic but with parallels in Samoyed or Ugric languages from which, directly or indirectly, they had to be borrowed. These include a word for "horse" (*yunt*), surely of capital importance in everyday usage. There is also the Chinese transcription of the word used by the Kirghiz to denote the special kind of iron said to be collected after rainfalls. It must have sounded **qaša*, a close parallel to the word **qošu* used for "iron" by Mongol-speaking Kitans which survived in the archaic Mongol dialect spoken by the Dahurs in Manchuria and the Selkup Samoyeds in Siberia. Clearly, it is a Paleosiberian substratum word, otherwise unknown in the Altaic languages, one which constitutes a valuable indication of the multilingual composition of the Türk state.

As witnessed by the Bugut inscription, the role of the Sogdians within the Türk state ensured a prominent status for their language. It is safe to assume that it was widely used in commerce and in other international contacts.

Türks and the Juan-juan

The Türks built their empire on the ruins of that of the Juan-juan. The destruction came from within, not in the wake of an invasion, and differentiation in concrete terms between victors and vanquished is by no means easy. Beyond providing the names of successive Juan-juan rulers and a dreary enumeration of military campaigns, both offensive and defensive, Chinese sources contain little information of real interest on the people that was the major power in Inner Asia for at least a century and a half. If for no other reason than that of better understanding the genesis of Türk power, a short conspectus of Juan-juan history must be given here.

We do not even know the real name of the Juan-juan. The form used here and in the majority of serious works dealing with them is but the conventional transcription of the Chinese characters most often used to transcribe their name. The variety of Chinese efforts to render the Juan-juan self-appellation shows the difficulty of the undertaking. Peremptory assertions to the contrary notwithstanding, no solid evidence exists concerning the language or lan-

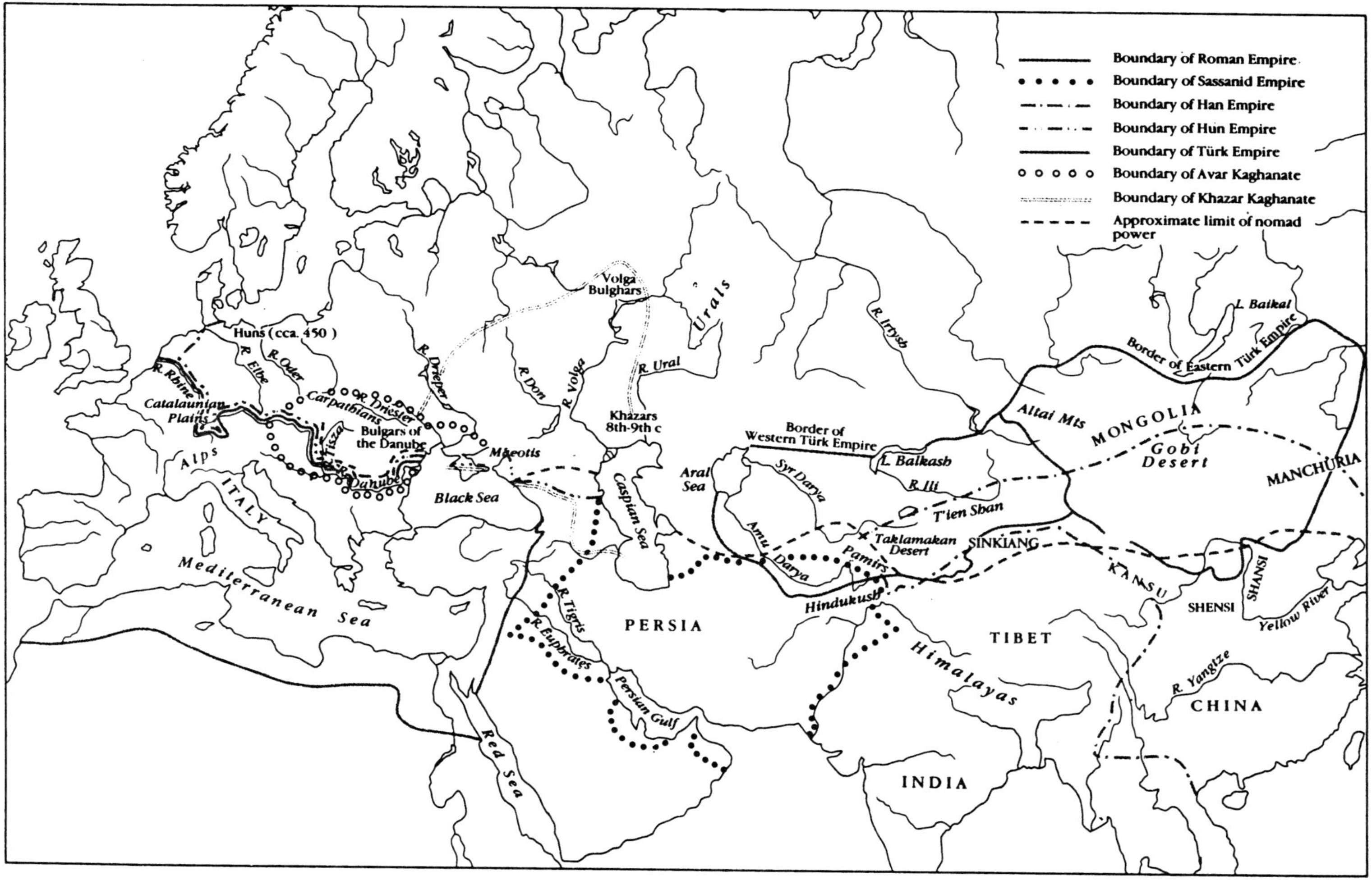
Boundary of Roman Empire
Boundary of Sassanid Empire
Boundary of Han Empire
Boundary of Hun Empire
Boundary of Türk Empire
Boundary of Avar Kaghanate
Boundary of Khazar Kaghanate
Approximate limit of nomad power
Huns (cca. 450)
R. Rhine
R. Elbe
R. Oder
Catalaunian Plains
Carpathians
R. Driester
R. Drieper
Tisza
Bulgars of the Danube
Danube
Alps
ITALY
Mediterranean Sea
Black Sea
Maeotis
R. Don
R. Volga
Volga Bulghars
Urals
R. Ural
Khazars 8th-9th c
Caspian Sea
R. Tigris
R. Euphrates
Persian Gulf
Red Sea
PERSIA
Aral Sea
Syr Darya
Amu Darya
Border of Western Türk Empire
L. Balkash
R. Ili
R. Irtysh
T'ien Shan
Taklamakan Desert
Pamirs
Hindukush
SINKIANG
Himalayas
TIBET
INDIA
Altai Mts
MONGOLIA
Gobi Desert
Border of Eastern Türk Empire
L. Baikal
MANCHURIA
KANSU
SHENSI
SHANSI
Yellow River
R. Yangtze
CHINA

guages used by the Juan-juan, and their ethnic appurtenance is equally obscure. Some Chinese sources view them as "another kind of Hsiung-nu" (and we have remarked on the value to be set on this type of a statement) while others attach them to the Tung Hu, i.e., the Eastern Barbarians.

Throughout their history the Juan-juan were locked in virtually unceasing combat with the Northern Wei dynasty of China (386–534). Contemporary hostilities may even have been projected into the distant past with the assertion that the ancestor of the Juan-juan was a slave taken prisoner by the ancestor of the Wei in 277. The Juan-juan emerged into the limelight during the reign of T'o-pa Kui, founder (386–409) of the Northern Wei, when their chief She-lun united into one federation the tribes obeying him and those commanded by his uncle. He then defeated the people of the "high chariots," the Kao-chü (or Kao-ch'ê) of north-western Mongolia, and established an empire which extended from Karashahr in the west as far east as northern Korea.

In subsequent years the Juan-juan repeatedly attacked the Wei, compelling them to erect a defensive wall some two thousand *li* long. In 429 an alliance between the Kao-chü and the T'o-pa (Tabgach) led to the defeat of the Juan-juan kaghan Ta-t'an (415–29) who, in consequence, seems to have lost his reason, dying soon afterward. In his name some wish to see the ethnonym Tatar. It was under his rule – and, apparently, because of the uncleanliness of his people – that the previously friendly relationship between the Juan-juan and their western neighbors, the Yüeh-pan, turned sour. The ruler of the latter, with his retinue, decided to pay a visit to Ta-t'an but, according to the *Wei shu*, as he entered Juan-juan territory he was horrified by the filth in which the people lived: they never washed their hands or their garments, and the womanfolk cleaned the plates by licking them. Expressing his disgust in insults, the Yüeh-pan ruler retraced his steps, and enmity resulted from this social call gone awry. The anecdote may well be the earliest mention of the dirtiness of some Inner Asian peoples that was to shock so many later travelers. It should, however, also be noted in this context that our sources emphasize the cleanliness of the Yüeh-pan, who are said to have taken three baths a day.

Following the traditions of Chinese diplomacy, always in search of an ally in the rear of the Inner Asian foe, the Wei attempted to look for one in the western regions. An embassy sent for this purpose by the emperor T'ai-wu, while crossing territory controlled by the Juan-juan, was forced to turn back. Perhaps to avenge themselves, in 438 the Chinese launched a major offensive which, however, achieved nothing. Following nomad strategies described

already by Herodotus, the Juan-juan ruler Wu-t'i (429–44) refused to engage his troops, and the enemy, plagued by drought and lack of fodder, had to withdraw without having achieved its purpose. In 443 a similar expedition met a similar fate, though on this occasion the Wei army advanced as far as the Orkhon river. This time the cold and not the heat was the cause of the heavy losses suffered by the invading army. More successful was the campaign led in 448 by the emperor T'ai-wu, who joined forces with the Yüeh-pan and inflicted a crushing defeat on the Juan-juan ruler T'u-ho-chen (444–50).

On the whole, and in spite of temporary setbacks suffered mainly when engaged in offensive warfare, the Wei contained Juan-juan encroachment upon Chinese land. Barred in this direction, the Juan-juan sought compensation in the Tarim basin, where they repeatedly interfered in the affairs of local kingdoms. Of particular interest is their attack in 460 against Kocho, which brought about the death of its ruler An-chou, and thus the end of the illustrious Chü-ch'ü dynasty said to be of Hsiung-nu origin. In 471 the Juan-juan occupied the city-state of Khotan, a most important station on the southern east–west trade route which they endeavored to control. The local ruler, well aware of the danger of an impending attack, had asked for Chinese help to avert it. Though sympathetic, the emperor in his reply insisted on the impossibility of offering effective help to a country so far away.

Early in the 6th century internal strife greatly weakened the cohesion of the Juan-juan state and led, ultimately, to its disintegration. Ch'ou-nu kaghan (508–20) – his position shaken because of his attachment to a female shaman – was murdered, apparently on the orders of his own mother, who then had her younger son A-na-kui enthroned. Not everyone welcomed the action and, having been attacked and defeated by partisans of the late Ch'ou-nu, A-na-kui fled to the Wei court, where he requested and obtained help. In the meanwhile, back at home, his uncle Brahman sat on the vacant throne. The name of the usurper, given in Chinese transcription as P'o-lo-men, is somewhat surprising and cannot readily be explained. In Wei times it was usually applied to the inhabitants of Northern India. After a renewed attack by the Kao-chü, Brahman had to seek refuge with the Wei, who thus provided asylum to two contending Juan-juan rulers. In a shrewd move they helped both. A-na-kui was given support to establish himself in the region of the Silver Mountain (Yin Shan), between Turfan and Karashahr, while Brahman was installed near the Kokonor. There was thus little danger of the two Juan-juan factions uniting. In an attempt to break his isolation Brahman established links with the Hephthalites, about whom much will be said later on. Their ruler married simultaneously three of Brahman's daughters, a rather surprising match in

view of the Hephthalites' alleged practice of polyandry. Displeased, the Chinese had him interned; he died in Lo-yang in 524, and A-na-kui remained the sole ruler of the Juan-juan. It is difficult to know how much real power he wielded, but he skilfully exploited the internal difficulties of the rapidly disintegrating Wei state. He established matrimonial relations with both the Eastern and Western Wei, and at times was an effective power broker between contending Chinese factions. In the process, A-na-kui probably neglected to pay sufficient attention to developments taking place in his own back yard.

In 546 the T'ieh-lê – a tribal confederation first mentioned in the fourth century – were about to attack the Juan-juan. According to the *Sui shu* they too were descended from the Hsiung-nu and, in the sixth century, their numerous tribes formed an uninterrupted chain reaching from the "Western Sea" to the Baikal. They were somehow connected with the Kao-chü and – as we shall see – the powerful Uighurs were themselves a T'ieh-lê tribe. There can be no doubt that the T'ieh-lê, girding themselves for battle, resided somewhere in the Altai region not far from the Türks whose chief Bumin, out of loyalty towards the Juan-juan, decided in favor of preemptive action. He inflicted upon them a crushing defeat and, encouraged by this victory, sued for the hand of A-na-kui's daughter.

By that time the Türks, or at least some of them, had lived for more than a century under Juan-juan rule. In 439, when the Northern Wei emperor T'ai-wu destroyed the small barbarian state of North Liang, established in Kansu by the Chü-ch'ü family, some five hundred Türk families sought refuge with the Juan-juan. The reasons that prompted this action remain unknown, but the sources report that the Türks, all of whom bore the surname A-shih-na, were settled by the Juan-juan in the Altai, where they worked on the manufacture of iron implements. The Gold Mountain (Chin shan) where they worked had the shape of a helmet which in their language was called *türk*. This is why the fugitive people adopted this name. No valid, scholarly explanation of this popular etymology has yet been proposed.

Although many questions remain unanswered concerning the end of Juan-juan rule in Mongolia, it can be taken for certain that in 552 it was replaced by that of the Türks and that the shift was not brought about by foreign conquerors. The disintegration of Juan-juan power was the result of an internal revolution engineered by a disgruntled faction that had lived within the empire and, linguistically as well as ethnically, may have been indistinguishable from the rest of the population. The only specific trait of the Türks is occupational, and it links them with the practice of metallurgy.

Evidence has already been cited to show that in the middle of the 5th

century the Türks manufactured iron implements within Juan-juan boundaries. A century later, A-na-kui's disdainful reference to such an occupation is said to have triggered the Türk revolt which, within a few years, led to the disintegration of the Juan-juan empire. There is no way of knowing whether the Türks were engaged in the mining or in the processing of iron ore, or possibly in both of these related activities. There are many references to caverns in which Türks had lived prior to their obtaining political power, and terms such as "ancestral" or "birth" caverns occur frequently. According to the *Chou shu*, the kaghan of the Türks "every year leads the nobles to the ancestral cavern to offer a sacrifice." The statement is repeated in several texts derived from the *Chou shu* and refers to the ruler of the Eastern Türks on whose territory the cavern – clearly a national shrine – was located. This, and also the practice of the annual ceremony, is confirmed by the *Sui shu*, which reports that every year the Western Türks send a high dignitary (or several dignitaries) to offer a sacrifice in the ancestral cavern. In the light of other evidence pointing to the mining or metallurgical activities of the Türks, there is reason to believe that these caverns were in fact mines. Semi-historical accounts of later date – which cannot here be examined in detail – firmly link "ancestral caverns" with metallurgy. Information provided by travellers of the 6th and 7th centuries contain some additional evidence. In 568 the Greek Zemarkhos, ambassador of Justin II to the Western Türks in Sogdiana, then under Türk rule, met a Türk who offered him iron for sale. The historian Menander, reporting this event, added his own commentary to the effect that it was in this way that the Türks wanted to make it known that they had iron mines. When the famous Chinese Buddhist pilgrim Hsüan-tsang called on one of the rulers of the Western Türks he noticed an iron bedstead in place of the usual wooden one. He found the object so unusual that he deemed it worthy of a mention in his travel account.

With some exaggeration and a touch of anachronism one might view Türk metallurgy as a powerful economic weapon, instrumental in securing the levers of political power. Since there is no sure way of distinguishing between defeated Juan-juan and victorious Türks (for all we know they might even have spoken the same language), the latter's "conquest" of the former may be likened to a hypothetical (and unlikely) bid by the United Steelworkers of America, or any other powerful labor union, to get hold of the reins of executive power in the United States. Though allowance must be made for the relatively modest scale of leverage metallurgists may have had in a pre-industrial society, the importance of the manufacture of arms, over which the Türks probably exerted some control, cannot be disregarded. There is even

some modest but quite straightforward evidence to show incipient attempts to monopolize production. It would appear that, once they became the rulers of the great empire, the Türks, to use a modern term, subcontracted the metallurgical production to their kin, the Kirghiz.

Located to the north of the Türks, the Kirghiz – whose language was very close to, perhaps indistinguishable from, that of the Türks – had gold, tin, and iron in their country. After rains, so our sources say, the Kirghiz collected an iron ore which they used for the manufacture of high quality arms. These they delivered to the Türks, one must assume not always with the best of grace. In 583 the Sui emperor Kao-tsu remarked that the Kirghiz were waiting with gnashing teeth for their chance to attack the Türks. But, as we shall see, the turn of the Kirghiz came much later, when in the mid 9th century they overthrew the Uighurs, successors in Mongolia of the Türks.

The founding of the first Türk kaghanate

The death of A-na-kui presented Bumin and his Türk people with the awesome task of ruling over a great empire. Some two centuries later, in the inscriptions of the Orkhon, the memory of these stirring times was thus remembered:[6]

> When high above the blue sky and down below the brown earth had been created, betwixt the two were created the sons of men. And above the sons of men stood my ancestors, the kaghans Bumin and Ishtemi. Having become the masters of the Türk people, they installed and ruled its empire and fixed the law of the country. Many were their enemies in the four corners of the world, but, leading campaigns against them, they subjugated and pacified many nations in the four corners of the world. They caused them to bow their heads and to bend their knees. These were wise kaghans, these were valiant kaghans; all their officers were wise and valiant; the nobles, all of them, the entire people were just. This was the reason why they were able to rule an empire so great, why, governing the empire, they could uphold the law.

Bumin, the founder of the Türk empire, died soon after his victory and was followed by his son Kuo-lo, who ruled for only a few months. There is evidence to suggest that from its very inception the Türk empire was to some extent bifocal. The eastern parts, centered on Mongolia, the traditional cradle

[6] It is a regrettable fact that no translation of the Orkhon inscriptions into idiomatic English exists. That given in Talât Tekin's otherwise very valuable *A Grammar of Orkhon Turkic*, (1968) cannot lay such claim. The three translations given in this chapter are my own, of passages taken from the Köl tegin and Bilge kaghan inscriptions. They are based on the editions prepared by V. Thomsen, 1896, S.E. Malov, 1951, and Talât Tekin in the aforementioned book. I have attempted to convey the meaning of the text but did not consider philological problems which should be, and have been, treated elsewhere.

of many nomad empires, had the primacy, if not the supremacy, of the two halves. It was ruled by Muhan (553–72), son of Bumin, whereas the western parts fell to Bumin's brother (Muhan's uncle), Ishtemi (553–?). Together, they are the founding fathers of what may be called the First Türk kaghanate.

The very size of the territory under Türk rule entailed the necessity of some administrative division, leaving considerable – perhaps complete – freedom of action to the local ruler. As reported by Menander – who based his information on what the Türks themselves said – the Türk state was quadripartite, governed by four rulers. As convincingly argued by Huan Wang[7] (apparently unaware of Menander's data), Chinese sources clearly show the existence of four major administrative units, namely the Central, Eastern, Western, and Western Frontier (*hsi mien*) Regions. The ruler of the Central Region was the Great Kaghan (*chung mien ta ko-han*). However important Ishtemi's role and authority may have been – it may be compared with that played by Batu in the Mongol empire of the thirteenth century – supreme power rested with Muhan, in whose territory lay the sacred Ötükän forest, focal point of Türk national consciousness. Ishtemi's domain was the Western Frontier Region.

Muhan embarked upon a series of military conquests. He wiped out what were probably the last identifiable military forces of the Juan-juan. In the east he defeated the Kitans, in the north he incorporated the Kirghiz into his realm, in the west he defeated the Hephthalites; his might extended from the Pacific to the "Western Sea" and to Lake Baikal in the north; he subdued "all the countries outside China," reports with admiration the *Chou shu*.

Although Muhan was nominally credited with the defeat of the Hephthalites, the campaign against them was probably led by Ishtemi, his uncle, who was in charge of the Western Frontier Region. The name Hephthalite, which appears in Chinese as well as Greek sources, was the dynastic appellation, adopted towards the end of the 5th century, either of a people or – less likely – of a country called Avar or Var. The Chinese transcription of the name (modern *hua* 滑) would allow both readings. According to the *Liang shu* these (A)vars were the subjects of the Juan-juan, a statement that can be interpreted in different ways. On the one hand it may be seen as indicating that the two names refer to two peoples, on the other – viewed from the vantage point of an outsider – it may mean that the (A)vars, though a distinct ethnic entity, became Juan-juan through being subjugated by the latter. The case would be similar to that of, say, the southern Irish being called British. Hephthalite rule was established in Tokharistan towards the end of the 5th century. In the absence of reliable information concerning their

[7] Wang, 1983.

previous abodes, it is likely that the Hephthalites were not invaders but had been, for some time, part of the region's population. Some Chinese sources consider them descendants of the Great Yüeh-chih. They sent their first embassy to the T'o-pa Wei in 456–7, and remained in touch with them until the destruction of their state. When speaking of the Hephthalites the Wei – just as the other northern dynasties – used a variety of transcriptions of that name instead of the (A)var appellation favored by the southern Liang.

At the time when the Hephthalites gained power, Tokharistan and Gandhara were ruled by the Kidarites, a local dynasty of ephemeral existence which for about half a century united under its rule the territories lying immediately to the north and to the south of the Hindukush. In the second or third decades of the fifth century they had carved their land from what used to be Kushan territory. Pressed by the Hephthalites, the Kidarites moved west and clashed with the Parthians and the Sassanids. Information on these conflicts reached Byzantium and, as we have seen (chapter 7, p. 200), Priscus viewed the Kidarites as a branch of the Huns.

A *terminus post quem* of the Hephthalite penetration into Tokharistan is provided by the report of two Wei ambassadors who in 437 visited the region but who in their detailed report make no mention of them.[8] Once established on the Iranian border, the Hephthalites were inevitably drawn into the sphere of Persian politics. Peroz, king of Persia (459–84), fled to them in search of an alliance which, once gained, allowed him to win back the throne from his brother, the usurper Hormizd III. As time passed, the relationship turned sour and Peroz lost his life in 484 in a vain attack on the Hephthalites. Ṭabarî, our principal source for all these events, calls the victor Akhshunvar, but it is uncertain whether this is a title or a personal name. As a corollary of the temporary weakening of Sassanid power, Hephthalite influence became stronger in Sogdiana, which in the first years of the 6th century became an integral part of the Hephthalite state.

Perhaps because of the stabilization of their western border area, the Hephthalites extended their influence to the northeast. Between 493 and 508 they led two campaigns against the Kao-chü, the aforementioned people of the "high chariots" and, almost simultaneously, they subdued several city states in Chinese Turkestan. Khotan, Kashgar, Kocho, Karashahr all had to suffer from their invasions. As a result of such expansion, the Hephthalites came into contact with the Juan-juan and tightened their relationship with the Wei, to whom, between 507 and 531, they sent thirteen embassies.

[8] Enoki, 1959, p. 24.

The relative abundance of data notwithstanding, we have but a very fragmentary picture of Hephthalite civilization. There is no consensus concerning the Hephthalite language, though most scholars seem to think that it was Iranian. The *Pei shih* at least clearly states that the language of the Hephthalites differs from those of the High Chariots, of the Juan-juan and of the "various Hu," a rather vague term which, in this context, probably refers to some Iranian peoples. Other sources speak of the necessity of using T'u-yü-hun interpreters when negotiating with the (A)var. Evidence concerning the script used by the Hephthalites is also contradictory. According to the Buddhist pilgrims Sung Yün and Hui Sheng, who visited them in 520, they had no script, and the *Liang shu* specifically states that they have no letters but use tally sticks. At the same time there is numismatic and epigraphic evidence to show that a debased form of the Greek alphabet was used by the Hephthalites. Equally inconsistent are references to the Hephthalites' religion. Somewhat surprisingly Sung Yün and Hui Sheng report that they do not believe in Buddhism, though there is ample archeological evidence that this religion was practiced in territories under Hephthalite control. According to the *Liang shu* the Hephthalites worshiped Heaven and also fire – a clear reference to Zoroastrianism. There are also indications that Nestorian Christianity was widespread within the Hephthalite empire. Burial in coffins is reported to have been the normal practice in disposing of the dead – a custom unthinkable among Zoroastrians. Procopius even adds the detail that companions of the deceased – presumably if he was a man of some importance – were buried alive (?) with him.

Particular attention should be paid to information concerning the Hephthalites' general lifestyle and physical appearance. According to Chinese sources – including the eyewitness accounts of Sung Yün and Hui Sheng – the Hephthalites have no cities, but roam freely and live in tents. In contrast, Procopius of Caesarea and Menander Protector both speak of Hephthalite cities taken over by Türks.

According to Procopius – writing in the mid 6th century – the Hephthalites "are of the stock of the Huns in fact as well as in name: however they do not mingle with any of the Huns known to us. They are the only ones among the Huns who have white bodies and countenances which are not ugly."[9] This statement may have been based on the Caucasoid appearance of at least some of the Hephthalites. Yet the fact that the same author refers to them as White Huns should not be connected with their physique. Color names are often

[9] Procopius of Caesarea, *History of the Wars*, ed. H.B. Dewing, I, iii, 2–4.

added to Inner Asian ethnonyms, we know, for instance, of "White" and "Black" Khazars. Color names appear also in yet another appellation of the Hephthalites. Pahlavi sources call them Xyōn(o) and distinguish between "white (*spēd*)" and "red" (*karmir*) Xyōns. The latter name, transcribed *Κερμιχίωνες*, occurs also in Byzantine sources and – according to at least one author (Theophanes Byzantios) – is said to be the Persian appellation of the Türks. A further difficulty is caused by the fact that the name Xyōn is probably identical with that of the Chionites who in the middle of the 4th century caused considerable trouble, first to the Persian king Shāpūr II, then – through a reversal of alliances – to the Romans. In 359, together with Shāpūr's troops, they victoriously besieged the city of Amida defended by a Roman garrison. While it would be difficult to see the Hephthalites in these Chionitae described by Ammianus Marcellinus, it could well be that, later on, some of their descendants were integrated in the latter's empire.

To summarize the essential elements of a complex and fragmentary presentation, the Hephthalites appear under many names spelt in a bewildering variety of ways. Yet it is reasonably certain that the ethnonyms Hephthalite, Avar or Var, Hyōn were, at one time or another, applied to at least some fractions of the population of the Hephthalite state, destroyed between 557 and 561 through the joint action of the Türk kaghan Ishtemi and Khosrow I Anushirvan, king of the Persians. Cooperation between the Sassanid king and the Türks was not uniformly harmonious, though their alliance was strengthened by Khosrow's marrying a daughter of the Türk ruler. Questions of prestige undoubtedly played a role in the worsening of their relations. A case in point may be that in their contacts with Byzantium, Persians and Türks both claimed suzerainty over the land of the defunct Hephthalite empire, the partition of which created a new situation in Central Asia.

Byzantine–Türk relations

Since 527, with some interruptions, Persia and Byzantium were engaged in a series of wars. The appearance of a major power and a potential ally on Persia's eastern border was a fact which Byzantine diplomacy could ill afford to ignore. In contrast, an alliance with Byzantium directed against the Persians would have held little political promise for the Türks, whose cooperation with Khosrow – as exemplified in the campaign against the Hephthalites – could be fruitful. It was through the machinations of Sogdian merchants bent on securing for themselves the lucrative silk trade with Persia and Byzantium that the deterioration of Türko-Persian relations came about.

The Sogdian merchants in whose hands, under Hephthalite rule, the silk-trade effectively rested, convinced their new lord, the Türk kaghan, to send – some time before 568 – a commercial mission to Persia, with a view to obtaining permission to engage in silk trade within that country. Although traveling under Türk auspices, the mission was in fact Sogdian, led by a Sogdian: Maniakh. The silk brought by this mission was duly purchased by the Persians and then publicly burnt. The most likely explanation of this insulting, though correct, action seems to be that acceptance of the Sogdians' offer would have entitled direct sale of the silk by them to the Persian customer or even to foreign merchants. Though dependent on Türk supplies, the Persians seem to have been determined to keep in their own hands the benefits resulting from silk trade. Possibly they also viewed with apprehension the prospect of Türk caravans criss-crossing their country. But the Sogdians were not to take no for an answer: a second mission – this time composed of Türks – made a renewed attempt to break the trade barrier. According to the explanation given by the Persians, the hot climate of the land proved fatal to them; the Türks suspected, not without good reason, that their envoys were poisoned. With a single-mindedness that must command some respect, Maniakh now conceived the plan of bypassing the Persians so as to get into direct touch with the most important customer: Byzantium.

The first Türk delegation we know of arrived in Constantinople in 563. According to Theophanes it had been dispatched by a certain Askel, king of the Kermikhions. As mentioned earlier, the Persians called the Türks by that name, a practice that may have its roots in the incorporation into the Türk empire of the "red" Hephthalites. Be that as it may, Askel is the original form of the name of the first tribe of the confederation called by the Chinese Nus-hih-pi. This was the westernmost tribal group of the Western Türks and the name Askel (A-hsi-chieh in Chinese transcription) was applied indifferently to the tribe or to its ruler.

The importance of Askel's mission pales beside that of the embassy led by Maniakh arriving in Constantinople at the end of 568 and presenting to Emperor Justin II its credentials written in "Scythian script." Though it was quite clear to all concerned that the aims of this embassy were more ambitious than those of a mere trade delegation, Justin II – who received the Türks with much attention – took care to have them see local sericulture, a possible hint that Byzantium was not all that much dependent on imports. According to Menander, the Türk ruler represented by Maniakh was Silziboulos (Σιλζίβουλος), a name for which no adequate explanation has been given. It is generally believed that Silziboulos and Ishtemi are one and the same person,

an opinion first expressed by J. Marquart.[10] But this identification is based on nothing more than the fact that at the time of Maniakh's mission Ishtemi was in charge of the Western Frontier Region of the Türk empire. Menander – on the testimony of Maniakh – asserts that Silziboulos was the most powerful among the four kaghans. If we are to believe him we must conclude either that Silziboulos is identical with Muhan or that, to boost the authority of his own ruler and at the same time to lend more weight to his own mission, Maniakh was guilty of gentle diplomatic exaggeration. As we shall see, the second alternative is probably the correct one.

In the course of Byzantine–Türk negotiations commercial questions were overshadowed by urgent political matters. Justin showed great interest in knowing more about the peoples conquered by the Türks, among them the Hephthalites and more particularly the Avars, with whom he had more than his due share of trouble. The Avars – it will be recalled (see Chapter 8) – first appear in Western sources in connection with a migration described by Priscus, which took place between 461 and 465. Living within the boundaries of the Hephthalite state, the Avars were affected by the Türk conquest. While some of them accepted it, others – according to information given by Maniakh to Justin some 20,000 (warriors?) – fled to the west and were considered by the Türks runaway subjects. Hostility towards the Avars was one more common bond between Romans and Türks who, in the words of Menander, "became friends" and entered into an alliance with each other. Maniakh's mission proved to be an unqualified success, and led to the dispatch of the first Byzantine embassy to the Türks.

In August 569, under the leadership of the *strategus* Zemarkhos, a group of Romans joined Maniakh's party returning to its homeland. Menander gives a detailed and, one likes to believe, trustworthy account of Zemarkhos' journey to Silziboulos, who received the envoy with much pomp and circumstance, displaying riches which did not fail to impress him. The contacts were most cordial, and the Türk ruler actually invited Zemarkhos – though not his suite – to accompany him on a, presumably minor, foray against the Persians. Zemarkhos was also present at an altercation between his host and a Persian ambassador. Persian hostility obliged Zemarkhos to make a considerable detour on his return journey. Unfortunately there is no way to locate with precision the place where he had met the Türk ruler, though it is clear that it was somewhere to the east, in the Talas valley. Maniakh having died, Zemarkhos was accompanied on his return journey by the *tarkhan* Tagma,

[10] Marquart, 1901, p. 216.

head of a new Türk mission to Constantinople. The pattern of diplomatic relations seems to have demanded that the embassies travel jointly, a new one escorting the one returning to its homeland.

In the period between 568 and 576 diplomatic contacts were frequent; Menander mentions five Roman embassies to the Türks. Beyond the names of their leaders little information is available on these routine contacts. They cannot compare in importance with the embassy headed by Valentine, who in 576 set out for what was his second mission to the Türks. He was accompanied by 106 Türks returning to their country.

Valentine was received by Turxath, son of the recently deceased Silziboulos, at whose funeral he was called upon to assist. The ceremony involved human sacrifice and, for the Romans, the painful obligation to lacerate their faces. According to Menander Turxath was one of the eight chiefs who shared rule over the Türks, Arsilas being the name of the most prominent among them. The meeting between Turxath and Valentine was stormy. The original purpose of Valentine's mission was to inform the Türks of Tiberius II Constantine's accession to the dignity of co-emperor with Justin II and to strengthen the anti-Persian alliance. Arriving as friends, the Romans were taken aback by Turxath's ill-tempered and menacing outbursts prompted – it would appear – by his rage at Byzantium's harboring the fugitive Avars. Turxath was not content with making idle threats. At his instigation – if not on his outright order – Anagai, prince of the Utigurs, and a certain Bokhan, led Türk and allied troops in an invasion which in 576 captured the Byzantine city of Bosporus in the Crimea.

It is not possible to establish with any precision the place occupied by Turxath within the Türk hierarchy, and it is not clear in what relation he stood to the other seven chiefs. It can, however, be taken for granted that he was not the head – not even a *primus inter pares* – of the Western Türks (at that time not yet a political entity) nor was he the highest ranking official of the Western Frontier Region. This appears clearly also from the fact that – his hostility towards the Romans notwithstanding – Turxath had their group proceed to the interior of the Türk territories to meet Tardu, without any doubt his superior. The eastward progress of Valentine resembles that of the monks of the 13th century on their way to Mongolia. John of Plano Carpini was first received by the chief Corenza, then, further east, by Batu, who sent him even further to the Great Khan Güyük.

Tardu's name is well attested in Chinese sources (as Ta-t'ou); he was the son of Ishtemi and kaghan of the Western Frontier Region (*hsi mien ko-han*). According to Menander, Turxath was the ὅμαιμος of Tardu. The Greek term

is usually translated with "brother," but it can be applied also to other close relatives. The matter is of some importance because if Turxath and Tardu had been brothers, Ishtemi would have to be identified with Silziboulos. I have already given some reasons why such an identification should be rejected. There is of course first of all the unbridgeable phonetic difference between the two names, and we have also seen that there was a perfectly good transcription into Greek letters of Ishtemi's name. There are other reasons for rejecting the equation of the two individuals. Chinese sources do not indicate that Ishtemi had, besides Tardu, another son. If Silziboulos had really been Ishtemi, one of the two founding fathers of the empire, whose name was still revered some two centuries later, his son Tardu would have certainly come to the obsequies. Chinese sources are mute on the dates of Ishtemi's death and Tardu's accession to power. In 576 when Valentine visited Turxath, Tardu was already kaghan of the Western Frontier Region, but there are no data on how and when he acceded to this position. It would then appear wise not to identify Ishtemi with Silziboulos. The latter must have been a minor potentate, one of the eight Türk chiefs, a dignity which his son Turxath inherited.

The partition of the Türk state

Tardu's rule extended over a long period of time (he died in 603) and over a vast tract of land comprising the Western Frontier Region of the Türk empire, authority over which lay, theoretically at least, in the hands of Bumin's second son Muhan (553–72) and, following his death, in those of Muhan's younger brother Taspar (572–81). Their names appear in the Sogdian inscription of Bugut, which testifies to the abiding role of the Sogdians within the empire and also to the presence of Buddhism in their midst.

The great rift between the eastern and western Türks – often thought of as having taken place during the reigns of Bumin and Ishtemi – occurred under Taspar's successor Nivar kaghan (581–7), whose name, formerly known only in Chinese transcription (She-tu or, by the title, Sha-po lüeh) appears in the Bugut inscription. It was brought about by Muhan's son Ta-lo-pien, who bore the title Apa kaghan, and who became actively involved in a family feud over the succession of Taspar. He sought and obtained the help of the powerful Tardu, ruler of the Western Frontier Region, who supported him with substantial forces – the sources speak of 100,000 troops – in his fight against Nivar. Highly successful in his military undertakings, Apa would probably have ousted Nivar had the latter not received help from his father-in-law, the Sui emperor Kao-tsu. Undaunted, bent on creating an empire of his own, Apa

turned his forces against his former protector Tardu, who had to seek refuge in the Sui court. By 583 Apa kaghan had established the state of the Western Türks. It was, as the *Sui shu* clearly states, the product of a quarrel between Nivar and Apa, and territorially it comprised the Western Region, Apa's home base as it were, and the Western Frontier Region wrested from Tardu. In 587 Apa kaghan fell into the hands of Ch'u-lo-hu, Nivar's short-lived successor at the head of the Eastern Türks (587–8), and was never again heard of. In his absence Ni-li (587–604) was elected kaghan of the Western Frontier Region. Theoretically at least this dignity was still held by Tardu, but he somehow eclipsed; after 585 for nine years the Chinese sources are mute on his activities.

Very little is known about Ni-li – even the date of his death is uncertain – though just before and during his reign Türk forces were very active in Persia where, in 588, they battled with Hormuzd IV and his famous general Bahram Chobin. According to the Armenian Sebeos, an arrow shot by Bahram himself killed the "Great King of the Türks." It is possible that the victim was no other than Ch'u-lo-hu who – according to the *Sui shu* – was killed by a stray arrow whilst campaigning in the West. Whoever he may have been, the death of the Türk leader did not put an end to Türk activity in Persia. A reversal of alliances brought them to support Bahram Chobin in his ultimately unsuccessful revolt against Khosrow II. Among the Türk prisoners of war captured by Khosrow's army some had on their foreheads the sign of the cross. They told their captors that in their childhood, to escape an epidemic and on the advice of some Christians, they were so marked by their mothers. It is clear that, besides Buddhism and Zoroastrianism (reported by Theophylactus Simocattes), Nestorian Christianity was also known to and practiced by at least some Türks.

In 594 Tardu reappeared in connection with a conflict which opposed him to Yung-yü-lü (alias Tu-lan), kaghan of the Eastern Türks (588–99). One cannot but admire the staying power and acumen of Tardu who, late in life, succeeded in staging a political comeback successful enough to allow him to seek sovereignty over at least the Eastern Türk state. It can be taken for certain that he was the Türk kaghan who in 598, styling himself "lord of the seven races, master of the seven climes" wrote a letter to Emperor Maurice. Theophylactus Simocattes, who records the fact, does not indicate why this letter was written, though he uses the occasion to give an extensive account of events in Inner Asia. Much of what he says is certainly based on the kaghan's letter but, repeated scholarly attempts notwithstanding, many of his statements remain unclarified and are in seeming contradiction with other sources.

However, he does record the name of Ishtemi in a form (Stembis) on which we have already commented (see p. 290). Tardu's attempt to impose his rule on all the Türks failed. In 603 the revolt of some of the tribes compelled him to flee and he was never heard of again.

For convenience of presentation, so far relatively little attention has been paid in this chapter to the role of China in Türk history, pervasive from the creation of the Türk state to its final destruction. Contacts between Türk and Chinese were first established at a time when the former were still under Juan-juan rule. The rise of the Türks coincided with a period of internal instability in China and the first contacts were with the ephemeral Western Wei (535–57) and Northern Chou (557–81) dynasties. Under the short-lived but strong Sui dynasty (581–618), Chinese power became a decisive factor in Türk politics, a tangle of personal and tribal conflicts. Though accustomed to the impermanence of "barbarian" power, the Chinese themselves seem to have been taken aback by the persistence and violence of Türk internal divisions. "The Türks" – according to the Sui Annals – "prefer to destroy each other rather than to live side-by-side. They have a thousand, nay ten thousand clans who are hostile to and kill one another. They mourn their dead with much grief and swear vengeance." Between Türks and Chinese, in time of hostilities, the pattern of intercourse included Türk raids on Chinese lands, Chinese expeditions against the troublesome neighbors, while in periods of peace matrimonial links were established between ruling houses, gifts (mostly silk by the Chinese, and horses by the Türks) exchanged. Such "presents" – "tribute" may be a word more appropriate in the circumstances – could be very substantial. Thus for instance for some time Muhan and Taspar received from the Northern Chou 100,000 pieces of silk a year and at the same time the Chinese had also to entertain on a lavish scale thousands of Türks living a parasitic life in the capital city. In his turn, in 573 and 574 Taspar sent horses to the Northern Chou, but their value was only a fraction of that of the Chinese presents. In contradistinction to the practices followed on the Byzantine borders of Inner Asia, money or gold were seldom used in these "foreign aid" payments.

While the order of things changed little with the founding of the T'ang dynasty, the balance of power shifted in favor of the Chinese. At an early stage of his struggle for power the future emperor Kao-tsu – founder of the dynasty – was supported by Ch'u-lo, kaghan of the Western Türks who, in 605, had taken refuge in the Sui court but who later joined the group supporting the pretender. But Ch'u-lo was but an émigré, unable to provide help as substantial as that given by his mortal enemy Shih-pi, kaghan of the Eastern Türks (609–19). Pressed by him, and against his own conscience and the advice of his

son the future emperor T'ai-tsung, Kao-tsu delivered his friend and ally to the Eastern Türks who put him to death. The story illustrates the nature of the triangular relationship between the Chinese and the two Türk states, a dominant factor of T'ang history.

It would seem that the Türks tended to cast themselves in the role of kingmakers and showed scant respect for the dynasty they had helped to power. Hsieh-li (619–34), the new kaghan of the Eastern Türks, made himself a thorough nuisance and a menace which only T'ai-tsung's cleverness and great personal courage could neutralize, on occasion with peaceful means. Even before his ascension to the throne he was the chief architect of Chinese policy *vis-à-vis* the Türks, and when in 627 he stepped into the place of his father, who had abdicated, he further strengthened the Chinese position. One element in the strategy initiated by Kao-tsu and followed by T'ai-tsung consisted in strengthening their ties with the Western Türks and fomenting discord between them and the Eastern Türks. The Chinese policy to "ally oneself with those who are far away so as to fight those who are close" dictated a rapprochement with T'ung yabghu kaghan (619–30) of the Western Türks, a potential enemy of Hsieh-li. But there was no need for the alliance to become active, the defeat of Hsieh-li was achieved by the direct military action of T'ai-tsung. Taking advantage of internal dissensions – which he had done his best to encourage – in 630 T'ai-tsung's troops launched an attack against Hsieh-li who, defeated, was taken a prisoner and transferred to China, where he died in 634.

The Western Türks

At the same time and for similar reasons, the Western Türk state faced a deep crisis. T'ung yabghu's reign had auspicious beginnings. He revived the occidental ambitions of his great-grandfather Ishtemi and became involved in the continuous drama of Byzantine–Persian relations. This time the principal *personae dramatis* were Heraclius (610–41) and Khosrow II (591–628) and a Türk supporting actor whom the chronicler Theophanes calls Ziebel (Ζίεβηλ). Ingenious efforts have been made to view this name as the Greek rendering of the name of T'ung yabghu. But, leaving on one side the phonetic difficulties of the equation, there remains the fact that Ziebel is said to be a general, not a ruler, "second in rank to the kaghan." The days of cooperation such as existed between Ishtemi and Muhan were long gone and it is unlikely that T'ung yabghu would have ranked himself second behind his antagonist and foe Hsieh-li. Nor is it likely that the proud T'ung yabghu would have

prostrated himself before his ally Heraclius, as reported on Ziebel by Theophanes. The two met at the initiative of the emperor who, probably in 626, sent a certain Andreas to T'ung yabghu with an offer of alliance which the latter eagerly accepted. Khosrow's plea – reported by the Armenian chronicle of Moses Dasxuranci – to remember the old ties of friendship between the Sassanids and Türks and to abstain from attacking, fell on deaf ears. After several campaigns of devastation, in 627 Romans and Türks stood before the walls of Tiflis – which they failed to conquer. Apparently on the advice of Heraclius the Türk forces "reared in a cool climate . . . and unable to endure the coming of summer in the sweltering land of Asorestan in which the capital of the Persian king lies"[11] withdrew. They returned repeatedly, taking advantage of the chaos following the murder of Khosrow II, to plunder the lands the Sassanids were no longer able to defend.

In 630 T'ung yabghu was a powerful man. The Chinese Buddhist pilgrim Hsüan-tsang, who crossed the vast territories under his direct or indirect control and who met the ruler himself, bears eloquent witness to his might and to the luxury of his entourage. The Tarim basin, the Ferghana valley, parts of present-day Afghanistan, and parts of the Indus valley were under Türk rule, the exact geographical limits of which cannot be established with accuracy. However, in his pursuit of glory and conquests – in the words of the Old T'ang Annals – T'ung yabghu was no longer "good to his people, and the tribes hated him." Led by the Turkic Karluks, they revolted and murdered him. Moses Dasxuranci, who also speaks of the plight of the "destructive lion of the north," puts these words of belated regrets in the mouth of T'ung yabghu, whom he calls Jebu kaghan: "Brigands have fallen upon me, and you shall never see my face again, for I did not consolidate my position but imprudently dissipated myself over kingdoms unsuited to me. My pride has thus caused me to fall from my exalted position."[12]

The death of T'ung yabghu created a political vacuum no one was able to fill; self-appointed rulers fought against each other with means inadequate for the fulfillment of their ambitions. The Western Türk confederation was disintegrating, though the five Nu-shih-pi tribes in the west and the five Tu-lu tribes in the east kept their respective cohesion. Jointly they were called in Türk On Ok "ten arrows," while the Chinese referred to them as the tribes of Ten Clans (Shih Hsing). Using for their benefit the incessant conflicts between tribes, the murderous quarrels that set their respective leaders against each other, T'ai-tsung and his successor, the equally gifted Kao-tsung (650–83), no

[11] Dowsett, 1961, p. 86. [12] Dowsett, op. cit. p. 106.

longer menaced by the Eastern Türks, gradually extended Chinese rule over the territories only lately under Türk domination. The agony of the Western Türk state was more prolonged than had been that of its eastern counterpart which – as we have seen – collapsed quite suddenly. The process of disintegration and absorption by the Chinese dragged on for a quarter of a century. In 657 Ho-lu – the last *de facto* ruler of the Western Türks – was made a prisoner and taken to the Chinese capital where, it would seem at his own request, he was symbolically sacrificed on the tomb of the emperor T'ai-tsung. His life was in fact spared, and he died two years later, in 659, to be buried beside the tomb of the kaghan Hsieh-li who, it will be remembered, also died a prisoner of the Chinese. The five Tu-lu tribes were the power base of Ho-lu. The yabghu Chen-chu, his erstwhile enemy and the last chief of the Nu-shih-pi faction of the Western Türks, fell in battle against the Chinese in 659. With his death, which followed by a quarter of a century that of Hsieh-li, last ruler of the Eastern Türks, and with its territory taken over by the Chinese, the Western Türk realm ceased to exist.

The second Türk Kaghanate

The Orkhon inscriptions recall in moving terms, not easy to render in English, the decay of Türk might, the period of Chinese servitude. They speak of a time when the

> younger brothers were unlike their elder brothers, sons were unlike their fathers. Kaghans unwise and incompetent succeeded on the throne, unwise and incompetent were their officials. Because of discord between the nobles and the commoners, because of the cunning and deceitfulness of the Chinese who set against each other younger and elder brothers, nobles and commoners, the Türk people caused the disintegration of the empire that had been their own, caused the ruin of the kaghan who had been their kaghan. The sons of the nobles became slaves of the Chinese, their ladylike daughters became servants. The Türk nobles demitted their Türk offices, accepted Chinese titles and offices, submitted to the Chinese emperor, and for fifty years they placed at his disposal their labor and their strength.

The short excerpt just cited shows what other passages of the inscriptions abundantly confirm, to wit, that the internal conflicts were not only tribal or personal but also social, opposing the upper class (the "nobles," *bäglär*) to the common people (the "commoners," *budun*). The treason of the former is bitterly resented and the renascence of the Türk state unequivocally attributed to the wish of *hoi polloi*, the "black" people (*qara budun*).

The man who united the distraught, disheartened patriots – one can hardly find a better word to describe them – was Elterish (682–92), scion of the A-

shih-na clan, a distant descendant of the late Hsieh-li kaghan. In the Orkhon inscriptions Elterish's son speaks thus of his father's deeds:

My father the kaghan set out with seventeen men, and as the word spread that he had set out and was advancing, those who were in the towns went up into the mountains and those who were in the mountains came down, they gathered, and there were seventy-seven men. Because Heaven gave them strength, the army of my father was like wolves and his enemies were like sheep. Leading campaigns to the east as to the west, he gathered the people and made them rise. And all together they numbered seven hundred men. When they were seven hundred, in accordance with the institutions of my ancestors my father organized those who had been deprived of their state, those who had been deprived of their kaghan, who had become slaves and servants, who had lost their Türk institutions. [. . .] He led forty-seven campaigns and fought in twenty battles. By the strength of Heaven he deprived of their state those who had a state, deprived of their kaghan those who had a kaghan, he subjugated his enemies and made them bend their knees and bow their heads.

Elterish's achievement, the whipping into shape of a ragtag, demoralized Türk fighting force, was considerable. In Chinese sources he carries the name Ku-to-lu, i.e. Turkic Kutlugh "the Fortunate." He is the founder of what modern historians call the Second Türk Kaghanate. Among his early successes the incorporation into his expanding realm of the Toquz Oghuz, known by the Chinese as the Nine Clans (Chiu hsing) – a confederacy of T'ieh-lê tribes – strengthened his hand. Through their submission Elterish acquired a considerable number of horses, an indispensable commodity for further warfare partially directed against China.

Elterish died of illness and – because of the youth of his sons, seven and eight years of age – his succession caused no problem. His younger brother Kapghan kaghan, called Mo-ch'o in Chinese sources, ascended the throne. His, by Inner Asian standards long, rule (691–716) saw the further strengthening of the Türk kaghanate. To begin with, Kapghan worked on a rapprochement with the Chinese, who bestowed on him a variety of honorific titles. In his turn, Kapghan dealt a devastating blow to the Kitan, who in 696 harassed China with their incursions. Of more historical significance is Kapghan's demand that those Türks who between 670 and 673, probably at their own request, had settled in the Ordos region be repatriated, or in blunter words, delivered to him. His attitude recalls that of Turxath demanding the extradition of the fugitive Avars. Unable to withstand the pressure, the Chinese extradited several thousand families; moreover, they gave the kaghan a substantial amount of grain and also three thousand pieces of farm implements. Understandably, the Chinese sources dwell mostly on Türk incursions, looting expeditions directed against China, activities which went hand in

hand with repeated demands to establish matrimonial links with the T'ang. Yet it would appear that most of Kapghan's energies were taken up with fighting or forming short-lived alliances with other Inner Asian peoples. There were campaigns against the Western Türks (On Ok), or at least their remnants, against the Nine (Toquz) Oghuz, the Bayirku; it is well-nigh impossible to establish with any amount of certainty who was friend or foe and when. The shifting of alliances was constant. Kapghan's glorious reign ended abruptly on 22 July 716 when – neglecting elementary precautions – he was ambushed and killed by a Bayirku.

Kapghan's son Bögü failed to take his father's place. He, his brothers and most of the close relatives of the defunct kaghan were swiftly dispatched as the reins of power were grabbed by two sons of Elterish, Prince Köl (Köl tegin) and the next Türk ruler Bilgä kaghan (716–34), called also Mo-chi-lien in Chinese sources. The sources state quite explicitly that of the two brothers it was the younger, Köl tegin, who was the more dynamic and that he was instrumental in his brother's elevation to the throne. Bilgä kaghan readily recognized his indebtedness to his younger brother and, unlike so many similar situations, the siblings worked in perfect harmony, aided by a remarkable man, one of the few Inner Asian statesmen (as distinct from rulers) whose career it is possible to follow. His name was Tonyukuk, and he served with distinction first under Elterish, then under Kapghan at whose death he joined the faction supporting Kapghan's son. This mistake did not cost him his life, he was spared in the general massacre partly, perhaps, because of his great authority and his age (at that time he must have been going on for seventy); partly also, one would like to think, because he was Bilgä kaghan's father-in-law. Tonyukuk was the embodiment of Türk polity, staunch but reasonable opponent of the Chinese, and fierce guardian of Türk national values, even to rejecting Buddhism and Taoism as unsuited to a people of warriors. Tonyukuk felt that because the Türks were few in numbers – less than a hundredth part of the Chinese, as he put it – the only way for them to maintain their national identity was "to follow the water and the grass" and have no permanent dwellings. If the Türks were to change their old customs, he argued, one day they would be defeated and annexed by the Chinese. If strong, the Türks could attack, if weak, they could withdraw into their mountains and forests. Tonyukuk was convinced that war was the stock-in-trade of his people, the only means to improve the living conditions of the *budun*. The funeral stele of Bilgä summarizes the long process:

I [Bilgä] did not reign over a people that was rich; I reigned over a people weak and frightened, a people that had no food in their bellies and no cloth on their backs. I

consulted with my younger brother Köl tegin. To preserve the reputation achieved by our father and our uncle, for the sake of the Türk people, I spent the nights without sleep and the days without rest [. . .] When I became kaghan, the people who had dispersed in different countries returned, at the point of death, on foot, and naked. To reestablish the nation I led twenty-two campaigns [. . .] Then, by the grace of Heaven, and because of good fortune and propitious circumstances, I brought back to life the dying people, the naked people I clothed, and I made the few many.

The glorious time mirrored in the inscriptions were not to last, Köl tegin died in the spring of 731. His death was a terrible blow for Bilgä, but even the emperor Hsüan Tsung seems to have been shocked by the passing of this truly great man. He ordered a funeral stele to be erected in his honor and sent six famous painters to depict on the walls of a temple built for the purpose the most memorable battles fought by Köl tegin. Also, he consented to the marriage of Bilgä kaghan with an imperial princess.

The Second Kaghanate was at the peak of its glory when internal conflicts caused it to fall. Bilgä kaghan was poisoned by a trusted member of his entourage and died on 25 November 734, not without having taken revenge on the murderer and his followers. His son had no difficulty in securing for himself the throne, but he was short-lived, and for the decade following Bilgä kaghan's death we cannot even establish with certainty the number of those who claimed to be rulers of the Türks. The rapid decline of the kaghanate was the result of disintegration, interior turmoil in which the Basmil, the Karluk, and the Uighur components of the state vied with each other and for the control of the levers of power. In 745 the head of the last Türk kaghan was presented to Hsüan Tsung on behalf of the new ruler of what had been the Türk empire, henceforth the state of the Uighurs, one of the Tokuz Oghuz tribes.

Epilogue

Türk civilization was exceptionally complex; it is difficult to analyze or to comprehend. The picture given of it in Chinese sources is less stereotypical than it would appear to a superficial observer. Although described as typical nomads, "following grass and water," many of the Türks do not fit well into this pattern. It can be taken for granted that some of them – perhaps the very core of the people – were forest-dwellers, and that only the politically and militarily active social upper-crust was supported by a pastoral economic infrastructure. The share of metallurgy in Türk economy cannot be precisely determined but, at least in the beginnings of specifically Türk history, it certainly was the basis of Türk political power.

Heterogeneity characterized Türk views of the supernatural. A "national" religion, the exact tenets of which cannot be documented, centered on Tängri, the Sky (or Heaven), to which in the fifth month of the year the Türks were wont to offer sheep and horses in sacrifice. As we have seen, there was also at least one yearly sacrifice connected with metallurgy and performed in the "ancestral cavern." At least some Türks – but certainly not all of them – had the wolf for totem, and no doubt some cult was attached also to the "sacred" forest Ötükän, the very name of which may be connected with words for "request, prayer." Numerous spirits were honored and shamans were used to communicate with them. The cult of the female spirit of goddess Umay – continued in some areas to the present day – is certainly of Mongol origin and testifies to the presence of a Mongol component in the body of Türk religious beliefs.

The words attributed to the wise Tonyukuk warning his people not to adopt Taoism or Buddhism are themselves proof that these religions were practiced in his country. But there is much more to show the strength and importance of Buddhism, which may not have had a large following but which had certainly made converts in important positions. Hsüan-tsang's testimony shows the pervasive presence of Buddhism under Türk rule. The most important event in the history of Buddhism among the Türks was the conversion by the Chinese monk Hui-lin of Taspar (572–81), who undertook the building of monasteries and asked the emperor of the Northern Ch'i for canonical works. Actually the first known attempt to render into Türk a *sūtra* (the Mahāparinirvāṇa) belongs to this period when the court of the kaghan of the Central Region became a center of Buddhist studies. Their chief promoter was the Gandharan monk Jinagupta (Jnānagupta?), who spent a little over ten years (575–85) in the entourage of Taspar and of his successor Nivar. In 581 ten Chinese monks, who had travelled to India in search of holy books but who were prevented from returning home by the persecution of Buddhists initiated by the Chou, joined Jinagupta, "who knew the languages of foreign countries and was familiar with the scripts of distant lands." Together they engaged in the study, cataloguing, and translation into Chinese (and perhaps also into Türk) of the 260 Sanskrit works they had brought from India. Thus these religions found shelter and asylum among the northern Barbarians, patrons of an intellectual undertaking of great importance for the spread of Buddhism. Most Buddhist activity took place within the domain of the Eastern or Northern Türks, but the western parts were also open to Buddhist missionary activities, as is witnessed by the friendly reception offered by T'ung yabghu to the Indian monk Prabhākaramitra. Although present,

Zoroastrianism, Christianity, and Manicheism (mainly among Sogdians) played minor roles compared with Buddhism. All in all, religious tolerance appears to have been as characteristic of the Türks as it was to become of the Mongols of the Chinggisid period.

The picture of Türk civilization as it emerges from the sources is neither uniform nor static. For instance, according to the *Sui shu*, the Türks know no script, the *Chou shu* likens their script to that of the Hu, but the runiform inscriptions of the Orkhon belie both of these statements.

As described in the sources, the process of electing the ruler reflects an archaic ceremonial probably ignored in real life. According to the *Chou shu*, when the Türks elect a ruler, the high dignitaries of the realm bundle him in a felt rug and spin him nine times from east to west. After each turn, they bow to him. Then the ruler-elect is put on horseback and has to ride – probably to ascertain whether he can still mount a steed in a dizzy state. After the ride he is strangled with a silken shawl until he almost chokes. When the shawl is loosened, those standing around fire at him the question "How long will you be our kaghan?" The kaghan, dazed, is unable to give a clear answer, but from his mutterings those assisting at the ritual take a clue as to the length of his reign. The Arab geographer Al-Istakhrī ascribes almost the same ritual to the Khazars: "When they wish to appoint a kaghan, they bring him and throttle him with a piece of silk till he is nearly strangled, Then they say to him, 'How long do you wish to reign?' He says 'So and so many years.' If he dies before then, well and good. If not, he is killed when he reaches the year in question."[13] Türks and Khazars were closely linked politically and linguistically, and the parallels between their rituals are not surprising. However, one wonders whether in the often bloody struggles for the throne such procedures were indeed followed.

Repeated attempts notwithstanding, no clear idea of the internal structure of the Türk state has emerged, we do not really know the precise meaning of the various dignitaries' titles, nor can we identify the bonds of solidarity that linked together – at least some of the time – the motley population of this great empire. It remains the task of future research to give a credible, reasonably comprehensive, not cliché-ridden description of Türk civilization. As for the Türk role in the history of Inner Asia, it can safely be termed pivotal. The Türks achieved and maintained for a period, long by Inner Asian standards, the political unification of a stretch of land that reached from the confines of China to the borders of Byzantium. They intervened with lasting effect in the

[13] Cf. D.M. Dunlop, 1957, p. 97.

destinies of China, Iran, Byzantium; they conveyed knowledge between the Greek, Iranian, Indian, and Chinese worlds. In the Western World, for centuries, their name was used as a common denomination of barbarians, irrespective of their language, whereas for the peoples of Inner Asia the name Türk became, and has remained, the hallmark of the unity of peoples sharing a common language.

12

The Uighurs

The second of the great nomad empires of Mongolia lasted from 744 to 840, and its capital was Karabalghasun on the High Orkhon River. For some years before its foundation, the Uighur leader, known to the Chinese as Ku-li p'ei-lo, had been consolidating the power of his own clan, the Yaghlakar, among the various Uighur tribes; and in 742, he led a coalition of Uighur, Karluk and Basmil forces in a successful attempt to drive the last important ruler of the Eastern Türks from the Mongolian steppes. This set the scene for further expansion of Ku-li p'ei-lo's power, and the Chinese historian tersely remarks that in 744 "he attacked and defeated the Basmil and took upon himself the title of Kutlugh bilgä Köl kaghan."[1] Shortly after this, the Karluk also became victims of the Uighur kaghan, and an easterly group of them was brought under subjection.

The empire's founder died in 747 and leadership devolved upon his son, Bilgä köl kaghan, called Mo-yen-ch'o in the Chinese sources. He was a brutal and ambitious man who carried forward his father's achievements by strengthening the monarchy and extending his people's domination over the Karluk and Basmil. He also added a further dimension to the historical importance of the Uighurs by ordering his eldest son to render to the great neighbouring T'ang empire in China invaluable military service against the An Lu-shan rebellion (755–63) which, despite its failure to overthrow the T'ang, dealt the dynasty a blow so heavy that it never fully recovered. Because of China's dependence on their military support, the Uighurs were in a position to dictate terms to the Chinese emperors, and some of their rulers exploited this advantage to the full.

Upon Mo-yen-ch'o's death in 759, his second son, called I-ti-chien or Mou-

[1] *Chiu T'ang-shu* (Old T'ang history), comp. Chao Ying et al. Po-na ed., 195:3. The first section of *Chiu T'ang-shu*, 195 has been translated in Edouard Chavannes, *Documents sur les Tou-kiue (Turcs) occidentaux*, pp. 87–94. All translations cited in these notes are into the language used in the title of the work where they occur.

yü in the Chinese sources, ascended the throne under the title Tängri kaghan and during his reign the Uighurs reached the height of their power. He continued his predecessor's policy of serving the T'ang upon Uighur terms, and in 762 went himself to the Central Kingdom to help the Chinese in the last battles against the rebellion, by this time under the leadership of Shih Ch'ao-i. For the Chinese, the final defeat of the An Lu-shan rebellion was of enormous significance. But for Mou-yü kaghan's own people the most important result of his stay in China was his conversion to Manichaeism. This religion was to exercise a profound influence on Uighur history and it will be necessary to deal with it in some detail later in this chapter.

One of the consequences of Mou-yü kaghan's adoption of Manichaeism was an increase in the influence of the Sogdians over the Uighur court; among this people, which was of vital importance in the history of Central Asia, were many Manichaean devotees fleeing persecution in their own country. In the end, Mou-yü kaghan's advisers were to be the cause of his downfall. In 779, the Sogdians recommended that the kaghan should take advantage of the state mourning which followed the death of the Emperor Tai-tsung (762–79) and invade China. Mou-yü kaghan agreed to the proposal but was opposed by his first cousin and chief minister Tun bagha. Seeing no other way to thwart the plan, Tun assassinated the kaghan and had many of his Sogdian allies murdered. He then set himself on the throne under the title Alp kutlugh bilgä kaghan and initiated an era of anti-Sogdian and pro-Chinese rule.

After Tun's death in 789, Manichaean and Sogdian influence was reinstated, even though relations with China remained friendly. By this time Uighur influence and prestige were declining sharply. At home, the power of the ruling clan passed into the hands of the general and chief minister entitled El ögäsi (adviser of the empire). This man acted as regent for the young kaghan, who was still in his teens. Abroad, the same general suffered severe humiliation in two unsuccessful attempts in 790 to rescue the Chinese and Uighur outpost Beshbalik from the Tibetans, who had for some time been making territorial gains at China's expense.

In 795 the kaghan died without a son and one of his ministers, who can probably be identified as the former regent El ögäsi, ascended the throne. The new ruler is described as follows in a Chinese source:

> He was originally of the Ädiz clan. He was clever in debate and brave in war. From T'ien-ch'in's [i.e. Tun bagha's] time on, he had been in command of an army and held great authority; the senior ministers and all the chiefs feared and obeyed him. When he became the kaghan, he took on the surname of the Yaghlakar clan and sent an envoy to the Chinese court to announce the death [of his predecessor]. All the sons, grandsons

and young members of the families of the kaghans from T'ien-ch'in on he sent in to the T'ang imperial court.[2]

This dynastic founder, who reigned under the title Tängridä ülüg bulmïsh alp kutlugh ulugh bilgä kaghan, can be accounted one of the greatest of Uighur monarchs. Even before he ascended the throne, he had succeeded in retaking Pei-t'ing from the Tibetans in 791–2,[3] thus reversing his earlier defeats there. Under this man the Uighur empire enjoyed a remarkable restoration,[4] and to some extent his accomplishments survived his death (808).[5] Yet by the late years of his successor's reign (808–21), it was clear that Uighur strength was beginning to dissolve. A sign of this decline can be seen in the ability of the Chinese court under Hsien-tsung (808–20) to hold out from 813 until 820 against a Uighur request for a Chinese bride.

The last twenty years of the Uighur empire show a story of continuing disintegration leading to an eventual *débâcle*. Court intrigue wasted the power of the ruling clan, rebellions broke out against the throne and in 839 a particularly severe winter killed much of the livestock on which the Uighurs relied so heavily. Meanwhile, the kaghans were confronted with an increasingly aggressive northern neighbour, the Kirghiz. In 840, at the invitation of a rebel Uighur chief, Kirghiz forces entered the much weakened empire in

[2] Ssu-ma Kuang, *Tzu-chih t'ung-chien* (Comprehensive mirror of government) 20 vols. (Peking, 1956 ed.), XVI, 7568.

[3] Most scholars have assumed that the Tibetans held Pei-t'ing on a long-term basis. The date given above is based on the convincing research of Moriyasu Takao in "Uiguru to Toban no Hokutei sōdatsusen oyobi sono nochino Seiiki jōsei ni tsuite" (The Uyghur-Tibetan struggle for Beshbalygh and the subsequent situation in Central Asia), *TG*, 55.4: 60–87 (1973).

[4] The achievements of this dynastic founder are described in lines 12ff. of the Chinese version of the Karabalghasun inscription, found by a Russian mission in 1889. There are three texts on the stone, in Chinese, Sogdian, and Old Turkic, the first of them being by far the best preserved. The Chinese version may be found, together with complete translations, in several works including W. Radloff, *Die alttürkischen Inschriften der Mongolei*, 3 vols. (Saint Petersburg, 1894–5), III, 286–91 and Gustav Schlegel, "Die chinesische Inschrift auf dem uigurischen Denkmal in Kara Balgassun," *Mémoires de la Société Finno-ougrienne*, 9: 127ff. (1896). In point of fact, scholars are divided over the identity of the kaghan whose exploits are described in lines 12ff. of the Chinese inscription. Following Abe Takeo in *Nishi-Uiguru kokushi no kenkyū* (Research on the history of the West Uighurs; Kyoto, 1958), pp. 182ff., I believe the relevant kaghan to be the founder of the second dynasty and have argued the case in *The Uighur empire according to the T'ang dynastic histories, A study in Sino-Uighur relations 744–840*, 2nd ed. (The Australian National University Asian publications series, no. 2; Canberra, 1972), pp. 184–7. However, some scholars ascribe the events described in that part of the stele to a slightly later date. See especially Haneda Tōru, "Tōdai Kaikotsushi no kenkyū" (Research on Uighur history in the T'ang), *Haneda hakushi shigaku rombunshū* (The collected historical writings of Dr Haneda), 2 vols. (Tōyō shi kenkyū sōkan, no. 3; Kyoto, 1957–8), I, 317ff.

[5] Most authorities claim that this dynastic founder died in 805. However, in his article "Kyūsei Kaikotsu kagan no keifu" (Qaghans of the Uighurs of Nine Clans), *TG*, 33.3–4: 95–108 (1950), Yamada Nobuo has demonstrated convincingly that 808 is the correct date and has been followed by Abe Takeo (*Nishi-Uiguru*, p. 189). I have presented the case for the later date in *The Uighur empire*, pp. 187–90.

strength. They delivered the *coup de grâce* by killing the kaghan and taking his capital, whereupon the Uighurs were forced to disperse.

Ethnic composition, territorial extent and administration

Let us turn from this brief sketch of Uighur history to a more detailed consideration of which peoples lived within the confines of the Uighur empire; how far the boundaries extended; and which persons or groups held power and prestige among the Uighurs.

At the time of its foundation, the nucleus of the population was a conglomeration of nine Turkic tribes, collectively known as the Toquz Oghuz (i.e. the Nine Oghuz) or Nine Surnames. They included the Uighurs, the Bukhu, the Khun, the Bayirku and the Tongra. The remaining four are called Ssu-chieh, Ch'i-pi, A-pu-ssu and Ku-lun-wu-ku in the Chinese histories. Of these nine, the first seven are listed there as separate tribes who lived north of the Gobi in the Period of Division. The A-pu-ssu and Ku-lun-wu-ku became accepted on an equal footing with the others only about 742. The A-pu-ssu was originally a subtribe of the Ssu-chieh, and the Ku-lun-wu-ku a combination of two tribes.

The Uighur chapter of the New T'ang history (*Hsin T'ang-shu*) records that an embassy of 788 was led by an official of the Ädiz tribe, indicating that the Ädiz belonged to the confederation by that time. However, the Chinese version of the Karabalghasun inscription, which was written after 808 and contains a great deal of valuable material on Uighur history, still calls the Uighur ruler "Kaghan of the Nine Surnames . . ." Apparently, the confederation still consisted of nine units, but the division was no doubt political rather than ethnical.

In 744, the ruling tribe was the Uighurs, who were themselves subdivided into ten clans, collectively called On-Uighur (i.e. the Ten Uighurs). Of these, the dominant one was the Yaghlakar and, until the second dynasty was founded in 795, the whole empire was ruled by kaghans drawn from the Yaghlakar family. Like that of the Nine Surnames, the identity of the On-Uighur was not fixed, and the division into the groups ceased to be ethnical.[6]

[6] The precise status of the various tribes within the Toquz Oghuz confederation has been the subject of much debate. A bibliography of contributions until 1956 may be found in E.G. Pulleyblank, "Some remarks on the Toquzoghuz problem," *Ural-Altaische Jahrbücher*, 28: 35 (1956). I have followed Pulleyblank's interpretation (pp. 35–42), which is very similar to that of the great Japanese sinologist Haneda Tōru. Dr Haneda's article on the subject, "Kyūsei Kaikotsu to Toquzoɣuz to no kankei o ronzu' (The relationship between the Nine Surname Uighurs and the Toghuzoghuz), was first published in *TG*, 9: 1–61 (1919) and reprinted in *Haneda hakushi*, 1, 325–94. The most significant contribution since Pulleyblank's is James Hamilton, "Toquz-Oɣuz et On-Uyɣur", *JA*, 250: 23–63 (1962). This article adds to, but does not upset, Pulleyblank's thesis.

All the units mentioned so far in this section are categorized in the Chinese sources as T'ieh-lê tribes, but several other ethnic groups lived within the Uighur empire as subjects. As we have seen, the earliest to be subjugated were the Basmil, who lived in the Beshbalik area, and an easterly splinter-group of the Karluk, the major part of which people inhabited a region between Lake Balkhash and Beshbalik. These two tribes were regarded as inferiors by the Uighurs, who relegated them to the forward guard in battle, the greater danger being accorded to the less important soldiers. It seems probable that many of the remaining Karluk were later absorbed into the Uighur empire. An inscription found at Shine-usu in Mongolia in 1909 describes in great detail a war against the Basmil and Karluk undertaken by Mo-yen-ch'o.[7] Moreover, a Chinese text referring to about 789 tells us that "the three tribes of the Karluk . . . were subject to the Uighurs."[8] However, with the loss of Beshbalik to the Tibetans in 790, the Uighurs forfeited the allegiance of the Karluk and Basmil until they retook the westerly regions not long after.

Apart from the Türks left over from the time when they had dominated Mongolia and the all-important Sogdians, the most significant minority under Uighur control was probably Chinese. Not only did several of the kaghans marry a Chinese princess, but there is evidence that other natives of the T'ang settled among the Uighurs. The standard dynastic histories note that in 792 the emperor honoured with official title a Chinese of the Lü family who had gone to Karabalghasun and become the adopted son of the kaghan, taking the surname Yaghlakar. The Shine-usu inscription also informs us (west side, line 5) that Mo-yen-ch'o kaghan ordered some Chinese and Sogdians to construct a city called Bay-Balik on the Selenga River, a tributary of the Orkhon. Presumably they were to act as supervisors rather than labourers.

This discussion will have given some idea of the territory within the Uighur empire. Yet a few further and more specific comments may be worthwhile. A Chinese source records the situation in 745 as follows: "The eastern extremity was [the territory of] the Shih-wei, the western, the Altai Mountains, and the southern controlled the Gobi Desert so it covered the entire territory of the ancient Hsiung-nu."[9] This passage shows that the Chinese emperor recog-

[7] See G.J. Ramstedt, "Zwei uigurische runeninschriften in der Nord-Mongolei," *Journal de la Société Finno-ougrienne*, 30.3: 24ff. (1913). The original text is presented with transcription and translation.

[8] Ssu-ma Kuang, *Tzu-chih t'ung chien*, XVI, 7520.

[9] *Hsin T'ang-shu* (New T'ang history), comp. Ou-yang Hsiu et al., Po-na ed., 217A: 3. I have translated those sections of the Uighur chapters in the Old and New T'ang histories dealing with the period 744 to 840 in *The Uighur empire*, pp. 54–125. Earlier translations of the Uighur chapter in the New T'ang history are noted p. 126. For annotated translations into Japanese of

nized the territorial gains which the kaghan had recently made. It is unfortunately a somewhat vague statement since the Altai Mountains and the Gobi both cover a large territory, but it certainly suggests that the extent of the Uighur empire was substantial. The Shih-wei lived south of the Kerulen River. A northern limit is not specified, but probably the kaghan assumed that his possessions ran at least as far as Lake Baikal, into which the Orkhon River flows.

The territory of the Uighurs was expanded west with the firmer conquest of the Basmil and Karluk and then remained constant at least until the death of Tun bagha. The loss of Beshbalik and its aftermath appear to have reduced the extent of the Uighur empire drastically. We are told that the Karluk "overcame [the territory round] the Fou-t'u Valley and seized it from the Uighurs."[10] This valley was probably northwest of Mt. Ötükän,[11] the sacred forest of the Turkic peoples, and dangerously close to Karabalghasun. In any case, the extent of Uighur alarm over the loss of the Fou-t'u may be gauged from the following comments of the Chinese historian: "The Uighurs trembled with fear and moved all the northwestern tribes, with their sheep and their horses, to the south of their royal camp in order to escape from them [the Karluk]."[12]

The recovery and extension of territory by the founder of the second dynasty was certainly impressive, and we know that he succeeded in extending his power as far west as Ferghana. Moreover, a list of dignitaries mentioned in a Manichaean hymnbook suggests that strong Uighur influence, if not necessarily outright domination, was felt in Beshbalik, Kocho, Kucha, Aksu, Kashgar and Karashahr. This text may well refer to a period as late as the reign of Ho-sa (824–32).[13]

the Uighur chapters in both T'ang histories see Saguchi Tōru, "Kaikotsu den" (The biographies of the Uighurs), in Saguchi Tōru, Yamada Nobuo and Mori Masao, *Kiba minzoku shi 2, Seishi hokuteki den* (The history of horse-riding peoples 2, The biographies of the northern races in the standard histories; Tōyō bunko 223; Tokyo, 1972), pp. 299–462.

10 *Chiu T'ang-shu*, 195: 10*b*.

11 See especially Tasaka Kōdō, "Chū Tō ni okeru seihoku henkyō no jōsei ni tsuite" (On the state of the north-western frontiers in the mid-T'ang), *Tōhō gakuhō*, 11.2: 588–9 (Tokyo, 1940). However, Abe Takeo has suggested in *Nishi-Uiguru*, pp. 165–7, that the Fou-t'u Valley lay in P'u-lei Subprefecture (*hsien*) east of Beshbalik.

12 *Chiu T'ang-shu*, 195: 10*b*.

13 The place-names given in the hymn-book (*Maḥrnāmag*) are discussed by W.B. Henning in "Argi and the 'Tokharians'," *Bulletin of the School of Oriental and African Studies* 9, 566–7 (1937–9). I have followed his correspondences here. The period to which the *Maḥrnāmag* refers is uncertain. F.W.K. Müller, who has published the text of a short section of the hymnbook together with transcription and translation, suggests the reign of *Ay tängridä qut bulmiš alp bilgä* kaghan (also called Ho-sa, 824–32) and gives good reasons for so doing. See "Ein Doppelblatt aus einem manichäischen Hymnenbuch (Maḥrnâmag)," *Abhandlungen der Preussischen Akademie der Wissenschaften*, 5, 29–30 (1912). However, Henning, "Argi and the

The focal point of the empire was naturally the capital, Karabalghasun. It was there that the kaghan maintained his court and that the policies of the empire were decided. The great majority of the officials under the kaghan fulfilled both a military and civil function. This is not surprising, since the Uighurs were a warlike people among whom administrators were, on the whole, expected to be competent soldiers.

Most of the official titles found among the Uighurs had been adopted from the Türks. A Chinese record states that in 647 the Uighur kaghan "set up the names of officials similar to those which had formerly existed among the Türks,"[14] and an examination of the Uighurs of the empire period shows no radical departure from this pattern. Moreover, there is no evidence that the functions of the various officials had changed much since earlier times.

There were also a few official titles of Chinese origin. Most of these had been used already by the Türks, and not taken over by the Uighurs directly from China. The most striking was the *tutuk* derived from the Chinese *tu-tu*. This title had been in use among the steppe people for centuries. According to one authority, it had perhaps "not been borrowed by the Turkic founders of the new [Türk] empire, but by their predecessors, the Juan-juans."[15] It is therefore not surprising that the word carried different meanings among the Uighurs and 8th-century Chinese. In the T'ang empire, a *tu-tu* was the leading official of a *tu-tu fu*, a title applied to certain major cities and their environs. Among the Uighurs, the *tutuk* were tribal leaders and there were eleven of them, one for each of the nine major tribes of the confederation and the Karluk and Basmil. A contemporary Chinese scholar writes that, apart from their political leadership they "were responsible for collecting taxes for the state treasury."[16] The *tutuk* of the Uighurs, that is the leading tribe of the nine, was normally a close relation of the kaghan, but not the kaghan himself. Presumably, the chieftains lived among their own people away from the capital, but they certainly held influence at court and maintained their own garrison there.

Information is lacking on whether the position of *tutuk* was hereditary. There is, however, ample evidence that the Yaghlakar kaghans normally succeeded from father to son, a pattern by no means universal among other

'Tokharians'," p. 566 and James Russell Hamilton, *Les Ouïghours à l'époque des Cinq Dynasties, d'après les documents chinois* (Bibliothèque de l'Institut des Hautes Études Chinoises, vol. 10; Paris, 1955), p. 141 suggest rather the reign of the more famous kaghan of the same title who ruled from 808 to 821.

14 *Chiu T'ang-shu*, 195: 1*b*. See also Chavannes, *Documents*, p. 91.

15 Hilda Ecsedy, "Old Turkic titles of Chinese origin," *AOH*, 18: 85 (1965).

16 Liu Chih-hsiao, *Wei-wu-erh tsu li-shih (shang-pien)* (The history of the Uighur nationality, vol. 1) (Beijing, 1985), p. 30. Liu's is a very important example of the numerous works published in the People's Republic of China in the 1980s about China's minority nationalities.

Turkic rulers. Indeed, we know from the Old T'ang history (*Chiu T'ang-shu*) that, when Mo-yen-ch'o kaghan died in 759, his younger son Mou-yü kaghan (759–79) succeeded to the throne only because the elder son was dead. This suggests that the Uighurs followed the rule of primogeniture.

The first kaghan to push this usage aside was Tun bagha, who came to the throne through a *coup d'état*. When he died in 789, his son came to the throne, but was killed the following year by his younger brother. It was probably partly because of the strength of the feeling for father-to-son succession that this action prompted an immediate rebellion in favour of the assassinated kaghan's son. The latter was set on the throne even though still hardly older than a child.

The sources give little information on the system of succession after the foundation of the second dynasty in 795. In only two cases are we told the relationship of kaghan to his predecessor, one being a first cousin or a younger brother, the other a nephew. Both instances occur towards the end of the dynasty and may indicate that the ruling family was losing its vitality rather than that the old principle of succession had been lost.

It is natural that the kaghans should have bestowed official functions and titles on their own relations, and several instances of this practice can be found recorded in the Chinese sources. On the other hand, power was by no means concentrated entirely in the ruling family. The founder of the second dynasty had been a minister at court under his predecessor. The great chief minister of Tun bagha and later Yaghlakar kaghans, El ögäsi, appears to have been unrelated to them. It is probable also that the *tutuk* of the various tribes were drawn from the tribes themselves.

There was another sector of the population with power at court, from whom ministers were doubtless chosen. This was the Sogdians, of whom most, if not all, were Manichaeans. The influence of the Sogdians at court dates at least from Mou-yü kaghan's acceptance of Manichaeism and remained strong from then on. Even under Tun bagha, who killed Mou-yü kaghan for heeding their anti-Chinese advice, Sogdians were not entirely lacking among Uighur officials. The New T'ang history mentions under the year 782 an Uighur ambassador and general named K'ang Ch'ih-hsin, whose surname suggests that he was a Sogdian.[17] No doubt Tun bagha recognized the trading skill of the Sogdians and valued their assistance in economic matters.

It is, however, principally during the 9th century that the political power of

[17] See E.G. Pulleyblank, "A Sogdian colony in Inner Mongolia," *T'oung Pao*, 41: 319–23 (1952).

Manichaeans and Sogdians becomes obvious. In 807 the first Uighur embassy to include Manichaeans arrived in the T'ang capital, Ch'ang-an. From this date onwards, the reports of several of the Uighur embassies tell us that they included Manichaeans and the Old T'ang history even notes, under the year 813, that "Manichaeans were trusted and respected among the Uighurs." The profusion of Manichaeans in the government from the beginning of the 9th century suggests strongly that, after the reaction under Tun bagha against Sogdians and their religion, the new dynasty which replaced his clan strove consciously to encourage and patronize them. There arose an increasingly formidable priesthood buttressed by an ethnic clique. It may be that there were even times when the kaghans found themselves too dependent for comfort on this largely foreign power-group.

If the monarchs' officials and advisers were drawn largely from the Manichaean Sogdians and the royal family, the katuns were often Chinese. The principal wife of at least seven of the thirteen Uighur rulers was a Chinese. One of Mo-yen-ch'o's katuns was actually the daughter of Emperor Su-tsung (756–63), the Princess of Ning-kuo. She returned to China in 759 upon her husband's death and the younger Princess of Ning-kuo, who had escorted her to Karabalghasun and became the concubine of Mo-yen-ch'o kaghan, was made the katun of his successor. Mou-yü kaghan also married in succession two daughters of a famous T'ang general, P'u-ku Huai-en, who in 764 rebelled against the dynasty he had served so long and died the following year. He was regarded as a Chinese, even though he was descended from the Uighur Bukhu tribe. Mou-yü kaghan's first Chinese wife, whom he had married before his accession to the throne, died in 768 and her sister became his bride the following year. Tun bagha's katun, the Princess of Hsien-an, was the daughter of Emperor Te-tsung (779–805). When Mo-yen-ch'o had married the Princess of Ning-kuo, it had been regarded as a great honor that the emperor should grant a foreign ruler one of his own daughters, for Su-tsung was the first T'ang emperor to take this course. But by Tun bagha's time, the Uighurs had come to expect such a favour, though the Chinese court by no means shared this attitude. The Princess of Hsien-an outlived her first husband by nineteen years, until 808, and is known to have become the katun of three of Tun's successors. There was only one other Chinese princess who became the wife of a kaghan, and that was the Princess of T'ai-ho, Hsien-tsung's daughter. She arrived in Karabalghasun in 822 and lived among the Uighurs until after the fall of their empire; and she may well have been the wife of more than one kaghan. The princesses named above provide a colourful side of the history of the Uighur empire, especially since, of the more than twenty women the T'ang

court bestowed as brides on foreign rulers, the Princesses of Ning-kuo, Hsien-an and T'ai-ho were the only ones who were actually the daughters of Chinese emperors.[18]

Over his wives, officials and people the kaghan was in theory all-powerful, simply by virtue of his royal status. The full title of seven out of the thirteen kaghans[19] includes one of the three phrases *tängridä*, *ay tängridä* or *kün tängridä*, showing that they believed their power was derived from "Heaven," "the God of the Moon," or "the God of the Sun" respectively. The beginning of the Sogdian version of the Karabalghasun inscription refers to one kaghan of the second dynasty as "the great Turkic ruler of the world who has received his splendor from Heaven."[20] This last eulogy suggests that the Uighur rulers claimed universal suzerainty over all nations. Certainly the titles they took upon themselves prove that, like most sovereigns of Mongolia both before and after the Uighurs, they considered themselves to exercise government by a more than human right.

The T'ang emperors naturally did not share the belief that the Uighur kaghans owed their majesty to Heaven. The Chinese histories record the ritual "appointment" of the successive kaghans, as if their right to rule was a favour granted by the Chinese emperor. The Uighurs themselves probably interpreted the ceremony merely as a formal act of recognition, for certainly they did not regard themselves as under Chinese guardianship. On the other hand, the Uighur rulers were no doubt happy over this outward sign of approval from the emperor. Despite the contempt in which some of them held the T'ang, the Chinese court retained a good deal of prestige among the peoples of Inner Asia.

In accordance with the divine authority they believed was theirs, the Uighur kaghans expected both their subjects and foreigners to show respect by an act of ritual. Nobody was exempt from this. When Mou-yü kaghan was in China in 762 assisting the T'ang forces against Shih Ch'ao-i, he demanded that the Chinese heir-apparent himself should make a ceremonial dance as a sign of reverence. An official subordinate to the prince refused on his behalf, but this proved a costly stand. The official and three other Chinese were savagely beaten and two of them died within a day. Another ceremonial sign of esteem

[18] See K'uang P'ing-chang, "T'ang-tai kung-chu ho-ch'in k'ao" (A study of the diplomatic marriages of T'ang princesses), *Shih-hsüeh nien-pao*, 2.2: 49ff. (1935).

[19] The Uighur kaghans are listed, together with all their names and titles, in Hamilton, *Les Ouïghours*, pp. 139–41. See also Liu Chih-hsiao, *Wei-we-erh tsu*, pp. 64–5, which gives the kaghans' relationship to their predecessor. However, the kaghan both list as ruling from 805 to 808 should, I believe, be excluded.

[20] See Olaf Hansen, "Zur sogdischen Inschrift auf dem dreisprachigen Denkmal von Karabalgasun," *JSFOu*, 44.3: 15 (1930).

for the kaghan was that his wives were buried with him when he died. This course was requested of the Princess of Ning-kuo when Mo-yen-ch'o kaghan died in 759. She refused, but succeeded in pacifying the Uighur courtiers by slashing her face, an ordinary sign of grief, loyalty or respect for the dead.

These illustrations suggest that, during some periods at least, even eminent Chinese could defy the wishes of the Uighur ruler only at great risk to themselves. This raises the more significant question of how complete the kaghans' power was among their own people. Certainly some of the Uighur inscriptions leave an impression of effective megalomania, but they are written in a highly rhetorical style and may be misleading. On the whole, the Chinese sources convey a similar feeling but in a far more reserved and unsympathetic way.

The degree of effective authority wielded by any kaghan naturally depended on the strength of his personality. There is no doubt that the first rulers of the Yaghlakar dynasty held undisputed power. They might ask the advice of their ministers, but certainly felt free to disregard it. As mentioned earlier, Mou-yü kaghan was advised by his Sogdian ministers to invade China. He chose to follow the suggestion. After a disgraceful incident in 780, in which an overenthusiastic Chinese official called Chang Kuang-sheng massacred about 1,000 Uighurs and Sogdians in north China in the hope of undermining Uighur power, Tun bagha was advised by all his ministers to take revenge on the Chinese by the simple expedient of killing the Chinese who came to Karabalghasun to apologize. Tun rejected the advice. It was only at the end of the dynasty that the kaghan's ministers gained ascendancy over him. In particular, El ögäsi undoubtedly had the last Yaghlakar kaghan completely under his thumb.

The second dynasty provides only one example of a ruler really strong by comparison with the first kaghans of the earlier period, namely the dynastic founder. Yet the impression conveyed in the sources is that the monarchs of the early ninth century were perfectly capable of controlling their own court. It was not until about 830 that the picture changed drastically. By that time the empire was fast crumbling and the last three rulers failed utterly to cope with the rebellious subjects of their empire. The pattern of decline was the same for both dynasties.

It may be added, too, that in general only the weak kaghans met with violent deaths because of attempts to overthrow them. Of the thirteen rulers of the Uighur empire, at least five were assassinated and a further one was either murdered or committed suicide following the success of a rebellion led by one of his ministers. Only one of the six, Mou-yü kaghan, had enjoyed a

successful reign, and the other five all died within eight years of the fall of their respective dynasties.

It is not unusual historically that the rulers of an empire should be obeyed in their own court and capital except at the end of a dynasty. It may be more useful to ask how far the rule of the kaghans extended beyond their immediate surroundings. Only scanty information is available, but it suggests that there were severe limitations on the implementation of the royal writ throughout most parts of the empire. The *tutuk* who ruled the tribes were certainly concerned in court affairs and acted as ambassadors or generals, but nowhere do we find any proof that the kaghans exercised any real control over the activities of the tutuk among their own tribes.

The testimony of the famous Arab traveller, Tamīm ibn-Baḥr al-Muṭṭawwi'ī, who visited the Uighur empire about 821, gives a more positive clue. He reports that Manichaeism was only one of the two religions practised by the people in the towns outside the capital, adding that "Among its population [Karabalghasun's], the Zindīq religion [Manichaeism] prevails."[21] This indicates clear limits to the effect of central control in the empire, since it was nearly sixty years since the edict which ordered every person in the empire to embrace Manichaeism.

The court's authority was still weaker in the distant parts of the empire. Beshbalik and other western cities appear to have been inside Uighur territory, yet at least until 790 the Chinese also maintained governors there and regarded them as Chinese protectorates. Tun bagha must have regarded Beshbalik as semi-independent since, according to the New T'ang history, he charged a toll on people coming through the main part of his territory from the city. A Buddhist pilgrim called Wu-k'ung passed through Uighur territory in 789, but left his Sanskrit books in Beshbalik for safety's sake because he knew the kaghan was not a Buddhist.[22] He clearly felt that the city was beyond Uighur jurisdiction.

To be within the boundaries of the empire did not exclude the possibility either of nearly complete autonomy or of Chinese protection.

[21] See V. Minorsky, "Tamīm ibn Baḥr's journey to the Uyghurs," *BSOAS*, 12.2: 283 (1948). Minorsky's article gives the original Arabic text and a translation. Minorsky discussed the travels of Tamīm briefly in his *Ḥudud al-'Ālam: 'The regions of the world' a Persian geography 372 A.H. – 982 A.D.* (E.J.W. Gibb Memorial New Series, vol. 11; London, 1937), pp. 268–70, but revised several of his conclusions in the later article cited above.

[22] See Sylvain Lévi and Ed. Chavannes, "Voyages des pélerins bouddhistes, L'itinéraire d'Ou-k'ong (751–790)," *Journal asiatique*, 9.6, 366 (1895). For further evidence on the the limitations of central control see Annemarie von Gabain, "Steppe und Stadt im Leben der ältesten Türken," *Der Islam*, 29: 58 (1949), where there are comments on a text given, with transcription and translation, in F.W.K. Müller, "Zwei Pfahlinschriften aus den Turfanfunden," *APAW*, 3: 6–13 (1915).

Religion

The doctrinal affiliations of the kaghans and their subjects have been of some importance in reaching this conclusion and a few others connected with the political life of the Uighurs. No account of these people can be complete without a treatment of their religion, especially as it related to the most striking aspect of their history during the period 744 to 840, their adoption of Manichaeism.

The founder of the religion, the Persian Mani (216?–76?) postulated two opposing principles, that of good or light and that of evil or darkness. He held that the souls of men shared in the divine, but that the material body, essentially the helpmate of the power of darkness, obstructed its development within the individual. To fight against this negative force and thus find relief from suffering, human beings must keep themselves as free as possible from the material world.

Mani saw time in three phases. In the first of them matter and spirit were separate, and in the second mingled. Man, as body and spirit, was the only place of mixture and existed in this form only in the second phase. By abstracting himself from matter, he could hasten the end of this evil stage and bring on a great purification which would introduce the third phase. Good and evil would then be once again and irrevocably separated.

Mani's religion divided mankind into two broad categories. The first was the elect, the clergy of Manichaeism, themselves subdivided into a clear hierarchy, led by the supreme head (Chinese *fa-wang*) and regional "archbishops" (Chinese *mu-she*). Of this group was demanded a life of celibacy and fasting, including a ban on meat and fermented liquid. The second category was the auditors, the laymen of Manichaeism. They were expected to be abstemious, kind and generous in giving alms, but were allowed to eat normally and to keep a wife. An auditor who had fulfilled his duties would be reincarnated, after death, as an elect. When the great purification was over, those who had triumphed over the material world would live in the region of absolute light, while those who had succumbed would be taken to the region of total darkness.

Mani's was a proselytizing faith, and spread to many parts of the Eurasian continent. There was a Manichaean population in the Byzantine empire from an early date and the religion attracted a considerable following in medieval Europe. The Manichaeans also sent missionaries east and in 694 a dignitary of the church arrived at the Chinese court. He was followed in 719 by a *mu-she*, who was welcomed in Ch'ang-an both for his knowledge of astronomy and

for his religion. Emperor Hsüan-tsung (712–56) even ordered that a temple be built for his guest's use. By 732, however, the emperor had undergone a change of heart and issued an edict condemning Manichaeism as "a basically evil doctrine which deceives the people by falsely calling itself Buddhism."[23] Despite these harsh words, the proclamation explicitly allowed non-Chinese to continue practising the Doctrine of Light (*ming-chiao*), as the Chinese called it, and this was to be of great importance for the Uighurs.

Among the places which maintained foreign Manichaean communities was Lo-yang. This city, the most important in China after Ch'ang-an, fell twice to the rebel forces of An Lu-shan and his successors, and both times it was retaken by the T'ang government with the help of powerful Uighur contingents. On the second of these occasions, Uighur forces under Mou-yü kaghan remained in the region of the city from November 762 until about February the following year. During that time the Uighur soldiers went round pillaging the neighborhood and treating the inhabitants with violence. However, it appears that the kaghan was making frequent visits to a group of Sogdians who were devotees of Manichaeism. These men were able to exercise a great influence over their guest and when he returned to Karabalghasun he took four of them with him. The most important was a certain Jui-hsi (lit. "Perspicacious serenity") whose name is similar to those found among Buddhist monks. The Chinese version of the Karabalghasun inscription is warm in its praise for him. "He was marvellously learned in the Doctrine of Light [. . .] and his eloquence was like a cascade. That is why he was able to initiate the Uighurs to the true religion."[24]

Shortly after the kaghan and his followers arrived back in Karabalghasun, a debate began at court over whether the Uighur state should adopt Manichaeism. A powerful faction led by a senior official was bitterly hostile to the innovation. However, Jui-hsi's group succeeded in persuading the kaghan to override this opposition, and he issued a decree that Manichaeism should be embraced by his subjects.

According to one report, this decision was greeted with great joy by the people, who "gathered in crowds of thousands and tens of thousands [. . .] and gave themselves over to joy until morning."[25] Yet despite these signs of popular approval, Mou-yü kaghan was apparently unconvinced that the zeal

[23] Tu Yu, *T'ung-tien* (Complete institutions), Wan-yu wen-k'u ed. (Shih-t'ung, vol. 1; Shanghai, 1935), p. 229c. See also the translation of Edouard Chavannes and Paul Pelliot in "Un traité manichéen retrouvé en China," *JA*, 11.1: 154 (1913).

[24] See Chavannes and Pelliot, "Un traité manichéen," pp. 191–2.

[25] See W. Bang and A. von Gabain, "Türkische Turfan-Texte II," *SPAW*: 416–17 (1929). A transcription of the original Old Turkic text is given together with a translation.

of the ordinary man would prove durable. He divided his people into groups of ten, in each of which one person was made responsible for the religious instruction and good works of the other nine. We see here echoes of an ancient military system, practised in Mongolia since the time of the Hsiung-nu, whereby one soldier was placed in charge of a unit of ten.

Mou-yü kaghan was one of the few monarchs in history to impose Manichaeism on his people and (apart from the later Uighur kaghans) the only one in East Asia. So curious and unique an event requires explanation, but this is unfortunately not forthcoming in the sources and we are reduced to speculation. Several possible motives for the kaghan's action suggest themselves. When the Sogdians in Lo-yang talked to him of their religion, it may have struck him as an ideal mixture between sophistication and rigour, an excellent tool for raising the cultural level of his people without in any way relaxing the discipline which he, as the leader of a warlike people, demanded of his subjects. Its contempt for the body and material goods must have appealed to his militaristic nature.

Mou-yü kaghan's choice of Manichaeism rather than Buddhism or other religions was motivated partly by a desire to show his independence of T'ang influence. This was a faith which the Chinese disliked. It could boast but few adherents in the Middle Kingdom and the emperor had even condemned it. The kaghan had ample reason to despise the Chinese, who must have seemed to him feeble and helpless. His behavior towards the heir-apparent not long before and his brutality towards the ordinary Chinese citizens show that it was not through love that he had agreed to help save the T'ang from destruction. To adopt a religion such as Manichaeism would demonstrate to the emperor that he cared nothing for China, and would help lessen its political and cultural impact in his empire. He possibly desired greater sophistication for his subjects, but it must come from peoples further west, not from the T'ang.

Even more important to Mou-yü may have been the financial strength of the Sogdians. The kaghan's own political power depended to a great extent on his economic supremacy and that of his clan. Alliance with the Sogdians through adopting their religion was an important way of securing this objective. Among other financial matters, the Sogdians were in an excellent position to help the kaghan trade in the western regions, exchanging silk from China for other goods such as gold and silver.[26]

Nevertheless, to place an interpretation of this sort on Mou-yü kaghan's

[26] I owe the points raised in this paragraph to personal correspondence with Moriyasu Takao.

conversion is not to deny that he could have felt a genuine fervor for Manichaeism. The cruelty of war has been known to inspire religious enthusiasm even in the most brutal of men. The aftermath of the savage battle which had expelled the last rebels from Lo-yang was an ideal opportunity for the Sogdians to exert their influence on the royal visitor. Although the few months the kaghan spent in the city seem scarcely adequate to produce a deep conversion, the impact of Manichaeism might well have strengthened in his mind after he returned with Jui-hsi to his own capital. Naturally, later Uighurs believed him sincere and one early text describes him as an "emanation of Mani."[27]

Mou-yü kaghan's decision to establish the Doctrine of Light in his empire was followed by friendly relations with dignitaries of the international Manichaean community. The supreme leader of the church sent a message of congratulations to the kaghan and also despatched some elects, both men and women, to spread and exalt the religion. Other Manichaeans in lands far from Karabalghasun also showed great interest in the Uighur sovereign's change of heart and recognized what an asset he could be to their church. This is suggested by the existence of an Iranian text discovered by Albert von Le Coq at Turfan. Not only does it refer to the kaghan as "the ruler of the East, preserver of religion and helpmate of truthful men,"[28] but also gives a detailed list of Uighur officials. Its author was clearly very well informed on developments in Karabalghasun and probably enjoyed close relations with the court there.

Meanwhile, Mou-yü kaghan was determined to use his influence for the benefit of his religion not only in his own empire but in China as well. According to one source, he "instructed some monks of the Religion of Light to take their doctrine to the T'ang."[29] In 768, an imperial order was issued that Manichaean temples be built, probably in Ch'ang-an and Lo-yang. Three years later the Uighurs asked permission to establish centers in four more cities, this time in south China. The emperor allowed the construction of a Manichaean temple in each of present-day Kingchow, Hupeh province, Nanchang in Kiangsi, Shaohsing in Chekiang and Yangchow, Kiangsu. It may be that the kaghan wanted these temples partly as a means of supervising Uighurs resident in China and keeping them to some extent free from the influence of Chinese culture.

[27] See F.W.K. Müller, "Uigurica II," *APAW*, 3: 95 (1910).

[28] F.W.K. Müller, "Der Hofstaat eines Uiguren-Königs," *Festschrift Vilhelm Thomsen zur Vollendung des siebzigsten Lebensjahres am 25 Januar 1912* (Leipzig, 1912), pp. 208–9. A transcription of the original text is given with translation.

[29] See Chavannes and Pelliot, "Un traité manichéen," p. 263.

Despite Mou-yü kaghan's vigorous actions on behalf of Manichaeism, the faction hostile to his religion was still alive at his court and gained ascendancy during the reign of Tun bagha. It has been suggested that Tun leaned towards Nestorian Christianity. One Latin record states that in the early 780s "a Turkic king" asked the Nestorian patriarch Timothy I (728–823) "to set up an archbishop in his region"[30] and that the latter complied with the request. However, the center of the archbishopric lay on the banks of the Syr Darya,[31] a long way west of Karabalghasun, and consequently the "king" in question cannot have been Tun bagha. His adherence was probably to the natural religion of the Türks. It takes a long time to eradicate an ancient way of thinking and a conservative movement against Mou-yü kaghan's innovation would not be unexpected. Moreover, there are signs of a connection between Tun and the Turkic natural religion. The T'ang histories report that he was a leader of an expedition in China in 765, during which he helped repulse a powerful contingent of Tibetans from China. The Uighur forces had brought magicians with them to the Middle Kingdom and paid great attention to what they said.

Although his successor reacted against it, Mou-yü kaghan's attitude towards Manichaeism had struck deep roots among the Uighurs. It was reinstated not long after Tun died and remained strong at court throughout the second dynasty. The titles of all the kaghans of that period except the last (for whom no title is recorded) are known to have included reference to "the God of the Moon" or "the God of the Sun," phrases not found in the kaghans' titles until 789. They are symbols of darkness and light in Manichaeism and strongly suggest affiliations with that doctrine on the part of the second dynasty's founder and his successors.[32] In 807, after a break of more than thirty years, Uighur embassies again began asking the T'ang court for permission to build Manichaean temples in China, a sign that interest in the church had completely revived in Karabalghasun. I have already mentioned the growth of Sogdian and Manichaean power at court. The priesthood was becoming an ever more influential professional group, with a social status probably no lower than the military.

In relating the arrival of the 807 embassy at court, the New T'ang history

[30] See Bang and von Gabain, "Türkische Turfan-Texte II," p. 420 and von Gabain, "Steppe und Stadt," pp. 47–8.

[31] See Jean Dauvillier, "Les provinces chaldéennes 'de l'extérieur' au moyen âge," *Mélanges offerts au R.P. Ferdinand Cavallera* (Toulouse, 1948), p. 285.

[32] See Tasaka Kōdō, "Kaikotsu ni okeru Manikyō hakugai undō" (An anti-Manichean movement among the Uighurs), *Tōhō gakuhō*, 11.1: 229–31 (Tokyo, 1940). This article puts forward the suggestion that there was a restoration of the traditional Turkic religion under *Tun bagha*.

tells us something of the habits of this powerful clergy. "Their laws prescribe that they should eat only in the evening, drink water, eat strong vegetables and abstain from fermented mare's milk."[33] The abstemiousness characteristic of western Manichaean elects seems to have applied also to those among the Uighurs. In other vital respects, also, Uighur Manichaeism appears to have followed orthodox patterns. The Karabalghasun inscription and Maḥrnāmag attest to a belief in the principles of light and darkness, the division of time into three phases, and to a recognition of the sanctity of scriptures held as canonical in other regions. Mani's followers among the Uighurs shared with their co-religionists further west the notion that after a person's death his soul could inhabit another body. We find the same distinction between elect and auditor; and, among the former, the same hierarchy and division into male and female.

The Uighur Manichaeans may have adopted a rigid code of morals and rules, but did not necessarily always live up to it, a failing common to the followers of all creeds in all centuries. Mani's hatred of material things did not prevent the Uighur court from becoming more and more immersed in luxury, and none of the kaghans appears to have been greatly troubled by this development. There is even evidence of a dissident sect in the west of the Uighur empire the monks of which were willing to forego some of the more extreme abstemious practices of orthodox Manichaean elects. Sogdian letters addressed to a Manichaean dignitary in Kocho and probably referring to this sect complain that certain monks are carrying on such banned activities as washing their bodies in flowing water, personally felling trees and digging in the garden.[34]

To expect perfection of any group of people would be unreasonable. Yet the deviations noted above underline the incomplete impact of Manichaeism on the Uighur empire. Despite Mou-yü kaghan's edict of 763, the old natural cults of the Turkic people, which had earlier been the prevailing religion among the Uighurs, remained strong among the Uighurs. The Karabalghasun inscription records part of the edict in favor of the new faith and notes some of the features the Manichaeans hoped to eliminate.

[33] See also Chavannes and Pelliot, "Un traité manichéen," pp. 264ff., where there are translations and a lengthy discussion of this and parallel passages. The characters I have translated "fermented mare's milk", they render as *de lait et de beurre*. The great Russian sinologist Father Iakinf Bichurin translated them as *kymis*, that is, "fermented mare's milk". See *Sobranie svedenij o narodakh, obitavshikh v Srednej Azii v drevnie vremena*, 3 vols. (Moscow–Leningrad, 1950–3 ed.), I, 331. This substance has been commonly consumed in Mongolia since time immemorial and is the most likely meaning of the characters in the present context.

[34] See W. Henning, "Neue Materialien zur Geschichte des Manichäismus," *Zeitschrift der Deutschen Morgenländischen Gesellschaft*, N.F. 15: 16–18 (1936).

Let all sculpted or painted images of the demon be entirely destroyed by fire; let those who pray to genies or prostrate themselves before demons all be [three characters missing] and let the people accept the Religion of Light. Let [the country] with barbarous customs and smoking blood change into one where the people eat vegetables; and let the state where men kill be transformed into a kingdom where good works are encouraged.[35]

In 765, two years after this edict, the Uighur generals consulted magicians and begged for an oracle before embarking on their military campaign in China. They also ordered these religious leaders to call up wind and snow; and when the weather changed to the decisive military advantage of the Uighurs, the magicians were given the credit for the support of the elements. I have already noted the probable restoration of the Turkic cults under Tun bagha, and it is likely that the savage tribes who dwelt within the precincts of the Uighur empire away from the capital continued the practice of their ancient religion.

Even among Manichaean Uighurs, features of the religion proscribed in 763 could still be found beneath the surface. Witness the following observation from Tamīm ibn-Baḥr.

And of the wonders of the country of the Turks are some pebbles they have, with which they bring down rain, snow, cold, etc., as they wish. The story of these pebbles in their possession is well known and widely spread and no Turk denies it. And these [pebbles] are especially in the possession of the king of the Toghuzghuz and no other of their kings possesses them.[36]

The kaghans themselves apparently took this old power seriously long after their conversion to Manichaeism. Another striking remnant from the past was the respect paid to Ötükän, the sacred forest of the traditional Turkic religion. Uighur Manichaean texts mention this divinity with due reverence,[37] giving no hint that its status might have been changed with the introduction of the Religion of Light.

Social change

Despite the persistence of the old ways, it is clear from their approach to religion that the Uighurs of the empire period were undergoing change more rapidly than at any time in their earlier history. They were definitely advancing towards a more sophisticated stage of civilization in their modes of thought, social patterns and economy.

[35] See Chavannes and Pelliot, "Un traité manichéen," pp. 193–4, 198.
[36] Minorsky, "Tamīm ibn Baḥr's journey," p. 285.
[37] See, for example, A. von Le Coq, "Türkische Manichaica aus Chotscho III," *APAW*, 2, 35 (1922), and the comments on this text by von Gabain in "Steppe und Stadt," pp. 61–2.

The Old T'ang history records that the Uighurs of the period before 744 "moved above in search of waters and pastures [. . .] and excelled in horsemanship and archery."[38] They had been in fact originally a typical nomadic people. Their livelihood had depended on stock-breeding and hunting; agriculture had been foreign to them. They had not constructed permanent buildings or cities and their art and culture had been of a very primitive kind.

To a large extent the Uighurs remained nomadic. All through the period of the empire, their economy was dominated by certain domestic animals, principally the sheep and the horse, but also the ox and the camel. The breeding of these animals involved the use of grazing lands, and since it was not possible to use one area indefinitely for this purpose, the breeders were forced to move from place to place. Of all the animals the Uighur nomads tended, sheep were the most valuable economically. They provided wool for the felt out of which tents could be made, their skin could be used as clothing, their dung burnt for warmth in winter, their flesh eaten; and they also yielded milk, some of which could be made into cheese. Horses and oxen were also sources of meat and milk, fermented mare's milk being particularly popular among all but the Manichaean elect. An added advantage of both animals was that they could function as beasts of burden. Horses were of particular value because they could move so quickly. They were, in addition, used extremely widely as articles of trade and played an important role in the military, religious and artistic life of the Uighurs.

At the time of the battles against An Lu-shan's son in 757, the daily rations given to the Uighur army of about 4,000 were 20 cattle, 200 sheep and 40 *shih* (about 2,900 kgms) of grain. The large supply of meat is not surprising considering the nature of Uighur society. Indeed, it is most unlikely that the ban on eating animal flesh in the edict of 763 was extensively obeyed and may even have been intended to apply only to the elect of the new faith. When the Chinese traveller Wang Yen-te visited the Uighurs of the Turfan region in the 980s, he reported that "all the poor eat meat," and spoke of "mediocre horses destined to be eaten."[39] There is, therefore, no doubt that the flesh of domestic animals remained part of the standard Uighur diet.

The reference to grain as part of the troops' rations is more striking. The generous quantity given was perhaps due to the enthusiasm of a Chinese. Yet

[38] See Chavannes, *Documents*, p. 88.

[39] See Stanislas Julien, "Notices sur les pays et les peuples étrangers, tirées des géographies et des annales chinoises, III, Les Oïgours," *JA*, 4.9, 64 (1847), a translation from Ma Tuan-lin, *Wen-hsien t'ung-k'ao* (Complete examination of old documents and various compositions), Wan-yu wen-k'u ed., 2 vols. (Shih-t'ung, vol. 7; Shanghai, 1936), II, 2639*c*.

agriculture cannot have been unknown among the Uighurs even in 757, and probably grew larger in scale with the injunction in the edict of 763 to eat vegetables. The clergy are known to have eaten onions and allied bulbs (the "strong vegetables" mentioned in connection with the 807 embassy), and these probably spread to some extent to other sections of the community. The reports of Tamīm ibn-Baḥr show clearly that, while the attention given to pasture since time immemorial was still very much alive in 821, settled cultivators were occupying an increasingly important place in Uighur society.

> He [Tamīm] journeyed twenty days in steppes where there were springs and grass but no villages or towns: only the men of the relay service living in tents [. . .] And then, after that, he travelled twenty days among villages lying closely together and cultivated tracts [. . .] After all these days he arrived at the king's town [Karabalghasun]. He reports that this is a great town, rich in agriculture.[40]

Tamīm's claim that the Uighurs practised agriculture has been strikingly confirmed by the discoveries of archeologists, who have found signs that the Uighurs used millstones, pestles and irrigation canals, and even evidence that grain, such as millet, was buried together with corpses of certain Uighurs.[41]

Associated with the growth of agriculture we find the development of towns, the presence of which is well attested in the passage just quoted. We know also two important cities built on the initiative of Uighur kaghans. One of them was Bay-Balik [lit. "Rich Town"], to which I referred earlier. Work on its construction was started in 757 upon an order from kaghan. The other was Karabalghasun, built at about the same time. Both, then, were completed under Mo-yen-ch'o kaghan, so that the process of urbanization must have begun very quickly after the empire was founded. Very little is known about Bay-Balik, and its precise significance for the Uighurs is unclear. It is certain, however, that Karabalghasun developed into quite an impressive city. It contained a royal palace, which appears from the Shine-usu inscription (south side, line 10) to have been built at about the same time as the city itself, and was completely walled. Tamīm records that "the town has twelve iron gates of huge size. The town is populous and thickly crowded and has markets and various trades."[42] He adds that it was dominated by a golden tent, which could be seen from some distance outside the city. It stood on the flat top of the palace and could hold 100 people.

At least part of the Uighur community had forsaken its nomadic past. Even outside the great cities of the west like Kocho and Beshbalik, a settled urban

[40] See Minorsky, "Tamīm ibn Baḥr's journey," p. 283.

[41] See L.R. Kyzlasov, *Istorija Tuvy v srednie veka* (Moscow, 1969), p. 85. See also Liu Chih-hsiao, *Wei-wu-erh tsu*, pp. 39–40.

[42] See Minorsky, "Tamīm ibn Baḥr's journey," p. 283.

civilization was being developed. The presence of "markets and various trades" shows that produce was brought from outside the capital and dispensed to the people through middlemen. Archeologists have found evidence of handicrafts in the Karabalghasun area at about the time of the Uighur empire.[43] The variety of occupations and professions had widened. The military was still important and Tamīm himself testifies that an enormous army was garrisoned in Karabalghasun, but it had to face far keener competition from other groups to retain its dominant social status.

Along with the partial urbanization of life went an expansion of foreign trade. The Uighurs needed fewer of the vast number of horses they bred, and they were more and more attracted to luxury goods. Earlier steppe people had exchanged some of their horses for Chinese silk, but the scale of the Sino-Uighur trade was unusually large. It reached impressive proportions about 760 and became one of the most important aspects of their mutual relations. A Chinese historian explains its development as follows:

> The Uighurs, taking advantage of their service to China [during the An Lu-shan rebellion], frequently used to send embassies with horses to trade at an agreed price for silken fabrics. Usually they came every year, trading one horse for forty pieces of silk. Every time they came they brought several tens of thousands of horses [. . .] The barbarians acquired silk insatiably and we were given useless horses. The court found it extremely galling.[44]

This was a forced trade, of far greater value to the Uighurs than to the Chinese, and continued throughout the period of the Uighur empire. Most of the vast quantity of silk involved could be re-exported to other countries or function as a form of currency. But some of it was possibly used among the urban rich, who were becoming accustomed to a softer life. Other commodities were exchanged besides those already noted. When a group of Uighur officials and princesses came to Ch'ang-an in 821 to welcome the Princess of T'ai-ho, "they presented the court with camel's hair, brocade, white silk, sable and mouse furs," and other things like jade belts as well as 1,000 horses and 50 camels.[45] These goods were no doubt sometimes traded by the Uighurs, but detailed information is nowhere recorded.

Not only were the Uighurs able to impose a forced trade on China, but they also established a money-market within the Middle Kingdom itself. After the An Lu-shan rebellion collapsed, certain Uighurs took up residence in China,

[43] See Liu Chih-hsiao, *Wei-wu-erh tsu*, p. 39.
[44] *Chiu T'ang-shu*, 195: 8*b*-9; Mackerras, *The Uighur empire*, p. 86.
[45] *T'ang hui-yao* (T'ang compilations), comp. Wang P'u et al., Ts'ung-shu chi-ch'eng ed., 16 vols. (Shanghai, 1936), XVI, 1748.

where some of them married and became significant property-owners, and lent out money to be repaid with interest. The T'ang government was uneasy over these activities and the influence foreigners were able to acquire in financial and consequently political circles, and tried to take measures against the Uighur moneylenders. These efforts, however, met with little success and, by the end of the 9th century, the Uighurs had developed an efficient machinery which gave them a significant degree of control over Chinese finance. The growth of this power had been made possible by the dependence of the T'ang on Uighur military might, but does not appear to have been hindered by the collapse of the empire in 840.

For the purposes of commercial relations, either within their empire or beyond it borders, the Uighurs used a simple system of transportation based on the horse and the camel. Tamīm ibn-Baḥr records that the fastest possible means of carriage in Uighur territory was a relay of horses, but seems to have been referring more to the transport of persons than of goods. This means of travel was possible for only six months of the year on account of the cold. When large numbers of people moved together, they journeyed in a caravan of camels, horses and, sometimes, carriages. The most magnificent caravan associated with the Uighurs of the period 744 to 840 was of Chinese origin. It was that which took the Princess of T'ai-ho and several thousand Chinese and Uighur attendants from Ch'ang-an to Karabalghasun. It left the former city on 28 August 821 and did not arrive in the Uighur capital until early the following year. Large caravans may have been able to travel all the year round, but they were an exceedingly slow means of carriage.

The system of transportation may have been more developed than in earlier times, but was essentially unchanged. The same is so of Uighur accommodation. Despite the growth of towns and cities, the tent appears to have remained by far the most important form of dwelling among the Uighurs. Naturally the rich owned at least two tents and sometimes many more. These may have been movable, but dwellings of this sort were not necessarily temporary. Even in Karabalghasun ministers and commoners lived in tents. The most significant example of all was the golden tent to which Tamīm refers. So famous did this structure become that the foreign enemies of the kaghans regarded it as the very seat of Uighur power; and this was not unexpected, since gold was an imperial symbol. In declaring his intention to overthrow the empire, the Kirghiz leader announced to the kaghan: "Your fate is sealed, for I shall certainly seize your golden tent."[46]

[46] Ssu-ma Kuang, *Tzu-chih t'ung-chien*, XVII, 7947.

The existence of such a splendid tent is but one symptom of a general rise in the sophistication of Uighur society. There were several reasons for this development.

The establishment of a strong and widespread administration, made necessary by the founding of an empire, tends to result in the construction of a permanent seat of government. The ruler aims to be in touch with happenings everywhere in his territory and in a period of poor communications everybody must know where to find him. Once a city is built, nomadism begins to decline. Agriculture appears and a settled urban population, dependent on food produced outside the town, emerges within a fairly short time. Conditions for intellectual pursuits improve, paving the way for the growth of a more developed civilization. All these trends are logical and each of them can be seen clearly in operation among the Uighurs.

Chinese influence had been felt among the nine tribes long before 744. Even in the 7th century the advanced political institutions of the Central Kingdom were creating an impact. It is not surprising that Chinese should have helped build cities such as Bay-Balik. The products of the Uighurs' great southern neighbor also proved desirable to them as the life of the city-dweller grew more comfortable.

Meanwhile, the Sogdians were exercising a further civilizing influence over the Uighurs. As it happened, the kaghans deliberately chose Sogdian rather than Chinese culture and the Sogdian impression upon Uighur society was consequently more pervasive. The Sogdians assisted their less sophisticated hosts in the development of trade and taught them much about the arts of living. Above all, this foreign community introduced the Uighurs to a religion which involved a settled clergy and temples and, as a result, the nomadic life became more and more difficult, less and less attractive. Certain select Uighurs could develop their intellectual and cultural capacities, and grapple with theological and other problems which would have been quite beyond the understanding of their ancestors.

The Uighurs would no doubt have developed a partly urban society of their own accord, but the twin influences of the more highly developed cultures of the Chinese and Sogdians contributed a great deal towards accelerating the process.

The part-nomad, part-settled empire of the Uighurs collapsed after less than a century of power. Let us conclude with a brief enquiry into the causes of its fall.

The Arab writer al-Jāḥiẓ, who died in 868 or 869, believed that the Uighurs'

conversion to Manichaeism had contributed to their decline. "The Toghuzghuz used to excel the Karluk, even if the latter were twice as numerous," he wrote, but after they adopted Manichaeism they began to suffer defeats.[47] Certainly, their newly adopted religion tended to turn the minds of the Uighurs and their rulers away from the love of war and encouraged more peaceful activities, and Jāḥiẓ's view is a reasonable one. But the influences associated with Manichaeism were also important factors. The Uighur empire was trying to absorb an entirely strange culture which necessitated a partial break with their past. The conflicts which this attempt created – between the settled, foreign-influenced city-dwellers and the still traditionally inclined nomads – must surely have resulted in considerable tensions among the Uighurs.

The discrepancies between life in the cities and away from them grew wider. Two quite distinct and utterly different societies grew up within the same empire. It became obvious with the passage of time that the two were politically, as well as socially, separate. The court's control outside the capital weakened, leaving opportunities for discontented local chiefs wide open. It has always been possible, under some circumstances, for a state to survive severe political and cultural fragmentation, but the Uighur empire had hardly been founded before the divisions set in and it did not have the strength to overcome them.

If Mou-yü kaghan believed that the emphasis in Manichaeism on personal discipline and restraint would help the Uighurs preserve their power, he was certainly to be proved wrong by events. In the central court itself, the soft life and luxury began to replace the rigor of the past. The speed with which the trend asserted itself must surely have sapped the capacity of the kaghans for hard work and for political and military conflict. Disloyal ministers saw their chance to seize power for themselves and it is scarcely surprising that the last decade of the empire witnessed several power struggles and rebellions in Karabalghasun itself.

The kaghans were lords over an enormous army, but with the coming of a less militaristic period many of the soldiers appear to have become redundant and therefore idle. The kaghans could never be sure that the army would remain loyal, especially since a substantial part of it was under the direct command of the tutuk leading the nonroyal tribes. An idle soldiery of uncertain loyalty can be extremely dangerous to a government at the best of times. When court power splits into factions, disaster usually follows.

[47] See Minorsky, "Tamīm ibn Baḥr's journey," p. 297 and W. Barthold, *Histoire des Turcs d'Asie Centrale*, tr. M. Donskis (Initiation à l'Islam, vol. 3; Paris, 1945), p. 43.

Another important reason for the Uighur fall was the increase in pressure from outside. T'ang China was hardly a cause for worry, but the Tibetans were a constant source of concern and in 816 came near to attacking Karabalghasun itself. An even more serious threat was posed by the Kirghiz to the north, with whom war broke out in about 820 and continued intermittently from then on. In the event they were able to take advantage of the disunity of the Uighurs and even secured an invitation to send in troops from one of the kaghan's generals.

Economic causes always play a part in the downfall of an empire. Unfortunately concrete information concerning the Uighur *débâcle* is limited to a statement in the New T'ang history, where we are told that in 839, "there was a famine and pestilence, and also heavy snowfalls; many of the sheep and horses died." It may be that this was simply the last straw in the breakdown of the Uighur economy. The silk/horse trade with China might have ceased some time earlier. The Chinese sources given detailed reports for the 820s, which suddenly break off in 829 and show nothing at all for the 830s (though the trade resumed in the post-empire period). Food and general production had probably been falling among the Uighurs for several years before the great famine of 839. It was to be expected that this last disaster, which coincided with an unstable situation both at home and abroad, was followed so quickly by total collapse.

The Uighurs never again succeeded in founding a powerful empire. Their future role in history lay primarily in cultural achievements, the foundations of which were laid between 744 and 840.

13

The Karakhanids and early Islam

It has been suggested, with some justice, that a *limes* system separating steppe from sown, barbarian from cultivated, urban society, spanned Eurasia.[1] This system of fortifications and natural barriers, however, was not impenetrable. When the societies sheltered by these walls were strong, incursions from the nomadic world beyond were repulsed or contained. When their defences proved inadequate, sedentary societies either had to tame the "barbarian" by converting him to their culture or be completely transformed themselves. Western Central Asia, an Eastern Iranian area increasingly coming under the cultural influence of neighboring, kindred Sassanid Iran before the advent of Islam and the recipient of cultural currents emanating from the Mediterranean, India and China, was one of those zones through which the steppe-dweller could enter sedentary society. Conversely, its mercantile urban centers also served as a gateway through which the cultural and material achievements of settled society could penetrate the steppe. In the period under discussion, Western Central Asia, having recently accommodated itself to the political and cultural buffetings administered to it by expanding Arab power, was about to enter into another period of intense and intimate contact with the nomadic, Turkic societies to its north and north-east. In this instance, it would serve as the transmission zone for the cultural fruits of one nomadic society to another. Its role in this process was not passive, for the Islamic culture which entered the steppe zone had been influenced and reworked by the Eastern Iranians.

The Eastern Iranian lands around the Oxus (Jayḥūn, modern Amu Darya), lacking political unity and effective leadership, were the natural targets of Arab raiding columns fresh from the conquest of Sassanid Iran. When eastern Iran, i.e. Khorasan, fell, it was quickly transformed into a staging place for the organized conquest of Western Central Asia. This included both those lands around the Oxus and those beyond, i.e. Transoxiana (in the Arab sources *Mā*

[1] W. Barthold, *Zwölf Vorlesungen über die Geschichte der Türken Mittelasiens* (1932–5, reprint Hildesheim, 1962), p. 42.

warā'n-nahr "that which lies beyond the river"). The Arab conquests began in earnest in the last quarter of the 7th century and were not really completed until the middle of the next century. The progress of Arab arms was as much halted by internal disputes between the rival tribal factions of the invaders as by the resistance proferred by local Iranian dynasts and their occasional Turkic allies. The latter, living in the twilight years of the Western Türk Kaghanate, had maintained an increasingly nominal overlordship over some Eastern Iranian principalities beyond the Oxus such as Chāch (Shāsh of Arabic sources, modern Tashkent) and Ferghana, and had supplanted some local dynasties. The murder of the Türgesh Kaghan called "Su-lu" in Chinese sources (the "Abu Muzāḥim" of the Muslim authors) in 738 by his subordinate Mo-ho (Bagha) Tarkhan and the subsequent internecine strife amongst the Türks, ensured the victory for the Islamic armies. Indeed, the Talas battle in 751 in which the Muslims aided by the Turkic Karluks stopped the Chinese and their Turkic allies was not, as Gibb noted,[2] the deathblow to Chinese imperial traditions in Western Central Asia. Rather, it was China's meddling in the murky politics of the Western Türk Kaghanate, a policy that contributed to the latter's destruction and thereby removed the only serious opposition the Muslims faced. The Arabs, however, did not seek to establish themselves deep in the steppe. Instead, they retired to the *ribāṭs* (border forts), oasis city-states and rich, urban trappings of the Khorasanian towns. Here the symbiosis between Arab and Iranian began and the resultant synthesis of cultures would be transmitted to the steppe.

The victorious Muslims encountered a mosaic of religions in their newly won territory. Recent archeological investigations at the site of medieval Ṭarāz (Talas, Aulie-Ata, modern Dzhambul), for example, indicate that its population and that of surrounding towns during this period professed Zoroastrianism, Christianity and Buddhism. In addition, there were a variety of local cults including a Sogdian-influenced Bacchic cult, a cult centering around the fertility goddess Anahit and the Turkic heaven cult.[3] Central Asian Zoroastrianism or Mazdaism was widespread in the Sogdian and Khorezmian cultural zones. Here, however, it evidenced many localisms and was, undoubtedly, qualitatively different from its state-dominated counterpart in Iran proper. The principality of Ustrushana (Usrūshāna in Arabic, modern Shakhristan in the Uzbek SSR) appears to have been particularly attached to Zoroastrianism, which held out there until the mid 9th century. Indeed, the region was so closely associated with Zoroastrianism that the

[2] H.A.R. Gibb, *The Arab Conquests in Central Asia* (1923, reprint New York, 1970), pp. 97–8.
[3] T.N. Senigova, *Srednevekovyĭ Taraz* (Alma-Ata, 1972), pp. 114–17.

caliphal government in 840 was able to try and execute its former *afshīn*, Ḥaidar, a major military and political figure in Baghdad's service, on the probably trumped up charge that he was conspiring to restore Ustrushana's independence and Zoroastrian faith.[4]

Manichaeism, which had traditionally sought shelter in Transoxiana during periods of persecution beginning in Sassanid times, also had its representatives here. Indeed, it was from here that it was brought by Sogdians to the Uighurs. As late as the 10th century, a Manichaean monastery still existed in Samarkand. Manichaean communities were known to Merv (modern Mary) in the 6th century and the Sogdian colonies in Western Türk lands (Arghu Talas, Yegenkent, Ordukent, Chigilbalik and Kashu) in the 8th century.[5]

Although al-Nadīm in the *Fihrist* states that "Shamanīya whose prophet is Buddha" was the religion of the "majority of the people of the land beyond the river [. . .] before Islam,"[6] Buddhism here was deeply mixed with shamanism or at least appeared as such to Muslim observers. A more orthodox Buddhism may have existed in Merv but had probably died out just before the Arab conquests. It was only in the southeastern corner of the Iranian world, Bactria, that Buddhism continued to flourish well into Islamic times.

Christianity, especially the adherents of the persecuted Nestorian heterodoxy, was also found in Iranian and Turkic Central Eurasia, coming to the latter through Iranian merchant intermediaries. In the Islamic period, the Catholicos of the Nestorians, Timotheos (780–823), having received from the Caliphate a kind of patriarchal jurisdiction over the entire Christian community in the Muslim orbit, embarked on an ambitious program of proselytization in the Turkic steppes with results that would be felt in Mongolia and China. Judaism also appears to have been relatively widespread in Eastern Iranian areas where its adherents are reported to have outnumbered the Christians.

[4] B.G. Gafurov, *Tadžiki* (Moskva, 1972), pp. 334–335; Ibn al-Athīr, *Al-Kāmil fi'l-Ta'rīkh: Chronicon quod perfectissimum inscribitur*, ed. C.J. Tornberg, 12 vols. (1851–76, reprint Beirut, 1965–6 with differing pagination), VI, 517–18; V.V. Bartol'd (Barthold), *Turkestan v êpokhu mongol'skogo našestvija* in *Akademik V.V. Bartol'd Sočinenija*, 9 vols (Moskva, 1963–73), I, 269; R.N. Frye, *The Golden Age of Persia. The Arabs in the East* (London, 1975), pp. 43–4.

[5] *The Fihrist of al-Nadim*, ed. trans. B. Dodge, 2 vols. (Records of Civilization: Sources and Studies, vol. 83, New York–London, 1970), II, 801–2; *Ḥudūd al-'Ālam*, trans. V.F. Minorsky (E.J.W. Gibb Memorial New Series, vol. 11, London, 1937, reprint 1970), p. 113; S.G. Kljaštornyĭ, *Drevnetjurkskie runičeskie pamjatniki kak istočnik po istorii Sredneĭ Azii* (Moskva, 1964), p. 131; T.N. Senigova, "Voprosy ideologii i kul'tov Semireč'ia (VI–VIII vv.)" *Novoe v arkheologii Kazakhstana*, ed. M.K. Kadyrbaev (Alma-Ata, 1968), p. 52; A von Le Coq, *Türkçe Mânī elyazıları*, trans. F. Köseraif (Istanbul, 1936), p. 21.

[6] Al-Nadīm, *Fihrist*, ed. trans. Dodge, II, 824.

The Islam brought to the Eastern Iranian frontier during the Umayyad period was still parochial and decidedly Arab in its outlook. It was, however, in this frontier zone, more open by nature to the mixing and cross-fertilizing of cultures, that Islamic ecumenism was born.[7] Not surprisingly, the revolution, as much one of a new consciousness as a political phenomenon, which brought the Abbasids to power was born in the east and represented not only the political aspirations of non-Arab converts but the new, increasingly ecumenical Islam of the Arabs of Khorasan as well. With Iranian and other *mawālī* now able to fully participate in the Islamic state, to influence and be influenced in turn, the foundation for an Islamic renaissance in the 9th and 10th centuries was laid. In the course of this renaissance the Islamicization of Eastern Iran was completed and the expansion of the "land of Islam" (*Bilād al-Islām*) deeper into Central Asia was undertaken. The Iranian peoples of the region, united now in the Islamic Commonwealth, were Persianized, rather than Arabized. The vernacular of the Sassanid court, Darī, became the *lingua franca* of the Muslim East, expanding with the borders of Islam. As a consequence, it was in its Irano-Islamic garb that Muslim culture penetrated the Turkic steppes. The Iranian East became not only a center of Arab and Islamic learning, but the birthplace of "New Persian" and the cradle of Perso-Islamic literature. These developments were, to varying degrees, fostered by the Muslim Iranian dynasties that emerged in the East of the Caliphate in the 9th century.

As the Abbasid Caliphate entered its "Golden Age" during the reign of Hārūn al-Rashīd (786–809), the early stirrings of those centrifugal forces which culminated in the political fragmentation of the Islamic world were coming to the fore. Faced with sectarian and popular revolts, Baghdad was increasingly forced to draw the islamicized or islamicizing remnants of the pre-existing governing elites into Caliphal service. Ṭāhir b. Ḥusain, a descendant of the rulers of Bushang in the Herat region, had won the favor of al-Ma'mūn (813–33) during the latter's successful struggle for the throne with his brother al-Amīn. In 821, he was named viceroy of Khorasan. The post was soon transformed into a virtually hereditary possession of the Ṭāhirid family until 873. Its holders ranged from governors with considerable autonomy to *de facto* independent rulers. From their residence at Nīshāpūr in Khorasan the active propagation of Islam in the pagan territories to the east was promoted. 'Abdallāh b. Ṭalḥa (830–845), the grandson of the dynasty's founder, sent his son Ṭāhir on a campaign deep into the Oghuz Turkic steppe. Ṭāhir, in the

[7] Frye, *Golden Age*, pp. 101–2.

words of al-Balādhurī, "conquered places which had not been reached by any before him.[8]" Raids such as this had economic motivations as well for they netted an important commodity: slaves. Ibn Khurdādhbih informs us that in this same 'Abdallāh's time, some 2000 Oghuz prisoners (perhaps the fruits of Ṭāhir's labor) brought a price of 600,000 dirhams. His successor was able to present the Caliph al-Mutawakkil with a gift of some 200 slaves in 847.[9] Later, under the Sāmānids, the slave trade became a major commercial enterprise. In time, the human cargoes from the east came to consist largely of Central Asian Turkic *ghulāms* ("military slaves") who increasingly came to dominate the Caliphal army and ultimately the state. Although initially they were favorably received because of their martial qualities and direct character, their introduction into the Near East had consequences of which the 9th-century Caliphate could hardly approve and about which it could do little. Henceforth, the dominating force in Middle Eastern politics, until the fall of the Ottoman Empire, would be Turkic or Turkicized military elites.

The Ṭāhirids were toppled by the Ṣaffārids in Khorasan in 873. Political power, however, here and in Islamic Central Asia fell not to them but to the Sāmānids. The founder of the dynasty, Sāmān, a native of Balkh and an alleged descendant of the Sassanian ruler Bahrām Chōbīn, was a convert to Islam sometime during the governorship of Asad b. 'Abdallāh al-Qushairī (d. 738). His son Asad and four grandsons, Nūḥ, Aḥmad, Yaḥyā and Ilyās, entered Caliphal service. The brothers, c. 819, were granted the governorships of Samarkand (Nūḥ), Farghana (Aḥmad), Shāsh (Yaḥyā) and Herat (Ilyās). Aḥmad (d. 864) was able to establish a secure base so that his son Naṣr, following the collapse of the Ṭāhirids, became master of Transoxiana. This was formally confirmed by the Caliph al-Mu'tamid in 875 following the takeover of Bukhara in the previous year by Naṣr's brother Ismā'īl. Fraternal dissension led to war between Naṣr and Ismā'īl which ended in the former's defeat in 888. Ismā'īl allowed his brother to retain the nominal leadership of the family, but actual power resided with him, a fact that was given official recognition by the Caliphate when he was appointed Naṣr's successor. Ismā'īl is reported to have boasted that "while I live, I am the wall of the district of Bukhara.[10] The forces against whom this wall stood were the steppe nomads.

[8] Al-Balādhurī, *Futūḥ al-Buldān*, ed. R.M. Raḍwān (Cairo, 1959), p. 420.

[9] Ibn Khurdādhbih, *Kitāb al-Masālik wa'l-Mamālik*, ed. M.J. de Goeje (Bibliotheca Geographorum Arabicorum, vol. 6, Leiden, 1889), pp. 37, 39; Al-Mas'ūdī, *Murūj adh-Dhahab wa Ma'ādin al-Jawhar*, ed. C. Pellat 7 vols. (Beirut, 1966–79), v, 42.

[10] Narshakhī, *Ta'rīkh-i Bukhārā: The History of Bukhara*, trans. R.N. Frye (The Medieval Academy of America Publications No. 61, Cambridge, Mass., 1954), p. 34.

The Turkic steppe in early Sāmānid times

The reconstruction from the fragmentary and frequently confused notices of our sources, of the ethnic and tribal composition of the steppes beyond the Muslim forts of Transoxiana, is still the object of intense scholarly investigation. With this *caveat* in mind, let us attempt to construct an admittedly imperfect picture of the Turkic steppe peoples in immediate propinquity to Sāmānid holdings in the late 9th century.

The Volga–Ural region was inhabited by the Turkic Pechenegs who were being driven westward by their neighbors the Oghuz and would soon leave the area entirely. The Oghuz tribes extended from the middle and lower course of the Syr Darya (Yaxartes, Saiḥūn) and Aral Sea region, where Khorezmian outposts kept watch on them, to Ispījāb (Isfījāb, Isbījāb, identified with Sairam near present day Chimkent in the Kazakh SSR). Here they bordered with the Karluks. They nomadized as far north as the Irtysh and the Kimek confederation. The Karluk encampments stretched from Ispījāb to the Ferghana valley and beyond in the east and extended to the Chu and Ili rivers in the north where the subject Chigil and Tukhsi tribes lived. The entire Oghuz–Karluk border with the Muslim world is described as being in a state of constant warfare, with the raids of the "Turks" reaching deep into Khorasan. South and east of the Karluks, and closely associated with them, were the Yaghma who extended towards Kashgar.

Beyond this first line of Turkic tribes and tribal confederations lay yet other groupings whose pressure on their southern neighbors undoubtedly accounted in part for the disturbances along the Sāmānid frontier. This ongoing warfare between the tribes is mentioned by a 9th century Muslim author al-Ya'qūbī in his geographical work the *Kitāb al-Buldān* where he notes that "each tribe of the Turks has a separate country and they war with one another."[11]

Paramount amongst the northern tribes was the Kimek confederation, a not very stable grouping that had been centered on the Irtysh, directly to the north and northwest of the Oghuz and Karluks. The Kimeks were slowly and steadily shifting to the southwest and west, with resultant pressure on the Oghuz in particular. One of their constituent elements, the Kipchaks, had already begun to break away in the early to mid 9th century and encroach on the Baskhir Uralian lands in their movement towards the Volga.

The land inhabited by these and lesser tribal groupings occasionally hinted at in our sources, had formed part of the territory of the Western Türk

[11] Al-Ya'qūbī, *Kitāb al-Buldān*, ed. M.J. de Goeje (BGA, vol. 7, Leiden, 1892), p. 295.

kaghanate the imperial traditions of which were still strong. Some of the tribes that had been members of the kaghanate appeared under new names reflecting a new political orientation. Some simply resurfaced under their old names. Still others were migrants from elsewhere. These nomads were not cultural savages. They had been in close contact with China, Byzantium and the oasis cities of Eastern and Western Turkestan. Their experience with empire had led to the creation of an elaborate, imperial ideology. Moreover, they considered their economic system, nomadism, and its lifestyle to be far superior to that of the agricultural lands.

The Karluks, consisting initially of three subgroupings, lived in the western Altai and had nomadized as far as the Irtysh prior to their coming to Semirech'e (the region of the Ili and several parallel smaller rivers, a translation of the Kazakh *Jeti su* "seven rivers"). They were thus in a position to participate in the affairs of both the Western and Eastern kaghanates. Their early orientation appears to have been more towards the latter. In 742, in alliance with the Basmïl and Uighurs, they overthrew Ozmïsh, scion of the Ashina house and ruler of the Türk. In the subsequent realignment of the hierarchy of the nomadic *imperium*, the Karluks were elevated from the status of a subject tribe led by an *el teber* to that of a *yabghu*-led people. The title *yabghu* was one of the highest dignities in the Turkic world. It implied, usually, membership in the charismatic Ashina clan in whom the "heaven-mandated" right to rule resided and command over a large tribal grouping or wing of the state. Within two years, the Karluks and Uighurs (whose ruler had become the senior or left *yabghu*) toppled the Basmïl Kaghan who had assumed the mantle of the Türk *imperium*. The Uighur *yabghu* now became kaghan and the Karluk the senior or left *yabghu*.[12] Within a year, however, hostilities irrupted between the erstwhile allies. Defeated in the contest, the Karluks, or at least sizable elements of them were compelled to migrate westward. In the boastful words of the Moyun Chur inscription "all those of the Karluks who remained alive fled to the Türgesh."[13]

The entrance of the Karluks into the Western Türk–Türgesh lands can hardly have been a pacific process. Karluk success here was undoubtedly aided by the fact that their opponents had been weakened by long wars with

[12] Liu Mau-tsai, *Die Chinesischen Nachrichten zur Geschichte der Ost-Türken (T'u-küe)*, 2 vols. (Göttinger Asiatische Forschungen, vol. 10, Wiesbaden, 1958), I, 230–1; O. Pritsak, "Von den Karluk zu den Karachaniden," *Zeitschrift der Deutschen Morgenländischen Gesellschaft*, 101, 272–4 (1951).

[13] See text in G. Aidarov, *Jazyk orkhonskikh pamjatnikov drevnetjurkskoĭ pis'mennosti VIII veka* (Alma-Ata, 1971), p. 351. The event is reflected in later Muslim sources, cf. *Sharāf al-Zamān Tāhir Marvazī on China, the Turks and India*, ed. trans. V.F. Minorsky (London, 1942), Arabic text, p. 19, trans. p. 30.

the Arabs and Chinese. In 766 the Western Türk–Türgesh tribes submitted to them and the Karluks established their capital at Suyab on the Chu river. The Chigil and Tukhsi tribes who appear in the early 12th-century author al-Marwazī as four of the nine tribal groupings (three of them Chigil) constituting the Karluk confederation, may well have been Türgesh tribes incorporated into the Karluk union at this time. Despite this westward shift, Karluk interest in Inner Asian affairs was maintained through an alliance with Tibet against China and the Uighurs in the struggle for control over Eastern Turkistan. Increasingly, however, the Karluks drew the attention of the Muslims who began to send out expeditions against them. This resulted ultimately in a further westward shift in the Karluk political orientation leading to a deeper involvement in the Muslim orbit and a lessening of the ties with Tibet. The last recorded formal visit of Karluk envoys to the Tibetan court appears to have taken place during the reign of Ral-pa-čan (817–36).[14]

The report of al-Ya'qūbī that the Karluk *yabghu* converted to Islam during the Caliphate of al-Mahdī (775–85) can hardly be historical. Nonetheless, the Karluks and allied tribes were undoubtedly coming under the cultural influence of Sogdian and Muslim traders and through them were becoming acquainted with Christianity and Islam. Muslim sources imply that in the early years of the 9th century, the Karluk *yabghu*, along with the "Khaqan" of Tibet and rulers of Kabul and Otrar, had accepted the overlordship of the Caliphate. The tributary relationship alluded to here may have been nothing more than gift-sending which, under the proper political circumstances, could be viewed as "tribute."

There are indications that hostilities with the Uighurs continued until the latter became totally absorbed in their struggle with the Kirghiz who ultimately destroyed their empire in Mongolia in 840. The fall of the Uighur state marks a clear turning point in Karluk history. The Kirghiz, after their conquest of the Uighurs, did not lay claim to the Türk nomadic *imperium*. They do not appear to have moved their capital to Mongolia nor to have taken possession of the sacred territories with which the imperial dignity in the steppe had hitherto been associated. This sharp departure from ideological tradition created, in effect, a vacancy in the supreme imperial office, one which the Karluks did not hesitate to fill.

The Muslim authors make mention of the Karluk Kaghanate. Ibn al-Faqīh (10th century) notes that supreme political power in the Turkic world rests with the Karluk Kaghan. Al-Mas'ūdī refers to the latter as the "Khāqān of

[14] H. Hoffmann, "Die Qarluq in der Tibetischen Literatur," *Oriens*, 3: 199 (1950).

Khāqāns" and states that the other Turkic rulers submitted to him. In the somewhat garbled accounts that Gardīzī (11th century) gives of the genesis of the Turkic peoples of his day, it is reported that **Khutoghlan*, the last Kaghan of the "Khāqānīyān" was killed in a revolt and the Kaghanate passed to the Karluk clan of *Chūnchān* or *Chūnpān*. The first Karluk ruler to attain the kaghanal dignity was "*ilmālm-s-n yabghu*" (perhaps a corruption of **Il-almïsh* "he who has taken political power").[15] The kaghanate could pass, thus, to the Karluks because they controlled the sacred lands of the Western Türks (the possession of which was one of the criteria signaling the mandate of heaven) and perhaps because of the Ashina affiliation of their ruling clan. Thus, by the mid 9th century, these eastern neighbors of the Sāmānids claimed a hegemony over the steppe peoples. The extent to which this was translated into real power beyond the confines of the Karluk confederation and its allies is open to question.

The western neighbors of the Karluks, the Oghuz, harbored no such imperial ambitions. Their origins are also somewhat more difficult to trace. The Türk kaghanate in Mongolia contained a number of tribal groupings appearing under the term *Oghuz* (usually with a prefixed numeral indicating the number of constituent tribes). The term is, for the most part, not transcribed in Chinese sources, but translated as "tribe." Indeed, the earliest meaning of this term, before it was frozen as an ethnonym, was probably "union of kindred tribes." Hence, we are not bound to view all the "Oghuz" of Central Eurasia as the necessarily unilinear descendants of the Oghuz of Mongolia since this technical term could be adopted by any sizable tribal union.[16] There are some indications, however, that elements of the Syr Darya Oghuz, or at least their ruling clan, originated in the ethnic milieu of the Eastern Türk kaghanate. The *yabghu* rank attested by Muslim authors from the mid 9th century as the title of the Oghuz ruler bespeaks such a tie. Ibn al-Athīr (a 13-century source) reports that the Oghuz who entered Transoxiana during the caliphate of al-Mahdī and joined the revolt of al-Muqanna' (c.776–83) migrated thither "from the borderlands of the most distant parts of the Turks," *i.e.* Mongolia.[17] This is the earliest date at which we can place them in Transoxiana.

Our data do not tell us much about their activities with respect to the Islamic lands during the next century. Oghuz legends indicate that they were

[15] Gardīzī in V.V. Bartol'd, "Izvlečenie iz sočinenija Gardizi *Zain al-Akhbār*" in Bartol'd, *Sočinenija*, VIII, Pers. Text, p. 26, Russ. trans. pp. 42–3.

[16] P.B. Golden, "The Migrations of the Oğuz," *Archivum Ottomanicum*, 4, 45–54 (1972).

[17] Ibn al-Athīr, ed. Tornberg (Beirut ed.), XI, 178.

engaged in conquering a new homeland and expelling the Pechenegs. The Oghuz in Kazakhstan and the Syr Darya-Ural river region faced continuing pressure from tribes to their east who were moving to join them. They were also engaged in what for us must remain ill-defined wars and raids with their Kimek and Karluk neighbors. The steppe was in turmoil, a reflection of the dislocations caused by the collapse of the Türk kaghanate and subsequent Karluk-Uighur and Kirghiz–Uighur wars. The migration of the tribes which ultimately came to form the Oghuz of the Syr Darya should be viewed in this context. The Oghuz conquests resulted in the westward migration of the Pechenegs. The latter, forced to cross the Volga towards the end of the 9th century, evicted the Hungarian tribal union from the Pontic steppes, driving it into Pannonia. These movements marked the first serious breaching of the Byzantino-Khazar defense line against nomadic incursions.

During this and subsequent periods, the Oghuz appear in our sources as one of the most anarchic and troublesome tribal groupings. Gradually, however, in the chaos that reigned beyond the Muslim *ribāṭs* and towns, elements of the Oghuz and Karluk tribes were drawn to Islam.

The Sāmānids and Islam in Central Asia

The early Sāmānid amīrs carried out an active policy with regard to their steppe neighbors. Nūḥ b. Asad, c. 840, organized a successful expedition against the Turks around Ispījāb. Naṣr b. Aḥmad campaigned against the nomads of Shawghar. The greatest Sāmānid undertaking, however, was the expedition led by Ismāʿīl (d. 907) in Muḥarram 280/March–April 893 in which he first toppled the Afshīn dynasty in Ustrushana and then marched into the steppe to Ṭarāz (Talas), one of the headquarters of the Karluk kaghan. They city was taken, after a difficult siege, along with some 10,000 (15,000 in some accounts) prisoners, including the katun, wife of the kaghan, A large church there was transformed into a mosque and, according to one report, the "amīr of Ṭarāz" embraced Islam. The ruler's name is given by al-Masʿūdī as *Ṭ nk s*, which is noted as "characteristic of each of the kings who rule this region." The name may be a garbling of **Ṭafkash* (Tabghach) which, as we shall see, frequently figures in Karakhanid titulature. The defeat was no mortal blow, for Ismāʿīl had to repulse, c. 903–4, a major Turkic invasion. This was, perhaps, the Karluk response to the Ṭarāz attack.[18]

[18] Al-Masʿūdī, *Murūj*, ed. Pellat, v, 150; Al-Ṭabarī, *Taʾrīkh al-Ṭabarī*, ed. Muḥammad Abu'l-Faḍl Ibrāhīm, 10 vols. (Dhakhāʾir al-ʿArab, vol. 30, Cairo, 1964–70), x, 34, 116; Ibn al-Athīr, ed. Tornberg (Beirut ed.), viii, 464–5; Narshakhī, trans. Frye, p. 86; see also Pritsak, "Von den Karluk," pp. 288–90.

Our sources now begin to mention sizable groupings of Oghuz and Karluk tribesmen who had gone over to Islam and constituted an important part of the Muslim border defenses. Ibn Ḥawqal, for example, reports the presence of islamicized Oghuz and Karluk warriors in Sütkend and a grouping of over "1,000 tents of the Turks" who have embraced Islam living in the pasturages between Fārāb, Kanjida and Shāsh. The circumstances in which they converted are unclear, but this was probably the result of ongoing attempts at proselytism, not always by orthodox members of the Muslim community. Thus, as early as the late Umayyad (or early Abbasid) period, Muslim sectarians such as Isḥāq of the "Muslimīyah," were active in the area. Ispījāb appears to have been one of the major centers for the propagation of Islam in the steppes. Large numbers of "fighters for the faith" gathered here attracted by "holy war" and the promise of booty. The influence of centers such as this radiated out into the steppe. Thus, al-Maqaddasī mentions a Muslim *Türkmen* ruler of the town *Ordu* who was, apparently, the vassal of the amīr in Ispījāb. Although the ethnic affiliation of the Ordu Turkmen is not mentioned, the term Türkmen, at this time, was associated with both Oghuz and Karluk groupings. Their chief distinguishing and shared feature was adherence to Islam.[19]

The major impetus for conversion to Islam, despite the evidence of considerable military activity, does not appear to have been the *jihād*. Rather, Islam penetrated the steppes in a more pacific fashion through Muslim merchant caravans and settlers. Increasingly, the towns of Transoxiana and beyond were gaining Muslim populations drawn there by commercial prospects. 10th century sources already report a large number of towns in the steppe which have mosques. The merchant and urban dweller brought the material achievements of the prosperous Islamic lands to the nomads. The lure of Islam as a civilization was strong, just as Rome had appealed to the Germanic tribes. As the full partaking of the benefits of Muslim society was predicated upon membership in the community of believers, social and economic rather than military pressure gained conversions. This pressure was reinforced by the activities of Muslim mystics, the *ṣūfī*s who journeyed to the steppe tribes to preach and propagate the new faith. These dynamic, charismatic and largely still anonymous personalities whose resemblance to the shamans of Turkic

[19] Al-Muqaddasī, *Aḥsan al-Taqāsīm fī Ma'rifat al-Aqālīm*, ed. M.J. de Goeje (BGA, vol. 3, Leiden, 1906), p. 25; Al-Bīrūnī, *Kitāb al-Jamāhir fī Ma'rifat al-Jawāhir*, ed. S. Krenkow (Ḥaidarābād, 1355/1936–7), p. 205; Maḥmūd al-Kāshgharī, *Dīwān Lughat al-Turk*, facs. ed. B. Atalay (Ankara, 1941), pp. 238, 622 ff.; Turk. trans. B. Atalay, *Dîvânü Lügat-it-Türk*, 3 vols. (Ankara, 1939–41), I, 473, III, 412 ff.; S.G. Agadžanov, *Očerki istorii oguzov i turkmen Srednej Azii IX–XIII vv.* (Ashkhabad, 1969), pp. 80–3; R.G. Kuzeev, *Proiskhoždenie baškirskogo naroda* (Moskva, 1974), p. 183; F. Sümer, *Oğuzlar* (Ankara, 1967), pp. 28–9, 50–2.

society may not have been entirely coincidental, won many converts with their fiery rhetoric. They were aided by the fact that their audience was already acquainted with Buddhism, Manichaeism, Christianity and possibly Judaism (from neighboring Khazaria) and was hence relatively sophisticated and receptive. Finally, there were larger political forces in operation. Conversion to Islam could and did symbolize a new political orientation the adoption of which may have been dictated by intra-tribal or intra-dynastic rivalries which had little reference to theology. It is in just such a context that our first report of a mass conversion may be placed. In the year 960, according to Ibn Miskawaih and Ibn al-Athīr, "200,000 tents of the Turks" went over to Islam. Although it is nowhere specified who these "Turks" were, circumstantial evidence points to the Karakhanid dynasty and its tribal followers. Subsequently, in Autumn, 1043, we learn that "10,000 tents of the Turks" living between Balasaghun and Bulghar had accepted Islam. The claim, however, by Ibn al-Athīr, in whose chronicle we find this notice, that after this of all the Turkic peoples "only the Tatar and Khiṭā [Khitai] who are in the region of China have not embraced Islam," is premature.[20] Of the major Turkic political units of the day, it is only with the Karakhanids that conversions on a grand scale (even allowing for considerable inflation of numbers) are associated.

The origins of the Karakhanids

The term *Karakhanid*, like the older *Ilek Khanid* is itself artificial. It is taken from the title *Qara khan* or *Qara Khāqān* which occupies a prominent place in the titulature of the rulers of this dynasty. Maḥmūd al-Kāshgharī, a scion of the dynasty, writes in the *Dīwān Lughat al-Turk*, that the "Khāqānīyah rulers are called *Qara*, e.g. Bughra Qara Khāqān."[21] Unfortunately, we do not know the actual name of the royal clan other than the usages employed by our Muslim authors (*Khāqānīyah*, *Āl-i Afrāsiyāb*). The available evidence points to a close association with the Karluk tribal confederation and the Yaghma grouping. The nature of the relationship between these two tribal unions has yet to be fully elucidated.

An examination of our material for the later Karluks reveals a complicated inner tribal structure. Al-Marwazī and 'Awfī report that they are divided into

[20] Ibn Miskawaih, *Tajārub al-Umam*, ed. H.F. Amedroz (Oxford, 1920, reprint Baghdad, n.d.), 3 vols., II, 181; Ibn al-Athīr, ed. Tornberg (Beirut ed.), IX, 520; Neshrī in his *Kitāb-i Cihân-nümâ*, ed. F.R. Unat, M.A. Köymen, 2 vols. (Ankara, 1949–57), I, 16–17, associates the origin of the term *Türkmen* with the 960 event.

[21] Maḥmūd al-Kāshgharī, *Dīwān*, ed. Atalay, p. 542; Turk. trans. Atalay, *DLT*, III, 221.

nine sub-groupings: three *Chigil*, three *B.gh.sk.l* (*H.skī* in 'Awfī) and one each of the *Bulāq* (*N.dā* or *B.dwā* in 'Awfī), the **Kökerkin* (*Külerkin* or *Küderkin*, the *K.wālīn* of 'Awfī) and *Tukhsi*. The *Ḥudūd al-ʿĀlam* also mentions the *L.bān* living in Kirmīnkath and three tribes nomadizing between Mirkī and Kūlān: *Bīstān*, *Khaym* and **Berish*. The Chigil and Tukhsi, remnants apparently of older Türgesh groupings as was noted earlier, were one of the most important of these sub-groups. The Chigil appear to have formed the nucleus of the Karakhanid army and loomed so large in the eyes of the Oghuz that the latter called all the Turkic peoples from the Syr Darya to China by this name.

The Chigil had a considerable history. A *Chigil Tutuq* is mentioned in the Moyun Chur inscriptions. A number of towns bearing their name and hence indicating areas of settlement, appear in Muslim authors and Turkic Manichaean texts (cf. *Chigil Balïq*, *Chigil Kent* etc.). Their ruler, according to Gardīzī and the *Mujmal al-Tawārīkh* bore the title *tüksin*.[22] Maḥmūd al-Kāshgharī places them in Quyas near Barsghan, Ṭarāz and in villages around Kashgar from which they had been evicted and scattered. They were concentrated, in strength, in the region north of Issyk-kul.

The Karluk confederation (including elements in Tokharistan) was not a static entity. Its tribal composition, in the period from the 9th to 12th centuries, probably underwent a number of changes. This mutability of the nomadic tribal unions is a factor which must always be taken into account when attempting to attribute the origins and ethno-political affiliations of the steppe dynasties to any particular grouping.

The Karluk center in the 9th and 10th centuries appears to have been at Balasaghun in the Chu valley. The city itself had a mixed population, as al-Kāshgharī reports, its inhabitants speaking both Sogdian and Turkic. In the local dialects it was also known as *Quz Ulush*. There are muted references in our sources to an attack on Balasaghun by "pagan Turks" sometime before 943. Barthold has associated these "pagan Turks," who were soon Islamicized (in 960?), with the Karakhanid dynasty.[23]

The Yaghma appear to have been of Toquz Oghuz origin or at least to have been closely affiliated with them. The *Ḥudūd al-ʿĀlam* notes that "their king is from the family of the Toghuzghuzz kings." Our anonymous author also remarks that the Yaghma "have numerous tribes" among whom are the *Bulāq*

22 Gardīzī in Bartol'd, "Izvlechenie," *Bartol'd Sočinenija*, VIII, Pers. Text, p. 31; *Mujmal al-Tawārīkh*, ed. M. Bahār (Tehran, 1939), p. 421. Kāshgharī in the *Dīwān* notes that *tüksin* is "the title of one from the common people who is in the third rank below the ruler" (*DLT*, ed. Atalay, pp. 219–20; Turk. trans. I, 437).

23 Barthold, *Zwölf Vorlesungen*, pp. 77–8 and his "Očerk istorii Semireč'ja" in *Bartol'd Sočinenija*, II/1, 40.

who elsewhere (see above) have been placed amongst the Karluk inner tribes. Their abode, in the 10th century, was in the western-central T'ien Shan and the northwestern part of Eastern Turkestan. Yaghma elements were also located in the Ili river–Issyk-kul region. The possession of Kashgar was, at one time, disputed by them and the Karluks. Gardīzī, in a somewhat muddled account, closely associates them with the "Turk Khāqān" who settled them between the Kimeks and Karluks. A remembrance of this western sojourn is perhaps to be found in the village *Yaghma* near Ṭarāz which al-Kāshgharī connects with them. Ultimately, they were forced back to the east. Their ruler was rewarded with the title *Yaghma Tutugh*, i.e. "military commander of the Yaghma territory." A later source, the *Mujmal al-Tawārīkh* reports, however, that the "ruler [*pādishāh*] of the Yaghma is called Bughra Khan."[24] The elevation of the Yaghma ruler to khanal status probably occurred after 840 and given the biological tie of the Yaghma ruling clan with the "Toghuzghuzz kings" may reflect a *translatio imperii*. What is important for us here, however, is the association of the *Bughra Khan* title with the Yaghma. In the period under discussion, this title appears to have been the monopoly of the Karakhanid ruling house.

Pritsak, in a series of studies, advanced the thesis that the Karakhanid dynasty sprang from the ruling clan of the Karluks which, in turn, was of Ashina origin. The Yaghma, in his view, along with the Chigil, formed the two most important tribal unions of the three Karluk tribal confederations. In this reconstruction, the first "Karakhanid" ruler was **Bilge Kür (Kül) Kadïr Khan* from whom the Sāmānid Nūḥ b. Asad took Ispījāb in 840. He is also to be identified with *Ilmālm s.n.*, the first Karluk kaghan mentioned in Gardīzī. The Karluk-Karakhanid kaghanate thus formed, followed the bipartite system of rule typical of the Türk imperial tradition. The eastern (and supreme) kaghan bore the title *Arslan Qara Khaqan* (*Arslan* "lion" = the totem of the Chigil) and his co-ruler in the western half of the state was called the *Bughra Qara Khaqan* (*Bughra* "male camel" = the totem of the Yaghma). Beneath them stood four sub-kaghanal rulers bearing the titles *Arslan Ilig*, *Bughra Ilig*, *Arslan Tegin* and *Bughra Tegin*.[25]

Our sources will not permit a more precise resolution of the question of Karakhanid origins. Nonetheless, it is clear that the dynasty that ultimately assumed power here had either Ashina or "Toghuzghuzz" affinities. The

[24] *Ḥudūd al-ʿĀlam*, trans. Minorsky, pp. 95–6, 277; Gardīzī in Bartol'd, "Izvlečenie," *Bartol'd Sočinenija*, VIII, Pers. text, p. 28, Russ. trans. pp. 45–6; *Mujmal*, ed. Bahār, p. 421.

[25] O. Pritsak, "Die Karachaniden," *Der Islam*, 31, 22–4 (1954); Idem, "Von den Karluk," pp. 282–5.

means by which they imposed themselves on these two or three tribal unions may be conjectured but not conclusively demonstrated. The faint references to a Karluk–Yaghma struggle for possession of Kashgar point to some major confrontation from which the Karakhanid kaghanate emerged. The Karluks and Yaghma continued to maintain a separate identity, just as the Oghuz tribes were to do after the foundation of the Saljuk Sultanate. Interestingly enough, Maḥmūd al-Kāshgharī, who was in a position to know, nowhere specifically ties the "Khāqānīyah" rulers to either of them.

Finally, we should note that the Karakhanids, like the Orkhon Türks and many of their own Turkic dynastic contemporaries, viewed this conglomeration of tribes, tribal unions and sedentary areas that recognized their overlordship, as a family possession. Thus, as various members of the expanding royal clan shifted to different offices and geographical areas of the realm, their titles changed in accordance with their relative position on the ladder of ranks in the ruling hierarchy. Thus, it is extremely difficult to follow the career of a given member of the family on the basis of his official Turkic titles. With their conversion to Islam (see below), however, various Islamic names and honorifics were added on. These names and titles, reflected on Karakhanid coins, when collated with our written sources, allow us to gain some notion of the inner workings of this often chaotic state.

Ismā'īl Sāmānī's opponent at Ṭarāz may have been Oghulchak Kadïr Khan, son of Bilge Kül Kadïr Khan and co-kaghan in the west according to Pritsak's reconstruction. This defeat (893) was perhaps responsible for his withdrawal to the Kashgar region. In any event, it was here that a Karakhanid prince, Satuk (perhaps his son or nephew) converted to Islam. The circumstances of the conversion and its exact date are far from clear. The Ottoman historian Münejjimbashï (d. 1702), basing himself on a tradition preserved in Baghdad historiography and ultimately stemming from a certain Abu'l Majd Maḥmūd b. 'Abd al-Jalīl, a Karakhanid emissary in 1105 to the Abbasid court, writes that Satuk Bughra Khan who came from a place called Artuch (identified in the *Ḥudūd* as a "populous village of the Yaghma") was the first of the khans to become a Muslim. This apparently took place under the influence of a *faqīh* from Bukhara. After conversion, he obtained a *fatwā* which, in effect, permitted him to commit patricide. Having dispatched his presumably still pagan father, he went on to conquer Kashgar. The mass conversion of the tribes under the Karakhanid dynasty was undoubtedly accompanied by considerable internal turmoil. It was not completed during Satuk's lifetime; he died in 955. The acceptance of Islam by "200,000 tents of the Turks" (see above) was probably one of the culminating points in this process. There is

some evidence to indicate that Muslim missionaries were also an active force in this.

The later Sāmānids and the steppe tribes

By the last quarter of the 10th century, the Karakhanids had begun to expand towards the Sāmānid holdings. Given the military potential of the tribes under Karakhanid rule, it is surprising that their conquests were so relatively modest and slow in realization. The Karakhanids, however, were as often at war with one another as with their opponents. Indeed, their great gains came only when their opposition proved weaker and even less cohesive than that segment of the Karakhanid confederation that attacked them. Thus, the Karakhanid conquests of Sāmānid territory were as much a reflection of the decline in the "House of Sāmān" as they were an indication of Karakhanid power.

Officially, the Sāmānids were the *amīrs* of Khorasan and *Mā warā'n-nahr*, with their capital in Bukhara. The inner core of their state was governed by various lieutenants appointed by the dynasty. Frontier zones were under the *mulūk-i aṭrāf* ("border kings") who were often the scions of ancient, local dynasties. When the power of the central government weakened, the centrifugal tendencies inherent in such a structure came to the fore. The Sāmānids, like their nominal overlords in Baghdad, had come to rely increasingly on *ghulām* armies with predictable results. Sāmānid raids into the steppes were as much for slaves as for conquest. The human booty thus obtained was then groomed and trained in special schools for military and administrative posts. Slaves were inexpensive, in the 10th century, and seemingly ubiquitous. As in the Caliphate, those *ghulāms* who had risen to the highest ranks possessed their own *ghulāms*. Their positions thus buttressed, they began to show signs of a decidedly non-servile attitude. Installed now in the most important and sensitive governmental posts, they were soon able to dictate policy. This was made easy by the fact that the successors of Ismā'īl were men of lesser stature. Aḥmad b. Ismā'īl was murdered by the Turkic palace guard in 914 after seven years of rule. His son and successor, Naṣr II (914–43), under whom Persian letters flourished despite the absence of domestic tranquility, was faced with rebellious relatives and religious strife. The latter was engendered by his dalliance with the Qarmaṭian movement and led to his forced abdication under pressure from an alliance of the *'ulamā'* and Turkic guard. His son Nūḥ (943–54) hastened to purge the realm of Ismā'īlī sectarians. He too was compelled, however, to spend much of his time contending with unruly relatives for the throne. To these clear signs of decline were added mounting

financial difficulties reflected in the government's delay in paying the troops, which led to still further instability. Thus, 'Abd al-Malik b. Nūḥ (d. 961) became little more than a figurehead for the ruling clique of powerful Turkic *ghulāms*. Upon his death, one of the *ghulāms*, Alp Tegin, commander of the army in Khurasan, unsuccessful in his bid to place his candidate on the throne, struck out on his own. He seized Ghazna in 962 and established himself there at a safe distance from the crumbling Sāmānid center.

Alp Tegin's *ghulāms* effected a reconciliation with the government in 965, but maintained their autonomy. After the death of Alp Tegin in 963 and that of his son Isḥāq in 966, they chose their leaders Bilge Tegin (966–975) Böri Tegin (975–7) and Sebük Tegin (977–97) from the ranks of their commanders. Sebük Tegin, a *ghulām* of Alp Tegin, while continuing to view himself as a Sāmānid "governor," began, together with his energetic son Maḥmūd, to gather up power within the Sāmānid orbit. The Sāmānids, in turn, faced with Karakhanid encroachments, came to rely on him more and more. By the time of his death, Sebük Tegin had come to view the burgeoning "Ghaznavid" state as a family possession, dividing it in the Turkic manner. His youngest son, Ismā'īl (in effect the *ot tegin* "prince of the hearth") received the "home" territories of Ghazna and Balkh.[26] Power, however, was in the hands of the capable Maḥmūd, commander of the Ghaznavid armies in Khorasan which were nominally under Sāmānid suzerainty. Under Maḥmūd this *ghulām* army and its attendant Persian bureaucracy was transformed into an empire.

Manṣūr b. Nūḥ al-Sāmānī (961–76) whose elevation had provoked the strategic withdrawal of Alp Tegin, was unable to arrest the disintegration of his state. This became even more evident during the reign of his son Nūḥ II (976–97) as military commanders and provincial governors began to carve out lands for themselves. A major crisis developed when the commander of the army, Abu'l-'Abbās Tash, who had been made governor of strategically vital Khorasan in 982, was drawn into a war with Abu'l-Ḥasan Simjūrī, the powerful governor of Kuhistan, and his ally the chamberlain Fā'iq. Tash lost, in 987, and fled west. Abu 'Alī Simjūrī, who succeeded his father in 989, now fought Fā'iq and defeated him, the latter fleeing to Merv in 990. It was in this chaotic context that the Karakhanid armies under Hārūn Bughra Khan marched on Bukhara in 992.

Nūḥ II, faced by treachery from Simjūrī, who had concluded a secret agreement with the Karakhanids, and Fā'iq, who defected to the enemy at

[26] In this I do not follow C.E. Bosworth's otherwise excellent account of Ghaznavid origins, see his *The Ghaznavids* (Edinburgh, 1963), pp. 27–45. On the *Ot tegin*, see B. Ögel, *Türk mitolojisi* (Ankara, 1971), I, 28–9, 596.

Kharjang, was forced to abandon Bukhara. The Karakhanid occupation of the city was short-lived as the Bughra Khan fell ill because of the climate and water, and withdrew in the direction of Balasaghun, whence he had come. He died en route thither. Nūḥ, now speedily returned to his capital, sought to deal with the traitorous Simjūrī and Fā'iq. He joined forces with the Ghaznavid Sebük Tegin. The latter defeated both rebels in 994. The Ghaznavids were richly rewarded, Maḥmūd being named governor of Khorasan. The Karakhanids, now under Naṣr Ilig, the Arslan Ilig or sub-kaghan of the western part of the realm, again moved on Bukhara in 996. Nūḥ initially turned to Sebük Tegin, but the two had grown suspicious of one another, resulting in a Ghaznavid thrust at Bukhara and a separate agreement dividing Transoxiana at the Qaṭwan steppe between Naṣr Ilig and Sebük Tegin. The latter was now master of all provinces south of the Oxus.

The Sāmānid domain was reduced to the areas around Bukhara and Samarkand. Manṣūr II (997–9), Nūḥ's desperate successor, turned once again to Fā'iq who was consistent only in his treachery. He conspired with the Karakhanids as well as with other Sāmānid commanders. In 999, allied with the general Beg Tuzun, Fā'iq deposed and blinded Manṣūr, placing 'Abd al-Malik II (999–1000) briefly on the throne. With this event, in the somber words of the Bukharan historian Narshakhī, "the rule of the house of Sāmān went from there."[27] On 23 October 999, Naṣr Ilig took Bukhara, meeting little resistance. 'Abd al-Malik tried to organize the local population for the defence of the dynasty, only to be met by indifference. The Karakhanids, as the local *'ulamā'* reasoned, were also orthodox Muslims and hence, if that were God's will, also worthy of rule. 'Abd al-Malik, together with the remnants of the dynasty, was packed off to Uzgend. The Karakhanids had clearly achieved respectability within the Islamic orbit, the first dynasty based on a Turkic ethnic base to do so. Meanwhile, the Ghaznavid Maḥmūd had firmly entrenched himself in Khorasan. The Oxus, as had been agreed upon earlier, was the border between the Karakhanid and Ghaznavid realms.

A gallant attempt by Ismā'īl II al-Muntaṣir (1000–5), who had escaped from Karahanid captivity, to restore the Sāmānid dynasty was doomed to failure, despite some brilliant moments. It ended ignominiously with his murder at the hands of an Arab bedouin chieftain. Without entering into the details of al-Muntaṣir's adventures, we should note that a key factor in his activities had been the Oghuz tribesmen whom he had managed to rally (or lure) to his support. In the oncoming contest for dominion in Western Central Asia, these

[27] Narshakhī, trans. Frye, p. 100.

Oghuz, particularly the bands associated with the family of Saljuk, would be a decisive element.

The Sāmānid achievement in Central Asia had been considerable. The islamicization of the area was due, in large measure, to their activities. The governmental and cultural styles set by them would be, in varying degrees, the legacy of every Muslim state in the region. Paradoxically, the early Sāmānids had been perhaps too successful. Confidence in the personal "wall" of men like Ismā'īl I had led to a weakening of the actual physical defences of the realm. Thus, when the steppe, ecologically and in the person of the nomads, began to make encroachments on the oasis cities, the feebler descendants of Ismā'īl were unable to hold it back. The eventual absorption of the nomads, their taming by the pre-existing civilization, however, was the product of the Irano-Arab-Islamic synthesis, one of the most enduring achievements of Sāmānid rule.

The Oghuz yabghu state and the Saljuk origins

The tribal and dynastic elements associated with the Syr Darya Oghuz probably entered this region from the east in the same period in which the Karluks were consolidating their hold over Semirech'e. The struggle for a new homeland undoubtedly reinforced the position of whatever "charismatic" clans existed in the loose Oghuz union. By the time of Ibn Faḍlān's visit to them, c. 921, the Oghuz were led by a *yabghu*. This title has frequently been confused in Arabic-script sources with *bayghu* (lit. "sparrow-hawk"), a lesser-ranking title of totemic origin. The *yabghu* appears to have had a "deputy," the *kül erkin*, as well as the rudiments of a state organization reflected in a number of lesser titles. He was in no sense an absolute ruler. Indeed, despite the surface continuity of a number of Orkhon Türk institutions and titles, these Oghuz were at a much lower level of development.[28]

Islam was beginning to make some headway, probably amongst the border tribes and those individuals or groups who had settled in the cities along the Syr Darya. The capital or winter residence of the *yabghu* was *Yangï Kent* – "New City" – (implying some older, earlier royal residence?) on this same river. These cities and border towns had Iranian colonists in them as well.

The Oghuz, as we have seen, were a source of trouble all along the Muslim frontier. Subjected to growing pressure from their northern neighbors, the Kipchaks and Kimeks, and restrained by the surrounding states, the Oghuz

[28] Agadžanov, *Ocherki*, pp. 133–6.

represented a powerful, pent up tribal force, ready to pour through any opening in the ring of containment about them. Their opportunity came in the second half of the 10th century. In 965 they participated in the destruction of the Khazar state with whom they had hitherto been allied. Indeed, the Oghuz *yabghu* was probably a Khazar vassal. Expansion in this direction, however, was for the most part blocked by the Rus' and Khorezm. Thus, when the Sāmānid hold loosened and then disappeared, the way south became open. The Oghuz here, however, were less masters of their own destiny than victims of larger forces. The mass migration of Oghuz tribes into the Near and Middle East had the quality of both an invasion and an eviction. The leadership that was able to harness and channel, but never fully control, this desperate force was provided by the Saljuks.

Saljuk, the son of Dokak Temir Yal̈igh ("Iron-Bow"), was the *Sü Bashï*, "war lord," of the Oghuz *yabghu* according to some of our accounts. In others, he is said to have been in Khazar service. Given the fact that three of his sons, before his conversion to Islam, bore the names Mīkā'īl, Isrā'īl and Mūsā, the family, clearly, must have been under Khazar-Judaic influence at one time. In or around the year 985, Saljuk was forced to flee from his overlord, either the Khazar kaghan or Oghuz *yabghu*. He took refuge in Jand, an important commercial city on the Syr Darya. Here, he converted to Islam. Together with his family, retainers and followers, he, like other "trucial Turks" took part in the wars and raids of the Muslim *ghāzīs* against the "pagan Turks." It was at this juncture that the band under his leadership became caught up in the Sāmānid-Karakhanid-Ghaznavid struggle for dominion in Muslim Central Asia. Thus, Oghuz elements harried the retreating Bughra Khan in 993 and later aided the ill-fated al-Muntaṣir. These Oghuz were probably the Seljuks.

The Karakhanid–Ghaznavid wars and the Saljuks

In 1001, the Karakhanid Naṣr Ilig and Maḥmūd came to terms. The Amu Darya was again delineated as the border between the two empires and the arrangement cemented by the marriage of Naṣr's daughter to the Ghaznavid ruler. This agreement was soon broken by Naṣr Ilig who attempted drives in Khorasan in 1006 and 1008. In the latter effort he was aided by his overlord the Tafghach Bughra Khan, Yūsuf Kadïr Khan. Oghuz groups were active in these campaigns on the side of the Ghaznavids. The Karakhanids, unsuccessful in both drives, now took up arms against each other, a consistent theme of their domestic history. Naṣr Ilig moved against his brother, the kaghan, Aḥmad b. 'Alī in 402/1011–12. Despite his death in the following year, the

feuding continued, ending only with the mediation of the Khorezmshah Ma'mūn b. Ma'mūn. The latter was more than an innocent bystander for he had been forced to carry on a delicate balancing act between his powerful and aggressive neighbors. Maḥmūd of Ghazna followed these events very closely, fearing an eventual Khorezmian-Karakhanid *entente* aimed at him. He had been subtly insinuating himself into Khorezmian affairs for some time and now applied intolerable pressure. In 1017, Ma'mūn, his brother-in-law, crumbled and perished in the flames of his palace in the aftermath of an army revolt, the product of Maḥmūd's pressure tactics. His nephew and successor Muḥammad was unable to ward off the inevitable Ghaznavid invasion sent to "avenge" Ma'mūn's untimely end. Khorezm was annexed by Ghazna and Maḥmūd's general, Altuntash, installed as Khorezmshah. The balance of power, given Khorezmian wealth, had tipped in favor of Ghazna.

The Karakhanid cousins Arslan Khan Manṣūr b. 'Alī and Kadïr Khan Yūsuf relented, briefly in 410/1019–20, in their feuding to stage an attack on Ghaznavid Khorasan. Defeated once again, Yūsuf, who in times past had not been averse to conspiring with Ghazna against his kinsmen, now did so once again. The Ghaznavid annexation of Khorezm would remain unchallenged.

These dynastic disturbances only added to what appears to have been a very unsettled situation in the steppes. In 408/1017–18, a large mass of nomadic tribes, "300,000 tents of the Turks" in the exaggerated language of our sources, set in motion probably by the activities of the Kitai, attacked the Karakhanid Toghan Khan Ahmad b. 'Alī. They were defeated in what Muslim sources describe as a great victory. This disturbance is most probably connected with the migration of the "*Qūn*" noted in al-Marwazī and later authors. According to these accounts, the "Qūn" had been forced out of the "land of Kitai" and compelled to seek new pasturages. They were then attacked by the "*Qāy*" and in their flight displaced the "*Sārī*". The latter then caused displacements amongst the "Türkmen" and Oghuz. The complete identification of all the *dramatis personae* in this event remains a source of debate amongst specialists. Nonetheless, there are a number of general points of agreement. The shock waves of this concatenation of migrations probably reached the westernmost regions of Central Asia in the second quarter of the 11th century. In its aftermath, the unstable Kimek tribal union collapsed to be replaced by that of the Kipchaks. The Oghuz, already faced with steady Kimek–Kipchak encroachments, were now subjected to tremendous pressures which resulted in the movement of some of them westward, towards the Pecheneg lands in the Pontic steppes. Others were pushed to the south. There can be little doubt that part of the tribal reservoir that the Saljuks were able to

tap, a reservoir of hungry, bedraggled, displaced and increasingly desperate Oghuz clans and tribes, was one of the final products of this chain of migrations. The migrations also further fueled the turbulence touched off by the intra-Karakhanid and Ghaznavid–Karakhanid wars. These too, as we shall see, had made the position of many Oghuz tribes in Transoxiana untenable.

In 1025, Maḥmūd of Ghazna and Kadïr Khan Yūsuf (who had become Supreme Kaghan the previous year), collaborated in an attack on Yūsuf's brother 'Alī Tegin. The latter had established himself in Bukhara as master of Mā warā'n-nahr c. 1020 and had become a thorn in the side of both. One of the principal sources of military strength on which 'Alī Tegin relied was the Saljuk band under the leadership of Isrā'īl Arslan Yabghu (it is unclear when and how Isra'il had obtained this title). This band was now attacked and defeated. Isrā'īl was led off into captivity in Ghaznavid India, from which he never returned. His followers were settled in Khorasan where their dire economic situation led them to raiding and brigandage. Maḥmūd, however, did not strike a mortal blow at 'Alī Tegin as he wished to keep him as a counterpoise to Yūsuf. His position was further strengthened by a brilliant diplomatic manoeuver in which the Ghaznavid Sultan was able to secure from the Caliphate the concession that all of the latter's dealings with the Karakhanids would be conducted through him. The Caliphate, however weak and debased at this time, was still an important source of political legitimization in the increasingly Islamic Turkic steppes. Control of this political lever gave Maḥmūd a dominating position in Central Asian affairs.

'Alī Tegin rapidly recovered and again demonstrated his independence by proclaiming himself the *Tamghach Bughra Qara Khāqān* in Transoxiana. The Ghaznavids, now under Maḥmūd's capable but erratic son Mas'ūd (1030–41) decided it was time to break 'Alī's power and sent the aging Khorezmshah Altuntash against him in 1032. The Khorezmian forces were defeated near Bukhara and Altuntash mortally wounded. The passing of the principal figures in these events (Kadïr Khan Yūsuf in 1032 and 'Alī Tegin in 1034) effected those changes that had thus far proved intractable to the force of arms. The Saljuks on whom 'Alī Tegin so relied now left the service of his sons and under the nominal leadership of Mūsā b. Saljuk (real authority was in the hands of the cousins Toghrul and Chaghrï), moved to join the new Khorezmshah Hārūn b. Altuntash. The latter, rightly suspicious of the intentions of Mas'ūd, was making rapid strides towards independence. This, of course, would have destroyed the elaborate web of containment around the Karakhanids spun by Maḥmūd and his successor was quick to thwart it.

Hārūn was killed in a Ghaznavid plot. Meanwhile, the Saljuks were badly mauled by Shāhmalik, the *yabghu* of Jand (son of the "Oghuz yabghu," Saljuk's arch-foe) in 1034. Now, truly in desperate straits, the Saljuks migrated to Northern Khorasan. Their raids and depredations here, adding to the chaos already engendered by earlier Oghuz movements to the region, forced a confrontation with the Ghaznavids. It is clear that this was the last thing that the Saljuks wanted, but abstention from raiding would have cut them off from the meager food supply on which they were just barely subsisting.

The dramatic dénouement took place at Dandānaqān near Merv in 1040. The Saljuks, fueled by desperation, won a resounding victory which permanently undermined Ghaznavid imperial ambitions. Mas'ūd was toppled and executed in a *coup* shortly afterwards. Henceforth, the shrinking Ghaznavid state largely withdrew from Central Asian affairs and focused its dwindling energies on India. Indeed, their earlier preoccupation with booty-laden India was undoubtedly one of the causes that contributed most to their neglect of their north western frontier and resultant loss of Khorasan. The Saljuks, channeling where they could the anarchic energies of the Oghuz tribes that had entered Iran, went on to become the leading Muslim power in the Near East. The conquest and occupation of Byzantine Anatolia after 1071, one of the factors that led to the Crusades, was really the work of the tribal raiders to which the Saljuk government had to give its reluctant consent. The rugged Saljuk chieftains, however, were transformed in their new habitat. When they reappeared in Central Asia it was as Sultans of the Islamic world.

The Saljuks in Central Asia

In contrast to Saljuk progress and consolidation, albeit imperfect at times, the Karakhanids were experiencing increasing fragmentation. The nominal unity of the mutually antagonistic members of the dynasty had been maintained until at least the death of Kadïr Khan Yūsuf. The sons of Naṣr Ilig of the 'Alid line had re-established themselves in Transoxiana putting an end to the brief interlude of Ḥasanid power associated with 'Alī Tegin and his successors. This familial division goes back to the two divergent lines of 'Ali b. Baytash Musa and Bughra Khan Hārūn (al-Ḥasan) b. Sulayman, the grandsons of Bughra Khan Satuk. The kaghanate was now moving strongly in the direction of a formal division into two separate kaghanates, one based in Transoxiana and the other in Eastern Turkestan with the borders meeting in Ferghana–Semirech'e, areas that were frequently contested. Although there is no una-

nimity in scholarly opinion as to the precise period to which this development should be attributed,[29] it probably reached fruition by the second half of the 11th century. In any event, it was the resurgent 'Alid line under Böri Tegin Ibrāhīm and his son Shams al-Mulk Naṣr who would have to face the awesome power of the Saljuks.

The Saljuk state represented something new amongst the early Turco-Islamic states. It occupied, in a sense, an intermediate position between the models represented by Ghaznavid and Karakhanid organization. The former was a largely personal and "artificial" creation, a mobile army or military caste (primarily Turkic but with sizable non-Turkic elements) and an accompanying Persian bureaucracy based on Sāmānid models imposed by conquest on a territory. It had an almost "colonial" and "robber baron" mentality. It was held together by conquest, booty and such legitimization as it could gather from the Caliphate. There was no ethnic base of loyal subjects tied to the dynasty by a common origin and history to which it could appeal. Even the religious bond was not universal. The Karakhanid kaghanate, on the other hand, was largely possessed of such a base, as disquieting as it could often be, buttressed by shared Turkic traditions and a notion of *translatio imperii*. Islamic legitimization, which it too eagerly sought, was helpful, but not necessarily decisive with the tribes, the extent of whose islamicization is open to question. The Saljuks, although they attempted to enlarge on the "charisma" of the royal house within the traditional, Turkic steppe context, were forced to rely more on the Islamic tradition as the Karakhanids had largely pre-empted and indeed had a better claim to the mantle of succession in the nomadic *imperium*. This, however, posed certain problems with their tribal followers whose consciousness in these matters remained at the tribal level. The Saljuk Sultans, transformed now into Islamic potentates, the spiritual heirs of the Sassanid Shāhanshāhs, were not able to impress their tribal kinsmen with their imperial grandeur nor, for that matter, firmly control them. Relying increasingly on Sāmānid models fostered by brilliant statesmen such as Niẓām al-Mulk, and a mercenary and *ghulām* army, they were soon estranged from the tribes that had brought them to power. The tension thus created had perilous consequences for the dynasty.

In 1042, Saljuk armies crushed their old foe Shāhmalik who had established himself in Khorezm at the expense of the Altuntashids. He fled only to be captured and executed in Makrān. Khorezm was now secured, but Seljuk

[29] O. Pritsak, "Karachanidische Streitfragen," *Oriens*, 3, 227–8 (1950) and his "Die Karachaniden," pp. 36–38; E.A. Davidovič, "O dvukh karakhanidskikh kaganatakh," *Narody Azii i Afriki*, 1968, No. 1, pp. 73–5.

attempts to re-establish a hold over the Syr Darya were probably blocked, at least in part, by the influx of Kipchak tribes who soon transformed the onetime "Desert of the Oghuz" into the "Desert of the Kipchaks" (*Dasht-i Qifchāq*). Alp Arslan (1063–72) extended Saljuk authority once again to Jand, where the dynasty's founder was buried, and to some of the neighboring Kipchak chieftains in 458/1065–6. The complaints of the Karakhanid Tamghach Khan Ibrāhīm about unprovoked aggression against a fellow Muslim ruler prevailed to prevent further encroachments at this time. His son, however, Shams al-Mulk Naṣr (1068–80) faced another Saljuk invasion in 1072 which was only temporarily halted by Alp Arslan's murder in its initial stages. The latter's successor Malikshāh (1072—92) then repulsed a Karakhanid counteroffensive and an uneasy peace was restored as the Karakhanids returned to internal strife.

A more decisive resolution of the question of overlordship in Transoxiana was not long in coming. Serious conflicts with the *'ulamā'* had now been added to the list of Karakhanid domestic woes. This, of course, given the proper invitation, provided the Saljuks with a religious justification for intervention. Thus, it was at the request of the *'ulamā'* of Transoxiana that Malikshāh marched into Karakhanid lands in 1089. Bukhara and Samarkand were quickly taken. The Karakhanid Aḥmad Khan (1081–9) was deposed and exiled to Saljukid Isfahan. The western Karakhanid kaghanate was now a Saljuk vassal state. The Eastern Kaghan, Hārūn b. Sulaymān (d. 1103), following a Saljuk campaign into Talas and Semirech'e, submitted as well. Difficulties continued in the western part of the newly won territory, particularly in Samarkand and with the Chigil tribesmen there. The area, however, was soon pacified and subsequent Karakhanid rulers here were little more than supporting players in the larger events. The Saljuks wisely did not annex these areas outright, wishing, no doubt, to avoid being drawn into the morass of local politics.

After Malikshāh's death, the Saljuks also fell prey to family rivalries and internecine strife. Their domestic preoccupations emboldened Kadïr Khan Jibrā'īl of the eastern, Ḥasanid line to attempt to end Saljuk dominance in Transoxiana. He was stopped by Sanjar b. Malikshāh at Tirmidh in 1102. Sanjar who was viceroy in the east and from 1118 the supreme Saljuk Sultan, now made the Karakhanid Muḥammad II b. Sulaymān, his kinsman, the Arslan Khāqān of the west (1102–30) and aided him when necessary against dynastic rivals. Compelled in 1130 to again intervene in local affairs, Sanjar ultimately placed his Karakhanid nephew, Maḥmūd II b. Muḥammad (1132–41) on the kaghanal throne. The latter proved to be completely loyal to Saljuk

interests. Despite the seeming ease with which Sanjar controlled affairs here, Saljuk power was on the wane. It was sapped by internal tensions and worrisome vassals, such as the Khorezmshahs, and would be unable to successfully meet a new challenge from the steppe, the Karakitai.

The entrance of the Karakitai into Karakhanid holdings in Turkestan was aided by the difficulties local rulers were experiencing with the turbulent Karluks and other tribes. One thrust of the Karakitai refugees from the collapse of the Liao dynasty in China was parried by "the ruler of Kashghar" in 522/1128. Another movement led by the Gür Khan, according to Muslim sources, went through Kirghiz lands and entered Karakhanid territory. It was joined by various Turkic tribal elements. The Karakhanid ruler of Balasaghun, according to Juvainī, faced with troublesome Karluk and Kangli tribes, appealed to the Gür Khan, in effect, offering his realm. The latter came and conquered the region, ascending a "throne that had cost him nothing."[30] From here attacks were launched east and west. Karluk tribesmen, dissatisfied with Sanjar and Maḥmūd, joined the Gür Khan and urged him to invade Transoxiana. This he did, defeating Maḥmūd at Khojanda in 1137.

Sanjar, of course, could not stand idly by. The great confrontation between Sanjar and the Karakitai took place in the Qaṭwān steppe in 1141. Sanjar was disastrously defeated and the Saljuk hold in Central Asia broken. The Karakitai, far milder masters than the Saljuks, established their authority in Transoxiana and Khorezm. Sanjar's fortunes, meanwhile, continued to decline. In 1153, he was defeated and captured by Oghuz tribesmen of Khuttal and Ṭukhāristān, themselves refugees from the unruly Karluks in Mā warā'n-nahr. He escaped from captivity in 1156 only to die a year later, a broken man.

Control of the region, the administrative and structural forms of which were left largely unchanged by the Karakitai, was not uncontested. A new power, that of the Khorezmshah state, was emerging. The latter, through earlier attempts to subvert Saljukid power, had helped pave the way for Sanjar's collapse. Khorezm had long been an important commercial emporium, one of the main conduits for the raw materials and products of the Slavic lands to their west into the Islamic world. This strong economic base made the acquisition of Khorezm a commercial as well as strategic *desideratum* of every major power in the region. It was just these factors, however, so easily translated into autonomy, if not outright independence, that made its reten-

[30] 'Ata Malik Juvainī, *Ta'rīkh-i Jahān-Gushā: The History of the World Conqueror*, trans. J.A. Boyle, 2 vols. (Cambridge, Mass. 1958), I, 354–6; Ibn al-Athīr, ed. Tornberg (Beirut ed.), Xi, 81–6; Abu'l Ghāzī Bahadur Khan, *Shajara-yi Türk: Histoire des Mongols et des Tatares par Aboul-Ghazi Béhadour Khan*, ed. trans. P.I. Desmaisons (St. Pétersbourg, 1871–4, reprint Amsterdam, 1970), text, pp. 48–9.

tion a frequently difficult task. Beginning with the Ghaznavid *ghulām* Altuntash (1017–32), the various holders of the Khorezmshah title had been Turks. This factor, buttressed by the presence in the surrounding steppelands of first Pecheneg and Oghuz and later Kipchak, Kangli, Köchet, Chighrak and other Turkic tribes, contributed to the gradual Turcization of the region, a process that was not completed until the 13th century.

In 1097, Quṭb al-Dīn Muḥammad Aybek, son of Anushtegin an earlier Saljuk governor of Khorezm, became the Khorezmshah. It was his son Atsïz (1127–56) who first gave clear signals of separatist tendencies. Although a tribute-paying Karakitai vassal after 1141, he allowed little outside interference in his affairs. Atsïz campaigned against the surrounding steppe tribes, annexed Jand and Mangishlak and thereby laid the groundwork for future expansion. These policies were continued by his son Il Arslan (1156–72), who lacked, however, the power sufficient to achieve independence. Tekesh (1172–1200), his successor, despite periodic difficulties with his brother and rival claimant to the throne, Sulṭānshāh, fared even better. He extended his authority to Khorasan, thereby doubling the size of his domain, and contested the supremacy in the eastern Islamic world with the semi-barbarian Ghūrids who had replaced the Ghaznavids and were seeking a foothold in eastern Iran. Tekesh, through marriage to a Kangli princess, Terken Katun, secured the support of some of the tribes. His wife's kinsmen and other tribal aristocrats now entered Khorezmian service. This, however, did not preclude further problems with the nomads. Indeed, this was the critical, weak spot of the Khorezmian state. Reliance on the often fickle tribal chieftains gave it a military force that could and did melt away. It was, however, on just such a force that Tekesh's son Muḥammad (1200–20) pinned his hopes of conquest.

Muḥammad's aspirations did not apparently stop at liberating his large and unstable holdings from Karakitai overlordship. He aimed at making himself the supreme potentate of the entire eastern Islamic world. His first steps were cautious and focused on shoring up his hold on areas in his possession and cooperating with the Gür Khan in areas where both would profit. Our sources are contradictory in their chronology of Muḥammad's "liberation" of Muslim Transoxiana from the "infidel" yoke. He exploited the revolt in Bukhara against the excesses of the theocratic *ṣadrs* to establish his authority there c. 1207. In this, he was still acting as the loyal vassal of the Gür Khan. Sometime later, he began to conspire with the Karakhanid ruler of Samarkand, 'Uthmān. The latter had been rebuffed in his request for the hand of a Karaitai princess and subsequently openly declared his allegiance to the Khorezmshah. This produced a predictable Karakitai invasion and occupa-

tion of Samarkand. The occupation was cut short, however, by the shock administered to the weakening fabric of Karakitai power by the Naiman refugee Küchlüg in 1210. Muḥammad and Küchlüg had, apparently, agreed to divide the Gür Khan's empire. The latter was successful against Küchlüg, his son-in-law, but was then taken prisoner by him when his own army revolted. Meanwhile, Muḥammad had defeated the *Tayangu*, the Karakitai army commander in the Talas region. The victory, though not decisive, gained him great prestige in the Muslim world. Samarkand's ruler, 'Uthmān, was now married to Muḥammad's daughter, while his city was occupied by Khorezmian troops. Their depredations provoked a popular revolt in 1212 which 'Uthmān joined. Muḥammad immediately marched on the city, took it and executed 'Uthmān, thus ending the western branch of the Karakhanid dynasty.

The collapse of the Karakitai in Transoxiana, thus engineered by Muḥammad, was fraught with dangers of which the latter was probably ignorant. The Persian historian of the Mongols, Juvainī, aided by the perspective of years, put into the mouth of the dying Atsïz the injunction to his sons not to fight the Gür Khan because "he was a great wall behind which were terrible foes."[31] The prevision of Atsïz may be doubted, but the prophecy, even if invented *post facto*, was true enough. The Gür Khan died in 1211 and Küchlüg was swept away in 1218 by those "terrible foes," the Mongols. The Khorezmian state that faced the Mongol armies, a state encompassing sizable parts of Iran, Iraq, the Oxus and Transoxiana, was devoid of true political unity. It was wary of its ambitious ruler, and wracked by internal dissension between the dynasty and the tribal armies on which it chiefly relied. Regardless of how one resolves the question of who really provoked the Mongol–Khorezmian war,[32] its outcome was as predictable as the war itself was inevitable. Muḥammad ended his days a refugee on a Caspian island and many of the lustrous cities of Central Asia lay in smoking ruins.

[31] Juvainī, trans. Boyle, 1, 357.

[32] I.P. Petrushevskiĭ, "Pokhod mongol'skikh vojsk v Srednjuju Aziju v 1219–1224 gg. i ego posledstvija" in S.L. Tikhvinskiĭ (ed.), *Tataro-Mongoly v Azii i Evrope* (Moskva, 1970), pp. 101–19.

14

Early and medieval Tibet

Pre- and early history

At our present level of knowledge, we cannot define with certainty the boundaries between pre- and early history. This is due, on the one hand, to the fact that systematic excavations in Tibet and bordering regions have not yet been possible, nor are they to be expected in the near future. On the other hand we have access to the ancient Chinese historical works which contain historical and ethnographical data on the "barbarian peoples," information which we must certainly use in spite of the fact that it is frequently adulterated with contemporary interpolations. In such sources one must also distinguish between the data which refer to those peoples who directly bordered the Chinese upland and had trade or military relations with the Chinese, and the data on those peoples who are merely mentioned from hearsay but had no direct contact with the Chinese and concerning whom certain "barbarian clichés" existed which, of course, have no historical value. Frequent mention is made for instance of the immorality of women who belonged to the various foreign peoples, information which simply shows that they had different sexual mores from those acceptable in China. Among the Tibetans and related peoples this would refer to the social institution of polyandry.

When we turn to the few available archeological finds, it is evident that their value is rather meager, consisting as they do of objects which have been found on the earth's surface or were unearthed by a slight scratching of the soil and that quite by chance.

The most important evidence of Tibetan prehistory are the megalithic monuments which extend in a broad belt from western Tibet across the plateau to the north of the trans-Himalayas, the region of the great salt lakes, and parts of the Byang-thang as far as Amdo in northeast Tibet. Because there has been no thorough study of these cairns, menhirs, and dolmens which

ethnologists connect with ancestor worship,[1] we simply do not know whether they can be traced back to the ancient Tibetans.[2] One fact, however, is of great interest: the range of distribution of the megaliths coincides with that of the Eurasian animal style, the artifacts of which have been found in a broad belt which extends from the lands of the Scythians in south Russia to the Chinese province of Kansu.

As the ethnological-anthropological works of W. Eberhard show, the culture of those groups which he terms "West Tibetans" is practically identical with the culture of the "Ch'iang" tribes, differences appearing only in the form of influences from other, primarily steppe, peoples. Whereas T'u-fan, the ancient name which the Chinese gave the Bod (the true Tibetans), appeared only at the time of the Sui dynasty and was especially prominent in the two T'ang annals, the collective name "Ch'iang" (written in one character consisting of "sheep" and "man") goes back to the most ancient Chinese documentation. Thus the Tibetans are closely related to the Ch'iang, who consisted of many tribes, and those folk-groups which were later known as "Tibetans" may have wandered from the Ch'iang homeland in what is now northeast Tibet, the Kukunor region, and the districts bordering Kansu, to the valley of the upper Brahmaputra in the southwest, obviously in many intermittent stages.

Among the Chinese the name Ch'iang is extremely ancient and appears, always written with the same character, on the oracle bones of the Shang Dynasty, in the *Bamboo Annals*, in the venerable *Shu-ching*, in the first great work of Chinese historiography, the *Shi-chi* by Ssu-ma Ch'ien, and in the annals of the first and second Han dynasties. The Ch'iang were sheep-breeding nomads without close political ties, a factor which in no way hindered them from constantly banding together in warlike brigandage, often in the tracks of other peoples such as the Hsiung-nu. During the Han period the Ch'iang settled further to the east in those regions which they would later incorporate into their own kingdom from the Chinese: Kansu and Shensi. Actually, parts of Shensi were even then inundated by the Ch'iang, as was western Szechwan (see map No. 1 in Eberhard, 1942).

As an appellation for the Western Barbarians the name Ti appears somewhat later than Ch'iang and Eberhard's ethnological description of the Ti (1942, p. 82) tends to identify the Ch'iang with the Ti who left their traces on the map of Tibet in place-names such as Dan-tig to the east of bsTong-kha

[1] Adam-Trimborn, 1958, p. 1.

[2] For sources concerning the Tibetan megaliths, see Roerich, 1930, and 1931 and Aufschnaiter, 1956–7.

(Wylie 1962, pp. 193 and 196). During the T'ang period the Ch'iang in the Nan Shan were also known as the Nam-tig,[3] hence Nan Shan probably did not originally mean "southern mountains" but the mountains where the Nam group of the Ti lived, the name being employed not only ethnically but geographically.

Mention has been made of the fact that the Ch'iang never created a real state but merely formed short-lived confederacies in order to carry out brigandage expeditions or protect themselves from the frequent encroachments of the Chinese officials. There are, however, examples of groups of the Ch'iang uniting in a real state under the overlordship of steppe warriors. A classic example of such a development was the T'u-yü-hun state which was destroyed later, in the 7th century, by the Tibetan King Srong-brtsan sgam-po. The Ch'iang of northeast Tibet, including the Kukunor region, came under the rule of a Hsien-pi group whose dynasty called itself A-ch'ai (found in Tibetan literature as A-zha) and the state was called T'u-yü-hun (Tibetan: Thogon, Tho-yo-gon). Information that the inhabitants of the T'u-yü-hun state raised horses and drank kumiss, but also had yaks and grew grain in favorable locations, indicates that their culture was a composite one, characteristic of the steppe peoples such as the Ch'iang.

Among the Tibetans themselves things were much the same. According to the Chinese sources the mythical ancestor of the Bod was called T'u-fa and was believed to have been the son of a T'o-pa (hence a Turk, whom the Northern Wei Dynasty, 386–534, called T'o-pa; Eberhard 1942, p. 51) and a Hsiung-nu woman, a probable indication of the subjugation of a Ch'iang people by a stratum of steppe warriors. Since the Chinese delight in toying with similar sounding names, suspicion is raised by the fact that the ancestor of the Tibetans is called T'u-fa (T'u-fan). Yet there is no reason to treat all Chinese data as inventions, the less so as the T'ang Annals give the name of the first mythological king of the Tibetans as Ho-t'i po-si-yeh in which it is only necessary to transpose two characters (Ho-t'i Si-po-yeh) to obtain an excellent transcription of the Tibetan form (O-lde spu-rgyal) of the name of the first king who, according to the oldest documents, is supposed to have descended from heaven. Among the Tibetans totem and tabu were twofold: the dog (which indicates a steppe people), and the monkey, which also appears among other Ch'iang peoples, such as the Tang-hsiang. According to other sources, the Tibetans originated in the Yung-pei region in north Yunnan

[3] Thomas, 1948, pp. 58–61.

[4] Concerning the T'u-yü-hun see Molè, 1979 and the data in Franke vol. 3, pp. 250 ff. Also Eberhard, 1942, pp. 61–2.

where the Mo-so now live and where, in the warm regions of the Yangtse, monkeys live among the luxuriant vegetation.

The assumption that the Ch'iang originally lived a nomad life in northeast Tibet and the neighboring regions which were to be later sinicized makes no provision for an explanation of the influences of the steppe-nomads in the overall cultural and ethnological makeup of the people. Even if the Tibetans (the Bod-pa as they call themselves) had, as mentioned above, come from so southerly a place as Yung-pei, we still must face the assumption that they had previously been forced to the south from the community of the Ch'iang in and around Amdo before they came under the overlordship of the steppe warriors. In the north, the later "Tibetans" who were called Ch'iang certainly came in contact with the Yüeh-chih, the upper stratum of which was Indo-European, i.e. Iranian. When the majority of these people were driven west by the Hsiung-nu under Motun (around 177 B.C.) a small group remained behind in the Nan Shan and may have mixed to a certain extent with the local Ch'iang.

The western migration of the Tibetans into their later homeland in the valley of the gTsang-po was a gradual process. This is evident from the fact that the first mythical king, who is called O-lde spu-rgyal rather than gNgya-khri btsan-po in the oldest sources, appears only as the ninth monarch by the name of sPu-lde gung-rgyal in the obviously frequently altered lists of the later historians, and from the fact that in the rKong-po country which borders the Ol-kha there is a mountain called O-de gung-rgyal. If we remember that the first king descended from heaven on to a mountain which was later located in the Yar-klungs valley, then consider the names O-lde spu-rgyal and sPul-lde gung-rgyal, it will be evident that the name of the mountain in Ol-kha rKong-po is similar to that of the king. The *rGyal-po bka'i thang-yig* (*Documents Concerning the Kings*) calls the mountain of descent the Byang-rdor in (r)Kong-po which, as the "mountain of the descent of the gods" (lha-bab-ri), was transferred to the Yar-klungs valley, the home of the later royal dynasty. (The pronunciation of Byang and Thang is identical.)

In an unusually informative article on the nomad tribes G.N. Roerich correctly points out that there occurred not only a southwesterly migration of the Ch'iang peoples of the Amdo region, i.e. the region where the true Tibetans lived, but also a migration directly to the west. These tribes migrated in the direction of the Tibetan highlands (Byang-thang) and, after reaching the northern spurs of the gNyan-chen thang-lha Range (at that time the northern border of Tibet), moved along the trans-Himalayas and thrust through the region of the great salt lakes into the Kailas–Manasarovar region and its

adjacent districts. These tribes were the Yang-t'ung (Tibetan: Zhang-zhung). The Chinese speak of the "Greater Yang-t'ung" and the "Lesser Yang-t'ung", whereas the chronicles and other texts of the Bon-po which have become available to us and were originally compiled in the Zhang-zhung language, speak of the "Upper" (*stod*) and "Lower" (*smar*) Zhang-zhung, the latter being the more ancient expressions and typical of mountain people. The Zhang-zhung were unquestionably the Ch'iang and spoke a language similar to, but not identical with Tibetan. The Zhang-zhung empire comprised all Western Tibet and included Gu-ge, Ladakh, Zangs-dkar, Lahul, Khu-nu, and the districts of Ru-thog, Da-rog, Guge, and the Manasarovar region in the east as well as the much-discussed Suvarṇagotra (Tibetan: gSer-rabs) which I hesitate to identify with Zhang-zhung, considering it rather their vassal state. Zhang-zhung power extended to the north as far as the mountains of Khotan and to the east the upper Yangtse (Tibetan: 'Bri-chu) formed the boundary of the sphere of influence of the Sum-pa (Chinese: Su-p'i) who carried on military and brigandage campaigns against Khotan. The Sum-pa were finally conquered by the Zhang-zhung. This was the situation when the Tibetans began their expansion, and we read in a religious Bon text (*sNyan-rgyud*) that the Tibetans waylaid the Zhang-zhung king in the vicinity of Dangra (Tibetan: gYu-mtsho) while he was on an inspection tour of the Sum-pa and killed him. The Sum-pa also spoke a Tibeto-Burmese language which differed from Tibetan and of which we have only a few uncertain glosses.

The residence of the Zhang-zhung king in western "Upper" Zhang-zhung was Khyung-lung dngul-mkhar in the upper valley of the Sutlej. That of the "Lower" Zhang-zhung was to the east of the sacred Dang-ra at gYu-mtsho Khyung-rdzong. That Tibet was surrounded by a crescent of Zhang-zhung at the time of the first Tibetan state is clearly seen from a commentary by Dran-pa nam-mkha in a Bon source (Tenzin Namdak 1966, pp. 19–20). At the time of the probably historical king whose reign cannot be dated but whom the later, mythical lists of kings of the Buddhist chronicles place seventh and, for etiological reasons, call Gri-gum btsan-po, there appeared a quite sober description of the kingdom of Tibet: "Downward from the myriarchy of the Upper Zhang-zhung, and upward from the chiliarchy of Lower Sum-pa, to the north and south between the Türk and the Mon [the peoples on the southern slopes of the Himalayas], was the territory of the Tibet of the four 'horns' or military districts [*ru*]".[5]

[5] Concerning the "Four Horns" see Uray, 1960.

The rise of the Tibetan empire

Although the late monastic chronicles provide only very general data on the prehistory of the Tibetan tribes along the Brahmaputra and confuse the mythical with the genuinely historical, we possess valuable documents, found in East Turkestan, which describe the period before their unification into a comparatively centralized state under an emperor (*btsan-po*). The later chronicles simply inform us that Tibet was ruled by various spirits until, as already mentioned, the first ruler descended from heaven to rule the land. The list of the twenty-seven kings was obviously altered many times to accord with various political and religious trends, and only the last four princes: Lha-tho tho-ri gnyan-btsan, Khri-gnyan gzung-btsan, 'Bro-gnyan lde'u, and sTag-ri gnyan-gzigs, who preceded gNam-ri Srong-brtsan could have exerted any authority as local princes from their castle of Phying-ba stag-rtse in Phyong-rgyas, a valley near Yar-klungs. The last-named of these princes was succeeded by gNam-ri srong-brtsan, who is called Slon-btsan rlung-nam in the ancient Tun-huang documents. He reigned from 570 to 620 and set himself to unite the Tibetans and the related Ch'iang peoples, a work which was to be completed only by his son.

The *Tun-huang Chronicle* provides us with interesting and evidently authentic information on the struggles of the rulers of Phying-ba stag-rtse, who apparently also ruled over Myang-ro (later Nyang-ro). It would seem that their two chief competitors were Zing-po-rje sTab-skya-bo, who resided in Nyen-kar rnying-pa (in the sTod-lung valley), and Zing-po-rje Khri-pangs-sum, who ruled over the sDur-ba'i yu-sna castle. Also important during this period were the noble families or clans of the Myang, mGar, dBa's, mNon, Tshe-spong, and Khyung-po. gNam-ri srong-(bslon) brtsan defeated his opponents and a Zhang-zhung noble, K'yung-po sPung-sad zu-tse, played an important role in these struggles until the time of the great Srong-brtsan sgam-po. He defeated and killed Mar-mun, the ruler of rTsang-bod (the later province of gTsang, or part of it), comprising some twenty-thousand families, earning thereby the special favor[6] of gNam-ri from whose hand he received as a fief the conquered parts of gTsang. It is quite possible that parts of gTsang, especially those districts to the north of the Brahmaputra, which even in our century were covered with Bon monasteries, were at that time inhabited by a Zhang-zhung people. A revolt of the Dags-po province to the east of Yar-klungs was put down by the bTsan-po's troops. According to an article in the

[6] Concerning the term *glo-ba-ñe* "in favor" and *glo-ba-ring* "in disfavor" see Li, 1959.

Chinese encyclopedia *Wen-hsien t'ung-kao* by Ma Tuan-lin (this report is not found in the older historical works), this first great ruler of Tibet defeated the barbarian tribes (certainly of Tibeto-Burmese origin) on the western borders of the Chinese province of Szechwan and in the as yet non-sinicized region of what would later be Yunnan.[7] The *La-dvags rgyal-rabs*[8] even asserts that gNam-ri conquered King gNya-zhur (Lig-gnya-šur was a title of the Zhang-zhung kings) and other states in the west as well as Gru-gu (Dru-gu) or the western Türks of Inner Asia.[9] This information would seem to anticipate the events which took place under gNam-ri's successor, Srong-brtsan sgam-po, although we cannot exclude the possibility that the growing might of the Tibetans, even then, had relations, peaceful or warlike, with the Zhang-zhung and the western Türks. Evidence for this might be found in an observation in the *Tun-huang Chronicle* which states that the Zing-po-rje fled to the land of the Türks (*dru-gu yul-du bros-so*) after the fall of his castle. Of historico-cultural interest is a statement in the *La-dvags rgyal-rabs* that, as far back as the reign of gNam-ri, medical science and astrology (*rtsis*) were imported from China. According to the *Tun-huang Chronicle*, gNam-ri srong-brtsan is believed to have been poisoned.

As was frequently to be the case later, the death of the bTsan-po provoked a general rebellion and the *Tun-huang Chronicle* numbers among the insurgents the regions of Dags-po, rKon-po, which was semi-autonomous although incorporated into the empire, the Myang-po region, and even Tshe-spong, the land which the wife of the poisoned king had brought with her. The confederated states of Zhang-zhung, which at most were semi-independent, also became hostile. In spite of his youth, the heir to the throne, Srong-brtsan sgam-po (about 620–49), provided a forewarning of his future power by having the unnamed traitor executed at court. The faithful "Great Minister" (Myang Mang-po-rje Zhang-snang) forced the Sum-pa to submission without a stroke of the sword; then the emperor (bTsan-po) personally led an army into the northwest and forced the A-zha and the "Chinese" to pay tribute, which evidently meant that several Chinese governors in Kansu were obliged to submit to Tibetan extortion.

The Tibetan campaign against the A-zha and the neighboring regions of China would seem to have been somewhat unexpected, since the A-zha had never been a Tibetan vassal-state nor subject to Srong-brtsan gam-po. The T'ang Annals provide an explanation for this: the Tibetans had heard that both the Türks and the T'u-yü-hun (A-zha) had obtained Chinese princesses

[7] See Petech, 1939, p. 35. [8] Francke, p. 82; p. 30, lines 27–9. [9] Francke, p. 82.
[9a] Concerning the mGar family, see my essay, Hoffmann, 1971.

as wives for their rulers, but that the emperor T'ai-tsung had refused the Tibetans, evidently owing to the intrigue and opposition of the T'u-yü-hun. One result of this war of revenge was that the Kokonor region of the A-zha became a part of the Tibetan empire; only a few of the conquered A-zha went over to the Chinese and were settled further to the east. Also, T'ai-tsung agreed in 641 to give the royal princess Wen-ch'eng to the Tibetan ruler as his bride. Srong-brtsan sgam-po lived with the princess (whose name the *Tun-huang Annals* transcribe as Mun-chhang Kong-cho) for nine years until his death in 649. On the domestic front the new ruler had many perils to face, especially those instigated by his father's favorite, Khyung-po sPung-sad zu-tse, who was a native of Zhang-zhung and apparently wished to restore Zhang-zhung power. He sowed mistrust between the emperor and the "Great Minister," Myang Zhang-snang, who entrenched himself in his castle of sDur-ba, an act which in itself seemed to prove to the emperor the minister's evil intentions. The stronghold was stormed, destroyed, and the minister killed. sPong-sad zu-tse now believed the time was propitious to do away with the emperor himself and he set a trap by inviting him to a banquet in his park. The emperor accepted the invitation but sent his minister mGar Stong-brtsan yul-bzung on ahead to observe. He noticed that a plot was being hatched, and reported this to the emperor. sPung-sad zu-tse, who realized why the emperor had sent on this mission his faithful minister, saw that he had failed and committed suicide. His own son decapitated his father's body and took the head to the emperor who, in turn, allowed him to retain his fief. mGar served the emperor until the latter's death, and his office of "Great Minister" was filled by his descendants for decades.

Srong-brtsan sgam-po also made use of other marriages to further his policies of empire. He married a princess from the Tibetan feudal aristocracy, Mong-bza Khri-mo mnyen-idong-steng, from sTod-lung, who presented him with an heir to the throne, and also a princess from the Mi-nyan (the later Tanguts) to the northeast of Kukunor. His marriage to the Nepalese princess, Khri-btsun, the daughter of Amshuvarman, has been questioned by Tucci, although internal evidence strongly indicates its historicity. Nepal was a vassal-state of Tibet at the time of the emperor, as is clear from the fact that when the Chinese envoy Wang Hsüan-ts'e on his way to India in 648 was mistreated by the local potentate of Tirabhukti he was protected by a bodyguard composed of Tibetans and Nepalis given him by Srong-brtsan sgam-po.

Wishing to improve the empire culturally and raise it from barbarism (later Buddhist sources describe the country at that time as the land of the red-faced

barbarians of the borderlands), the emperor sent one of his nobles, Thon-mi Anu-i bu Sambhoṭa, to India to study the Indian scripts and adapt one of these to the Tibetan language. He traveled over much of India and finally returned with one script, presumably the Gupta script of Kashmir, which he adapted to the writing of Tibetan. The sources report that Thon-mi compiled eight treatises on Tibetan grammar, only two of which have come down to us. The new script was first used in a state chancery set up by the Chinese, a factor of great importance for that period, as was the importation of paper, tea, and alcoholic beverages from China. Srong-brtsan sgam-po constructed a fortified, walled capital, Ra-sa (walled-about place) for the princess which was later called Lha-sa (place of the gods). The *Tun-huang Annals* tell us that succeeding Tibetan emperors resided alternately in various castles and strongholds, especially in the vicinity of the later bSam-yas.

In things pertaining to spiritual culture the Indians were the Tibetans' teachers. It is possible that several Buddhist teachings became known during the time of Srong-brtsan sgam-po, although the emperor was more interested in the cultural than the purely religious aspects of the Indian religion. Legendary adornment notwithstanding, the influence of the Chinese and Nepalese wives of the emperor was of great importance in that the first Buddhist temples were built: the Jo-khang in Lhasa, the holiest temple in Tibet and the "navel," i.e. centre of the empire, and the Ra-mo-che. The chapels for the civilizing of the borderlands also go back to this period. Among these the Khra-'brug temple has remained intact and practically unaltered and shows that Tibetan temple architecture developed from that of the ancient fortresses; in both we find defensive bulwarks with thick, inward-sloping walls and narrow, crenelated windows.

When, at the age of 13, the heir to the throne, Gung-srong gung-brtsan, attained his majority, he was appointed co-regent, but died five years later. When the emperor died in 649 he was succeeded by his grandson Mang-slon (srong) mang-brtsan, at that time still a minor.

The period of the regency

As the grandson of Srong-brtsan sgam-po was still a child when he succeeded his grandfather, the administration of the government was in the hands of the faithful "Great Minister", mGar sTong-brtsan, until his death in 667. The new emperor, and later his son, deferred to the mGar family which during the remainder of the century held the reigns of government. That the sons of mGar sTong-brtsan made no attempt to overthrow the reigning dynasty was

probably due to the fact that the Tibetan subjects, whose minds were dominated by magic, saw in the majesty (mnga-thang) and magic powers (mthu) of the legal dynasty a guarantee for the existence of the state which not even the mighty mGar family could take lightly.

When in 659 the Chinese began treacherous negotiations with the A-zha, mGar sTong-brtsan appeared in the northeast and attacked and killed the vassal king, although the latter's successor was allowed to retain his special position over his closely united people. On his father's death, mGar bTsan-snyal Ldom-bu became "Great Minister" and at the beginning of his administration in 669 the Chinese suffered a great defeat in East Turkestan. Their short-lived colonial rule over the whole territory lasted from 670 until 692. It is of interest to note that in the summer of 673 bTsan-snyal dom-bu summoned the great State Assembly in conjunction with his brother, mGar Khri-'bring brtsan-brod who, until the end of the century, was the most powerful man in Tibet and "Great Minister" from 685 until 698. Another son of the elder mGar, bTsan-po yon-tan rgyal-bzung, was a general (dmag-dpon).[10]

In 677 under the new emperor, Khri'dus-srong Mang-po-rje (676–704), the Zhang-zhung in the west also attempted an uprising. The leader of the revolt, Ra-sangs-rje sPung-rye-ryung, was unsuccessful and "fell into disfavor," i.e. was killed. As may be deduced from his name, the former Zhang-zhung kingdom had been given by the Tibetans a native administration; "Ra-sangs" is the Zhang-zhung word for minister or official to which the Tibetans added "rje" which bears the same meaning.[11]

In 698 Khri-dus-srong succeeded in ridding himself of his steward, mGar Khri-'bring, who then committed suicide, and the role of regent was assumed by his mother, Khri-ma-lod. Khri-dus-srong now assumed command of the army, but his campaigns were unsuccessful and he was defeated by the Chinese. He died in 704, at an early age, during a campaign against the 'Jang (the Mo-so kingdom in present-day Yunnan), the same year in which a son was born to him.

Two things were worthy of note following the death of Khri-'dus-srong: for the next few years there is no mention of a "Great Minister" nor is there any indication of the summer and winter residences of the empress dowager and

[10] In the later Bon literature which has retained many Zhang-zhun names, *rje* is not found after *Ra-sangs*, a title which evidently indicates a master in the Bon religion. See *Ra-sangs kLu-rgyal* in the historical work published by Karmay, 1972, p. 54.

[11] Se-rib may have been the region which comprises present-day Dol-po, bLo-bo (Mustang) and bordering regions in northwest Nepal, and it must have been in direct contact with Zhang-zhun. The assumption made by F.W. Thomas, 1935, p. 152, note 1 and shared by Pelliot, 1963, II, p. 711, which identifies Se-rib with gSer-rigs (Suvarṇa-gotra) is quite dubious and by no means probable. See also Stein 1972, p. 60.

the royal child. During these years Khri-ma-lod was at the height of her powers and was the real regent of Tibet as is evident from the fact that her grandson, Khri-lde-gtsug, who was merely "heir to the throne" was enthroned only eight years later in 712 with the full dynastic title of Khri-lde-gtsug-brtsan (also called Mes-ag-tshoms in the later chronicles). That his father's campaigns in 'Jang (Nan-chao) were not entirely in vain, although they cost that ruler his life, can be seen from the chronicle which reports that Kag La-bong (Chinese: K'o Lo-fêng), the ruler of Nan-chao, became a vassal of Tibet during the reign of Khri-lde gtsug-brtsan. A Nan-chao princess, 'Jeng Me-khri-btsun, was given to the emperor in marriage and bore him an heir to the throne, Lhas-bon, who, however, died before his father. The report in the annals of uprisings in 705 (evidently in Tibet proper) can be explained as the normal consequences of a change in the dynasty. In the same year Khri-gzigs zhang-nyen of the Dba's clan became prime-minister, and the country Serib[12] on the southern border of the empire rose in a revolt which ended only in 709 with the capture of its king.

The anticipated unrest in Zhang-zhung came only later. In 719 the anti-Tibetan party there and in Mard (the lower part of Ladakh, Mar-yul) had to be kept at bay, and even in 721 the minister Khri-gzigs had to prove the power of Tibet by holding the winter Council of State in 'Ryan-shi-gar, although the same year "numerous emissaries from sTod-phyogs [i.e. Zhang-zhung] had professed their loyalty."

For a decade following the death of Khri-'dus-srong the Chinese border was comparatively quiet. Chinese emissaries came and went and negotiations were under way for another marriage with a Chinese princess. But when in 710 Princess Chin-ch'eng (Tibetan: Kim-sheng) arrived in Ra-sa (Lha-sa) with a Tibetan honor guard, Khri-'dus-srong was dead and Mes-ag-tshoms, his successor, a six-year old child. The wedding had to be postponed and the Chinese remained in Tibet until the death of the princess in 739 when relations between the two countries again deteriorated into open warefare. In 729 the Tibetans captured the fortified city of Kua-chou. During the princess's last years Chinese and Tibetans competed for the possession of Gilgit (Tibetan: Bru-sha), important because of its strategic position on the road leading to the passes to East Turkestan. In 737 things came to a head. In the summer of that year a Tibetan official appeared in Bru-sha, the country accepted the rule of

[12] "The Prophecy of the Arhat Sangha-vardhana" in F.W. Thomas, 1935, pp. 41–69, and "The Prophecy concerning Khotan," *ibid.*, pp. 73–87. Several copies of the second of these prophecies, dating from the period of the Tibetan universal monarchy are available and may be found in the India Office Library in London, and in the Fonds Pelliot Tibétain of the Bibliothèque Nationale, Paris.

the Tibetan bTsan-po, and in the following winter the local prince paid a visit to Khri-lde gtsug-brtsan. But while a Chinese emissary was negotiating at the Tibetan court, the Chinese army destroyed Bru-sha. Ultimately Tibetan influence returned to Bru-sha and a new agreement was reached involving a matrimonial alliance: the king of Bru-sha married a Tibetan princess. Later, under the son of the then bTsan-po, the possession of this land was to lead to great troubles. During this entire period the diplomatic and military activities of the Tibetan empire were unusually energetic: attempts were made to get in touch with other opponents of Chinese expansion to the west, such as the Turkic Türgesh (Tibetan: Dur-gyis) and the Caliphate (Ta-chig). In 732 and 744 emissaries of both powers were at the Tibetan court. In 732 the Tibetan princess, 'Dron-ma-lod, became the bride of the kaghan of the Türgesh. In 742 an heir was born to Mes-ag-tshoms who, at his enthronement in 756, took the name Srong-lde-brtsan. It was under this man that the Tibetan empire would reach the zenith of its power.

Mention should be made of one event in connection with the death of the Chinese wife of Mes-ag-tshoms in 739 when there was a smallpox epidemic to which the princess herself succumbed. A description of this terrible epidemic in Tibet is found in a religious work: *The Prophecy Concerning the Land of Li*, i.e. Khotan. The events inserted here within the framework of an older prophecy[13] describe the banishment of the Buddhist clergy from the kingdoms of Khotan, Kashgar, Gilgit and Kashmir, their wanderings, and finally their admission into Tibet at the urgings of Mes-ag- tshoms' Chinese wife. Three or four years later the smallpox broke out in Tibet and the anti-Buddhist ministers and nobles took advantage of this opportunity to drive out the unwanted guests. A good example of the feudal nobles' dislike of the increasing Buddhist influence even before there were Buddhist clergy or monasteries in Tibet.

The zenith of the Tibetan empire: Khri-srong lde-brtsan (755–97)

Although the new bTsan-po ostensibly observed a strict neutrality and supported both the Buddhists and Bon-po, in fact he favored the Buddhists and sent his confidants to India and China to obtain Buddhist scriptures and invite outstanding teachers to Tibet. He also relied on the Buddhist clergy as allies against the nobles in order to consolidate his position as emperor. When one of his emissaries, sBa gSal-snang, brought scriptures from China he found

[13] Lokesh Chandra, fol. 261, lines 2–3.

it was necessary to conceal them. Fearing for the safety of his accomplice, he provisionally removed him from the intrigue-ridden centre of the empire and appointed him governor of the southern province of Mang-yul on the Nepalese border. From Nepal gSal-snang was able to travel to India, visit Bodh-Gaya, and make the first contacts with the outstanding Buddhist philosophers of the time. In the meantime the emperor, with the aid of his influential and compliant minister, 'Gos Khri-bzang, prepared a plot to rid himself of his most powerful enemies among the nobles. It was arranged for soothsayers to prophesy that in order to assure the safety of the empire and the emperor, two prominent officials should remain for three months in a tomb. The choice fell on Ma-zhang Khrom-pa and 'Gos Khri-bzang. The latter was able to escape, but Ma-zhang Khrom-pa was sealed in and perished miserably. At the same time the leader of the nobles, sTga-agra kLu-ḳhong, was banished to the northern deserts. As these domestic events were taking place the external expansion of the empire continued. The *Tun-huang Annals*-fragment reports a legation of allegiance sent from the west in 756, including one from Shig-nig (Shignân or Shugnân) in the Pamirs. A hitherto neglected Bon source[14] describes how the "King of the Arabs" (sTag-gzig) promised, following his defeat, to construct and defend a bridge of wooden beams at a place where the trade-route crossed a large stream on the western border of the Tibetan empire. This evidently refers to a bridge over the Upper Oxus in a locality called Dar-i Tubbat (the "Gate of Tibet") in the Muslim geographical work entitled *Ḥudūd al-Ālam.*[15]

For the same year 756 the *Annals* report the reconquest of Se-cu, the Turfan region, (Chinese: Hsi-chou). In 758 Tibetan troops captured Leng-cu (Chinese: Liang-chou) along the Chinese front. In 762 the Tibetan generals took Keng-shi or King-shi,[16] the region surrounding and including the Chinese capital of Ching-chao or Ch'ang-an. As the Chinese emperor fled at the approach of the Tibetan army, the Tibetans set up a prince, Guang-bu huant-ti, who was able, however, to hold out for only three weeks.

The Tibeto-Chinese peace treaty of 783 confirmed Tibetan dominion over East Turkestan, Kansu, and a large part of Szechwan. During this period Tibetan influence also extended to the south and the Buddhist king of Magadha and Bengal, Dharmapāla, (circa 760–815) acknowledged Tibetan

[14] Bacot-Toussaint, 1940, pp. 46 and 153, (citation from the *Tunhuang Chronicle*). Cf. the inscription of 783 erected below the Potala, and the text on an obelisque of the short-lived Tibeto-Chinese peace treaty. See Richardson, 1952, p. 2.

[15] Minorsky, p. 350.

[16] Tucci, 1958 pp. 12–22 discusses this problem.

overlordship – the reason why the Muslim writers refer to the Bay of Bengal as the "Tibetan Sea."

Khri-srong lde-brtsan's long series of political and military victories show that he was increasingly able to establish his authority in domestic affairs, especially in religious policies. The Buddhist teacher Shāntirakshita was now actually invited to Tibet, but as the opposition proved too strong, his visit lasted only four months. At his departure he advised the Emperor to invite the famous Tantricist and exorcist, Padmasambhava, who would be better able to cope with the Bon and their magic. Thus it happened that Padmasambhava drove out from the country the "evil spirits," i.e. the refractory followers of the folk religion and the Bon faith. The emperor now began the construction of bSam-yas, the first monastic complex, and Padmasambhava prevented the evil spirits from destroying at night what had been built during the day. The monastery enclosure with its monks' quarters and numerous temples which symbolized the Buddhist universe, was designed by Shāntirakshita who had been recalled to Tibet where he ordained the first seven young Tibetans called "probationary monks." The sources do not agree as to their number or names.[17] These first monks, who were soon to be joined by others, immediately began the translation of Buddhist texts from various languages into Tibetan in the "House of Translators." That the Bon still had to be taken into consideration is seen from the fact that Bon priests were invited from the districts of the former Zhang-zhung state to translate their sacred texts from Zhang-zhung into Tibetan. One of the disciples of Shāntirakshita, Vairocanarakshita, or simply Vairocana, showed unusual versatility by translating both Buddhist and Bon texts. He dedicated himself not only to Shāntirakshita's teaching of the Ten Perfections (*pāramitā*) as the basis for the gradual ascent to Liberation but, as a disciple of Padmasambhava, he also translated magic-mystical Tantric texts which were based on "sudden" Enlightenment, a doctrine shared by the Chinese Ch'an school. Recalling that Chinese monks who upheld the doctrine of "sudden" Enlightenment were also at work in bSam-yas, it is evident that grounds for conflict were forming.

The struggle between the "Gradualists" and the "Subitists" eventually led to catastrophe. From 792 to 794 a debate took place between the two schools, ordered and presided over by the emperor. He declared the arguments of the Chinese invalid and ordered them to leave the country. Their school, although repressed from time to time, did not disappear in Tibet, but still continued as a branch of the rNying-ma-pa and is called the "Great Perfection."

In 779 Buddhism was declared the state religion and an Imperial Edict

[17] Schlegel, 1896.

commanded that support be provided for religion and the monastery, and that allowances were to be given for food and clothing, paper and ink, and special grants were to be made to meditative hermits. A specific number of Tibetan families was obliged to supply the requisites of one monk, an arrangement which led to increased expenses under the emperor's successors and bore within it latent trouble.

The last years of the emperor's reign were less fortunate than the early ones. This was due more to a concatenation of various events in the country's foreign affairs and a revival of the hostility of the nobles than to any lessening of his energy. Most importantly, Tibet, a thinly-populated land, had reached the limits of its military capabilities and constant warfare on several fronts could not be continued indefinitely. The peace treaty of 783 with China proved to be fragile and in 787 Tibetan armies again advanced against the Chinese capital, when a serious defeat near T'ai-te in 789 forced them to abandon the campaign. In 789 the Arabs under Caliph Hārūn al-Rashīd (786–809), as they had become uneasy over Tibetan expansion, repudiated their traditional alliance with the Tibetans and entered into negotiations with the Chinese. This caused the Tibetans to deploy a considerable portion of their troops in the west as a defense against the Muslim armies. A Chinese advance into East Turkestan was halted at the great battle of Pei-t'ing (Turkic: Beshbalik) in 791 in which the Tibetans and their Karluk allies faced the Chinese and the Uighurs. In spite of initial Chinese victories recorded in the inscription of Karabalghasun,[18] the Tibetans and their allies were able to destroy the enemy and even the Turkic Sha-t'o[19] who were friendly to the Chinese were driven out of Kansu. The result of this was that East Turkestan remained under Tibetan rule until the middle of the 9th century.

The end of the reign of the great Khri-srong lde-brtsan (797) is clouded by a veil of uncertainty. Although it is assumed that he abdicated in that year, many circumstances suggest that his first wife, Tshe-spong-bza rMa-rgyal ldon-skar, who was a member of the Bon nobility and his enemy, murdered him just as she later poisoned his son, Mu-ne bTsan-po, whom she herself had put on the throne.

The decline and disintegration of the empire

If the events relating to the death of Khri-srong lde-brtsan are unclear, even more unclear is the information we have concerning his son, Mu-ne btsan-po.

[18] See the discussion of these events in Otto Franke, 1937, II., p. 482.

[19] According to our present knowledge the interpretation given by Haarh 1969a would seem to be the best.

The ancient chronicle of the Sa-skya hierarch, Grags-po rgyal-mtshan, mentions a Mu-khri btsan-po who died as a youth, and who may be the same person as Mu-ne btsan-po. He was placed on the throne by his mother, and had a short reign, probably only from 797 to 799. He continued the policies of his predecessor and did all he could to deprive the nobles of their power. He struck at their economic basis, and in three law-suits confiscated their properties, part of which he added to the crown-lands, part of which he distributed among the peasants. Although this action dealt a mortal blow to the nobles, it had not been well planned. Because their personal and political existence was at stake, the formerly disunited nobles now joined together, and with his own mother taking the initiative, the emperor was poisoned.

The dowager empress now wished to place another son, Mu-rug btsan-po, on the throne but was hindered in this by an act of violence committed by the prince himself. According to the *bLon-po bka'i thang-yig*, the prince had brought down upon himself the hatred of the powerful sNa-nam clan by killing the minister sNa-nam bTsan-po 'U-ring, son of the "Great Minister" Zhang rGya-tsha Lha-snang. According to the account, the "Great Minister" was having a private discussion with the emperor and 'U-ring had been ordered to guard the door. When he attempted to stop the prince from entering, the latter killed him. The dowager now enthroned yet another of her sons, Mu-tig btsan-po, who reigned from 799 until 815 under the imperial title of Khri-lde Srong-btsan, though Mu-rug btsan-po, who was obedient to his mother and an obliging helper of the nobles, actually ruled in the background until he was killed by a sNa-nam noble in 804. The chronology of these rulers is extremely confused; Tibetan and Chinese data are difficult to harmonize.[20]

Like his father, Khri-lde srong-btsan (also called mJing-yon Sad-na-legs) was favorable to Buddhism. Under his rule the translation of Buddhist texts was continued, even intensified, and it is probable that work on the *Mahāvyutpatti*, a bi-lingual lexicon the purpose of which was to unify Tibetan Buddhist terminology, was begun at this time and completed under his son, Ral-pa-can. It was during this period that there occurred on the domestic scene exactly what the nobility had feared: the Tibetan Buddhist monks attained increased influence in the affairs of the state. Especially important roles were played by the monks Myang Ting-nge-'dzin and Bran-ka dPal-yon, the latter even becoming "Great Minister" and, from 810 was the leading figure in Tibetan politics. It is believed that this monk retained his office even under Ral-pa-can, the emperor's son and successor.

[20] R.A. Stein, 1961, p. 87.

Fighting continued on the Chinese border with varying success, but the Chinese were still unable to reconquer East Turkestan. In the west, feudal strife between al-ᶜAmin and al-Ma'mūn, the sons of Hārūn al-Rashīd, had crippled the Caliphate and the Tibetans were able to make incursions into Muslim territory. At one time they even besieged Samarkand and Sogdiana. Somewhat later, in 840, the Uighurs, who had presented a danger to the Tibetans in the north, lost their steppe empire to the Kirghiz. At this time the Buddhist "Great Minister" attempted to conclude a permanent peace treaty with the T'ang, but was unable to achieve this until the reign of the next emperor.

Sad-na-legs left three sons: bTsad-ma, who became a Buddhist monk, gLang-dar-ma (whose name is obviously a sobriquet), and the youngest who, as Emperor from 815 to 838, was known by the reign-title of Khri-gtsug lde-brtsan although Tibetan historians call him Ral-pa-can ("he who has curls") as he supposedly fastened streamers to his hair upon which he invited the Buddhist monks to sit in order to demonstrate his piety. Ral-pa-can was a weak ruler who suffered from poor health, paid little attention to the affairs of state which he left to his advisors, and was primarily interested in the propagation of Buddhism and, of much greater danger to the State, in granting privileges to the clergy. The translations of Buddhist texts multiplied, temples and monasteries were endowed, and new religious buildings were erected. The minister, Bran-ka dPal-yon succeeded in concluding an agreement with the Chinese which guaranteed the Tibetans both peace and the ratification of their conquests. The agreement was signed in the Chinese capital in 821, in Lhasa in 822, and the text inscribed on obelisks (*rdo-ring*) which were set up in the Chinese capital, on the border at Me-ru, and in Lhasa, the latter standing before the Jo-khang until 1959.

The domestic situation finally reached a crisis; the nobles and the common people revolted at the continuing and increased privileges of the clergy. The emperor had made the serious mistake of attempting to force Buddhist virtues on a people who still clung to their ancient code of ethics. The monks were made responsible for enforcing these changes and if they were met by angry glances or pointing fingers, the offenders were punished by having their eyes torn out or their fingers chopped off. The Bon nobles now thought the time propitious to overturn things. A conspiracy was hatched, the emperor's chambers broken into, and his head was twisted off his body. The conspirators put gLang-dar-ma on the throne who reigned from 838 to 842 under the reign-title of 'Ui-dum-brtan, and the leader of the conspirators, dBa's rgyal-to-re, became "Great Minister." Understandably, Buddhist historians de-

scribe the minister as a monster and even the later T'ang Annals describe his fondness for wine, women, and hunting, and report that he was cruel and perverse, lacking in generosity, and conclude that the disintegration of the state was inevitable. Now it was the turn of the nobles and the Bon priests to control the new ruler just as the Buddhists had controlled Ral-pa-can, although a note in the Chronicle of Grags-pa rgyal-mtshan indicates that the terrible persecution of the Buddhists began only six months after gLang-dar-ma ascended the throne. In its course temples and monasteries were desecrated, translation-work brought to a halt, and the foreign monks banished. Tibetan religious were given the choice between returning to lay life or death, and they were forced to participate in hunting expeditions with bows and arrows. This was obviously a period of wild confusion and disorder and the Chinese sources report catastrophes, earthquakes, epidemics and famine. Buddhism was extirpated throughout Central Tibet; the power of the government did not extend to the distant provinces of the east or west. The empire of Srong-brtsan sgam-po was now completely disintegrating and the murder of gLang-dar-ma in 842 by a Tantric hermit heralded further trouble.

The *Hsin T'ang-shu* makes it clear that gLang-dar-ma left no heir. The ancient noble families were not interested in a continuation of the dynasty, and a great domestic war seems to have broken out bringing the empire to an end. Apparently the successors of the great emperors ruled as minor kings in Central Tibet and Yar-klungs and as feudal lords in the old imperial lands around bSam-yas. It is more or less uniformly reported that dPal-khor-btsan, a descendant of the Yar-klungs Dynasty, built Buddhist temples and was murdered by his subjects. His eldest son seems to have remained in Yar-klungs and his youngest son, Khri-skyid-lding, called sKyid-lde Nyi-ma-mgon by later historians, went to the west where he founded a new kingdom above Ladakh. A late edition of the *sBa-bzhed*[21] tells of a minor dynasty in the neighborhood of bSam-yas called bTsan-po Khri in connection with the activity, around 950–1025, of a certain kLu-mes who, from Amdo, began to re-establish Buddhism in Central Tibet.

A final attempt to save the empire was made by an outstanding administrator of the eastern region bordering on China. Zhang Khong-bsher of the Dba's clan struggled with another pretender from the 'Bro family whom he defeated in 949. Judging the situation in Lhasa hopeless, he made himself bTsan-po, raised a large army, and harassed the western borders of China until, as the last representative of Tibetan unity, he was defeated in 966 by an Uighur

[21] Pelliot, 1961, p. 139.

general from Pei-t'ing. The Uighurs beheaded him and forwarded his head to the Chinese capital.[22]

Administration and social structure during the empire

Before the unification of Tibet under gNam-ri srong-brtsan and Srong-brtsan sgam-po, the individual tribes were independent and, as the Chinese sources indicate, had practically no political organization beyond brief alliances for such limited activities as brigandage. With the unification of Tibet, all this changed, and instead of tribal chieftains who from their fortifications ruled over their nomadic or sedentary subjects, a centralized government was gradually established by the emperor which, through his officials, reached to the furthest outposts of the empire. That the feudal principle was still firmly maintained by the tribal chieftains is shown by the fact that they regarded the ruler as a *primus inter pares*, and only strong personalities such as Srong-brtsan sgam-po and Khri-srong lde-brtsan were able to preserve the empire from feudal anarchy and employ the tribal chieftains who exercised military and administrative powers in their own districts as ministers and imperial officials.

If the Buddhist clergy's intrusion into state politics did not lead to a break between the nobles and the dynasty, or if the often refractory nobles did not do away with the imperial regime even under weak rulers (as the mGar family might easily have done in the 7th century), the cause for it must be seen in the sacral nature of the bTsan-po which, in the Bon religion, could not be questioned. That the dynasty was well aware of this is shown by the fact that even the later emperors, who were inclined toward Buddhism, observed the sacral customs when ascending the throne, in funeral rites, and when signing treaties. It was the magico-charismatic factor in the office of the universal monarch, the sacred nature of his rule, that protected the dynasty.[23] There were four powers inherent in the monarch which ensured the welfare of the state: majesty (*nMga-thang*), magic (*dBu-ring*) – literally, "helmet" which the bTsan-po wore at sacral functions – the religious law (*chos*) which originated with the Bon but was later claimed by the Buddhists – and political authority (*chab-srid*) which the ruler exercised through his officials. The Tibetan emperors as well as the kings of Zhang-zhung had their own Bon priests (*sku'tsho-bai gshen*, or *sku-gshen*)[24] who protected their vital powers, and we

[22] Tucci, 1955–6.

[23] Information on this will be found in a commentary by the Bon priest Dran-pa nam-mkha (8th century), in Namdak, 1966, p. 22, line 15.

[24] According to the manuscript *rGyal-rabs bon-gyi byung-gnas* in my possession.

even know the names of several of these priests, such as Khri-srong lde-brtsan't sku-gshen, who was called Khri-snyan rgyal-chung.[25] On ceremonial occasions the bTsan-po was seated in the center of the throne room, the Bon priest sat in the place of honor on his right, and the "Great Minister" sat on his left.

Directly under the bTsan-po stood the vassal-princes, the Dar-rgyal of the T'u-yü-hun, and the princes of rKong-po and Myang who were of higher rank than the Tibetan ministers. These were followed in order of rank by the "Great Minister" or "Great Ministers" who usually came from the most illustrious of the feudal families. If a monarch married into such a family these nobles took the title of Zhang, or "maternal uncle." These were followed by the "inner" (*nang-blon*) and "outer" (*phyi-blon*) ministers, the adjectives referring to their position in the palace.[26] Then came the chiliarchs, i.e. the commanders of a military "district of a thousand," the military officers (*dMag-dpon*), and the overseers of the royal stables (*lo-ngam rta-rdzi*).

Originally Tibet proper was divided into military districts and the military governors eventually took over the civil administration. In ancient times Tibet was divided into three horns or banners (*ru*):[27] dbU-ru (later dbUs-ru) in the center including Lhasa, the capital; gYo-ru (later gYon-ru) to the east, including the important provinces of Yar-klungs, Phyin-lung, Dags-po, gNyal, and Lho-brag; and gYas-ru in the west which included Lower gTsang and Upper gTsang. Each horn was under a Ru-dpon (commander of a banner) who was assisted by two dPa'zla (adjutants). Later Ru-lag, a fourth horn, was created – first mentioned in the *Tun-huang Annals* of 709 – which included the districts to the south of the Brahmaputra, i.e. Mang-mKhar, Lha-rtse, and Myang-ro. Each banner had a various number of chiliarchs.

The conquered regions in East Turkestan, China, and the west had special colonial administrations. East Turkestan was administered from Khotan where the king of the hereditary dynasty was allowed to reside and oversee the domestic affairs of his district. The Tibetan governor bore the title of Nang-rje-po and it was he who was referred to as the "King of Tibet" by the Muslim sources as they had no knowledge of Lhasa or Tibet proper. This high official directed both civil and military affairs and the peoples in the west had to deal with him on matters of peace and tribute.

The various documents from Tun-huang and East Turkestan show that there were other officials in the colonial districts: the Brung-pa and the

[25] See Tucci, 1950, pp. 61–5. [26] See Tucci, 1956, pp. 77–90; Uray, 1960.
[27] See Uray, 1962.

mNag.[28] Both seem to have been connected with finance, and the office of mNag was evidently the higher of the two. The office of the Brung-pa ceased to exist at the beginning of the eighth century when it was either amalgamated with another office or the title was changed. The "Great mNgans" seem to have been connected with the levelling of taxes and the *Tun-huang Annals* report that in 726 their number was reduced from eight to four and that taxation then became the function of the Khab-so (court officials or palace guards).

Concerning the social structure of Tibet during the universal monarchy (and here we must disagree with Bogoslowskij who believes that the same structure obtained in the many petty states before the unification),[29] there were, first of all, the members of the noble clans (*phu-nu*) who were free citizens (*dMangs* or *'Bangs*)[30] and the serfs (*bran*) who were usually attached to the land and worked for the landowners. Later the Buddhist monks joined these groups and at least equaled the feudal nobility or (especially under Ral-pa-can) occupied even higher positions. Apart from the clergy, the positions of the classes were not fixed and were subject to change.[31] For example, two nobles of the important Myang clan, Nam-ro-re khru-gu and sMon-to-re, father and son, were given as *bran* to mNyan Ji-Zung,[32] and at a later date gNam-ri srong-brtsan gave his father the landed holdings of mNyan Ji-zung, his former lord. Nor, as Róna-Tas points out, were such cases isolated ones. As may be seen from the ancient sources, (annals, chronicles, and inscriptions), the status of a family could become totally altered by a grant from the bTsan-po. Such grants in land were known as *khol-yul* and were fiefs which the emperor awarded for special services. Under certain circumstances these could become inherited property on condition that the fief-holders did not disobey the state or emperor. If he did, the land and the families of the *bran* (bran-khyim) reverted to the state. The landed property of the state, i.e. of the emperor, was called *rje-zhing*. All newly-conquered districts outside Tibet automatically became state property which the emperor might grant to favored officers and officials.

When, in 779, Buddhism was declared the state religion the clergy obtained many privileges. Lands bequeathed to the monasteries were tax-free, a mea-

[28] Bogoslovskij, 1972, pp. 26 and 102. The kingdoms of the minor dynasties also had rulers and subjects. The development of a "class society" is postulated from the standpoint of orthodox Marxism.

[29] Bogoslovskij, 1972, p. 82 understands *'bangs* to be "serfs." For many of the ancient sources this is out of the question. *'Bangs* were "subjects" as opposed to the imperial dynasty.

[30] Róna-Tas, 1955, p. 262. [31] Róna-Tas, *ibid.* [32] Bogoslovskij, 1972, pp. 157–73.

sure taken by the emperor to counterbalance the power of the feudal nobles, and temples and monasteries regularly received grants. Important in this connection as well as generally for a state which carried on wars of expansion, was the fixed tax system which in Tibet proper was called *khral* and which might be reduced or postponed in the event of a poor harvest or war damage. Taxes in kind were called *khva*.[33] *Chad-kha* was a special tax levied at irregular intervals, according to special circumstances, and a tax called *dpya* was levied only in the conquered regions. It is interesting to note that in the 9th century rKong-po, whose prince held a special position in the empire, refused to pay the *khral* tax levied by the Khab-so officials and that the rKong-po inscription[34] contains a document which confirms the privileges of the principality, to wit that only the prince of that land could levy taxes.

The "dark period" (850–1000) and the "second introduction of Buddhism"

In the breakdown of the monarchy there were no victors, only vanquished. The reduction of the heirs of the imperial dynasty to insignificant principalities in Central Tibet resulted in an absence of state archives, hence there was no official historiography until the time of the later monasteries. The Chinese sources, because of the slow agony of the T'ang Dynasty, are mostly silent concerning this period and make only incidental mention of the eastern Tibetan principalities.

If, following the destruction of Buddhism in Central Tibet, the sources say nothing about any Bon activity or about the formation of a state Bon Church, this is so because not religious wars, but the egoism of the nobles caused the ruin of the empire. Yet, the great feudal princes reaped no benefit from the changed state of affairs. Without being able to establish why this was so we merely point to the facts that the ancient noble families of the dBas, sNa-nam, 'Bro, Tshe-spong, etc., simply disappeared from history and were replaced by a new generation of local princes, and that Tibetan history as a whole altered its course and became the history of religious groups and sects.

An interesting question now arises: did Buddhism which, according to its opponents, was forced upon the people by decree, disappear in the overall decline, or were there Tibetans who accepted the religion voluntarily? The

[33] Richardson, 1954.

[34] All the dates from the time of the Buddhist renaissance are rather uncertain. I have relied on Richardson 1957, the only comprehensive study of this period, where tentative chronological tables will be found on p. 62.

question must be answered in the affirmative because, as we shall see, in centuries to come there were to be idealists who banded together, observed the traditions, and finally again propagated the Doctrine throughout the entire land. New centres of propagation were formed in Amdo in the east and later in the kingdom of Gu-ge.

The persecution of Buddhists in central Tibet was obviously a serious blow, but even in 841, the year of the persecution, three "learned men" (Tibetan: *mkhas-pa-mi-gsum*) who were surprised in their hermitage to the southwest of Lhasa, escaped and made their way to the vicinity of Mt. Dan-tig on the Upper Huang-ho in Amdo, taking with them by mule transport religious books (Vinaya and Abhidharma). There, in a cave, they devoted themselves to meditation. A young man from a Bon family by the name of Mu-zu gSal-'bar heard of the hermits, searched for them, and was so impressed that he requested admission to the Order. He was accepted and eventually became the celebrated Buddhist scholar known as dGongs-pa rab-gsal (832–915).[35] This man became the pivot of a renewed collective movement and his works and those of his disciples constitute the first stage in the re-introduction of Buddhism into Tibet. Because of contradictions in the sources, it is still not certain whether there were one or two links in the chain of transmission between him and kLu-mes Shes-rab Tshul-khrims (c. 950–1025), but there was, at any rate, a direct connection which went back to the time of the emperor. In ever-increasing numbers young men were ordained in Amdo and returned to the central provinces of dbUs and gTsang, to propagate what they had learned, and to create the beginnings of the oldest school of Tibetan Buddhism, the rNying-ma-pa. It would be quite wrong to underestimate, as has frequently happened, the work of these men. As is clear from the *Deb-ther sNgon-po*,[36] they transmitted not only the Tantras which went back to Padmasambhava, but also the unbroken tradition of the Vinaya.

The monks who came from Amdo either took over the closed and neglected temples and monasteries, or founded new ones. kLu-mes himself repaired the first Tibetan monastery of bSam-yas which had been founded in 786 by Khri-srong lde-brtsan and had fallen into disrepair. Sum-pa ye-shes blo-gros[37] who belonged to the group of the "ten men from dbUs and gTsang," encountered the Indian teacher Atīsha who had arrived in Western Tibet in 1042, and the monks who had been ordained in Amdo met those from the west. The western Tibetan renovators of Buddhism thus appeared several decades after the rise of the Amdo group.

[35] *The Blue Annals*, Roerich, 1949, vol. 1, pp. 77–87.
[36] Roerich, 1949, vol. 1, pp. xv and 65; Obermiller, 1932, p. 202. [37] Francke, 1926, p. 276.

As already mentioned, a great-grandson of gLang-dar-ma made his way to Western Tibet where he established a small kingdom. The Ladakh Chronicle[38] reports that a certain dGe-bshes-bstan of sPu-hrangs invited him to this region to the south of Manasarowar and gave him 'Bro-bza 'Khor-skyong in marriage, and that he was able to establish a capital, Nyi-zungs, from which he would conquer all Western Tibet. His queen belonged to the Zhang-zhung lineage, the 'Bro, which had been important during the universal monarchy. G. Tucci's sources[39] agree that this king divided his kingdom among his three sons and that the eldest received Mar-yul (Ladakh). The older monastic chronicles are at variance concerning the two younger brothers. According to Grags-pa rgyal-mtshan and 'Phags-pa, the second son, bKra-shis-mgon, received the heart of the Zhang-zhung region: Pu-hrangs and Ya-rtse (Seṃjā in present-day Nepal)[40] while the youngest, lDe-gTsug-mgon, was given the districts of Mon, a rather vague term applied to the tribes on the southern slopes of the Himalayas. However, according to Bu-ston, the *Deb-ther sNgon-po*, and the *dPa-bo gtsug-lag 'phreng-ba*, the eldest son received sPu-hrangs and the younger brother inherited Zhang-zhung. Although we find later discrepancies in the genealogy of the Western Tibetan kings, it is certain that the kingdom of Gu-ge and sPu-hrangs were later united although we are not certain when or from which king the dynasty of Gu-ge descended.

The sons of the king of Gu-ge were named 'Kor-re and Srong-nge. The eldest, 'Khor-re, eventually became a Buddhist monk without, however, totally renouncing his royal functions, and is known as the "royal-monk" Ye-shes-'od. The later line of the Gu-ge Dynasty descended from his brother, Srong-nge who, even during the time of the royal monk, was in charge of governmental affairs. The kings of Gu-ge resided at rTsa-brang on a cliff overlooking the Sutlej valley.

Ye-shes-'od wished to reform the degenerate Buddhism of his realm and endeavored to bring outstanding Indian teachers to his capital, as for instance, Dharmaphāla, the great master of the Vinaya, who became the king's personal guru and founded a special Vinaya school. Hearing of the fame of Dīpankara Shrījnāna (usually known as Atīsha), Ye-shes-'od did everything in his power to bring him to the capital. When a first invitation produced no results, he organized expeditions throughout the country to collect gold to send as a gift to Atīsha's monastery. In the meantime Srong-nge, the royal monk's brother, had died and his son, Lha-lde, ruled in his place. On one of his expeditions in search of gold, Ye-shes-'od fell into the hands of the Karluks

[38] Tucci, 1956, pp. 51–63. [39] Tucci, 1956, p. 107.
[40] Translated by Tucci, 1949, I, pp. 10–12.

who at that time ruled the eastern part of East Turkestan. Their conditions for releasing the royal monk were either conversion to Islam or a ransom consisting of his weight in gold. When Byang-club-'od, the king's nephew, brought the gold, the equivalent of the weight of the head was lacking the Karluks refused to free him. A touching dialogue between the royal monk and his nephew has come down to us in which the nephew promises to obtain the rest of the gold but the uncle refuses, saying that he is now old and that it would be better to use the already-collected gold to invite the teacher Atīsha. In tears, the prince obeys, and Ye-shes-'od, broken and ill by his long captivity, is executed by the Karluks. A telling example showing the difference between this Buddhism and that of the imperial era.

The learned translator Nag-tsho Tshul-khrims rgyal-ba was sent to Vikramashīla and Atīsha now agreed to go to Tibet. He left his monastery in 1040, traveled through Nepal, and arrived at the Western Tibetan capital in 1042 where he fulfilled Ye-shes-'od's expectations, purifying the tantric rituals, cultivating Buddhist teachings, stressing Vinaya, and introducing the Mahāyāna Sutras and Vajrayana doctrines. As a guide, he left the Tibetans his Bodhipathapradīpa with a voluminous commentary. Atīsha taught in various parts of dbUs, and finally died there in 1054. His disciple, 'Brom-ston, founded the school of the bKa-gdams-pa and its first monastery, Rva-sgrengs, was established in 1057 and was rapidly followed by many more. Atīsha's work continued to live on in the later school of the dGe-lugs-pa. The great council of Tabo in Gu-ge (1076) in which monks from dbUs, gTsang, and Eastern Tibet as well as from Western Tibet participated, must be regarded as the crowning point of the "later introduction" of Buddhism from the west.

As is evident from the above, the schools of the rNying-ma-pa and the bKa-gdams-pa were established in direct connection with the "later introduction" of Buddhism. It is also important to point out that the other great schools whose hierarchs were to play an important role in Tibet politically were formed, with the exception of the dGe-lugs-pa, in the 11th and 12th centuries as a result of the severing of communications with India after the Muslims destroyed the last Buddhist stronghold there.

Development of the theocratic state: Tibet and the world empire of the Mongols

The proliferation of monasteries greatly altered the overall situation in Tibet. As pious laymen made rich donations, the monasteries quickly accumulated vast tracts of land which were cultivated by the lower orders of monks. The

leaders of the various sects and the abbots of the monasteries soon formed a religious aristocracy which was not always distinct from the lay nobility or inimical to it. As it was usual for the son of a propertied family to enter the religious life, the lines between the religious and secular aristocracy were frequently crossed and close economic and political ties often linked a certain noble family to a monastery. There was even open warfare between rival monasteries in which armies of the nobles fought on either side.

While the nomads of the northern plateau were bound to the past and no longer played a role in the course of events as they had in Imperial times, the eastern nomads were notorious brigands. Political and economic life went on only in the districts of the agricultural oases, the small cities, and the great monasteries, and only Western Tibet enjoyed a stable government, feudal anarchy still being rife in Central Tibet. Influential at this time were the Tshal-pa family, several clans in Yar-klungs, and, among the religious, the abbots of Sa-skya and 'Bri-bung.

The emergence of the Mongols in the northeast in 1207 demanded an answer to the question of who actually exercised power in Tibet. It had been a member of the Tshal-pa family who had reported to Chinggis Khan the capitulation of the Tibetans and who had promised tribute, whereupon the Mongol khan abandoned his proposed campaign and turned westward. By 1227 the Mongols, after the final destruction of the Hsi-Hsia Tangut state in the vicinity of Kansu and Kokonor, had moved uncomfortably close to the Tibetans and it remained to be seen whether the expanding Mongol world empire would again bother with Tibet, especially since the nobles had ceased paying tribute while the Great Khan had been in Khorezm in the west. In 1239 a Mongol expeditionary corps was sent to the northern frontier and went through the land plundering and destroying. This thrust extended to the venerable monasteries of Rva-sgreng and rGyal-lha-khang, which were mercilessly sacked.

These events terrified the Tibetans. They knew that they could not withstand the Mongols and that negotiations would be necessary if they were to escape the worst. A council of Tibetan magnates showed that the Sa-skya abbot, Kun-dga rgyal-mtshan, was the most important political figure in Tibet, and he was ordered by the Mongol prince Godan to appear in his camp near Lan-chou. When he arrived there in 1247, he recognized the overlordship of the Mongols and was able to cure the prince of an illness. He was then appointed *darughachi*, or governor, of Tibet, awarded a golden diploma, and recognized as the supreme authority in Tibet, directly responsible to the Mongols. A letter which the abbot sent to the religious dignitaries of dbUs,

gTsang, and Western Tibet upon his return trip is an unusual historical document, giving, as it does, copious details which fill in the overall picture. The Mongols did not station an army of occupation in Tibet, but sent officials to supervise the payment of tribute. Although Sa-skya Pandita's letter had contained entreaties and serious warnings to the Tibetan hierarchs and nobles, many of these soon repudiated their submission and refused to recognize the Sa-skya abbots as the suzerains of Tibet. This led to another Mongol invasion in 1251 and to further plundering.

Following Godan's death, Khubilai became supreme commander in Lanchou until he was elected Great Khan and Emperor of China (1259–1294). 'Phags-pa (1235–1280) succeeded his uncle, Sa-skya Pandita, as governor of Tibet and Sa-skya abbot, and although Khubilai also favored the second Karma-pa hierarch, Karma Bakshi, in the end the new Sa-skya abbot became the emperor's spiritual teacher. 'Phags-pa was frequently commanded to appear at the court in Khanbalik and he not only gave the Mongols the so-called square script (*dörbeljin üsüg*) which was used for official documents until the end of the Yüan Dynasty, but he also conferred upon the emperor an esoteric initiation. In gratitude, Khubilai confirmed him in the office of his uncle as representative of the thirteen "ten-thousand districts" (Khri-sde) or, according to another classification, the three *chol-ka* (dbUs, gTsang, and Upper and Lower Amdo). Following a preliminary census, the Mongols took a second, exact census in Tibet and created new administrative units for purposes of taxation. Although the office of the Sa-skya abbots was hereditary, a Chief in Command (*dPon-chen*) who was appointed by the emperor was attached to it; thus the rule of the Sa-skya-pa was dependent upon the Yüan dynasty. As the power of the dynasty declined, the position of the Sa-skya-pa became increasingly contested and ineffectual. One of the first revolts of this time originated in the 'Bri-gung monastery and was put down in 1290 jointly by Sa-skya and Mongol troops, who razed the rebellious monastery.

Decline of the Sa-skya power and the rule of the Phag-mo-gru-pa

About the year 1300 an explosive situation developed in Central Tibet. Mongol influence (after Khubilai's death there was no more question of dominion) has always been resented and this dislike was increasingly extended to the Sa-skya hierarchs whose hold over the myriarchs decreased as the Mongols became less able to come to the military aid of their representatives. The leadership of the movement against the Sa-skyas was still in the hands of the 'Bri-gung-pa who were supported by the abbots of another

monastery, gDan-sa-mthil, which had been founded by Phag-mo-gru-pa, the disciple of sGam-po-pa. Over the generations the power of these abbots had gradually increased and was eventually wielded by a single family, the rLangs, who had provided the abbots of the monastery since 1208. Rivalry had also arisen over the years between gTsang, which was represented by the Sa-skya-pa, and dbUs, which still gloried in the imperial heritage – a rivalry which continued to exist until the time of the foundation of the Yellow Church.

The man who was to raise the power of the Phag-mo-gru-pa to its zenith was Byang-chub rgyal-mtshan (1302–73). He had received a religious education in Sa-skya and had no differences with the Grand Lama, although he did with the dPon-chen. These differences led to tensions which caused him to return to the Phag-mo-gru-pa district where he became myriarch in 1338. He did everything in his power to improve the military strength and administration of his myriarchy, but lived in constant discord with the neighboring myriarchs of gYa-bzang and Tshal-pa. His enemy, the dPon-chen of Sa-skya, took advantage of this situation to remove him, and after a resort to arms he was captured and convicted, but escaped. He still had to answer to the Sa-skya, however, and, fearing another arrest, left instructions to his followers for all eventualities. He was again incarcerated and tortured, but refused to abandon his claims. Dissension among the high Sa-skya officials allowed him to return to his administrative district where he carried on further warfare with the Sa-skya troops and the other myriarchs and was finally victorious. He conquered one province after another, attacked gTsang, led an army against Sa-skya, and removed the hierarchs. Sa-skya was consequently deprived of its overlordship and its territory added to the victor's domains. The last Mongol emperor of China, Toghon Temür, could only acknowledge the *fait accompli* and appoint Byang-chub rgyal-mtshan *darughaci*. As the ruler of an empire which included all Central Tibet, he now assumed the title of *sde-srid*. He attempted to restore the ancient monarchy but, because of the increased independence of the provincial governors, failed in this – as would his successors, none of whom remotely approached his greatness. His creation of an enlarged law-code, based upon the ancient laws of Srong-brtsan-sgam-po, is indicative of the intentions of this unusual man under whom Tibet underwent something approaching a national renaissance. He was succeeded in 1373 by his grandson, 'Jam-dbyand Shâkya rgyal-mtshan, who reigned but a short time.

The problem of Phag-mo-gru-pa's succession is a complex one and more research remains to be done on the events of this period. Although it produced many capable rulers, the power of the house declined, the reasons for this

being twofold: rivalry between the abbots of gDan-sa-mthil and the political-military leaders, and the fact that Byang-chub rgyal-mtshan had made the offices of officials and military leaders hereditary. This was an innovation which allowed the principalities to break away from the central authority, thus opening the door to feudal anarchy. The most powerful rivals were the Rin-spungs-pa who held the same positions of power under the Phag-mo-gru-pa as the latter had held under the Sa-skya-pa, and were symbolic of the independence and equality of gTsang against dbUs. This meant that the ancient rivalry between the two provinces was again making itself felt. From 1435 the Rin-spung princes of bSam-grub-rtse (present-day Shigatse) ruled over all gTsang and far outranked the Phag-mo-gru-pa. Of great importance was the fact that the Rin-spung princes joined the Red-Hat sect, thus adding religious to political conflict between dbUs and gTsang. In 1368 the Mongol Yüan Dynasty was replaced by the Ming, who were in no position to interfere in Tibet although they did perpetuate the illusion of overlordship by receiving the so-called "tribute emissaries" and granting titles to several of the guard lamas.

The small importance attached to these visits to the Chinese court is shown by their limited number – once every three years – and by the obligation the emissaries had to follow specific travel routes.

15

The forest peoples of Manchuria: Kitans and Jurchens

The political fragmentation of China in the 10th century A.D. and most of her history under the Sung dynasty (960–1234) was coeval with the emergence of states on her borders which were founded by non-Chinese peoples but largely patterned on Chinese models. Of these peoples the Kitans and the Jurchen are of special importance because they both succeeded in extending their domination over large parts of Northern China. In this respect they were the precursors of the Mongols whose final subjugation of the entire Chinese territory in the 13th century was made possible, or at least easier, because they were no longer faced with a unified China but by a Sung China which had been severely weakened by the Kitan and Jurchen conquests on her northern border. Another factor of general historical interest is that both for the Liao state of the Kitans and the Chin state of the Jurchen we have detailed dynastic histories written in Chinese. Unlike earlier invaders who settled for a while on Chinese soil such as Hsiung-nu, Hsien-pi and other tribal groups whose history is known only through Chinese eyes, we have for the 10th to 13th centuries historical sources which provide a very full documentation on states founded by non-Chinese peoples. The multi-state system of those centuries can therefore be studied not only from the Chinese angle but also from the Kitan and Jurchen viewpoints as well. For the first time in Inner Asian history we have in that period a wealth of information on "barbarian" peoples and their history that can be paralleled with the purely Chinese (and therefore necessarily China-centred) sources. Moreover, the name of the Kitan people has had quite a history by itself. During the 13th century China, or rather Northern China, became known in the Near East and in Europe as Cathay or Catai, a name derived from the ethnic term Kitan. From the 14th century on Cathay as a name for China was gradually forgotten in Europe and only rediscovered by the Jesuit missionary Matteo Ricci towards the end of the 16th century. Although the name China supplanted in modern times the older designation in the Western languages of Europe, the name of the Kitans

survives to this very day as the general name for China in most Slavonic languages (e.g. in Russian *Kitai* = "China"). The following brief history of both Kitans and Jurchen will concentrate more on their histories as peoples and not so much on their dynastic history as a part of the Chinese world which will find its proper place in the *Cambridge History of China*. This period of their history is obviously the best documented one; but in spite of the sinicisation to which both peoples were exposed for centuries much valuable information on their pre-dynastic past and ways of life can be found in sources dealing with the Liao and the Chin states.

The Kitans

As indicated above, a natural periodization for Kitan history suggests itself: first, their history as one of the Manchurian populations, second, their history as a dynasty of conquest in China (907–1125), and third, their subsequent history both in China under the Jurchen (1125–1234) and as rulers of the Central Asian Karakitai empire (1124–1211). For the first two periods our historical information comes almost exclusively from Chinese sources. These are the dynastic histories from the *Wei-shu* (covering the period of the Wei dynasty, 386–556) on to the *Liao-shih* ("History of the Liao") itself. This work which has altogether 116 chapters was compiled in 1343–4 under the Mongol Yüan dynasty and printed soon after in 1345.[1] Another Chinese work dealing with the Liao is *Ch'i-tan kuo-chih* ("Records of the Kitan state") in 27 chapters attributed to the Sung author Yeh Lung-li.[2] The *Ch'i-tan kuo-chih* is important because it contains, in addition to annals and biographies of Liao personalities, interesting data on rites and folklore of the Kitan not to be found in the dynastic history *Liao-shih*. It also contains four travelogues written by Chinese envoys who visited the Liao state. Chapters 23 and 27 of the *Ch'i-tan kuo-chih* (those dealing with Kitan tribes, administrations and folk-traditions) have been transmitted separately under the title of *Liao-chih* ("Records of Liao").[3] The serious study of Liao history and of the Kitan people has begun relatively late in China, Japan and the West, but is, as far as Western languages are concerned, now made relatively easy by the monumen-

[1] Many reprints are available among which the punctuated and annotated edition of the *Chung-hua shu-chü* (Peking, 1974, 5 volumes) should be mentioned. A comprehensive collection of primary sources and secondary literature in Chinese has been published in Taiwan: *Liao-shih hui-pien*, 10 volumes, (Taipei, 1971–3).

[2] On the intricate problems of authorship and data of the *Ch'i-tan kuo-chih* see Pelliot, 1959, I, pp. 369–71. A complete annotated Russian translation of the work is Taskin, 1979.

[3] There exists an excellent French translation of *Liao-chih* with much additional information: Stein, 1940.

tal work of Karl A. Wittfogel and Feng Chia-sheng, who, assisted by a host of other competent scholars, have produced a comprehensive and virtually exhaustive manual of Liao society and history. Since its publication (1949) not much has been added to our knowledge, apart from a number of shorter studies on minor problems.

Early history prior to the founding of the Liao state

The original habitat of the Kitans was Manchuria where they are first recorded in what is now the north of Jehol province, near the upper course of the Liao River and its tributary Laoha Muren. This country, known to the Chinese as Sung-mo, consists of river plains with abundant grass and more mountainous parts clad with forests of pine, elm, willow and other trees. Summer rains provided the necessary moisture for pasturing grounds; the forests (which, more than one thousand years ago, will certainly have been more extensive than they are today) teemed with game, chiefly deer, but also wild pigs, tigers and bears. This country where we first find the Kitan people mentioned therefore lent itself to cattle-raising and hunting, but some agriculture was also possible in the fertile river plains and marshes. The Kitans inhabited a land which was situated between the steppe country in the West and the exclusively mountainous parts of Eastern Manchuria; it bordered in the South on Northern China and those parts of Manchuria on the lower course of the Liao river that had always been a convenient area for Chinese agricultural settlers. The name Kitan seems to go back to the 4th century A.D. when several chieftains of the Yü-wen branch of the Hsien-pi had names that may have been related to the tribal name Kitan. The Chinese rendering of the name from the 5th century on has consistently been Ch'i-tan. In the Orkhon inscriptions (732–5) their name appears as Qitay. The Kitans formed for some time a federation with the K'u-mo-hsi tribe but in 388 broke away and became an independent unit. In the 5th century A.D. they began to send tribute embassies to the Wei state of the T'o-pa in Northern China; the first embassy is recorded for 468. They were troublesome neighbors and not infrequently invaded Chinese territory in smaller groups. On the western borders of their homeland the Kitans had to withstand the pressure of the Türks who for some time in the second half of the 6th century made the Kitan a part of their steppe empire. A large group of Kitans therefore took refuge in Korea whereas a smaller group tried to be admitted by the Chinese as immigrants but were refused entry.

During the T'ang period (618–906) the relations between Chinese and

Kitans varied between temporary alliances and periods of Kitan invasions. Under the early emperors of the T'ang the Kitans were allies of the Chinese. In 644 they assisted the Chinese, together with their former kinsmen, the Hsi, descendants of the K'u-mo-hsi, in their campaign against Korea. In recognition of their achievements some Kitan tribal chiefs were honoured with Chinese titles and organized into small principalities in the Jehol region under nominal Chinese sovereignty. But in 696 a Kitan leader turned against his Chinese overlords and assumed the title of kaghan, thus putting himself on the same level as the rulers of the Türk empire. The Chinese reaction was a campaign against the Kitans, but several attempts to subdue them failed and it was not until 714 that a new alliance was formed. This time the Kitan ruler was given the title of "Regional King of Sung-mo" and received a Chinese princess in marriage. This diplomatic move on the part of the Chinese, however, did not prevent the Kitan rulers from trying their luck again with the Türks. Inevitably a Chinese punitive expedition resulted and a new agreement was concluded in 745, again solemnized by marriage with a Chinese princess.

The Kitan policy of allying themselves alternatively with Chinese and Türks was also continued after the Turkic people of the Uighurs became a predominant factor in Eastern Inner Asia. At first the Kitan declared themselves vassals of the Uighurs but in 842 joined the Chinese side. At that time the power of the T'ang empire was already on the decline, and when Chinese central control virtually broke down, the Kitans seized upon the opportunity to extend their dominions at the expense of the Chinese. The rise of the Kitans from a pastoral tribe to the leading group of a huge empire was chiefly due to their ruler A-pao-chi (872–926) with whom a new period in Kitan history begins, a transition from tribal society to a dynastic pattern of domination.

The social organization of the Kitan people was quite complex, even before they absorbed by their conquests other ethnic groups and extended their domination over a largely agricultural Chinese population. Even in predynastic times we have to reckon with a variety of ethnic and occupational groups who in one way or another were dependent on the Kitans, the nucleus of the whole federation. The very number of tribes into which the Kitan people was subdivided changed considerably over time. Most sources agree that there were eight basic Kitan tribes in the 9th century, each headed by a chieftain, called *ta-jen* (lit. 'great man') in Chinese. Every three years the ruler of the federation was selected from among the eight tribes. Each tribe was at the same time a military unit, but it seems that originally there existed no clan groups within the tribes and, consequently, no family names. The fluidity of social organization may also be gathered from the fact that we can see from

the sources how new tribes came into existence, either from small frontier garrisons and similar settlements or occupational groups transferred to a new location. Two families that reached prominence during the 9th century and indeed became the leading clan groups were the Yeh-lü and the Hsiao clans. The Yeh-lü (or I-la in a different Chinese orthography),[4] from which A-pao-chi, the empire-builder, came, were of pure Kitan extraction, whereas the Hsiao clan (which received this Chinese name as late as 947; earlier name forms are Shih-mo and Shen-mi) was of Uighur ancestry. The two families formed an alliance in the 9th century and replaced the earlier kaghans of the Yao-lien tribe. This alliance lasted throughout the history of the Liao state; the emperors came from the Yeh-lü clan and took their empresses from the Hsiao clan. The important position of the Hsiao clan with its Uighur elements accounts for the presence of some Turkic traits in Kitan society and administration (some administrative tribal terms can be linked with Turkic ones), together with the fact that also the Hsi, descendants of the K'u-mo-hsi are generally regarded as Turks.

A typical feature of Kitan social organization was the military camps. The Kitan word is *ordo*, a term which occurs in many languages of Inner Asia. Each ruler had his own ordo which functioned as bodyguard in peacetime and elite corps in war. The number of warrior households attached to a single ordo might be as high as 15,000. After the death of a ruler the ordo families were kept together and functioned as tomb guards. Not all ordo members belonged to the Kitan people; not infrequently other tribal groups and even prisoners were attached to the camp. It is not quite clear if this organization goes back to the predynastic period or was a creation of later times. There are no statistics available on the total number of Kitans at any given time, but for the early 12th century, towards the close of the dynasty, the total number of Kitans is estimated at 150,000 households with something like 750,000 individuals; out of these, c. 60,000 households (300,000 individuals) were organized in the imperial military camps, the rest remaining with their original tribes. The population figure must have been accordingly much smaller for the early period of Kitan history, perhaps not more than 300,000 individuals.

Another characteristic of Kitan social structure is the absence of a fixed residence for the chieftains. They had seasonal residences between which they moved according to the hunting and fishing seasons. The Kitan term for seasonal residence is *na-po*, a word that was, like the institution itself, later taken over by the Jurchens and even occurs in Yüan China under the Mongols.

[4] It seems that the name I-la is related to an old Mongolian word for "stallion." See Rachewiltz, 1974.

The marriage system of the Kitans differed in many respects from that of their Chinese neighbors. Kitan girls were freer to marry a man of their own choice than their Chinese contemporaries, and in dynastic times many women of higher social status were wealthy, powerful and took an active interest in politics. Not only the husband but also the wife could ask for a divorce. Sororate (the custom of jointly marrying several sisters) was not infrequent, and in pre-dynastic times even compulsory. Levirate was equally common. The Kitans did not share the Chinese aversion, or rather taboo, against marrying outside their generation. The Chinese exogamic clan-system was adopted under the Liao only for the ruling Yeh-lü clan and the Hsiao clan of the imperial consorts; as a consequence the Kitan commoners and tribesmen had no family names and seem to have had no clan-ancestors' worship. Intermarriage with Chinese occurred but was generally discouraged, even in dynastic times. Another un-Chinese feature was marriage by abduction (*Raubehe*) which became, however, over the years a ritualized game for the initiation of matrimonial relations.

Religion and customs

We are not too badly informed about Kitan religion, rites and ceremonies because the *Liao-shih* and other Chinese sources include many data, which, though mostly fragmentary, show that tribal beliefs and customs were still alive in dynastic times. A particularly curious tradition is the ancestral legend of the Kitan people.

An old tradition handed down from antiquity relates that there was a man who descended the course of the Muddy River, riding on a white horse, and also a woman who, riding on a small cart drawn by an ash-coloured ox, descended the course of the Huang River. They met at the Mu-yeh Mountain. And as the rivers united they became man and wife. These were the first ancestors. They engendered eight sons who each took up a separate residence at a certain place [. . .] Their statues were set up on Mount Mu-yeh where their descendants worshiped them, and it was their duty to sacrifice a white horse and an ash-colored ox. Thus they sacrificed the beings on which their ancestors had come.

Later there was a chief called Nai-ho. This chief was nothing but a skull hidden under a rug in a round felt tent, and was invisible to everybody. Only when there was a great affair of the state, and after the sacrifice of a white horse and a gray ox, he took on human shape and came out to show himself. After the affairs were settled he returned to the tent and became again a skull. When a man from that country went to have a close look, he disappeared. Then there was another chief whose name was K'ua-ho, who wore a boar's head and was clad in pig-skin. He too lived in a round felt tent. When there was an action he came out, then he retired and hid himself again. Later it happened that his wife looked at him as he was wearing his pig-skin; he abandoned her

and nobody knows where he went. Then there was another one called Hua-li-hun-ho. He had raised twenty sheep. Each day he ate nineteen and had only one left, but the following day there were twenty again.[5]

These legends contain certain elements which are also reflected in Kitam rituals. Mount Mu-yeh was the holy mountain of the whole people where regular worship took place in the ninth month of every year. The union of the two rivers and the hierogamy of the two ancestors meeting at a holy place are an age-old theme which occurs also in Chinese traditions. White, the color of the ancestor's horse, remained the sacred color of the Kitans, a tradition apparently also carried on by the Mongols who also had white as their holy colour. The eight sons of the ancestral pair became the founders of the eight original Kitan tribes. The strange legends connected with the three chiefs may be connected with traditions of theriomorphous ancestors. Such animal ancestry legends are well attested for Turks and Mongols, by whom wolf and hind were regarded as ancestors of the tribe; in the case of the Kitans there may have existed a legend of dog-ancestor and a wild-boar-ancestor, whereas the legend of the inexhaustible sheep points to the role of sheep in the early Kitan economy.

The ancestral pair were, at a later stage of Kitan religious beliefs, regarded as incarnations of the God of Heaven and the Goddess of the Earth. The Earth-goddess of the Kitans was thought to appear as an old woman riding on a cart. Other gods were imagined to live on certain mountains. Shamanism was an integral part of Kitan religion. A chief-shaman had to preside over the rites connected with the Fire God at the end of the year; the following day shamans danced singing, ringing bells and holding arrows among the tents in order to excorcise the evil spirits of the past year.

Our sources allow us to reconstruct a calendar of seasonal rites and ceremonies observed by the Kitans. Some of the ceremonies are of Chinese origin but many others were certainly a part of Kitan tradition. To this category belong all customs connected with hunting and fishing. Seasonal hunting and fishing expeditions were a normal part of the emperor's and the Kitan nobles' life. A special ritual surrounded the catching of the first fish (in spring) and the first wild goose (in autumn). This occasion was taken as an augury for the whole season and celebrated with a luxurious banquet. To shoot at willow branches during the fourth month of the year was a ceremony for obtaining plentiful rain in summer. Many festive rituals also included sporting contests (wrestling, arrow-shooting, polo). The investiture of a new

[5] The translation has been made after the French version of Stein, 1940, pp. 11–13.

ruler was solemnized by rituals that certainly go back to the tribal period of the Kitans. Magical "rebirth" and "recognition" ceremonies are described in detail by Chinese observers. An age-old custom of the Kitans was to bury favourite animals and valuable property together with the deceased chieftain; in later times the sacred objects that had belonged to a deceased emperor were burned. The grim custom of killing and burying persons together with a chieftain or noble persisted into the 10th century, but was abandoned later under Chinese influence.

Language and script

The linguistic affiliation of the Kitans is to a certain extent still a matter of scholarly debate. Some 200 words of their language have been preserved in Chinese transcription together with their meaning, but many among these are titles which are as a rule easily borrowed from one language into another and can therefore hardly be used as evidence. Some Kitan tribal titles seem to have a counterpart in Turkic languages. Other words are certainly related to Mongolian, and it has been supposed that the Kitan language was a branch of Mongolian ("Old South Mongolian"). There are also some words which might be of Tunguz origin, and a few have resisted so far all attempts of finding an etymology. All this reflects to a certain degree the character of the Kitan league as a federation comprising several ethnic and linguistic elements. It has even been argued that Kitan was not an Altaic language at all but was an isolated language that has died out since.[6]

In dynastic times the Kitans developed two script systems of their own. The first was invented in A.D. 920 under A-pao-chi and was called "large script." Another script, the so-called "small script" was invented in A.D. 924, and according to the *Liao-shih* followed the model of the Uighur script. Specimens of both types of script have survived on stone and on bronze objects; some inscriptions are bilingual in Kitan and Chinese so that decipherment was facilitated. A certain degree of confusion has been caused by the fact that the characters of the "small script" were combined into quite large units which have for a long time been regarded as the "large script." It would be helpful if we were to call the characters of the script invented in A.D. 924 "composite script" and others "non-composite." The decipherment of the composite script, first by Russian scholars and later by the Chinese, has made consider-

[6] For a survey of earlier studies of the Kitan language see Sinor 1963, pp. 248–249 and also Franke 1969. The opinion that Kitan was not an Altaic language at all has been voiced by Doerfer, 1969. The majority of scholars in East and West is at present in favor of the "Mongolian" theory.

able progress during the last few years.[7] The graphic elements of the composite script seem to have been developed from abbreviated forms of Chinese characters, not unlike the *kana* syllabaries in Japanese. Altogether 378 basic characters have been distinguished so far, out of which c. 130 have been identified either for their sound value ("phonograms") or their meaning ("semantograms"). These researches have also shown that the Kitan language had suffixes; some of these have been tentatively identified with grammatical endings in Mongolian. The number of Kitan words which could be reconstructed is, however, still quite small and is limited mostly to names, calendar terms and numbers.

Most extant Kitan texts are in composite script. Only very few specimens of the non-composite characters ("large script") have survived. The characters of this script have been adapted from Chinese characters, and many of them seem to have been the prototypes of Jurchen characters. Their decipherment is still in the initial stage.[8]

The Liao state of the Kitans

In 907 A-pao-chi assumed the title of emperor and began to transform his state by introducing a Chinese-type formalized administrative system. The essential feature of the Kitan state remained, however, a dichotomy between a bureaucracy for governing the sedentary population (chiefly Chinese), and a more tribal administration for the Kitans themselves and other ethnic groups. Different laws existed for Kitans and non-Kitans. A further step towards integration into the Chinese political orbit was made when the name of the Kitan state was changed to Great Liao in 947. This followed Chinese precedents, because, as in China, the name of the state and dynasty was a geographical one, in this case taken from the Liao River in Southern Manchuria. The expansion of the Kitans was first directed against Northern China. In 938 they obtained the cession of 16 prefectures including what is now Peking from the Chinese state of Chin (not to be confounded with the later Chin state of the Jurchens). A few years later (947) the Chin dynasty had to surrender. The following decades brought intermittent border warfare with the Chinese state of Sung which had been founded in 960 and attempted to reunify China.

7 For the Russian attempts at decipherment see *Materialy*, 1970 and the review by Gy. Kara of this work in *AOH*. 26 (1972), pp. 155–157. The latest comprehensive study by Chinese scholars is *Ch'i-tan hsia-tzu yen-chiu*, representing the efforts of a team of scholars at the University of Inner Mongolia.

8 For a Japanese study of the "large script" (non-composite characters) see now Toyota, 1963, where a specimen of the script (a tomb inscription) is reproduced.

Kitan military superiority forced the Sung to agree to a peace treaty in 1005 which confirmed the *status quo* along Sung's northern border against the promise of an annual payment of 100,000 taels of silver and 200,000 bolts of silk to the Liao state. A period of coexistence followed, but in 1042 a new war broke out between Sung and Liao, which ended in a new treaty raising the Sung payments to 200,000 taels of silver and 300,000 bolts of silk. These payments which were considered "tribute" (a term obviously avoided by the Sung Chinese) contributed a great deal to the economic strength of the Liao state. In addition to the enforced payments there was a constant state-controlled trade at Sung's northern borders where the Kitans, or rather their Chinese subjects, sold horses, animal products, furs and certain minerals to China proper.

The other states bordering upon the Liao, the Tangut empire of Hsi-Hsia and the kingdom of Korea had, in order to assure peace of their borders, at one time or other recognized the formal suzerainty of the Liao, and there existed regularized diplomatic relations between these powers and the Kitans. But throughout Liao's existence the Kitans were troubled with minor insurrections of various tribal groups. The Hsi were unruly allies, and so were other ethnic groups belonging to the non-Chinese part of the Kitan federation. In what is now Mongolia, the Tsu-pu Tatars repeatedly invaded territory held by Kitans. But the greatest menace to the Liao state came from their Jurchen subjects. Early in the 12th century the Jurchens began to break away from Kitan domination and in 1114 a full-scale war between the Kitan and their former subjects broke out. In 1120 the Supreme Capital of the Liao was taken and in the following years the whole Liao empire was overrun by the Jurchens acting in alliance with the Sung. The last Liao emperor was captured in 1125, and the dynasty of the Yeh-lü clan that had dominated Manchuria and parts of Northern China for over two hundred years came to an end.

This period showed a slow but inexorable change of the Kitan people through Chinese cultural influence. Many Kitan emperors and their court aristocrats adopted Buddhism and became pious protectors of the Buddhist faith. The desire to make the Kitan nobility and office-holders familiar with Chinese literature beyond Buddhist texts resulted in many translations from Chinese into Kitan. Unfortunately none of the Kitan translations has survived, but we know at least which texts were translated. Apart from Chinese calendars, medical books and similar works of immediate practical use there existed a Kitan translation of the T'ang work *Chen-kuan cheng-yao* ("Essentials of Rule of the Chen-kuan period"), a handbook of statecraft that was held in high esteem by all non-Chinese dynasties because it was regarded as a

ruler's vade mecum. Also a part of the *Wu-tai shih* ("History of the Five Dynasties") was translated into Kitan, no doubt because it gave them information on their Chinese neighbors in the 10th century. Other books translated into Kitan were political essays by the Chinese T'ang author Po Chü-i (772–845) and a Taoist treatise dealing with the forces of the Universe, the *Yin-fu ching* ("Harmony of the Seen and the Unseen").[9] It is significant that apparently no Confucian classics were translated and that the interest of the Kitan in Chinese literature was limited to books concerning statecraft in its widest sense. The Kitan upper class certainly showed no great desire to compete with the Chinese in literary or artistic pursuits. The attitude corresponds with the dual character of the Liao state where two types of civilization coexisted side by side.

The Kitans after the fall of the Liao state

The fall of the Liao empire, however, did not mean the end of the Kitans as a people. Already prior to the death of the last emperor one of his kinsmen, Yeh-lü Ta-shih, had fled west in 1124, accompanied by a host of followers not exceeding ten thousand warriors. He crossed the Tarim basin and finally invaded the steppe country east of the T'ien Shan mountains. There he conquered not only the Karakhanid empire but also defeated the Saljuq armies. These victories made him the ruler of a semi-nomad empire in Western Asia which was known to the Chinese as Western Liao (Hsi-Liao) and to the Islamic world as Karakitai: "Black Kitans." The center of his empire was Balasaghun in the valley of the River Chu; he adopted the title of *gür khan*, "Universal Khan." Indeed, his dominions stretched from the Chinese border in the East to the Aral Sea in the West.

Unfortunately, the history of the Karakitai empire, which lasted until 1211 when it was divided between the Naimans, then allies of Chinggis Khan, and the Khorezm shah Muḥammad, is not too well known. The Chinese sources give only fragmentary information and Muslim sources are not always reliable and hard to reconcile with the Chinese data.[10] The basic characteristic of Karakitai rule seems to have been the domination of a sedentary, agricultural and trading oasis culture by a predominantly nomad Kitan minority. The Kitans, even in a country which had great cities such as Samarkand,

[9] This relatively obscure text has served in China also as a handbook on statecraft and strategy; see the translation and discussion of the text by Rand, 1979. This can perhaps explain why it was translated into Kitan.

[10] A convenient annalistic history of the Karakitai state may be found in Wittfogel-Fêng, 1949, pp. 627–57.

preferred to live in tents, but they realized the importance of agriculture and promoted the production of grain, wine, fruit and cotton, whereas horses, sheep and camels were bred in the steppe parts of the empire. Kitan domination differed, however, from a Chinese-type domination insofar as local political systems and rules were left more or less intact, and no attempt was made to impose a uniform system of government upon the diversified countries that constituted the Karakitai empire. Neither was the empire an imitation of a Near Eastern type of state with an omnipotent despot at its head. Kitan rule in Inner Asia therefore can be described as a separate type of government which may be termed "Central Asian," a loose domination over a great variety of ethnic groups and civilizations. Yeh-lü Ta-shih and his immediate successors retained some of the cultural traits inherited from the Liao empire; the Karakitai coins followed the Chinese pattern and Buddhism continued to be the main religion of the Kitans even in Inner Asia. Other religions (Islam, Nestorian Christianity) were tolerated and, contrary to the later Mongol conquerors, no Kitan "Universal khan" ever adopted Islam. Yeh-lü Ta-shih's victories over Islamic rulers became known in Europe and gave rise to the belief in a Christian, or at least non-Islamic, kingdom in Asia which in European legends appears as Prester John's Kingdom, a state which was thought to help eventually the hard-pressed crusaders in Palestine and to crush the Muslims. In later years the Prester John legend was transferred to the Mongol rulers, regarded as potential allies against the Islamic states in the Near East.

The majority of Kitans had not followed Yeh-lü Ta-shih on his move to Western Asia. They became subjects of the Jurchens and their Chin state, where they were considered and treated as a separate ethnic group along with Chinese and other non-Jurchen peoples. There existed purely Kitan military units, chiefly in the north-west of the Chin empire. Some Kitans even rose to high rank in the Chin bureaucracy, but generally the Jurchen rule seems to have been resented by most Kitans, who continued to regard the Jurchens as upstarts. A major rebellion broke out in 1161 when the Chin ruler had embarked on a campaign against the Sung. This dangerous revolt in the hinterland of the Chin state was quelled, however, and many unruly Kitan tribesmen were transferred from their original units to Jurchen units. Some Kitans even defected to the Sung, their former adversaries. A limited amnesty was granted in 1164 when Kitan leaders who had remained faithful to the Jurchen were reinstated. But new rebellions broke out in 1169 and 1177, followed each time by a dispersal of Kitans among other tribal units. There must have existed a sense of ethnic identity between all Kitans because a few

fled to Western Liao. The cultural role of educated Kitans under the Chin is shown by the fact that Kitan script continued to be used long after the fall of Liao and that many Jurchen learned Kitan in addition to Chinese. The use of the Kitan script was forbidden in 1191, and the translation from Jurchen language into Kitan was prohibited.

When the Mongol armies began to attack the Chin state in 1211 a few Kitans looked upon the Mongols as friends, not enemies. Yeh-lü Liu-ko, a scion of the former Liao ruling dynasty, rebelled and declared his allegiance to Chinggis Khan in 1212. When the Mongols took Peking in 1215, they recruited Kitans for their new regime. Among them was Yeh-lü Ch'u-ts'ai (1189–1243), the famous statesman who helped Chinggis and his successors establish a stable government, and who must be regarded as one of the great statesmen in the 13th century. Some Kitans also distinguished themselves under the Mongol Yüan dynasty as literati and administrators, although they had long lost their cultural identity and become thoroughly Chinese. But even as late as about 1300 there must have existed a feeling among the Mongol–Chinese bureaucracy that the Kitans were a group apart from the other ethnic groups in the Mongol empire, because a census taken in Chen-chiang lists Kitans separately along with Tanguts and Jurchens. It is only during the 14th century that the Kitans disappear from the scene in China and Inner Asia, after a history of their own which is truly remarkable for its military, political and cultural vitality.

The Jurchens

The same historical periodization as for the Kitans suggests itself for the Jurchen people: predynastic, dynastic and post-dynastic. Their dynastic period coincides with the existence of the Chin state from 1115 to 1234, and is evidently the best documented part of their history because of the *Chin-shih* ("History of the Chin"). The *Chin-shih* contains also many valuable data on the pre-dynastic period. It was compiled in 135 chapters from earlier sources in 1343–4 and printed in 1345 along with the *Liao-shih*. Another important source is the *Ta-Chin kuo-chih* ("Records of the Great Chin State") in 40 chapters. It is attributed to a certain Yü-wen Mou-chao but the authorship remains doubtful. Some of the chapters dealing with the customs of the Jurchen have been transmitted separately under the title of *Chin-kuo chih* ("Records of the Chin State"), a version that is important because it contains a detailed account of early Jurchen history missing in the current editions of *Ta-*

Chin kuo-chih.[11] The military and diplomatic contacts between the Sung state and the Jurchen are amply documented in the monumental compilation *San-ch'ao pei-meng hui-pien* ("Collected Documents on the Treaty Violations under Three Emperors"), covering the period from c. 1115 to 1161 in its 250 chapters. The author is the Sung Historian Hsü Meng-hsin (1126–1206).[12] These sources are supplemented by a number of travelogues written by Sung envoys to the Chin court. A wealth of information on the pre-dynastic history of the Jurchen is contained in the *Liao-shih* and other Liao sources. Chinese authors living under the Chin state have also written valuable accounts, some of them, like the *Kuei-ch'ien chih* ("Records written in Retirement") by Liu Ch'i, based on personal evidence.[13] For the later history of the Jurchen people, after the fall of the Chin state in 1234, we have to rely equally on Chinese sources of Yüan and Ming date, and, to a certain extent, also on Sino-Korean sources. The scholarly study of Jurchen and Chin history has been chiefly a domain of Japanese historians until quite recently, but now some comprehensive works in Western languages are available.[14]

The ethnic designation of the Jurchen people presents some thorny problems because it seems that their name was recorded differently at different periods. The original name was apparently Chu-li-chen (Jurčen). This form is met also in Mongolian sources from the 13th century on as *Jürca* or *Jürcid* (*-d* is a Mongolian plural), in Persian texts as *Jūrča* or *Jūrčä*. Marco Polo has *Ciorcia* which goes back to the same ethnicon. From the 10th century on, another name occurs in Liao sources, Nü-chen, which was changed later into Nü-chih because of a taboo on the Liao emperor Hsing-tsung's (r. 1031–1054) personal name Tsung-chen. Nü-chen may have been the Kitan designation of the Jurchen people. The spelling Jurchen adopted here is, in a way, a compromise between several forms of the name; it is warranted by the fact that the character *nü* in Nü-chen has also the pronunciation *ju*. In the 16th century the name was Jusen, a form derived from an earlier Juchen which in turn comes from the original Jurchen.[15]

The linguistic affinity of the Jurchen is clear. Their language belongs to the Tunguz family and is closely related to Manchu. Many Jurchen words and names in Chinese transcription have been preserved in Chinese works of the 12th and 13th centuries. They constitute the earliest recorded Tunguz materi-

[11] On the dating and authorship of the *Ta-Chin kuo-chih* see Pelliot, 1959, I, pp. 369–70.

[12] Chapter 3 of the *San-ch'ao pei-meng hui-pien* contains much valuable information on the Jurchen and their original way of life. For a translation see Herbert Franke, 1975.

[13] On Liu Ch'i and Chin historiography in general see Chan, 1970.

[14] Vorob'ev 1975, Tao, 1976.

[15] See article "Ciorcia" in Pelliot, 1959, I, pp. 366–90.

als. A later stage of the language is reflected in Jurchen vocabularies of the 16th century, where the Jurchen equivalent to Chinese words is noted in Chinese characters used phonetically. The close affinity between Jurchen and Manchu was already discovered in Europe in the 18th century by Claude Visdelou (1656–1737). The Manchus themselves have always been aware of their relationship with the Jurchen people and their language.

The Jurchens prior to the founding of the Chin state.

The Jurchen people, which was to become such a paramount political power in China's northern borderlands, had been considered for a long time by Chinese authors as an ethnic group of which the Mo-ho tribe in Southern Manchuria had been a constituent. For a long time the Mo-ho and also the later Jurchens had been subjects of the Po-hai state that had existed in the countries adjoining the Gulf of Liaotung between Korea and China. Their name, however, is mentioned comparatively late in Chinese sources, unless we regard the Great and Little Ju-che, who sent embassies to the T'ang court in A.D. 748, as early Jurchens. When the Kitans under A-pao-chi rose to power, the Jurchen became subjects of the Kitans. The Kitan ruler transferred a large group of Jurchen to Liaotung in Southern Manchuria where they engaged in agriculture and cattle-breeding. They were called "Civilized Jurchen" by the Chinese and by sinicized Kitans. The majority of the people, however, continued to live in the wooded country southeast of modern Kirin in Manchuria and on the Sungari river. This part of the Jurchen was called "Uncivilized Jurchen," a terminology that reflects not only political attitudes but also a different way of life: life on the open plains and life in the forest. The forest Jurchen too were vassals of the Kitans and from 928 on continued to send embassies to the Kitan court. The Jurchen living near the coast, on the other hand, regarded themselves as tributary vassals of the Sung court, and in the late 10th century repeatedly sent embassies to the Sung by boat, thus bypassing the Liao state of the Kitans. Already in 991 they offered the Sung an alliance against the Kitans, a political move which was not carried into effect until much later. After c. A.D. 1000 the clan of the Wan-yen which lived along the An-ch'u-hu River in Manchuria rose to prominence. The clan ancestor was Han-p'u, originally a man from the Hei-shui ("Black Water") Mo-ho. According to thc ancestral legend, as related in the *Chin-shih*, he was already over sixty years old when he left the Mo-ho tribe and came to the Jurchen where he settled among the Wan-yen clan and succeeded in quelling a feud between two families. In recognition, he was betrothed to a worthy unmarried

woman also sixty years old. This marriage was solemnized by the gift of a dark ox. From this rather belated union came one daughter and three sons. After this Han-p'u and his descendants were formally received into the Wan-yen clan. This legend has certainly a historical basis; it points to the fact that the Wan-yen clan, at some time during the 10th century, had absorbed immigrants from Korea and Po-hai. The mention of the dark ox also has some significance. Oxen played a great role in Jurchen economy and folklore. For a long time the various Jurchen clans lived as neighbors and vassals of the Kitans and not a few of their chieftains were granted honorary titles by the Liao court. During the 11th century the different Jurchen groups merged into larger units, and under Wu-ku-nai (1021–74), a fifth-generation descendant of Han-p'u, became a real power in Manchuria. But the Kitans continued to treat them as primitive and boorish people, whose duty was to supply them with tribute gifts, such as pearls, falcons for hunting, furs and other commodities. Extortion and usurious practices were as it seems, quite common. One of the practices that infuriated the Jurchen was the customary right of the Kitan messengers to sleep with Jurchen girls; sometimes they even took married women. There were some minor rebellions against the Kitan overlords, but a thorough attempt to achieve independence took place only under A-ku-ta (1068–1123), a grandson of Wu-ku-nai. A-ku-ta too had been appointed as a local prefect by the Liao and in 1113 was elected as supreme chief of his tribe. A full-scale war broke out in 1114 when A-ku-ta led 2,500 soldiers against the Liao garrisons. Barely one year later he felt secure enough to declare himself emperor. His state was called Chin ("Gold"), probably because the name of the An-ch'u-hu River where his people lived also means "golden" in Jurchen (cf. Turkic *altun*, Mong. *altan*, Manchu *aisin* "gold").[16] The state name was therefore derived from a river name, in the same way as the Kitan state was named Liao after the Liao River in Manchuria.

The Jurchen way of life

It is difficult to generalize about the Jurchen way of life, their primitive economy and trade relations. As we have seen, the Jurchen lived in various habitats with distinctive economic features. One thing, however, is certain: neither the "civilized" nor the "wild" Jurchen were pastoral nomads, and the nomad element was much stronger within the Kitan federation than among the Jurchen. One reason, apart from the characteristics of their forested

[16] The Jurchen word for "gold" is differently reconstructed by contemporary scholars. Some prefer *ancun*, other *alcun*. The former word is perhaps to be connected with Manchu *ancun* "earrings for women" and is not related to Manchu *aisin* "gold."

homelands, was that the ox, their principal domestic animal, is not suited for long-range treks. In addition to horned cattle they raised horses and sheep and bred pigs but, unlike the Kitans, they had no camels. Their agriculture was quite developed. In addition to cereals, such as grain or millet, they also cultivated flax from which linen was manufactured. For climatic reasons sericulture was unknown among the Jurchen. Some of the products of their country came from the forest: wax, honey, pine seeds, and the root of the ginseng plant which played a great role in the Chinese pharmacopeia as a stimulant and aphrodisiac. Hunting and fishing were the chief occupations. Deer, wild boar, pheasant, ermine, and sable were hunted. Jurchen hunters had a special technique of imitating the cry of the stag and thus luring other deer. Such hunters were even given in "tribute" to the Kitans who appreciated their skills. Other products of the Jurchen country which were traded with the Kitans and Chinese were marine and river pearls and even crude gold; however, hunting-falcons seems to have been the chief export good cherished by their neighbors. The Jurchen were accomplished blacksmiths and even exported iron helmets and armor. Trade between the Jurchen and their partners was chiefly effected through barter; money was unknown to them and the first attempt to produce a currency of their own took place long after the foundation of the Chin state. It seems that Jurchen–Kitan trade in particular had taken semi-ritualized forms. During seasonal hunting and fishing expeditions of the Kitan court the Jurchen tribesmen gathered at the licensed border-markets in Manchuria presenting tribute and trading their goods. These occasions were celebrated by feasting and drinking, and the Jurchen seem to have had to suffer frequent humiliations from their overlords. Some sources relate that A-ku-ta finally revolted because the Liao emperor ordered him to dance before the Kitan nobles at one of these feasts.

The dwellings of the Jurchen were adapted to the climatic conditions of their homeland with its severe winter cold. They did not normally use bricks but built log cabins or semi-subterranean dwellings covered with birch bark or wooden planks. Their houses frequently had an oven-bed made of clay which was heated from below and served for eating, sleeping and household work during the winter months, similar to the huge tile-stoves to be found in traditional Russian peasant huts. These heatable couches are even today a normal feature of Northern Chinese houses where they are called *k'ang*.[17] The Jurchen dress was likewise suited to the climate. Even in the summer, they were clad in furs, worn over linen garments. Rich people sometimes had silk

[17] Russian archeologists have brought to light in the Far Eastern coastal province many finds which illustrate the predynastic Jurchen way of life. See Medvedev, 1977, and Lenkov, 1974.

gowns imported from China or Korea. As colors, the Jurchens preferred red and yellow. They were fond of jewelry and liked to wear earrings, made of gold in the case of well-to-do tribesmen; pearl embroidery also seems to have been practiced. The hair-style of the male Jurchen was to have the hair bound together with colored bands into a "pigtail"; this same custom was later, in the 17th century, imposed on the Chinese by the victorious Manchus. The "pigtail" was so much a distinctive feature of the Jurchen that in the 12th century some Chinese insurgents adopted this hair-style in order to disguise themselves as Jurchen and thereby to spread terror among the population and the loyalist soldiery.

Life in these Jurchen villages, with their underground caves and log-cabins, was frugal and simple. The diet consisted of pap made from cereals, roast meat, fish and such vegetables as could be grown in the climate of the Manchurian forest-lands. From millet or imported rice they distilled a kind of wine of which they were inordinately fond. Heavy drinking remained, throughout their dynastic period, a national characteristic. "They are fond of wine and love to kill. They ferment rice in order to make wine [...] When they are drunk, they are fettered with a rope until they have become sober so that they cannot kill other people. They would not recognize even their father or mother [when drunk]."[18] This unflattering description of Jurchen mores comes, of course, from a Chinese source and may be tainted by the ethnographic cliché of the ferocious savage, but excessive drinking is reported frequently also in Chin sources and by Chinese envoys. After the establishment of the Chin state, wine-making became in theory a state-monopoly, but private distilling remained widespread in spite of legislation. Wine produced in the Jurchen homelands was inferior to the Chinese brands. Emperor Shih-tsung (r. 1161–90) once stayed a whole year in the old Jurchen capital of Hui-ning in Manchuria and found the local wine rather bad.

The same ferociousness which the Jurchen displayed – if we are to believe the Chinese source – in their domestic drinking was also apparent in their military actions. They were excellent horsemen and skilled archers, as one would expect from a people in whose economy and ritual hunting played a prominent role. Jurchen military organization was simple but, as the conquests of the early 12th century showed, effective. Their military units consisted of groups of 5, 10, 100 and 1,000 warriors, a decimal system which can be found in most Inner Asian army organizations. Leadership, originating perhaps from tribal chieftainship, was mostly hereditary. The larger units

[18] *Ta-Chin kuo-chih* ch. 39, p. 299. See also Franke, 1974.

were called *Meng-an mou-k'o* which means "units of thousand or hundred," *meng-an* being the Jurchen numeral for "1,000" (a loan word from Mongolian) and *mou-k'o* a word which seems to be related to the Manchu word *mukūn* "family, herd" but which the Chinese glosses explain by "one hundred man." In the early 12th century these semi-tribal units, under hereditary leaders, became also a kind of agricultural organization because the Jurchens settled in the conquered territories in *meng-an mou-k'o* villages, which might also be described as military colonies. A curious military custom is reported of the Jurchen: whoever brought the corpse of a killed soldier home inherited the property of the deceased.

Other features of social organization among the primitive Jurchen were a high degree of local independence and considerable fragmentation. The clan groups lived in the early times without a formal common overlord. Small groups consisted of a few hundred families only, and only some of the larger groups had a few thousand. Only in later times, from the 11th century on, did these groups develop into structured tribes ruled by a prominent family or clan, and one of the achievements of leaders like Wu-ku-nai and A-ku-ta was to unite them into what may be called a nation. Chieftainship even of the smaller groups was hereditary, but succession was not patrilineal; instead, younger brothers followed their elder ones. The Jurchen word for chieftain was *po-chi-lieh*, a word that can be reconstructed as *bogile* and may be related to the Turkic term *bäg* ("chief"). The word occurs as *beile* in Manchu where it designated an aristocratic, later a court, rank and as such survived into the early 20th century. The Jurchen chieftains, however, had no absolute power over their tribesmen; important decisions, such as warfare, were referred to the tribal council. The council members (clan and village elders) painted their faces with black soot and sat down in a circle in the open field where they discussed an issue. The chieftain selected from among the suggested alternatives; after agreement had been reached the faces of the councilors were cleaned again. The end of the meeting was invariably a feast with heavy drinking. Open and free discussion of politics remained a feature of government in the Chin state after Chinese bureaucratic structures had been adopted and the *bogile* system supplanted by a ministerial bureaucracy. In predynastic times the Jurchen had no script; it is said that they used incised arrows for noting and memorizing important decisions.

The Jurchen had, of course, no written laws. Their customary law was very simple and straightforward. A murderer was executed, and his family enslaved. Enslavement could, however, be redeemed by paying cattle or money to the victim's family. In cases of theft the convicted thief had to pay a

compensation ten times the worth of the stolen goods, six parts of which went to the legal owner and four to the clan community. Other offences were punished by *bastonnade*. A strange custom existed among the Kitans as well as among the Jurchen: on a certain day of the year (16th day of the first month for the Jurchens, 13th day of the fifth month for the Kitans) free theft was allowed. This was a kind of contest in which ingenuity and skill could be tested, both on the part of the wary owners and of the "thiefs." Objects that people tried to steal could be worthless things (if owners were on the guard), or precious property such as horses, and even daughters or wives. But the stolen objects or persons could be redeemed by giving a huge party. If a girl was stolen and her parents did not try to redeem her, their behavior was viewed as tacit consent to her marrying the man who had stealthily abducted her. Another characteristic of the Jurchen family system which seemed strange and objectionable to the Chinese was levirate: a man could marry the wives of his deceased brother, or a son those of his father, with the exception of his own mother.

Unfortunately, little is known about primitive Jurchen religion, much less than about that of the Kitan. The Jurchen had, like the Kitans, many seasonal feasts and rituals, mostly connected with hunting and fishing. The scanty data of our sources show, however, that in many respects Jurchen religious ceremonies and rituals were taken over from the Kitans. Shamanism was very common. Indeed the very word shaman can be traced back to the Jurchen language. A Chinese text of the 12th century records that *shan-man* is a Jurchen word meaning "sorceress." This word or its cognates occur in practically all Tunguz languages; in Manchu it is *saman*.[19] But even in predynastic times Buddhism had reached the Jurchens, probably from Korea, because already the brother of Han-p'u, the tribal ancestor, is said to have been a pious Buddhist.

The Chin state of the Jurchen

Within a few years after his enthronement A-ku-ta succeeded in overthrowing the Liao state and conquering its entire territory. In this he had been encouraged and to a certain extent assisted by the Sung. When he died in 1123 A-ku-ta was the uncontested ruler of Manchuria, a part of the Mongolian steppes and those parts of Northern China in present Hopei, including Peking, that had already formed a part of the Liao state. Under his younger brother and

[19] Pelliot, 1913.

successor Wu-ch'i-mai (canonized as T'ai-tsung, r. 1123–35) Chin power was further consolidated. The confrontation with the Sung over the eventual fate of the Peking region, and the Jurchen claim that the annual tribute payments of Sung to Liao should be paid to them, led to a long period of fierce campaigns. Between 1126 and 1128 the Jurchens conquered the greater part of Northern China including the Sung capital of K'ai-feng. Stabilization took place only in 1142 when a formal peace treaty was concluded that made the Huai River the border between Chin and Sung and entitled the Jurchen to annual payments in silver and textiles. From then on, uneasy coexistence characterized the Sung–Chin relations, with repeated attempts from the one or the other party to reverse the balance of power. One such attempt was the campaign of the Jurchen usurper Hai-ling (r. 1149–61) against Sung, which failed disastrously and resulted in Hai-ling's overthrow. His successor, emperor Shih-tsung (r. 1161–89), restored the balance and was able to maintain external peace and internal security. His long reign marks the apex of the Chin state. Under his successors the central power of the court declined; moreover, the rising power of the Mongols gradually placed the Chin into a buffer-state situation to which it finally succumbed in 1233–4 through a combined attack of the Mongols and the Sung Chinese.

Admittedly this is an overly brief sketch of the 120 years of Chin history. The following remarks attempt to outline some of the internal developments of the Chin state insofar as they concern the history of the Jurchen as a people. One characteristic of these developments is apparent at first glance: the absorption into Chinese civilization was quicker and more thorough than in the case of the Kitans. But in spite of sinicization some features of predynastic Jurchen society and culture were preserved. This is particularly true for the *meng-an mou-k'o* system. Already under A-ku-ta this military organization had been formalized (in 1114) and was later made to serve the integration of the subjugated populations. Not only Jurchen were members of the organizations, but also Chinese and Po-hai settlers in Manchuria. After the conquest of the Liao state the Kitans too formed their own *meng-an mou-k'o* units; other tribal units retained their separate status as semi-military bodies but on organizational lines similar to the *meng-an mou-k'o* – for example the Tangut and Tieh-lê tribes. Only those parts of the population that remained outside these organizations were subjected to a Chinese-type civilian administration. The proportion of the Chinese within the *meng-an mou-k'o* increased drastically after the inclusion of Northern China into the Chin state. One reason for this inclusion of non-Jurchen elements was the need for huge armies in the many campaigns against Sung. In 1187, the total *meng-an*

mou-k'o population was about 6 million people, including more than a million slaves attached to Jurchen and non-Jurchen households. Only a part of these many millions can have been genuine Jurchen. Understandably the Kitans remained an element of unrest, and there were not a few Kitan rebellions against Jurchen rule. But on the whole this system showed a remarkable stability throughout the existence of the Chin state. The ancient *bogile* administration was gradually supplanted by Chinese-type chanceries and bureaucracies; it already had become obsolete under T'ai-tsung. Altogether the Jurchen state of Chin is characterised by multinationality, with a large Chinese majority. The total population figures of the Chin under Shih-tsung was about 40 million people – many times that of the Liao state.[12]

Under these conditions the preservation of nationaldentity of the Jurchen became a problem. Again and again laws against Jurchen adoption of Chinese dress, family names and customs were issued, and emperor Shih-tsung himself was one of the chief advocates of preserving Jurchen national culture. His predecessor Hai-ling represents the opposite alternative. He tried to transform the Jurchen into Chinese, and his attempt to conquer Sung China can be interpreted as a realization of his claim that the Jurchens and the Chin state were the "real Chinese" and therefore entitled to rule over the whole of China. It characterizes Hai-ling that he gave orders to burn down Hui-ning, the ancient Jurchen capital of Manchuria, the "Supreme Capital," as it used to be called, and to move the center of the state to Yen-ching (Peking) instead. He wanted the Jurchen to become Chinese, unlike his successor Shih-tsung who cherished a nostalgic memory of the good old simple Jurchen way of life as he saw it. He even spent a whole year in the Supreme Capital in Manchuria which he had partly rebuilt.

The use of the Jurchen language at the Chin court had progressively decreased during the 12th century, so much so that one day Shih-tsung was very pleased to hear a birthday poem in Jurchen language recited by an imperial prince. This shows that knowledge of Jurchen could not be taken for granted even for members of the imperial clan. But the Jurchen language had to compete not only with Chinese; the Kitan language and scripts continued to be used for a long time after the founding of the Chin state. The Jurchens also created scripts of their own. In 1119 an imperial clan member invented a script system based on Kitan, the so-called "large characters," and in 1138 a simpler writing system ("small characters") was designed. This script is attested by a few inscriptions on stone dating back to the 12th and early 13th centuries, and by inscriptions on seals and mirrors. The decipherment of a great part of these characters was greatly facilitated by an early-16th-century glossary which

gives the Jurchen characters, their sound transcribed in Chinese, and their meaning. The pioneer work in deciphering the Jurchen script was done by Wilhelm Grube at the end of the last century, and great progress has been made since then by scholars from various countries. It is now possible to read with a high degree of certainty inscriptions of the Chin period.[20] The Jurchen language of the 12th and early 13th century has also served as a medium of translation for Chinese classical and historical texts. We know from the *Chin-shih* that there existed a rather voluminous corpus of Jurchen translations from Chinese. These works served as textbooks for the state examinations and included Confucian classics such as the *Analects*, the *Meng-tzu* and the *Hsiao-ching* and some minor philosophical works. Chinese historical writing is represented by Jurchen versions of *Ch'un-ch'iu* ("Spring and Autumn Annals") *Shih-chi* ("Records of the Historian"), *Han-shu* ("Han History") and the *Hsin T'ang-shu* ("New History of the T'ang Dynasty"). The *Chen-kuan cheng-yao* ("Essentials of Rule of the Chen-kuan period") was also translated, as well as a few Chinese handbooks on military strategy. The great number of translations into Jurchen shows the desire of the Chin state to make the Jurchen intellectuals and officials acquainted with Chinese thought and traditions. But unfortunately not a single line from these old Jurchen books has been preserved. A unique document on paper has been discovered recently. It seems to be in the "large" script and was found among the Tangut manuscripts kept in Leningrad. It is, however, still undeciphered.[21] Although the deciphered texts supply some additional information on the internal structure of the Jurchen state in the 12th and 13th centuries, the greatest part of our knowledge of Jurchen life has come from Chinese sources.

The Jurchens under the Yüan and Ming dynasties

The end of the Chin state in 1234 did not lead to an extinction of the Jurchen as a people. It is true that a great number of Jurchen had by the early 13th century been absorbed into Chinese civilization and lost their national identity. But when the Mongols invaded Manchuria and Northern China, after 1211, some Jurchen decided to serve the Mongols rather than to attempt a hopeless fight against them. The Jurchen were treated by the Mongols as *Han-jen*, a word

[20] The bilingual glossary with appended texts edited in Grube, 1896 has been the subject of a modern study by Kiyose, 1977. A very comprehensive study is Chin Kuan-p'ing and Chin Ch'i-ts'ung, 1980. This book contains also reproductions of recently discovered Jurchen inscriptions and the decipherment of some of these texts.

[21] See Kara–Kychanov–Starikov, 1972.

that originally means "Chinese" but was used in Mongol legislation to designate the non-Mongol populations in Northern China and Manchuria. The Jurchen therefore ranked on a par with native Chinese, Kitans and Po-hai. It seems that after the Mongol conquest a part of the Jurchen people returned to their native grounds in Manchuria where they continued or resumed their traditional occupation as hunters and fur-traders. Some hereditary myriarchies were established the leaders of which were responsible for the tributes to the Mongols. On the whole there was not much Mongol interference with the Jurchen in Manchuria. The homeland of the Jurchen was a very remote corner of the Mongol empire, and indeed so far away from the centers of Mongol power that Nurkan, a small place north of Vladivostok, was a sort of "Botany Bay" for the Mongol administration of China, a place where offenders were banished. The Mongols themselves had certainly not much to fear from the inhabitants of the Manchurian forests and, although the Jurchen had sometimes reason to complain of the corvées and tributes exacted by their Mongol overlords, there was comparatively little discontent. Only twice, in the 1340s and 1350s, were there minor rebellions.

One reason why the Mongols did not concern themselves very much with the Jurchen was that they were not dependent on the products of Manchuria such as horses, cattle, furs and falcons. This changed after the national Chinese dynasty of the Ming was founded in 1368. The Ming state after 1368 was engaged in almost continuous struggle with the Mongols and therefore looked to Manchuria as a source for horses. In 1406 licenced horse markets were established. The Ming also created a garrison system, using the existing military organizations of the Jurchen to act as frontier guards. The Jurchen therefore were in name vassals of China, and their leaders held Chinese military and civilian ranks. But *de facto* the Jurchen were independent and, during the 15th century, became a power of their own. This development was due partly also to their flourishing economy, which in these years was based not only on hunting, fishing and some agriculture, but also on a considerable iron industry. The population began to grow and gradually, through intermarriage and absorption of other ethnic elements, a new nation emerged, that of the Manchus, which in the 17th century succeeded in conquering China just as their Jurchen forefathers did five hundred years earlier. The degree to which the Manchus considered themselves the successors of the mediaeval Jurchen is also illustrated by the name which the Manchu chieftain Nurhaci gave to his dynasty in 1616, Hou Chin, "Later Chin."

Bibliography

Abbreviations

AAH.	*Acta Archaeologica Academiae Scientiarum Hungaricae*
ABAW.	*Abhandlungen der Bayerischen Akademie der Wissenschaften*
AE.	*Archeológiai Értesitő*
AF.	*Asiatische Forschungen*
AH.	*Archaeologia Hungarica*
AKDM.	*Abhandlungen für die Kunde des Morgenlandes*
ALH.	*Acta Linguistica Academiae Scientiarum Hungaricae*
AM.	*Asia Major*
AO.	*Arkheologicheskie otkrytija*
AOF.	*Altorientalische Forschungen*
AOH.	*Acta Orientalia Academiae Scientiarum Hungaricae*
APAW.	*Abhandlungen der Preussischen Akademie der Wissenschaften*
ASGE.	*Arkheologicheskij sbornik Gos. Ermitazha*
BEFEO.	*Bulletin de l'Ecole Française d'Extrême Orient*
BGA.	Bibliotheca Geographorum Arabicorum
BMFEA.	*Bulletin of the Museum of Far Eastern Antiquities*
BSOAS.	*Bulletin of the School of Oriental and African Studies*
BSOS.	*Bulletin of the School of Oriental Studies*
BZ.	*Byzantinische Zeitschrift*
CAJ.	*Central Asiatic Journal*
GAF.	*Göttinger Asiatische Forschungen*
HJAS.	*Harvard Journal of Asiatic Studies*
JA.	*Journal asiatique*
JRAS.	*Journal of the Royal Asiatic Society*
JSFOu.	*Journal de la Société Finno-ougrienne*
JAOS.	*Journal of the American Oriental Society*
KCsA.	*Kőrösi Csoma Archivum*
KSIA.	*Kratkie soobshchenija Instituta arkheologii Ak. nauk SSSR*
KSIE.	*Kratkie soobshchenija Instituta êtnografii Ak. nauk SSSR*
KSIIMK.	*Kratkie soobshchenija o dokladakh i polevykh issledovanijakh Instituta istorii material'noj kul'tury*
KSINA.	*Kratkie soobshchenija Instituta narodov Azii*
MGM.	Monumenta Germaniae Historica

MGM.AA.	Monumenta Germaniae Historica, Auctores Antiquissimi
MIA.	Materialy i issledovanija po arkheologii SSSR
MRDTB.	*Memoirs of the Research Department of the Toyo Bunko*
MS.	*Monumenta Serica*
MSFOu.	*Mémoires de la Société Finno-ougrienne*
NS.	New Series
NyK.	*Nyelvtudományi Közlemények*
OE.	*Oriens Extremus*
OZ.	*Ostasiatische Zeitschrift*
PPV.	Pamjatniki pis'mennosti Vostoka
RE.	*Realenzyklopädie der klassischen Altertumswissenschaft*, begründet von A.F. von Pauly, neu bearbeitet von G. Wissowa u.a.
SA.	*Sovetskaja Arkheologija*
SE.	*Sovetskaja Êtnografija*
SO.	*Studia Orientalia. Edidit Societas Orientalis Fennica*
SPAW.	*Sitzungsberichte der Preussischen Akademie der Wissenschaften*
SV.	*Sovetskoe vostokovedenija*
TDAYB.	*Türk Dili Arastırmaları Yıllıgı Belleten*
TG.	*The Toyo Gakuho*
TGIM.	*Trudy Gosudarstvennogo istoricheskogo muzeja*
TIE.	Trudy Instituta êtnografii
TIV.	Trudy Instituta vostokovedenija
TP.	*T'oung Pao*
TVOIRAO.	Trudy vostochnago otdêlenija Imperatorskago Russkago Arkheologicheskago Obshchestva
UAJ.	*Ural-Altaische Jahrbücher*
UJ.	*Ungarische Jahrbücher*
UZGLU.	*Uchenye zapiski Leningradskogo gosudarstvennogo universiteta*
VDI.	*Vestnik drevnej istorii*
VI.	*Voprosy istorii*
WZKM.	*Wiener Zeitschrift für die Kunde des Morgenlandes*
ZDMG.	*Zeitschrift der Deutschen Morgenländischen Gesellschaft*
ZIV.	*Zapiski Instituta vostokovedenija Akademii nauk SSSR*
ZS.	*Zentralasiatische Studien*

General

The following, skeletal bibliography is divided into two sections. The first of these lists the very few, and mostly unsuccessful, attempts to present a comprehensive synthesis of Inner Asian history.

The second section presents a selection of works which, for one reason or another, could find no place in the bibliographies of the individual chapters. The

Editor just could not allow this volume to appear with a bibliography in which, for instance, Berthold Laufer's name does not occur. Most of the publications listed in this section deal with cultural rather than historic topics and thus transcend the chronological framework of any single chapter. Also, archeological remains are often attributed without sufficient reason to a people known from written sources. To avoid the perpetuation of such false attributions a selection of such archeological publications are better listed in this general section.

Section 1

Barthold, W., 1935, *12 Vorlesungen über die Geschichte der Türken Mittelasiens*, Deutsche Bearbeitung von Theodor Menzel, (Berlin).

Daffinà, Paolo, 1982, *Il nomadismo centrasiatico*, Parte prima, Istituto dell'India e dell'Asia Orientale, (Roma). The title does not reflect accurately the content of the book which is probably the best and most up-to-date presentation of Inner Asian history and civilization up the end of the Hsiung-nu period.

Deguignes, 1756–8, *Histoire générale des Huns, des Turcs, des Mongols et des autres Tartares occidentaux . . . avant et depuis Jésus-Christ, jusqu'à présent.* I-IV (in 5 volumes), (Paris).

Grousset, René, 1939, *L'Empire des Steppes*, 1939. The English translation by Naomi Walford, *The Empire of the Steppes. A History of Central Asia*, 1970, (Rutgers University Press), very weak on the transliteration of proper names and losing much of the original's superb style, presents the great advantage of having an index.

Hambly, Gavin, editor, 1966, *Zentralasien, Fischer Weltgeschichte*, Band 16. There is an English version: 1969, *Central Asia, Delacorte World History*, volume XVI, (New York).

Geschichte Mittelasiens, 1966, Handbuch der Orientalistik, Erste Abteilung, Fünfter Band, Fünfter Abschnitt, (Leiden). Cf. Haussig 1966, Jettmar 1966, Petech 1966, Spuler 1966.

Haussig, Hans Wilhelm, 1966 "Awaren, Shuan-shuan und Hephthaliten," in *Geschichte Mittelasiens*, pp. 106–23.

1983, *Die Geschichte Zentralasiens und der Seidenstrasse in vorislamischer Zeit*, (Darmstadt).

Jettmar, Karl, 1966, "Mittelasien und Sibirien in Vortürkischer Zeit," in *Geschichte Mittelasiens*, pp. 1–105.

Klaproth, J., 1826, *Tableaux historiques de l'Asie depuis la monarchie de Cyrus jusqu'à nos jours*, (Paris).

Parker, E.H., 1895, *A Thousand Years of the Tartars*, (London). An oft quoted book, to be shunned at all costs.

Petech, Luciano, 1966, "Tibet," in *Geschichte Mittelasiens*, pp. 311–47.

Pletneva, S.A., (Editor), 1981, *Stepi Êvrazii v êpokhu srednevekov'ja*, (Moscow). An archeological approach to the history of Inner Asia from the 5th to the 14th century.

Sinor Denis, 1969, 2nd revised edition 1971, *Inner Asia. History – Civilization – Languages. A Syllabus*, Indiana University Uralic and Altaic Series volume 96. A very skeletal syllabus for college teaching. The first edition – printed from uncorrected proofs – should be avoided.

Spuler, Berthold, 1966, "Geschichte Mittelasiens seit dem Auftreten der Türken," in *Geschichte Mittelasiens*, pp. 123–310.

Visdelou, 1779, *Observations sur ce que les historiens arabes et persiens rapportent de la Chine et de la Tartarie dans la Biliothèque Orientale de Mr d'Herbelot* on pp. 7–366 of d'Herbelot, Bibliothèque orientale, (La Haye).

Section 2

Abramzon, S.M., 1971, *Kirgizy i ikh ėtnogeneticheskie i istoriko-kul'turnye svjazy*, (Leningrad).

Barthold, W., 1968, *Turkestan Down to the Mongol Invasion*, New Edition, (London).

Eberhard, W., 1942a, *Kultur und Siedlung der Randvölker Chinas*, (Leiden). Still very important.

1942b, *Lokalkulturen im alten China*, (Leiden).

1949, *Das Toba-Reich Nordchinas*, (Leiden).

1965, *Conquerors and Rulers. Social Forces in Medieval China*, 2nd, revised edition, (Leiden).

1978, *China und seine westlichen Nachbarn. Beiträge zur mittelalterlichen und neueren Geschichte Zentralasiens*, (Darmstadt).

Gabain, A.v., 1973, *Das Leben im uigurischen Königreich von Qočo (850–1250)*, I–II, Veröffentlichungen der Societas Ural-Altaica, Bd.6, (Wiesbaden).

Jettmar, Karl, 1964, *Die frühen Steppenvölker. Der eurasiatischer Tierstil. Entstehung und sozialer Hintergrund*, Kunst der Welt, (Baden-Baden). [Mainly on Scythians, Sarmatians, and Hsiung-nu. Beautiful illustrations, accurate, selective bibliography.]

Kjuner, N.V., 1961, *Kitajskie izvestija o narodakh Juzhnoj Sibiri, Central'noj Azii i Dal'nego Vostoka*, (Moskva).

Laufer, Berthold, 1914, *Chinese Clay Figures*. Part I, *Prolegomena on the History of Defensive Armor*, Field Museum of Natural History, Publication 177, Anthropological Series XIII, No. 2, (Chicago).

1919, *Sino-Iranica, Chinese Contributions to the History and Civilization in Ancient Iran*, Field Museum Anthropological Series XV, 3, (Chicago).

Liu, Mau-tsai, 1969, *Kutscha und seine Beziehungen zu China vom 2.Jh.v. bis zum 6.Jh.n.Chr.*, I–II, *AF*. 27, (Wiesbaden).

Mahler, Jane Gaston, 1959, *The Westerners Among the Figurines of the T'ang Dynasty of China*, Serie Orientale Roma XX, (Rome).

Miquel, André, 1975, *La géographie humaine du monde musulman jusqu'au milieu du 11e siècle. Géographie arabe et représentation du monde: la terre et l'étranger*, École Pratique des Hautes Étrudes, Civilisations et Sociétés 37, (Paris).

Nowgorodowa, Eleonora, 1980, *Alte Kunst der Mongolei*, (Leipzig). An archeological approach to the history of Mongolia from the Paleolithic to the end of the Türk empire.

Pinks, Elisabeth, 1968, *Die Uiguren von Kan-chou in der frühen Sung-Zeit (960–1028)*, *AF* 24, (Wiesbaden).
Rudenko, S.I., 1969, *Die Kultur der Hsiung-nu und die Hügelgräber von Noin Ula*, Antiquitas Reihe 3, Band 7, (Bonn). An improved version of the Russian original published in 1962. There is no proof that the Noin Ula site belonged to the Hsiung-nu.
1970, *Frozen Tombs of Siberia, the Pazyryk Burials of Iron Age Horsemen*, (University of California Press).
Schafer, Edward H., 1963, *The Golden Peaches of Samarkand. A Study in T'ang Exotics*, (University of California Press).
Zürcher, E., 1959, *The Buddhist Conquest of China. The Spread and Adaptation of Buddhism in Early Medieval China*, (Leiden). Contains many references to Inner Asia.

1. Introduction: the concept of Inner Asia

The following bibliography is divided into two sections. The first gives references to the works cited in the footnotes of Chapter 1. The second contains other references of importance to the subject of the chapter.

Section 1

Boyce, Mary, 1975, *A History of Zoroastrianism*, vol. 1, Handbuch der Orientalistik, Erste Abteilung, 8. Band, Erster Abschnitt, Leiferung 2, Heft 2A (Leiden).
Dawson, Christopher (editor), 1966, *The Mongol Mission*, Harper Torchbook (1966).
Dolgikh, B.O., 1960, *Rodovoj i plemennoj sostav narodov Sibiri v XVII v.*, TIV. 55.
Jagchid, S., 1970, "Trade, Peace and War Between the Nomadic Altaics and the Agricultural Chinese," *Bulletin of the Institute of China Border Studies* 1, pp. 35–80 (Taiwan).
Jagchid, S.–Bawden, C.R., 1965, "Some Notes on the Horse-Policy of the Yüan Dynasty," *CAJ.*, pp. 246–68.
Kothe, Heinz, 1970, "Apollons ethnokulturelle Herkunft," *Klio* 52, pp. 205–30.
Lattimore, Owen, 1938, "The Geographical Factor in Mongol History," *The Geographical Journal* 91, reprinted in Owen Lattimore, *Studies in Frontier History. Collected Papers 1928–1958*, pp. 241–58 (Oxford 1962).
Lechner, Kilian, 1954, *Hellenen und Barbaren im Weltbild der Byzantiner*, (München).
Meserve, Ruth I., 1982, "The Inhospitable Land of the Barbarian," *Journal of Asian History* 16, pp. 51–89.
Meuli, K. 1935, "Scythica," *Hermes* 70, pp. 121–76.
1960, "Scythica Vergiliana. Ethnographisches, Archäologisches und Mythologisches zu Vergils Georgica 3, 367ff.," *Beiträge zur Völkerkunde* (Basel), pp. 88–200.
Moravcsik, Gy.–Jenkins, J.R.H., 1967, *Constantine Porphyrogenitus. De administrando imperio*, new, revised edition (Dumbarton Oaks).

Murphey, Rhoads, 1961, *An Introduction to Geography* (Chicago).
Richard, Jean, 1965, *Simon de Saint-Quentin. Histoire des Tartares* (Paris).
Rossabi, Morris, 1970, "The Tea and Horse Trade with Inner Asia During the Ming," *Journal of Asian History* 4, pp. 136–68.
Serruys, Henry, 1975, *Sino-Mongol Relations during the Ming*. III, *Trade Relations: The Horse Fairs (1400–1600)*, Mélanges chinois et bouddhiques XVII (Bruxelles).
Sinor, Denis, 1946–7, "Autour d'une migration des peuples au Ve siècle," *JA*. pp. 1–78.
1957, "The Barbarians," *Diogenes* 18, pp. 47–60.
1965, "Some Remarks on the Economic Aspects of Hunting in Central Eurasia," in *Die Jagd bei den altaischen Völkern, AF* 26 (Wiesbaden).
1975, "Horse and Pasture in Inner Asian History," *Oriens Extremus* 19, pp. 171–83.
1978, "The Greed of the Northern Barbarian," in *Aspects of Altaic Civilization* II, edited by Larry V. Clark and Paul Alexander Draghi, Indiana University Uralic and Altaic Series, vol. 134, pp. 171–82.
1988, "The Problem of the Ural-Altaic Relationship," in *Handbook of Uralic Studies* edited by Denis Sinor, (Leiden) 1, pp. 706–41.

Section 2

Alföldi, A., 1950, "Die ethische Grenzscheide am römischen Limes," *Schweizer Beiträge zur Allgemeinen Geschichte* 8, pp. 35–50 – the following entry is an English version of the same article:
1952, "The Moral Barrier on Rhine and Danube," in *Congress of Roman Frontier Studies*, edited by E. Birley, pp. 1–16 (Durham).
Grecs et Barbares. Six exposés et discussions, 1961, Entretiens sur l'Antiquité Classique VIII (Genève).
Jagchid, S., 1970, "Trade, Peace and War Between the Nomadic Altaics and the Agricultural Chinese," *Bulletin of the Institute of China Border Studies* 1, pp. 35–80 (Taiwan).
Jones, W.R., 1977, "Le mythe du Barbare à travers l'histoire et la réalité," *Cultures* IV, 2, pp. 104–24.
Khazanov, A.M. 1981a, "Myths and Paradoxes of Nomadism," *Archivum europ. sociol.* 22, pp. 141–53.
1981b "The Early State among the Eurasian Nomads," in *The Study of the State*, edited by Henri J.M. Claessen and Peter Skalnik, pp. 155–75 (The Hague).
1984, *Nomads and the Outside World* (Cambridge).
Lattimore, Owen, 1940, *Inner Asian Frontiers of China*, American Geographical Society, Research Series No. 21 (New York).
Studies in Frontier History. Collected Papers 1928–1958 (Oxford 1962).
Mackinder, H.J., 1904, "The Geographical Pivot of History," *The Geograpical Journal* 23, pp. 424–37.
Sinor, Denis, 1954, "Central Eurasia," in Denis Sinor (editor), *Orientalism and History*, pp. 82–103 (Cambridge), 2nd edition (Bloomington, Indiana), pp. 93–119.

1977, "Le Mongol vu par l'Occident," *1274, Année charnière. Mutations et continuité*, Colloques internationaux du Centre National de la Recherche Scientifique, No. 558, pp. 55–72 (Paris).

2. The geographic setting

Anuchin, V.A., 1948, *Geograficheskie ocherki Man'chzhurii* (Moscow).
Berg, Lev, 1950, *Natural Regions of the USSR*, translated from the Russian by Olga Titelbaum and edited by John A. Morrison (New York).
Borisov, A.A., 1970, *Klimatografija Sovetskogo Sojuza* (Leningrad).
Boulnois, Luce, 1966, *The Silk Road*, translated from the French by Dennis Chamberlain (New York).
Ginsburg, Norton (editor), 1958, *The Pattern of Asia* (Englewood Cliffs, N.J.).
Grigorev, A.A. and Budyko, M.I., 1960, "Classification of the Climates of the U.S.S.R.," *Soviet Geography* 1, pp. 3–23.
Hooson, David, 1966, *The Soviet Union: People and Regions* (Belmont, CA.).
Huntington, Ellsworth, 1917, *Pulse of Asia* (Boston).
Institute of Geography, U.S.S.R., Academy of Sciences, 1969, *The Physical Geography of China*, translated from the Russian, 2 volumes (New York).
Koeppen, W. and Geiger, R., 1930, *Handbuch der Klimatologie*, 4 volumes (Berlin).
Lattimore, Owen, 1940, *Inner Asian Frontiers of China*, American Geographical Society Research Series No. 21 (New York).
Lydolph, Paul, 1970, *Geography of the U.S.S.R.*, 2nd edition (New York).
Meigs, Peveril, 1953, "World Distribution of Arid and Semi-Arid Homoclimates," in *Arid Zone Hydrology*, pp. 202–10 (Paris, UNESCO).
Murzaev, E.M., 1954, *Die Mongolische Volksrepublik: Physisch-geographische Beschreibung*, translated from the Russian (Gotha).
1958, *Srednjaja Azija* (Moscow).
1966, *Priroda Sin'czjana i formirovanie pustyn' Central'noj Azii*, (Moscow).
Petrov, M.P., 1966, *Pustyni Central'noj Azii*, 2 volumes (Moscow).
1973, *Pustyni Zemnogo Shara* (Leningrad).
Pounds, Norman, J.G., 1961, "Land Use on the Hungarian Plains," in Norman J.G. Pounds (editor), *Geographical Essays on Eastern Europe*, Indiana University Russian and East European Series vol. 24, pp. 54–74 (Bloomington, Indiana).
Suslov, S.P., 1961, *Physical Geography of Asiatic Russia*, translated from the Russian by Noah Gershevsky and edited Joseph Williams (San Francisco).
Wang, Chi-wu, 1961, *The Forests of China with a Survey of Grassland and Desert Vegetation* (Cambridge, Mass.).
Wernstedt, Frederick V., 1972, *World Climatic Data*, vol. IV (Lemans, PA.).

Atlases

Academy of Sciences, U.S.S.R., 1974, *Fiziko-geograficheskij atlas mira* (Moscow).
Basilevich, K.V., et al. (editors), 1950, *Atlas istorii SSSR*, vol. 1 (Moscow).
Hsieh, Chiao-min, 1973, *Atlas of China* (New York).

Institut êtnografii, Academy of Sciences U.S.S.R., 1964, *Atlas geograficheskikh otkrytii v Sibiri i severo-zapadnoj Amerike XVII–XVIII vv.* (Moscow).

3. Inner Asia at the dawn of history

The references provided by the deceased author refer to the sources used to write his chapter but do not provide sufficient information for further readings. Because of the vastness of the subject, a complete bibliography would have to include, at the very least, several hundred references. For a serious study the volumes so far published of the *Sovetskaja arkheologicheskaja literatura* are indispensable. They are: 1941–57 (Moskva, 1959); 1958–62 (Leningrad, 1969); 1963–7 (Leningrad, 1975); 1968–72 (Leningrad, 1980); 1973–5 (Leningrad, 1983); 1976–8 (Leningrad, 1986).

The somewhat dated collective work edited by P.N. Tret'jakov and A.L. Mongajt, *Pervobytno-obshchinnyj stroj i drevnejshie gosudarstva na territorii SSSR*, (Moskva, 1956) which is the first volume of the great synthesis of the history of the USSR, *Ocherki istorii SSSR*, is still useful; the ideological bias can easily be detected. The relevant chapters of V.M. Masson–V.I. Sarianidi, 1972, Frumkin, 1970, Belenitsky (= Belenickij), 1968, or Jettmar, 1966 are important not only on account of their being written in a language other than Russian, but, also, the first three of these deal with the southern regions of Inner Asia, somewhat short-changed in Professor Okladnikov's chapter in which heavy emphasis is given to the northern and eastern parts of Inner Asia.

In the following bibliography the editor has introduced a few works which either were published after the author completed his manuscript, or which were considered particularly suitable for further reading. These additions are marked with an asterisk *. It is hoped that some personal comments, given in [ ] square brackets will be helpful. [D.S.]

Adamenko, O.M., 1970, "O geologicheskikh nizhnepaleoliticheskikh orudijakh na r. Ulalinke (g. Gorno-Altajsk)," in: *Sibir' i ee sosedi v drevnosti*, (Novosibirsk), pp. 57–62.

**Arkheologicheskie pamjatniki Jakutii, bassejny Aldana i Olekmy*, 1983, edited by Mochanov, Ju.A., (Novosibirsk). [Important, recent publication.]

*Belenitsky (= Belenickij), Aleksandr, 1968, *Central Asia*. Translated from the Russian by James Hogarth (Geneva). [Only some parts relevant to this chapter.]

Chard, C.S. 1958a, "An Outline of the Prehistory of Siberia. Pt. I. The Pre-Metal Periods," *Southwestern Journal of Anthropology* 14.

1958b, "The Oldest Sites of Northeastern Siberia," *American Antiquity* 21, No. 4.

Chernecov, V.N. 1953, *Drevnjaja istorija Nizhnego Priob'ja*, MIA 35.

Chernikov, S.S., 1949, *Drevnjaja metallurgija i gornoe delo Zapadnogo Altaja* (Alma-Ata).

1960, *Vostochnoj Kazakhstan v êpokhu bronzy*, MIA 88.

Chlenova, N.L., 1962, "Ob olennykh kamnjakh Mongolii i Sibiri," *Mongol'skij arkheologicheskij sbornik* (edited by S.V. Kiselev), (Moskva), pp. 27–35. [The same topic was studied more in detail by the same author in "Skifskij olen'," MIA 115 (1962), pp. 167–203. See also Jacobson 1983.]

1964, "Karasukskaja kul'tura v Juzhnoj Sibiri," in *Drevnjaja Sibir* (Ulan-Udê), pp. 263–78.

1972, **Khronologija pamjatnikov karasukskoj êpokhi* (Moskva).

Coon, C.S., 1951, *Cave Exploration in Iran 1949*, University Museum, University of Pennsylvania (Philadelphia).

*Debec, G.F., 1948, *Paleoantropologija SSSR*, Trudy Instituta êtnografii AN SSSR, Novaja serija IV.

1956, "Problema proiskhozhdenija kirgizskogo naroda v svete antropologicheskikh dannykh," *Trudy kirgizskoj arkheologo-êtnograficheskoj êkspedicii* I, pp. 3–17.

Derevjanko, A.P., 1970a, Gromatukhskaja kul'tura, In: *Sibir i ee sosedi v drevnosti* (Novosibirsk).

1969, "The Novopetrovka Blade Culture on the Middle Amur," *Arctic Anthropology*, No. 1, pp. 119–127.

1970b, *Novopetrovskaja kul'tura Srednego Amura* (Novosibirsk).

Derevjanko, A.P.–Okladnikov A.P., 1969, "Drevnie kul'tury vostochnykh rajonov MNP (k itogam arkheologicheskikh issledovanij 1949 i 1967 gg.)," *SA* 1969, 4, pp. 141–56.

Dikov, N.N., 1958, *Bronzovyj vek Zabajkal'ja* (Ulan-Udê).

1964, "Kamennyj vek Kamchatki i Chukotki v svete novejshikh arkheologicheskikh dannykh," in *Istorija i kul'tura narodov severo-vostoka SSSR* (Magadan). [There is an English version: *"The Stone Age of Kamchatka and the Chukchi Peninsula in the Light of New Archaeological Data," *Arctic Anthropology* (1965), 3, No. 1, pp. 10–25.]

*1977, *Arkheologicheskie pamjatniki Kamchatki, Chukotki i Verkhnej Kolymy. Azija na styke s Amerikoj v drevnosti* (Moskva). [With English table of contents.]

*1979, *Drevnie kul'tury Severo Vostochnoj Azii* (Moskva). [Continuation of Dikov 1977, with English table of contents.]

Fedoseeva, S.A., 1968, *Drevnie kul'tury verkhnogo Viljuja* (Moskva).

*Frumkin, Grégoire, 1970, *Archaeology in Soviet Central Asia* (Leiden, Brill). [Only some parts relevant to this chapter.]

Garrod, D.A.–Bate, D.M., 1937, *The Stone Age of Mount Carmel* (Oxford).

Gerasimov, M.M., 1958, "Mal'ta, paleoliticheskaja Mal'ta (raskopki 1956–1957 gg.)," *SE*. 1958, 3.

Griffin, J.B., 1960, "Some Prehistoric Connections Between Siberia and America," *Science* 131, pp. 801–12.

Grjaznov, M.P. 1929, "Bronzovyj kinzhal s ozera Kotokel'," *Burjatievedenie* 9–10 (Verkhneudinsk).

1952, "Pamjatniki karasukskogo êtapa v Central'nom Kazakhstane," *SA*. 1952, 12.

1956, *Istorija drevnykh plemen Verkhnej Obi*, MIA 48.

1961, *Drevnjaja bronza minusinskikh stepej*, Trudy otdela istorii pervobytnoj kul'tury Gos. Ermitazha, I (Leningrad).

Grjaznov, M.P.–Shnejder, E.R., 1929, "Drevnie izvajanija minusinskikh stepej," *Materialy po Etnografii*, tom 4, vyp. 2.

Guljamov, Ja.G.–Islamov, C.–Askarov A., 1966, *Pervobytnaja kul'tura i vozniknovenie oroshaemogo zemledelija v nizov'jakh Zaravshana* (Tashkent).

Istorija Sibiri, 1968, I, *Drevnjaja Sibir* (Leningrad).

*Jacobson, Esther, 1983, "Siberian Roots of the Scythian Stag Image," *Journal of Asian History* 17, pp. 68–120.

*Jettmar, Karl, 1966, "Mittelasien und Sibirien in Vortürkischer Zeit," in *Geschichte Mittelasiens, Handbuch der Orientalistik* edited by Bertold Spuler, Erste Abteilung, 5. Bd., 5. Abschnitt, pp. 1–105.

Kiselev, S.V., 1950, *Drevnjaja istorija Juzhnoj Sibiri* (Moskva).

Klapchuk, I.N., 1970, "Galechnye orudija mestonakhozhdenija Muzbel' 1–2 v Central'nom Kazakhstane," in: *Po sledam drevnikh kul'tur Kazakhstana* (Alma-Ata), pp. 217–26.

Krader, L. 1952, "Neolithic Finds in the Chukchi Peninsula," *American Antiquity* Vol. 3.

Krivcova-Grakova, O.A., 1952, "Alekseevskoe poselenie i mogilnik," *TGIM* 17, pp. 57–172.

Larichev, V.E., 1969, *Paleolit Severnoj, Central'noj i Vostochnoj Azii*, I (Novosibirsk).

Maksimenkov, G.A., "Okunevskaja kul'tura v Juzhnoj Sibiri," in *Novoe v Sovetskoj arkheologii* (Moskva), pp. 168–74.

Maringer, J., 1950, *Contribution to the Prehistory of Mongolia*, The Sino-Swedish Expedition, Publication 34 (Stockholm).

Martynov, A.I., 1964, "Andronovskaja kul'tura," in *Drevnjaja Sibir*, first version of *Istorija Sibiri* (Ulan-Udê), pp. 249–61.

*Masson, V.M.–Sarianidi, V.I., 1972, *Central Asia. Turkmenia Before the Achaemenids* (London).

Matjushchenko, V.I.–Lozhnikova, G.B., 1969, Raskopki mogil'nika u derevni Rostovka bliz Omska v 1966–1969 gg. Predvaritel'noe soobshchenie," in *Iz istorii Sibiri* (Tomsk).

Medoedov, A.G., 1970, "Arealy paleoliticheskikh kul'tur Sary-Arka," in: *Po sledam drevnikh kul'tur Kazakhstana* (Alma-Ata), pp. 200–16.

Mochanov, Ju.A., 1969a, *Mnogoslojnaja stojanka Bel'kachi 1 i periodizacija kamennogo veka Jakutii* (Moskva).

1969b *"The Early Neolithic of the Aldan," and "The Bel'kachinsk Culture on the Aldan," *Arctic Anthropology* 6, no. 1, pp. 95–103 and 104–14.

Movius, H.L. 1944, "Early Man and Pleistocene Stratigraphy in Southern and Eastern Asia," *Papers of the Peabody Museum of American Archaeology and Ethnography*, vol. XIX, No. 3.

*1953, "Palaeolithic and Mesolithic Sites in Soviet Central Asia," *Proceedings of the American Philosophical Society* 94, No. 4, pp. 383–421.

Novgorodova, E.A., 1969, *Central'naja Azija i Karasukskaja problema* (Moskva).

Okladnikov, A.P., 1946, 1950, 1955, *Lenskie drevnosti*, I, II, III, (Jakutsk; vol. III, Leningrad).

1949a, "Issledovanija must'erskoj stojanki i pogrebenija neandertal'ca v grote Teshik-Tash Juzhnyj Uzbekistan (Srednjaja Azija)," in: *Teshik-Tash* (Moskva), pp. 7–85.

1949b, *Istorija Jakutii* (Jakutsk), 2nd edition Moskva 1955. [See also English version, 1970.]

1950, *Neolit i bronzovyj vek Pribajkal'ja*, MIA. 18.

1951, "Novye dannye po drevnejshej istorii Mongolii," *VDI*, 1951, 4, pp. 162–74.

1954, "Olennyj kamen' s r. Ivolgi," *SA*. 19, pp. 207–20.
1956, "Ancient Cultures and Cultural and Ethnic Relations on the Pacific Coast of North Asia," *Proceedings of the Thirty-Second International Congress of Americanists* (Copenhagen).
1957, "Iz istorii êtnicheskikh i kul'turnykh svjazej neoliticheskikh plemen srednego Eniseja," *SA* 1957, l. pp. 26–55.
1959a, *Dalekoe proshloe Primor'ja* (Vladivostok).
1959b, "Tripody za Bajkalom," *SA* 1959, 3, pp. 114–36.
1959c, *Ancient Populations of Siberia and its Cultures*, Russian Translation Series of the Peabody Museum of Archaeology and Ethnology, vol. 1 (Cambridge, Mass.).
1961, "Khodzhikentskaja peshchera – novyj pamjatnik Uzbekistana," *KSIA* 82, pp. 68–76.
1962, "Paleoliticheskie nakhodki v rajone Orok-Nor," *Materialy po istorii i filologii Central'noj Azii* (Ulan-Udê), Serija vostokovedenija vyp. 8, pp. 169–75. [English version: Okladnikov, 1965b.]
1963, *Drevnee poselenie na poluostrove Peschanom u Vladivostoka*, MIA 112.
1964a, "K voprosu drevnejshej istorii Mongolii. Pervobytnaja Mongolija," *Studia Archaeologica* (Ulan Bator) t. 3, fasc. 8.
1964b, *O pervonachal'nom zaselenii chelovekom Sibiri i novykh nakhodkakh paleolita na reke Zee* (Moskva). English version published simultaneously in Moscow: *The Peopling* [sic!] *of Siberia and New Paleolithic Finds at the Zea River*.
1965a, *Petroglify Angary* (Moskva–Leningrad).
1965b, "Paleolithic Finds in the Region of Orok-Nor," *Arctic Anthropology*, 3, No. 1, pp. 142–5. [See Above, 1962.]
1966, "K voprosu o mezolite i êpipaleolite aziatskoj chasti SSSR," in MIA. 126.
"Arkheologija Doliny Zei i Srednego Amura," *SA*, 1966, 1, pp. 32–41.
1966b, "Drevnee poselenie na r. Tadushi u der. Ustinovka i problema dal'nevostochnogo mezolita (v svjazi i raskopkami 1964 g.)," in: *Chetvertichnyj period Sibiri*, (Moskva), pp. 352–72.
1966c, "Poselenie u s. Voznesenovka vblizi ust'ja r. Khungari," *AO* 1966, pp. 175–8.
1966d, "Central'no-Aziatskoj ochag pervobitnogo iskusstva (k itogam Sovetsko-mongol'skoj arkheologicheskoj êkspedicii 1966 g.)," *Vestnik Akademii Nauk SSSR*, 1966, pp. 96104.
1969a, *Liki drevnego Amura* (Novosibirsk).
1969b, "Ulalinka – drevnejshee paleoliticheskoe mestonakhozhdenie Sibiri," *AO*, 1969, pp. 185–6.
1969c, "Ancient Cultures in the Continental Part of North-East Asia," *Actas del XXXIII Congreso Internacional de Americanistas* (San José de Costa Rica).
1970, *Yakutia Before its Incorporation into the Russian State*, Arctic Institute of North America, Anthropology of the North. Translations from Russian Sources, editor Henry N. Michael, No. 8, (Montreal). [Translation of the second edition (1955) of Okladnikov 1949b.]

Okladnikov, A.P.–Derevjanko, A.P., 1968, "Paleolit Dal'nego Vostoka (tipologija i stratigrafija)," Problemy izuchenija chetvertichnogo perioda. Tezisi (Khabarovsk).

1969, "Paleolit Amura," *Izvestija Sibirskogo otdelenija AN SSSR*, 1969, No. 1, p. 1.
Okladnikov, A.P.–Kirilov, I.I., 1968, "Paleoliticheskoe poselenie v Sokhatno (Titovskaja sopka)," *Izvestija Sibirskogo Otdelenija AN SSSR*, serija oshchestvennykh nauk, No. 6, pp. 111–14.
Okladnikov, A.P.–Troickij, S.L. 1967, "K izucheniju chetvertichnykh otlozhenij i paleolita Mongolii," *Bjulleten komissii po izucheniju chetvertichnogo perioda*, No. 33, pp. 4–30.
Okladnikov, A.P.–Zaporozhskaja, V.D., 1970, *Petroglify Zabajkal'ja*, I–II (Leningrad).
Ranov, V.A., 1970, "Galechnaja tekhnika v kul'turakh kamennogo veka Sibiri i Srednej Azii," in: *Sibir' i ee sosedi v drevnosti*, edited by V.E. Larichev (Novosibirsk), pp. 17–26.
Rudenko, S.I. 1947, *Drevnjaja kul'tura Beringova morja i êskimosskaja problema* (Moskva–Leningrad). [English translation: 1961.]
1961, *The Ancient Culture of the Bering Sea and the Eskimo Problem*, translated by Paul Tolstoy. Arctic Institute of North America, Anthropology of the North. Translation from Russian Sources, editor Henry N. Michael, No. 1 (Montreal).
Sorokin, V.S., 1962 *Mogil'nik bronzovoj êpokhi Tasty-butak 1 v Zapadnom Kazakhstane*, MIA 120.
Sosnovskij, G.P., 1941, "Plitochnye mogily Zabajkal'ja," *Trudy Otdela istorii pervobytnogo obshchestva. Gos. Ermitazh*, I, pp. 273–309.
Teploukhov, S.A., 1927, "Drevnie pogrebenija v Minusinskom krae," *Materialy po êtnografii*, vyp. 2–3.
Tolstov, S.P., 1948, *Drevnij Khorezm* (Moskva).
Vadeckaja, E.B. 1967, *Drevnie ljudi Eniseja* (Leningrad).
Vasil'evskij, R.S., 1961, "Drevnjaja korjakskaja kul'tura (po arkheologicheskim raskopkam na Okhotskom poberezh'e)," in *Voprosy istorii Sibiri i Dal'nego Vostoka. Trudy konferencii po istorii Sibiri i Dal'nego Vostoka. [. . .] Mart 1960* (Novosibirsk), pp. 321–5.
Volkov, V.V., 1967, *Bronzovyj i rannyj zheleznyj vek Severnoj Mongolii* (Ulan-Bator).

4. The Scythians and Sarmatians

Scythian historiography began with Herodotus; no other Inner Asian people has been dealt with so often and in so much detail in European scholarship. Denis Sinor, *Introduction à l'étude de l'Eurasie Centrale* (Wiesbaden 1963), pp. 210–15 gives useful, commented data on the secondary literature up to, approximately, 1962. The testimony of the written sources must be completed by archeological data to which the volumes so far published of the *Sovetskaja arkheologicheskaja literatura* give limited access. They are: 1941–57 (Moskva, 1959); 1958–62 (Leningrad, 1969); 1963–7 (Leningrad, 1975); 1968–72 (Leningrad, 1980); 1973–5 (Leningrad, 1983); 1976–8 (Leningrad, 1986). However, this excellent bibliography lists only Soviet works, and is of no help for tracing Hungarian and Romanian publications. See e.g. Párducz 1941–50, Roska, 1937, Fettich, 1931.

The principal written source on the Scythians is Book IV of Herodotus. Most of the commentaries on this famous work are just about useless, woefully inadequate in what touches Inner Asia. Dovatur et al., 1982, and Rybakov, 1979 (see below) are important

steps in the right direction. The former book contains the original text, translation and commentary of the Herodotian passages dealing with Inner Asia. Nejkhardt, 1982, contains much useful and relevant information. To familiarize oneself with the Classical references to the Scythians, one may turn to the articles "Skythen" in *Ebert Reallexikon der Vorgeschichte* (XII, 1928, pp. 230–51) and K. Kretschmer, "Scythae", in Pauly-Wissowa, *Realencyclopaedie der Altertumswissenschaften* (2e Reihe, II, 1923, pp. 923–46). The oft-quoted work of Tomaschek, 1888, is basically flawed.

In the following bibliography the editor introduced a few works which either appeared after the author completed her manuscript, or which were considered particularly suitable for further reading. These additions are marked with an asterisk *.

Abaev, V.I., 1949, *"Skifskij jazyk," [The Scythian Language], in: *Osetinskij jazyk i fol'klor* I, pp. 147–244 (Moscow).

1965, *Skifo-evropejskie izoglossy*, [Scythian-European Isoglosses] (Moscow).

Abramova, M.P., 1952, "Kul'tura sarmatskikh plemen II v. do n.ê.–I v. n.ê.," [The Culture of the Sarmatian Tribes from the 2nd century B.C. to the 1st century A.D.], *SA*, 1959, 1, pp. 52–71.

Anokhin, V.A., 1965, "Monety skifskogo carja Atei," [The Coins of the Scythian King Atheas], *Numizmatika i sfragristika* (Kiev), 2, pp. 3–15.

Artamonov, M.I., 1949, "Etnogeografija Skifii" [The ethno-geography of Scythia], *UZLGU*, issue 13, No. 85, pp. 129–71.

1950, "K voprosu o proiskhozhdenii skifov" [On the question of the Origin of the Scythians], *VDI* 2, pp. 37–47.

1966, *Sokrovishcha skifskikh kurganov* [Treasures of Scythian Kurgans], (Praha–Leningrad).

1972, "Skifskoe carstvo" [The Scythian Kingdom], *SA*, 1972, 3.

*Balcer, Jack M., 1972, "The Date of Herodotus IV. l. Darius' Scythian Expedition," *Harvard Studies in Classical Philology* 76, pp. 99–132.

Bongard-Levin, G.M.–Grantovskij E.A., 1974, *Ot Skifii do Indii. Zagadki istorii drevnikh ariev* [From Scythia to India. Riddle of the History of the Ancient Aryans] (Moscow).

Brashinskij, I.B.–Marchenko, K.K. 1980, "Elizavetovskoe gorodishche na Donu – poselenie gorodskogo tipa," [Elizavetovskoe Gorodishche – a settlement of urban type], *SA*, 1980, 1, pp. 211–18.

Chernenko, E.V., 1968, *Skifskii dospekh* [Scythian armor] (Kiev).

1981, *Skifskie luchniki* [Scythian archers] (Kiev).

*Diakonoff, I.M. 1981, "The Cimmerians," *Acta Iranica*, 2nd Series, vol. VII, pp. 103–40. [Very important.]

"Diskussionye problemy otechestvennoj skifologii" [Debatable Problems Concerning the Native Land of the Scythians], 1980, *Narody Azii i Afriki* 5, pp. 102–30 and 6, pp. 67–102.

*Dovatur, A.I.–Kallistov, D.P.–Shisova, I.A., 1982, *Narody nashej strany v "Istorii" Gerodota* [The peoples of our land in the "Histories" of Herodotus] (Moscow).

Drevnosti stepnoj Skifii, 1982 [Antiquities of the Scythian Steppes) (Kiev).

*N. Fettich, 1931, "Bestand der skythischen Altertümer Ungarns," in Rostovcev, 1931, pp. 494–529.

Galanina, L.K., 1980, *Kurdzhipskij kurgan* [The Kurkzhipsk Kurgan] (Leningrad).
Grakov, B.N., 1947, "Perezhitki matriarkhata u sarmatov" [Survivals of matriarchate among the Sarmatians] *VDI*, 3.
1954, *Kemenskoe gorodishche na Dnepre*, [The Kamenskoe Gorodishche on the Dnieper], MIA, 36.
1971, *Skify* [The Scythians] (Moscow).
Il'inskaja, V.A., 1966, "Skifskie kurgany okolo g. Borispolja", [Scythian kurgans near Borispol], *SA*. 1966, 3, pp. 152–71.
1968, *Skify dneprovskogo lesostepnogo Levoberezh'ja* [The Scythians of the Forest-Steppe on the Left Bank of the Dnieper], (Kiev).
1975, *Ranneskifskie kurgany bassejna r. Tjasmin* [Early Scythian Kurgans from the Tasmin Basin] (Kiev).
Jacenko, I.V., 1959, *Skifija VII–V vv. do n.ê.* [Scythia in the 7th to 5th centuries B.C.], (Kiev).
Jakovenko, E.V., 1974, *Skifi Skhidnogo Krimu v V–III st. do n.ê.*, [The Scythians of East Crimea in the 5th–3rd Centuries B.C.] (Kiev).
*Jettmar, Karl, 1964, *Die frühen Steppenvölker. Der eurasiatischer Tierstil. Entstehung und sozialer Hintergrund*, Kunst der Welt (Baden-Baden). [Mainly on Scythians, Sarmatians, and Hsiung-nu. Beautiful illustrations, accurate, selective bibliography.]
Khazanov, A.M., 1971, *Ocherki voennogo dela sarmatov* [Essays on the Military Affairs of the Scythians] (Moscow).
1975, *Social'naja istorija skifov*, [A Social History of the Scythians] (Moscow). [There is an English resume on pp. 334–41.]
Kovpanenko, G.T., 1967, *Pam'jatki skif'skogo chasu v basejni Vorskla* [Sites of the Scythian Period in the Vorskla Basin] (Kiev).
1981, *Kurgany ranneskifskogo vremeni v bassejne r. Ros*, [Kurgans of the Early Scythian Period in the Vorskla Basin] (Kiev).
Latyshev, V.V. 1893–1947, *Izvestija drevnikh pisatelej grecheskikh i latinskikh o Skifii i Kavkaze = Scythica et Caucasica e veteribus scriptoribus graecis et latinis*, I. *Scriptores Graeci* (Sanktpeterburg 1893), II. *Scriptores Latini*, 1–2 (Sankpeterburg 1904–1906), III. "Izvestija drevnikh pisatelej o skifii i Kavkaze," *VDI* 4 (1947), pp. 230–348.
Leskov, A.M., 1974, *Die skythischen Kurgane, Zeitschrift für Archäologie und Urgeschichte* 5 (special edition).
1981, *Kurgany: nakhodki, problemy* [Kurgans: Finds and Problems] (Leningrad).
Liberov, P.D., 1965, *Pamjatniki skifskogo vremeni na Severnom Donu* [Sites of the Scythian Period in the North Don area] (Moscow).
Maksimova, M.I., 1954, "Serebrjanoe zerkalo iz Kelermesa" [A Silver Mirror from Kelermes] *SA*, 21, pp. 281–305.
Mancevich, A.P., 1964, "O plastine iz kurgana Karagodeuashkh" [On the Plate from the Karagodeuashkh Kurgan], *ASGE*. 6, pp. 128–38.
1966, "Derevjannye sosudy skifskoj êpokhi," *ASGE*. 8, pp. 23–38.
Machinskij, D.A., 1972, "O vremeni pervogo aktivnogo vystuplenija sarmatov v Pridneprov'e po svidetel'stvam antichnykh pis'mennykh istochnikov" [On the Time of the First Active Appearance of the Sarmatians in the Dnieper Area, According to the Testimony of Ancient Written Sources], *ASGE*. 13, pp. 30–54.

*Meuli, K., 1935, "Scythica," *Hermes* 70, pp. 121–76.
Meljukova, A.I., 1964, *Vooruzhenie skifov*, [The Arms of the Scythians], *Arkheologija SSSR. Svod arkheologicheskikh istochnikov*, D 1–4, (Moscow).
1979, *Skifija i frakijskij mir* [Scythia and the Thracian World] (Moscow).
1981, *Krasnokutskij kurgan* [The Krasnokutsk Kurgan] (Moscow).
*Minns, E.H., 1913. *Scythians and Greeks. A Survey of Ancient History and Archaeology on the North Coast of the Euxine from the Danube to the Caucasus* (Cambridge).
Moshkova, M.G., 1963, *Pamjatniki prokhorvskoj kul'tury* [Sites of the Prokhorovka Culture] (Moscow).
1974, *Proiskhozhdenie rannesarmatskoj (prokhorovskoj) kul'tury* [The Origins of Early Sarmatian (Prokhorovka) Culture] (Moscow).
Mozolev'skij, B.M., 1979, *Tovstva Mogila* [The Tovsta Burial Mound] (Kiev).
*Nejkhardt, A.A., 1982, *Skifskij rasskaz Gerodota v otechestvennoj istoriografii* [The Scythian Account of Herodotus in Soviet historiography] (Leningrad).
Onajko, N.A., 1966, *Antychnij import v Pridneprov'e i Pobuzh'e v VII–V vv. do n.ê.* [Ancient Imports into the Dnieper and Bug areas in the 7th to 5th centuries B.C.] (Moscow).
1970, *Antychnij import v Pridneprov'e i Pobuzh'e v IV–III vv. do n.ê.*, [Ancient imports into the Dnieper and Bug Areas in the 4th to 3rd centuries B.C.] (Moscow).
**Or des Scythes, Trésors des Musées Soviétiques*, 1975 (Paris).
*Párducz, M. 1941–50, *Denkmäler der Sarmatenzeit in Ungarn*, *AAH*, vols. XXV, XXVIII, XXX.
Petrenko, V.G., 1967, *Pravoberezh'e Srednego Pridneprov'ja v V–III do n.ê* [The Right Bank of the Middle Dnieper in the 5th to 3rd centuries B.C.] (Moscow).
1978, *Ukrashenija Skifii v VII–III vv. do n.ê* [Ornaments of Scythia in the 7th to 3rd Centuries B.C.] *Arkheologija SSSR. Svod arkheologicheskikh istochnikov*, D 4–5 (Moscow).
Piotrovskij, B.B., 1954, "Skify i Drevnij Vostok" [The Scythians and the Ancient East], *SA*, 19.
Pogrebova, N.N., 1958, "Pozdneskifskie gorodishcha na Nizhnem Dnepre" [Late Scythian Sites in the Lower Dnieper Area], MIA, 64, pp. 103–247.
1961, "Pogrebenija v mavzolee Neapolja skifskogo" [Burials in the Mausoleum at Scythian Neapolis], MIA, 96, pp. 103–213.
Pokrovskaja, E.F., 1955, "Melitopol'skij skifskij kurgan" [The Melitopol Scythian Kurgan], *VDI*, 2, pp. 191–9.
*Potratz, A.H., 1963, *Die Skythen in Südrussland* (Basel).
Pridik, E.M., 1914, "Mel'gunovskij klad 1763 g." [The Melgun Treasure of 1763], *Materialy po arkheologii Rossii* (St. Petersburg).
Problemy skifskoj arkheologii, 1970 [Problems of Scythian Archeology] (Moscow).
Raevskij, D.S., 1977, *Ocherki ideologii skifo-sakskikh plemen* [Essays on the ideology of Scytho-Sacian Tribes] (Moscow).
Rikman, E.A., 1975, *Pamjatniki sarmatov i plemen chernjakhovskoj kul'tury* [Sites of the Sarmatians and of the Tribes of the Chernjakhiv Culture] (Kishinev).
Rolle, Renate, *1979, *Totenkult der Skythen*, I–II, Vorgeschichtliche Forschungen Bd. 18 (Berlin–New York).

1980, *Die Welt der Skythen* (Luzern, Frankfurt a.M.).
*Roska, Martin von, 1937, "Der Bestand der skytischen Altertümer Siebenbürgens," *Eurasia Septentrionalis Antiqua*, 11, pp. 167–203.
Rostovcev, M.I. 1918, *Ellinstvo i iranstvo ne juge Rossii* [Hellenism and Iranism in South Russia], (Petrograd) = Rostovcev 1922.
*1922 [Rostovtzef], *Iranians and Greeks in South Russia*, (Oxford).
1925, *Skifija i Bospor* (Leningrad). = Rostovcev 1931.
*1931, *Skythien und der Bosporus*. 1, *Kritische Übersicht der schriftlichen und archäologischen Quellen* (Berlin).
Rutkivs'ka, L.M., 1969, "Kochovki ta zemlerobi na territorii stepovoj Ukraini v seredini I tysjacholittja n.ê" [Nomads and Agriculturalists on the Territory of the Ukrainian Steppes in the Middle of the 1st Millenium A.D.], *Arkheologija* (Kiev), 22, pp. 149–60.
Rybakov, B.A., 1979, *Gerodotova Skifija* [The Scythia of Herodotus] (Moscow).
Shelov, D.B., 1965, "Car Atei" [King Atheas], *Numizmatika i sfragistika* (Kiev), 2, pp. 16–40.
Shilov, B.P., 1961, "Raskopki Elizabetovskogo mogil'nika v 1959 g." [The 1959 Excavations of the Elizavetovskij burial], *SA*, 1961, 1, pp. 150–68,
Shramko, B.A. 1962, *Drevnosti Severskogo Donca* [Antiquities of the Severskij Donec Area] (Kharkov).
1975, "Nekotorye itogi raskopok Bel'skogo gorodishcha i gelono-budinskaja problema" [Some results of the excavations at Belsk Gorodishche and the Geloni-Budini Problem], *SA*, 1975, 1, pp. 65–84.
Shul'c, P.N. 1946, "Skul'pturnye portrety skifskikh carej" [Sculptural portraits of Scythian Kings] *KSIIMK*, 12, pp. 44–56.
1967, "Skifskie izvajanija Severnogo Prichernomor'ja" [Scythian Sculptures of the Northern Black Sea Area], *Antichnoe obshchesvto* (Moscow), pp. 225–36.
Skifskie drevnosti, 1973 [Scythian Antiquities] (Kiev).
Skifo-sibirskij zvernyj stil' v iskusstve narodov Evrazii, 1976 [The Scytho-Siberian Animal Style in the Art of the Peoples of Eurasia] (Moscow).
Skify i sarmaty, 1977 [The Scythians and Sarmatians] (Kiev).
Skifskij mir, 1975 [The Scythian World] (Kiev).
Skifija i Kavkaz, 1980 [Scythia and the Caucasus] (Kiev).
Smirnov, K.F., 1961, *Vooruzhenie savromatov* [The Arms of the Sauromatae] MIA, 101.
1974, *Savromaty* [The Sauromatae] (Moscow).
1975, *Sarmaty na Ilek*, [The Sarmatians on the Ilek], (Moscow).
1977, "Savromaty i Sarmaty", [The Sauromatae and the Sarmatians," *Problemy arkheologii Evraziii i Severnoj Ameriki*, (Moscow), pp. 129–138.
*Sulimirski, T., 1970, *The Sarmatians* (London).
*1981, "The Scyths," in *The Cambridge History of Iran* vol. 2 (edited by Ilya Gershevitch), pp. 149–99.
*Szemerényi, Oswald, 1980, "Four Old Iranian Ethnic Names: Scythian – Skudra – Sogdian – Saka," *Sitzungsberichte der Österreichischen Ak. d. Wiss. Phil. -hist. Kl*. 371 = *Veröffentlichungen der iranischen Kommission*, Bd. 9, (Wien). [On the wider geographic distribution of the Scythians.]
Terenozhkin, A.I., 1961, *Predskifskij period na dneprovskom Pravoberezh'e* [The Pre-

Scythian Period on the Right Bank of the Dnieper] (Kiev).
1966, "Ob obshchestvennom stroe skifov" [About the Social System of the Scythians], *SA*, 1966, 2, pp. 33–49.
1971, *Kimmeriicy* [The Cimmerians] (Kiev).
*Tomaschek, W., 1888, "Kritik der ältesten Nachrichten über den skythischen Norden," *Sitzungsberichte der Wiener Akademie der Wissenschaften*, 116, pp. 715–80; 117, pp. 1–70. [This oft-cited work is now completely outdated.]
Vinogradov, V.B., 1963. *Sarmaty Severo-Vostochnogo Kavkaza* [The Sarmatians of the Northeastern Caucasus] (Grozny).
Vjazmitina, M.I., 1962, *Zolota Balka* [Zolota Balka] (Kiev 1962).
1972, *Zoloto-Balkovskij kurgan* [The burial place of Zoloto-Balkovskij] (Kiev).
Voprosy skifo-sarmatskoj arkheologii, 1954 [Questions of Scytho-Sarmatian Archeology], (Moscow).
Vysotskaja, T.N., 1979, *Neapol' – stolica gosudarstva pozdnikh skifov* [Neapolis – Capital of the Late Scythian State] (Kiev).
Zaseckaja, I.P., 1971, "Osobennosti pogrebal'nogo obrjada gunnskoj êpokhi na territorii stepej Povol'zhja i Severnogo Prichernomo'rja" [Characteristics of the Burial Rite in the Volga Steppes and in the Region North of the Black Sea during the Hun Epoch] *ASGE*, 13, pp. 61–72.

5. The Hsiung-nu

Hsiung-nu history must almost entirely be reconstructed on the basis of Chinese written records. The very great majority of these primary sources are now available in competent, often well commented translations. Because of some spectacular advances in the study of the Hsiung-nu, the chapter devoted to the secondary literature in Denis Sinor, *Introduction à l'étude de l'Eurasie Centrale* (Wiesbaden, 1963), pp. 217–21, is of use only in so far as it concerns the earlier literature. In the following bibliography items marked with an asterisk * were added by the editor. Some of these were not yet available to the author when he prepared his manuscript.

Works in Chinese and Japanese

The Archaelogical Team of Inner Mongolia and the Museum of the Inner Mongolia Autonomous Region, "Ho-lin-ke-erh fa-hsien i-tso chung-yao ti Tung-Han pi-hua mu," *Wen-wu*, 1974:1.

Chang Hsing-t'ang, *Shih Chi Han Shu Hsiung-nu ti-ming chin-shih*. Taipei, 1963.

Chang Wei-hua, *Lun Han Wu-ti*, Shanghai, 1957.

Ch'en Shou, *San Kuo Chih*, Po-na edition.

Cheng Ch'in-jen, "Hsiung-nu," *Hsin Shih-tai*, vol. 9, No. 4 (1969).

Chia I, *Hsin Shu*, collated by Lu Wen-chao, Ts'ung-shu Chi-ch'eng edition.

Chung-kuo K'o-hsüeh Yüan K'ao-ku Yen-chiu So, *Hsin Chung-kuo ti K'ao-ku Shou-huo*, Peking, 1961.

Egami Namio, *Kita Ajiya Shi*, Tokyo, 1956.

Yūrashiya Kodai Hoppō Bunka, Kyoto, 1948.

Fan Yeh, *Hou Han Shu*, Shanghai, Commercial Press, 1927.

Hsieh Jiann, "Hsiung-nu tsung-chiao hsin-yang chi ch'i liu-pien," *Chung-yang Yen-chiu Yüan Li-shih Yü-yen Yen-chiu So chi-k'an*, vol. 42, Part 4 (1971).

"Hsiung-nu she-hui tsu-chih tè ch'u-pu yen-chiu," *Chung-yang Yen-chiu Yüan Li-shih Yü-yen Yen-chiu So chi-k'an*, vol. 40, Part 2 (1969).

"Hsiung-nu cheng-chih chih-tu tè yen-chiu," *Chung-yang Yen-chiu Yüan Li-shih Yü-yen Yen-chiu So chi-k'an*, vol. 41, Part 2 (1969).

Huang Lin-shu, *Ch'in Huang Ch'ang-ch'eng K'ao*, revised edition, Hong Kong, 1972.

Inoue Yasushi and Iwamura Shinobu, *Seiiki*, Tokyo, 1963.

Ise Sentarō, *Seiiki Keiei-shi no Kenkyū*, Tokyo, 1962.

Ishiguro Tomio, "Senpi Yūboku kokka no ryōiki," *Hokudai Shigaku*, Oct., 1957.

Kubo Yasuhiko, "Bo Ki Kō setchi no mokuteki ni tsuite," *Shien*, vol. 26, Nos. 2–3 (Jan., 1966).

Kuwabara Jitsuzō, *Chang Ch'ien Hsi-cheng K'ao*. Translated into Chinese by Yang Lien, Shanghai, Commercial Press, 1934.

Lin Lü-chih, *Hsiung-nu Shih*, Hong Kong, Chung-Hua Wen-Hua, 1963.

Lü Ssu-mien, *Yen-shih Cha-chi*, Shang-hai, 1937.

Ma Ch'ang-shou, *Pei-Ti yü Hsiung-nu*, Peking, 1962.

Wu-huan yü Hsien-pi, Shanghai, 1962.

Matsuda Hisao, *Kodai Tenzan no Rekishi Chirigaku Teki Kenkyū*, Tokyo, revised edition, 1970.

Sabaku no Bunka, Tokyo, 1966.

Mori Masao, "Iwayuru 'Hoku-Tei-Rei' 'Sei-Tei-Rei' ni tsuite," *Takigawa Hakase*

Kanreki Kinen Ronbunshu, vol. 1: *Tōyōshi hen*, 1957.

"Kyōdo no Kokka," *Shigaku Zasshi*, vol. 59, No. 5 (May, 1950).

"On 'Die 24 Ta-ch'en' of Professor Pritsak," [In Japanese] *Shigaku Zasshi*, Vol. 80, No. 1 (Jan., 1971).

Pan Ku, *Han Shu*, Shanghai, Commercial Press, 1927.

Shiratori Kurakichi, *Hsiung-nu Min-tsu K'ao*, translated into Chinese by Ho Chien-min, Shanghai, 1936.

Seiiki Shi Kenkyū, two volumes, Tokyo, 1944.

Tung-Hu Min-tsu K'ao, translated into Chinese by Fang Chuang-yu, Shanghai, Commercial Press, 1934.

Ssu-ma Ch'ien, *Shih Chi*, Peking, Chung-Hua Shu-chu, 1972.

Ssu-ma Kuang, *Tzu-chih T'ung-chien*, Ku-chi Ch'u-pan She edition, 1957.

Sun Shou-tao, "Hsiung-nu Hsi-ch'a-kou Wen-hua Ku-mu ch'ün ti fa-hsien," *Wen-wu*, 1960: 7/8.

Tamura Jitsuzō, *Kita Ajiya ni okeru Rekishi Jekai no Keisei*, Tokyo, 1956.

Tezuka Takayoshi, "Kansho Kyōdo to no Washin Jōyaku ni Kansuru ni san no mondai," *Shien*, vol., 12, No. 2 (Dec., 1948).

"Kyōdo Bokkō Shiron," *Shien*, vol. 32, No. 2 (March, 1971).

"Kyōdo no Jōkaku ni tsuite," *Shien*, vol. 16, No. 1 (June, 1955).

"Kyōdo Zenu Sōzoku Kō," *Shien*, vol. 20, No. 2 (Dec., 1959).

"Minami Kyōdo no koko to Shinkō to no tsuite," *Shien*, vol. 27, No. 1 (June, 1966).

"Nitchikuō Hi no dokuritsu to Minami Kyōdo no Zenu Keishō ni tsuite," *Shien*, vol. 25, No. 2 (Nov., 1964).

Ting Ch'ien. *Hsiung-nu Chuan K'ao-cheng*, P'eng-lai Ti-li ts'ung-shu edition, Chekiang Shu-chü, 1915.

Tseng Yung, "Liao-ning Hsi-ch'a-kou ku-mu ch'ün wei Wu-huan i-chi lun," *K'ao-ku*, 1961:6.

Uchida Gimpū, "Gokanjo Minami Kyōdo Den no Kitazenu Ojoken Kiji ni tsuite," *Iwai Hakase Koki Kinen Ronbunshū*, Tokyo, 1963.

"Gōkan Kōbutei no tai-Minami Kyōdo seisuku ni tsuite," *Shirin*, 17:4 (October, 1932), and 18:1 (Jan., 1933).

"Gōkan makki yori Gokoran boppatsu ni itaru Kyōdo gobu no josei ni tsuite," *Shirin*, 9:2 (Apr., 1934).

Kodai no Mōko, Tokyo, 1940.

"Kyōdo Jujuden Chimei Kō," *Takigawa Hakase Kanreki Kinen Ronbunshū*, vol. 1: *Tōyōshi hen*, 1957.

Kyōdo shi Kenkyū, Osaka, 1953.

"Zenu no shōgō to Kyōdo Zenutei no ichi ni tsuite," *Tōhōgaku*, No. 12 (1956).

Wang Kuo-wei, *Kuan-t'ang chi-lin*, Taipei, Shih-chieh Shu-chü, 1961.

Wen Ch'ung-i, "Han-tai Hsiung-nu tè she-hui tsu-chih yü wen-hua hsing-t'ai," *Pien-chiang Weh-hua Lun-chi*, edited by Ling Shun-sheng et al., vol. 2, Taipei, 1953.

Yang K'uan, *Chan-kuo Shih*, Shanghai, 1955.

Yüan Hung, *Hou Han Chi*, Ssu-pu ts'ung-k'an edition,

Works in Western languages

*Barfield, Thomas J., 1981, "The Hsiung-nu Imperial Confederacy: Organization and Foreign Policy," *Journal of Asian Studies* 41, 1, pp. 45–61.

Bielenstein, Hans, 1956, *Emperor Kuang-wu and the Northern Barbarians*, The 17th Ernest Morrison Lecture in Ethnology, Canberra, The Australian National University.

*Boodberg, Peter A., 1936, "Two Notes on the History of the Chinese Frontier," *HJAS*, 1, pp. 283–307.

*Daffinà, Paolo, 1982, "The *Han shu Hsi yü chuan* retranslated. A Review Article," *TP*, 68, pp. 309–39.

Dubs, H.H., 1938–55, *The History of the Former Han Dynasty. A Critical Translation with Annotations*, (Baltimore, Md.).

Haloun, Gustav, 1937, "Zur Üse-Ṭsi Frage," *ZDMG*, 91, pp.243–318.

*Harmatta, J. 1971, "Eine neue Quelle zur Geschichte der Seidenstrasse," *Jahrbuch für Wirtschaftsgeschichte* 2, pp. 125–43.

*Henning, W.B., 1948, "The Date of the Sogdian Ancient Letters," *BSOAS* 12,

pp. 601–15. [Discovers the Sogdian name of the Hsiung-nu. On the conclusions to be drawn from this discovery see Maenchen-Helfen, 1955, and for a new interpretation see Harmatta, 1971.]

*Hulsewé, A.F.P., 1979, *China in Central Asia. The Early Stage: 125 B.C.–A.D. 23. An Annotated Translation of the Chapters 61 and 96 of the History of the Former Han Dynasty. With an Introduction by M.A.N. Loewe*, Sinica Leidensia XIV. [A masterpiece of capital importance. For important discussions see Daffinà 1982, and Pulleyblank 1981.]

Jettmar, Karl, 1951, "The Altai Before the Turks," *BMFEA*, 23, pp. 135–223.

1951–2, "Hunnen und Hiung-nu – ein archäologisches Problem," *Archiv für Völkerkunde* 6/7, pp. 166–80.

1964, *Die frühen Steppenvölker. Der eurasiatischer Tierstil. Entstehung und sozialer Hintergrund*, Kunst der Welt (Baden-Baden). [Mainly on Scythians, Sarmatians, and Hsiung-nu. Beautiful illustrations, accurate, selective bibliography.]

Kao Ch'ü-hsün, 1960, "The Ching Lu Shen Shrines of Han Sword Worship in Hsiung-nu Religion," *CAJ* 5, pp. 221–32.

Lattimore, Owen, 1940, *The Inner Asian Frontiers of China*, American Geographical Society, Research Series No. 21 (New York).

Levin, M.G.–Potapov, L.P., 1956, *The Peoples of Siberia*, edited by Stephen Dunn (Chicago).

Maenchen-Helfen, Otto, 1939, "The Ting-ling," *HJAS* 4, pp. 77–86.

*1944–5, "Huns and Hsiung-nu," *Byzantion* 17, pp. 222–43.

*1955, "Pseudo-Huns," *CAJ*. 1, pp. 101–6.

1961, "Archaistic Names of the Hiung-nu," *CAJ* 6, pp. 249–61.

McGovern, W.M., 1939, *The Early Empires of Central Asia: A Study of the Scythians and the Huns and the Part they Played in World History* (Chapel Hill, N.C.).

Minns, Ellis H., 1942, "The Art of the Northern Nomads," *Proceedings of the British Academy* 28.

*Pritsak, Omeljan, 1954, "Die 24 T'a-chên. Studie zur Geschichte des Verwaltungsaufbaus der Hsiung-nu Reiche," *OE* 1, pp. 178–202.

Pulleyblank, E.G., *1963, "The Consonantal System of Old Chinese, Pt. II. Appendix: The Hsiung-nu Language," *AM* NS. 9, pp. 239–65.

1966, "Chinese and Indo-Europeans," *JRAS*. pp. 9–39.

*1970, "The Wusun and Sakas and the Yüeh-chih Migration," *BSOAS* 33, pp. 154–60.

*1981, "Han China in Central Asia," *International History Review* 3, pp. 278–86.

Sinor, Denis, *Inner Asia. A Syllabus*, 2nd, revised edition, Indiana University Uralic and Altaic Series vol. 96 (Bloomington, IN.).

Suzuki Chusei, 1968, "China's Relations with Inner Asia: the Hsiung-nu, Tibet," in *The Chinese World Order*, edited by John K. Fairbank (Cambridge, Mass.).

*Taskin, V.S., 1968–73, *Materialy po istorii sjunnu. (Po kitajskim istochnikom)*, I–II (Moscow).

Tarn, W.W., 1938, *The Greeks in Bactria and India*, (Cambridge).

Watson, Burton, 1961, *Records of the Grand Historian of China*, translated from the *Shih-chi* of Ssu-ma Ch'ien (New York).

Yü, Ying-shih, 1967, *Trade and Expansion in China. A Study in the Structure of Sino-Barbarian Economic Relations* (Berkeley and Los Angeles).

6. Indo-Europeans in Inner Asia

The chapter "Les Yue-tche, les Tokhares, les Wou-souen" devoted to the secondary literature in Denis Sinor, *Introduction à l'étude de l'Eurasie Centrale*, (Wiesbaden 1963), pp. 221–3 is still of use for an assessment of the earlier literature, but it does not include works pertaining to the study of the northern part of the Indian subcontinent. The interested reader would be well advised to consult the bibliographies in Litvinskij–Sedov, 1984, in Staviskij, 1977, and in Narain 1987. In the following bibliography items marked with an asterisk * were added by the editor. Many of these were not yet available to the author when he prepared his manuscript.

Agrawala, V.S. 1950, "Catalogue of the Mathura Museum," *The Journal of the Uttar Pradesh Historical Society*, 23, pts. 1–2.
Andersson, J.G., 1943, "Researches into the Pre-History of the Chinese", *BMFEA* 15.
Bailey, H.W., 1937, "Ttaugara," *BSOS* 8, pp. 883–921.
1947, "Recent Works on Tokharian," *Transactions of the Philological Society*, pp. 126–53 (London).
1970a, "Saka Studies: The Ancient Kingdom of Khotan," *Iran. Journal of the British Institute of Persian Studies* 8, pp. 65–72.
1970b, "Tokharika," *JRAS*, pp. 121–2.
1971, "The Kingdom of Khotan," *Papers on Far Eastern History* 4, pp. 1–16.
Banerjea, J.N., 1962, "The Rise and Fall of the Kushana Empire," in *Comprehensive History of India* edited by K.A. Nilakanta Sastri, vol. 2, chapter 7, pp. 156–221 (Calcutta).
Basham, A.L. (Editor), 1968, *Papers on the Date of Kaniṣka, submitted to the Conference on the Date of Kaniṣka, London, 20–22 April, 1960* (Leiden 1968).
Beal, S., 1906, *Si-Yu-Ki, Buddhist Records of the Western World*, 2 volumes (London).
Benveniste, E., 1961, "Inscriptions de Bactriane," *JA*, pp. 113–51.
Bivar, A.D.H., 1956, "The Kushana-Sassanian Coin Series," *Journal of the Numismatic Society of India*, 18, pp. 13–42.
1963, "The Kaniṣka Dating from Surkh Kotal," *BSOAS* 26, pp. 498–502.
Brough, John, 1965, "Comments on Third-Century Shan-shan and the History of Buddhism," *BSOAS* 28, pp. 582–612.
1970, "Supplementary Notes on the Third-Century Shan-shan," *BSOAS* 31, pp. 39–45.
Burrow, T., 1935, "Tokharian Elements in the Kharoṣṭhī Documents from Chinese Turkistan," *JRAS*, pp. 667–75.
**Central'naja Azija v kushanskuju êpokhu = Central Asia in the Kushan Period*, I–II, 1974–1975, (Moskva). Proceedings of the International Conference on the History, Archaeology and Culture of Central Asia in the Kushan Period, Dushanbe, September 27 – October 6, 1968. [As is usual in similar publications, the quality of the contributions is uneven, but, all the same, the volumes contain much of what is of great value. The articles are in English, French and Russian; the latter have an English summary.]

Chang, Kwang-chih, 1963, *Archaeology of Ancient China* (New Haven and London).

Cheng, T'e-kun, 1973, "The Beginning of Chinese Civilization," *Antiquity* 47, pp. 197–209.

Chavannes, E., 1907, "Les pays d'Occident d'après le Heou Han Chou," *TP* 6, pp. 149–234.

Cunningham, A., 1888, "Coins of the Indo-Scythian King Miaus or Heraus," *The Numismatic Chronicle and Journal of the Royal Numismatic Society* 3rd Series, 8, pp. 47–58.

1889, "Coins of the Tochari, Kushans or Yue-ti," *Numismatic Chronicle and Journal of the Royal Numismatic Society* 3rd Series, 9, pp. 268–311.

1892, "Coins of the Kushanas or Great Yueti," *Numismatic Chronicle and Journal of the Royal Numismatic Society* 3rd Series, 12, pp. 40–82, 95–159.

1893, 1894, "Later Indo-Scythians," *Numismatic Chronicle and Journal of the Royal Numismatic Society* 3rd Series, 13, pp. 93–128, 166–202; 14, pp. 243–93.

Curiel, R. and Schlumberger, D., 1953 *Trésors monétaires d'Afghanistan*, Mémoires de la Délégation Archéologique Française en Afghanistan 14.

*Daffinà, Paolo, 1982, "The *Han shu Hsi yü chuan* retranslated. A Review Article," *TP* 68, pp. 309–39.

Enoki Kazuo, 1955, "The Origin of the White Huns or Hephtalites," *East and West* 6, pp. 231–7.

1959, "On the Nationality of the Ephtalites," *MRDTB* 18, pp. 1–58.

1963, "The Location of the Capital of Lou-lan and the Date of Kharoṣṭhī Inscriptions," *MRDTB*. 22, pp. 125–171.

1965, "On Sino-Kharoṣṭhī Coins," *East and West*, 15, pp. 231–276.

1968, "Hsieh (謝), Fu-wang (副王) or Wang (王) of the Yüeh-shih," *MRDTB* 26, pp. 1–13.

1969, "On the Date of the Kidarites (1)," *MRDTB* 27, pp. 1–26.

1970, "On the Date of the Kidarites (2)," *MRDTB*. 28, pp. 13–38.

Frye, R.N., 1966, *The Heritage of Persia* (New York).

Gardner, Percy 1886, *The Coins of the Greek and Scythic Kings of Bactria and India in the British Museum* (London). Reprinted: Chicago 1966.

Girshman, R., 1946, *Begram. Recherches archéologiques et historiques sur les Kouchans*. Mémoires de la Délégation Archéologique Française en Afghanistan 12 (Cairo).

*Göbl, Robert, 1967, *Dokumente zur Geschichte der iranischen Hunnen in Baktrien und Indien*, I–III (Wiesbaden). [Controversial in its conclusions, it is an impressive catalogue of coins attributed to the Hephthalites, Kidarites and some other peoples.]

Haloun, Gustav, 1937, "Zur Ŭe-ṭsi Frage," *ZDMG* 91, pp. 243–318.

Han shu, [History of the (Former) Han], compiled by Pan Ku [A.D. 32–92], Ssu-pu pei yao edition, vols. 49–52 (Shanghai, 1936).

Henning, W.B., 1938, "Argi and the 'Tokharians'," *BSOAS* 9, pp. 545–71.

1939, "The Great Inscription of Šāpūr I," *BSOS*. 9, pp. 823–49.

1948, "The Date of the Sogdian Ancient Letters," *BSOAS* 12, pp. 601–15.

1960, "The Bactrian Inscription," *BSOAS* 23, pp. 47–55.

1965, "Surkh-Kotal und Kaniṣka," *ZDMG* 115, pp. 75–87.

Herzfeld, E., 1924, *Paikuli. Monument and Inscription of the Early History of the Sasanian Empire*, Forschungen zur Islamischen Kunst, vol. IV (Berlin).
Hou Han shu, [History of the Later Han], compiled by Fan Yeh [A.D. 398–446], Ssu-pu pei-yao edition, vols. 53–5 (Shanghai, 1936).
Hsin T'ang shu [The New T'ang History], Ssu-ou pei-yao edition (Shanghai 1936).
Hsüan-tsang, *(Ta T'ang) Hsi-yü chi* [Record of the Western Region of the Great T'ang Dynasty], see: Zücher 1968, Watters 1904, Beal 1906.
*Hulsewé, A.F.P., 1979, *China in Central Asia. The Early Stage: 125 B.C.–A.D. 23. An Annotated Translation of the Chapters 61 and 96 of the History of the Former Han Dynasty. With an Introduction by M.A.N. Loewe*, Sinica Leidensia XIV. [See the important reviews by Daffinà 1982, and Pulleyblank 1981.]
I Chou shu [History of the Chou Dynasty], compiled by K'ung Chao. Ssu-u pei-yao edition, vol. 130, 7, 11–13.
Konow, Sten, 1929, *Kharoṣṭhī Inscriptions with the Exception of those of Aśoka*, Corpus Inscriptionum Indicarum II, Pt. 1 (Calcutta).
Krause, W. 1955, "Tocharisch," *Handbuch der Orientalistik*, edited by B. Spuler, Vol. 4, *Iranistik*, Abschnitt 3.
Lane, George S., 1958, "The Present State of Tocharian Studies," *Proceedings of the VIIIth International Congress of Linguists*, pp. 252 ff. (Oslo).
1964, "On the Significance of Tocharian for Indo-European Linguistics," in *Classical, Mediaeval and Renaissance Studies in Honor of Louis Ullman*, edited by Charles Henderson Jr., vol. 1, pp. 283–92 (Roma).
1970, "Tocharian: Indo-European and Non-Indo-European Relationships," in *Indo-European and Indo-Europeans*, edited by George Cardona, Henry M. Hoenigswald and Alfred Senn, pp. 73–88 (Philadelphia).
*Litvinskij, B.A.–Sedov, A.V., 1984 *Kul'ty i ritualy kushanskoj Baktrii pogrebal'nyj obrjad* (Moskva 1984).
Loewe, Michael, 1969, "Chinese Relations with Central Asia," *BSOAS*. 32, pp. 91–103.
MacDowall, D.W., 1960, "The Weight Standards of the Gold and Copper Coinages of the Kushana Dynasty from Kadphises to Vasudeva," *Journal of the Numismatic Society of India* 22, pp. 63–74.
Maricq, André, 1958a, "La grande inscription de Kaniṣka et l'étéo-tokharien, l'ancienne langue de la Bactriana", *JA* pp. 345–440.
1958b, "Classica et Orientalia, 5, Res Gestae Divi Saporis," *Syria*, pp. 295–360.
1968 in Basham 1968.
Marshall, John, 1951, *Taxila. An Illustrated Account of Archaeological Excavations Carried out at Taxila under the Orders of the Government of India between the Years 1913 and 1934*, 3 volumes (Cambridge).
Martin, M.F.C., 1937–38, "Coins of Kidara and the Little Kushans," *Numismatic Supplement of the Journal of the Asiatic Society of Bengal* 47, pp. 23–50.
Masson, M.E., 1968, "K voprosu o severnykh granicakh gosudarstva 'velikikh kushan'," *Obshchestvennye nauki v Uzbekistane* 8, pp. 14–25.
Mukherjee, B.N., 1967, *The Kushana Genealogy* (Calcutta).
Narain, A.K., 1962, *The Indo-Greeks* (Oxford 1962).
1969, "The Early Movement of the Sakas and the Pahlavas," *Studies in Asian*

History, Proceedings of the Asian History Congress 1961, pp. 62–76 (Delhi).
1987, *On the "First" Indo-Europeans. The Tokharian – Yuezhi and their Chinese Homeland*, Papers on Inner Asia, No. 2, Indiana University Research Institute for Inner Asian Studies (Bloomington, IN).
Pargiter, F.E., 1962, *The Purāna Text of the Dynasties of the Kali Age*, The Chowkamba Sanskrit Studies, vol. 49 (Varanasi).
Pei shih [History of the Northern Dynasties], Ssu-pu pei-yao edition (Shanghai 1936).
*Pelliot, Paul, 1934, "Tokharien et Koutchéen," *JA* I, pp. 23–106.
Prušek, J., 1971, *Chinese Statelets and the Northern Barbarians in the Period 1400–300 B.C.* (Dordrecht).
Pugachenkova. G.A., 1966, "Diskussii o 'Sotera Megase'," Trudy Gosudarstvennyj Universitet Tashkent 295, pp. 15–25.
Pulleyblank, E.G., 1966, "Chinese and Indo-Europeans," *JRAS*, pp 9–39.
*1981, "Han China in Central Asia," *International History Review* 3, pp. 278–86.
Puri, B.N., 1965, *India under the Kushanas* (Bombay).
Reichelt, Hans, 1931, *Die sogdischen Handschriftenreste des Britischen Museums*, II. *Die nicht-buddhistischen Texte* (Heidelberg).
Rosenfield, John M., 1967, *The Dynastic Arts of the Kushans* (Berkeley–Los Angeles).
San Kuo chih [Memoirs of the Three Kingdoms] compiled by Ch'en Shou, Po na pen edition (Taipei 1967), Wei Chih 3: 6a; Cf. Zürcher 1968, p. 371.
Schlumberger, Daniel, 1952–1964, "Le temple de Surkh Khotal en Bactriane," *JA* 1952, pp. 433–53; 1954, pp. 161–205; 1955, pp. 269–80; 1964, pp. 303–26.
1961, "The Excavations of Surkh Khotal and the Problem of Hellenism in Bactria and India," *Proceedings of the British Academy* 47, pp. 77–95.
Shih chi, by Ssu-ma Ch'ien [145–86 B.C.?], Chapter 123, Ssu-pu pei-yao edition, vols. 46–48. Cf. Watson 1961.
**Sovetskaja arkheologija Srednej Azii i kushanskaja problema*, 1968 (Moskva).
Staviskij, B.Ja., 1966, *Mezhdu Pamirom i Kaspiem. (Srednjaja Azija v drevnosti)* (Moskva).
1977, **Kushanskaja Baktrija: problemy istorii i kul'tury* (Moskva).
Stein, Sir M.A., 1900, *Kalhana's Rājataranginī, a Chronicle of the Kings of Kashmir*, translated by -, 2 vols. (Westminster). Reprinted Delhi–Varanasi, 1961.
Tarn, W.W. 1951, *The Greeks in Bactria and India*, 2nd edition, (Cambridge).
Thomas, F.W., 1944, "Sino-Kharoṣṭhī Coins," *The Numismatic Chronicle and Journal of the Royal Numismatic Society*. 6th Series, vol. 4, pp. 83–98.
Vorob'ev-Desjatovskij, V.S., 1958, "Pamjatniki central'no-aziatskoj pis'mennosti," *UZLGU*, 16, p. 280–308.
Watson, Burton, 1961, *Records of the Grand Historian of China*, translated from the *Shih-chi* of Ssu-ma Ch'ien (New York).
Watson, William, 1971, *Cultural Frontiers in Ancient East Asia* (Edinburgh).
Watters, Th., 1904, *On Yuan Chwang's Travels in India, 629–645 A.D.* (London).
Wei shu [History of the Wei], Ssu pu pei-yao edition, vols. 65–67 (Shanghai 1936).
Whitehead, R.B., 1914, *Catalogue of the Coins in the Punjab Museum, Lahore*, vol. I, *Indo-Greek Coins* (Oxford).
Yü, Ying-shih, 1967, *Trade and Expansion in China. A Study in the Structure of Sino-Barbarian Economic Relations* (Berkeley and Los Angeles).
Zejmal, E.V., 1971, "Sino-kharoshtijskie monety. (K datirovke khotanskogo

dvujazychnogo chekana)," *Strany i narody Vostoka* 10, pp. 109–120.
Zograf, A.N., 1937, *Monety Geraj* (Tashkent).
Zürcher, E., 1968, "The Yüeh-chih and Kaniska in the Chinese Sources," in Basham, 1968, pp. 358–90.

7. The Hun period

No work dealing with the history of either the East or the West Roman empires in the 4th or 5th centuries can ignore the Huns. There would be no point in listing here even a selection of the historical syntheses dealing with either of the two empires, but Bury, 1958 and Stein, 1968 should be mentioned because of their usefulness in setting the Huns within the frameworks of, respectively, the West and the East Roman empires.

Among the primary Latin sources, Ammianus Marcellinus and Jordanes are the most important. Aalto-Pekkanen I, pp. 199–255 assembles the Latin texts in which the name of the Huns (*Hunni*, *Unni*, etc.) occur, but care should be taken, since many of these references are not to the Huns themselves but rather to other peoples to whom the name was transferred. Thompson, 1948, pp. 4–14 and Maenchen-Helfen, 1973, pp. 1–17 survey the most important Classical, Greek or Latin, sources. For further information on individual Byzantine authors reporting on the Huns one should refer to Moravcsik, 1958, I. Czeglédy, 1954, 1957 and 1971 are of great help for the assessment of Syriac sources.

The following bibliography does not include all the entries of the chapter "Les Huns" of Denis Sinor, *Introduction à l'étude de l'Eurasie Centrale* (Wiesbaden 1963), pp. 261–5.

Aalto, Pentti–Pekkanen, Tuomo, 1975, *Latin Sources on North-Eastern Eurasia*, I–II, Asiatische Forschungen vol. 44 (Wiesbaden).
Altheim, Franz, 1962–75, *Geschichte der Hunnen*, I–V (Berlin). [This work has been written with the collaboration of many scholars. Extreme caution is recommended in its use, since it is replete with gratuitous hypotheses.]
Ammianus Marcellinus, 1939, With an English Translation by John C. Rolfe, I–III (Loeb Classical Library).
Bachrach, Bernard S., 1973, *A History of the Alans in the West* (Minneapolis). [The histories of the Huns and Alans are closely intertwined.]
Bökönyi, S., 1974, *History of Domestic Mammals in Central and Eastern Europe* (Budapest).
Buchanan, James J.–Davis Harold T., 1967, [translators] *Zosimus: Historia Nova. The Decline of Rome* (Trinity University Press).
Bury, J.B., 1889. Reprinted 1958, *History of the Later Roman Empire from the Death of Theodosius I. to the Death of Justinian*, I–II (Dover Publications).
Chabot, J.B., 1899–1924, *Chronique de Michel le Syrien, patriarche jacobite d'Antioche*, I–IV (Paris).
Claudian, 1922, With an English translation by Maurice Platnauer, I–II (Loeb Classical Library).
Croke, Brian, 1977, "Evidence for the Hun Invasion of Thrace in A.D. 422," *Greek, Roman, Byzantine Studies* 18, pp. 347–68.
1981, "Anatolius and Nomus: Envoys to Attila," *Byzantinoslavica* 42, pp. 159–70.

Czeglédy, K., 1954, "Monographs on Syriac and Muhammadan Sources in the Literary Remains of M. Kmoskó," *AOH* 4, pp. 19–90.

1957, "The Syriac Legend Concerning Alexander the Great," *AOH* 7, pp. 231–49.

1971, "Pseudo-Zacharias Rhetor on the Nomads," in *Studia Turcica*, edited by L. Ligeti, pp. 133–48. (Budapest).

De Crespigny, R., 1984, *Northern Frontier. The Policies and Strategy of the Later Han Empire*, Faculty of Asian Studies Monographs, NS. 4 (Canberra).

Dewing, H.B. See Procopius of Caesarea.

Doerfer, Gerhard, 1973, "Zur Sprache der Hunnen," *CAJ* pp. 1–50. [Cf. on the same topic Pritsak 1982.]

Dowsett, C.J.F. [translator], 1961, *The History of the Caucasian Albanians by Mvsès Dasxurançi* (Oxford).

Gordon, C.D., 1960, *The Age of Attila. Fifth Century Byzantium and the Barbarians* (Ann Arbor, Michigan). [Chapter 3. (pp. 57–111) is devoted to the Huns. Long translations of the *Fragments* of Priscus are linked by short narrative passages.]

Gregory of Tours, *Historica Francorum*, edited by B. Krusch, W. Levison, MGM. SSRM. 1937–51 (Hannover).

Harmatta, J. 1976, "L'apparition des Huns en Europe Orientale," *AAH* 24, pp. 277–83.

Haussig, Hans-Wilhelm, 1977 "Das Problem der Herkunft der Hunnen," *Materialia Turcica* 3, pp. 1–15.

Henning, W.B., 1948, "The Date of the Sogdian Ancient Letters," *BSOAS* 12, pp. 601–15. [Discovers the Sogdian name of the Hsiung-nu. On the conclusions to be drawn from this discovery see Maenchen-Helfen, 1955.]

Homeyer, H., 1951, *Attila der Hunnenkönig von seinen Zeitgenossen dargestellt* (Berlin).

Iordanes, *Getica*. See Mierow, C.C., 1915.

Lindner, Rudi Paul, 1981, "Nomadism, Horses and Huns," *Past and Present* 92, pp. 3–19.

Maenchen-Helfen, Otto, 1944–5, "Huns and Hsiung-nu," *Byzantion* 17, pp. 222–43.

1955, "Pseudo-Huns," *CAJ* 1, pp. 101–6.

1961, "Archaistic Names of the Hiung-nu," *CAJ* 6, pp. 249–61.

1973, *The World of the Huns* (University of California Press). [Without any doubt the major synthesis on the history of the Huns, but it should be borne in mind that it was published posthumously, without the final polish the author would, no doubt, have given to his *magnum opus*.]

Markwart, J., 1930, *Südarmenien und die Tigrisquellen nach griechischen und arabischen Geographen* (Wien).

Marquart, J., 1901, *Ērānšahr nach der Geographie des Ps. Moses Xorenac'i*, Abhandlungen der königl. Gesellschaft der Wissenschaften zu Göttingen, Phil. hist. Kl. NF. Bd. III, Nr. 2. [The names Marquart and Markwart refer to the same person. Both works display a dazzling erudition but contain only passing references to the Huns. They are not mentioned in the Hun chapter of Sinor, *Introduction*.]

Mierow, C.C., 1915, *The Gothic History of Jordanes* (Princeton).

Moravcsik, Gyula, 1926, "Attilas Tod in Geschichte und Sage," *Kőrösi Csoma*

Archivum 2, pp. 83–116.
1946, "Byzantine Christianity and the Magyars in the Period of their Migration," *The American Slavic and East European Review* 5, pp. 25–45. Reprinted in Gyula Moravcsik, *Studia Byzantina* (Budapest 1967), pp. 245–59.
1958, *Byzantinoturcica* I, *Die byzantinischen Quellen der Geschichte der Türkvölker*, II, *Sprachreste der Türkvölker in den byzantinischen Quellen*, 2nd edition (Berlin). [Volume I gives an excellent bibliography on the Huns (pp. 60–5) and provides an indispensable guide to the Byzantine authors in whose works this people is mentioned.]
Németh, Gyula, (editor), 1940a (reprinted 1986) *Attila és húnjai* (Budapest). [Still very useful.]
1940b "A húnok nyelve," in Németh 1940a, pp. 217–26.
Párducz, Mihály, 1959, "Archäologische Beiträge zur Geschichte der Hunnenzeit in Ungarn," *AAH* 11, pp. 309–98.
1963, *Die ethnischen Probleme der Hunnenzeit in Ungarn*, Studia Archaeologica I (Budapest).
Paulus Diaconus, *Historia Langobardorum*, edited by Bethmann and Waitz MGM 1878, pp. 45–187.
Pigulevskaya, N., 1969, "Notes sur les relations de Byzance et des Huns au VIe s.," *Revue des études sud-est européennes* 7, pp, 199–203.
Pritsak, Omeljan, 1982, "The Hunnic Language of the Attila Clan," *Harvard Ukrainian Studies* 6, pp. 428–76. [Cf. on the same topic Doerfer 1973.]
Procopius of Caesarea, *History of the Wars* (1914) edited and translated by H.B. Dewing, vol. I, (Loeb Classical Library).
Platnauer, Maurice, see: *Claudian.*
Prosper Tiro Aquitanus, *Epitoma chronicorum*, edited by T. Mommsen, MGM. IX, *Chron.min.* I, pp. 385–499.
Rolfe, John C., see: *Ammianus Marcellinus.*
Sidonius, *Poems and Letters* (1936), edited and translated by W.B. Anderson, vol. I (Loeb Classical Library).
Sinor, Denis, 1946–47, "Autour d'une migration de peuples au Ve siècle," *JA* pp. 1–78.
1978, "The Greed of the Northern Barbarian," in *Aspects of Altaic Civilization* II, edited by Larry V. Clark and Paul Alexander Draghi, Indiana University Uralic and Altaic Series, vol. 134, pp. 171–82.
Sozomenos, *Ecclesiastical History*, in Henry Wace and Philip Schaf, *A Select Library of Nicene and Post-Nicene Fathers*, Second Series, vol. II (Oxford and New York 1891).
Stein, Ernest, 1968, *Histoire du Bas-Empire*, I–II (Amsterdam).
Thompson, E.A., 1946, "Christian Missionaries among the Huns," *Hermathena* 67, pp. 73–9.
1948, *A History of Attila and the Huns* (London).
Werner, Joachim, 1956, *Beiträge zur Archäologie des Attila-Reiches*, Abhandlungen der Bayerischen Akademie der Wissenschaften, NF. 38, A. [Gives good references to the earlier archeological literature.]
Zosimus, *Historia Nova*, see Buchanan 1967.

8. The Avars

Bibliographies and other research aids

Aalto, Pentti–Pekkanen, Tuomo, 1975, *Latin Sources on North-Eastern Eurasia*, I–II, Asiatische Forschungen vol. 44 (Wiesbaden). [Vol. I, pp. 79–98 gives the Latin texts in which the name of the Avars occur.]

Banner, János–Jakabffy, Imre, 1954–68, *Archäologische Bibliographie des Mittel-Donaubeckens*, I–III (Budapest). [A complete bibliography up to 1966.]

Bibliographia Archaeologica Hungarica, compiled by E. Németh, Mária F. Fejér, Imre Jakabffy, published in *AE*, 98 (1971), pp. 122–38; 99 (1972), pp. 132–48; 100 (1973), pp. 129–52; 101 (1974), pp. 161–83; 102 (1975), pp. 155–85; 103 (1976), pp. 147–70; 104 (1977), pp. 121–44; 104 (1978), pp. 140–60; 105 (1978), pp. 140–62; 106 (1979), pp. 152–74; 107 (1980), pp. 137–51.

Bóna, I., 1971, "Ein Vierteljahrhundert Völkerwanderungsforschung in Ungarn (1945–1969)," *AAH*. 23, pp. 265–336.

Csallány, Dezsó, 1956, *Archäologische Denkmäler der Awarenzeit in Mitteleuropa* (Budapest). A complete bibliography up to 1955. To be complemented by Kollautz, 1965.

Glossar zur frühmittelalterlichen Geschichte im östlichen Europa. Herausgegeben von Jadran Ferluga, Manfred Hellmann, Herbert Ludat (and for Serie B also Klaus Zernack) (Wiesbaden).

Serie A. *Lateinische Namen bis 900*, Bd. I, 1977. [On pp. 187–257, 403–7 are reproduced those passages found in Latin sources in which the name of the Avars occur. To some extent the coverage of Aalto–Pekkanen and the *Glossar* overlap but texts in which the name of the Avars is applied to another people are listed separately in the *Glossar*.]

Serie B. *Griechische Namen bis 1025*, Bd. I, 1980. [On pp. 23–200, 297–302 are given those Greek texts in which the name of the Avars occur. On pp. 195–200 an excellent bibliography has the added advantage of not including works dealing with the Juan-juan. The *Glossar* is an indispensable tool for the study of the Avars.]

Jakabffy, Imre, 1981, *Archäologische Bibliographie des Mitteldonaubeckens 1967–1977*, (Budapest).

Kollautz, Arnulf, 1965, *Bibliographie der historischen und archäologischen Veröffentlichungen zur Awarenzeit Mitteleuropas und des fernen Ostens mit Berichtigungen und Ergänzungen zu der von Dezsö Csallány in der "Archäologischen Denkmälern der Awarenzeit in Mitteleuropa," Budapest 1956, angeführten Literatur* (Klagenfurt). [Complete bibliography up to 1964.]

Moravcsik, Gyula, 1958, *Byzantinoturcica* I, *Die byzantinischen Quellen der Geschichte der Türkvölker*, II, *Sprachreste der Türkvölker in den byzantinischen Quellen*, 2nd edition (Berlin). [Volume I contains a useful bibliography on the Avars (pp. 72–6) which, however, contains many items not directly relevant to this people. This same volume provides an indispensable guide to the Byzantine authors in whose works the Avars are mentioned.]

Sinor, Denis, 1963, *Introduction à l'étude de l'Eurasie Centrale*, (Wiesbaden) [pp. 265–267 on the Avars].

Szádeczky-Kardoss, Sámuel, 1972, *Ein Versuch zur Sammlung und chronologischen Anordnung der griechischen Quellen der Awarengeschichte nebst einer Auswahl von anderssprachigen Quellen* (Szeged).

Historical studies

Avenarius, A., 1974, *Die Awaren in Europa* (Amsterdam–Bratislava).

Bakay, K., 1973, "Az avarkor időrendjéről," *Somogyi Múzeumok Közleményei* 1, pp. 5–86.

Barišić, F., 1953, *Čuda Dimitrija* (Beograd). [French summary.]

1954, "Le siège de Constantinople par les Avares et les Slaves," *Byzantion* 24, pp. 371–95.

Beševliev, Veselin, 1963, *Die protobulgarischen Inschriften* (Berlin).

Böhmer, J.F.–Mühlbacher, E.–Lechner, J. 1908, *Regesta Imperii*, I. *Die Regesten des Kaiserreichs unter den Karolingern: 751–918* (Innsbruck).

Charanis, P. 1953, "On the Slavic Settlement in the Peloponnesus," *BZ*, 46, pp. 91–103.

Comşa, M., 1972, "Directions et étapes de la pénétration des Slaves vers la Péninsule Balkanique aux VIe–VIIe siècles (avec un regard spécial sur le territoire de la Roumanies," *Balcanoslavica* 1, pp. 9–28.

Czeglédy, K., 1983, "From East to West: the Age of Nomadic Migrations in Eurasia," *Archivum Eurasiae Medii Aevi* III, pp. 25–125. Translated from Hungarian by P.B. Golden.

Deér, Joseph, 1965, "Karl der Grosse und der Untergang des Awarenreiches" in *Karl der Grosse*, herausgegeben von W. Braunfels, vol. 1, pp. 719–91 (Düsseldorf).

Dujčev, Ivan, 1976, *Cronaca di Monemvasia* (Palermo). [An important work concerning the penetration of the Avars and Slavs into Hellas.]

Fontes Graeci Historiae Bulgaricae, 1954–69, 8 volumes (Sofia).

Fontes Latini Historiae Bulgaricae, 1958–65, 3 volumes (Sofia).

Fritze, W.H., 1963, 1965, 1967, "Slaven und Awaren im angelsächsischen Missionsprogramm," *Zeitschrift für Slavische Philologie* 31, pp. 316–38; 32, pp. 231–51; 33, pp. 358–72.

1979, "Zur Bedeutung der Awaren für die slawische Ausdehnungsbewegung im frühen Mittelalter," *Zeitschrift für Ostforschung* 28, pp. 498–545.

Fülöp, Gy., 1978, "La survivance des Avars au IXe siècle," *Alba Regia*, 16, pp. 87–97.

Grafenauer, B., 1950, "Quelques problèmes relatifs à l'époque des Slaves du Sud," *Zgodovinski Casopis* 4, pp. 23–126. [In Slovenian with a French summary.]

Hartmann, *Geschichte Italiens im Mittelalter*, 1900, 1903, II, 1, II, 2 (Leipzig).

Haussig, H.W., 1953, "Theophylakts Exkurs über die skythischen Völker," *Byzantion* 23, pp. 275–462.

1956, "Die Quellen über die zentralasiatischen Herkunft der europäischen Awaren," *CAJ* 2, pp. 2–43.

Herrmann, E., 1965, *Slawisch-germanische Beziehungen im südostdeutschen Raum von der Spätantike bis zum Ungarnsturm. Ein Quellenbuch mit Erläuterungen* (München).

Horedt, K., 1958, "Das archäologische Fundgut Siebenbürgens von 450–650 u. Ztr.," in *Untersuchungen zur Frühgeschichte Siebenbürgens*, pp. 87–111 (Bucharest).

1968, "Das Awarenproblem in Rumänien," *Studijné Zvesti Archeologického Ustavu Slovenskoj Akadémie Vied* 16, pp. 103–120.

1975, "The Gepidae, the Avars and the Romanic Population in Transylvania," in: *Relations Between the Autochtonous Population and the Migratory Populations on the Territory of Romania* edited by M. Constantinescu et al., pp. 111–22 (Bucharest).

Kőhalmi, Katalin U, 1972, *A steppék nomádja lóháton, fegyverben* (Budapest).

Kollautz, A. 1965, "Awaren, Langobarden und Slaven im Noricum und Istrien," *Carinthia* I, pp. 619–45.

1966, "Awaren, Franken und Slawen in Karantanien und Niederpannonien und die fränkische und byzantinische Mission," *Carinthia* I, 156, pp. 232–75.

1970, *Denkmäler byzantinischen Christentums aus der Awarenzeit der Donauländer* (Amsterdam).

1979, "Völkerbewegungen an der unteren und mittleren Donau im Zeitraum von 558/562 bis 582 (Fall von Sirmium)," *Zeitschrift für Ostforschung* 28, pp. 448–89.

Kollautz, A.–Miyawaka, Hisayuki, 1970, *Geschichte und Kultur eines völkerwanderungszeitlichen Nomadenvolkes. Die Jou-jan der Mongolei und die Awaren in Mitteleuropa*, I–II (Klagenfurt).

Kovačević, J., 1966, "Avari na Jadranu," in *Materijali* III, *Simpozijum praistorijske i srendjevekovne sekcie Arkheološkog Društva Jugoslavie, Novi Sad 1965*, pp. 53–81, (Beograd).

1977, *Avarski Kaganat* (Beograd).

Kuznetsov, V.A., 1984, "The Avars in the Nart Epos of the Ossets," *AOH*, 38, pp. 165–169.

László, Gyula, 1944, *A honfoglaló magyar nép élete* (Budapest).

1970a, *A népvándorláskor művészete Magyarországon* (Budapest).

1970b, *Steppenvölker und Germanen. Kunst der Völkerwanderungszeit* (Wien–München–Budapest).

1975, "Inter Sabariam et Carnuntum . . .," *Studia Slavica* 21, pp. 139–57.

Lemerle, Paul, 1979–81, *Les plus anciens recueils des miracles de Saint Démétrius*, 2 volumes (Paris).

*Ligeti, Lajos, 1986, "A pannóniai avarok etnikuma és nyelve," *Magyar Nyelv* 82, pp. 129–51. [Essential contribution to the study of the ethnicity and language of the Avars.]

Magnae Moraviae Fontes Historici, edited by L. Havlik, 1966, 1967, 1969, 1971, 4 volumes (Praha–Brno).

Makk, Ferenc, 1975, *Traduction et commentaire de l'homélie écrite probablement par Théodore le Syncelle sur le siège de Constantinople en 626* (Szeged).

Mohay, A., 1979, "Priskos' Fragment über die Wanderungen der Steppenvölker. (Übersicht über die neueren Forschungen)," in *Studies in the Sources of Pre-Islamic Central Asia*, edited by J. Harmatta, pp. 129–144 (Budapest).

Nagy, T., 1947–8, "Studia Avarica," [in Hungarian!] *Antiquitas Hungarica* I, pp. 56–63; II, pp. 131–49.

Németh, Gyula, 1930. *A honfoglaló magyarság kialakulása* (Budapest).

Nystazopoulou-Pelekidou, M., 1970, *Συμβολὴ εἰς τη'ν χφουολο'γησιν τῶν 'Αβαϱινῶυ καὶ Σλαβικῶν ἐπιδϱομῶν ἐπὶ Μαυϱικίου* (582–602), *Symmeikta* 2, pp. 145–205.

Olajos, T., 1969, "Adalék a (H)ung(a)ri(i) népnév és a késői avarkori etnikum történetéhez," *Antik Tanulmányok* 16, pp. 87–90.

1976, "La chronologie de la dynastie avare de Baian," *Revue des études byzantines*, 34, pp. 151–58.

1977, "Megjegyzések Maurikios császár avar háborujának utolsó éveihez Theophylaktos Simokattes elbeszélésében," *Acta Universitatis Szegediensis de Attila József Nominatae, Acta Historica* 58, pp. 3–12. [Russian résumé.]

1985, "Quelques remarques sur les évènements des dernières années de la guerre avaro-byzantine sous l'Empereur Maurice," in *From Late Antiquity to Early Byzantium*, edited by V. Vavřinek, pp. 161–5, (Praha).

Popović, V., 1975, "Les témoins archéologiques des invasions avaro-slaves dans l'Illyricum byzantin," *Mélanges d'Archéologie et d'Histoire de l'Ecole Française de Rome* 87, pp. 445–504.

Pritsak, Omeljan, 1982, "The Slavs and the Avars," *Settimane di studio del Centro italiano di studi sull'alto medioevo* XXX, *Gli Slavi occidentali e meridionali nell'alto medioevo*, pp. 353–435 (Spoleto).

Rusu, M., 1975, "Avars, Slavs, Romanic Population in the 6th–8th Centuries," in *Relations Between the Autochtonous Population and the Migratory Populations on the Territory of Romania* edited by M. Constantinescu et al., pp. 123–153 (Bucharest).

Simson, Bernhard–Abel, Sigurd, 1888, 1883, *Jahrbücher des fränkischen Reiches unter Karl dem Grossen*, I–II (Leipzig).

Sinor, Denis, 1946–7, "Autour d'une migration de peuples au Ve siècle," *JA*, pp. 1–78.

"Qapqan," 1954, *JRAS*, pp. 174–84.

Stein, Ernst, 1919, *Studien zur Geschichte des byzantinischen Reiches vornehmlich unter den Kaisern Justinus II und Tiberius Constantinus* (Stuttgart).

1968, *Histoire du Bas-Empire*, I–II (Amsterdam).

Stratos, Andreas N., 1968–72, *Byzantium in the Seventh Century*, I (602–634), II (634–641) (Amsterdam).

Szádeczky-Kardoss, S., 1968, "Kuvrat fiának, Kubernek a története és az avarkori régészeti leletanyag," *Antik Tanulmányok* 15, pp. 85–7.

1970a, "Kutriguroi," *RE*, Supplementband XII, 516–20.

1970b "Onoguroi," *RE*, Supplementband XII, 902–6.

1975, "Über die Wandlungen der Ostgrenze der awarischen Machtsphäre," in *Researches in Altaic Languages*, edited by L. Ligeti, pp. 267–274 (Budapest).

1978 – "Az avar történelem forrásai – Die Quellen der Awarengeschichte (Auszug)," *AÉ*, 105 (1978), pp. 78–90; II, 106 (1979), pp. 94–111, 231–43; 107 (1980), pp. 86–97, 201–13; 108 (1981), pp. 81–8, 218–32; 109 (1982), pp. 136–44; 110 (1983), pp. 89–99; 111 (1984), pp. 53–70; 113 (1986), pp. 83–112. [To be continued.]

1986, *Avarica. Über die Avarengeschichte und ihre Quellen*. Mit Beiträgen von Therese Olajos (Szeged).

Tirr, D.A., 1976, "The Attitude of the West Towards the Avars," *AAH*, 28, pp. 111–21.

Tomka, P., 1971, "Le problème de la survivance des Avars dans la littérature archéologique hongroise," *AOH*, 24, pp. 217–52.

Vásáry, I., 1972, "Runiform Signs on Objects of the Avar Period," *AOH* 25, pp. 335–47.
Waldmüller, Lothar, 1976, *Die ersten Begegnungen der Slawen mit dem Christentum und den christlichen Völkern vom VI. bis VIII. Jahrhundert. Die Slawen zwischen Byzanz und Abendland* (Amsterdam). [An important work concerning the connections between the Avars and the Slavs.]
Zástěrová, Bohumila, 1971, *Les Avares et les Slaves dans la Tactique de Maurice* (Praha).
Zöllner, E., 1950, "Awarisches Namensgut in Bayern und Österreich," *Mitteilungen des Instituts für österreichische Geschichtsforschung* 58, pp. 244–66.

Archeological publications (mainly excavations)

Barkóczy, L., 1968, "A Sixth-Century Cemetery from Keszthely-Fenékpuszta", *AAH*, 20, pp. 275–311.
Bóna, I., 1971a, "Ein Vierteljahrhundert Völkerwanderungsforschung in Ungarn (1945–1969)," *AAH*. 23, pp. 265–336.
1971b, *A népvándorlás kora Fehérmegyében* (Székesfehérvár).
1973 *VII. századi avar települések és Árpád-kori magyar falu Dunaujvárosban* (Budapest).
1979, "A Szegvár-sápoldali sír," *AE*, 106, pp. 3–30.
Csallány, Dezsö, 1939, "Kora-avarkori sirleletek – Grabfunde der Frühawarenzeit," *Folia Archeologica* 1–2, pp. 121–80.
1956, *Archäologische Denkmäler der Awarenzeit in Mitteleuropa* (Budapest). [A complete bibliography up to 1955. Complemented by Kollautz 1965, cited above, p. 000.]
Eisner, J., 1952, *Devinske Nová Ves* (Bratislava).
Erdélyi, István, 1982, *Az avarság és kelet a régészeti források tükrében* (Budapest). [Russian summary.]
Gerevich, L.–Erdélyi, I.–Salamon, A. (editors), 1972, *Les questions fondamentales du peuplement du bassin des Carpathes du VIIIe au Xe siècle* (Budapest).
Hampl. F. 1964, "Neue awarenzeitliche Funde aus Niederösterreich," *Archaeologia Austriaca* 35, pp. 66–86.
Huszár, L., 1954–1955, "Das Münzmaterial in den Funden der Völkerwanderungszeit im Mittleren Donaubecken," *AAH*, 5, pp. 61–109.
Kovrig, I., 1955, "Contribution au problème de l'occupation de la Hongrie par les Avars," *AAH*, 6, pp. 163–184.
1963, *Das awarenzeitliche Gräberfeld von Alattyán* (Budapest).
Kürti, Béla, 1980, "Avarkori sírleletek a Békés megyei Gerláról," *Muzeumi kutatások Csongrád megyében*, pp. 145–152.
László, Gy., 1955, *Études archéologiques sur l'histoire de la société des Avars*, Archaeologica Hungarica, NS. XXXIV (Budapest).
1965, "Les problèmes soulevés par le groupe à la ceinture ornée de griffons et de rinceaux de l'époque avare finissante," *AAH*, 17, pp. 73–5.
Lipták, P. 1957, "Awaren und Magyaren im Donau–Theiss Zwischenstromgebiet.

(Zur Anthropologie des VII–XIII Jahrhunderts)," *AAH*, 8, pp. 199–268.
1959, "The 'Avar Period' Mongoloids in Hungary," *AAH*, 10, pp. 251–79.
Sós, A.Cs., 1973, "Zur Problematik der Awarenzeit in der neueren ungarischen archäologischen Forschung," *Berichte über den II. International Kongress für Slawische Archäologie* II. pp. 85–102.
Szőke, B.M., 1980, "Zur awarenzeitlichen Siedlungsgeschichte des Körös-Gebietes in Südostungarn," *AAH*, 32, pp. 181–95.
Wenger, S., 1975, "Paleoanthropology of the Population Deriving from the Avar Period at Fészerlakpuszta," *Anthropologia Hungarica* 14, pp. 57–100.

9. The peoples of the Russian forest belt

Collections of sources

Bendefy, L., *Fontes authentici itinera (1235–1338) Fr. Iuliani illustrantes*, Archivum Europae Centro-Orientalis, III, (Budapest, 1937).
Györffy, Gy. (ed.), *A magyarok elődeiről és a honfoglalásról* (Budapest, 1958).
Istorija Tatarii v materialakh i dokumentakh (Moskva, 1937).
Lewicki, Tadeusz (ed. trans.), *Źródła arabskie do dziejów słowiańszczyzny*, I–II (Wrocław-Kraków-Warszawa, 1956–77).
Pauler, Gy., Szilágyi, S. (ed. trans.), *A magyar honfoglalás kútfői* (Budapest, 1900).
Szentpétery, E. (ed.), *Scriptores rerum Hungaricarum* (Budapest, 1937).

Arab sources

Abu'l-Fidā, *Taqwīm al-Buldān* ("Geography of the Lands"): *Géographie d'Aboulféda*, ed. R. Reinaud, M. Le Bon MacGuckin de Slane (Paris, 1840).
Al-Bakrī: Kunik', A, Rozen', V., "Izvestija al-Bekri o Rusi i lavjanakh i, "*Zapiski Imperatorskoi Akademii Nauk*," 32 (1878).
Abu Ḥāmid al-Gharnāṭī, *Tuḥfat al-Albāb wa Nukhbat al-'Ajā'ib* ("The Gift of the Hearts and Selection of the Wonders"): *Abu Ḥāmid el-Grenadino y su relación de viaje por tierras eurasiáticas*, ed. trans. C.E. Dubler (Madrid, 1953).
Ibn Faḍlān, *Risāla*: A. Zeki Validi Togan (ed. trans.), *Ibn Faḍlān's Reisebericht AKDM*, XXIV, 3 (Leipzig, 1939).
Risāla: Kovalevskiĭ, A.P. (facs. ed., trans.), *Kniga Ibn Fadlana o ego putešestvii na Volgu v 921–922 gg.* (Khar'kov, 1956).
Risāla, ed. S. Dahān (Damascus, 1379/1960).
Ibn Ḥawqal, *Kitāb Ṣurat al-Arḍ: Opus Geographicum auctore Ibn Ḥaukal "Liber Imaginis Terrae,"* ed. J.H. Kramers (Bibliotheca Geographorum Arabicorum, II^2, Leiden, 1938–9), 2 vols.
Ibn Rusta, *Kitāb al-A'lāq al-Nafīsa* ("The Book of Precious Gems"), ed. M.J. de Goeje (*BGA*, VII, Leiden, 1892).
Al-Idrīsī, *Kitāb Nuzhat al-Mushtāq fī Ikhtirāq al-Afāq: Opus Geographicum sive "Liber ad eorum delectationem qui terras peragrare studeant,"* ed. E. Cerulli, F. Gabrieli et al. fasc. 1–7 (Leiden, 1970–8).

Al-Iṣṭakhrī, *Kitāb Masālik al-Mamālik: Viae regnorum*," ed. M.J. de Goeje (*BGA*, I Leiden, 1870).

Al-Marwazī, *Ṭabā'i al-Ḥayawān* ("The Nature of Animals"): *Sharaf al-Zamān Ṭāhir Marwazī on China, The Turks and India*, ed. trans. V.F. Minorsky (London, 1942).

Al-Mas'ūdī, *Kitāb al-Tanbīh wa'l Ishrāf* ("The Book of Admonition and Recension"), ed. M.J. de Goeje (*BGA*, VIII, Leiden, 1894).

Al-Mas'ūdī, *Murūj al-Dhahab wa Ma'ādin al-Jawhar* ("Meadows of Gold and Mines of Precious Stones"), ed. C. Pellat (Beirut, 1966–79) 7 vols.

Al-Mas'ūdī (?), *Akhbār al-Zamān wa man abādahu'l-Ḥidthān wa 'Ajā'ib al-Buldān wa Ghāmir bi'l-Ma' wa'l-'Umrān* ["The History of Times Past (lit. 'The Information of Times which Events have exterminated) and the Wonders of the Lands and Wastes on Water and Cultivated Lands"] (Beirut, 1966).

Al-Muqaddasī, *Aḥsan al-Taqāsīm fī Ma'rifat al-Aqālīm* ("The Best of Divisions Regarding Knowledge of the Climes"), ed. M.J. de Goeje (*BGA*, III, Leiden, 1906).

Yāqūt, *Mu'jam al-Buldān* ("Geographical Dictionary"), 5 vols. (Beirut, 1957).

Byzantine sources

Dexippi, Eunapii, Petri Patricii, Prisci, Malchi, Menandri historiarum quae supersunt, ed. I. Bekker, B.G. Niebuhr (Corpus Scriptorum Historiae Byzantinae, Bonn, 1829).

Georgios Monakhos: *Georgii Monachi chronicon*, ed. Carl de Boor, I–II (Leipzig, 1904).

Konstantinos Porphyrogennetos: *Constantine Porphyrogenitus, De Administrando Imperio*, ed. Gyula Moravcsik, trans. R.J.H. Jenkins (Corpus Fontium Historiae Byzantinae, I, Dumbarton Oaks, Washington, D.C., 1967).

Symeon Logothetes: *Theophanes Continuatus, Ioannes Cameniata, Symeon Magister, Georgius Monachus*, ed. I. Bekker (Corpus Scriptorum Historiae Byzantinae, Bonn, 1838).

Hebrew sources

Kokovcev, P.K. (ed., trans.), *Evreĭsko-khazarskaja perepiska v X veke* (Leningrad, 1932).

Latin sources

Adamus Bremensis, *Gesta Hamburgensis Ecclesiae Pontificum*, ed. B. Schmeidler (MGH. Scriptores in usum scholarum, Hannover–Leipzig, 1917).

Annales Admuntenses (MGH. Scriptores, XXX/2, Hannover, 1934).

Annales Fuldenses, ed. F. Kurze (MGH. Scriptores in usum scholarum, XIII, Hannover, 1891).

Jordanes, *Getica, Iordan, O proiskhoždenii i dejanijakh getov* (ed. trans.) E. Č, Skržinskaja (Moskva, 1960).

Persian sources

Gardīzī, *Zain al-Akhbār* ("Adornment of Information"), excerpts in: Bartol'd, V.V., "Izvlečenie iz sočinenija Gardizi zain al-Akhbār, in *Akademik V.V. Bartol'd Sočinenija*, 9 vols (Moskva, 1963–73), vol. 8.

Ḥudūd al-'Ālam, ("The Regions of the World"), trans. V.F. Minorsky (Gibb Memorial Series, New Series, XI, London, 1937, 2nd rev. ed. London, 1970).

Mujmal al-Tavārīkh ("Compendium of the Histories"), ed. M. Bahār (Tehran, 1939).

Slavic sources

Begunov, Ju.K., *Pamjatnik russkoĭ literatury* XIII veka "Slovo o pogibeli russkoĭ zemli" (Moskva–Leningrad, 1965).

Constantinus et Methodius Thessalonicenses, Fontes (Konstantin i Metodije Solunjani, Izvori), ed. F. Grivec, F. Tomšić (Radovi Staroslavenskog Instituta, IV, Zagreb, 1960).

Ipat'evskaja letopis': Polnoe sobranie russkikh letopiseĭ, II, 2nd ed. (Moskva, 1962).

Lavrent'evskaja letopis': Polnoe sobranie russkikh letopiseĭ, I, 2nd. rev. ed. (Leningrad, 1926).

Patriaršaja ili Nikonovskaja letopis': Polnoe sobranie russkikh letopiseĭ, IX–XIII (Sanktpeterburg, 1862–1904, reprint Moskva, 1965) 3 vols.

Secondary sources

Alikhova, A.E., "K voprosu o burtasakh," *Sovetskaja Êtnografija*, no. 1 (1949).

Aininiskiĭ, S.A., "Izvestija vengerskikh missionerov XIII–XV vv. o Tatarakh i Vostočnoĭ Evrope," *Istoričeskiĭ Arkhiv*, III (1940).

Ašmarin, N.I., *Bolgary i Čuvašy* (Kazan', 1902).

Bárczi, G., Benkő, L., Berrár, J., *A magyar nyelv története* (Budapest, 1967).

Bárczi, Géza, *A magyar nyelv életrajza* (Budapest, 3rd ed., 1975).

Bartha, Antal, *Hungarian Society in the 9th and 10th Centuries* (Budapest, 1975).

Bartha, Antal, Czeglédy, Károly, Róna-Tas, András (eds.), *Magyar őstörténeti tanulmányok* (Budapest, 1977).

Bartol'd, V.V., "Basdžirt," *Akademik V.V. Bartol'd Sočinenija*, 9 vols (Moskva, 1963–73) v (*Enzyklopedie des Islam*, 4 vols, Leiden–Leipzig, 1913–36, I).

"Bolgary," *Akademik V.V. Bartol'd Sočinenija*, 9 vols (Moskva, 1963–73) (*Enzyklopaedie des Islam*, 4 vols., Leiden-Leipzig, 1913–36, I).

"Burtasy," *Akademik V.V. Bartol'd Sočinenija*, 9 vols (Moskva, 1963–73) (*Enzyklopaedie des Islam*, 4 vols., Leiden-Leipzig, 1913–36, I).

Benkő, Loránd, *Tanulmányok a magyar nyelv életrajza köréből* (Nyelvtudományi Értekezések, 40, Budapest, 1963–6).

et al., *A magyar nyelv történeti-etimológiai szótára*, 4 vols. (Budapest, 1967–84).

Boba, Imre, *Nomads, Northmen and Slavs* Slavo-Orientalia, II, (The Hague–Wiesbaden, 1967).

Čekalin, F., "Meščera i Burtasy po sokhranivšimsja o ikh pamjatnikam," *Trudy VIII Arkheologičeskago s"ezda*, III (Moskva, 1897).

Čermecov, V.I., "Nižnee Priob'e v I tysjačeletii n.e.," MIA 58 (1957).
Csallány, D., "Rovásirásos gyűrűk Magyarországon," *Archaeológiai Értesítő*, 82 (1955).
Czeglédy, Károly, "Magna Hungaria," *Századok*, 75 (1943).
"A magyarság Dél-Oroszországban" in L. Ligeti(ed.), *A magyarság őstörténete* (Budapest, 1943).
"A IX századi magyar történelem főbb kérdései," *Magyar Nyelv*, XLI (1945).
IV–IX századi népmozgalmak a steppén (A Magyar Nyelvtudományi Társaság Kiadványai, 84, Budapest, 1954).
Hajdú, Péter (eds.), *A magyar őstörténet kérdései* Nyelvtudományi Értekezések, 5, (Budapest, 1955).
"Pseudo-Zacharias Rhetor on the Nomads," in L. Ligeti (ed.), *Studia Turcica* (Budapest, 1971), pp. 133–48.
"Etimológia és filológia (Bulgár-török jövevényszavaink átvételének történeti hátteréről)," in L. Benkő, E.K. Sál (eds.), *Az etimológia elmélete és módszere* (Nyelvtudományi Értekezések, 89, Budapest, 1976).
Dąbrowski, Krzysztof, Nagrodzka-Majchrzyk, Teresa, Tryjarski, Edward, *Hunowie Europejscy, Protobułgarzy, Chazarowie, Pieczyngowie* (Wrocław-Warszawa-Kraków-Gdańsk, 1975).
Décsy, Gyula, *Einführung in die Finnisch-Ugrische Sprachwissenschaft* (Wiesbaden, 1965).
Deér, József, *Pogány magyarság keresztény magyarság* (Budapest, 1938).
Dienes, István, *The Hungarians Cross the Carpathians*, trans. B. Balogh (Budapest, 1972).
Ducellier, A., "Les sources byzantines et l'apparition des Hongrois en Europe," *Études Finno-Ougriennes*, 1 (1964).
Yegorov, V.T., "Êtnogenez čuvašeĭ po dannym jazyka," *Sovetskaja Etnografija*, no. 3 (1950).
Erdélyi, István, "Bol'šaja Vengrija," *AAH*, 13 (1961).
"Teorii vengerskikh učenykh o povolžskom proiskhoždenii drevnikh vengrov," *Arkheologija i Etnografija Baškirii*, 4 (1971).
"Fouilles archéologiques en Bachkirie et la préhistoire hongroise," *AOH*, 25 (1972), 301–12.
Fedotov, M.R., *Istoričeskie svjazi čuvašskogo jazyka s jazykami finno-ugrov Povolž'ja i Pecmi*, Čuvašsko-mariĭskie jazykovve svjazi, pt. 1 (Čeboksary, 1965).
Istoričeskie svjazi Čuvašskogo s volžskimi i permskimi finno-ugroskimi i jazykami (Čeboksary, 1968).
Fehér, Géza, *A bolgár-törökök szerepe és műveltsége* (Budapest, 1940).
"Zur Geschichte der Steppenvölker von Südrussland 9–10 Jhr.," *Studia Slavica Academiae Scientiarum Hungaricae*, 5 (1959).
Fodor, István, "K voprosu o pogrebal'nom obrjade drevnikh vengrov," A.P. Smirnov (ed.), *Problemy arkheologii i drevneĭ istorii ugrov* (Moskva, 1972).
Verecke híres útján . . . (Budapest, 1975).
Garipov, T.M., Kuzeev, R.G., "Baškiro-Mad'jarskaja problema," *Arkheologija i Etnografija* 1 (1962).

Gening, V.F., Khalikov, A.Kh., *Rannie bolgary na Volge* (Moskva, 1964).

"Etnogenez udmurtov po dannym arkheologii," *Voprosy finno-ugorskovo jazykoznanija* IV (1967).

Ginagi, Kh.G (ed.), *Istorija Tatarskoĭ ASSR*, 2 vols (Kazan', 1955–60).

Göckenjan, H., *Hilfsvölker und Grenzwächter im mittelalterlichen Ungarn* (Quellen und Studien zur Geschichte des östlichen Europa, v, Wiesbaden, 1972).

Golden, Peter B., "The People نوكردة," *Archivum Eurasiae Medii Aevi*, I (1975).

"The Q'azaro-Hungarian Title∼Personal Name يلك ∼ 'Ἰέλεχ,'" *Archivum Eurasiae Medii Aevi*, I (1975).

Gombocz, Zoltan, "Die Bulgarisch-Türkischen Lehnwörter in der ungarischen Sprache," *MSFOu.*, 30 (1912).

"Árpádkori török személy neveink," *Magyar Nyelv*, XI (1915).

Honfoglalás előtti bolgártörök jövevényszavaink, ed. L. Ligeti (Budapest, 1960).

Grekov, Boris D., "Volžskie bolgary v IX–X vv.," *Istoričeskie Zapiski* 14 (1945).

Gyóni, M., "Kalizok, kazárok, kabarok, magyarok," *Magyar Nyelv* XXXIV (1938).

Magyarország és a magyarság a bizánci források tükrében, (Magyar–Görög Tanulmányok – *Οὐγγροεκκηνικαὶ Μελέται*, 24, Budapest, 1943).

Győrffy, György, "Besenyők és magyarok," *KCsA*. Supplement vol. I (1939) pp. 397–500.

Tanulmányok a magyar állam eredetéről (Budapest, 1959).

"Magyarország népessége a honfoglalástól a XIV sz. közepéig" in J. Kovacsics (ed.), *Magyarország történeti demográfiája* (Budapest, 1963).

"Système des résidences d'hiver et d'été chez les nomades et les chefs hongrois du Xe siècle," *Archivum Eurasiae Medii Aevi* I (1975).

Autour de l'état des semi-nomades: le cas de la Hongrie Studia Historica Academiae Scientiarum Hungaricae, 95, Budapest, 1975).

Hajdú, Péter, "K etnogenezu vengerskogo naroda," *ALH* 2 (1952).

A magyarság kialakulásának előzményei. Nyelvtudományi Értekezések, 2; (Budapest, 1953).

Finnugor népek és nyelvek (Budapest, 1962), Eng. trans.: *Finno-Ugrian Languages and Peoples*, trans. G.F. Cushing (London, 1975).

"Finnougrische Urheimatforschung," *UA*. 41 (1969), 252–64.

Bevezetés az uráli nyelvtudományba (Budapest, 1966).

Halasi-Kun, Tibor, "A magyarság kaukázusi története" in L. Ligeti (ed.), *A magyarság őstörténete* (Budapest, 1943).

"Kipchak Philology and the Turkic Loanwords in Hungarian, I," *Archivum Eurasiae Medii Aevi*, I, (1975).

Hrbek, I., "Ein arabischer Bericht über Ungarn (Abū Ḥāmid al-Andalūsī al-Ġarnāṭī 1080–1170)," *Acta Orientalia Hungarica*, 5 (1955).

Jamguzin, R.Z., "Istorija i sovremennoe sostojanie izučenija etnogeneza i etničeskoĭ istorii Baškir," in I.K. Akmonov (ed.), *Iz istorii Baškirii* (Ufa, 1968).

Itkonen, Erkki, "Zur geographischen Ausdehnung der finnisch-ugrischen Urheimat," *UAJ*, 41 (1969), 303–6.

Jenkins, Romilly J.H. (ed.), *Constantine Porphyrogenitus, De Administrando Imperio*, Volume II, *Commentary* (London, 1962).

Káldy-Nagy, Gyula, (ed.), *Hungaro-Turcica. Studies in Honour of Julius Németh* (Budapest, 1976).
Khakimzjanov, F.S., "Sledy dialektov v jazyke pamjatnikov volžskoĭ Bulgarii," *Sovetskaja Tjurkologija* 4 (1974).
Khalikov, A.Kh., "K voprosu o načale tjurkizacii naselenija Povolž'ja i Priural'ja," *Sovetskaja Etnografija* no. 7 (1972).
Khalikova, E.A., "Pogrebal'nyĭ obrjad Tankeevskogo mogil'nika i ego vengerskie paralleli," in A.P. Smirnov (ed.), *Problemy arkheologii i drevneĭ istorii ugrov* (Moskva, 1972).
Kokhavskiĭ, I., *Proiskhodenie čuvašskogo naroda* (Čeboksary, 1965).
Kristó, Gyula, Róna-Tas, András (eds.), *Bevezetés a magyar őstörténet kutatásának forrásaiba*, I–II, 3 vols. (Budapest, 1976–7).
Kuzeev, R.G. (ed.) *Baškirskie šežere* (Ufa, 1960).
Proiskhoždenie baškirskogo naroda (Moskva, 1974).
Laščuk, L.P., *Formirovanie narodnosti Komi* (Moskva, 1972).
László, Gyula, "K voprosu o formirovanii finno-ugrov," in A.P. Smirnov (ed.), *Problemy arkheologii i drevneĭ istorii ugrov* (Moskva, 1972).
A honfoglalókról (Budapest, 1973).
A "kettős honfoglalás" (Budapest, 1978).
Lewicki, Tadeusz, "Türkische Stadt Dānā nach einem Bericht des Arabischen Geographen Ibn al-Faqīh," *Folia Orientalia*, 13 (1971).
"Les noms des Hongrois et de la Hongrie chez les médiévaux géographes arabes et persans," *Folia Orientalia*, 19 (1978).
Ligeti, Lajos, "Kündü," *Nyelvtudományi Közlemények*, 48 (1931).
"Régibb török jövevényszavaink magyarázatához," *Magyar Nyelv*, XXIX (1933), XXX (1934), XXXI (1935), XXXIII (1937).
(ed.), *A magyarság őstörténete* (Budapest, 1943).
"Az uráli magyar őshaza," in L. Ligeti (ed.), *A magyarság őstörténete* (Budapest, 1943).
"A török szókészlet története és török jövevényszavaink, Gyöngy," *Magyar Nyelv*, XLII (1946).
Ligeti, Louis (Lajos), "À propos des éléments altaïques de la langue hongrois," *ALH* 11 (1961), 15–42.
Ligeti, Lajos, "Gyarmat és Jenő," *Nyelvtudományi Értekezések*, 40 (1963), 230–9.
"A magyar nép mongol-kori nevei" *Magyar Nyelv*, LX (1964), 385–404.
Ligeti, Louis (Lajos), "Quelques problèmes étymologiques des anciens mots d'emprunt turcs de la langue hongroise," *AOH.*, 29 (1975), 279–88.
Ligeti, Lajos, "Régi török jövevényszavaink etimológiai problémái" in L. Benkő, E.K. Sál (eds.), *Az etimológia elmélete és módszere* Nyelvtudományi Értekezések, 89, (Budapest, 1976).
"A magyar nyelv török kapcsolatai és ami körülöttük van," *Magyar Nyelv*, LXXII (1976), pp. 11–27, 129–36.
A magyar nyelv török kapcsolatai és ami körülöttük van, ed. E. Schütz, E. Apor (Budapest Oriental Reprints, Series A 1 and 2, vol. I–II, Budapest, 1977–9).
"Régi török eredetű neveink," *Magyar Nyelv*, LXXIV (1978) pp. 257–274, LXXV (1979) pp. 26–42, LXXV (1979) pp. 259–273.

Lotz, János, "Etymological Connections of *magyar* Hungarian," in *For Roman Jakobson* (The Hague, 1956).

Lytkin, V.I., "Einige ostseefinnische Lehnwörter in komi-syrjänischen Mundarten," *UAJ*, 31 (1959), 164–8.

"K etimologii slov ugry i jugra," *Etimologija* (1968).

et al. (eds.), *Osnovy finno-ugrovskogo jazykoznanija/Voprosy proiskhoždenija i razvitija finno-ugrovskikh jazykov* (Moskva, 1974).

et al. (eds.), *Osnovy finno-ugrovskogo juzykoznanija/Mariĭskiĭ, permskie i ugrovskie jazyki* (Moskva, 1976).

Macartney, C.A., *The Magyars in the Ninth Century* (Cambridge, 1930, reprint: 1968).

Manninen, I., *Die Finnisch-Ugrischen Völker* (Leipzig, 1932).

Marquart, Josef, *Osteuropäische und Ostasiatische Streifzüge* (Leipzig, 1903, reprint: Hildesheim, 1961).

"Ein arabischer Bericht über die arktischen (uralischen) Länder aus dem 10. Jahrhundert," *UJ*. 4 (1924), 261–334.

Merkuškin, G. Ja., "Vkhoždenie mordovskogo naroda v sostav russkogo centralizovannogo gosudarstva," in B.A. Rybakov (ed.), *Etnogenez mordovskogo naroda* (Saransk, 1965).

Molnár, Erik, *A magyar nép őstörténete* (Budapest, 1953).

A magyar társadalom története az őskortól az Árpádkorig (Budapest, 2nd ed. 1949).

Mongaït, A.L., *Rjazanskaja zemlja* (Moskva, 1961).

Moór, Elemér, "Die Ausbildung des urungarischen Volkes im Lichte der Laut- und Wortgeschichte," *ALH*., 6 (1956), 7 (1957), 8 (1958), 9 (1959), 10 (1960).

"Die Benennungen der Ungarn in den Quellen des IX und X Jahrhunderts," *UAJ*. 31 (1959), 191–229.

Moravcsik, Julius (Gyula), "Zur Geschichte der Onoguren," *Ungarische Jahrbücher*, X (1930), 53–90.

Moravcsik, Gyula, *Byzantinoturcica²* (Berliner Byzantinistische Arbeiten, 10–11, 2 vols., Berlin, 1958).

Byzantium and the Magyars, trans. S.R. Rosenbaum, rev. trans. Mihály Szegedy-Maszák, rev. Miklós Szenczi, Zsigmond Ritoók (Amsterdam, 1970).

Moskalenko, A.A., "Slavjano-vengerskie otnošenija v IX v. i drevnerusskoe naselenie srednego i verkhnego Dona," in A.P. Smirnov (ed.), *Problemy arkheologii i drevneĭ istorii ungrov* (Moskva, 1972).

Mukhamedova, R.G., *Tatary-Mišari* (Moskva, 1972).

Németh, Gyula, *A honfoglaló magyarság kialakulása* (Budapest, 1930).

"A magyar rovásírás," *A Magyar Nyelvtudomány Kézikönyve*, II (1934).

"A magyar népnév, a magyar törzsnevek, a kazár népnév," *Magyar Nyelv*, XXXIV (1938).

Németh, Julius (Gyula), "Ungarische Stammesnamen bei den Baschkiren," *ALH* 16 (1966).

Németh, Gyula, "A baskírföldi magyar őshazáról," *Élet és Tudomány*, 13 (1966).

Pais, Dezső, "A Gyula és a kündüh," *Magyar Nyelv*, XXVII (1931).

A magyar ősvallás nyelvi emlékeiből (Budapest, 1975).

Palló, Margit K., "Hungaro-Tschuwaschica," *UA*., 31 (1959), 239–58.

Pauler, Gyula, *A magyar nemzet története Szent Istvánig* (Budapest, 1900).

Pekkanen, Tuomo, "On the Oldest Relationship between Hungarians and Sarmatians: From Spali to Asphali," *UAJ*, 45 (1973).

Pengitov, N.T., *Proiskhoždenie mariĭskogo naroda* (Jaškar-Ola, 1967).

Perényi, J., "A 'Magna Hungaria' kérdéséhez," *Magyar Nyelv*, LV (1959), pp. 385–391, 488–99.

Popov, A.I., "Burtasy i mordva," *UZLGU* no. 105, serija vostokovedčeskikh nauk z, 1948.

Pritsak, Omeljan, "Bolgaro-Tschuwaschica," *UAJ.*, 31 (1959), 274–314.

"From the Säbirs to the Hungarians," in Gy. Káldy-Nagy (ed.), *Hungaro-Turcica. Studies in Honour of Julius Németh* (Budapest, 1976), pp. 17–30.

Räsänen, Martti, "Die tschuwassischen Lehnwörte im Tscheremissischen," *MSFOu*. LXVII (1920).

Uralaltaische Wortforschungen (Studia Orientalia edidit Societas Orientalis Fennica, XVIII: 3, Helsinki, 1955).

"Gibt es im Baschkirischen etwas Ugrisches," *AOH.*, 12 (1960), 73–8.

Rásonyi, László, "Başkurt ve Macar yurtlarındaki ortak coğrafî adlar üzerine," *X Türk Dil Kurultayında Okunan Bilimsel Bildiriler, 1963* (Ankara, 1964).

Rédei, K., *Die syrjänischen Lehnwörter im Wogulischen* (Budapest, 1970).

Róna-Tas, A., "A bolgár-török permi érintkezések néhány kérdése," *Nyelvtudományi Közlemények*, 77 (1975).

Róna-Tas, A., "A permi nyelvek őspermi bolgár-török jövevényszavai," *Nyelvtudományi Közlemények*, 74 (1973).

Rohan-Csermak, Géza, "La patrie primitive des Finno-Ougriens sous l'aspect ethnologique," *UAJ*, 41 (1969), 265–72.

Róheim, G., *Hungarian and Vogul Mythology* (Monographs of the American Ethnological Society, XXIII, 1954).

"A kazár nagyfejedelem és a Turulmonda," *Ethnographia*, XXVIII (1917).

"A kazár és magyar nagyfejedelem," *Ethnographia*, XXIX (1918).

Róna-Tas, András, – Fodor, S., *Epigraphica Bulgarica. A volga bolgár-török feliratok* (Studia Uralo-Altaica, I, Szeged, 1973).

"Some Volga Bulgarian Words in the Volga Kipchak Languages," in Gy. Káldy-Nagy (ed.), *Hungaro-Turcica. Studies in Honour of Julius Németh* (Budapest, 1976), pp. 169–75.

Rudenko, S.I., *Baškiry. Istoriko-etnografičeskie očerki* (Moskva-Leningrad, 1975).

Rybakov, B.A. (ed.), *Etnogenez mordovskogo naroda* (Saransk, 1965).

Safargaliev, M.G., "Zametka o burtasakh," *Učenye Zapiski Mordovskogo Naučno-Issledovatel'skogo Instituta Jazyka, Literajury i Istorii* 13 (1951).

Schönebaum, H., "Die Kenntnis der byzantinischen Geschichtsschreiber von der ältesten Geschichte der Ungarn vor der Landnahme," *Ungarische Bibliothek*, first series, 5 (Berlin–Leipzig, 1922).

Sebestyén, Irén N., "Zur Frage des alten Wohngebietes der uralischen Völker," *ALH.*, I (1951–2).

Serebrennikov, B.A., *K voprosu o svjazi baškirskogo jazyka s vengerskim* (Ufa, 1963).

Šušarin, V.T., "Russko-vengerskie otnošenija v IX v.," *Meždunarodnye svjazi Rossii do XVII veka* (Moskva, 1961).

Sinor, Denis, "Autour d'une migration de peuples au V siècle," *JA.*, 235 (1946–7), pp. 1–78.

"Un voyageur du treizième siècle; le dominicain Julien de Hongrie," *BSOAS*, XIV pt. 3 (1952), 589–602.

The Outlines of Hungarian Prehistory," *Cahiers d'histoire mondiale/Journal of World History*, IV (1958), pp. 513–40.

"Geschichtliche Hypothesen und Sprachwissenschaft in der ungarischen, finnisch-ugrischen und uralischen Urgeschichtsforschung," *UAJ.*, 41 (1969), 273–81.

Smirnov, A.P., "Očerki po istorii drevnikh bulgar," *Trudy Gosudarstvennogo Istoričeskogo Muzeja* XI (Moskva, 1940).

"Očerk drevneĭ istorii Mordvy," *Trudy Gosudarstvennogo Istoričeskogo muzeja* XI (Moskva, 1940).

Volžskie bulgary (*Trudy* Gosudarstvennogo Istoričeskogo Muzeja XIX, Moskva, 1951).

"K voprosy o burtasakh," *Kratkie Soobščenija o Dokladakh i Polevykh Issledovanijakh Instituta Istorii Material'noĭ Kul'tury AN SSSR* XL (1951).

Očerki drevneĭ i srednevekovoĭ istorii narodov Povolž'ja i Prikam'ja (Moskva, 1952).

Železnyĭ vek čuvašskogo Povolž'ja (*Materialy i Issledovanija po arkheologii SSSR* 95, Moskva, 1961).

"Etnogenez mordovskogo naroda po dannym arkheologii I–XV vv. n.e.," in B.A. Rybakov (ed.), *Etnogenez mordovskogo naroda* (Saransk, 1965).

"Ob etničeskom sostave Volžskoĭ Bolgarii,' in V.L. Janin (ed.), *Novoe v arkheologii* (Moskva, 1972).

(ed.), *Problemy arkheologii i drevneĭ istorii ugrov* (Moskva, 1972).

Les populations finnoises des bassins de la Volga et de la Kama, trans. O. Boyer (École des languages orientales vivantes, Publications, 4rth series, vol. 8, Paris, 1898).

Stepanov, P.D., "Burtasy i Mordva," in B.A. Rybakov (ed.) *Etnogenez Mordovskogo naroda* (Saransk, 1965).

Tatiščev, V.N., *Istorija rossiĭskaja*, ed. M.N. Tikhomirov et al., 7 vols. (Moskva–Leningrad, 1962–8).

Toivonen, Y.H., "Zur Frage der Finnisch-Ugrischen Urheimat," *JSFOu.* LVI (1952).

Tomka, P., "Le problème de la survivance des Avars dans la littérature archéologique hongroise," *AOH*, 24 (1971).

Trefilov, G.N., *Proiskhoždenie udmurtskogo naroda* (Iževsk, 1956).

Trer'jakov, P.N., *Finno-ugry, balty i slavjane na Dnepre i Volge* (Moskva-Leningrad, 1966).

de Vajay, Sz., *Der Eintritt des ungarischen Stämmebundes in die europäischen Geschichte* (München, 1968).

Vásáry, István, "The Hungarians or Možars and the Meščers/Mišers of the Middle Volga Region," *Archivum Eurasiae Medii Aevi*, 1 (1975).

Vasil'ev, B.A., "Problema burtasov i mordvy," *Voprosy etničeskoĭ istorii mordovskogo naroda* (*Trudy Mordovskoĭ Etnografičeskoĭ Ekspedicii* 1, Trudy Instituta Etnografii, 63, Moskva, 1960).

Vernadsky, George, de Ferdinandy, M., *Studien zur ungarischen Frühgeschichte*

(Südosteuropäische Arbeiten, 47, München, 1957).
Vorob'ev, N.I., Khisamutdinov, G.M., *Tatary srednego Povolž'ja i Priural'ja* (Moskva, 1967).
Vuorela, T., *The Finno-Ugric Peoples*, trans. J. Atkinson (Indiana University Publications, Uralic and Altaic Series, vol. 39, Bloomington–The Hague, 1964).
Wichmann, Y., "Die tschuwassischen Lehnwörter in den permischen Sprachen," *MSFOu*. XXI (1903).
Wladikin, W.E., "Die frühen Perioden der Ethnogeschichte der Udmurten (Wotjaken)," *Acta Ethnographica Hungarica*, 21 (1972).
Zolotareva, I.M. (ed.), *Etnogenez finno-ugorskikh narodov po dannym antropologii* (Moskva, 1974).
Zsirai, Miklós, "Finnugor népnevek. I. Jugria" *Nyelvtudományi Közlemények*, XLVII (1928–30), XLVIII (1931–4).
Finnugor rokonságunk (Budapest, 1937).
A finnugorság ismertetése (Budapest, 1958).

10. The peoples of the south-Russian steppes

Collections of sources

Chavannes, Edouard, *Documents sur les Tou-kiue (Turcs) Occidentaux, recueillis et commentés suivi de Notes Additionnelles* (Sbornik trudov Orkhonskoĭ ekspedicii, VI, Sanktpeterburg, 1903; *T'oung Pao*, series II, 4, 1904, both reprinted as one volume: Paris, 1941).
Garkavi, A. Ja., *Skazanija musul'manskikh pisateleĭ o slavjanakh i russkikh* (Sanktpeterburg, 1870).
Skazanija evreĭskikh pisateleĭ o khozarakh i Khozarskom carstve (Sanktpeterburg, 1874).
Karaulov, N.A., "Svedenija arabskikh geografov IX i X vekov po R. Kh. o Kavkaze, Armenii i Aderbeĭdžane," *Sbornik Materialov dlja Opisanija Mestnosteĭ i Plemen Kavkaza* 38 (1908).
Kupfer, Franciszek, Lewicki, Tadeusz, *Źródła hebrajskie do dziejów Słowian i niektórych innych ludów środkowej i wschodniej Europy* (Wrocław-Warszawa, 1956).
Lewicki, Tadeusz, *Źródła arabskie do dziejów Słowiańszczyzny*, I–II,[1-2] 3 vols. (Wrocław–Kraków–Warszawa, 1956, 1969, 1977).
Liu Mau-tsai, *Die Chinesischen Nachrichten zur Geschichte der Ost-Türken (T'u-küe)*, 2 vols Göttinger Asiatische Forschungen, vol. 10, Wiesbaden, 1958).
Pigulevskaja, N.V., *Siriĭskie istočniki po istorii narodov SSSR* (Moskva–Leningrad, 1941).
Turkic Orkhon inscriptions: Aidarov, G., *Jazyk orkhonskikh pamjatnikov drevnetjurkskoĭ pis'mennosti* (Alma-Ata, 1971).
Abu'l-Fidā, *Taqwīm al-Buldān* ("Geography of the Lands"): *Géographie d'Aboulféda*, ed. R. Reinaud, M. Le Bon MacGuckin de Slane (Paris, 1840).

Al-Bakrī: Kunik, A., Rozen, V., "Izvestija al-Bekri o slavjanakh i ikh sosedjakh," *Zapiski Imperatorskoĭ Akademii Nauk* 32 (1878).

Al-Balādhurī, *Kitāb Futūḥ al-Buldān* ("The Book of the Conquest of the Lands"), ed. M.J. de Goeje (Leiden, 1895).

Al-Dimashqî, *Nukhbat al-Dahr fī 'Ajā'ib al-Barr wa'l-Baḥr: Cosmographie de Chems ed-din abu Abdallah Mohammed ed Dimachqui*, ed. F. Mehren (St. Petersbourg, 1866), trans.: *Manuel de la cosmographie du Moyen Age*, trans. F. Mehren (Copenhagen, 1874).

Abu Ḥāmid al-Gharnāṭī, *Tuḥfat al-Albāb wa Nukhbat al- 'Ajā'ib* ("The Gift of the Hearts and Selection of the Wonders"): *Abu Ḥāmid el Grenadino y su relación de viaje por tierras eurasiáticas*, ed., trans. C.E. Dubler (Madrid, 1953).

Ibn A'tham al-Kūfī, *Kitāb al-Futūḥ*, ed. M. 'Abu'l-Mu'id Khan and Sayyid 'Abdu'l-Wahhāb Bukhārī, 8 vols. thus far (Da'iratu'l-Ma'arif il-Osmania Publications, New Series, IX/xii/i–viii, Hyderabad, 1968–75).

Ibn al-Athīr, *Al-Kāmil fī'l-Ta'rīkh: Chronicon quod perfectissimum inscribitur*, ed. C.J. Tornberg, 12 vols. (Leiden, 1851–76, reprint: Beirut, 1965–6).

Ibn Faḍlān, *Risāla*: A. Zeki Validi Togan (ed. trans.), *Ibn Faḍlān's Reisebericht* (Abhandlungen für die Kunde des Morgenlandes, XXIV, 3, Leipzig, 1939).

Risāla: Kovalevskiĭ, A.P. (facs. ed., trans.) *Kniga Akhmeda ibn Fadlana o ego putešestvii na Volgu v 921–922 gg.* (Khar'kov, 1956).

Risāla, ed. S. Dahān (Damascus, 1379/1960).

Ibn al-Faqīh, *Kitāb al-Buldān* ("The Book of the Lands"), ed. M.J. de Goeje (Bibliotheca Geographorum Arabicorum, V, Leiden, 1885).

Ibn Ḥawqal, *Kitāb Ṣurat al-Arḍ: Opus Geographicum auctore Ibn Ḥauḳal "Liber Imaginis Terrae,"* ed. J.H. Kramers (BGA., II², 2 vols., Leiden, 1938–9).

Ibn Miskawaih, *Tajārub al-Umam* ("The Experiences of the Nations"): *The Eclipse of the 'Abbasid Caliphate*, ed. H.F. Amedroz, trans. D.S. Margoliouth, 5 vols. (Oxford, 1920–1).

Ibn Rusta, *Kitāb al-A'lāq al-Nafīsa* ("The Book of Precious Gems"): Khvol'son, D., *Izvestija o khozarakh burtascekh, bolgarakh, mad'jarakh, slavjanakh i russakh Abu-Alî Akhmeda ben Omar ibn Dasta* (Sanktpeterburg, 1868).

Kitāb al-A'lāq al-Nafīsa ("The Book of Precious Gems"), ed. M.J. de Goeje (BGA., VII, Leiden, 1892).

Ibn Khurdādhbih, *Kitāb al-Masālik wa'l-Mamālik: Liber viarum et regnorum*, ed. M.J. de Goeje (BGA., VI, Leiden, 1889).

Al-Idrīsī, *Kitāb Nuzhat al-Mushtāq fī Ikhtirāq al-Afāq: Opus Geographicum sive "Liber ad eorum delectationem qui terras peragrare studeant,"* ed. E. Cerulli, F. Gabrieli et al. fasc. 1–9 (Leiden, 1970–1984).

Al-Iṣṭakhrī, *Kitāb Masālik al-Mamālik: Viae regnorum*, ed. M.J. de Goeje (BGA., I, Leiden, 1870).

Jehuda hal-Levi, *Kitāb al-Khazar: Book of Kuzari*, trans. H. Hirschfeld (New York, 1946).

Al-Kāshgharī, Maḥmūd, *Divanü Lûgat-it-Türk*, facs. ed. Besim Atalay (Türk Dil Kurumu, Ankara, 1941).

Al-Maqdisī, *Kitāb al-Bad' wa'l-Tawārīkh* ("The Book of Creation and the Histories"), ed. C. Huart, 6 vols. (Paris, 1899–1919, reprint: Tehran, 1962).

Al-Marwazī, *Ṭabā'i al-Ḥayawān* ("The Nature of Animals"): *Sharaf al-Zamān Ṭāhir Marwazī on China, the Turks and India*, ed. trans. V.F. Minorsky (London, 1942).
Al-Mas'ūdī, *Kitāb al-Tanbīh wa'l-Ishrāf* ("The Book of Admonition and Recension"), ed. M.J. de Goeje, (BGA., VIII, Leiden, 1894).
Murūj al-Dhahab wa Ma'ādin al-Jawhar ("Meadows of Gold and Mines of Precious Stones"), ed. C. Pellat (Beirut, 1966–79) 7 vols.
Al-Muqaddasī, *Aḥsan al-Taqāsīm fī Ma'rifat al-Aqālīm* ("The Best of Divisions regarding Knowledge of the Climes"), ed. M.J. de Goeje (BGA., III, Leiden, 1906).
Al-Nadīm, *Kitāb al-Fihrist* ("The Index"), ed. G. Flügel (Leipzig, 1871–2, reprint: Beirut, 1964).
The Fihrist of al-Nadīm, trans. B. Dodge (Records of Civilization: Sources and Studies, LXXXIII, 2 vols., New York–London, 1970).
Al-Ṭabarī, *Ta'rīkh al-Ṭabarī* ("The History of al-Ṭabarī"), ed. Muḥammad Abu'l-Faḍl Ibrāhīm, 10 vols. (Dhakhā'ir al-'Arab, 30, Cairo, 1962–1967).
Al-Ya'qūbī, *Ta'rīkh* ("The History") (Beirut, 1390/1970).
Yāqūt, *Mu'jam al-Buldān* ("Geographical Dictionary"), 5 vols. (Beirut, 1957).

Armenian sources

Asołig: *Histoire universelle par Etienne Açoghig de Daron*, trans. E. DuLaurier, 2 vols., (Paris, 1883–1917).
Movsēs Daskhurants'i, *Patmut'iwn Ałuanits': Movsisi Kałankatuats'woy Patmut'iwn Ałuanits' asharhi*, ed. M. Emin (Moskva, 1860, reprint: Tiflis, 1912).
The History of the Caucasian Albanians by Movsēs Dasxuranç̣i, trans. C.J.F. Dowsett (London, 1961).
Ełishe (Eghishe): Egiše, O Vardane i voĭne armyanskoe, trans. (into Russian) I.A. Orbeli (Erevan, 1971).
(Pseudo-)Movsēs Khorenats'i: *Géographie de Moïse de Corène*, ed., trans. A. Soukry (Venise, 1881).
Łewond (Ghevond), *Patmut'iwnłevondeay metsi vardapeti Hayots'*, ed. I. Ezeants' (St. Peterburg, 1887).
Ghévond, *Histoire des guerres et des conquêtes des Arabes en Arménie*, trans. V. Chahnazarian (Paris, 1856).

Ethiopian sources

John of Nikiu, *The Chronicle of John, Bishop of Nikiu*, trans. R.H. Charles (London, 1916).

Greek sources

Agathias, *Agathiae Myrinae, Historiarum libri quinque*, ed. R. Keydell (Corpus Fontium Historiae Byzantinae, II, Berlin, 1967).
Comnena, Anna: *Anne Comnene, Alexiade*, ed., trans. B. Leib, 3 vols. (Paris, 1937–45).
Dexippi, Eunapii, Petri Patricii, Prisci, Malchi, Menandri historiarum quae supersunt, ed. I. Bekker, B.G. Niebuhr (Corpus Scriptorum Historiae Byzantinae, Bonn, 1829).

Malalas, Ioannes, *Chronographia*, ed. L. Dindorf (Corpus Scriptorum Historiae Byzantinae, Bonn, 1831).
Nikophoros Patriarkhos, *Nicephori Archiepiscopi Constantinopolitani opuscula historica*, ed. C. de Boer (Bibliotheca Scriptorum Graecorum et Romanorum Teubneriana: Scriptores Graeci, Leipzig, 1880, reprint, 1975).
Konstantinos Porphyrogennetos: Constantinus Porphyrogenitus, *Excerpta de Legationibus*, ed. C. de Boer (Berlin, 1903).
Constantine Porphyrogenitus, De Administrando Imperio, ed. Gyula Moravcsik, trans. Romilly J.H. Jenkins (Corpus Fontium Historiae Byzantinae I, Dumbarton Oaks, Washington, D.C., 1967).
Prokopios, *De Bello Gothico*, ed. W. Dindorf (Corpus Scriptorum Historiae Byzantinae, Bonn, 1883–1838).
Simokattes, Theophylaktos, *Historiae*, ed. C. de Boer, rev. ed. P. Wirth (Stuttgart, 1972).
Skylitzes, Ioannes: *Georgius Cedrenus Ioannis Scylitzae ope*, ed. J. Bekker (Corpus Scriptorum Historiae Byzantinae, 2 vols., Bonn, 1839).
Theophanes, *Chronographia*, ed. C. de Boer 2 vols. (Leipzig, 1883, reprint, Hildesheim, 1963).
Theophanus Continuatus, *Historiae*, ed. J. Bekker (Corpus Scriptorum Historiae Byzantinae, Bonn, 1838).

Georgian sources

K'art'lis Ts'khovreba ("The Life of Georgia"), ed. S. Qaukhch'ishvili, 2 vols. (T'bilisi, 1955, 1959).

Hebrew sources

Golb, Norman, Pritsak, Omeljan, *Khazarian Hebrew Documents of the Tenth Century* (Ithaca, 1982).
The Khazar Hebrew Correspondence: Kokovcov, P.K., *Evereĭsko-khazarskaja perepiska v X veke* (Moskva-Leningrad, 1932).
"Khazar Cambridge Document": Cambridge University Library, T-S Loan 38, see also: Kokovcov, *Evreĭsko-Khazarskaja perepiska.*
Petaḥia of Ratisbon: *Travels of Rabbi Petachia of Ratisbon*, ed., trans. A. Benisch (London, 1856).
Schechter, S., "An Unknown Khazar Document", *Jewish Quarterly Review*, new series, 3 (1912).

Latin sources

Annales Bertiniani: Annales de Saint-Bertin, ed. F. Grat, J. Vielliard, S. Clémencet, intro. notes by L. Levillain (Paris, 1964).
Jordanes, *Getica: Iordan, O proiskhoždenii i dejanjakh getov* (ed., trans), E.Č. Skržinskaja (Markva, 1960).
Ravennatis anonymi Cosmographia, ed. J. Schnetz (Itineraria Romana, II, Leipzig, 1940).

Persian sources

Bal'amī, *Tārīkh-i Ṭabarī: Chronique de Abou Djafar Mohammad ben Djarir ben Yezid Tabari (traduite sur la version persane d'Abou 'Ali Mohammed Bel'amī*, trans. H. Zotenberg, 4 vols. (Paris, 1867–74).

Tarjuma-i Tārīkh-i Ṭabarī, Lithographic ed. M. Minovi of MS. 7481 of Jerusalem, al-Aksa Mosque Library (Teheran, 1345/1926–7, reprint: 1966).

Gardīzī, *Zain al-Akhbār* ("Adornment of Information"), excerpts in: Bartol'd, V.V., "Izvlečenie iz Sočinenija Gardizi *Zaīn al-Akhbar*," in *Akademik V.V. Bartol'd, Sočinenija*, 9 vols. (Moskva, 1963–73), vol. 8.

Ḥudūd al-'Ālam ("The Regions of the World"), trans. Vladimir Minorsky (Gibb Memorial Series, New Series, XI, 2nd rev. ed., London, 1970).

Slavic sources

Ipat'evskaja letopis': Polnoe sobranie russkikh letopiseĭ, II, 2nd. ed. (Moskva, 1962).

Lavrent'evskaja letopis': Polnoe sobranie russkikh letopiseĭ, I, 2nd. rev. ed. (Leningrad, 1926).

Patriaršaja ili Nikonovskaja letopis': Polnoe sobranie russkikh letopiseĭ, IX – XIII (Sanktpeterburg, 1862–1904), reprint (Moskva, 1965), 3 vols.

Syriac sources

Bar Hebraeus, *The Chronography of Gregory Abū'l Faraj Bar Hebraeus*, trans. E.A.T.W. Budge (London, 1932).

Michael Syrus: *Chronique de Michel le Syrien*, ed. trans. J.B. Chabot, 4 vols. (Paris, 1899–1910).

Zacharias Rhetor, *Die Sogennante Kirchengeschichte des Zacharias Rhetor*, trans. K. Ahrens, G. Krüger (Leipzig, 1889).

Turkic sources

Codex Cumanicus in Faksimile herausgegeben, ed. Kaare Grønbech (Monumenta Linguarum Asiae Maioris, I, Kopenhagen, 1936).

Grønbech, Kaare, *Komanisches Wörterbuch* (Monumenta Linguarum Asiae Maioris, Subsidia, I, København, 1942).

Secondary literature

Aliev, S.M., "O datirovke nabega rusov upomjanutykh Ibn Isfandijarom i Amoli," In A.S. Tveritinova (ed.), *Vostočnye istočniki po istorii narodov jugo-vostočnoĭ i central'noĭ Evrope*, 2 vols. (Moskva, 1964, 1969), vol. II.

Altheim, F., Stiel, R., "Michael der Syrer über die erste Auftreten der Bulgaren und Chazaren", *Byzantion*, XXVIII (1958).

Ančabadze, Z.B., "Kipčaki severnogo Kavkaza po dannym gruzinskikh letopiseĭ XI – XIV vekov," in I.V. Treskov et al. (eds.), *Materialy naučnoĭ sessii po probleme proiskhoždenie balkarskogo i karačaevskogo narodov* (Nal'čik, 1960).

Angelov, D., Gjuzelev, V., 'Izvestija v armjansk izvori za srednevekovnata istorija na Bŭlgarija," *Istoričeski Pregled*, 22.1 (1966).
Obrazuvanie na bŭlgarskata narodnost (Sofija, 1971).
Ankori, Zvi, *Karaites in Byzantium* (New York – Jerusalem, 1959).
Artamonov, M. I. *Očerk drevneĭšeĭ istorii Khazar* (Leningrad, 1936).
"Belaja Beža," *SA* 16 (1952), pp. 42–76.
Istorija khazar (Leningrad, 1962).
Ašmarin, N.I., *Bolgary i čuvaši* (Kazan', 1902).
Bacot, Jacques, "Reconnaisance en Haute Asie Septentrionale par cinq envoyés Ouïgours au VIII siècle," *JA*. 1956, pp. 137–153.
Barnea, I., "Predvaritel'nye svedenija o kamennykh pamjatnikakh v Bessarabii (obl. Dobrudža)," *Dacia*, NS 7 (1962).
Bartol'd, V.V., "Novyĭ trud o polovcakh," *Russkiĭ Istoričeskiĭ Žurnal* – (1921), reprinted *Akademik V.V. Bartol'd Sočinenija*, 9 vols., (Moskva, 1963–73), V.
Mesto prikaspiĭskikh oblasteĭ v istorii musul'manskogo mira (Baku, 1925), reprinted *Akademik V.V. Bartol'd Sočinenija*, 9 vols. (Moscow, 1963–73) II/1.
"Kipčaki," *Akademik V.V. Bartol'd Sočinenija*, 9 vols (Moskva, 1963–73), V (*Enziklopaedie des Islam*, 4 vols., Leiden–Leipzig, 1913–36, II).
"Khazary," *Akademik V.V. Bartol'd Sočinenija*, 9 vols. (Moskva, 19 63–73), V (*Enziklopaedie des Islam*, 4 vols., Leiden–Leipzig, 1913–36) II.
"Arabskie izvestija o rusakh," *SV*. 1 (1940): *Akademik V.V. Bartol'd Sočinenija*, 9 vols. (Moskva, 1963–73) II/1.
Barthold, W. (V.V. Bartol'd), Golden, Peter B. "K͟hazar", *Enclopaedia of Islam*[2] (Leiden–London, 1960–1978, still in progress), VI.
Baskakov, N.A., "Poloveckie otbleski v 'Slove o polku Igorove'," *UAJ* 48 (1976).
Battal-Taymas, Abdullah, *Kazan Türkleri* ("The Turks of Kazan") (Ankara, 1966).
Benzing, Johannes, "Das Hunnische, Donaubolgarische und Wolgabolgarische," in J. Deny et al. (eds.), *Philologiae Turcicae Fundamenta* (Wiesbaden, 1959 – still in progress), I.
Beševliev', V., Verata na pŭrvobŭlgarite/*Die Religion der Protobulgaren* (Sofia, 1939).
Die protobulgarischen Inschriften (Berliner Byzantinistische Arbeiten, 23, Berlin, 1963).
Boba, Imre, *Nomads, Northmen and Slavs* (Slavo-Orientalia, II Wiesbaden–The Hague, 1967).
Boswell, A. Bruce, "The Kipchak Turks," *The Slavonic Review*, 6 (1927).
Bratianu, Georges, *La mer Noire. Des origines à la conquête ottomane* (Societas Academica Dacoromana, Acta Historica, IX, München, 1969).
Burmov, A., "Vŭprosi iz istorijata na prabŭlgarite," *Godišnik na Sofiĭkija Universitet, istoriko-filologičeski fakultet*, 44.2 (1947).
Burmov, A., "Kŭm vŭprosa za proizkhod na prabŭlgarite," *Izvestija na Istoričeskot družestvo v Sofija* 22–4 (1948).
Czebe, Gy., "Turco-byzantinische Miszellen, I. Konstantinos, De administrando Imperio 37. Kapitel über die Petschenegen," *KCsA*., I (1921–5) pp. 209–19.
Czeglédy, Károly, Egy bolgár török *yiltavar* méltóságnév," *Magyar Nyelv*, XL (1944).
"Egy kazár méltóságnév," *Magyar Nyelv*, XLIII (1947).

"A kunok eredetéről," *Magyar Nyelv*, XLV (1949), pp. 43–50.
"A kazár *kil-kel* eredete," *Magyar Nyelv*, XLIX (1953), pp. 175–8.
"Herakleios török szövetségesei," *Magyar Nyelv*, XLIX (1953), pp. 319–23.
"Monographs on Syriac and Muhammadan Sources in the Literary Remains of M. Kmoskó," *AOH.*, 4 (1954) pp. 19–91.
IV–IX századi népmozgalmak a steppén (A Magyar Nyelvtudományi Társaság Kiadványai, 84, Budapest, 1954).
"Kaukázusi hunok, kaukázusi avarok", *Studia Antiqua Hungarica*, 2 (1955) pp. 123–40.
"Khazar Raids in Transcaucasia in A.D. 762–764," *AOH.*, 11 (1960) pp. 75–88.
"A korai kazár történelem forrásainak kritikájához," *A Magyar Tudományos Akadémia nyelv-és irodalomtudományi osztályának közleményei*, 15 (1960) pp. 107–28.
"Bemerkungen zur Geschichte der Chazaren," *AOH.*, 13 (1961) pp. 243–51.
"*ΤΕΡΜΑΤΖΟΥΣ*," *Acta Antiqua Hungarica*, 10 (1962).
A nomád népek vándorlása napkelettől napnyugatig (Kőrösi Csoma Kiskönyvtár, 8, Budapest, 1969).
"Pseudo-Zacharias Rhetor on the Nomads," in L. Ligeti (ed.), *Studia Turcica* (Budapest, 1971), pp. 133–48.
"Ogurok és türkök Kazáriában" in A. Bartha *et al.* (eds.), *Magyar őstörténeti tanulmányok* (Budapest, 1977).
Dąbrowski, Krzysztof, Nagrodzka-Majchrzyk, Teresa, Tryjarski, Edward, *Hunowie Europejscy Protobułgarzy, Chazarowie, Pieczyngowie* (Wrocław-Warszawa-Kraków-Gdańsk, 1975).
Diaconu, P., *Les Petchenègues au Bas-Danube* (Bibliotheca Historica Romaniae, 27, Bucarest 1970).
Dunlop, Douglas M., *The History of the Jewish Khazars* (Princeton, 1954).
Džanašvili, M., "Izvestija gruzinskikh letopiseĭ i istorikov o severnom Kavkaze i Rossii," *Sbornik Materialov dlja Opisanija Mestnosteĭ i Plemen Kavkaza*, 22 (1897).
Eremjan, S.T., "Juriĭ Bogoljubskiĭ po armjanskim i gruzinskim istočnikam," *Naučnye Trudy Erevanskogo Gosudarstvennogo Universiteta* 23. (1946).
Gening, V.F., Khalikov, A.Kh., *Rannie bolgary na Volge* (Moskva, 1964).
Gjuzelev, B. *Knjaz Boris Pŭrvi. Bŭlgari prez vtorata polovina na IX vek* (Sofija, 1969).
Golden, Peter B., "Hazar Dili" ("The Khazar Language"), *TDAYB.* (1971).
"The Migrations of the Oğuz," *Archivum Ottomanicum*, 4 (1972), pp. 45–84.
"The Question of the Rus' Qağanate," *Archivum Eurasiae Medii Aevi*, 2 (1982) pp. 77–97.
"Imperial Ideology and the Sources of Political Unity Amongst the Pre-Činggisid Nomads of Western Eurasia," *Archivum Eurasiae Medii Aevi*, 2 (1976).
Khazar Studies. An historico-philological inquiry into the origins of the Khazars (Bibliotheca Orientalis Hungarica XXV, Budapest, 1980).
"Khazaria and Judaism", *Archivum Eurasiae Medii Aevi*, 3 (1983), pp. 127–56.
Golubovskiĭ, P., *Pečenegi, Torki i polovcy do našestvija tatar. Istorija južnorusskikh stepeĭ IX – XIII* vv. (Kiev, 1884).

Grekov, B.A., Čerepnin, L.V., Pašuto, V.T., *Očerki istorii SSSR: period feodalizma IX – XV vv.* (Moskva, 1953).

Grigor'ev, V.V., *Rossija i Azija* (Sanktpeterburg, 1876).

Gumilev, L.N. *Otkrytie Khazarii* (Moskva, 1966).

Drevnie Tjurki (Moskva, 1967).

Gyárfás, István, *A jász-kúnok története*, 4 vols. (Kecskemét–Szolnok–Budapest, 1870–85).

Györffy, György, "Besenyők és magyarok," *Kőrösi Csoma Archivum*, 1, Supplement vol. 1 (1939), pp. 397–500.

Tanulmányok a magyar állam eredetéről (Budapest, 1959).

"Monuments du lexique petchénègue", *AOH*, 18 (1965).

"Sur la question de l'établissement des Petchénègues en Europe," *AOH*, 25 (1972).

"Système des résidences d'hiver et d'été chez les nomades et les chefs hongrois du Xe siècle," *Archivum Eurasiae Medii Aevi*, 1 (1975).

Halasi-Kun, Tibor, "Orta Kıpcakca *q*-, *k*- ~ O meselesi" ("The Problem of Middle Kipchak *q*-, *k* ~ O") *Türk Dili ve Tarihi Hakkında Araştırmalar*, ed. H. Eren, T. Halasi-Kun (Ankara, 1950), 1.

Harmatta, János, "The Dissolution of the Hun Empire", *Acta Archaeologica Hungarica*, 2 (1952).

Haussig, H.W. "Theophylakts Exkurs über die Skythischen Völker," *Byzantion*, 23 (1953).

Henning, W.B., "A Farewell to the Khaghan of the Aq-Aqatärān," *BSOAS* 14 (1952), pp. 501–22.

Gruševskiĭ (Gruševs'kiĭ), M. *Očerki istorii Kievskoĭ zemli ot smerti Jaroslava do konca XIV st.* (Kiev, 1891).

Hruševs'kiĭ, M., *Istorija Ukraïni-Rusi* 10 vols. (L'viv–Kiiv, 1903–37, reprint New York, 1954–8).

Istvánovits, M., "Georgian Data Bearing on the Petchenegs", *AOH.*, 16 (1963).

Jakubovskiĭ, A. Ju., "Rasskaz ibn Bibi o pokhode maloaziĭskikh turok na Sudak, polovcev i russkikh v načale XIII v.," *Vizantiĭskiĭ Vremennik* 25 (1928).

"O russko-khazarskikh i russko-kavkazskikh otnošenijakh v IX – X vv.," *Izvestija Akademii Nauk SSSR serija istorii i filosofii*, 3.5 (1946).

Kakabadze, S., "Operedviženijakh pečenegov v VII – VIII vv.," *Bjulleten' Kavkazskogo Istoriko-Arkheologičeskogo Instituta v Tiflise. No. 8 (1931)*

Karaulov', N.A., "Bolkary na Kavkaze," *Sbornik Materialov dlja opisanija mestnosteĭ i plemen Kavkaza* (1908).

Kargalov, V.V. *Vnešnepolitičeskie faktory razvitija feodal'noĭ Rusi. Feodal'naja Rus' i kočevniki* (Moskva, 1967).

Každan, A.P., "Ioan Mavropod: pečenegi i russkie v seredine XI v.," *Sbornik Radova Vizantološkog Instituta* 8.1 (1963).

Khabičev, M.A., "O drevnetjurkskikh runičeskikh nadpisjakh v alanskikh katakombakh," *Sovetskaja Tjurkologija* 2 (1970).

Kiss, Attila, "11th Century Khazar Rings from Hungary with Hebrew Letters and Signs", *AAH.*, 22 (1970).

Kljaštornyĭ, S.G., *Drevetjurkskie runičeskie pamjatniki kak istočnik po istorii Sredneĭ Azii* (Moskva, 1964).

Kmoskó, Mihály, "Araber und Chazaren," *KCsA* 1 (1921–5) pp. 280–92.
Koledarov, P.S., "Naïranni spomenovanija na Bŭlgarite vŭpkhu starinnite karti," *Izvestija na Instituta za Istorija, Bŭlgarska Akademija na Naukite* 20 (1968).
Kollautz, Arnulf, Miyakawa, Hisayuki, *Geschichte und Kultur eines völkerwanderungszeitlichen Nomadenvolkes. Die Jou-Jan der Mongolei und die Awaren in Mitteleurope*, 2 vols. (Aus Forschung und Kunst, Herausgegeben vom Geschichtsverein für Kärnten, vols. 10–11, Klagenfurt, 1970).
Kononov, A.N., "K etimologii etnonimov kypčak, kuman, kumyk," *UAJ* 48 (1976).
Kossányi, Béla, "Az úzok és kománok történetéhez a XI–XII században," *Századok*, 57–8 (1923–4), pp. 519–37.
Kudrjašov, K.V., *Poloveckaja step'* (Zapiski Vsesojuznogo Geografičeskogo Obščestva, novaja serija, vol. 2, Moskva, 1948).
Kumekov, B.E., *Gosudarstvo kimakov IX–XI vv. po arabskim istočnikam* (Alma-Ata, 1972).
Kumykov, T.Kh., "Etnogenez balkarskogo i Karačaevskogo narodov v istoričeskoĭ literature," in I.V. Treskov et al. (eds.), *Materialy naučnoĭ sessii po probleme proiskhoždenija balkarskogo i Karačaevskogo narodov* (Nal'čik, 1960).
Kurat, Akdes Nimet, "Peçeneklere dair arastirmalar" ("Researches on the Pechenegs"), *Türkiyat Mecmuası*, 5 (1935).
Peçenek tarihi ("History of the Pechenegs") (Istanbul, 1937).
"Bulgar," *Islâm Ansiklopedisi* (Istanbul-Ankara, 1940 to present), fasc. 20.
"Muḥammad bin A'ṣam al-Kufi'nin *Kitâb al-Futûḥ*'u" ("The *Kitāb al-Futūḥ* of Muḥammad b. A'tham al-Kufī"), Ankara Üniversitesi Dil ve Tarih-Coğrafya Fakültesi Dergisi, 7 (1949).
IV–XVIII yüzyıllarda karadeniz kuzeyindeki Türk kavimleri ve devletleri ("The Turkic Tribes and States in the North of the Black Sea in the 4th to 18th Centuries"), (Ankara Üniversitesi Dil ve Tarih-Coğrafya Fakültesi Yayınları, 182, Ankara, 1972).
Kuz'min, A.G., *Rjazanskoe letopisanie* (Moskva, 1965).
Lewicki, Tadeusz, *Polska i kraje sąsiednie w świetle 'Księgi Rogera' geografa arabskiego z XII w. al-Idrīsī'ego*, 2 vols. (Kraków–Warszawa, 1945, 1954).
"Źródła hebrajskie do dziejó w środkowej i wschodniej Europy w okresie wczesnego średniowiecza (IX–XIII ww.)," *Przegląd Orientalistyczny*, 15.3 (1955).
"Źródła arabskie i hebrajskie do dziejów Słowian w okresie wczesnego średniowiecza," *Studia Źródłoznawcze*, 3 (1958).
"'Arisu. Un nom de tribu énigmatique cité dans le lettre du roi Khazar Joseph (Xe siècle)", *Cahiers du Monde Russe et Soviétique*, 3.1 (1962).
"Écrivains arabes du IXᵉ au XVIᵉ siècle traitant de l'ambre jaune de la Baltique et de son importation en pays arabes," *Folia Orientalia*, 4 (1962–3).
"Ludy Daghestanu i północnego Kaukazu w oczach średniowiecznych pisarzy arabskich (IX–X ww.)," *Przegląd Orientalistyczny*, 46.2 (1963).
Ligeti, Lajos, "A kazár Σάρκελ név jelentéséhez," *Magyar Nyelv*, XXXIII (1936).
"Sur deux mots comans," *AAH* 10 (1962).
"À propos du 'Rapport sur les rois demeurant dans le Nord'," *Études Tibétaines dediées à la mémoire de Marcelle Lalou* (Paris, 1971).

Macartney, C.A., "The Petchenegs," *Slavonic Review*, 8 (1929), pp. 342–55.
"The End of the Huns," *Byzantinisch-neugriechische Jahrbücher*, 10 (1934).
Maenchen-Helfen, Otto, "Akatir," *CAJ*, 11 (1966).
The World of the Huns, ed. Max Knight (Berkeley, 1973).
Marquart, Joseph, *Die Chronologie der alttürkischen Inschriften*. Mit einem Vorwort und Anhang von Prof. W. Bang in Löwen (Leipzig, 1898).
"Historische Glossen zu den alttürkischen Inschriften," *Wiener Zeitschrift für die Kunde des Morgenlandes* 12 (1898).
Ērānšahr nach der Geographie des Ps. Moses Xorenac'i (Abhandlungen der kgl. Gesellschaft der Wissenschaften zu Göttingen. Phil.-hist. Klasse, Neue Folge, vol. III N.2, Berlin, 1901).
Osteuropäische und Ostasiatische Streifzüge (Leipzig, 1903, reprint: Hildesheim, 1961).
Über das Volkstum der Komanen – in Bang. W. and Marquart, J., *Osttürkische Dialektstudien* (Abhandlungen der kgl. Gesellschaft der Wissenschaften zu Göttingen, phil.-hist. Klasse, New Series, vol. 13, N.1, Berlin, 1914).
Menges, Karl H., "Etymological Notes on Some Päčänäg Names", *Byzantion*, 17 (1944–5) pp. 256–80.
"Altaic Elements in the Proto-Bulgarian Inscriptions," *Byzantion*, 21 (1951).
"The Oriental Elements in the Vocabulary of the Oldest Russian Epos, the Igor' Tale," Supplement to *Word* (Monograph No. 1, New York, 1951).
"Tmūtorkan',", *Zeitschrift für Slavische Philologie*, 29 (1960).
Minorsky, Vladimir, "The Khazars and the Turks in the *Akām al-Marjān*," *BSOAS* 9 (1937–9).
Studies in Caucasian History (London, 1953).
A History of Sharvān and Darband (Cambridge, 1958).
Miskolczy, Gy., "A kúnok ethnikumához", *Történeti Szemle*, 7 (1918).
Moravcsik, Julius (Gyula), "Zur Geschichte der Onoguren," *Ungarische Jahrbücher* 10 (1930).
"Proiskhoždenie slova *TZITZAKION*," *Seminarium Kondakovianum* IV (1931).
Byzantinoturcica,[2] 2 vols. (Berliner Byzantinistische Arbeiten, vols. 10–11, Berlin, 1958).
Mošin, V., "Les Khazares et les Byzantins d'après l'anonyme de Cambridge," *Byzantion*, 6 (1931), pp. 309–25.
"Rus' i Khazarija pri Svjatoslave," *Seminarium Kondakovianum*, 6 (1933).
Németh, Julius (Gyula), "Zur Kenntnis der Petschenegen," *KCsA*. 1 (1921–5) pp. 219–25.
Németh, Gyula, *A honfoglaló magyarság kialakulása* (Budapest, 1930).
"Die Petschenegischen Stammesnamen," *UJ*. 10 (1930), pp. 27–34.
"Die Volksnamen *quman* und *qūn*," *KCsA*, 3 (1940). pp. 95–109.
Die Inschriften des Schatzes von Nagy-Szent-Miklós (Bibliotheca Orientalis Hungarica, 2, Budapest, 1932).
"The Runiform Inscriptions from Nagy-Szent-Miklós and the Runiform Scripts of Eastern Europe" *ALH*., 21 (1971).
Németh, Péter, "Obrazovanie pograničnoĭ oblasti Boržavy," in A.P. Smirnov (ed.) *Problemy arkheologii i drevneĭ istorii ugrov* (Moskva, 1972).

Ögel, Bahaeddin, *Islâmiyetten önce Türk kültür tarihi* ("The History of Pre-Islamic Turkic Culture") (Türk Tarih Kurumu Yayınlarından, VII series, 42, Ankara, 1962).
(Orkun), Hüseyin Namik, *Peçenekler* ("The Pechenegs") (Istanbul, 1933).
Pálóczi-Horváth, A., "Situation des recherches archéologiques sur les Comans en Hongrie," *AOH*, 27 (1973), pp. 201–9.
"L'immigration et l'établissement des Comans en Hongrie," *AOH*, 29 (1975) pp. 313–33.
Parkhomenko, V., "Rus' i Pečenegi,' *Slavia* 8 (1929–31).
Pashuto, V.T., *Vnešnjaja politika Drevneĭ Rusi* (Moskva, 1968).
Patkanoff, S., "Über das Volk der Sabiren," *Keleti Szemle* 1 (1900), 258–77.
Pelliot, Paul, À propos des Comans," *JA* 1920, I, pp. 125–185.
Notes sur l'histoire de la Horde d'Or suivies de Quelques noms turcs d'hommes et de peuples finissant en 'ar' (Oeuvres Posthumes de Paul Pelliot, II, Paris, 1949).
Pletneva, S.A., *Pečenegi, torki i polovci v juznorusskikh stepjakh* (MIA 62, Moskva-Leningrad, 1958).
Ot kočeviĭ k gorodam (Moskva, 1967).
"Ob etničeskoĭ neodnorodnosti naselenija severo-zapadnogo khazarskogo pograničʹja," in V.L. Janin (ed.), *Novoe v Arkheologii* (Moskva, 1972).
Drevnosti černykh klobukov (Svod Arkheologičeskikh Istorikov, El–19, Moskva, 1973).
Khozary (Moskva, 1976).
Polovoĭ, N. Ja., "O maršrute pokhoda russkikh na Berdaa i russko-khazarskikh otnošenijakh v 943 g., "*Vizantiĭskiĭ Vremennik* 25 (1961).
Ponomarev, A.L., "Kuman-polovcy," *Vestnik Drevneĭ Istorii* 3–4 (1940).
Popov, A.N., "Kipčaki i Rus'," *UZLGU set. istor nauk. 14 (1949).*
Pritsak, Omeljan, *Die bulgarische Fürstenliste und die Sprache der Protobulgaren* (Ural-Altaische Bibliothek, I, Wiesbaden, 1955).
"يوار Yowār und *Κάβαρ* Kāwar," *UAJ.*, 36 (1964).
"Polovtsiana, 1–2," *Reşid Rahmeti Arat için*, ed. M. Ergin (Ankara, 1966).
"Non-'Wild' Polovtsians," *To Honor Roman Jakobson*, 2 vols. (The Hague–Paris 1967), II. pp. 1615–23.
"The Pechenegs. A Case of Social and Economic Transformation," *Archivum Eurasiae Medii Aevi*, 1 (1975).
"The Polovcians and the Rus'," *Archivum Eurasiae Medii Aevi*, 2 (1982), pp. 321–380.
Rachewiltz, Igor de, *Papal Envoys to the Great Khans* (Stanford, 1971).
Rásonyi, László, "Der Volksname *Berendey*," *Seminarium Kondakovianum* VI (1933).
"Contributions à l'histoire des premières cristallisations d'état des Roumains. L'origine des Basarabas," *Archivum Europae Centro-Orientalis*, 1 (1935).
Rasovskiĭ, D.A., "Pečenegi, torki i berendeĭ na Rusi i v Ugrii," *Seminarium Kondakovianum* 6 (1933).
"Polovcy," *Seminarium Kondakovianum* 7 (1935), 8 (1936), 9 (1937), 10 (1938), 11 (1940).
"Les Comans et Byzance," *Actes du IVe Congrès International des Études*

Byzantines (Bulletin de l'Institut Archéologique Bulgare, IX, Sofia, 1935).
"Khinova," *Seminarium Kondakovianum*, 8 (1936).
"Tūlkoviny," *Seminarium Kondakovianum*, 8 (1936).
"Rus' i kočevniki v êpokhu Svjatogo Vladimira," *Vladimirskiĭ Sbornik v pamyat' 950-letija Kreščenija Rusi* (Belgrad, 1938).
"Rol' polovcev v voĭnakh Aseneĭ c vizantiĭskoĭ i latinskoĭ imperijami v 1118–1207 godakh," *Spisanie na Bŭlgarskata Akademija na Naukite* 58 (1939).
"Rus', černye klobuki i Polovcy v XII' v.," *Izvestija na Bŭlgarskoto Istoričesko Družestvo* 16–18, *Sbornik v pamet' prof. Petŭr Nikov* (Sofija, 1940).
Róna-Tas, András, Fodor, István, *Epigraphica Bulgarica. A volgai bolgár-török feliratok* (Szeged, 1973).
Sallaville, S., "Un peuple de race turque christianisé au XIIIe siècle: Les Comans," *Echos d'Orient* 18 (1914).
Ščerbak, A.M., "Neskol'ko slov o priemakh čtenija runičeskikh nadpiseĭ naĭdennykh na Oonu," *SA* 19 (1954).
"Znaki na Keramiki i kirpičakh iz Sarkela-Beloĭ Vežy," *MIA* No. 75 (1959).
"Les inscriptions inconnues sur pierres de Khoumara (au Caucase du Nord) et le problème de l'alphabet runique des Turcs Occidentaux," *AOH*, 15 (1962).
Schönebaum, H., "Zur Kabarenfrage," *Aus der byzantinistischen Arbeit der Deutschen Demokratischen Republik* 1 (*Berliner Byzantinistische Arbeiten* 5, Berlin, 1957).
Šanijazov, K.Š., *K êtničeskoĭ istorii uzbekskogo naroda (Istoriko-êtnografičeskie istedovanija na materialakh kipčakskogo komponenta)* (Taškent, 1974).
Šekera, I.M., *Mižanarodni zv'jazk kiïvs'koï Rusi* (Kiïv, 1963).
Sinor, Denis, "Autour d'une migration de peuples au Ve siècle," *JA*.235 (1946–7) pp. 1–78.
Soloviev, A.V., "Domination byzantine ou russe au nord de la Mer Noire à l'époque des Comnènes?," *Akten des XI Internationalen Byzantinisten-Kongres* (München, 1960).
Szokolay, Margit, "A magyarországi besenyőtelepekről," *Föld és Ember* IX. 2 (1929).
Thúry, J., "A khazar *isa* méltóságnévről," *Keleti Szemle* 4 (1903).
Togan, Ahmed Z.V., "Völkerschaften des Chazarenreiches im neunten Jahrhundert," *KCsA* 3 (1940).
Tolstov, S.P., "Khorezmiĭskaja genealogija Samuila Aby. Ešče raz k voprosu o kavarakh-khorezmiĭcakh," *SE* 1 (1947).
Po sledam drevnekhorezmiĭskoĭ civilizacii (Moskva-Leningrad, 1948).
Vajda, L., "Zur Frage der Völkerwanderungen," *Paideuma*, 19/20 (1973–4).
Vasil'evskiĭ, V.G., *Vizantija i Pečenegi* in *Trudi V.G. Vasil'evskago*, 4 vols. (Sankt-peterburg, 1908, reprint: Russian Reprint Series LXIX/1, The Hague, 1968), I.
Vasiliev, Alexander A., *The Goths in the Crimea* (Monographs of the Medieval Academy, 11, Cambridge, Mass., 1936).
Zajączkowski, Ananiasz, *Ze studiów nad zagadnieniem chazarskim* (Polska Akademia Umiejętności, Prace komisji orientalistycznej, 36, Kraków–Warszawa, 1947).
Związki językowe połowiecko-słowiańskie (Prace Wrocławskiego Towarzystwa Naukowego, series A, 34, Wrocław, 1949).

Karaims in Poland (Warszawa–Le Haye–Paris, 1961).
Zakhoder, B.N., *Kaspiĭskiĭ svod svedeniĭ o vostočnoĭ evrope*, 2 vols. (Moskva, 1962, 1967).
Zlatarski, V., *Istorija na Bŭlgarskata dŭržava prez srednite vekove*, 2 vols., ed. Khr. Petrov (Sofija, 1970).

11. The Türk empire

In comparison with the general paucity of primary sources of medieval Inner Asian history, the corpus of material dealing with the Türks is extraordinarily rich. On occasion, it is possible to coordinate the testimonies of Chinese, Byzantine, Greek and Türk sources – a real delight for the expert, but one which often leads to unwarranted conclusions.

Among the Chinese sources the dynastic Annals (mainly the *Chou shu*, *Sui shu*, *T'ang shu* and *Chiu T'ang shu*, *Liang shu*) provide ample information but there are also many data to be culled from Chinese encyclopaedias, travel accounts, inscriptions. Most of the texts found in the Annals and dealing with the Türks have been translated in the magnificent work of Chavannes, 1903, and by Liu, 1958. Among Byzantine sources, the *Excerpta de legationibus* of Menander and the *Histories* of Theophylactus Simocattes are of particular importance. For a description of these texts viewed from the Inner Asian point of view, see Moravcsik, 1958, I, pp. 422–6 and 544–8. A German translation of the passages relating to the Türks in Menander's work can be found in Doblhofer, 1955. Chavannes, 1903 not only gives translations of several Byzantine texts but also accompanies these with masterful, historical analyses.

Czeglédy, 1954, 1958 are good guides in the labyrinth of Iranian, Armenian, Syriac sources which shed, often indirect, light on Türk history. For the Armenian sources see Ter-Mkrtichjan, 1979. Sinor, 1963, pp. 203–4 may be of some help. See also Pigulevskaja, 1941, 1946, Ahrens-Krüger, 1899, Hamilton–Brooks, 1899, Payne-Smith, 1860.

Of extraordinary importance are the sparse historical data found in the inscriptions left by the Türks themselves. The very short bibliography given below (I) is limited to the editions of the texts and ignores the numerous linguistic and philological studies devoted to them. Recent publications are reviewed by Tryjarski, 1981.

The general bibliography (II) is limited to publications which are either very important for the study of Türk history or, though of limited utility, had to be included as justifications of statements made in the chapter. They complement rather than supplant the references given in Sinor, 1963, pp. 231–9. It is essential to remember that remarks of great importance are often hidden in footnotes of publications dealing mainly with other subjects.

Türk inscriptions

(*Note*. With the exception of Kljashtornyj–Livshic, 1972, all these texts are in Old Turkic.)

Batmanov, I.A.–Kunaa, A.Ch., 1963, *Pamjatniki drevnetjurkskoj pis'mennosti Tuv̯* (Kyzyl).

Bazin, Louis, 1976, "Eine Inschrift vom Oberen Jenissei als Quelle zur Geschichte Zentralasiens," *Materialia Turcica* 2, pp. 1–11.

Clauson, Sir Gerard, 1971, "Some Notes on the Inscription of Toñuquq," *Studia Turcica* edited by L. Ligeti, pp. 125–32, (Budapest).

Hovdhaugen, Even, 1974, "The Relationship between the two Orkhon Inscriptions," *Acta Orientalia.* 36, pp. 55–82.

Kljashtornyj, S.G., 1964, *Drevnetjurkskie runicheskie pamjatniki kak istochnik po istorii Srednej Azii* (Moskva).

1971, "Runicheskaja nadpis' iz vostochnoj Gobi," in *Studia Turcica* edited by L. Ligeti, pp. 249–258 (Budapest). and Livshic, V.A., 1972, "The Sogdian Inscription of Bugut Revised," *AOH.* 26, pp. 69–102.

Malov, S.E., 1951, *Pamjatniki drevnetjurkskoj pis'mennosti* (Moskva–Leningrad).

1952, *Enisejskaja pis'mennost' Tjurkov* (Moskva–Leningrad).

1959, *Pamjatniki drevnetjurkskoj pis'mennosti Mongolii i Kirgizii,* (Moskva–Leningrad).

Thomsen, V., 1896, *Inscriptions de l'Orkhon déchiffrées,* MSFOu v. 1924, "Alttürkische Inschriften der Mongolei," *ZDMG,* 78, pp. 121–75. Translated from Danish by H.H. Schaeder.

Tekin, Talât, 1968, *A Grammar of Orkhon Turkic,* Indiana University Uralic and Altaic Series vol. 69 (Bloomington, Indiana). On pp. 259–95, translation of the inscriptions.

Trijarsky, Edward, 1981, "Die alttürkischen Runen-Inschriften in den Arbeiten der letzten Jahre. Befunde und kritische Übersicht," *Altorientalische Forschungen* 8, pp. 339–352.

General

Ahrens, K.–Krüger, G., 1899, *Die sogenannte Kirchengeschichte des Zacharias Rhetor,* Bibliotheca Teubneriana (Leipzig).

Barthold, W., 1899, *Die alttürkischen Inschriften und die arabischen Quellen,* in W. Radloff, *Die alttürkischen Inschriften der Mongolei,* Zweite Folge (St. Pétersbourg)

1935, *12 Vorlesungen über die Geschichte der Türken Mittelasiens,* Deutsche Bearbeitung von Theodor Menzel (Berlin).

Bazin, Louis, 1974, *Les calendriers turcs anciens et médiévaux* (Lille).

1981, "Kül Tegin ou Köl Tegin?," *Scholia. Beiträge zur Turkologie und Zentralasienkunde. Annemarie von Gabain zum 80. Geburtstag am 4. Juli 1981 dargebracht von Kollegen, Freunden und Schülern.* Veröffentlichungen der Societas Uralo-Altaica, Bd. 14, pp. 1–7.

Beckwith, Christopher I., 1979, "The Tibetan Empire in the West," in *Tibetan Studies in Honor of Hugh Richardson,* pp. 30–8 (Oxford).

Bombaci, Alessio, 1964–1965, "Qutluɣ bolzun! A Contribution to the History of the Concept 'Fortune' among the Turks," *UAJ.* 36, pp. 284–91; 38, pp. 13–14.

1970a, "Qui était Jebu xak'an?," *Turcica* 2, pp. 7–24.

1970b, "On the Ancient Turkic Title *eltäbär,*" *Proceedings of the IXth Meeting of the Permanent International Altaistic Conference,* pp. 1–16 (Napoli).

1971, "The Husbands of Princess Hsien-li Bilgä," *Studia Turcica*, edited by L. Ligeti, pp. 103–23 (Budapest).

1974, "On the Ancient Turkish Title '*šaδ*'", Gururājamañjarikā. *Studi in onore di Giuseppe Tucci*, pp. 167–93 (Napoli).

1976, "On the Ancient Turkish Title *šadapït*", *UAJ* 48, pp. 32–41.

Cannata, Patrizia, 1981, *Profilo storico del I° impero turco (metà VI–metà VII secolo)*, Istituto di Studi dell'India e dell'Asia Orientale (Roma). [Possibly the best modern presentation of the Türk empire.]

Chabot, J.B., 1899–1924, *Chronique de Michel le Syrien, patriarche jacobite d'Antioche*, I–IV (Paris).

Chavannes, Edouard, 1903, *Documents sur les Tou-kiue (Turcs) Occidentaux*, (St. Pétersbourg). (Reprint 1941?)

1904, "Notes additionnelles sur les Tou-kiue (Turcs) Occidentaux", *TP*. 5, pp. 1–110. (Reprinted in the reprint of the *Documents*.)

1905, "Jinagupta, (528–605 après J.C.)," *TP* 6, pp. 332–56.

1912, "Epitaphes de deux princesses turques des T'ang," *Festschrift V. Thomsen*, pp. 78–87 (Leipzig).

Czeglédy, K., 1954, "Monographs on Syriac and Muhammadan Sources in the Literary Remains of M. Kmoskó," *AOH*. 4, pp. 19–90.

1958, "Bahrām Čōbīn and the Persian Apocalyptic Literature," *AOH* 8, pp. 21–43.

1962, "Coγay-quzï, Qara-qum, Kök-öng," *AOH* 15, pp. 55–69.

1972, "On the Numerical Composition of the Ancient Turkish Tribal Confederation," *AOH* 25, pp. 275–81.

1973, "Gardizi on the History of Central Asia (746–80 A.D.)," *AOH* 27, pp. 257–67.

1980, "Zur Geschichte der Hephtaliten," *AAH* 28, pp. 213–17.

1983, "From East to West: the Age of Nomadic Migrations in Eurasia," *Archivum Eurasiae Medii Aevi* III, pp. 25–125. [Translated from Hungarian by P.B. Golden.]

Daffinà, Paolo, 1985, "La Persia sassanide secondo le fonti cinese," *Rivista degli Studi Orientali* 57, pp. 121–70.

Doblhofer, E., 1955, *Byzantinische Diplomaten und östliche Barbaren. Aus den* Excerpta de legationibus *des Konstantinos Porphyrogennetos ausgewählte Abschnitte des Priskos und Menander Protektor* (Graz).

Doerfer, Gerhard, 1962, "Zur Bezeichnung der Westtürken", *CAJ* 7, pp. 256–63.

Dowsett, C.J.F. (trans.), 1961, *The History of the Caucasian Albanians by Movsēs Dasxurançi* (Oxford).

Dunlop, D.M., 1957, *The History of the Jewish Khazars* (Princeton).

Ecsedy, H. 1965, "Old Turkic Titles of Chinese Origin," *AOH* 18, pp. 83–91.

1972, "Tribe and Tribal Society in the 6th Century Turk Empire," *AOH* 25, pp. 245–62.

1977, "Tribe and Empire, Tribe and Society in the Turk Age," *AOH* 31, pp. 3–15.

Enoki Kazuo, 1955, "The Origin of the White Huns or Hephtalites," *East and West* 6, pp. 231–7.

1959, "On the Nationality of the Ephtalites," *MRDTB*, 18, pp. 1–58.

1969, "On the Date of the Kidarites (1)," *MRDTB* 27, pp. 1–26.

1970, "On the Date of the Kidarites (2)," *MRDTB* 28, pp. 13–38.

Gabain, A. von, 1950, "Steppe und Stadt im Leben der ältesten Türken," *Der Islam* 29, pp. 30–62.
1953, "Inhalt und magische Bedeutung der alttürkischen Inschriften," *Anthropos*, pp. 537–556.
Gumilev, L.N., 1967, *Drevnie tjurki* (Moskva).
Hamilton, F.J.–Brooks, E.G., 1899, *The Syriac Chronicle of Zachariah of Mitylene* (London).
Hamilton, James, 1962, "Toquz-oγuz et On-uyγur," *JA*, pp. 23–63.
1972, "Le nom de lieu *k.č.n* dans les inscriptions turques runiformes," *TP* 60, pp. 294–303.
Hannestad, K., 1955–7, "Les relations de Byzance avec la Transcaucasie et l'Asie Centrale aux 5e et 6e siècles," *Byzantion* 25–7, pp. 421–56.
Harmatta, J., 1962, "Byzantinoturcica," *AAH* 10, pp. 131–50.
1970, "Irán és Kina kapcsolatának történetéhez," *Antik Tanulmányok* 17, pp. 232–61.
1972, "Irano-Turcica," *AOH*, pp. 263–73.
1982, "La médaille de Jeb Sahansah," *Studia Iranica* 11, pp. 167–80.
Haussig, H.W., 1953, "Theophylakts Exkurs über die skythischen Völker," *Byzantion* 23, pp. 275–462.
Jisl, Lumir, 1968, "Wie sahen die alten Türken aus?," *UAJ* 40, pp. 181–9.
Khudjakov, Ju. S., 1980, *Vooruzhenie enisejskikh kyrgyzov* (Novosibirsk).
Kljashtornyj, S.G., 1962, "Problemy rannej istorii plemeni türk (ashina)," in *MIA* 130, pp. 278–81.
1964, *Drevnetjurkskie runicheskie pamjatniki kak istochnik po istorii Srednej Azii* (Moskva).
1977, "Mifologicheskie sjuzheti v drevne turkskikh pamjatnikakh," *Tjurkologicheskij sbornik*, pp. 117–38.
Ligeti, Louis, 1971, "A propos du 'Rapport sur les rois demeurant dans le nord'," in *Etudes tibétaines dédiées à la mémoire de Marcelle Lalou*, pp. 166–89 (Paris).
Liu, Mau-tsai, 1958. *Die chinesischen Nachrichten zur Geschichte der Ost-Türken (T'u-küe)*, I–II, Göttinger Asiatische Forschungen 10 (Wiesbaden).
Maljavkin, A.G., 1981, *Istoricheskaja geografija Central'noj Azii* (*Materialy i issledovanija*) (Novosibirsk).
Marquart, J., 1898, *Die Chronologie der alttürkischen Inschriften* (Leipzig).
1901, *Ērānšahr nach der Geographie des Ps. Moses Xorenac'i*, Abhandlungen der königl. Gesellschaft der Wissenschaften zu Göttingen, Phil. hist. Kl. NF. Bd. III, Nr. 2.
Moravcsik, Gyula, 1958, *Byzantinoturcica* I, *Die byzantinischen Quellen der Geschichte der Türkvölker*, II, *Sprachreste der Türkvölker in den byzantinischen Quellen*, 2nd edition (Berlin). [Volume I contains a useful bibliography on the Türks (pp. 77–81) which, however, lists many publications not directly relevant to these people. This same volume provides an indispensable guide to the Byzantine authors in whose works the Türks are mentioned.]
Mori, Masao, 1965, "On Chi-li-fa, Eltäbär/Eltäbir and Chichin (Irkin) of the T'ieh-lê tribes," *Acta Asiatica* 9, pp. 31–6.

1967, *Historical Studies of the Ancient Turkic Peoples*, I (Tokyo). [In Japanese, with English titles and summaries.]

Nagrodzka-Majchrzyk, Teresa, 1978, *Geneza miast u dawnych ludów tureckich (VII–XII w.)* (Polska Akademia Nauk). [French summary: "La genèse des villes chez les anciens peuples turcs," pp. 144–8.]

Nöldeke, Th., 1879, *Geschichte der Perser und Araber zur Zeit der Sasaniden. Aus der arabischen Chronik des Tabari übersetzt* (Leiden).

Olajos, T., 1979, "Theophylaktos Simokattés és történetíró elődje Menandros Protéktór', *Acta Universitatis Szegediensis de Attile József Nominata, Acta Historica* 66, pp. 3–17.

Payne-Smith, H., 1860, *The Third Part of the Ecclesiastical History of John of Ephesus* (Oxford).

Pelliot, Paul, 1912, "La fille de Mo-tch'o qaghan et ses rapports avec Kül-tegin," *TP* 13, pp. 301–6.

1915, "L'origine de T'ou-kiue, nom chinois des Turcs," *TP* 16, pp. 687–9.

1929, "Neuf notes sur des questions d'Asie Centrale," *TP* 26, pp. 201–66.

Pigulevskaja, N., 1941, *Sirijskie istochniki po istorii narodov SSSR, TIV* vol XLI. (Moskva).

1946, *Vizantija i Iran v rubezhe IV i VII vekov* (Moskva–Leningrad).

Pritsak, Omeljan, 1954, "Stammesnamen und Titulaturen der altaischen Völker," *UAJ* 24, pp. 49–104.

Pulleyblank, E.G., 1956, "Some Remarks on the Toquz-oghuz Problem," *UAJ* 28, pp. 35–42.

Róna-Tas, András, 1982, "A kazár népnévről," *Nyelvtudományi Közlemények* 84, pp. 349–80.

Roux, J.P. 1962, "La religion des Turcs de l'Orkhon des VIIe et VIIIe siècles," *Revue de l'histoire des religions* 161, pp. 1–24, 199–231.

Sinor, Denis, 1963, *Introduction à l'étude de l'Eurasie Centrale* (Wiesbaden).

1981, "The Origin of Turkic *balïq* 'town'," *CAJ* 25, pp. 95–102.

1982, "The Legendary Origin of the Türks," in: *Folklorica: Festschrift for Felix J. Onias*, edited by Egle Victoria Zygas and Peter Voorheis, Indiana University Uralic and Altaic Series vol. 141, pp. 223–45 (Bloomington, Indiana).

1984, "Some Components of the Civilization of the Türks (6th to 8th Century, A.D.)," in: *Altaistic Studies. Papers Presented at the 25th Meeting of the Permanent International Altaistic Conference at Uppsala, June 7–11, 1982*, edited by Gunnar Jarring and Staffan Rosén, Kungl. Vitterhets Historie och Antikvitets Akademien Konferenser 12, pp. 145–159 (Stockholm).

Sertkaya, Osman F., 1977, "Probleme der köktürkischen Geschichte: Muss es 'Inel kagan' oder 'Ini il kagan' heissen?," *Materialia Turcica*, 3, pp. 16–32.

Stebleva, I.V., 1965, *Poêzija tjurkov VI–VIII vekov* (Moskva).

Tezcan, Semih, 1977, "Eski türkçe *buyla* ve *baya* sanları üzerine," *TDAYB* pp. 55–69.

Ter-Mkrtichjan, L.Kh., 1979, *Armjanskie istochniki o Srednej Azii V–VII vv.* (Moskva).

Uray, G., 1979, "The Old Tibetan Sources of the History of Central Asia up to 751 A.D.: A Survey," in: *Prolegomena to the Sources on the History of Pre-Islamic Central Asia*, edited by J. Harmatta, pp. 275–304 (Budapest).

Wang, Huan, 1983, "Apa Qaghan Founder of the Western Turkish Khanate, the Splitting up of the Turkish Khanate and the Formation of the Western Turkish Khanate," *Social Sciences in China* 2, pp. 124–54.
Widengren, Geo, 1952, "Xosrau Anōšurvān, les Hephtalites et les peuples turcs. Etude préliminaire des sources.," *Orientalia Suecana* 1, pp. 69–94.
Zadneprovskij, Ju. A.–Mokrynin, V.P., 1984, "Rannefeodal'nye gosudarstva VI–X vv.," chapter IV, pp. 219–89 in *Istorija Kirgizskoj SSSR* 1 (Frunze).

12. The Uighurs

Abe Takeo, *Nishi-Uiguru kokushi no kenkyū* (Research on the history of the West Uighurs; Kyoto, 1958).
Bang, W. von and Gabain, A. von, "Türkische Turfan-Texte II," *SPAW*, 411–30 (1929).
Barthold, W., *Histoire des Turcs d'Asie Centrale*, tr. M. Donskis (Initiation à l'Islam, vol. 3; Paris, 1945).
Bičurin, N. Ja. (Iakinf), *Sobranie svedeniĭ o narodakh, obitavšikh v Sredneĭ Azii v drevnie vremena*, 3 vols. (St. Petersburg, 1851), 2nd ed., 2 vols. (Moscow–Leningrad, 1950–3).
Chavannes, Edouard, *Documents sur les Tou-kiue (Turcs) Occidentaux*, (St. Petersbourg, 1903).
Chavannes, Edouard and Pelliot, Paul, "Un traité manichéen retrouvé en Chine," *JA* 10.18: 499–617 (1911), 11.1: 99–199, 261–394 (1913).
Chiu T'ang-shu (Old T'ang history), comp. Chao Ying et al. Po-na ed.
Dauvillier, Jean, "Les provinces chaldéennes 'de l'extérieur' au moyen âge," *Mélanges offerts au R.P. Ferdinand Cavallera* (Toulouse, 1948), pp. 261–316.
Ecsedy, Hilda, "Old Turkic titles of Chinese origin," *AOH*. 18: 83–91 (1965).
Gabain, Annemarie von, "Steppe und Stadt im Leben der ältesten Türken," *Der Islam* 29: 30–62 (1949).
Hamilton, James Russell, *Les Ouïghours à l'époque des Cinq Dynasties, d'après les documents chinois* (Bibliothèque de l'Institut des Hautes Études Chinoises, vol. 10; Paris, 1955).
Hamilton, James, "Toquz-Oγuz et On-Uyγur," *JA* 250: 23–63 (1962).
Haneda Tōru, *Haneda hakushi shigaku rombunshū* (The collected historical writings of Dr Haneda), 2 vols. (Kyoto, 1957–8).
Haneda Tōru, "Tōdai Kaikotsushi no kenkyū" (Research on Uighur history in the T'ang), *Haneda hakushi shigaku rombunshū*, 1, 157–324.
Haneda Tōru, "Kyūsei Kaikotsu to Toquzoγuz to no kankei o ronzu" Toquzoγuz", (The relationship between the Nine Surname Uighurs and the Toghuzoghuz), *Haneda hakushi shigaku rombunshū*, 1, 325–94.
Hansen, Olaf, "Zur soghdischen Inschrift auf dem dreisprachigen Denkmal von Karabalgasun," *JSFOu*, 44.3: 1–39 (1930).
Henning, W., "Neue Materialien zur Geschichte des Manichäismus," *ZDMG*, n.F.15: 1–18 (1936).
Henning, W.B., "Argi and the 'Tokharians'," *BSOAS*, 9: 545–71 (1937–9).

Hino Kaizaburō, "Tōdai no Kaikotsusen" (*Hui-ho ch'ien* in the time of the T'ang dynasty), *Tōhōgaku*, 30: 38–49 (1965).
Hsin T'ang-shu (New T'ang history, comp. Sung Ch'i et al., Po-na ed.
Julien, Stanislas, "Notices sur les pays et les peuples étrangers, tirées des géographies et des annales chinoises, III, Les Oïgours," *JA*, 4.9: 50–66 (1847).
Kyzlasov, L.R., *Istorija Tuvi v srednie veka* (Moskva, 1969).
K'uang P'ing-chang, "T'ang-tai kung-chu ho-ch'in k'ao" (A study of the diplomatic marriages of T'ang princesses), *Shih-hsüeh nien-pao*, 2.2: 23–68 (1935).
Le Coq, A. von, "Türkische Manichaica aus Chotscho III", *APAW*, 2: 1–49 (1922).
Lévi, Sylvain and Chavannes, Éd., "Voyages des pélerins bouddhistes, L'itinéraire d'Ou-k'ong (751–790)," *JA*, 9.6: 341–84 (1895).
Liu Chih-hsiao, Wei-wu-erh tsu li-shih (shang-pien) (*History of the Uighur Nationality, Volume 1*), Min-tsu chu-pan-she (Nationalities Press), Peking, 1985.
Ma Tuan-lin, *Wen-hsien t'ung-k'ao* (Complete examination of old documents and various compilations), Wan-yu wen-k'u ed., Shih-t'ung, vol. 7, 2 vols. (Shanghai, 1936).
Mackerras, Colin, *The Uighur empire according to the T'ang dynastic histories. A Study in Sino-Uighur relations 744-840*, 2nd ed. (The Australian National University Asian publications series, vol. 3; Canberra, 1972).
Marquart, Jos., 'Ǧuwainī's Bericht über die Bekehrung der Uiguren,' *SPAW* 27: 486–502 (1912).
Minorsky, V., *Ḥudūd al-'Ālam 'The regions of the world' a Persian geography 372 A.H. 982 A.D.* (E.J.W. Gibb Memorial New Series, vol. 11; London, 1937).
"Tamīm ibn Baḥr's journey to the Uyghurs," *BSOAS* 12.2: 275–305 (1948).
Moriyasu Takao, "Uiguru to Toban no Hokutei sōdatsusen oyobi sono nochino Seiiki jōsei ni tsuite" (The Uyghur–Tibetan struggle for Beshbalygh and the subsequent situation in Central Asia), *TG* 55.4: 60–87 (1973).
Müller, F.W.K., "Uigurica II," *APAW* 3: 1–110 (1910).
"Ein Doppelblatt aus einem manichäischen Hymnenbuch (Maḥrnâmag)," *APAW* 5: 1–40 (1912).
"Der Hofstaat eines Uiguren-Königs," *Festschrift Vilhelm Thomsen zur Vollendung des siebzigsten Lebensjahres am 25 Januar* (Leipzig, 1912), pp. 207–13.
"Zwei Pfahlinschriften aus den Turfanfunden," *APAW*. 3: 1–38 (1915).
Pulleyblank, E.G. "A Sogdian colony in Inner Mongolia," *TP*. 41: 317–56 (1952).
"Some remarks on the Toquzoghuz problem," *UAJ*. 28: 35–42 (1956).
Radloff, W., *Die alttürkischen Inschriften der Mongolei*, 3 vols. (Saint Petersburg, 1894–5).
Ramstedt, G.J., "Zwei uigurische Runeninschriften in der Nord-Mongolei," *JSFOu*. 30.3: 1–63 (1913).
Saguchi Tōru, "Kaikotsu den" (The biographies of the Uighurs), in Saguchi Tōru, Yamada Nobuo and Mori Masao, *Kiba minzoku shi 2, Seishi hokuteki den* (The history of horse-riding peoples 2; the biographies of the northern races in the standard histories; Tōyō bunko 223; Tokyo, 1972), pp. 299–462.
Schlegel, Gustav, "Die chinesische Inschrift auf dem uigurischen Denkmal in Kara Balgassun," *MSFOu*. 9: i–xv, 1–141 (1896).

Ssu-ma Kuang, *Tzu-chih t'ung-chien* (Comprehensive mirror of government), 20 vols. (Peking, 1956 ed.).
T'ang hui-yao (T'ang compilations, comp. Wang P'u et al., Ts'ung-shu chi-ch'eng ed., 16 vols. (Shanghai, 1936).
Tasaka Kōdō, "Kaikotsu ni okeru Manikyō hakugai undō" (An anti-Manichean movement among the Uighurs), *Tōhō gakuhō*, 11.1: 223–32 (Tokyo, 1940).
"Chū Tō ni okeru seihoku henkyō no jōsei ni tsuite" (On the state of the north-western frontiers in the mid-T'ang), *Tōhō gakuhō*, 11.2: 585–625 (Tokyo, 1940).
Tu Yu, *T'ung-tien* (Complete institutions), Wan-yu wen-k'u ed., Shih-t'ung, vol. 1 (Shanghai, 1935).
Yamada Nobuo, "Kyūsei Kaikotsu kahan no keifu" (Qaghans of the Uighurs of Nine Clans), *TG.* 33.3–4: 90–113 (1950).

13. The Karakhanids and early Islam

Collections of sources

E. Bretschneider, *Medieval Researches from Eastern Asiatic Sources*, 2 vols. (London, 1888, reprint 1967).
E. Chavannes, *Documents sur les Tou-kiue (Turcs) Occidentaux* (St. Petersbourg, 1903).
Liu, Mau-tsai, *Die Chinesischen Nachrichten zur Geschichte der Ost-Türken (T'u-küe)*, 2 vols. (Göttinger Asiatische Forschungen, vol. 10, Wiesbaden, 1958).
O. Karaev, *Arabo-persidskie istočhniki o tjurkskikh narodakh* (Frunze, 1973).
V.A. Romodin (ed.), *Materialy po istorii Kirgizov i Kirgizii*, vyp. 1 (Moskva, 1973).
S.L. Volin et al. (ed.), *Materialy po istorii Turkmen i Turkmenii*, 2 vols. (Moskva–Leningrad, 1938–9), vol. 1.

Arab sources

Ibn al-Athīr, *Al-Kāmil fī'l-Ta'rīkh: Chronicon quod perfectissimum inscribitur*, ed. C.J. Tornberg, 12 vols. (1851–76, reprint Beirut, 1965–6).
Al-Balādhurī, *Futūḥ al-Buldān*, ed. R.M. Raḍwān (Cairo, 1959).
Al-Bīrūnī, *Athār al-Baqīyah*, ed. E. Sachau (1876, reprint Leipzig, 1923).
Kitāb al-Jamāhir fī Ma'rifat al-Jawāhir, ed. S. Krenkow (Ḥaidarābād, 1355/1936–7).
Ibn Faḍlān, *Risālah*, ed. S. al-Dahān (Damascus, 1960).
A.Z.V. Togan (ed. trans.), *Ibn Faḍlān's Reisebericht* (Abhandlungen für die Kunde des Morgenlandes, 24.3, Leipzig, 1939).
A.P. Kovalevskij (trans.), *Kniga Akhmeda ibn Fadlana o ego putešestvii na Volgu v 921–922 gg.* (Khar'kov, 1956).
Ibn Ḥawqal, *Kitāb Ṣūrat al-Arḍ*, J.H. Kramers, 2 vols. (Bibliotheca Geographorum Arabicorum, 2, Leiden, 1938–1939[2]).
Al-Idrīsī, *Kitāb Nuzhat al-Mushtāq fī Ikhtirāq al-Āfāq: Opus Geographicum*, ed. R. Rubinacci *et al.*, fasc. 1–9 (Leiden–Rome–Naples, 1970–84).

Al-Iṣṭakhrī, *Kitāb Masālik al-Mamālik*, ed. M.J. de Goeje (Bibliotheca Geographorum Arabicorum, 1, Leiden, 1927[2]).
Maḥmūd al-Kāshgharī, *Dîwân Lûghat al-Turk*, facs. ed. B. Atalay (Ankara, 1941) Turkish translation by B. Atalay, *Dîvânû Lügat-it-Türk*, 3 vols. (Ankara, 1939–1941).
Ibn Khurdādhbih, *Kitāb al-Masālik wa'l-Mamālik*, ed. M.J. de Goeje (Bibliotheca Geographorum Arabicorum, 6, Leiden, 1889).
Al-Marwazī: *Sharāf al-Zamān Tāhir Marvazī on China, the Turks and India*, ed. trans. V.F. Minorsky (London, 1942).
Al-Mas'ūdī, *Murūj adh-Dhahab wa Ma'ādin al-Jawhar*, ed. C. Pellat, 7 vols. (Beirut, 1966–1979).
Ibn Miskawaih, *Tajārub al-Umam*, ed. H.F. Amedroz, 3 vols. (Oxford, 1920, reprint, Baghdad, n.d.).
Münejjimbashï: text available only in Turkish translations: *Ṣaḥā'if al-Akhbār*, Turk. trans. Aḥmed Nedim, 3 vols. (Istanbul, 1285/1868), II.
Müneccimbaşı Şeyh Ahmed Dede Efendi'nin "Cami' üd-Düvel" adlı eserinden: Karahanlılar, Turk. trans. N. Lugal (Istanbul, 1940).
Al-Nadīm, *The Fihrist of al-Nadim*, trans. ed. B. Dodge, 2 vols. (Records of Civilization: Sources and Studies, 83, New York–London, 1970).
Al-Ṭabarī, *Ta'rīkh al-Ṭabarī*, ed. Muḥammed Abu'l Faḍl Ibrāhīm, 10 vols. (Dhakhā'ir al-'Arab, 30, Cairo, 1964–70).
Al-'Utbī, *Ta'rikh al-Yamīnī* with commentary of Shaykh Aḥmad b. 'Alī al-Manīnī (Cairo, 1268/1869).
Al-Ya'qūbī, *Kitāb al-Buldān*, ed. M.J. de Goeje (Bibliotheca Geographorum Arabicorum, 7 Leiden, 1892).
Ta'rīkh (Beirut, 1390/1970) 2 vols.
Yāqūt, *Mu'jam al-Buldān*, 5 vols. (Beirut, 1957).

Persian sources

Anonymous, *Ḥudūd al-'Ālam*, trans. V.F. Minorsky (E.J.W. Gibb Memorial New Series, 11, London, 1937, reprint 1970).
Abu'l Faḍl Baihaqī, *Ta'rīkh-i Baihaqī*, ed. Q. Ghanī, 'A. Fayyāḍ (Tehran, 1324/1945; Russ. trans. K. Arends, *Abu-l Fazl Baihakī, Istoriia Mas'ūda (1030–1041)*, 2nd rev. ed. (Pamjatniki Pis'mennosti Vostoka, 22, Moskva, 1969).
Gardīzī, *Zain al-Akhbār*, ed. M. Nāzim (Berlin, 1928).
V.V. Bartol'd, "Izvlečenie iz sočinenija Gardizi *Zain al-Akhbār*" in V.V. Bartol'd, *Sočinenija*, 9 vols. (Moskva, 1963–73), VIII.
Al-Ḥusainī, *Akhbār al-Dawlah al-Saljuqīyah* (Lahore, 1933); Turk. trans. N. Lügal, *Ahbar üd-devlet is-Selçukıyye* (Türk Tarih Kurumu yayın-larından, 2nd series, vol. 8, Ankara, 1943).
'Ata-Malik Juvainī, *Ta'rīkh-i Jahān Gushā: The History of the World-Conqueror*, trans. J.A. Boyle, 2 vols. (Cambridge, Mass., 1958).
Juzjānī, *Ṭabakāt-i Nāṣirī, A General History of the Muḥammadan Dynasties of Asia, including Hindūstān from A.H. 194 (810 A.D.) to A.H. 658 (1260 A.D.) and the*

Irruption of the Infidel Mughals into Islām, trans. H.G. Raverty, 2 vols. (Bibliotheca Indica, New Series, vols. 272–3, London, 1881, reprint 1970).

Mujmal al-Tawārīkh, ed. M. Bahār (Tehran, 1318/1939).

Narshakhī, *Ta'rīkh-i Bukhārā: The History of Bukhara*, trans. R.N. Frye (The Medieval Academy of America, Publication No. 61, Cambridge, Mass., 1954).

Niẓām al-Mulk, *Siyāsat-Nāmah*, ed. M. Qazwīnī, M. Chahārdihī (Tehran, 1334/1956); *The Book of Government or Rules for Kings*, trans. H. Darke (London, 1960).

Rashīd al-Dīn, *Jāmi' al-Tawārīkh* ed. A.A. Romaskevich, A.A. Khetagurov, A.A. Ali-zade, vol. I/I (Moskva, 1965); *Sbornik letopiseĭ*, Russ. trans. A.A. Khetagurov, vol. I/I (Moskva–Leningrad, 1952); *Die Geschichte der Oġuzen des Rashīd ad-Dīn*, Germ. trans. K. Jahn (Wien, 1969).

Turkic sources

G. Aidarov, *Jazyk orkhonskikh pamjatnikov drevnetjurkskoj pis'mennosti VIII veka* (Alma-Ata, 1971).

A. von Le Coq, *Türkçe Mânî elyazıları*, trans. F. Köseraif (İstanbul, 1936).

S.E. Malov, *Pamjatniki drevnetjurkskoj pis'mennosti* (Moskva–Leningrad, 1951).

G. Jarring, *Uzbek Texts from Afghan Turkistan* (Lunds Universitets Årsskrift, N.F. Avd. 1, vol. 34, Nr. 2, Lund–Leipzig, 1938).

R.B. Shaw, "A Grammar of the Language of Eastern Turkistan" Part 1, *Journal of the Royal Asiatic Society*, Bengal, 1877.

P.I. Desmaisons, *Histoire des Mogols et des Tatares par Aboul-Ghazı Béhadour Khan* (St. Pétersbourg, 1871–4, reprint Amsterdam, 1970).

Neshrī, *Kitab-i Cihan-nüma*, ed. F.R. Unat, M.A. Köymen, 2 vols. (Ankara, 1949–57).

Secondary literature

C.M. Abramzon, *Kirgizy i ikh ėtnogenetičeskie i istoriko-kul'turnye svjazi* (Leningrad, 1971).

S.G. Agadžanov, *Očerki istorii oguzov i turkmen Srednej Azii IX–XII vv.* (Ashkhabad, 1969).

S.M. Akhinžanov, "Kipchaki i Khorezm v kanun mongol'skogo našestvija," *Vestnik Akademii Nauk Kazakhskoj SSR* (1970), No. 1.

J. Bacot, "Reconnaissance en Haute Asie Septentrionale par cinq envoyés Ouigours au VIIIe siècle," *JA*, 244 (1956), pp. 137–53.

V.V. Bartol'd, "Balasagun", *Akademik V.V. Bartol'd Sočinenija*, 9 vols. (Moskva, 1963–1973), vol. III.

"Bogra Khan," *Sočinenija*, vol. II, pt. 2.

"Ilek-Khany," *Sočinenija*, vol. II, pt. 2.

Istorija kul'turnoi žizni Turkestana, Sočinenija, vol. II, pt. 1.

Istorija Turkestana, Sočinenija, vol. II, pt. 1.

"Karluki," *Sočinenija*, vol. V.

"Kimeki," *Sočinenija*, vol. V.

"Kipchaki," *Sočinenija*, vol. v.
"O khristianstve v Turkestane v domongol'skii period," *Sočinenija*, vol. II, pt. 2.
Očerk istorii Semirech'ja, Sočinenija, vol. II, pt. 1.
Očerk istorii turkmenskogo naroda, vol. II, pt. 1.
Turkestan v epokhu mongol'skogo našestvija, Sočinenija, vol. I.
Dvenadcat' lekcii po istorii tureckikh narodov Srednej Azii, Sočinenija, V: Germ. vers. (W. Barthold), *Zwölf Vorlesungen über die Geschichte der Türken Mittelasiens* (1932–5, reprint Hildesheim, 1962).
C.E. Bosworth, *The Ghaznavids* (Edinburgh, 1963).
"The Political and Dynastic History of the Iranian World (A.D. 1000–1217)," *The Cambridge History of Iran* ed. J.A. Boyle, vol. 5 (Cambridge, 1968).
C. Cahen, "Le Malik-nameh et l'histoire des origines Seljoucides," *Oriens*, 2 (1949), pp. 31–65.
Pre-Ottoman Turkey, trans. J. Jones-Williams (New York, 1968).
G. Clauson, "À propos du Manuscrit Pelliot Tibétain 1283," *JA* 245 (1957).
K. Czeglédy, "A karluk törzsek nevei," *Magyar Nyelv* 45 (1949), pp. 164–168.
"Kāšġarī földrajzi neveihez," *Bárczi Géza – Emlékkönyv*, ed. L. Benkö (Budapest, 1963).
"Gardīzī on the History of Central Asia (745–780 A.D.)," *Acta Orientalia Hungarica* 27.3 (1973).
E.A. Davidovič, "Numizmatičeskie materialy dlja khronologii i genealogii sredneaziatskikh Karakhanidov," *Trudy Gosudarstvennogo Istoričeskogo Muzeja*, 26, Numizmatičeskiĭ sbornik, pt. 2 (1957).
Idem, "O dvukh karakhanidskikh kaganatakh" *Narody Azii i Afriki* (1968), No. 1.
D.E. Eremeev, *Êtnogenez Tjurok* (Moskva, 1971).
E. Esin, "Ṭabarī's Report on the Warfare with the Türgiš and the Testimony of Eighth Century Central Asian Art," *Central Asiatic Journal* 17.2–4 (1973).
M.N. Fedorov, "Novye fakty iz istorii Karakhanidov pervoĭ četverti XI v. v svete numizmatičeskikh dannykh," *Iz Istorii Kul'tury Narodov Uzbekistana* (Tashkent, 1965).
"Očerk istorii Karakhanidov vtori četverti XI v. (po numizmatičeskim dannym)," *Istorija Material'noj Kul'tury Uzbekistana* 7 (1966).
"Ferganskiĭ klad karakhanidskikh dirkhemov 1034–1043 gg.," *Sovetskaja Arkheologija* (1968), No. 3.
R.N. Frye, *The Golden Age of Persia. The Arabs in the East* (London, 1975).
B.G. Gafurov, B.A. Litvinskiĭ, *Istorija tadžikskogo naroda*, 3 vols. (Moskva, 1963–5).
B.G. Gafurov, *Tadžiki* (Moskva, 1972).
P.B. Golden, "The Migrations of the Oğuz," *Archivum Ottomanicum*, 4 (1972).
"Imperial Ideology and the Sources of Political Unity Amongst the Pre-Činggisid Nomads of Western Eurasia," *Archivum Eurasiae Medii Aevi*, 2 (1976).
F. Grenard, "La légende de Satok Boghra Khan et l'histoire," *JA* 1900, I, pp. 5–79.
Ia. G. Guliamov, S.P. Tolstov et al., *Istorija Uzbekskoj SSR*, vol. I (Tashkent, 1967).
L.N. Gumilëv, *Drevnie Tjurki* (Moskva, 1967).
Poiski vymyšlennogo carstva (Moskva, 1970).
H. Hoffmann, "Die Qarluq in der tibetischen Literatur," *Oriens*, 3 (1950) pp. 190–208.

I. Kafesoğlu, *Harezmşahler devleti tarihi* (Ankara, 1956).
Sultan Melikşah devrinde büyük Selçuklu imparatorluğu (Istanbul, 1953).
S.G. Kljaštornyĭ, "Sogdijcy v Semirech'e," *Sovetskaja êtnografija* (1959), No. 1.
Drevnetjurkskie runičeskie pamjatniki kak istočnik po istorii Srednej Azii (Moskva, 1964).
M.F. Köprülü, *Türk edebiyatında ilk mutasavvıflar* (Istanbul, 1919, reprint, Ankara, 1966).
M. Köymen, "Büyük Selçuklular imparatorluğunda Oğuz isyanı", *Ankara Üniversitesi Dil ve Tarih-Coğrafya Fakültesi Dergisi*, 5 (1947).
"Büyük Selçuklu imparatorluğu tarihinde Oğuz istilası," *Ankara Üniversitesi Dil ve Tarih-Coğrafya Fakültesi Dergisi* 5 (1947).
Selçuklu devri Türk tarihi (Ankara, 1963).
B.E. Kumekov, *Gosudarstvo Kimekov IX–XI vv. po arabskim istočnikam* (Alma-Ata, 1972).
R.G. Kuzeev, *Proiskhozhdenie baškirskogo naroda* (Moskva, 1974).
L. Ligeti, "Egy karluk törzs neve kínai átírásban," *Magyar Nyelv* 45 (1949) pp. 168–70.
"À propos du 'Rapport sur les rois demeurant dans le Nord'," *Études Tibétaines dédiées à la mémoire de Marcelle Lalou* (Paris, 1971).
J. Marquart, *Über das Volkstum der Komanen* in W. Bang, J. Marquart, *Osttürkische Dialektstudien* (Abhandlungen der königlichen Gesellschaft der Wissenschaften zu Göttingen, philologisch-historische Klasse, n.F., vol. 13, Berlin, 1914).
A.N. Mikhailova, "Novye Epigrafičeskie dannye dlja istorii Srednej Azii IX v.," *Êpigrafika Vostoka*, 5 (1951).
B. Ögel, *Islâmiyetten önce Türk kültür tarihi* (Ankara, 1962).
Türk mitolojisi (Selçuklu tarih ve medeniyeti enstitüsü yayınları, vol. 1), vol. 1 (Ankara, 1971).
K.I. Petrov, *Očerk proiskhoždenija kirgizskogo naroda* (Frunze, 1963).
I.P. Petruševskij, "Pokhod mongol'skikh vojsk v Srednjuju Aziju v 1219–1224 gg. i ego posledstvija," *Tataro-Mongoly v Azii i Evrope*, ed. S.L. Tikhvinskiĭ (Moskva, 1970).
L.P. Potapov, *Êtničeskiĭ sostav i proiskhoždenie Altaicev* (Leningrad, 1969).
O. Pritsak, "Karachanidische Streitfragen," *Oriens*, 3 (1950), pp. 17–68.
"Von den Karluk zu den Karachaniden," *Zeitschrift der Deutschen Morgenländischen Gesellschaft*, 101 (1951).
"Āl-i Burhān," *Der Islam*, 30 (1952).
"The Decline of the Empire of the Oghuz Yabghu," *The Annals of the Ukrainian Academy of Arts and Sciences in the United States*, 2.2 (1952): "Der Untergang des Reiches des Oğuzischen Yabğu," *Fuad Köprülü Armağanı* (İstanbul, 1953).
"Die Karachaniden," *Der Islam*, 31 (1953–4).
"Qara. Studien zur türkischen Rechtssymbolik," *Symbolae in Honorem Z.V. Togan* (Istanbul, 1950–5).
Idem, "The Polovcians and Rus'," *Archivum Eurasiae Medii Aevi* 2 (1982).
W. Samolin, *East Turkistan to the Twelfth Century* (The Hague, 1964).
T.N. Senigova, "Voprosy ideologii i kul'tov Semireč'ja (VI–VII vv.)," *Novoe v Arkheologii Kazakhstana*, ed. M.K. Kadyrbaev (Alma-Ata, 1968).
Srednevekovyi Taraz (Alma-Ata, 1972).

K. Sh. Shaniiazov, *Uzbeki-Karluki, istoriko-êtnografičeskij očerk* (Tashkent, 1964).
"Uzy", *Obščestvennye Nauki v Uzbekistane* (1970), No. 2.
"K voprusu rasselenija i rodovykh delenii Kangly," in Kh. Z. Ziiaev (ed.), *Êtnografičeskoe izučenie byta i kul'tury Uzbekov* (Tashkent, 1972).
K êtnicheskoj istorii uzbekskogo naroda (Istoriko-êtnografičeskoe issledovanie na materialakh kipčakskogo komponenta) (Tashkent, 1974).
F. Sümer, *Oğuzlar* (Ankara, 1967).
A.Z.V. Togan, *Umumî Türk tarihine giriş*, 2nd ed. (İstanbul, 1970) vol. I (all published).
S.P. Tolstov, *Drevnij Khorezm* (Moskva, 1948).
Idem, *Po sledam drevnekhorezmijskoj civilizacii* (Moskva–Leningrad, 1948).
O. Turan, *Selçuklular tarihi ve Türk-İslâm medeniyeti* (Türk Kültürünü Araştırma Enstitüsü yayınları, 7, Ankara, 1965).
S.L. Volin, "Svedenija arabskikh istočnikov IX–XVI vv. o doline reki Talas i smezhnykh rajonakh," *Trudy Instituta Istorii, Arkheologii i Êtnografii Akademii Nauk Kazakhskoj SSR* (1960).

14. Early and medieval Tibet

Adam, Leonhard und Trimborn, Hermann, 1958, *Lehrbuch der Völkerkunde* (Stuttgart).
Aufschnaiter, P., 1956–57, "Prehistoric Sites Discovered in Inhabited Regions of Tibet," *East and West* 7, pp. 74–95.
Bacot, Jacques, 1935, "Le mariage chinois du roi Sron bcan sgan po (extrait du Mani bka' 'bum)," *Mélanges Chinois et Bouddhiques* III, pp. 1–10.
1940–1946, *Documents de Touen-houang relatifs à l'histoire du Tibet*, Annales du Musée Guimet, tome 51 (DTH) (Paris).
Bogoslovskij, V.A., 1972, *Essai sur l'histoire du peuple tibétain, ou la naissance d'une société de classes* (Paris).
Demiéville, Paul, 1952, *Le concile de Lhasa. Une controverse sur le quiétisme entre bouddhistes de l'Inde et de la Chine au VIIIe siècle de l'ère chrétienne*, Bibliothèque de l'Institut des Hautes Etudes Chinoises, Vol. VII (Paris).
Eberhard, W., 1942, *Kultur und Siedlung der Randvölker Chinas, T'oung Pao*, supplément au vol. 36 (Leiden).
1942–3, "Die Kultur der alten zentral- und west-asiatischen Völker nach chinesischen Quellen," *Zeitschrift für Ethnologie* 73 pp. 215–75.
Ferrari, Alfonsa, 1958, *Mk'yen brtse's Guide to the Holy Places of Central Tibet*, completed and edited by Luciano Petech, with the collaboration of Hugh Richardson, Serie Orientale Roma XVI (Rome).
Francke, A.H., 1926, "Antiquities of Indian Tibet," *Archaeological Survey of India*, New Imperial Series, Vol. L, II (Calcutta).
Franke, O., 1936–7, *Geschichte des Chinesischen Reiches*, Vols. 2 and 3 (Berlin/Leipzig).
rGyal-rabs bon-gyi 'byung-gnas, (Manuscript owned by the author).
Haarh, Erik, 1969a, "The Identity of Tsu-chi-chien, the Tibetan 'king' who died in 804 A.D.," *Acta Orientalia*, 25, pp. 121–70.
1969b, *The Yar-lun Dynasty, A study with particular regard to the contribution by*

myths and legends to the history of Ancient Tibet and the origin and nature of its kings (Copenhagen).
Hoffmann, Helmut, 1950, *Quellen zur Geschichte der tibetischen Bon-Religion*, Akademie der Wissenschaften und der Literatur, Abhandlungen der geistes- und Sozialwissenschaftlichen Klasse, Jahrgang 1950, Nr. 4 (Wiesbaden).
1967, "Žaṅ-žuṅ: the Holy Language of the Tibetan Bonpo," *ZDMG* 117, pp. 376–81.
1971, "The Tibetan Names of the Saka and the Sogdians," *Asiatische Studien* 25, pp. 440–55.
1972, *Tibet. A Handbook*, Indiana University Oriental Series, vol. 5 (Bloomington, Indiana).
Ḥudūd al-ʿĀlam, 1937, "*The Regions of the World*," A Persian Geography, translated and explained by V. Minorsky, E.J.W. Gibb Memorial Series, New Series XI (London).
Karmay, Samten G., 1972, *The Treasury of Good Sayings: A Tibetan History of Bon*, London Oriental Series, Vol. 26 (London).
Li, Fang-kuei, 1959, "Tibetan glo-ban-'dring," *Studia Serica Bernhard Karlgren Dedicata*, pp. 55–9 (Copenhagen).
Lokesh Chandra and Tenzin Namdak (editors), 1968, *History and Doctrine of Bon-po Nispanna-Yoga* (Tibetan Text), Satapitaka Series 73 (New Delhi).
Molè, G., 1970, *The T'u-yü-hun from the Northern Wei to the Time of the Five Dynasties*, Serie Orientale Roma XLI (Rome).
Namdak, Tenzin, 1966, *Mdzod phug: basic verses and commentary by Dran-pa nam-mhha'* (Delhi) [Tibetan text only].
Obermiller, E., 1932, *History of Buddhism by Bu-ston* (Heidelberg).
Pelliot, Paul, 1961, *Histoire ancienne du Tibet*, Oeuvres posthumes de Paul Pelliot, Vol. 5 (Paris).
1963, *Notes on Marco Polo*, II (Paris 1963).
Petech, Luciano, 1939, *A Study on the Chronicles of Ladakh, Indian Tibet* (Calcutta).
1946, "Alcuni nomi geografici nel La-dvags-rgyal-rabs," *RSO* XXII (Rome 1947), 1–10.
Richardson, Hugh E., 1952, *Ancient Historical Edicts at Lhasa and the Mu Tsung/Khri Gtsug Lde Brtsan Treaty of A.D. 821–822 from the Inscription at Lhasa*, Prize Publication Fund, Vol. 19 (London).
1954, "A Ninth Century Inscription from Rkon-po," *JRAS*, pp. 157–73.
1957, "A Tibetan Inscription from Rgyal-lha-khan, and a Note on Tibetan Chronology from A.D. 841 to A.D. 1042," *JRAS*, pp. 57–78.
1958–9, "The Karma-pa Sect. A Historical Note," *JRAS*, 139–64; pp. 1–17.
1971, "Who was Yum-brtan," *Études Tibétaines dédiées à la mémoire de Marcelle Lalou*, pp. 433–9 (Paris).
Roerich, George N., 1930, *The Animal Style among the Nomad Tribes of Northern Tibet* (Prague).
1931, "Problems of Tibetan Archaeology," *Urusvati Journal* I, pp. 27–34.
1949–53, *The Blue Annals*, 2 vols., Royal Asiatic Society, Monograph Series Vol. VII (Calcutta).
Róna-Tas, A., 1955, "Social Terms in the List of Grants of the Tibetan Tun-huang Chronicle," *AOH* pp. 249–70.

Schlegel, G., 1896, *Die chinesische Inschrift auf dem uigurischen Denkmal in Kara Balgassun, MSFOu*, v.
Shakabpa, Tsepon W.D., 1967, *Tibet. A Political History*, (Yale University Press).
Snellgrove, David and Richardson, Hugh, 1968, *A Cultural History of Tibet* (New York and Washington).
Stein, R.A., 1961, *Une chronique ancienne de bSam-yas: sBa-bzed*, Edition du texte tibétain et résumé français, (Publications de l'Institut des Hautes Etudes Chinoises, Textes et documents Vol. I (Paris).
1972, *Tibetan Civilization*, translated (from the original French) by J.E. Stapleton Driver (London).
Thomas, F.W., 1948, *Nam. An Ancient Language of the Sino-Tibetan Borderland* (London).
1935, 1951, 1953, 1963, *Tibetan Literary Texts and Documents*, 4 vols. (London).
Tucci, Giuseppe, 1949, *Tibetan Painted Scrolls*, Vol. I (Rome).
1950, *The Tombs of the Tibetan Kings*, Serie Orientale Roma I (Rome).
1955–6, "The Sacral Character of the Kings of Ancient Tibet," *East and West* 6, pp. 197–205.
1956, *Preliminary Report on two scientific expeditions in Nepal*, Serie Orientale Roma X, I (Rome).
1958, *Minor Buddhist Texts*, part II, Serie Orientale Roma IX, 2 (Rome).
1962, "The wives of Sron-btsan-sgam-po," *Oriens Extremus* 9, pp. 121–126.
1973, *Transhimalaya*, translated from the French by James Hogarth (London).
Uray, G., 1960, "The Four Horns of Tibet according to the Royal Annals," *AOH* 10, pp. 31–57.
1962, "The Offices of the Brun-pas and Great Mnans and the Territorial Division of Central Tibet in the Early 8th Century," *AOH* 15, pp. 353–60.

15. The forest peoples of Manchuria

Denis Sinor, *Introduction à l'étude de l'Eurasie Centrale*, (Wiesbaden 1963), pp. 160, 248–250 gives critical references to the earlier secondary literature. In the following bibliography items marked with an asterisk * were added by the editor. Some of these were not yet available to the author at the time when he prepared his manuscript.

Chan, Hok-lam, 1970, *Chin Historiography. Three Studies*, Münchener Ostasiatische Studien (München).
*1984, *Legitimation in Imperial China. Discussions under the Jurchen-Chin Dynasty (1115–1234)* (Seattle–London).
Chavannes, Edouard, 1897–8, "Voyageurs chinois chez les Khitans et les Joutchen," *JA* 1897, I, pp. 377–422, 1898, I, pp. 361–439.
Ch'i-tan hsiao-tzu yen-chiu 1985, [Study of Kitan small characters] (Peking).
Chin Kuang-p'ing and Chin Ch'i-ts'ung, 1980, *Nü-chen yü-yen wen-tzu yen-chiu*, [A Study of the Jurchen Language and Script] (Peking).
Derevjanko, E.I., 1975, *Mokhêskie pamjatniki Srednego Priamur'ja* (Novosibirsk).
Doerfer, Gerhard, 1969, "Altaische Scholien zu Herbert Frankes Artikel," *ZS* 3, pp. 45–9.

Franke, Herbert, 1969, "Bemerkungen zu den sprachlichen Verhältnissen im Liao-Reich," *ZS* 3, pp. 7–43.

1974, "A Note on Wine," *ZS* 8, pp. 241–5.

1975, "Chinese Texts on the Jurchen. I. A Translation of the Jurchen Monograph in the San-ch'ao pei-meng hui-pien," *ZS* 9, pp. 119–86.

1978a, "Chinese Texts on the Jurchen. II. A Translation of Chapter One of the Chin-shi," *ZS* 12, pp. 413–52.

1978b, *Nordchina am Vorabend der mongolischen Eroberungen: Wirtschaft und Gesellschaft unter der Chin-Dynastie (1115–1234)*, Rheinisch-Westfälische Akademie der Wissenschaften, Vorträge G 228 (Opladen).

1979, "Some Folkloristic Data in the Dynastic History of the Chin (115–1234)," in *Legend, Lore and Religion in China. Essays in Honor of Wolfram Eberhard on his Seventieth Birthday*, edited by Sarah Allan and Alvin P. Cohen, pp. 135–53 (San Francisco).

1981, "Jurchen Customary Law and Chinese Law of the Chin Dynasty", in *State and Law in East Asia*, edited by Dieter Eikemeier and Herbert Franke, pp. 215–233 (Wiesbaden).

1982, "Randnotizen zu einigen Worten der Khitansprache im Lichte neuerer Arbeiten," *AOH* 36, pp. 173–82.

1985, "Fremdherrschaften in China und ihr Einfluss auf die staatlichen Institutionen (10–14 Jahrhundert)," *Anzeiger der Österreichischen Akademie der Wissenschaften*, 122, No. 3 pp. 47–67.

Franke, Otto, 1948, 1952, *Geschichte des chinesischen Reiches*, vols. 4 and 5 (Berlin).

Gibert, Lucien, 1934, *Dictionnaire historique et géographique de la Mandchourie* (Hong Kong).

Grube, Wilhelm, 1896, *Die Sprache und Schrift der Jučen* (Leipzig).

Ho, Ping-ti, 1970, "An Estimation of the Total Population of Sung–Chin China," *Etudes Song In Memoriam Étienne Balázs*, Ser. 1 (Histoire et institutions), No. 1, pp. 35–53 (Paris).

Kane, Daniel, 1988, *The Sino-Jurchen Vocabulary of the Bureau of Interpreters*, Indiana University Uralic and Altaic Series, vol. 153 (Bloomington, Indiana).

Kara, Dzh.–Kychanov, E.I. – Starikov, V.S., 1972, "Pervaja nakhodka chzhur-chzên'skikh rukopisnykh tekstov na bumage," *Pis'mennie pamjatniki Vostoka. Istoriko-filologicheskie issledovanija 1969*, pp. 223–8.

Kara, György, 1975, "À propos de l'inscription khitane de 1150," *Annales Universitatis Budapestiensis. Sectio Linguistica 6*, pp. 163–7.

*1986–7, "On the Khitan Writing Systems," *Mongolian Studies* 10, pp. 19–24.

Kiyose, Gisaburo, 1972, *A Study of the Jurchen Language and Script, Reconstruction and Decipherment* (Kyoto).

Ligeti, L., 1952, "Note préliminaire sur le déchiffrement des 'petits caractères' joutchen," *AOH* 3, pp. 211–28.

Lenkov, V.D., 1974, *Metallurgija i metallo-obrabotka u chzhurchzhênej v XII veke (po materialam issledovanii Majginskogo gorodishcha)* (Novosibirsk).

Liao-shih hui-pien, [Comprehensive collection of Liao History], 1971–3, 10 volumes (Taipei).

Materialy po deshifrovke kidan'skogo pis'ma., 1970, 1. Starikov, V.S., *Formal'nyj*

analiz funkcional'noj struktury teksta; II. Arapov, M., Karapet'jan, A., Malinovskaja, Z., Probst, M., *Opyt morfologicheskogo analiza tekstov malogo kidan'skogo pis'ma*, (Moscow).
Medvedev, V.E., 1977, *Kul'tura amurskikh chzhurchzhênej konec X–XI vek (po materialam gruntovykh mogil'nikov)* (Novosibirsk).
Menges, Karl A., 1968, *Tungusen und Ljao, AKDM* 38, 1 (Wiesbaden).
Mikami, Tsugio, *Kinshi kenkyū*, 1970, 1972, 1973, [Researches on Chin History], 3 volumes (Tokyo).
Murayama, S., 1975, "Der Zusammenhang der Kitan-Schrift mit der türkischen Runenschrift," in *Proceedings of the Twenty-Second Congress of Orientalists*, edited by Zeki Velidi Togan, vol. 2, pp. 386–98 (Leiden).
Pelliot, Paul, 1913, "Sur quelques mots d'Asie Centrale," *JA* 1913, I, pp. 451–69.
1959, 1963, *Notes on Marco Polo*, 2 volumes. Article "Catai," vol. 1, pp. 216–29; article "Ciorcia," vol. 1, pp. 366–90 (Paris).
Rachewiltz, Igor de, 1974, "Some Remarks on the Khitan Clan Name Yeh-lü – I-la," *Papers on Far Eastern History* 9, pp. 187–204.
Rand, Christopher C., 1979, "Chinese Military Thought," *HJAS* 39, pp. 120–37.
Serruys, Henry, 1955, *Sino-Jürched Relations during the Yung-lo Period (1403–1424)*, Göttinger Asiatische Forschungen vol. 4 (Wiesbaden).
Shavkunov, E.V., 1968, *Gosudarstvo Bokhai i pamjatniki ego kul'tury v Primor'e* (Leningrad).
Shiratori, Kurakichi (ed.), 1912–14), *Beiträge zur historischen Geographie der Mandschurei*, 2 volumes (Tokyo). [N.B. Volume 1 appeared in 1914 and vol. 2 in 1912!]
Stein, Rolf, 1940, "Leao-tche," *TP* 35, pp. 1–154.
Ta-Chin kuo-chih, 1936, Basic Sinological Series (Shanghai).
Tamura, Jitsuzo and Kobayashi, Yukio, 1953, *Keiryo* [Tombs and Mural Paintings of Ch'ing-ling. Liao Imperial Mausoleum of Eleventh Century A.D. in Eastern Mongolia], 2 volumes (Kyoto).
Tao, Jing-shen, 1976, *The Jurchen in Twelfth-Century China. A Study in Sinicization* (Seattle–London).
Taskin, V.S., 1979, *E Lun-li, Istorija gosudarstva kidanej (Cidan'go chzhi)*, PPV 35 (Moskva).
Toyama, Gunji, 1964, *Kinchōshi Kenkyū* [Researches into the History of the Chin Dynasty] (Kyoto).
Toyota, Goro, 1963, "Kitan reiji ko," [A Study of the Simple Kitan Characters], *Toyo gakuho* 39 pp. 1–39.
Vasil'ev, V.P., 1857, *Istorija i drevnosti vostochnoj chasti Srednej Azii ot X do XIII v. s prilozheniem perevoda kitajskikh izvestij o kidanjakh, chzhurchzhênjakh i mongolo-tatarakh, TVOIRAO.* 4, (St. Petersburg).
Vorob'ev, M.V., 1975, *Chzhurchzhêni i gosudarstva Czin' (X v.–1234 g.). Istoricheskij ocherk* (Moskva).
1983, *Kul'tura Chzhurchzhênej i gosudarstva Czin'* (Moskva).
Wittfogel, K.A.,–Fêng, Chia-shêng, 1949, *History of Chinese Society. Liao (907–1125)*, Transactions of the American Philosophical Society N.S. 36 (Philadephia).

Index

'Bro-gnyan lde'u (Tibetan prince) 376
'Brom-ston (Tibetan Buddhist) 395
Bronze Age 79–92, 94–5; China 83; Far East 90–2; Siberia 79–90, *see also under individual areas and cultures*
Bruno of Querfurt 275
Bru-sha (Gilgit) 381, 382
Buddhism: Eastern Iranian 345, 354; Fourth Council 166; Jurchens 419; Karakitai 411; Kitans 409, 411; Kuṣāṇa 162, 166, 168; literature 152, 168, 174, 314, 386; Sarvāstivāda School 166; Sogdians 175, 305; Tokharians 151; translators 168; Türks 305, 314–15; Yüeh-chih, Great 154; *see also* Tibet
Bug river 102, 107–8, 109
Bughra Khan, Hārūn 355, 359, 362
Bugut inscription 291, 305
Bulkhara 38, 174, 347, 358, 360, 367, 369
Bukhu people 320, 325
Bulāq people 355–6
Bulgan Somon, Mongolia 52
Bulgaria, Byzantine 272, 274
Bulghar (capital of Volga Bulgharia) 238
Bulgharia, Magna (Palaia) 214, 261–3, 264–5
Bulgharian Prince-List 257, 261, 262
Bulghars 262; and Avars 210, 214, 215, 220, 222–3, 224, 262–3; Bavarian massacre of 214, 263; and Burṭās 248; and Byzantium 220–1; Christianity 262; Danubian state 214–15, 263; Hungarians and 221, 243, 247; and Huns 202; in Kazakh kaghanate 264; and Khazars 235, 262; and Mongols 242; Oghur 198–9, 224, 234–5; and Slavs 214–15, 262; on steppes 258; Tetüz 241; *see also*: Bulgaria; Volga Bulgharia
Bumin *see* Tu-men
Burchevichi (Burch-oghlu, Borchol) 280
Buret' Palaeolithic site 55–6, 60, 93
Burgundians 187, 189
burials: Neolithic 69, 71: Bronze Age 79, 81–2, 84, 86, 87, 88; *see also under individual peoples*
Buriat region 86–90, 95
Burṭās people 248–9, 251, 264, 265
Burun-urt area, Mongolia 44
Buty people 277
Byang-chub-'od (Gu-ge prince) 395
Byang-chub rgyal-mtshan (Tibetan leader) 398
Byzantium: Manichaeism 330; Peloponnesian state 220; relations with other states; Arabs 215; Avars 11, 207–14, 215, 223, 303; Bayan 208–9, Bulgharia, Magna 262; Bulghars 220; Cumans 275, 281–2; Franks 212; Hephthalites 303; Hungarians 267; Huns 179, 184, 187–8, 189–90, 191–2, 205; Khazars 260, 264, 265, 267, 269, 352; Kutrighurs 258–9; Oghuz 276; Pechenegs 5, 267, 274; Persia 200, 209, 210, 213, 259–60, 301, 304, 308–9, (nomads as allies against) 200, 258, 259–60, 308–9: Rus' 267–9; Sabirs 200, 260; Saljuks 274, 276, 365; Saraghurs 258; Scythians 106; Sogdians 175–6; Türks 208, 260, 296, 301–5, 315–16; *see also* Constantinople
Callipidae (Graeco-Scythians) 101
Calos Limen, Crimea 108
Cambodia, Palaeolithic 46
Carantan people 217, 220–1
Carpilio (son of Aetius) 187
Carthage, Council of (411) 186
Castra Martis (Kula) 185
Catalaunian Plains; battle 194, 197, 204
cattle breeding 7, 37; Neolithic 71, 73; Bronze Age 80, 83, 85, 87
Caucasus 24, 34; Alans 113; Huns 200, 201, 202, 260; Palaeolithic 49; Sarmatians 113, 114, 116; Scythians 100
cave frescoes, Palaeolithic 57
Celts 107, 110
Chabum, Crimea 107
Chāch (Tashkent) 38, 54, 344, 347
Chadir (Wu-lei) 133
Chagrï (Saljuk leader) 364
Chalmat(a) 241
Chang Ch'ien (Han envoy to Yüeh-chih) 131, 155–6, 157, 159–60, 174
Chan-kuan chang-yao 409–10, 422
Chang Kuang-sheng (Chinese official) 327
Chan-shih-lu ('Boy *shan-yü*') 136, 137–8
Chao (state); and Hsiung-nu 118–19
Chao-chün (queen of Hsiung-nu) 141
Chao Hsin fort 129
Chao P'o-nu (Han general) 132
Charlemagne, Emperor, king of Franks 217–20
Che-lan (Hsiung-nu king) 129
Cheng Chi (Han general) 133
Ch'en Hsi (Tai prime minister) 122
Ch'en T'ang (Han general) 141
Chen-yu (Nu-shih-pi yabghu) 310
Cheremis people 231, 236, 249, 252
Chernyakhiv culture 115
Chërnye Klobuki 274, 276–7, 281
Chersonese 107–8, 209
Chertomlyk; Scythian kurgan 103, 107
Chia I (Chinese statesman and scholar) 124
Ch'iang people 127, 130, 148, 157, 161, 372–5
Chia-ni-se-chia *see* Kaniṣka

Mstislav, prince of Rus' 269
Muḥammad, Khorezmshah 363, 369–70, 410
Muḥammad II b. Sulaymān (Karakhanid) 367
Muhan (Türk kaghan) 298, 303, 305, 307
Mujmal at-Tavārīkh 248–9
Mu-ne btsan-po (Tibetan emperor) 385–6
al-Muntaṣir (Ismā'īl II, Sāmānid ruler) 360, 361, 362
al-Muqaddasī 238
al-Muqanna', revolt of 351
Murom 240, 240, 250
Muroma people 250
Mu-rug btsan-po (Tibetan prince) 386
Mūsā b. Seljuk 364
al-Mu'tamid (Caliph of Baghdad) 347
Mu-tig btsan-po (Tibetan emperor) 386
Mu-yeh, Mount 405, 406
Mu-zu gSal-'bar (Buddhist scholar) 393
Myang (Tibetan clan) 376, 390, 391
Myang Mang-po-rje Zhang-snang (Tibetan 'Great Minister') 377, 378
Myang-po, Tibet 377
Myang-ro (Nyang-ro, Tibet 376
Myang Ting-nge-'dzin (Tibetan monk) 386
mythology 15, 65–6

Naga dynasty 169
Nag-tsho Tshul-khrims rgyal-ba (Tibetan Buddhist translator) 395
Nagyszentmiklós treasure 225
Naimans 370, 410
Nakhodka 20, 58, 77
Nalaikha area, Mongolia 55
Namazga-depe, Turkmenistan 64
gNam-ri srong-brtsan (Tibetan king) 376–7
Nam-ro-re khru-gu (Tibetan noble) 391
Nam-tig (group of Ch'iang people) 373
Nanaivandak (Sogdian merchant) 175, 178–9
sNa-nam (Tibetan clan) 386
sNa-nam bTsan-po 'U-ring (Tibetan minister) 386
Nanay people 77
Nang-rje-po (Tibetan governor) 390
Naṣr b. Aḥmad (Sāmānid) 347, 352
Naṣr II (Sāmānid) 358
Naṣr *Ilig* (Karakhanid) 360, 362
Naṣr, *Shams al-Mulk* (Karakhanid) 366, 367
Neapolis (Olbia) 107, 108, 110, 115
Nedao river 198, 257
Nenets people 230
Neolithic era 14, 63–79, 94; Baikal 66–70; bow and arrow 61, 62, 68–9; Far East 71–4; Mongolia 70–1; Pacific islands 77–9; taiga 63–70; *see also under* pottery
Nepal 378, 379
nephrite tools 66, 67
Nestorian Chronicle 214
Neuri people 103
Nganasan people 94, 230
gNgya-khri btsan-po (first mythical king of Tibet) 373, 374, 376
Nicephorus, Patriarch 215, 261, 262
Nieh Weng-i (Chinese merchant) 128
Ni Li (Türk kaghan) 306
Ning-Kuo, Princesses of 325, 326, 327
Nivar kaghan (Türk kaghan) 305–6, 314
Niẓām al-Mulk (Saljuk statesman) 366
Nizhnaya Tambovka station, Amur 76
Nizhnii Novgorod 241, 251–2
Nomus (Byzantine statesman) 192
Notitia episcopatuum 201
Novgorod 253, 254
Novopetrovka area, Amur 73, 74–5
Novopetrovsk 72
Nü-chen 413
Nūḥ b. Asad (Sāmānid) 347, 352, 356, 358
Nūḥ II (Sāmānid) 359–60
Nurhaci (Manchu chieftain) 423
Nurkan (Chinese penal settlement) 423
Nu-shih-pi (Türk group) 265, 289, 302, 309, 310
mNyan Ji-Zung (Tibetan noble) 391
gNya-zhur (Zhang-zhung king) 377
rNying-ma-pa (Tibetan Buddhist school) 393
Nyi-zungs (Western Tibetan capital) 394

oases 22–3, 26–7, 36, 37–8, 38–9
Ob region 23; Bronze Age 82, 84, 86; Neolithic 68, 72, 73, 94
Ob-Ugrians 66, 230, 244, 245, 253–5
Octar (Hun ruler) 187, 188, 189
Oghulchak Kadïr Khan (Karakhanid) 357
Oghurs 222; and Avars 206, 222–3, 224, 262; composition 257–8; and Finno-Ugrians 229, 233; fur trade 233, 235; language 258, 264; and Hungarians 224, 242–3; and Khazars 263, 264; migrations 234–5, 257–8; on south Russian steppes 257–9; and Türk Kaghanate 260, 261; and Volga Bulgharia 234–5; *see also*: Kutrighurs; Onoghurs; Saraghurs; Utrighurs
Oghuz people: and Arabs 346–7; and Byzantium 276–7; and Cumans 274, 276, 281; and Ghaznavids 362, 364; Islam 276, 353; and Karluks 352, 368; and Khazars 262, 269, 275–6, 276, 361–2; and Khorezm 362, 369; and Kimek-Kipchaks 278, 348, 352, 361–2; migration 274, 352, 361–2, 363; origins and history 351–2; and Pechenegs 247, 271, 272, 274, 275–6, 348, 351–2; and Rus' 276, 276–7, 362; and

LaVergne, TN USA
07 October 2009

160131LV00002B/144/A

9 780521 243049